INTERNET OF EVERYTHING

Key Technologies, Practical Applications and Security of IoT

INTERNET OF EVERYTHING

Key Technologies, Practical Applications and Security of IoT

Hang Song

National University of Defence Technology, China

清華大學出版社
TSINGHUA UNIVERSITY PRESS

World Scientific

Published by

World Scientific Publishing Co. Pte. Ltd.
5 Toh Tuck Link, Singapore 596224
USA office: 27 Warren Street, Suite 401-402, Hackensack, NJ 07601
UK office: 57 Shelton Street, Covent Garden, London WC2H 9HE

Library of Congress Cataloging-in-Publication Data
Names: Song, Hang (Computer scientist), author.
Title: Internet of everything : key technologies, practical applications and security of IoT / Hang Song, National University of Defence Technology, China.
Description: Tuck Link, Singapore ; Hackensack, NJ : World Scientific Publishing Co. Pte. Ltd, [2023] | Includes bibliographical references and index.
Identifiers: LCCN 2021046879 | ISBN 9789811246265 (hardcover) | ISBN 9789811246272 (ebook for institutions) | ISBN 9789811246289 (ebook for individuals)
Subjects: LCSH: Internet of things.
Classification: LCC TK5105.8857 .S68 2023 | DDC 004.67/8--dc23/eng/20211115
LC record available at https://lccn.loc.gov/2021046879

British Library Cataloguing-in-Publication Data
A catalogue record for this book is available from the British Library.

For any available supplementary material, please visit
https://www.worldscientific.com/worldscibooks/10.1142/12526#t=suppl

Desk Editors: Balasubramanian Shanmugam/Steven Patt

Typeset by Stallion Press
Email: enquiries@stallionpress.com

For my parents

Foreword by Yi Pan

The Internet of Things (IoT) is an inseparable part of our lives. IoT can dramatically improve medical efficiency, healthcare, education, energy, security, and many other aspects of the daily life of consumers; IoT solutions can improve decision-making and the productivity in retail, service (pre-/after-sale), logistics, and other sectors for enterprises. Cloud/Edge with virtualized storage media by way of IoT platforms, enables data storage, data analysis via machine learning and artificial intelligence techniques, and provides facilities for multiple stakeholders, including users/providers/integrators in the generalized or specific platforms. As for smart manufacturing and Industrial 4.0, the advances of IoT practice and application delivering real-time services further push forward the development in automation, management and super connectivity, which is essential for the evolution of industries, new commercial models, and in all aspects of everyday life. Now is it is the moment for us to get to know and go deeper into the IoT world.

Perhaps you can find a pile of books on IoT, yet few of them provide easy accessibility, comprehensible description of a developmental vision for the connected world in a constructive way, the layered technical architecture and the basic building blocks necessary to turn the vision into reality. However, this book goes beyond those fundamentals to share specific examples of layers of perception, communication & network, platform & service, and the application of IoT. Through his practices over the past 10 years, the author has published two related books on IoT before this one. The recent Chinese book, *IoE: Core Technology and Security of IoT*, has attracted the attention of tens of thousands of readers since its publication in 2019. So far, this book has had seven consecutive reprints in China. The author takes it as his imminent mission to launch another masterpiece for readers worldwide, with new ideas, new concepts, new technologies, new modalities, and new practices of the IoT world.

The technical descriptions, which begin with the layered architecture and progress deeper through the book chapter by chapter, aim to make the IoT and its technical specifications of it easily understandable. For a student, a researcher, or an engineer working with IoT, it is expected that the book will provide a good technical introduction to the framework, understanding and applications of IoT. It should serve as a complement to the IoT specifications, and provide a background and an explanation for both "know-why" and "know-how" in the design and practice when developing these technologies.

Finally, in the Internet of Everything era, we still have a long way to go in optimizing the industrial processes and progress toward a symbiotic, collaborative, and secured economy (especially in the post-pandemic era). Fortunately, the technologies, infrastructures, multi-sectors, and new models of IoT, together with the upgrading distributed cloud/edge infrastructure, allow resource sharing by means of perception, network, computing, memory, and analytics capabilities, and bring forth more opportunities as well as challenges.

Yi Pan
Dean and Chair Professor, Shenzhen Institute of Advanced Technology, Chinese Academy of Sciences, China;
Regents' Professor Emeritus Georgia State University, USA;
and
Fellow of American Institute for Medical and Biological Engineering (AIMBE), Institute of Engineering Technology (IET) and Royal Society for Public Health (RSPH)

Foreword by Jeng-Shyang Pan

This book gives a generic description of the technologies of IoT, summarizes the new structural IoT trends from a layered vision, and discusses the security issues of the state-of-the-art IoT systems. We are stepping into the new digitalization era, i.e., the IoE (Internet of Everything) era. The advances of autonomous IoT applications delivering services in real-time encompass development in numerous sensors in mobile devices, communication infrastructure, machine-to-machine (M2M), and smart applications have connected us to IoT technologies, which affect us most for the rapid evolution of industrial (enterprises) aspects, commercial aspects and every corner of our daily work and life.

With over 10 years research and practice of IoT, the author has authored two IoT-related books in China, which have won tens of thousands of readers. The favorable comment rate of his recent Chinese book *IoE: Core Technology and Security of IoT* (published in 2019) @ Dangdang.com is 99.9% currently. So this book continues his introspection on the recent technical trends in order to cater to more readers around the world, including e.g., the rise of 5G, Industrial IoT, digital twins and Tactile IoT. Tactile Internet integrated into the diversity of IoT platforms as fully interactive elements embedded into the optimization and application environment, as well as the embedment of AI/Machine Learning techniques and methods, enhances the accuracy and performance of models in the various IoT solutions and Industrial 4.0 applications.

Finally, the book is among the best IoT tutorial books available in the market and it is worth reading. Since building blocks of IoT are available today, when they can not only be developed and deployed for the benefit of society and industry, but also serve us at length in our daily lives, the challenge now is to educate people, including you and me.

Jeng-Shyang Pan
Professor of Shandong University of Science and Technology
and
Special Expert of the 5th National Thousand Talents Program of China

Preface

At one side, the new times is calling for new information and communication technology, in ubiquitously perceiving and expressing the real world over the super networked world, at the other side, there are rich of data, information and services from the virtual representation world in catering to realize their value for things, devices, you and me. The so called legacy digital gap between them needs the bridging and upgrading technology to unite both as integration.

The Internet of things (IoT) emerges as the times required, and it gives us a refreshing landscape throughout our daily lives, from working to consuming, and every aspect of IoT is trying to make our lives more convenient and our jobs more efficient. After the Internet, it is another important technological innovation and application innovation, which bring profound convenience, and at the same time, as a changer of the rules of the game, especially in the post-epidemic era.

Worldwide, at the end of 2019, there were 7.6 billion active IoT devices, a figure which is expected to grow to 24.1 billion in 2030, a compound annual growth rate (CAGR) of 11%, according to the research published by Transforma Insights. These devices range from digital TV, air conditioner, refrigerator, washing machine, tablets, mobile phones/handsets and those devices can be identified, monitored and controlled in industrial IoT.

This attracts the number of new players and partners to join the field and contribute to manifest and extend the IoT. Business interest and novel ideas drive now the deployment. For example, new products and services in selected IoT sector such as Industrial IoT (IIoT), and the existence of open platforms across vertical silos, helping developers' communities to innovate and not causing lock-in situations for users. Another example of new technology driven IoT is edge computing. According to IDC's worldwide IT predictions for 2021, COVID-19's impact on workforce and operational practices will be the dominant accelerator for 80% of edge-driven investments and business model change across most industries. This exposes more opportunities for industry-related as IIoT and V2X(Vehicle to everything) applications (e.g., real-time) and services are moving the developments toward the edge and, as a consequence, most of IoT data generated and processed by enterprises will exist at the edge rather than in the traditional centralized data center in the cloud.

Besides this, versatile IoT of protocols, architectures, and implementations in various platforms, applications and sectors, together with technologies and solutions are introduced in this book. The book also covered developments stemming from new market demands in systems, products, and technologies such as personal communications services, RFID and WSN (wireless sensor network) systems, enterprise networks, M2M/Satellite communications, and 5G.

Nowadays, artificial intelligence (AI) or machine learning (ML) is playing a more and more important role, with advances in edge computing processing/analyzing, new sensing capabilities and autonomous functions accelerating progress towards the ability to self-develop, self-maintain and self-optimize. According to the statistics in 2019, 5% of global organizations have fully adopted Artificial Intelligence/Machine Learning, and the penetration is expected to increase rapidly before 2025. This book also introduces AI/ML crossing each chapter, such as perception technology in IoT senses, AR/VR and location awareness of Chapter 4, ML as a service of 5G infrastructure in Chapter 5 and so on.

This book provides a systematic and high-level analysis for anyone wishing to learn about the state-of-art of IoT today. When the first book of the author was being written around 2012–2013, the concepts of IoT was competing for fame in the world and a piece of the market. In the "old" book the author gave the IoT Grid and IoT 2.0 as new words that time, which were opened in Baidu encyclopedia on-line.

When the second book of the author was written in 2018, which has been printed for seven times so far and attracted the attention of tens of thousands of readers (with high favorable comment rate reaching 99.9% in Dangdang.com), "things" changed dramatically, together with the rapid development of IoT. The public attention was transferred from "pieces" of

IoT, such as Wireless Sensor Networks, RFID, and M2M, to the whole. Small market segment grew up and integrated into IoT sectors, and pieces of technologies including perception, communication, service and platform, and application are united into addressing solutions for reaching each corner of IoT.

Along with the embarking on this book in 2020, more enabling technologies emerged in large numbers affecting or pushing IoT upgrading, such as Edge/Fog, AI/ML, Big data, LPWAN, 5G, IIoT, TIoT, IoV/V2X, automated driving, WiFi6 etc. All the aspects (included in the book) extended IoT vertically and horizontally, into a new words or a new times-Internet of everything (IoE) era. The rapid development of IoT and the expanding progress of use cases amazed us and draw more interest of academic research, analyst and practiser. Even some of them began to re-consider what IoT is on earth or what it should be. The question leads us into the first three chapters of this book. From the Chapters 4 to 7, we begin to explore IoT according to its natural layered architecture, i.e., technologies of perceptual layer, communication and networking layer, service and platform layer, and application layer.

"Rome was not built in a day". Today we do no longer question what IoT covers or not, but more what benefits and solutions it can bring and what still needs to be done for a full blossom. So open the book and find what we need step by step, and page by page.

Hang Song

About the Author

Dr. Hang Song is a chief scientist on the Industrial IoT of Nanjing Qiyuan Information Technology Inc. and an expert of the Shenzhen Internet of Things Industry Association (SZIOT).

He has worked as a postdoctoral researcher at NUDT (the National University of Defense Technology, China) and as a project scientist on the automated driving project in a Fortune 500 company.

He is also a special advisor of the "YUTU Forum" (held by the Henan Provincial Library of China), where he contributes more to the science and technology popularization of the Internet of Things (which has been reported by mainstream newspapers and magazines many times, such as *Henan Daily*), and has served in many conferences as keynote speaker as well as presented session talks internationally.

With about 20 years' research and practice of IoT, the projects he has devoted to are funded by the Postdoctoral fund of China and ICT enterprises. He has authored over 40 papers, and two IoT-related books. The recent book has attracted tens of thousands of readers since it was published in 2019. His research area includes Internet of Things, Industrial IoT, V2X, Cloud/Edge Computing, Wireless Sensor Network (WSN), 5G/6G, IoT security and reinforcement learning.

He has enjoyed special allowance for scientific and technological personnel, and also been awarded the outstanding professional and technical personnel by the ministries and commissions of China twice. Projects that he devoted to have obtained the First, Second and Third Provincial and Ministerial Awards for Science and Technology Progress, respectively, and one of them has obtained the Second Award for National Technological Invention of China.

Acknowledgments

I would like to gratefully thank Academician Binxing Fang, and Academician Yi Pan for their support in the planning and preparation of this book.

I would like to acknowledge the suggestion of Professor Xin Xu, Professor Chunhua Zhang, Dr. Zhaozhi Li. Dr. Haitao Liu, Dr. Jiangyuan Zhu, and Yuncheng Jiang for their constructive advice in Sections 7.3, 5.6 and 3.7, respectively, and many of my colleagues at NUDT or across industry and academia, as well as Balasubramanian Shanmugam, who is the copyeditor of this book.

This is a new book and some idea is accumulated from another my book *IoE: Core technology and Security of IoT* published in 2019. In addition to the acknowledgments in that book, I would also like to thank Academician Binxing Fang, for his continuous direction in my writing, the Postdoctoral fund of China, and the editor Jian Qin of Tsinghua Press.

I would also like to thank my readers of the previously published two IoT related books for their support that made this book possible. Ten of thousands readers and numerous favorite comments encourage me writing days by days and months by months.

I would also like to acknowledge my colleagues or friends for many good discussions, in particular: Yalan Mi, Zhe Zhao, Jing Dang, Hehong Li, Yuniang Cai (Jade), Dr. Tao Hu, Shuang Deng, and Hongqiao Li, as well as Xiaoming Bian, Wei Zhao and Weiguo Zhong.

I would also like to thank my families as writing this book would not have been possible without their generosity and support throughout this process.

I would also like to thank the China Postdoctoral Science Foundation funded project 4246z3.

This book has quoted a lot of the latest information, newspaper reports and literatures on the Internet all over the world. I would like to thank the original author and the publishing organization, especially when some of them may not specify the source of the quotation in details.

Hang Song

Contents

Chapter 1

What is IoT on Earth

"While embarking on a journey, the first step is important". — translation of the Chinese saying *"千里之行, 始于足下"*.

This chapter is a beginning for us to take a glance at Internet of Things (IoT) and start to think about what IoT on earth is.

1.1 Smart Coffee Pot

In 1991, when the scientists at the Troy Computer Laboratory of Cambridge University were working, they went downstairs to see if the coffee was ready in the pot but often returned empty-handed, which annoyed the scientists. To solve this problem, they installed a portable camera next to the coffee pot. The camera was aimed at the coffee pot, and the images were transmitted to the laboratory computer at a rate of three frames per second to enable the staff to see if the coffee was ready at any time, as shown in Fig. 1.1.

In 1993, this simple local "coffee observation" system was connected to the Internet via the laboratory website. Dramatically, a lot of Internet users around the world flocked to the coffee pot site just to see if the coffee was ready or not. In addition, tens of thousands of emails poured into the Cambridge University Travel Office, hoping to get a chance to see the magic coffee pot personally. The most dramatic result was that the coffee pot, which was under watch around the world and famous for the network, was finally sold at a high price on a certain auction site. Following the

Figure 1.1 Schematic diagram of coffee pot and remote monitor.

same thought, I wish such an IoT kindergarten should be built, and parents could see the status of their child in the kindergarten using their smart phones at any time or remind the teacher through the behavior of the child that "my baby wants to go to the toilet". Of course, it can also be used for the aged or in a gerocomium. If the electronic tag is embedded in the sole (e.g., in the "anti-losing" shoes), he or she can be prevented from getting lost, which extends the usage as a wearable device.

Auto vending machines or other automatic facilities were usually described as IoT devices or machines in the original era of IoT.

Whether the coffee is ready or not will become inadequate in the coming Internet of everything (IoE) era. For example, a cup of coffee from a heated vending machine may be sold at a supermarket, library/restaurant, or even online. An IoT solution, however, will be used to create new information or knowledge within a corporate environment — the service scope examples include more detailed scheduling of maintenance based on real-world information, and in particular, the coffee taste changing every two weeks and its impact on the sales (for details, see a use case of the artificial taste system in Section 4.4 of Chapter 4) and improved taste/product design due to feedback from the IoT after sales. As to the auto-coffee seller, tracking each user's taste buds (by crowdsourcing taste) and supplying improvement for an individual or a group is an IoE way of thinking.

1.2 Implanted Tags

One of the 007 films, "Casino Royale" (2006) shows a scene: Mrs. M asked someone to plant an electronic chip in the arm of 007 (Bond) by using a big implanting tool which looks like an impact drill, then an identity tag was embedded in the chip (for ID verification later).

"You want to spy on me?" said 007, Mrs. M calmly replied, "Yes". But thanks to the chip (in the following story), which is used to identify and position Bond through sending the SOS message during an emergency, Bond is saved.

This electronic chip is a radio frequency tag that can be connected anywhere and anytime (as the story in the film demonstrates), but in real life, people do not need to be embedded but just need to carry the chips with them, such as identity cards (e.g., Chinese ID of Generation 2), bus (subway) smart cards/zone cards, access cards, and a variety of paying tools that support Radio Frequency Identification (RFID) or Near Field Communication (NFC). When ID cards can be stored electronically in smart phones, people can go outside just with their phones. The tags or labels can not only be "implanted", they are widely used in commodities, such as the bar code in supermarket goods (Fig. 1.2), the identity of the author's book and the publisher website ID (see Fig. 1.2), and the two-dimensional code of the train ticket. Among them, the two-dimensional (QR) code can not only represent a commodity or a shopping mall, which can be physical or virtual, but also can be used for marking a person, such as a two-dimensional ID code in WeChat apps. Now, the two-dimension code can be used for the payment of taxi, shopping, etc. Of course, the implementation of the tag function can also occur in a whole set of systems and devices, such as in a GPS positioning system. That is, attaching a location ID to the device equipped with the positioning chip (by the map service apps of a smart phone, and the position information may be shown as a set of longitude, latitude, etc.).

Now, in China, the arrival of the electronic train ticket offers the travelers great convenience. After buying the train ticket (by the seller apps or website), we only need to download the ticket QR code to the smart phone, which avoids the trouble of picking up tickets at the railway station. More convenience in the Metro station of Zhengzhou city of China is available by means of face-recognition system. Of course, you can just stand and then pass through the gate of the access control system (ACS) of the Metro.

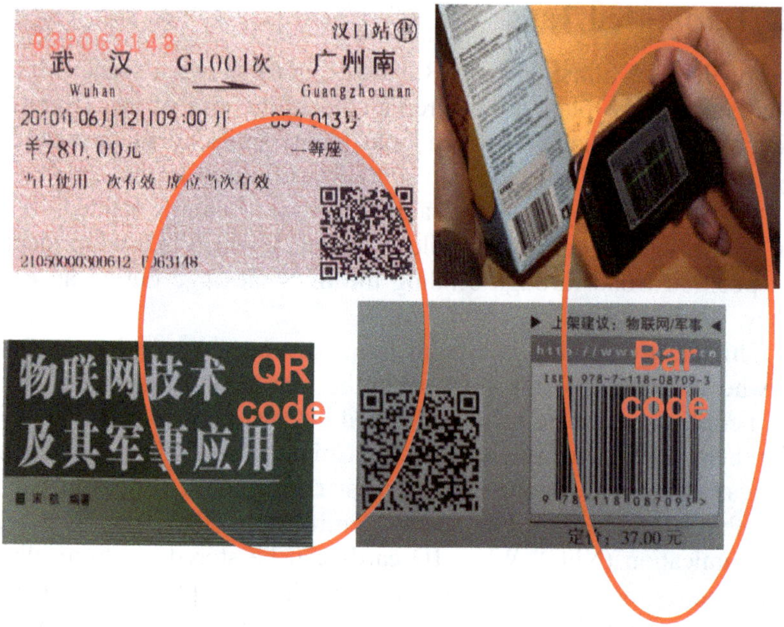

Figure 1.2 Bar code and two-dimension (QR) code.

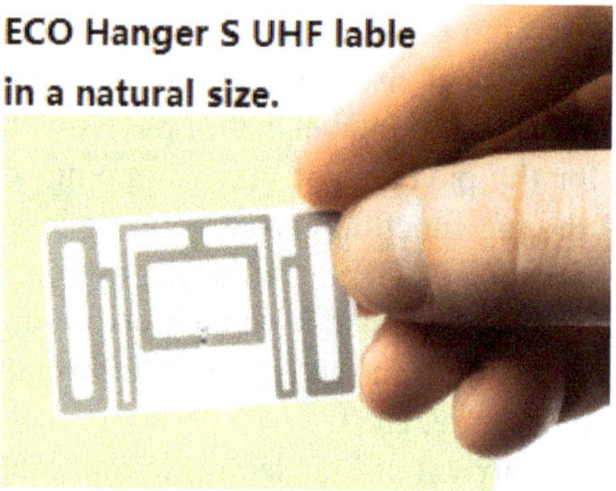

Figure 1.3 Paper stuff tag.

Figure 1.3 shows mini-size labels, such as ECO RFID (tags technology by Stora Enso) tags for trademark or cloth ID, and even tags that can be implanted in tablets (developed by Motorola company).

Electronic tattoos, made up of ultra-thin electrodes, electronic components, sensors, wireless power supplies, and communication systems, can measure the wearer's heart rate, blood pressure, skin temperature (tension), and other data, helping professionals to track the wearer's health indicators (wound healing, etc.). The corresponding "small capsule" of subcutaneous RFID chip is 12 mm long and 2 mm in diameter. It is made of SCHOTT 8625 glass with biological adaptability. Its built-in communication chip can combine NFC communication and RFID well together. At the same time, it also supports ISO14443A protocol of RFID for data transmission, which can be used in the ACS, e.g., in a car.

1.3 Electronic Toll Collection

Electronic toll collection (ETC) aims to eliminate the delay on expressway (or toll lanes, bridges, and tunnels) by collecting user fee electronically. ETC determines whether the passing vehicle is enrolled in the system back-end program, electronically debits the accounts of registered vehicle owners, and opens the gates automatically without requiring them to stop and manually pay the toll with cash or a card.

In most ETC wireless systems, vehicles using the system are equipped with an automated radio transponder device. When the vehicle passes a roadside toll reader device (sometimes integrated into a Road Side Unit, RSU), a radio signal from the reader triggers the transponder, which transmits back an identifying number which registers the vehicle's use of the road, and an electronic payment system, which requires users to sign up in advance and load money into a declining-balance account, charges the user the toll each time they pass a toll point (see Fig. 1.4).

The ease of varying the amount of the toll makes it easy to implement road congestion pricing, including for high-occupancy lanes, toll lanes that bypass congestion, and city-wide congestion charges.

Vehicles without transponders are either excluded or pay by plate — a license plate reader takes a picture of the license plate to identify the vehicle, and a bill may be mailed to the address to which the car's license plate number is registered, or drivers may have a certain amount of time to pay online or by phone.

The "Double-chip type ETC electronic tag"[1] independently designed ETC system by the Chinese has won the second prize of the National Science and Technology Progress Award in 2014. The vehicle identity

[1]This refers to the vehicle recognition ID and user information stored in two chips. For example, a microwave RFID card and a pre-bound IC card relative to bank account. The ETC system is popular in China for improving traffic efficiency.

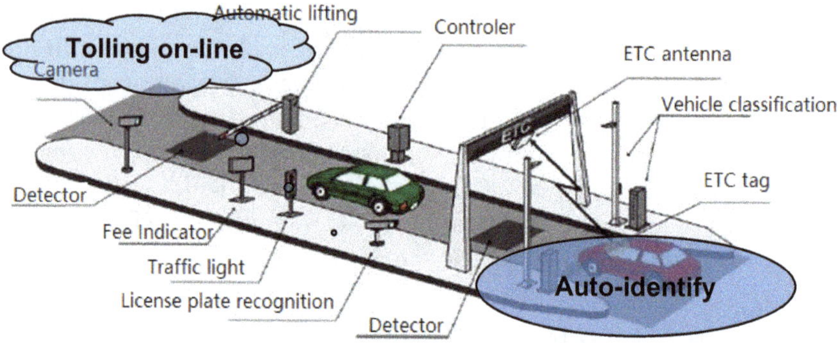

Figure 1.4 Schematic diagram of ETC traffic.

management and the integration of the road electronic toll subscriber card can realize the automatic check of the vehicle information by the toll gate management system when the vehicle enters the ETC range, which may enable entry to the vehicle network.

1.4 Enlightens

Through the above examples, let's think step by step, as shown in Table 1.1.

Following the "Things" column in Table 1.1, we extend the object of the Things to make it smart enough to communicate with us through tagging, embedding, high-speed connection (wired/wireless) technology, and so on.

Following the column of "net" in Table 1.1, we need to upgrade the net so that the network can become a tool for carrying and exchanging information, translating meaning or expression between people and things, with the protocols as communicable language even between different species.

"Contact/contactless" communication extends to combine intelligent identification, positioning, tracking, monitoring, and management of everything into a ubiquitous network. In short, in the IoT, things can communicate with us, e.g., Question: Is coffee ready? Coffee pot can answer: Ready.

In this way, we can unravel the mystery of the IoT and understand it as a technical system that allows us to communicate with things. By

Table 1.1 Progressive analysis of the concept of IoT.

Examples	Things	Networks	Communication	Key technology	Extended application
A smart coffee pot	Coffee pot	Laboratory network, Internet	Net observes whether the coffee is ready or not	Video sensors (smart sensors, such as thermometer)	Smart home/household, surveillance robot
Embedded tags	Bond is treated as a labeled "object" by Mrs. M	Ubiquitous network of intelligence agencies	Label signals the headquarters about Bond's critical situation through the intelligence network, and the headquarters allows nearby people to rescue through network and positioning	RFID, RFID–tag, GNSS (e.g., GPS)	Disaster search and rescue, commodity management (Walmart), logistics, personal management
ETC system	Vehicles, toll gates (entrance and exit), banks (online)	Charging system for networked bills and bank networks	Vehicle identification: The vehicle is automatically recognized at the entrance, cost of driving through the exit calculated, and fees are automatically debited through the banking network	Microwave RFID	Anti-fake, supermarket charges, parking lot management, vehicle networking, intelligent transportation
Object extension	Any object or person	Universal network	A universal connection between things	Huge IoT technology groups	Intelligent identification of everything, position, tracking, monitoring, and management

Note: Pay attention to the application extension of key technologies horizontally and enumerate typical application scenarios vertically.

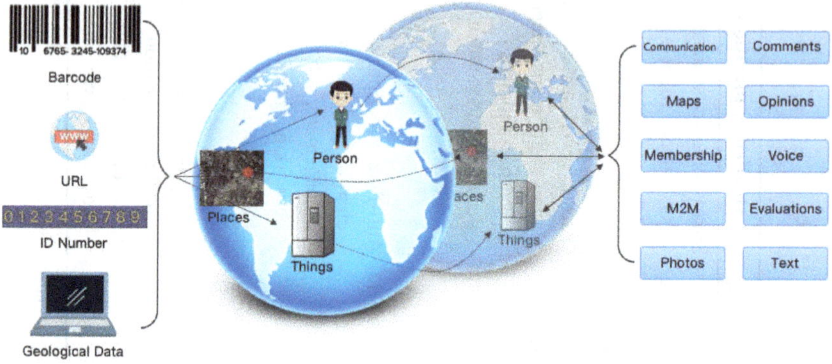

Figure 1.5 Schematic diagram of the IoT, from the IoT to the WoT, then to IoE.
Source: ITU.

implanting a chip or an electronic tag into a variety of daily supplies, loading the GNSS positioning system, or sensing the state of the surroundings by a sensor such as a camera, the human can acquire a new communication dimension in the information and communication world, in which the communication connection among people is extended to the interconnection between the person and things, and between things and things at any place with a rich set of applications, as shown in Fig. 1.5.

If each physical entity can be part of the IoT after it is marked in the real world and become a part of the virtual world by virtual representation, the integration of the physical world with the virtual world offers opportunities to enable ubiquitous computing applications and pervasive Web Service (or Web of Things (WoT)), as shown in Fig. 1.5.

Imagine one day in IoE era: When the driver fails to operate, the car will automatically give an alarm, and when the driver does not want to drive, the self-driving car (automated driving) can take us to the destination; a briefcase will remind the master that he forget something; clothes will "tell" the washing machine their requirements for water temperature; air conditioners, refrigerators, and televisions will play their part in communicating with us; frying robots will prepare dinners according to the family's or guests' tastes; drone couriers can deliver goods on our balcony quietly.

People and things in the IoT can coexist in order and harmony, whether working or living, in today's super-connected and super-coordinated world. The concept of the IoT derived from the above examples at an early stage, and the literal meaning of the IoT is: by using RFID, laser scanners, infrared sensors, positioning systems, geographic information systems, and other sensing devices, the interconnection of objects is achieved in the network, then according to the protocols, information exchanging, and communication over the network, the smart management of objects, positioning, identification, monitoring, tracking, and other functions and service are realized by the integration of the physical world with the virtual world.

Chapter 2

Development of Internet of Things

Life —

A net.

Zhenkai Zhao

Chapter 1 was just a preparation for us to find the door of the Internet of things (IoT) world and to imagine what awaits us in an IoT world. This chapter introduces the development of IoT as we step into the IoT world and into the Internet of Everything (IoE) era. Some scenarios and imagination will help us "merge" into the facilities of IoT. As comprehensive, developmental, and social views are analyzed in this chapter, we may transfer easily to the following chapter, where temporal, architectural, and technical descriptions of IoT will be given.

The rapid development of the IoT has brought about a new generation of devices and services in smart metering, smart buildings, environmental monitoring, in each aspect of our life, in every corner around us. Over the past years (after 2017, according to *Gartner IoT Forecast* in 2017), more than 5 million new devices have been connected to and integrated into our daily lives. Since the birth of the Internet, these rapidly upgrading devices and services have indicated that a new era of IoT which brings us more innovation and progress that serves as the symbol of a new epoch — IoE — is coming.

The network technology, represented by the Internet, mobile Internet, and the new-generation 5G cellular communication network, is a great achievement of information and communication technology (ICT) in the 21st century, which has brought about profound changes in various fields. With a more powerful network and richer information, the number of IoT-connected devices installed worldwide is increasing exponentially, and it is expected to reach 24.6 billion in 2025, including 19.1 billion short-range IoT connections and 5.5 billion wide-area connections (Ericsson Mobility Report, 2020; Ticlo, 2017).

IoT is an upgrading technology based on the rapid development of technology and the ubiquitous network coverage. It combines the technology of sensing, network technology, and various kinds of applications which subvert human thinking. The IoT, with its strong vitality, "induced" governments and enterprises around the world to pay full attention and give the soil for its growth.

Whether you are ready or not, the era of the IoE has come!

2.1 Formation of IoT Concepts

In the spring of 1998, Professor Kevin Ashton, working in the Auto-ID[1] Center of the Massachusetts Institute of Technology, put forward the concept[2] of IoT during a public speech. The "things" began to refer to various objects/devices, such as power meters, railways, bridges, tunnels, highways, buildings, water supply systems, dams, oil and gas pipelines, and other city facilities equipped with radio frequency identification (RFID), GPS/GNSS, QR code (one- or two-dimensional), and other sensors.

Through the connected devices, remote control or communication between things and human can be realized; then, the "dialogue" between people (e.g., an operator or a smart device user) and objects can be achieved via bi-directional communication, which provided data,

---

[1] The Auto-ID Center was renamed as Auto-ID Lab on November 1, 2003, providing technical support for EPC global. The purpose of the EPC global is to build a global network that can automatically identify anything with RF-tags in an open global network, i.e., the "IoT" prototype we mentioned earlier.

[2] With regard to the origin of the IoT, there is another claim that originates from online vending machines: In 1990, on the campus of Carnegie Mellon University, there were a group of programmers who used to buy an iced coke from the coke vending machine downstairs every time they knocked on the code, but often they had to face empty machines with coke sell-out. So, they connected the vending machine downstairs to the Internet and wrote a code to monitor how many cokes there were. This is very similar to the smart coffee pot in the previous article.

information, and service to us. Gradually, more and more devices and services are linked to buildings, transportations, public infrastructures, industries, commercials, and our society.

The actual term "IoT" coined by Ashton during his study of RFID was initially envisioned for supply-chain optimization. By aggregating data information from one-item RFID tags, we can track and count all items. He believed that the IoT has great potential to change the world. At that time, the concept of the IoT was limited to RFID and sensor networks.

In 2005, the International Telecommunication Union (ITU) held the World Summit on the Information Society in Tunis and released "ITU Internet Report 2005: The IoT", in which the IoT is described as follows:

Through embedding short-range mobile transceivers into a wide array of additional gadgets and everyday items, enabling new forms of communication between people and things, and between things themselves, a new dimension has been added to the world of information and communication technologies (ICTs): at any time, any place, for anyone, we will now have connectivity for anything (ITU Report, 2015).

In 2008, "IoT in 2020" (EU report) defined "things" of IoT as "having identities and virtual personalities, operating in smart spaces, using intelligent interfaces to connect and communicate within social, environmental, and user contexts". A different definition that puts the focus on the seamless integration could be formulated as "Interconnected objects having an active role in what might be called the Future Internet".

In 2009, IBM introduced the "Smart Planet" strategy, which outlined the premise of a smarter planet and the coming of age of a whole new generation of intelligent systems and technologies — more powerful and accessible than ever before. After that, the IoT solutions in various fields gradually became abundant, including smarter power grids, smarter food systems, and smarter water, healthcare, and traffic systems, as shown in Fig. 2.1.

In China, in the 2010 government work report, the IoT was interpreted as a kind of network which connected many items with the Internet according to the technologies and protocols through information sensing devices, information exchange, and communication in order to realize identification, positioning, tracking, monitoring, and management. IoT was an extended network on the basis of the Internet.

Therefore, the concept of IoT gradually developed and improved. China and the European Union have similar definitions for IoT at that time, both of which are characterized by applications, and the IoT is described in combination with specific sectors or applications. As a result,

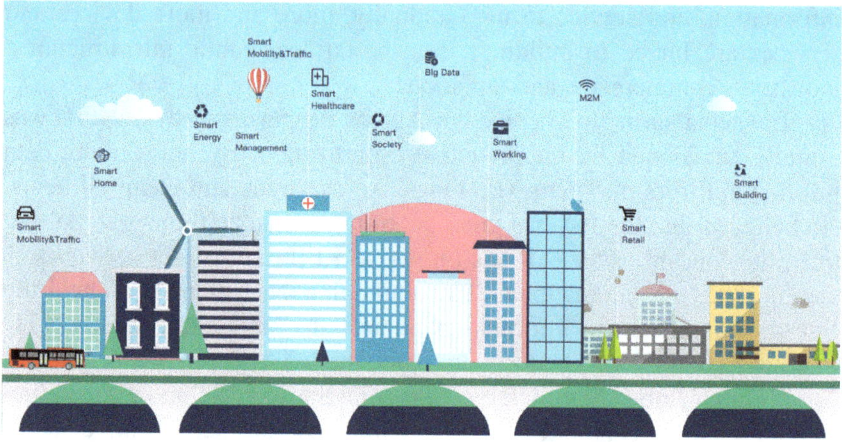

Figure 2.1 Conceptual map of smart earth technology application.

at this early stage, IoT refers to the data exchange paradigm among a large number of wired or wireless devices, sensors, and connected things around us but without much human interference.

By now, some definitions of IoT do not explicitly highlight the industrial IoT (IIoT) enough. Leading companies around the world are giving special attention and making significant investments in the IoT for their industrial solutions (IIoT). Although they use different terms, such as "Smarter Planet" by IBM, "IoE" by Cisco, and "Industrial Internet" by GE, their main objective is to use IoT to improve industrial production by reducing unplanned machine downtime and significantly reducing energy costs along with a number of other potential benefits. The IIoT refers to industrial objects or "things", instrumented with sensors, automatically communicating over a network, without human-to-human or human-to-computer interaction, to exchange information and take intelligent decisions with the support of advanced analytics.

After the first industrial wave represented by computers and the second industrial wave represented by Internet and mobile communication, the IoT is leading the new wave of the information industry, and its broad application prospect has been widely valued by governments all over the world. The IoT industry is booming, and its role in promoting economic development and social progress is gradually emerging. Worldwide, many countries are facing the opportunity and challenge of speeding up the transformation of economic development modes and adjusting the structure of economic growth. As a new industrial force, the IoT, with its great potential reform and development space, is bound to play a huge role in promoting economic transformation.

2.2 IoT and Human Society

2.2.1 *Population and connected devices*

The development trend of the relationship between population size and the number of connected devices is shown in the comparative analysis as in Fig. 2.2.

Figure 2.2 is derived from Cisco's statistical analysis. Cisco argues that the IoT was "born" between 2008 and 2009, when the number of connected devices exceeded the global population for the first time. As shown in Fig. 2.2, as per the forecast at that time, there would be 50 billion IoT devices in 2020, as predicted by Forrester. As shown in Fig. 2.3, by 2025, there will likely be more than 75 billion IoT-connected devices. According to Juniper Research's latest report, the number of IoT devices will reach 46 billion by 2021. But Fig. 2.2 suggests a trend of positive correlation

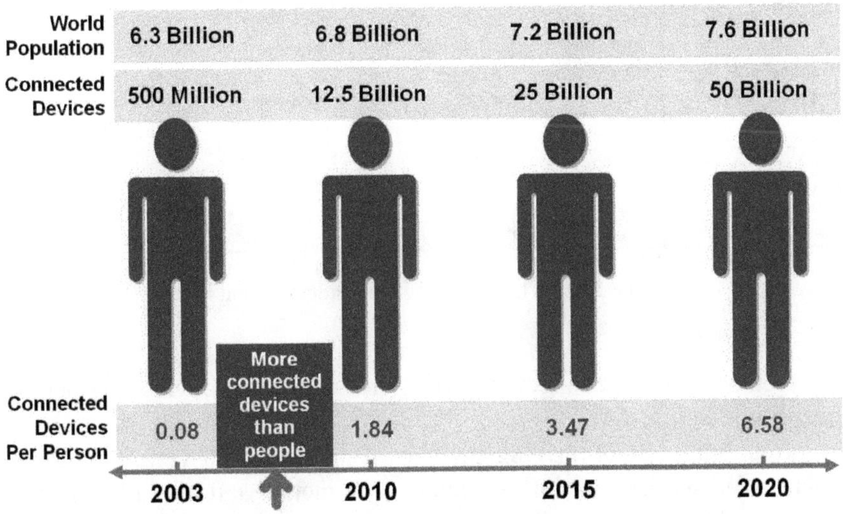

Figure 2.2 Trends in the relationship between population size and the number of connected devices.

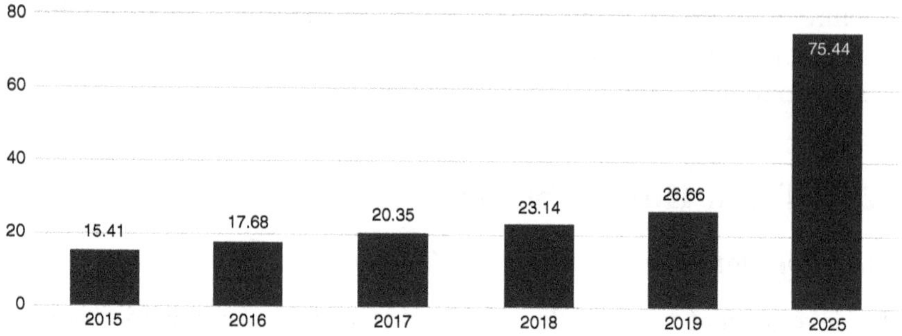

Figure 2.3 Number of IoT-connected devices installed worldwide.

Retail	Consumer and Health	City	Mobility and Transport	Infrastructure and Platform

•E-payments •Customized Media •Wearable •Retail logistics •Location and shopping assistance	•Smart Sensors and identification •Healthcare •Assisted living and fitness •Convenience • Robotics	•Building •Home/Office •Environmental protection and sustainability •Utilities • Energy •Traffic prediction of alleviation	•Logistics and supply chain •Pollution •On- board Unit (OBU) •Vehicle to Everything (V2X) •Intelligent Transportation System (ITS)	•Socioeconomics •Roads and Road side Unit (RSU) •Information Service Provider (ISP) •Metering •Industrial and optimised operation •Dangerous prediction and alarm

Figure 2.4 IoT is changing our production and life.

between population, connected devices, and connected devices per person over time.

Today, the IoT is thriving. As shown in Fig. 2.4, a variety of smart devices and services are influencing our production and life in companies (e.g., media, information, and ISPs), retail, cities, and healthcare. Figure 2.4 highlights the tight relationship between IoT and you and me, as customers, users, and citizens.

The emergence of the IoT not only contributed to the integration and development of contemporary high-tech cross-domain technologies but also gave humans a new vision for the harmonious development between nature and society. With regard to some comments about "IoT: Technology and Military Applications" (another book of the author) in Amazon, viewpoints of readers are shared as follows:

> The emergence of "IoT" in the new stage of scientific and technological development is not an accidental series of inventions and creations, but a choice of history, a necessity for the development of science and technology and the progress of human civilization. It's a historical opportunity for human beings to re-examine and reflect on the concept of harmony between people and things, social development and natural environment.
>
> — IoT enthusiasts on July 3, 2013

Another viewpoint is as follows:

> The book tells us by thinking about the transformation forces that the IoT is generating for human society as a new generation of information technology: the "IoT" that emerged when science and technology developed to a new stage. It is not a series of accidental inventions, it is the choice of history, it is the necessity of the development of science and technology and the progress of human civilization. It's a historical opportunity for human beings to re-examine and reflect on the concept of harmony between people and things, social development and natural environment. The concept of "IoT grid" is the description of the current development of the IoT!
>
> — Anonymous

These book reviews made the author consider "things", and the Chinese traditional saying, "the unity of nature and man and the mutual understanding between things and me" is enlightenment to us:

The ultimate goal of the development of the IoT is to realize the high integration and scientific planning of natural resources and social resources in the harmonious coexistence and friendly harmony between nature and society and to realize fine social management through scientific prediction, judgment, and analysis.

2.2.2 *Reflection on the unity of nature and human*

From the perspective of the development history of the thought of the relationship between man and nature, the thought of man and nature as unity has always been the mainstream in China. In the pre-Qin period of China, philosophers regarded nature (Tian), Tao, Tai Chi, and so on as the origin of all existence.

Neo-Confucianism in the Song and Ming Dynasties regarded "reason" (or Lee in Chinese) as the logical starting point of the unity of man and nature, and then, "the unity of nature and man, the mutual understanding between things and me" referred to the relationship between man and nature, which further extended the relationship between man and nature to the relationship between an individual and group in society.

In primitive societies, human beings survived passively, constantly trying to create means of production, adapting to nature under the drive of survival instinct, and their life was very short.

The communication between people is realized through simple codes, and the struggle between man and nature condition is very hard. At that time, man was incapable of changing the natural world, and every human being existed to maintain the continuity of life. In the game of man and nature, although human beings are obviously at a disadvantage, they possess the subjective ability to transform nature in the game. Man began to explore how to impose his will on nature for his own survival.

In feudal societies, human beings gradually mastered the laws of nature, e.g., using "slash-and-burn agriculture" in farming, explored "right place, right time" over the four seasons for knowing how to plant, and developed traditional agriculture. Agriculture can be regarded as "the first step in the game of man and nature", but also let human beings understand the principle of "leaving the green mountains in, no worry about burning firewood" as a small step from absolute obedience to nature to active adaptation to nature.

At this time, the relationship between man and nature belongs to the understanding of natural law, and the initial agriculture and animal husbandry have no ability to change the characteristics of natural law. With the increase in population, humans are becoming more and more dynamic in their interactions with nature. The advent of the era of fire farming and the era of large-scale animal husbandry made people acquire a certain degree of initiative over nature so that man has the ability to change the objective existence of nature across a wider range. At this time, classical oriental philosophy such as "humanity, justice, etiquette, wisdom, and faith" regulates the behavior of oriental human beings.

"If somebody has enough money, then he will think of honor and shame, if he has plenty food and clothes, he will consider what should be done and what should not be done with courtesy and etiquette".[3] The practical idea of "drain the pond to get all the fish" reflects the improvement of human cognition of nature. However, from the perspective of time axis, this cognition is restricted by a relatively short time cycle, which is in the order of magnitude of individual life time.

After entering the modern society, the great development of science and technology has gradually become an important force to change the human society and nature. With the increase in population, human beings have established the dominant position on Earth. The level of human productivity has been increasing. The arrival of the colonial era and the use of mineral resources began to change the balance between man and nature, and human beings began to transform the original being of nature with great ability. The industrial revolution and the birth of the capitalist system have made a qualitative leap in the ability of human beings to transform nature. Einstein's theory of relativity broke the upper limit of the human cognition of space–time, and it is possible for humans to try to reflect on the current social process at some point in time. Finally, the consistency and compatibility of human and nature are likely to be reflected in a longer historical cycle.

2.2.3 *IoT and sustainable development*

"Transformation" is a double-edged sword,[4] which gives us what we want and what we never desire. When human beings begin to transform nature according to their own will, they are doomed to be punished. Now the problem of environmental pollution and excessive transformation make human beings in their own "sole city" sadly look up at the sky (haze) and bow their head watching a pit (e.g., excessive mining underground).

---

[3]Chinese traditional saying: 仓廪实则知荣辱,衣食足则知礼节.

[4]Science and technology are not double-edged swords, but the transformation of humans using science and technology is a double-edged sword. — Noted by the author. An analogous saying is "Guns don't kill people, people kill people".

Mankind has to face climate change, depletion of resources, and other unavoidable problems. At the end of the 20th century, people of insight, represented by Joe Helen Bruntland, began to find a way for the sustainable development of mankind and began to explore new models of the relationship between man and nature.

In the relationship between human beings and nature, when "transformation" is expected to be replaced with "harmony", when science and technology develop to a new stage, when the Eastern philosophy of "the unity of nature and man" needs reflection again, and when the economic crisis calls for new technology and new ideas, the IoT has emerged. The IoT incorporated "things" into the network and changed the human-centric viewpoint from the original Internet purpose of serving us by sharing and transmitting information.

The emergence of the IoT is not only the result of the development of science and technology but also the result of the progress of human civilization. When it comes to the historical time to re-examine the status of things, it is also necessary to bring things into our era of the network. Respect for nature, equaled by sustainable development, all began with connected "things".

The IoT began to try to give "things" the right to dialogue, even if, in the early stage, human beings still want to control "things", but began to bring "things" into the vision of equality, which reflected the importance of "nature" that should be paid more attention to. "Originally", human and nature should be one. This idea is not fully expressed in Fig. 2.5; it can only be an introduction.

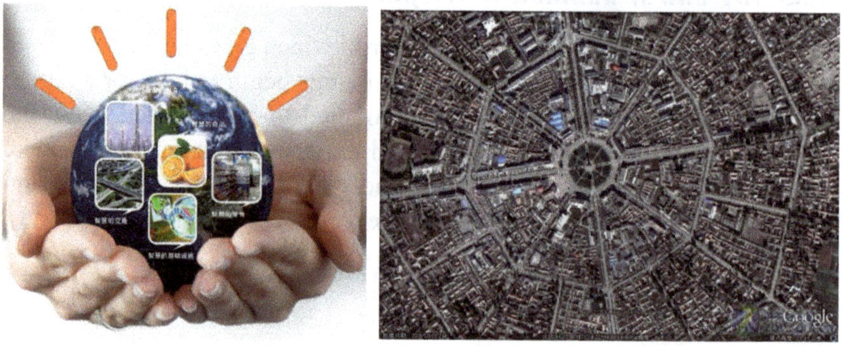

Figure 2.5 The unity of nature and human where things-centered or human-centered, environment-centered, or development-centered systems are treated equally.

Respect the nature not only because we are facing the natural resource constraints, and we need to increasingly do more with less from raw materials to energy, water, or food; but the natural resource is limited and even decreasing if averaged by the growing global population. The global economic growth demands put increasing constraints on the use of resources, including the introduction of regenerative systems as in the circular economy. The use of IoT to increase yields, improve productivity, and decrease loss or waste across global supply chains and consumer chains is therefore escalating.

Looking forward to the IoE era, human and nature are expected to stop gaming and to develop in harmony with mutual respect and double win.

2.3 Definition of the IoT at This Stage

The first definition of the IoT was from a "connectivity-oriented" perspective, where RFID tags were considered as things, with their connectivity to RFID readers/transponders (Atzori *et al.*, 2010). As IoT developed, functionally, the IoT is deemed as physical connectivity-oriented networks, which has threefold meanings: first, the IoT at its early stage is based on the Internet or on the paradigm of the expansion of the networks; second, its communication is extended to cover the information exchange between people and things and between things and things; third, on the basis of the first two points, it can realize the real-time perception and control of the physical world, accurate management, and decision-making assistance.

Figure 2.6(a) illustrates the European research cluster of IoT (IERC) definition, where "The IoT allows people and things to be connected anytime, anyplace, with anything and anyone, ideally using any path/network, and any service"; and data/information/service is provided through their mutual creation, cognition, computation, collecting, connecting, and caching, as shown in Fig. 2.6(b), where the latter/inner six aspects push IoT into its next generation — IoE.

Technically, in the 2016 RFID World Congress, the essence of the IoT is described as follows:

One of the new generations of information technology is highly integrated and deeply applied through the close combination of perceptual ability and information processing ability with the physical world.

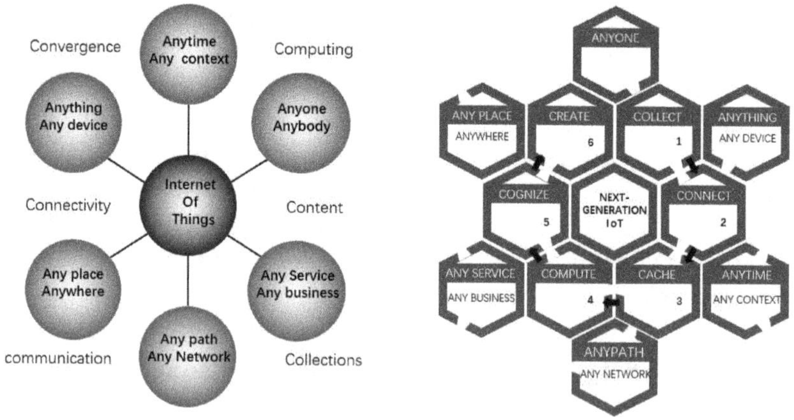

Figure 2.6 IoT vs. IoE. (a) IoT definition by IERC and (b) the enriched IoT definition. *Source*: CERP-IoT.

For the understanding of "thing" in the IoT, "thing" includes not only the electronic devices in our daily lives, such as mobile phones, vehicles, and equipment, but also non-electronic "things" in the traditional sense, such as food, clothing and tents, materials, parts and accessories, landmarks, boundaries, and road tablets. By "embedding", "marking", or "linking", we make it readable, recognizable, localized, addressable, perceptible, and controllable, enabling access to the IoT. In general, the conditions (five basic attributions) for one thing that can be incorporated into the "IoT" are listed as follows:

- **"Language" of things:** Data transmission (receiving/transmitting) for access;
- **Memory of things:** Having a certain storage function (even a barcode as No.);
- **Thinking:** Things have CPUs or others alike for computational process;
- **Communication of things:** There should be an operating system, application, and communication protocol;
- **Name of the object:** There is a unique ID number that can be identified.

The things include fridges, street lamps, buildings, vehicles, production machinery, rehabilitation equipment, and everything else imaginable. Although a "thing" is often referred to as an object equipped with sensors or RFID tags, sensors are not in all cases physically attached to the things.

As discussed in Chapter 1, the evolving things in IoT world include higher or lower capabilities, such as processing speeds, and the higher capabilities allow a multitude of applications to run autonomously. Their respective examples are the ACS of a metro station and the tag or the smart card as the "thing" with less capabilities in Section 1.2. At the early stage, an RFID tag with embedded processing is deemed as a traditional thing of (RF-) IoT.

Nowadays, the emerging things range from devices, marked physical embodies or things with embedded processors, to even a virtual program segment with a name/address/IP/ID (e.g., the agent in a program segment) for easily recognized/location or being aware/controlled of in accessing the IoT by contributing the resources such as flash memory (RAM), embedded processors, I/O capabilities, and networking interfaces. The latter also includes the virtual data/information/command within the things or just an ID with a simple service (e.g., a location tag).

A little different to "things", the definition of "devices" in the IoT vision is also wide and includes a variety of physical elements. These include personal objects we carry around such as smart phones, tablets, and digital cameras. These also include elements in our environments (e.g., home, vehicle, or work), industries (e.g., machines, motor, robot), and things fitted with tags (e.g., RFIDs), which become connected via a gateway device (e.g., a smart phone). Based on this view of devices, an enormous number of connected and heterogeneous devices, as shown in Fig. 2.7, will provide data and information and services in the IoT world.

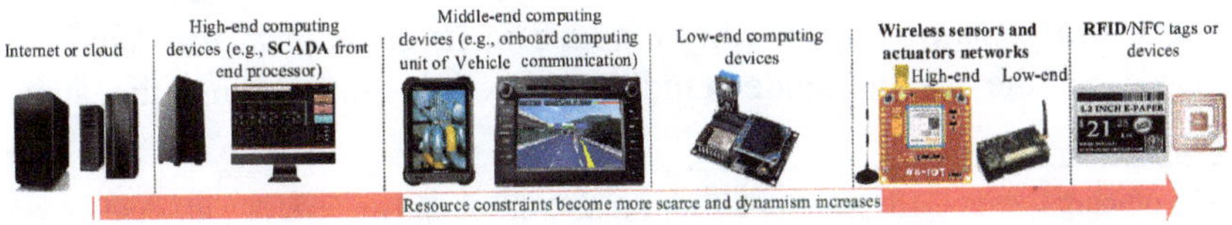

Figure 2.7 Examples of device heterogeneity in IoT.

Typically, a device has an embedded computer and several properties that are listed as the following (Tsiatsis *et al.*, 2018):

- **Computational capability:** Typically, 8-, 16-, or 32-bit microcontrollers[5] with on-chip working memory and storage.
- **Power supply:** Wired, battery, energy harvester, or hybrid.
- **Sensors and/or actuators:** Used to sample an environmental variable and/or exert control (e.g., flicking a switch, tuning a motor).
- **Communications interfaces:** Wireless or wired technologies (such as IEEE 802.15.4, Bluetooth, and Wi-Fi, which are increasingly integrated as tiny system-on-a-chip solutions) are used to connect devices to one another, the Internet/cloud, and remote servers.
- **Operating system (OS):** Main-loop, event-based, real-time, or full-featured OS.
- **User interface:** Display, buttons, or other functions for user interaction.
- **Device management:** Provisioning, firmware, bootstrapping, and monitoring.
- **Execution environment:** Application lifecycle management and application programming interface (API).

As shown in Fig. 2.7, device resource capacity (e.g., computational, connectivity capabilities and memory requirements shown above) decreases, moving from left to right.

From the discussion above, we can see that the understanding of IoT exists as a result of scientific knowledge and research progress in different cognitive relative stages. So, the above is only the definition of the IoT by now. The concept of the IoT is constantly developed and extended in practice.

The author believes that under the advocacy of the Paris Agreement (2018), in the new background of the emergence of the energy Internet, industrial IoT, and other ICTs and from the perspective of development, one of the goals of IoT should be added in its concept at this stage, as "based on the mutual understanding of people and things, the super

[5]The on-chip tiny SoC (System-on-a-Chip) enable the design of devices with small physical footprints of a few mm_2 with very low power consumption, e.g., in the milli- to micro-watt range, but which are capable of hosting complete communication protocol stacks, including small web servers.

connected world of intelligent interaction, and harmonious coexistence, IoT should help us to achieve efficiency improvement and environmental protection and energy sustainability improvement in coordinated development of human and nature".

At the same time, there are inextricable links between the IoT and the Internet, but from a development point of view, understanding IoT needs to grasp its description from the following three aspects.

First, the IoT cannot be simply regarded as an extension of the "network". The IoT is a series of new independent systems based on the developing infrastructure. Of course, the application of the IoT cannot be separated from the network as part of the infrastructure; second, the IoT is brewing (gestation) new business (new demand), with new business (new demand), common development, and improvement; third, the IoT embodies the closed-loop process of "from the physical world, through perceptual technology, network transmission and intelligent application, and finally back to the improved physical world". The ultimate goal is to achieve "the perception of nature and its power of efficient integration, the harmonious coexistence of human and nature, and the fusion and mutual growth between human wisdom and nature wisdom in a sustainable environment."

2.4 Understanding IoE

2.4.1 *IoE pyramid*

In the face of the increasing amount of data needed for human development, the transformation ability for data processing (abstracted in a model or a similar thinking way of human beings) into information has gone beyond the ability of the "human sensory and human brain" in the new IoE era.

Figure 2.8 illustrates the goals of enabling IoT applications with advanced analytics capabilities. Humans cognitive load requires an innovative model to relieve a part of themselves, to share benefits, and to focus on the upper stages of Fig. 2.8, as the sublimation steps from information to knowledge and to wisdom. As shown in Fig. 2.8, the IoT can assist human to process data in the upper process (from data processing/abstracting to information) and then promote information sharing and knowledge accumulation.

From the bottom to the top of the pyramid in Fig. 2.8, layers include data, information, knowledge, and wisdom. Data are processed in the

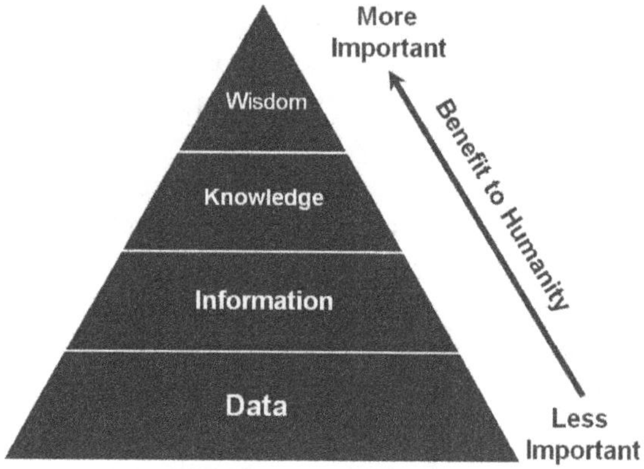

Figure 2.8 Pyramid of Wisdom, where IoT helps humans climb to the top of the pyramid.

form of raw material for information, and separate data are less important by itself, but in an information model or frame, it can identify trends and patterns and provides us information and service after being refined. The accumulating information from one generation to another brings sources to form human knowledge, and wisdom is born from knowledge and experience. Knowledge (more beneficial to mankind than information) changes with time, and wisdom will maybe last forever.

Data economics is an issue in the IoT market because the primary developers (the data level in Fig. 2.8) deploy systems in the field and own the resulting data, and the secondary developers (the information level in Fig. 2.8) are third parties that access the data to create new and innovative applications. Incentives need to be created for the primary owners of data to allow access to and use of the data by secondary developers. Creating and maintaining these incentives over time is potentially a complex technical and business undertaking.

Figure 2.9 shows another upside-down pyramid, including the IoT connection numbers in different stages. From 2010s to 2020s, the IoT greatly increases the amount of data available and the communication ability for connection, which obviously assists people to move toward more wisdom, according to the correlation between direct input (data) and output (wisdom) embodied in the wisdom pyramid of Fig. 2.8. The two pyramids indicated that the more data and information are created, the more opportunities of knowledge and wisdom people acquire. The increasing connections and the average number of devices per person give

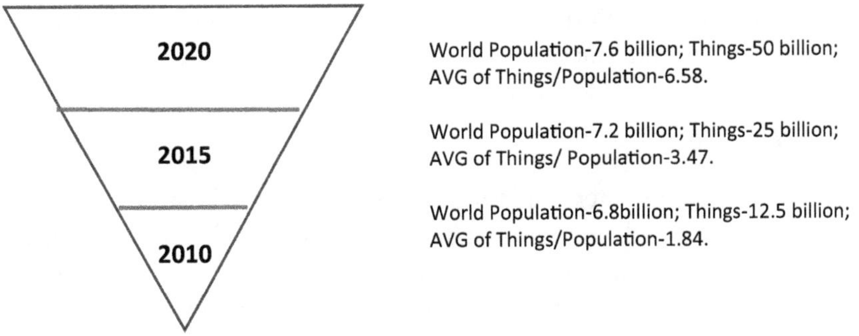

Figure 2.9 Pyramid of the IoTs in the past decade.

us more opportunities to know the things, the world, and ourselves (from the time dimension in Fig. 2.9). But from cognition dimension in Fig. 2.8, it is very different to achieve knowledge or wisdom even by the acquired of science and technology. Things of IoT may give us a hand. The interlinks among data, information, knowledge, wisdom, and artificial intelligence (AI) are analyzed as following.

In short, wisdom for a deep understanding and a trend forecasting scenario of our world is on the top of the pyramid. The acquirement and accumulation of it are based on the sets of tools/stages/experience which are required to process data, aggregate information, and create knowledge.

Knowledge representation across domains and heterogeneous systems are also important, as are semantics and linked data tools/models. As a result, we can expect to see an increased usage of cognitive technologies, such as AI/machine learning (ML), self-learning systems, and experience simulation (just as the way we practice and think, before we do it; so, IoT data can be treated both off-line and in mission critical real-time online applications). AI is one of the technical tools that helps us from data to information and maybe to knowledge. ML is an important branch of AI, and both are artificial and enlightened from the human cognitive process and activities.

To determine the information value of IoT data, the data will have to be combined with other information (context awareness or time-space information) from internal cooperating databases or in a given data/information integrated model, for example, to see whether the data received required any action. The information would be recognizable to the end users, either in the form of visualizations or other expressions of human–machine interfaces.

2.4.2 *IoT 2.0*

IoT looks like a new term that mimics the internet, which in fact is used in many pillars and sectors of industrial, commercial, government, and business scope. From the view of this book, there are four main pillars including consumers, businesses, governments, and industries. Now these IoT pillars are moving into sectors and capillary use cases.

For example, for IoT + (plus with) agriculture, we will think of soil, temperature, and humidity sensors, greenhouse control systems for automatic watering fertilization, and food quality control. For IoT + (plus) industry, we will think of sensors and actuators, mechanical arms or devices, wheeled robotic things, and industrial robots in the production line freely. For IoT + energy, we will think that almost all "things" have to use energy, and the value chain ranges from energy (re-)generation, supply, distribution, energy storage, to EVs. For IoT + logistics, we will think of the supply chain and the whole process from production to consumers. For IoT +city management, we will think of smart transportation, metering, smart building/home/office, and V2X. For IoT + environmental protection, we will think of the PM index, emission reduction and sustainability (IoT sense as smell in Section 4.4), and so on.

All of the above shows a pattern or trend that will have a fundamental and global impact on society at a macro level and micro level over several generations. It is something that will have a significant impact on the world in the foreseeable future. Accordingly, a mind shift from IoT 1.0 to IoT 2.0 is required. If IoT 1.0 is an extension of informatization/digitalization to include things or objects over Internet, then IoT 2.0 is a new concept of innovation, which brings us i-Watch, Baidu Box, Google Glass, fitness trackers and other smart devices, and augmented reality/virtual reality, 3D printing, and other technologies including 5G, LPWAN, TIoT, IIoT, and mobile IoT (not only a smart phone but also a pad with rich apps). In some reference books, the trend is described as a megatrend toward every corner covered, innovation driven, and the full blossom of IoT 2.0.

Some of the features of the IoT 2.0 era are as follows:

- New connection mode, wired or wireless, initiates the further demand for the desired communication (e.g., 5G, WiFi6, LPWAN, and satellite IoT);

- Connected objects into the grid (functionalization, industrial interconnection, and horizontal connection) and primitive IoT for better context awareness, flexible service, and sector integration;
- Each industry application forms the specific demand for the platform and service layer, and gradually, the industry platform develops into standardization;
- Application of the upper layer gradually separated from the IoT network layer, by diversities of communication and network technology (NB-IoT, LoRa, cellular and short range, etc.) fully developed, together with middleware, APIs blooming, and AI accelerated;
- More perception technologies flush, including but not limited to "sensor and actuator"(details in Chapter 4);
- IoT security will be a relatively independent research field and gets enough attention and development.

IoT 2.0 can also be understood as IoE as an alternative word, and obviously, the scope is larger than that of IoT. IoE emphasizes the concept of the interconnection of all things that any device or thing can be connected through the network and can communicate with each other in the network.

From an industrial aspect, IoT data involve numerous and very different and heterogeneous sources and also numerous and very different usages of the data. The analysis of IoT data may be viewed as a complex set of interactions related to time (i.e., when the data are received) and relevance (i.e., the overall relevance of the piece of data to the question in hand). Managing these interactions is critical to the success of IoT solutions. Decision support or even decision-making systems will therefore become very important in different application domains for IoT, which is included as AI/ML-accelerated development, e.g., in IIoT.

From an automation aspect, the information dimension is represented by actionable services as realized by actuators (instead of action by ourselves). There is a duality in sensing and actuation in terms of fusion and aggregation. However, data analytics is employed to find insights or information as mentioned earlier; basically by aggregation, one can consider complex multimodal actuation services that need to be resolved down to the level of individual atomic actuation tasks (which will be described as primitive IoT service in Chapter 5). IoE calls more for intelligence in the form of closed control loops of sensing and actuation, which can be simple or very complex. This duality and the closed control aspect will put new requirements on technologies that stretch the boundaries from what can be achieved based on data-only-oriented technologies used in the prevalent approach of “analytics”, which will be instead for the sensing, analytics, and action at the same time, as those earlier mentioned online applications (just like the exploitation while sensing/actuating and at the same time, exploring as human do). This mode of automation in closed control loops often is deemed as AI in contrast to human intelligence.

From a grid aspect, IoT grid places an emphasis on the openness and exposure of services and information at different levels. What is important is to be able to share information and services across organizations in the horizontal dimension as well as being able to aggregate and combine services and information to reach higher degrees of refinement and values in the vertical sectors. The open and collaborative nature of IoT means methods are required to publish and discover data and services as well as to achieve information interoperability, but also that care needs to be given to trust, security, and privacy.

Information interoperability requires semantics of data so that data can be shared across systems without too much humans interpreting the data from one system to another. What is also needed is provenance of information so that the information can be trusted and the source can be identified for the sake of any liability issues. It also dramatically increases the required capability of system integration and the management of large-scale complex systems across multiple stakeholders and multiple organizational boundaries. As we come to increasingly rely on ICT solutions to monitor and control assets and physical properties of the real world, we also require increased levels of cybersecurity, which is an important aspect when considering IoT security. Other aspects that can be used to describe this megatrend are included in Table 2.1.

This transition consists of a few main steps, namely moving away from isolated solutions to an open environment, from B2B to B2B and B2C and then to B2B2X; when it is compatible or open (in some degree) but complex enough (e.g., IIoT sectors), IoT solutions will be back to the grids (refer Section 6.2) and the trend of cloud computing back to the edge.

The general move towards a horizontal layering of both technology and business, by using of IP, web or platform as a technology toolbox (e.g., OPC UA, TSN in Chapters 5 and 6), and the use of the current Internet as a foundation for enterprise and government operations, multimodal sensing, actuation, and data sources, together with insight and

Table 2.1 Characteristics and approaches of IoT 1.0 and IoT 2.0/IoE practices.

Aspect	IoT 1.0 (past and now)	IoE (IoT.2.0)	Notes
Application	B2B Human centric Function driven Value chain Data and management driven	B2B, B2C, B2B2X Device/service centric Innovation driven Value grid Wisdom and automation driven	From the scale up (e.g., consumers, businesses, industries, and governments) to capillary use cases and to full fields. From enterprise integration (application specific) to sector subdividing and expansion by the assistance of facility-driven IoT grids/PIoT style.
Platform and service	Loose couple Procedure/integration based Business objective driven Connection as a service	Platform as a service SOA/middleware based Collaborative driven Everything as a service	From vertical sectors to industry-specific and generalized platforms; accelerated AI or ML as a service; context awareness
Communication and networks	Capillary Specific or heterogeneous connections Cloud Vertical or horizontal	Capillary and pillar collaboration Generalized and open Cloud/Edge collaboration Ubiquitous	From cloud to edge, then to the collaboration of both; new technology examples such as: 5G/satellite, LowPAN/WPAN, Web of things (web service)
Perception (technology)	RFID, WSN/WSAN, SCADA, GNSS,	IoT sense, biometric ID, tiptap, tactile, SLAM; location awareness/LBS, none — GNSS indoor	Composition of vertical systems/horizontal services into the coordination of time–space; medical and assisted living, fitness and tracking, AGV/UAV, and in-vehicle automated driving as examples.

automation technologies, will be planted into the main differing characteristics and shift of mindset between past and future. IoT 2.0/IoE practices with respect to IoT technology, connections, platforms, and applications are summarized in Table 2.1.

2.5 Summary

The rapid rise in the IoT has brought forth a new generation of devices and services representing the most significant era of innovation and growth since the launch of the Internet. IoT solutions are game changers offering consumers, businesses, and governments across the globe countless benefits. From coffee pots, fitness trackers to "smart" thermostats and connected devices to connected cities and healthcare services, society is on the cusp of a new technological era.

There is no doubt that the IoE era is really forthcoming! In the refreshing new IoT, cloud computing, big data, industry 4.0/IIoT and other new concepts blend, together with enabling technologies, which we not only should know but also should understand how to use. Such problems should not bind the "younger" generation's thinking.

Hope this book helps us to soberly understand the high-tech rush today to find our own way in the history and decide how to proceed and how to accomplish the tasks involved. The internal cause of the arrival of the IoT era may be the integration and application demands of various new technologies in the same way, while the external cause could be the historical drive of the harmonious development of man and environment, nature, and society. It is time to reflect as Hawking predicts that only 1000 years are left for the planet.

Let us hope that in the IoE era, the IoT will be understood in depth as follows: metaphysical knowledge + the unity of nature and man. Earlier, the number+ may be the internal cause: human beings are inspired by IoT and can climb the technological peak; afterwards, the number+ may be the external cause.

This chapter is only the beginning of what you can do with the IoT! Look forward to seeing the IoT from the basis of science and humanity.

Chapter 3

Characteristics of Internet of Things

"Logic will take you from A to B. Imagination will take you everywhere". — Albert Einstein

3.1 Architecture of Internet of Things and Beyond

Internet of Things (IoT) technology has a wide variety of applications and use of IoT is growing rapidly. Depending upon different application areas of IoT, it works as according to what it has been designed/developed for. But it does not have a standard defined architecture of working which is strictly followed universally. The architecture of IoT depends upon its functionality and implementation in different sectors. Still, there is a basic process flow based on which IoT is built.

What is reference architecture? IoT reference architecture is in reality the functional structure of a genetic IoT that is composed of several elements: sensors, actuators, protocols, communications, networks, cloud/edge infrastructure, etc. and often organized in layer-by-layer views.

Despite its sophistication, according to the data collection performance, transmission, (storage) processing, and application, IoT architecture exists in four layers to reliably combine these various kinds of components into an advanced and understandable network. The four layers of the IoT architecture (the technical picture will be introduced in the next section) conforms to the ITU IoT four-layer reference model, as shown in Fig. 3.1, and in the following part, the perception layer is used instead of the device layer.

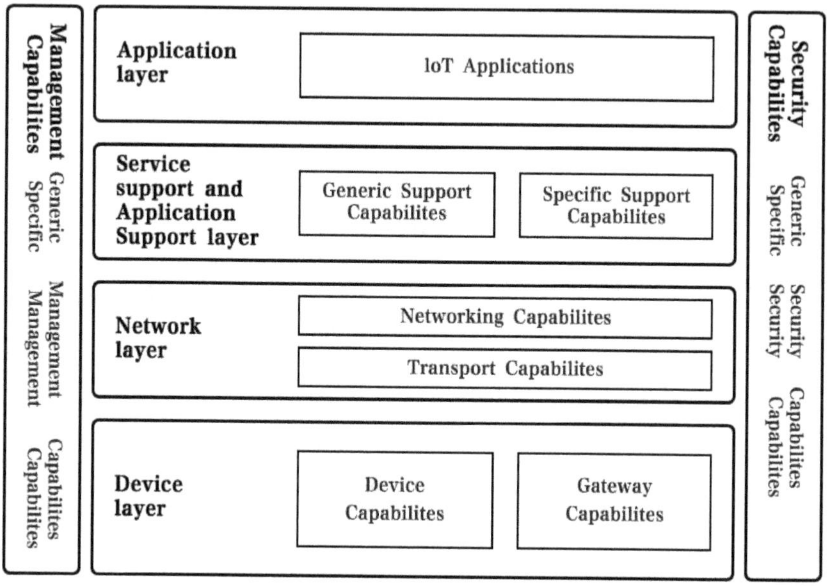

Figure 3.1 ITU IoT four-layer reference mode.

In this book, it is clear that there are four layers present: perception layer, communication and network layer, service and platform layer, and application layer. There will be an architectural description of Fig. 3.1 in the following section. These are explained as follows.

1. Perception Layer: Sensors, actuators, and other man-made devices are present in the lowest level as the perception Layer, where sensors gather data (e.g., parameters from physical environment) which will be transferred over a network and actuators allow things to act (e.g., to switch on or off the light, to open or close a door, to increase or decrease engine rotation speed, and more).

This layer represents the linking of indoor bridge for things into the IoT world. As discussed above, things of interest are either the real-world objects (of the nature), or man-made entities that are subjected to monitoring and controlling, or even virtual objects having digital representations and identities. Functionally, the perception layer can be further divided into two sub layers.

First is the device (or data acquisition) sub layer, where the data of the external physical world is collected by sensors, digital cameras, and other devices for data acquisition, together with the execution and control of an actuation.

In this sub layer, the main functional capabilities of sensing, actuation, and embedded identities are provided, for the evolved things to be identified, monitored, and controlled (in a given physical infrastructure). The sensors and actuators in various devices may work as smartphones or WSANs, smart meters, or other sensor/actuator nodes, which play the resources role that can be abstracted and integrated into higher-level data processing capabilities, and hence they represent the sources and sinks of monitored and controlled data. For example, the abstraction (in an information model) is provided by a sink node in this sub layer. As to RFID (radio frequency identification), identification of assets can be provided by different types of tags; such as RFID tags in ISO/IEC 18000 family of standards or optical codes, such as bar codes or quick response (QR) codes.

Second is the aggregator (or gateway) sub layer, where the data is cleaned, refined, or preprocessed after the original data is acquired by RFID, barcode, industrial fieldbus, infrared, and other short-distance transmission technologies (WSN, NFC, or Bluetooth). In this sub layer, a gateway or gateway device (e.g., sink node in WSN or coordinator in Zigbee) provides connectivity between things (often locally), enables data filtering before moving it to the upper layer (to reduce the volume of data for detailed processing and storing), and transmits control commands going from the upper layer (e.g., cloud/edge, platform layer or other IoT layers) to things. Things then execute commands using their actuators. Finally, a series of software functions can be designed here to manage these things, such as the information acquisition middleware (to be introduced in Chapter 6).

The two sub layers correspond to the device capability and gateway capability, respectively. In some occasions, the two sub layers are often designed as an integrator, e.g., in an RFID system, tags, readers, and gateways are managed by one back-end computer. In practice, it is sometimes difficult to distinguish the two sub layers clearly. The key technologies of perception layer include identification technology (e.g., RFID), short distance wired and wireless communication technology (e.g., WSN), and IoT senses. The topics of gateways and edge (device) are further dealt with in Sections 5.6 and 6.4.

2. Communication and Networks Layer: The main function of communication and network layer (in short, network layer) is to realize the communication of sensing data and controlling information ensure effective transition of perception layer data to a data lake or upwards, and control applications (downwards) without data lost or corruption. The simplest communication is the streaming data moving from one point to another (as an example of transport capability in Fig. 3.1).

From a comprehensive view, the network layer is to provide the ways for connectivity between the devices and resources on one end and the different computing infrastructures that host and execute service support logic and application logic on the other end. Through various networks, the relevant data or information obtained from the perception layer is processed by the functions of storage, analysis, transmission, query, and management. The networking includes not only the global network in the form of wired, wireless, satellite, and Internet but also the communication technology to realize the short-range wireless (wired) connections. The latter is often referred to as local area networks (LANs) in contrast to a wide area networks (WANs). WANs can be realized by different wired or wireless technologies, for instance, fiber, digital subscriber line (DSL) and cellular mobile networks, satellite, or microwave links for the global connections.

When it comes to LANs, there are many examples of different types, and there is also no stringent definition of what might be considered a LAN or a WAN. Basic examples of LANs include wireless personal area networks (WPANs; also known as body area networks, BANs) for fitness or healthcare applications, home or building area networks (HANs and BANs, respectively) used in automation and control applications, and neighborhood area networks (NANs) or field area networks (FANs) which are used in the distribution grid of a smart electricity grid.

From the views of WAN, the network layer solves the problem that the data obtained by the perception layer locally or the connections of things are limited in a certain range. Usually, long-range transmission in the network layer not only includes the WANs, such as mobile or cellular communication network, Internet, intranet, all kinds of private networks, and cable TV network, but also Lora and Sigfox in low-power wide area (LPWA) networks.

It is worth mentioning that even satellite network and 5G non-public networks (NPN) are booming, the integration of all the technologies above makes up for each other's weak points and is laying a solid network foundation for the IoT.

With the acceleration of the next-generation information and communication technology (ICT), there may be more suitable network forms (such as virtual network, slicing in 5G/B5G) for IoT in the future. The key technologies of communication and network layer mainly include long-/short-range communication technology, networking technology, and so on, which will be detailed in Chapter 5.

3. Service and Platform Layer: After the exploitation of perception and network layers (the above-introduced two layers of IoT) including identification, data capture, processing, and communication capabilities, the IoT makes full use of things to offer services to all kinds of applications in the service and platform layer, while ensuring that security and privacy requirements are fulfilled.

IoT platforms will be strongly driven by wireless, cellular (e.g., 5G and beyond) technologies, which will generate massive amounts of information as input for hyper computing processing capabilities and enabling new applications in services, such as robotics, autonomous vehicles, Artificial Intelligence (AI), and intelligent systems. Some key enabling points in this layer (important for designers) are discussed as follows:

- ***Service***: From an IoT perspective, services in this layer include the means to access IoT resources, how to publish and discover resources, tools for modeling contextual information, and information related to the real-world entities that are of interest, and capabilities that provide different levels of abstracted and complex services (e.g., data analytics). The dynamic service composition and automation involving control loops of sensing and actuation are usually organized into a service platform or a middleware by SOA (service-oriented architecture) or other tools.

- ***SOA and middleware***: SOA is a software methodology extending the web paradigm to IoT devices/service. SOA constructs a natural component of building any application and facilitate an easy integration of IoT device services into any enterprise system that is based on the SOA (e.g., ERP, MES that use web services or RESTful interfaces).

An IoT middleware often refers to platform-independent IoT service architecture for interoperability, e.g., an open sensor web architecture (OSWA) for developing sensor applications, and OPC-UA (see Section 6.1). IoT applications can then become technology- and programming language–independent by the middleware. Functionally, middleware service requirements for the IoT range from the registration and capture of the services (e.g., abstractions, resource management) to data analytics, and to some non-functional requirements (e.g., reliability, security, availability, and QoS supporting). Take data (or information) acquisition middleware (DAM) system as an example, which is presented in this layer or pre-located between the networks layer and the perception layer. DAM performs data aggregation and conversion function (collecting and aggregating data may include converting analog data of sensors to digital data, etc.). Usually, the same data processing function bearer can be called as processing unit or data processing sub layer for the application integration of IoT ecosystem, where data is accessed and service is provided. With the middleware, advanced gateways which mainly opens up connection between sensor networks (SNs) and Internet also performs many basic gateway functionalities, such as malware protection, events filtering, and data management services.

• ***Heterogeneity*:** Heterogeneous services originate from the heterogeneous devices (see Fig. 2.7) and heterogeneous networks, and the device heterogeneity emerges not only from differences in capacity and features but also for other reasons including multivendor products and application requirements. SOA and middleware help boost the IoT application development market as application development for IoT is not different from building applications for the web, when dealing with the heterogeneity. For example, a set of web services and protocols for web developers are easily available.

• ***Application Programming Interfaces*:** A key component in establishing the application supporting platforms towards development market is open APIs. By well-defined service interfaces, application programming interfaces (APIs) are required to facilitate application development, as are the appropriate software development kits (SDKs). Some application-specific and x-facilitated middlewares are introduced in Section 6.1, where "x" means a certain vertical domain or a development tool.

• ***Machine Learning*:** Based on the data analytics, event filtering, and service generating algorithms and methods, advanced techniques such as AI or Machine Learning (ML) are required to get further insight, which is often related with Big Data. At a beginning level of data analytics, massive data from the original massive devices, or from a data lake, or from human (e.g., behavior or other biometric characters in Section 4.3), exists in a big data warehouse.[1] Traditionally, an action command is from the application layer by an end-user, or a pre-designed mode in the data warehouse. But situations change when data analytics are used to find trends and gain actionable insights. When analyzed (e.g., in many cases — visualized in schemes, diagrams, infographics), data show some trends for prediction, e.g., the performance of devices help identify inefficiencies and work out the ways to improve an IoT system (make it more reliable, more customer-oriented). Also, the correlations and patterns found manually can further contribute to creating algorithms for control applications.

At a ML level, with the models ML generated, there is an opportunity to create more precise and more efficient models for control applications. Models are regularly updated (e.g., once in a week or once in a month) based on the historical data accumulated in a big data warehouse and the pattern insight of our minds. When the applicability and efficiency of new models are tested and approved by data analysts, new models are used by control applications.

- ***Collaboration and platform*:** IoT solutions can involve a large number of different devices, heterogeneous communication and service, and they can involve a large set of different actors providing services and information that need to be composed/re-composed and accessed at different levels of aggregation. The actors include not only service providers, but third parties (e.g., developers). In order to achieve the collaboration and facilitate the design for the heterogeneity (e.g., a platform-type middleware as OPC-UA for different abstraction levels that hide underlying complexities), a lot of organizations are dedicated to the services abstraction and platform-enabling from a set of different architectural views.

ITU establishes a proposed terminology, IoT-A gives a set of unified requirements, 3GPP defines the machine-type communications (MTCs) and services (see Section 5.8), and oneM2M regulates some horizontal/vertical frameworks.

A platform design will greatly benefit from providing the necessary abstractions both of underlying technologies and of data and service representations, as well as granularity of information and services, including

[1] Data warehouse stores context information about things and sensors (e.g., where sensors are installed) and the commands control applications send to things.

cross-domain interoperability and security. RAMI4.0 (reference architectural model industrie 4.0) proposes a methodology for how to arrive at a concrete architecture based on use cases and requirements. The OPC-UA is discussed in Section 6.1, industrial IoT (IIoT) architecture approach is discussed in Section 6.5. Tactile IoT (TIoT) propositions, MTC, and Internet of Vehicles (IoV) are covered in more detail in Chapter 5. Other architecture approaches or platforms will be introduced along with cloud/edge computing or 5G services architecture. Furthermore, a micro-granularity service in a proposed primitive IoT view is presented in Section 6.2.

- ***Open*:** Openness is important for ensuring interoperability between different components within a particular IoT system, as well as between different IoT systems, and for ensuring collaboration between different IoT platforms. Opening the IoT doors for stakeholder actors (developers, system integrators, users, and third-party service providers, such as ISP, MNO) takes on different roles of providing and using services. For example, openness eases the cloud provider independence by decoupling device, cloud, and applications with open interfaces. OpenIoT (https://openiot.network/) is a cloud services provider for virtual sensors, with its open community online. By the open-source middleware frameworks of OpenIoT, virtual sensors can be deployed and reconfigured in containers at runtime. The GSN middleware (integrated into OpenIoT) creates highly dynamic processing environments and allows the system to quickly react to changing processing needs and environmental conditions and virtual sensors are used to control processing priority, management of resources, and stored data.

Kaa (https://www.kaaproject.org/) is an open-source platform for building IoT solutions by offering a broad array of IoT features: device management, data collection, data processing and analytics, alerts, and so on. Anjay (https://www.avsystem.com/products/anjay/) includes an open-source version which supports LwM2M (light weight M2M standard developed by OMA) 1.0.2. Other open-source projects include OpenWSN (http://openwsn.atlassian.net), KSpot+, and IoTivity (https://iotivity.org). The latter is a Linux Foundation collaborative project, which is sponsored by the consortium, Open Connectivity Foundation (OCF) that develops specifications and certifications based on the IETF standards (will be introduced in Section 5.5).

These sorts of open and collaboration scenarios will become increasingly important for industries, individuals, and government and organizations work together to solve complex problems involving multiple stakeholders. For more details see the book *Collaborative IoT (C-IoT)*.

• ***Security***: While there is huge potential for the IoT in different domains, there are also concerns for the security of applications and networks. The IoT needs global connectivity and accessibility, which means that anyone can access it anytime and anywhere. This tremendously increases the attack surfaces for the IoT's applications and networks. The inherent complexity of the IoT further complicates the design and deployment of efficient, interoperable, and scalable security mechanisms.

4. Application Layer: This is the last layer in our architecture outline. The data centers or cloud is management stage of data where data, information, and workflow are managed and used by end-user applications; the application layer in turn provides the specific IoT applications, such as agriculture, healthcare, aerospace, farming, and defense. There is an open-ended array of different applications from various sectors across the industry, enterprise, consumer, and society domains, vertically or horizontally, as laid out in Chapter 7.

Chapter 6 also discusses some of them as IIoT, TIoT, IoV. and Sat IoT (in Chapter 5) vertically. The examples in this layer are devoted to providing some insights and use cases for different IoT applications.

• ***Business supporting***: From a horizontal view, a business sub layer or business supporting function is discussed in many literatures (mostly it can be included in OpenAPI or middleware), which focuses on supporting the core business or operations of any enterprise, organization, or individual that is interested in IoT applications. This is where any integration of the IoT applications into a given business domain or specific enterprise processes/systems takes place.

The enterprise systems may be enterprise resource planning (ERP), customer relationship management (CRM), or other business support systems (BSSs). From industrial views, manufacturing execution systems (MES), supervisory control and data acquisition (SCADA), and distributed control systems (DCS) are used to control industrial processes, such as electric power generation, oil refineries, water and wastewater treatment, and chemical, food, and automotive production. Product and process control are usually achieved by deploying feedback or feed-forward control loops whereby key product and/or process conditions are automatically maintained around a desired set point.

The business supporting system also provides exposure via APIs (or an open middleware with upwards API interfaces) for third parties to get access to data and information and can also contain support for direct access to applications by human users, such as location-based services (LBS) or city portal services for citizens in a smart city context, providing necessary data visualizations to the workforce in a particular managing view. The business supporting function relies on IoT applications as one set of enablers and needs necessary orchestration and composition to support a business process workflow. Some use cases discussion on business integration is provided in Chapters 6 and 7.

- ***Semantic interoperability***: In this layer, semantic interoperability across domains is essential for achieving many business applications. Semantic interoperability enables data and information to be shared across domains and understood by systems without needing manual interpretations on top of technical details or protocol and syntactic interoperability. Semantic interoperability requires mapping methods that can be predefined or self-learning. The latter requires algorithms that consider structural, terminological, and semantic differences and similarities.

- ***LBS***: Object localization needs to be tailored according to the IoT needs and deployment scenarios (such as indoor or outdoor environments). Typical indoor localization technologies include video or image processing, beacons of Bluetooth/Zigbee/WiFi, WiFi access points, or UWB ranging. Outdoor, GPS-based localization is typically relied on. For any localization solution, the required accuracy, size of area covered, and real timeliness of location must be considered.

A catalog function can also be required, together with localization of objects or assets of IoT. This function works as a repository of all assets of interest and includes other properties of the asset. EPCIS is an example in Section 4.1.3. As for object identification of RFID reader, because the location of the readers is given, tags based on optical or RF-technologies (e.g., QR codes or RFID tags) are located at the same time of identification. The purpose is to uniquely identify and name objects, also it works for a human identification by the same principle (RFID/BLT beacon details in Section 4.5.4). A prominent example is electronic product code information services (EPCIS), which will be detailed in Section 4.1.

• ***Agent*:** An agent is often referring to as a substitute of learner and worker in a piece of program, and after being trained online or offline, it works as a controller. A controller is a core automation point in any IoT system involving actuators. Control software commands the assets' desired behavior. Common to all controllers is the deterministic behavior of controlling operations based on input from priority desired and defined operational behavior. The use of different controller types is based on functional and non-functional characteristics meeting application needs.

Whereas many control systems in robotics and other real-world continuous and industrial systems use proportional, integral, and derivative (PID) controls, other IoT use cases, such as home automation, often use rule-based systems for event-driven control.

A PID controller is a control loop feedback mechanism using a mathematical function that takes the deviation between the desired state and the measure state as input for control.

Proportional control means that proportional feedback of the deviation is provided to determine the control value. A derivative part of the deviation dampens the error. An integral part of the deviation provides errors to be removed over time. Examples include inverse kinematics for robot control and temperature control of a fluid system. This requires knowledge about the physical behavior and properties of the asset controlled.

Rule-based controllers are based on a set of predefined rules that are trigger-action pairs, where a trigger is a condition and an action is a predefined workflow typically containing commands to the devices or related services — e.g., following the simple logic of "if this, then that". In complex, dynamic, and non-deterministic situations, one can enhance the usability and maintainability of both PID and rule-based control systems by making them use task planning technologies to help infer the actions to be taken. Optimization and task planning can be defined as the process of generating a sequence of actions with certain objectives, using various techniques.

3.2 From Multi-Layers Technical Vision

After having a basic understanding of the architecture and capabilities of its layers, we can identify implications for both the technology and business perspectives. When considering the support technologies of IoT, the technology architecture of IoT can be unfolded as four groups of evolving

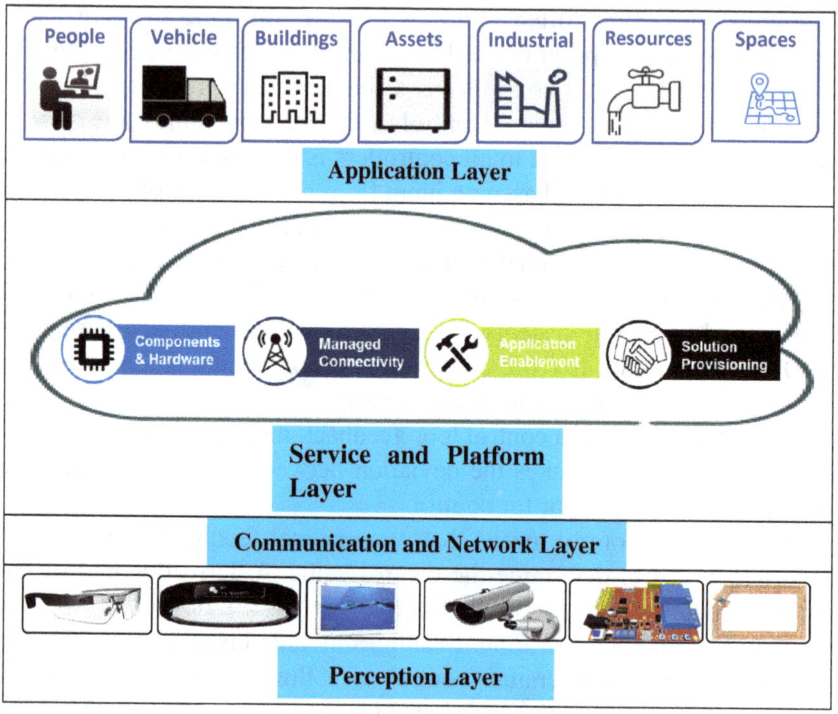

Figure 3.2 Overviews of IoT architecture in this book.

technologies and practices, and each group corresponds to a four-layered architecture aforementioned; see Fig. 3.2. The picture also gives a layered market perspective from horizontal view, which implies the decomposition and transition from vertically oriented systems or application-specific silos.

The steps of the book, also conform to the layered technology structure, which will be covered from Chapters 4 to 7. In Fig. 3.3, many of these layered technologies also have proof points of what is already ongoing, towards both horizontal combination (e.g., horizontal platform) and vertical cohesion, for a better selection within a given industrial sector.

1. Technologies in the Perception Layer: Combining ICTs, microcontrollers, micro-system (e.g., embedded SOC) and low power solutions,

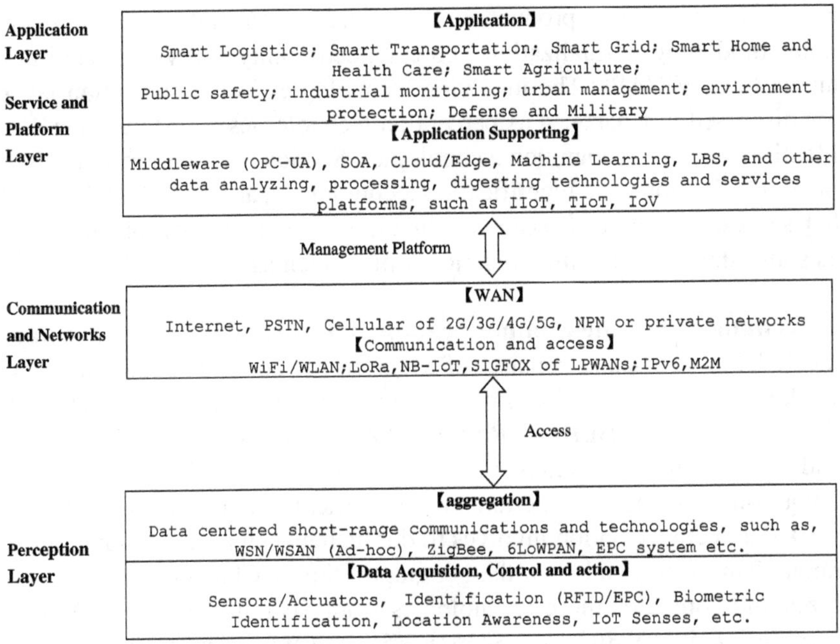

Figure 3.3 Technology architecture of IoT.

Note: The four-layer technology architecture corresponds to the four chapters from Chapters 4 to 7.

and distributed short-range communication technologies, the IoT perception layer creates a distributed intelligent world of things consisting of a wide range of sensing/actuating things, things to be located or accessed by multi perception technologies or other IoT senses (in particular, Section 4.4), and things with tags.

Some of the things just help to realize local usage, e.g., RFID things, but they can be extended to WAN application by EPC (electronic product code) system. Some of the things, known as devices, are linked in a dynamic connection (e.g., ad-hoc meshing) by a set of distributed and federated edge devices (e.g., gateways) and services. The significant advances of LPWA/M2M are the access solutions either to the public/non-public cloud by a cellular gateway or to the private cloud directly by the proprietary technologies (see Chapter 5). Hyper autonomous things include collaborative robotic things integrated into real-time industrial and intelligent business processes across different layers or sectors (e.g., TSN in network layer and IIoT sectors) that create a multi experience combining product design, visualization, field service, operations, modelling, virtualization into extended reality and virtual environments (e.g., VR/AR). The involving technologies in the perception layer are discussed in Chapter 4 as perception technologies of IoT. Section 4.1: Identification and recognition technologies, Section 4.2: Sensors and WSN, Section 4.3: Biometric Identification technologies, and Section 4.4: H2M/IoT senses, etc. These also can be found in the beginning part of Chapter 5, as some short-range communication topics, such as Zigbee/WPAN.

2. Technologies in the Communication and Networks Layer: The fragmented IoT landscape consists of a variety of communication and networking technologies. Leading technologies such as WiFi (WLAN), Zigbee, Bluetooth (BLE), LoRa/LoRaWAN, NB-IoT, Cellular IoT/M2M, and 5G dominate the industry; however, no single IoT technology has ubiquitous coverage and pertains to all vertical IoT use cases. Each network connectivity option involves tradeoffs between power consumption, range, bandwidth, and even the geography limits. Chapter 5 mainly analyzes and compares these technologies from Section 5.3 WLAN/WiFi6, Section 5.4 WPAN/802.15.4, Section 5.5 gateways and protocols, Cellular IoT/M2M/5G associated sections to Satellite IoT and TIoT.

3. Technologies in the Service and Platform Layer: In order to achieve a high degree of interoperability between various IoT solutions at the different system, technologies, open services and platforms are required to ease the burden of each stakeholder (including application developers). Then, hiding device-side technologies and providing simple abstractions of the sensing and actuation services is one target of IoT middleware, which is introduced in Section 6.1 of Chapter 6, including SOA. Also, IoT middleware can include data and event filtering and analytics as well as dynamic service composition and automation involving control loops of sensing and actuation. A SOM-type middleware can either provide different levels of automation and at different time scales ranging from real-time robot control to long-term forecasting or planning, or perform aggregation of information or knowledge, which helps the human-level wisdom realization.

In Section 6.2, the question focuses on how to decompose a IoT unit/cell from a grid level or more granular vision, for the service re-composed or integrated into a more general horizontal platform. For example, when the needed service design/deployment across functional programs in an application, or across applications is taken care of, primitive IoT and IoT grids give some kinds of service-centered methods. At the end of this section, some use cases are given.

In the introduction of Sections 6.3 and 6.4, edge/cloud provides data management and data analytics that are key functions for IoT systems where data and events generated by large amounts of sensor must be logged, stored, and processed to generate new insights or events, ML-based processing on which business decisions can be made. (Further, the service layer functions are provided at the edge or cloud level.

Several cloud service providers are extending the offerings to implement IoT solutions by using the existing "infrastructure as a service (IaaS)" ecosystems to provide new IoT services. In many cases, these systems are not optimized.)

Sections 6.5, 6.6, and other sections, unfold IoV, industrial IoT, and digital twin from vertical industrial views (the same views of M2M, 5G TSN, and TIoT in some sections of Chapter 5).

4. Technologies in the Application Layer (in Chapter 7): The application layer is offering the software components and specific functions that are suitable to deliver the key components for implementing various IoT applications that are connecting users, business partners, devices, machines, and enterprise systems with each other to provide information interpretation to different applications from industrial sectors.

Industrial sector refers to the procedures and associations within a given industrial vertical usage. It describes the structure and achievement with the goals of a particular industry. This is the key difference between the M2M, always being referred to as a vertical solution (but not an industrial sector), and the IoT market-oriented industrial sector. The latter cares more about how the industrial structures will be formed around these solutions (all above-mentioned technologies), despite very similar technology implementations. This is covered in more detail in Sections from 7.1 to 7.6, which discuss the decomposition and transition from vertically oriented systems or application-specific silos.

In the application layer, the SW/HW components at this layer interact with the service layer, while the software applications are based on vertical markets, the nature of device data, and business needs. At this layer, many applications are addressed, such as mission-critical business applications, specialized industry solutions, mobile applications, and analytic applications that interpret data for business decisions. The optimization for energy efficiency and green IoT requires the use of federation and orchestrations techniques that create dynamic and distributed energy control frameworks for IoT applications that need large capacity, higher delivery efficiency, reduced energy consumption, and low costs. The implementation of energy-efficient search engines, the cooling systems and use of energy harvesting techniques and of renewables must be considered when the HW/SW components of the IoT application layer are evaluated. New IoT applications including AR/VR, digital twins, virtual simulations, real-time searching engines, and discovery services will bring new challenges to optimizing the energy efficiency.

5. Security Issues: Chapter 8 discuss the security, i.e., how to enhance security defense, e.g., predicting the scenarios of security attackers and creating techniques for quarantining (information partly anonymous or third-party guaranteed) the IoT devices as well as solutions preventing the attack from a layered view.

However, the opening and interconnecting many "things" also means the possibility of interconnecting many different threats and attacks. For example, a malware virus can easily propagate through the IoT at an unprecedented rate. In the four layers IoT architecture, there may be various threats and attacks in each layer of the IoT system, as follows:

(1) Perception: In this aspect, typical attacks and issues include data leakage, sovereignty, breach, authentication, and other mechanics for protecting inter connections by point to point or point to gateway.
(2) Communication: Possible attacks include channel attacks, session hijacks, routing attacks, flooding, and so on. Apart from attenuation, theft, loss, breach, and disaster, data can also be fabricated and modified by the compromised sensors.
(3) Service: In this aspect, there may exist computational attacks that aim to generate wrong data processing results and even dangerous command or service.
(4) Application: The following attacks may occur: denial-of-service attacks (attacks on availability), access control attacks, integrity attacks, impersonation, modification of sensitive data, and so on.

IoT brings along new types of concerns on top of the safety aspects that exist in any consumer product or service. Moreover, the life cycle of some of the connected devices varies considerably and this can be a source of additional complexity when clarifying questions of security, upgradeability, liability, and others. Finally, as the recent cyber-attacks have shown, consumer IoT vulnerabilities can be the source of damage in critical infrastructures and industrial IoT.

3.3 Internet of Everything and Characteristics

3.3.1 *IoT and Internet of Everything*

We are currently experiencing the IoT, where millions of new devices are regularly being connected to the Internet. As these "things" add capabilities such as context awareness, increased processing power, and energy independence, and as more people and new types of information are connected, we will enter the Internet of Everything (IoE) era, when things that were silent will have a voice. Those elements ready for everyone to leverage from industrial views, are included by Qualcomm Huawei and GE, as visionary solutions to deliver the connectivity and communication are needed to support the IoE opportunity industry-wide. Cisco defines IoE as bringing together people, process, data, and things to make networked connections more relevant and valuable than ever before — turning information into actions that create new capabilities, richer experiences, and unprecedented economic opportunities for businesses, individuals, and countries.

When smart things everywhere are connected together, more and more opportunities and solutions arise in smart cities, smart building, smart industry, etc., as shown in Fig. 3.4.

This is the IoE, a paradigm shift that marks a new era of opportunity for everyone, from consumers and businesses to cities and governments. IoE is changing our world, but its effect on daily life will be most profound. We will move through our days and nights surrounded by connectivity that intelligently responds to what we need and want — what we may call the digital sixth sense. Dynamic and intuitive, this experience will feel like a natural extension of our own abilities. We will be able to discover, accomplish, and enjoy more, not only with each other but also with things in collaborative IoT. Smart devices, such as smart phones and other high-end or low-end things, are natural tools to deliver IoE experiences, and networks, a fundamental layer of IoE connectivity, are integrated around the globe.

The advent of IoT is taking place in an ICT environment affected by several major trends. "Scale" is one of them: the number of connected

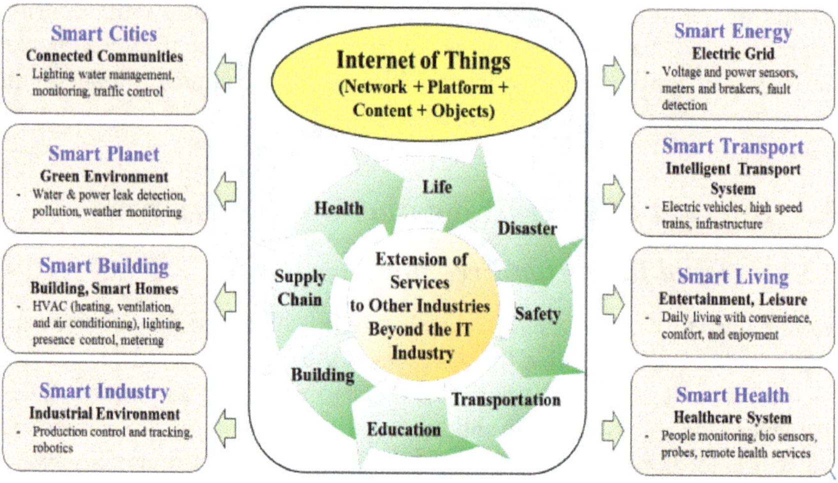

Figure 3.4 Smart everything.

Source: Heller. A. (2015). "The Sensing Internet — A Discussion on Its Impact on Rural Areas." *Future Internet*.

devices is increasing, while their size is reduced below the threshold of visibility to the human eye. "Mobility" is another: objects are ever more wirelessly connected, carried permanently by individuals, and geo-localizable. "Heterogeneity and complexity" is a third trend: IoT will be deployed in an environment. Other trends will be discussed in the following section.

3.3.2 *Analysis of the characteristics towards IoE*

Towards the IoE era, smart things want to live with humans in a mutually understanding environment. From the view of IoT world, the coming new IoE era is endowed with more features.

- **Heterogeneity of IoT Infrastructure:** Heterogeneity in relative aspects of things ranges from devices, data source (from things and the accompanying process), services, systems (underlying communication systems or communication networks), which result in heterogeneous devices and data: The embedded and sensor computing nature of many IoT devices means that low-cost computing platforms are likely to be used. In fact, to minimize the impact of such devices on the environment and energy consumption, low-power radios are likely to be used for connection to the Internet. If such low-power radios are not well-established for the usage of cellular network technologies may be instead of WPAN devices. But when they are interworked by a gateway or mediator, more coverage can be achieved both in the ranges and the quantities. However, the IoT will not be composed only of embedded devices and sensors, it will also need higher-end computing devices to perform heavier duty tasks (routing, switching, data processing, etc.).

Device heterogeneity emerges not only from differences in capacity and features but also for other reasons including multivendor products and application requirements.

Heterogeneous data not only includes data sources from heterogeneous things/devices but includes the middle processing of their transmissions (data clustering/refining/processing and service/information aggregating), and their adaption to the solutions/usages or APIs into the application layer. The latter adaption differs from SNs (including WSN/WSAN/RFID) to the use of control systems to operate industrial processes in cyber-physical systems (CPS) that intertwine software and physical components of various machines; to the manufacturing and Industry 4.0/ISMA(Intelligent Manufacturing in China); and to M2M solutions.

As a new trend of automation, Industrial 4.0 can further be viewed as a part of a larger concept dubbed the Industrial Internet, which can be seen as the combination of information technology (IT) and operational technology (OT). Containing software of industrial machinery relative and common to all of IT/OT approaches, there is a centricity on data and information about the things and the associated processes. In parallel, technologies to process data of different types and characteristics have been evolving as a new source of data generators, and the data generating include means to analyze data, handling of large amounts of data, popularly referred to as Big Data, and lately from ends-to-ends by edge/frog/cloud computing to provide automation and smartness to the things, together with their data transmission and utilization.

Final point comes with the perspective of heterogeneous services in heterogeneous connection of all the devices with the software systems (including heterogeneous OSs and middleware). The orchestration and reorganization, reconstruction that contained in the necessary application logic, algorithms, and data processing, provide the "soft" flexibility in the environment where necessary connectivity is needed and made up for across application domains.

Originally, one simple and isolated "thing" in a primitive IoT uses the form of service as it interlinks with other "things" while spreading/declaiming its characteristic as a server (sometimes also as a client); the "thing" will be in the circumstance of sharing services with other "things" for resources, collaboration and corresponding subject contents (i.e., exchanging information by communication). The things can be represented as (or attached with as a sub-functional part) sensors/actuators as integrity, so that they can execute certain function, complete certain action, interact with each other and with the environment, across sensor data types, actuation services, and underlying communication systems.

• **Pervasive Connection:** Easy access to the Internet/IoT is available virtually everywhere by utilizing modern communications and networking technologies, mainly thanks to wired/wireless and cellular technologies and the rapid deployment of cellular LTE/4G, 5G, and coming SatCom (satellite communication) supported B5G systems on a global scale. These systems provide ubiquitous and relatively cheap connectivity with the right characteristics for many applications and their optional deployment, including low latency and the capacity to handle large amounts of data with high reliability or massive machine type communication (mMTC) access. Some of these systems can be further complemented with last-hop technologies such as IEEE 802.11, IEEE 802.15.4, Bluetooth low energy, and power line communication (PLC) solutions, if necessary; in order to reach many cost-sensitive deployments and cover more things (including devices either light-weight or heavy-weight, as their different resource requiring in IoT). Technologies like 6LoWPAN allow IP connectivity to be provided end-to-end, stretching into the capillary network domain, and legacy and proprietary protocols like ZigBee PRO can be avoided with the benefit of IP and the web anywhere. 3GPP are also extending 5G towards different slices of the lower end of the scale as mMTC, providing very low latency but highly reliable connections (URLLC) for time-sensitive devices and other low-power extensions like NB-IoT targeting specific IoT applications including more constrained devices, New-Light 5G NR for embracing more types of coming pervasive connections.

M2M communications extend the internet-based technologies to a more broad and generalized connection in IoT, (M2M and RFID-based EPC networks are two of the IoT origins.)

The focus of M2M has been and still is to provide the necessary connectivity to various devices across application domains, primarily using the mobile network infrastructures. It is a family both close and distant, including not only legacy device-to-device, M2M (e.g., MTC by 3GPP), but regulations by OneM2M and other organizations.

• **Open Architectures and Services:** One of the evolution directions of IoT software architectures towards the "soft" but flexible and ubiquitous IoE is SOA paradigm, by which the web services can be extended to IoT devices. The natural open SOA architecture encourage more open component of building any application and facilitate an easy integration of IoT device services into any enterprise system (e.g., that uses HTTP/REST or RESTful interfaces). IoT development and applications can then become technology- and programming language–independent, especially by introducing middlewares and open APIs. This helps boost the IoT application development market as application development for IoT is not different from building applications for the web, and web developers are easily available. A key component in establishing the application development market is open APIs.

From a simplistic perspective, we can view openness in architectures, software, platform and services development techniques from what were originally closed environments towards platforms, where middlewares and open APIs provide a simple mechanism for developers to access the functionality of the platform. These platforms, due to the increasing use and power of the Internet, have become open platforms — ones that do not depend on certain programming languages or lock-in between platform developers and platform owners.

While the advocated IoT grids/primitive IoT (in Chapter 5) belong to SOA approach and they pertain to rather long-term disassembling of services into cell-level (towards a detailed and long-term integration) and assembling structures (or well-organized as tissues and organ), it forms the foundation for IoT evolving towards IoE, which will become apparent in the subsequent Section 6.2, after the introduction of the middleware in Section 6.1. From an analogy of bio-science views, the middleware works as the inner environment of bodies around cell-level services, and the diversity of middlewares with different kinds of cells embrace the capillarity functions of organs in our body with dual-direction exchange to/from cells, and to/from APIs ("APIs" as pre-designed functionalities of human tissues analogous to "IoT solutions"). So, "open" and "close" integration are both important, especially in dealing with security and privacy issues. Security consideration includes the information over an open architecture (as much as possible) but with information security and privacy protection in a safe IoT platform.

- **Intelligence:** One of the enabling trends for IoE is the AI, which helps to control and understand the things in a much better way. According to Intel's IoT vision, intelligent devices or things and intelligent systems (of systems) are the two key elements of IoT. In IoT's dynamic and open network, these intelligent entities along with other entities, such as web services (WSs), SOA components, and virtual objects, will be interoperable and able to act independently based on the context, circumstances, or environments. The intelligent software applying to reach various business objectives and key performance indicators (KPI) are often needed to be considered. Intelligence grows up in an open communication environment and nourished by the relation/connection to nature. (as language/patterns, knowledge/know how, wisdom/prediction). It is also planting into every detail and link of IoT.

  With the increase in practical applications of AI, e.g., integration of control systems logic with ML and other AI technologies, new opportunities are ahead. As different IoT systems are becoming more widely deployed, these systems will form systems of systems for collaborative efforts. Data and information will increasingly be shared across systems and across domain boundaries. Automation will require collaboration between different AI-powered systems but also increasingly call for seamless human–machine collaboration. This will also enable intelligent infrastructures that are adaptive to context awareness, self-learning, self-optimizing, and semantic functions.

- **Ultra-Large-Scale Interaction:** In an IoT environment, thousands of devices or things may interact with each other even in one local place (e.g., in a building, supermarket, and 5G mMTC scenario), which range from large number of constrained and embedded computing and sensors, to a router or sever with more processing, memory, and communication capacity.

  Overall, significant innovations are expected by the mere interactions among the different machines and their environments at large scale, e.g., at the smart city level or in global business networks. In addition, as IoT technology capabilities are expanding and being adopted across a number of industries, this will bring transformation of both business processes and business models.

  In IoT applications, sudden events and interactions can take place as objects move around and come into other objects' communication range, leading to the spontaneous generation of events. For instance, a smartphone user can come in close contact with a TV/fridge/washing machine at home, which can generate events without the user's involvement. Typically, in IoT, an interaction with an object means that an event is generated and is pushed to the system without much human attention. Security and privacy protection are accordingly of more importance because we humans can well hold a good/right/evil idea before we speak out and do it, but things cannot. Nevertheless, The regulator's role then would be setting limits to protect low-end devices as the vulnerable demographic part of our societies from predatory behaviors of data collectors.

3.4 Value Chain Towards an New Ecosystem

The main thrust of the legislation is establishing clear rules and a governance framework that would allow setting for the cyber security certification of ICT products, services, and processes in many European schemes. The framework allows also the potential development of labels accompanying a specific scheme. This would allow, e.g., the creation of a trusted IoT label for a particular type of IoT products, services, or processes. So, IoT security gives a baseline for the VALUE CHAINS.

In order to improve the mutual understanding of the context of globalization on these activities, steps and elements that contained within them are "focusing on the sequences of tangible and intangible value-adding activities, from conception and production to end use. Global value chain analysis therefore provides a holistic view of global industries — both from the top down and from the bottom up". Based on the construction of IoT security and trusted environments, a full range of activities that firms and workers perform to bring a product from its conception to end use and beyond, include design, production, marketing, distribution, and support to the final consumer are described in a value chain. These activities as simplified and illustrated in the following aspects, by which separate activities that work together to create a finalized product, may be contained within a single firm or divided among different firms.

Although in the context of the technology industries, the useful value chain can help identify the boundaries between existing industrial structures, such as M2M solutions and emerging industrial structures, as seen in Fig. 3.5, from the view of IoT market and the following Industry 4.0 value chain (in Chapter 6); some new demands in the coming IoE era arise. In the design/pre-design stage, including not only a production or a set of IoT suits (for particular usage) but the security demand/SLA or

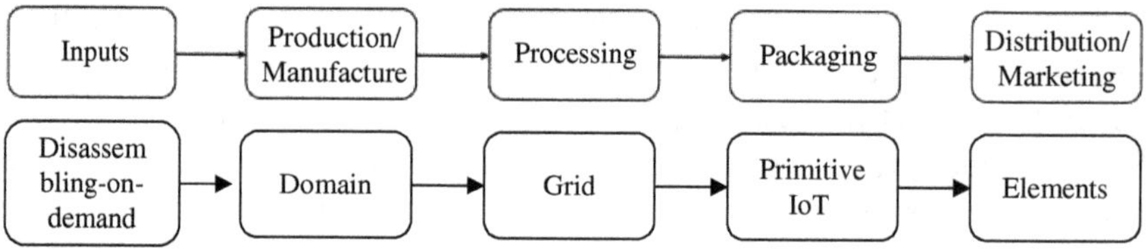

Figure 3.5 Two directions of IoT value chain.

Notes: Each minimized IoT cell with just a service gear in one kettle, is explained as PIoT. Each IoT Grid is composed of things, relations (communication bearer or service supply interface), and a set of services (from PIoT). The three elements push the transformation from systems levels to service-oriented micro-ecosystems.

even the moral issues, should be prepared well (as possible) before they become a prototype (or well-defined idea). The reverse chain is illustrated in Fig. 3.5, which is comprised of five separate activities that work together to create a product-oriented element in IoT (such as a service, a device, a relation, and even a name or an address).

Sometimes, the grid analysis and processing are working in parallel, as well as the primitive IoT creation and information packaging. In addition, on some industrial or commercial occasions, the two chains may influence each other at the same time. Take an important production concept in IoE era as an example, "Flexible Manufacturing System" requires the two chains to work at the same time. On the one hand, know-how from raw material inputs to production/processing/packaging and to distributing/marketing is needed in the first chain; on the other hand, both knowing how and knowing when from the disassembling (or producing)-on-demand for to the changing domain/grid/PIoT, to the upgrading elements from a consumer or a group of consumers, whose social requirements are changing almost in real time (e.g., when one needs an upgraded SLA or production, the other may request more privacy protection or other service on the compromise of SLA and payments).

The twisted two chains create a new ecosystem of IoE, and they are making impact on more industries, from both micro- and macro-economic, to individual perspective, which permits new opportunities as follows.

Other viewpoints of value chain that arise nowadays are listed as follows:

• The unleashing of the potential of the connected products or services (including a good idea or a representation online show of individual, or a borrowed bike/car/room (sharing for resident, teaching, live broadcasting for selling) are changing from buying to once-a-payment. For instance, the IoT economy is no longer driven by the purchase and use of products but by services (pay as you need). The value is shifting from the purchase/consumption of products to "pay for once usage" services. The connection that produces value is also changing from macro connection to micro connection.

• The micro and real-time adjustment ability of IoT makes the user-ship splitting from the ownership and pay-per-times for usages/services without buying the whole. From the views of ecosystems, separation of ownership and use right by the IoT technology push the idea "pay per usage of product or service" into our minds.[2] Dynamic adjustment of production, according to the diversity of quantity and quality of products/service or supplying chain) leads to the smart preparation of raw materials and technical deployment as one of the advantages.

Another lies in the real-time adjustment for the changing markets and the upgraded demands (including the design idea and the (re-)grading/upgrading of products/services). More instances can be found in the sharing bike/car, sharing kitchen/restaurant (e.g., carry-out food), and sharing education through online class or webinar/seminar.

• An open and flexible chain in supplying/distribution. Customizable production and distribution, taking China as an example, range from the source of agricultural products to family/dining table. The examples of APPs include Meituan.com, Jingxi (an APP) of JingDong.com, DuoDuo vegetables of Pinduoduo.com, which reduce the contact between people in the post-epidemic era. Not to mention that blockchains enhance and share the trust chain between/among the producer and consumers.

• The producer/manufacturer and the consumer are online at the same time, and they are changing each other by real-time demand (DiDi, Uber). These scenarios are also coming into the industry/agriculture and covering more details around our daily lives. More participants or stakeholders may find new opportunities (including new jobs) among the inter-links of the two twist chains.

---

[2]As the author mentioned, supplying improvement for individual or a group, a product or service, is an IoE thinking way, such as crowdsourcing service, from/to and for individuals; and time-sharing usages of a bike or a car.

• The more connections and more service/production options reveal more opportunity of accessing our privacy/security and details/clues about us, which are challenging each stage of the two chains in Fig. 3.5.

• IoT solutions with automation and integration help stakeholders move from primarily product-centered business models to service-oriented business models, also known as "servitization". More and more traditionally product-centered companies or organizations are realizing the revenue opportunities offered by developing an ongoing, service-oriented relationship with customers, e.g., organizing a customer relationship on the basis of a service contract whereby the customer is paying for a negotiated business outcome rather than a piece of equipment. In fact, automakers are increasingly talking about "mobility as a service" as a result of connected, and increasingly autonomous, vehicles as opposed to the traditional vehicle sales model. For example, Robot Taxi in China and Car-to-go/Carcare-to-go in Europe or US.

By now, we have started to see the full potential of IoT and the broad spectrum of different use cases. We have also seen the economic potential across the global economy including the industrial, enterprise, consumer, and public sectors. There are different ways to structure and size the market and also to structure the different applications and use cases. As can be seen, there are indeed recurring applications from across sectors, such as resource optimization, predictive maintenance of equipment, and autonomous operations. Further drivers and enablers for IoT are covered in Chapters 4 to 7, and use cases are the subject of Chapter 7 of this book.

Chapter 4

Perceptual Technologies Layer of IoT*

Eyes, ears, mouths, noses, and tongues allow humans to perceive the physical world, so do "smart things" want. Perceptual technologies do them the favor by being a bridge to our world.

Chapter 3 gave a layered vision with temporal characteristics and market conditions for the Internet of Things (IoT). This chapter emphasizes on perceptual technologies and their related new directions taken by the developing IoT world, such as radio frequency identification technology (RFID)/wireless sensor network (WSN), biometric identification, human-sensory-like details of IoT senses (e.g., augmented reality (AR)/virtual reality (VR)), location awareness, and some new sensing methods.

The perception layer, located at the bottom of the four-layer IoT reference architecture described in the previous chapter, shows the organized "sensory system" as well as the foundation of the IoT. Things in IoT perceive the whole physical world with their "sensory functions", where the perception information from various objects and environments are transmitted to the IoT network layer through communication module and access gateway.

If the related technologies involved in perception layer are collectively called as the perception technologies, as the basis of the IoT (indoor bridge technologies), the perception technologies provide the initial information source for perceiving the physical world, and integrate the physical and

* For this chapter, the author would like to specifically thank Mr. Jiang-yuan Zhu, who is a PhD scholar at the University of Nice, France, for his assistance.

information dimensions of our world, thus opening up a new cognitive way of transcending human beings' consciousness among objects/things. Things become connected by getting assigned an identifier and a means to be connected to other objects or to the network. The combination of physical world information collected by perceptual technology and network facilities can provide comprehensive services for human society and achieve the sublimation of the cognitive level of the physical world.

The essence of perceptual technology is information collection, a bit like the function of human sensory organs. There are many technologies involved in the perceptual layer of the IoT. In this chapter, the technology system of the perceptual layer of the IoT is briefly analyzed by means of identification technology, sensing technology and WSN, identification and biometric technology, interaction technology, and location awareness technology.

4.1 Identification and Recognition Technology

The IoT is not a single new technology or phenomenon. It includes a set of technologies that delivers the vision of IoT. RFID is a typical Identification technology, which has been around for some 60 years, and technologies to build sensor networks with it are not new, neither are capabilities to process data that originate from RF sensing things. The IoT perception capabilities can be viewed as a coming together of the sets of different technologies and usages. Now, let's begin with the identification and recognition technology.

Sometimes, recognition technology is a pattern in which a string of characters is represented as a barcode; sometimes, it is an electronic tag that only the reader can communicate with; sometimes, it works as the "digital pointer" in the information world. However, identification and recognition technology is one of the core technologies in the perceptual layer, which links "things" to the IoT world at the perception layer through their "congenital" characteristics or "marked by man-made" identifications (IDs).

4.1.1 *Automatic recognition technology*

Automatic recognition (or identification) is used to represent the connected object in the IoT, which has unique digital encoding or identifiable features. Automatic recognition technology is regarded as identification acquisition and feature extraction technology. It is embodied in barcode recognition, RFID, magnetic identification technology, and IC (integrated circuit) technology by means of data coding, data identification, data acquisition, data management, data transmission, and other standardized methods.

Barcode is a graphical representation of information, which can be read by a specific scanning device, converted into binary and decimal information compatible with the computer. Barcodes are divided into two kinds: one-dimensional barcode and two-dimensional barcode (i.e., QR code).[1]

One-dimensional barcode expresses information only in one direction by using multiple unequal widths "strip" and "empty", which are arranged in parallel according to a certain coding rule, and the rule aims to show a set of graphical information identifier. One-dimensional barcode can mark the country of manufacture, manufacturer, name of commodity, date of production and information of book classification number, place of start and end of mail, category, and date. So, it is widely used in many fields, such as commodity circulation, book management, postal management, and banking systems.

Barcode is usually used to identify items of a product, but it does not contain descriptive information of the product itself. When it is scanned and interpreted, it needs support from the backend database. One-dimensional barcode itself has limited information, as small amount of data (about 30 characters) with only letters, numbers, and some special characters.

Two-dimensional barcode can represent letters, numbers, ASCII characters, and binary numbers, with a maximum data content of 1850 characters. It can restore lost information through error correction codes, even if a part is damaged in some extent. From December 2009, train tickets in China have been upgraded with this two-dimensional code by the Ministry of Railways of China. In order to avoid information leakage, in December 2012, the Ministry of Railways adopted a special strong encryption technology to carry out a unified encryption of all information (including passenger identity information) in the two-dimensional code of train tickets, which further improved the ability of anti-counterfeiting.

In addition to the automatic and contactless recognition technology of barcode, contact recognition technology of magnetic card and IC card is commonly used in daily life. Magnetic card/stripe is a card-like magnetic recording medium, which uses magnetic carriers to record characters and

[1]There may be "three-dimensional code" in some later day. As an illusion, three-dimensional code may be combined with gene technology. The author of this book believes that DNA with a double helix structure of three-dimensional code can be used in the future to solve the rapid coding, identification of genes, and heredity. Among them, the third dimension is not only a spatial dimension but also a pointer to specific content.

Table 4.1 Characteristic of some automatic recognition technologies.

Automatic recognition technology	**One-dimensional barcode**	**Two-dimensional barcode**	**Magnetic stripe/card**	**IC card**	**RFID tag/card**
Information amount	Small	Medium	Medium	Large	Large
R/W	R	R	R/W	R/W	R/W
Coding standard	Y	Y	Self-defined	Self-defined	Y
Marking cost	Low	Low	Medium	High	Medium
Recognition cost	Low	Medium	Low	Medium	Medium
Advantages	Cheaper	Cheap, more available and information than one-dimensional barcode	Cheap, R/W	Secure by way of contact recognition, with medium cost	R/W contactless, recognition with high speed
Disadvantages	Small amount of information, close reading	Small amount of information, close reading, high equipment cost	Small amount of information, close reading, general confidentiality	Contact reading	Remote reading, high-cost

digital information for identification or other purposes. IC card, also known as smart card, is recognized by the data written on IC chips. These cards, card readers, and backend computer management system constitute the application system. Characteristic analysis and comparison of barcode and other commonly used automatic recognition techniques are shown in Table 4.1.

In Table 4.1, it can be seen that the barcodes (one-dimensional and two-dimensional) and magnetic bar/card have small information capacity and cannot provide more accurate information of items, such as location, status, by itself and with less anti-counterfeiting ability. In addition, photoelectric recognition technology is used to identify barcodes closely, and card identification must be in contact with the reader. So, barcode, magnetic stripe/card, and IC card are unable to achieve long-distance reading, which brings inconvenience to the application.

As a cheap and practical technology, barcode, magnetic bar/card, or IC card are still applied in various industries and commercial scenarios continuously. However, the information that these tags can represent is very limited, and the close identification limits the dynamic and fast reading, large amount of data acquisition, and the operation distance requirements. Therefore, RFID tags based on wireless technology are needed.

4.1.2 *RFID*

RFID is a typical identification technology as well as one of the key technologies of the IoT. RFID was extensively used during the period of the World War II, as "Identification Friend or Foe (IFF)", by using aircraft radar detection technology to distinguish the transmitted ID signals. The technology originated in 1950s, as it was achieved in the long-rang transponder system for aircrafts (as shown in Fig. 4.1). RFID technology has been widely used up to now.

During the 1970s and 1980s, the development of IC, microprocessor, and other technologies accelerated the development of RFID. RFID technology and products entered the stage of "explosion", and then early large-scale applications appeared. Since the 1990s, the standardization of RFID technology has been paid more and more attention, and RFID products have been widely used. Especially, in the late 1990s, because the standardization of electronic product code (EPC) system, which is based on the wide application of RFID in networking, RFID products became a part of people's lives gradually.

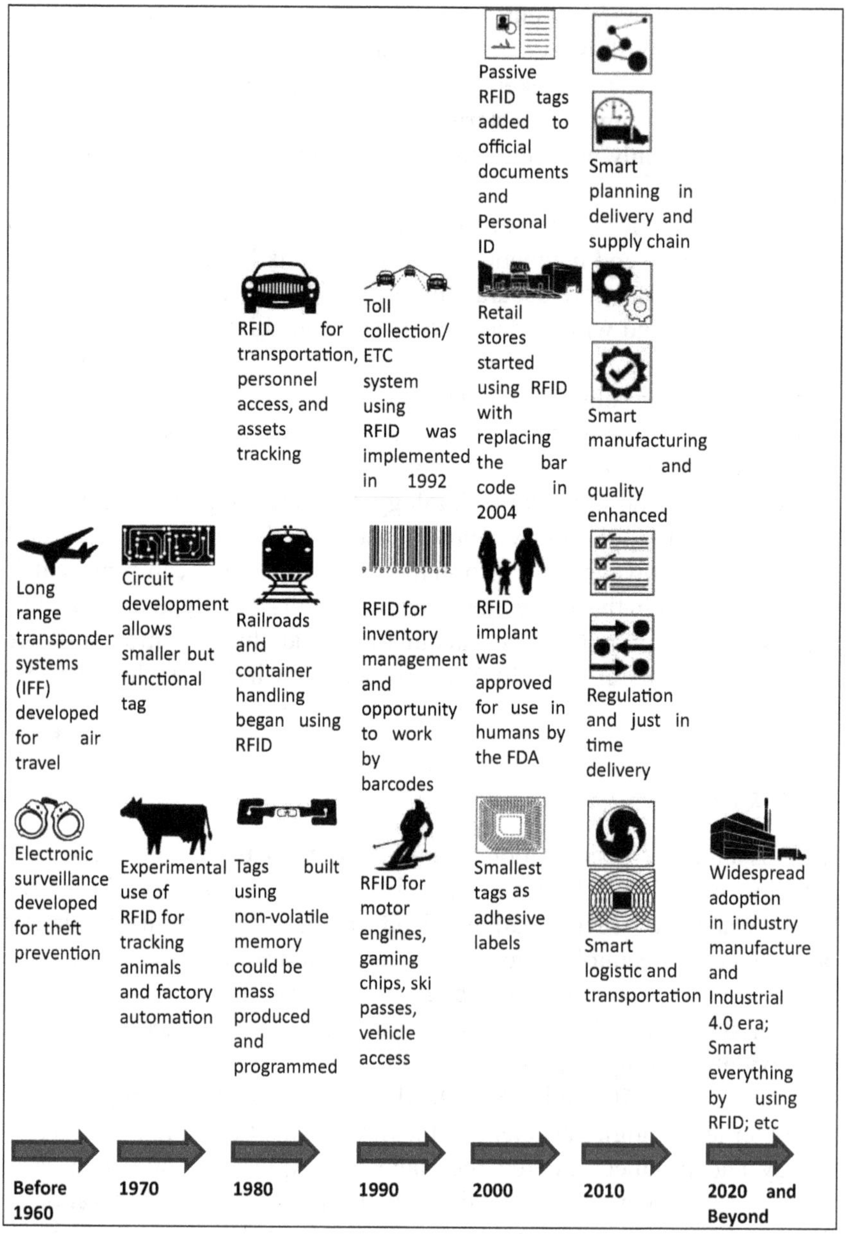

Figure 4.1 History of RFID.

Source: Wiki.

On November 5, 2003, Walmart, which accounted for 60% of the annual turnover of the retail industry in the US, at that time, announced that all goods supplied to Walmart store required RFID to be installed on their packing boxes before the spring of 2007. From then on, major retail stores started using RFID with a goal of replacing the barcode, as shown in Fig. 4.1.

At present, many famous research universities and well-known enterprises in the world are involved in the research and development of RFID. So far as the development of RFID market in China is concerned, the application of RFID includes Chinese identity card, electronic tickets (including bank ID, electronic access control, electronic ticket of railway, bus and other public transports, etc.), dangerous goods management, social security, health insurance, and so on.

Entering the 21st century, as the variety of RFID products becomes richer, different kinds of active, passive, and semi-passive electronic tags have been developed. At the same time, the cost of RFID has been continuously reduced with the application expanding continuously. Single-chip tag, multi-purpose reading, passive electronic tag, and long-range recognition RFID which is suitable for high-speed moving objects (such as electronic tolling collection (ETC) in Chapter 1) are becoming more and more popular.

1. Composition and principle of RFID: RFID is a kind of non-contact automatic identification technology, mainly used to establish unique identification for various items. RF signal and its spatial coupling transmission characteristics are used to identify stationary or moving objects automatically. A typical RFID system consists of a reader, a transponder or a tag which are attached to objects that need to be identified, and a computer or network system. The electronic tag is also called RF tag, contactless smart card, or ID tag. The electronic device consists of coupling elements (such as antennas) and RFID chips (including control modules and memory modules).

A reader unit contains a transceiver that is used to communicate wirelessly with the tags. When the reader transmits a specific frequency electromagnetic signal to the electronic tag, the electromagnetic signal is used to drive the electronics and read the ID code inside the transponder. Electronic tags appear as cards, buttons, and other styles. Some of them are made resistant to dirt or water, and the chip ID is unique which cannot

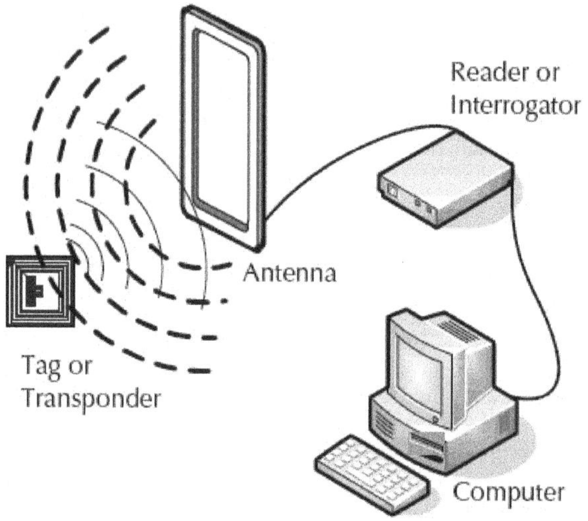

Figure 4.2 Typical application scenario of RFID system.

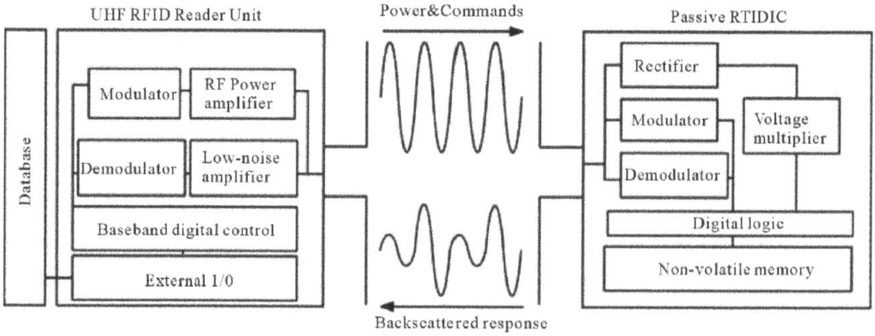

Figure 4.3 Composition of RFID system.

be copied, meeting some security mechanisms and other characteristics according to special standards, such as ISO and EPC.

As shown in Fig. 4.2, either a USB or an ethernet port is connected to the reader, in order to communicate with the application in the back-end, e.g., a database or program running in a computer.

RFID tags can be affixed to or installed on different objects, which facilitate the reader installed in different geographical locations to read and store the data in the tags automatically. RFID technology can also identify high-speed moving objects, which is introduced in the beginning chapter as ETC, where there is a global unique ID code in each RFID tag chip.

After affixing the object with RFID tag, it is necessary to establish the relevant description information of the object in the back-end database, which corresponds to the ID code one by one. As shown in Fig. 4.3, when a reader is used to operate on an item tag, the reader antenna sends an electromagnetic signal to the tag, the tag receives the electromagnetic signal from the reader, and the product information stored in the tag chip is sent out to the reader (passive tag works with the energy obtained by the induced current from the reader), or the tag sends signal actively with its energy. The reader reads the information and decodes it, then it is transmitted to the system server, where the description information of the item is queried according to the ID code.

According to the type of energy supplied to the tag, RFID tags can be divided into active, semi-active, and passive tags. As for passive tags, the distance between the tag and the reader is short enough for the tag to extract energy from the electromagnetic field, which is emitted by the reader. The right part of Fig. 4.3 is a passive tag, which contains two components, an antenna and an IC. The IC consists of a rectifier, modulator, and non-volatile memory banks. The memory stores an EPC that is the electronic fingerprint, such as a unique 96-bit long identification code.

Readers can be used to send and receive radio frequency signals to/from tags. They are hand-held (portable) or fixed, even embedded in other electronic systems as a component, with the functions of reading and writing, display and data processing, or transmitting data to back-end systems.

After the back-end computer obtains the data (or information in electronic tag) collected by distributed readers at different locations in real time and accurately, the data can be processed locally or in distributive database of clouds, according to the needs of the service.

So, the software components of RFID in the computer network system (along with the database in the back-end system of RFID, in the left part of Fig. 4.3) are also important, and these are the interfaces between different hardware of the reader/tag and various specific application requirements.

2. Classification of RFID: According to the power supply mode, tags are divided into active, semi-active, and passive tags. According to the carrier frequency at which the RFID works, it can be divided into low frequency, mediate frequency, high frequency, ultra-high frequency (UHF), and microwave frequency of working radio. According to the operation distance, it can be divided into close-distance coupling, long-distance coupling, and remote-distance coupling. According to the different forms of tag, it can be divided into card tag, linear tag, paper tag, glass tube tag, circular tag, and special purpose profiled tag (such as SIM-RFID, nano-SIM, and credit card). Here, passive, active, and semi-active RFID systems are discussed as follows:

(i) ***Active RFID system*****:** The active tag can actively send data in the form of RF signals to the reader with its own energy, which is powered by the internal battery of the tag itself. Active tag includes microprocessor, sensor, input/output port, and circuit. It has high working reliability and long signal transmission distance, with about 30 m and almost 100 m at the farthest.

With the degradation of battery energy in the tag, the data transmission distance becomes shorter and stability of the tag is also reduced.

The active RFID system is mainly used in applications with obstacles or high transmission distance between tag and reader because its working life depends on the continuous power supply capacity of the battery, so the volume of active tag is large and the cost is relatively high. The active RFID system is mainly used for remote detection of valuables or when long distance is necessary.

(ii) ***Semi-active RFID*****:** In semi-active RFID systems, although the electronic tag itself has a battery, it does not actively send data to the reader through its own energy, the battery is responsible for supplying power to the internal IC of the tag. Tags need to be activated by the energy of the reader before transmitting their own data. Then, when the tag enters the reading area of the reader, it is excited to work by the RF signal and power from the reader. The energy supporting the information exchange between the tag and the reader is mainly supplied by the RF energy of the reader.

The energy of the battery inside the semi-active tag doesn't convert into RF energy except when the tag cannot get enough power from the RF energy of the reader.

Before the tag enters the working state, it remains in low-power consumption state in order to save battery energy. Under ideal conditions, the working distance between readers and semi-active tags is less than 30 m. The typical effective working range is generally 10 m with high accuracy.

(iii) ***Passive RFID system*****:** The operation of passive RFID systems is also based on the coupling of electromagnetic waves, and the electronic tag of passive RFID has no power supplies inside. The reader unit generates a high frequency signal that is transformed into a wireless electromagnetic wave by the reader antenna. This signal is sent out for the tag antenna, which receives it and forwards it to the tag IC. Since passive tags do not contain any dedicated power supplies, e.g., batteries, the signal from the reader unit is used to provide operation power for the IC. Once the IC has rectified enough power to activate itself, the IC enables its modulator that switches between two loads in its input, a matched load and a non-matched load, to generate a backscattered response containing the tag's ID code.

The reading and writing distances of passive tags are smaller than those of active and semi-active tags. But they are relatively cheaper because the passive tags do not have a battery. The typical valid reading range is generally within 4 m.

RFID systems, along with their electronic tags, working in different RF bands have different characteristics. The frequency bands occupied by RFID are internationally limited and recognized within the ISM[2] bands. Their typical operating frequencies are 125 kHz, 133 kHz, 13.56 MHz, 27.12 MHz, 902–928 MHz, 2.45 GHz, 5.8 GHz, etc. According to the working frequency, RFIDs can also be divided into low frequency, mediate frequency, high frequency, UHF, and microwave radio frequency identification. Some of them are analyzed in Table 4.2.

3. Characteristics of RFID: The identification information can be transmitted by electromagnetic coupling, then the object tracking and data exchange can be carried out quickly. Because RFID needs to make use of radio frequency resources, it must abide by many specifications of radio frequency management. Compared with the recognition technology at the same or earlier time, RFID also has the following characteristics:

- *R/W function*: As long as the RFID reader is used, the data or information in the tag can be read contactless into the database, and multiple tags can be read by one reader at once. On the other hand, the processed data from back-end can also be written to the electronic tag by the writing function of the reader (or interrogator).

[2] Industry, science, and medicine.

Table 4.2 Main characteristics of different RFID frequencies.

Characteristic	Low frequency (LF)	High frequency (HF)	Ultra-high frequency (UHF)	Super-high frequency (SHF) (microwave)
Operating frequency	125–134 kHz[a], 131–450 kHz 30–50 kHz	7.4–8.8 MHz, 13.56 MHz, 27 MHz	433 MHz, 868–915 MHz	2.45–5.8 GHz
Typical reading distance	Less than 1 m	Less than 1 m	Passive tags: US~0–6 m, EU~0–4 m; Active tag:0–100 m	0–1000 m/Active tag
Operating data transmission rate	Low	Medium	Fast	Very Fast
Multiple tag reading	Limited	Up to 50 tags/sec	Up to 200 tags/sec	Up to 300 tags/sec
Wet environment	No significant impact	No significant impact	Significant impact	Significant impact
Direction	No	No	Part of	Yes
Standards/Protocol air interface	ISO/IEC18000-2, ISO11784/85, ISO14223, IEEEP1902.1/ RuBee EM4100	ISO/IEC 18000-3, ISO/IEC 15693, ISO/IEC 18092/ NFC, ISO/IEC 10536	ISO/IEC 18000-7, ISO/IEC 18000-6, EPCglobal C1G2, IEEE 802.11, IEEE 802.15 RFID and WPAN-low rate	ISO/IEC 18000-5 (withdrawn) IEEE 802.15 WPAN UWB
Availability	>30 years (RuBee-2 years)	>10 years	US > 9 years, EU > 7 years	>10 years
Power source	Passive-inductive coupling; active battery; RuBee considers active and passive tags	Passive/Inductive or capacitive coupling	Active battery; Passive-capacitive or E-field coupling	Active battery; Passive-capacitive or E-field coupling
Applications	Attendance system, access control system and so on; Fixed assets management and enterprise ID card or “one-card-pass” system	Post, air transportation, medicine, freight, library, product tracking	Vehicle identification and tracking, warehousing and logistics managements, remote control locks, shelf, and truck trailer.	ETC in highway, transportation, and parking lot, freight container

[a]According to Annex 9 of the ERC Rec 70-03, inductive RFID Reader systems primarily operate either below 135 kHz or at 6.78 MHz or 13.56 MHz. Therefore, the correlated transponder data return frequencies reside in the following ranges: LF range transponder frequencies: $f = < 135$ kHz, $f_{TRP} = 135$ to 148.5 kHz; HF range transponder frequencies: $f = 6.78$ MHz; $f_{TRP} = 4.78$ to 8.78 MHz; $f = 13.56$ MHz; $f_{TRP} = 11.56$ to 15.56 MHz.

- *Multi-styles*: RFID tags do not need to match the fixed size and printing quality of the paper (such as barcodes) in order to be read accurately. In addition, RFID tags can be miniaturized and made easy to be embedded in different items. Therefore, the production with tags can be controlled more flexibly, especially in the production line.
- *Environmental tolerance*: Tags can be read and written without contact, in dark or dirty environments. Some of them have environmental tolerance, including anti-moisture, anti-dust, and anti-smoke in harsh environment. Their anti-fouling characteristic includes anti-water, anti-oil, and protection against metal and other substances.
- *Penetrating communication*: RFID can read data from the tags even if it is coated with non-metallic, non-transparent materials, such as paper, wood, and plastics, so penetrating communication can be carried out. However, it is impossible to communicate through metal objects such as iron.
- *Convenience*: Some of the tags can be reused because information in a tag can be read and written repeatedly. If tags are defined and made as recyclable tags, their usage improves utilization and reduces electronics pollution. Furthermore, passive UHF RF-tags can be inkjet-printed directly on wood, paper, and cardboard substrates.
- *Security*: Transferring product data from back-end computer to reader will be provided with information security methods. The storage data in radio frequency tags can be guaranteed by means of cyclic redundancy check (CRC) and other checking methods in communication. More details will be discussed later.

Finally, some new trends are discussed as two use cases:

(1) *In-vehicle usage*: The application of RFID has been very extensive in smart transportation or smart city. For example, in Chinese highways, an ETC system was designed by the combination of microwave RFID of vehicle and user ID, which won the first prize of National Science and Technology Progress of 2015 in China, as shown in Fig. 4.4. The microwave RFID system aims at three major traffic scenarios.

The first is the highway ETC (passing without stopping) and charging scenario, where the microwave RFID is used to realize wireless communication; the mobile vehicle recognition RFID and system-level applications are analyzed in Fig. 4.4.

The second scenario is electronic license plate of vehicles, which is mainly used for traffic management and charging in smart cities, such as

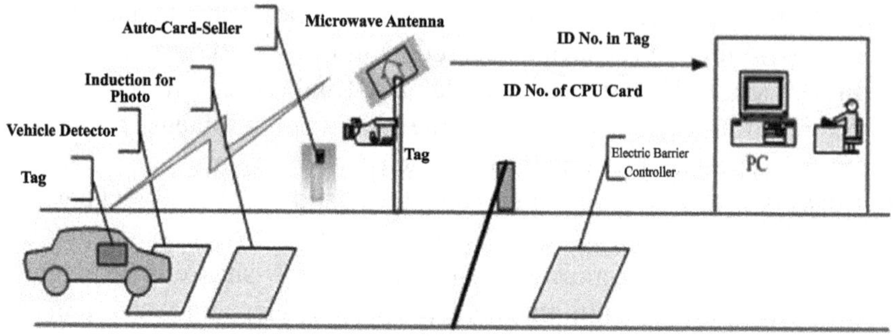

Figure 4.4 Chinese design and application of ETC system which won in the first prize of National Science and Technology Progress in 2015.

Stockholm, which is one of the famous smart cities in Sweden, for traffic control.

The third is toward an intelligent transportation scenario of Internet of everything (IoE), if the vehicle electronic ID system is combined with real-time individual information, such as vehicles speed, road conditions, location, and other LBS services. Then, more services can be achieved from macro-traffic view, including not only prediction of congestion analysis and active avoidance but also more services based on the vehicles to everything (V2X)[3] network.

(2) *In-cloth usage*: Nowadays, some clothing brands have begun to introduce the technology from ECO RFID, for its environmental-friendly materials — sustainable, renewable, no impact on existing waste streams, or recycling. As shown in Fig. 4.5, by printing an RFID label on a renewable paper, without plastic layers and harmful chemicals, the patented ECO technology gives us an innovative and feasible alternative to traditional inlay manufacturing processes.

4.1.3 *EPC system*

With the acceleration of global economic integration and the rapid technological innovation enlightened around IoT, the AutoID Center of

[3]V2X is a special kind of IoTs, and it will be discussed in Chapter 6.

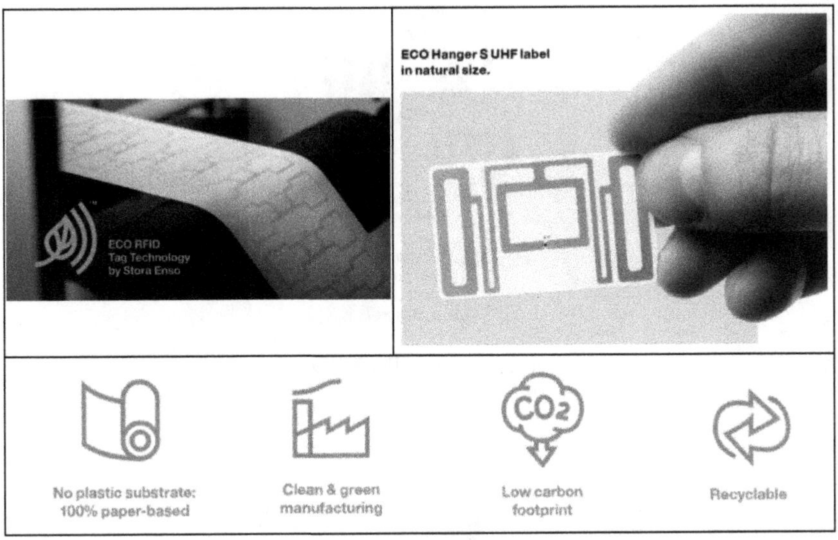

Figure 4.5 Green ECO RFID by Stora Enso.

Source: https://www.storaenso.com/.

Massachusetts Institute of Technology (MIT), with the support of the Unified Code Commission of the US, proposed the concept of EPC,[4] which was designed to providing a unique identity for every physical object anywhere in the world. Now, global trade item number (GTIN) coding system is perfectly combined with the concept of EPC, and EPC is integrated into the global unified identification system, thus making EPC become a truly revolutionary technology.

1. Introduction of EPC: In 1984, the first large-scale commercial application of EPC's introduction to industry was by General Motors Inc., who took the lead in adopting EPC and RFID technologies on its automobile production line. Since then, more and more retailers and manufacturers are concerned about and supporting the application of EPC. For example, Walmart (Inc.), the retail giant of the US, demanded for product identification and management that are requested to install RFID for goods purchased from suppliers.

[4]EPCglobal. EPC Radio-Frequency Identity Protocols Class-1 Generation-2 UHF RFID Protocol for Communications at 860 MHz-960 MHz Version 1.0.9.

Figure 4.6 An EPC RFID tag.

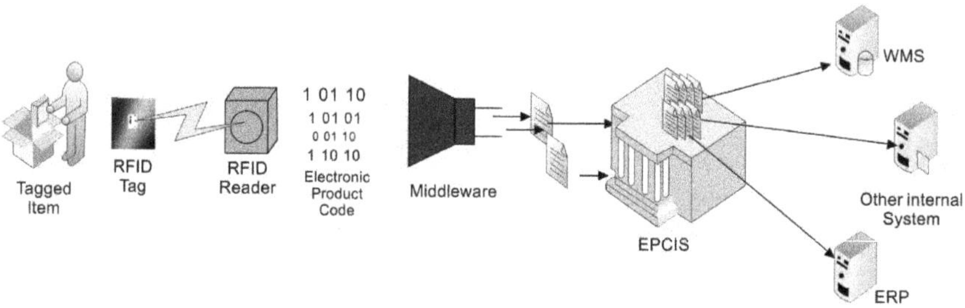

Figure 4.7 EPC structure includes EPC coding standard, EPC tag, EPC code, reader, middleware, object naming service (ONS), EPC information service (EPCIS), and others.

The biggest advantage of RFID is that it can manage the supply chain efficiently. So far as the application of supply chain management is concerned, RFID is a very suitable technology to reduce the logistic cost. But due to the non-uniform standards, the technology has not been widely used until EPC arose. Figure 4.6 shows **an EPC RFID tag used by Walmart**.

The main objective of EPCglobal is to provide an architecture to collect vast amounts of raw data from a heterogeneous RFID environment, filter them, compile them into usable data structures, and send them to computational systems (Fig. 4.7).

At present, EPCglobal, established by the International European Article Number and Uniform Code Council (EAN/UCC), is responsible for the global promotion and application of EPC. EPCglobal has established branches in Canada, Japan, China, etc., and the branches specialize in the distribution and management of EPC code segments and the promotion and application of EPC-related technologies in these countries.

The EPC is designed to meet the needs of various industries while guaranteeing uniqueness for all EPC-compliant tags. Some of the existing global standard one (GS1) identification keys (such as the Global Returnable Asset Identifier (GRAI)) already provide for unique identification.

In brief, EPCglobal defines the following components: (i) RFID readers (also denoted as RFID sensors); (ii) application-level events (ALE) for filtering and collecting EPC data; (iii) EPC information services (EPCIS) to store EPC data as well as to exchange this data along the EPCglobal network; (iv) middleware, which is as a capturing application between ALE and EPCIS, regulating how the former sends data to the latter. Each company has its own set of components, so the idea is to generate value by providing a standard way of capturing data from objects between the partners involved in a particular application field (including, for example, suppliers, enterprises, resellers, clients, buildings, and users).

2. EPC coding standard: The EPC coding structure is defined by the EPCglobal tag data standard (TDS), which is an open standard freely available for download from the website of EPCglobal, Inc. The canonical representation of an EPC is an URI, namely the "pure-identity URI" representation that is intended for use when referring to a specific physical object in communications about EPCs among information systems and business application software.

TDS in EPC aims to give each entity object a unique code and constructs a physical link to realize the real-time sharing of global item information. So, it defines relevant information of entities and establishes a universal information exchange language through unified and standardized coding. According to its ID coding bit length, the EPC coding structure is usually divided into three categories: 64 bit, 96 bit, and 256 bit. There are different coding formats for different applications, and the latest Gen2 standard EPC coding can be compatible with other codes. These three categories can continue to be divided into seven types, namely EPC-64-I, EPC-64-II, EPC-64-III, EPC-96-I, EPC-256-I, EPC-256-II, and EPC-256-III.

For example, the format of EPC-64 is as follows:

As shown above, four fields of EPC encoding are:

- Version number, which is used to identify the version number of the coding standard, so that the coding of electronic products can be of different lengths and types.
- EPC manager, which includes manufacturer information related to this EPC.

- Object **class**, to which the product belongs.
- Object **number**, which is the unique number of the object.

EPC code does not contain any product describing information, such as product name, location, and on-shelf cycle. Information stored in EPC code includes embedded information and reference information. Embedded information can include weight, size, validity, destination, and so on.

The basic idea is to use the existing computer network with its current information resources to store code data as a pointer, so that EPC code becomes a network pointer with the smallest amount of information. But the information the pointer referred to, which is stored in the computer or network, is actually enough to cover all the attributions or the items of one object (or product). So, this character overcomes some shortages of barcodes, such as small amount of information stored, reading closely, broken and information lost easily.

In the coding standard of EPC, the EPCglobal TDS also defines additional representations of an EPC identifier, such as the tag-encoding URI format and a compact binary format suitable for storing an EPC identifier efficiently within RFID tags (for which the low-cost passive RFID tags typically have limited memory capacity available for the EPC/UII memory bank). The EPCglobal TDS defines the structure of the URI syntax and binary format, as well as the encoding and decoding rules to allow conversion between these representations. The EPC is designed as a flexible framework that can support many existing coding schemes, including many coding schemes currently in use with barcode technology. More EPC standards by GS1 are shown in Table 4.3.

3. EPC Principle: EPC tries to provide almost perfect solution for supply chain management. In the IoT era, the connections built with EPC is realizing that every product of the world can be connected to each other at anytime and anywhere, and making fundamental changes in the whole process of product production, warehousing, procurement, transportation, sales, and consumption. It is an extension of the application of barcodes technology. The working principle of EPC is shown in Fig. 4.8. The logical structure and relationship of each part in the EPC working are shown in detail, and the main parts in it include EPC tag, reader, middleware, and EPC network, where ONS server, PML, and so on are defined as shown in Fig. 4.8.

Table 4.3 EPC/RFID standards list.

EPC/RFID Standards							
Identification	Tag data standard (TDS)	Tag data translation (TDT)					
RFID Air Interfaces	UHF Gen2 air interface	HF air interface					
RFID Software Interfaces	Low-level reader protocol (LLRP)	Discovery configuration & initialization (DCI)	Reader management (RM)	Application-level events (ALE)			
Implementation guidelines	Interoperability of barcodes, EPCIS, and RFID	Transport and logistics industry user group — Implementation guide — TLS pilots	Returnable transport item (RTI/Pallet tagging) guideline	GS1 EPCglobal standards in the consumer electronics supply chain	RFID-based electronic article surveillance (EAS) technical implementation guide	RFID-based electronic article surveillance (EAS) — strategic overview	Tagged-item performance protocol (TIPP) guidelines

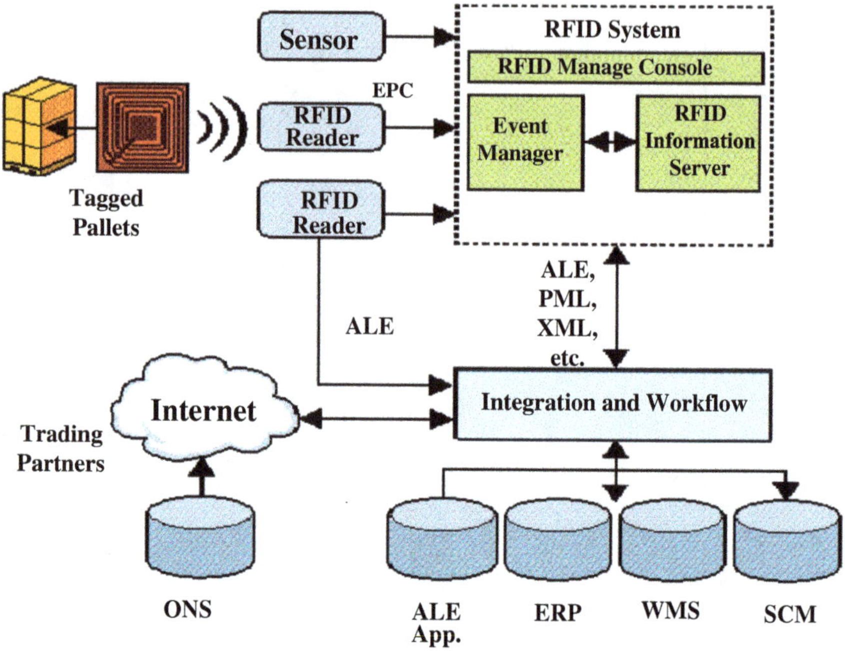

Figure 4.8 Working principle of the EPC network.

Table 4.4 EPC data format.

2-bit version number	21-bit EPC manager	17-bit object class	24-bit object number
XX	XXX...XXX	XXX...XXX	XXX...XXX

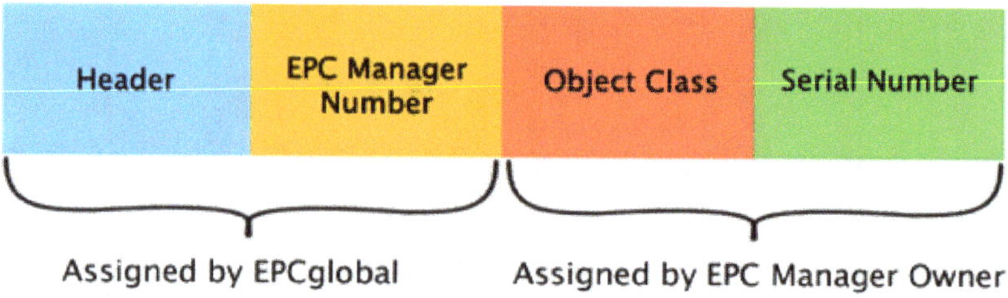

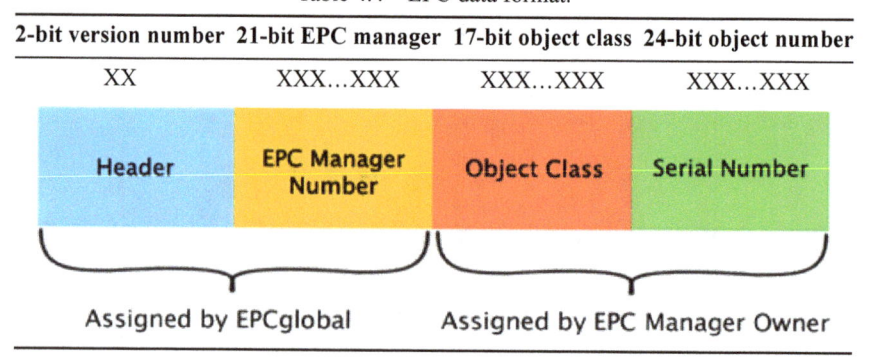

(1) ***EPC data format*****:** The standardized EPC data format consists of an EPC (sometimes called an EPC identifier or EPC ID) that uniquely identifies an individual object, and may include an optional filter value when it is necessary to enable the effective and efficient reading of the EPC tags. The EPC encoded in an RFID tag can identify the manufacturer, product, version, and serial number, as listed in Table 4.4.

The major part of the standard EPC data field is the EPC identifier. The optional filter value field within the EPC can supplement the basic EPC tag readings. For various applications and industries, the EPC version 1.1 standard specifies the following coding schemes:

General identifier (GID);
A serialized version of the EAN.UCC Global Trade Item Number (GTIN);
EAN.UCC Serial Shipping Container Code (SSCC);
EAN.UCC Global Location Number (GLN);
EAN.UCC Global Returnable Asset Identifier (GRAI);
EAN.UCC Global Individual Asset Identifier (GIAI).

For any given RFID tag with an EPC data format, an entry in its header field indicates which coding scheme can be applied.

(2) ***EPC tag*****:** As discussed previously, the information retrieval or querying of objects can be carried out based on EPC ID in the EPC tag. EPC tag is composed of special chip and tag antenna (coupling element), and it works as a RFID tag. The code inside is an identification scheme for universally identifying physical objects using RFID tags and other means, thus connecting each item of the physical world to a unique information communication address.

(3) ***Reader*****:** Reader is a device to read or write information data from/to EPC tags. According to the setting mode, the reader can be divided into hand-held mobile reader and fixed reader.

According to the function of reading and writing, it can be divided into read only, read/write, and programmer reader.

If handheld mobile readers support protocols such as Wi-Fi or ZigBee to achieve seamless communication, mobile reader can connect directly to the back-end communication network through the wireless access point (AP).

(4) ***Middleware*****:** Middleware in EPC, earlier called Savant, is distributed operating software, which is responsible for managing and transmitting EPC code-related data. It is in the middle between reader and Internet (or local area networks) and is responsible for data cache, data filtering, data processing, and so on.

EPC data is transmitted to local area network or Internet, after it is processed by Savant. The distributed structure of Savant is mainly reflected in hierarchical organization and management of data. The Savant at each level of the hierarchy will collect, store, and process information with other Savant systems, and it has the functions of data proofreading, reader coordination, selective data transmission, data storage, and task management.

First, the Savant system at the edge of the network directly exchanges information with the reader, proofreads the missed or misread information, and then redundant filters the same EPC code information transmitted by multiple readers. After preprocessing the data collected from the reader, the data is cached.

Take the supply chain as an instance. Savant queries the supply chain for special applications to see what necessary information needs to be passed on the supply chain, other information will be filtered in order to reduce the burden of the networks. The management of the Savant refers to user-defined monitoring management implemented only by a single Savant. For example, a warehouse middleware can write a program alone to alert the warehouse administrator when the number of goods in the warehouse is reduced to a threshold.

(5) ***EPC network system*****:** EPC network includes EPCIS, ONS, PML, and so on.

EPC Information Server (EPCIS) is the server that provides the information associated with the ID, and the object naming system (ONS) server is used to resolve the link between the EPC ID and the corresponding EPCIS server, which acts like the domain name server (DNS in the Internet.).

As for ONS, there are two kinds of information in the ONS: the embedded information and the reference information of the item. The reference information of the item is stored in the EPCIS maintained by the manufacturer.

After reading the code by the middleware (such as Savant), the ONS server is used to address the EPCIS server, where it stores the corresponding item information in the LAN or Internet, and then the item ID is used to obtain the reference information of the product in the product information server maintained by the manufacturer, and finally return it to the middleware. The process-related parts are as follows:

ALE[5] is a part of EPC software. ALE is also called as the RFID event manager and it gathers information from RFID readers, filters the

[5]As introduced formerly, application-level events is for filtering and collecting EPC data.

information, and provides the processed information to the EPCIS server or to a third-party enterprise resource planning (ERP) system, if necessary.

Physical Markup Language (PML) is an XML-based specification for describing the information format of an item. EPC product electronic code identifies a single product, but all the information about the product is written in PML.

URI Format aims to give a pure identity that is independent from underlying physical media, such as RFID tags or barcodes. The EPC standard provides this definition for a pure identity: "The identity associated with a specific physical or logical entity, independent of any particular encoding vehicle, such as an RF tag, barcode, or database field". The EPC standard further defines identity URI as "a representation of a pure identity as a uniform resource identifier (URI). A URI is a character string representation that is commonly used to exchange identity data between software components of a larger system". The standard URI representation of EPCs has four categories:

URIs for pure identities (also called canonical forms), which contain only the EPC fields to identify a physical object. For example, a pure identity URI for GID can be "urn:epc:id:gid:10.1002.2". A URI for GRAI can be "urn:epc:id:grai:0652642.12345.1234".

URIs for EPC tags, which represent the tag encodings. These URIs can be used by application software to write a tag. An example for a serialized GTIN 64-bit encoding is "urn:epc:tag:sgtin-64:3.0652642.800031.400".

URIs for raw bit strings, which represent invalid bit-level patterns as a single decimal number. For example, "urn:epc:raw:64.20018283527919".

URIs for EPC patterns, which refer to a set of EPCs for the purpose of EPC filtering. A pattern of "urn:epc:pat:sgtin-64:3.0652642"[6] refers to any SGTIN identifier 64-bit tag with a filter value of three, a company prefix of 0652642.

Finally, an encoding identity layer can also be conceptualized as a sub-layer of perceptual layer in IoT, and it would comprise a pure identity together with additional information, such as the filter value, rendered into a specific syntax (typically consisting of value fields of specific sizes).

---

[6]An item reference value is in [1024-2047].

A given pure identity may have a number of possible encodings, such as various tag encodings and various URI encodings.

Furthermore, encodings may also incorporate additional data besides the identity such as the filter value used in some encodings, in which case the encoding scheme specifies what additional data it can hold.

From an IoE vision, **a physical realization** of an encoding is an encoding rendered in a concrete implementation suitable for a particular machine-readable form (such as a specific kind of radio frequency tag, code in barcode, or specific database field). This encoding can be conceived as a lower layer, like the ISO's Open System Interconnect with its modeling of physical entities near the bottom of the stack.

The EPC system based on Internet and RFID constructs a network for real-time sharing of global item information. It becomes a new technology to change the retail settlement, logistics distribution, and product tracking management mode after barcode technology.

In EPC, the open questions that need to be considered are as follows:

What are the RFID inheritable problems in manufacturing/logistics/products?
Does it help to form a consistent and compatible identity system?
What about the governance in certain scenario or industrial application of RFID, other than the EPC network? Any new forms or securing methods?
Why human beings are more willing to name "things"?

4.1.4 *The analysis of EPC security*

The security of EPC system includes not only the security issues of RFID applications but also the front-end and back-end security issues of EPC and personal information security, as we called, security and privacy protection in IoT. As for RFID, the European Network and Information Security Agency (ENISA) has undertaken to identify emerging risks affecting trust and confidence, in 2009. Toward trust, acceptance, and security of IoT, a first step in the understanding of the privacy and security risks, particular regarding RFID, is constituted by ENISA. By the way, the "silence of the chips"[7] is concerned by ENISA, which

[7] Commission of the European Communities. Internet of Things — An action plan for Europe 2009.P6.

maybe has some relation with the function of "killing a tag" in EPC. This will be discussed later in this part. Here, the EPC deficiencies are analyzed in terms of security transmission mechanism and personal privacy protection scenarios:

- Due to the unpredictability of RFID readers installed locations and the interface between readers and tags is open to the air, the information of the RFID tag items will be read and recorded by the reader without enough user awareness. Especially, when their personal items in a tag were not protected adequately, unauthorized intruders may set up hidden readers of a similar nature nearby to gain access to the information being transmitted by the readers, or even compromise the readers themselves, thus affecting their integrity. The leaked information of RFID tags and readers facilitates the attacker's attack on the extra privacy lately.
- In some cases, RFID readers are installed in locations without adequate physical protection. It is vulnerable to various types of attacks, such as eavesdropping attacks, replay attacks, denial of service (DoS) attacks in the channel, man-in-the-middle attacks, and server attacks in the EPCIS when querying items information in internet or intranet.
- As the DNS in the Internet, ONS in the EPC system also has security threats, such as software vulnerabilities, cache poisoning, domain hijacking, DoS[8] attacks, and unauthorized access.

1. EPC C1G2 security analysis: In order to foster and promote the adoption of RFID technology and to support interoperability, EPCglobal[9] and the International Organization for Standardization (ISO) have been actively engaged in the standards for tags, readers, and the communication protocols between them. For example, EPC Class[10] 1 Gen 2 (EPC G2, indicating that the specification refers to the second major release) is a communication standard that gives a platform on which to build

[8] DoS, or distributed-DoS (DDoS).

[9] The security of EPC Gen2 compliant RFID protocols.

[10] Class 1 tags contain a write-once memory for storing an EPC. Class 2 tags add additional memory that can be changed frequently for storing additional data. Class 3 tags add batteries for longer read ranges and higher reliability but are fundamentally passive backscatter tags. Class 4 tags are essentially active tags that can communicate with other Class 4 tags as well as readers. Class 5 tags are not really tags at all — they are essentially wireless networked readers.

interoperable RFID protocols. EPC G2 standard was introduced by EPCGlobal and passed the certification of the ISO in 2006, which furthered its global application.

This standard specifies the EPC G2–compatible readers, the logical and physical requirements of the tags, and the communication protocols between them. It supports efficient tag reading, flexible bandwidth use, multiple read/write capabilities, and basic security guarantees, provided by an on-chip 16-bit pseudo-random number generator (RNG) and a 16-bit cyclic redundancy code (CRC-16).

As applications, it is important to employ protocols that offer a different level of security within the constraints of the specification. Several RFID authentication protocols address security issues using lightweight cryptographic mechanisms. Most of these use hash functions and complex cryptography, which are beyond the capability of most low-cost tags and are not supported by EPC G2. Some protocols use pseudo-RNGs, a mechanism that is supported by EPC G2, but these are not optimized for EPC G2 compliance. Other protocols use timestamps that are not supported by EPC G2. EPC G2 is designed to strike a balance between cost and functionality, with less attention paid to security. Some features of the EPC G2 standard are as follows:

- *Passive RFID tag*: It is specified by the EPC Class 1 Generation 2 UHF Air Interface Protocol that the operation and functionality are based on passive RFIDs, and that their physical and logical requirements for interrogator-talks-first systems that operate in the 860–960 MHz frequency range. Readers (interrogators) transmit information to tags by modulating an RF signal. Tags receive both transmitted information and operating energy from the RF signal. The readers receive information from the tags by transmitting a continuous-wave RF and their communication distances is up to 10 m.
- *Low cost*: EPC G2 supports efficient tag reading, flexible bandwidth use, multiple read/write capabilities, and basic security guarantees. But the low-cost tag relies on a simple 16-bit pseudo- RNG and a CRC-16 validation to complete the authentication process. EPC G2 cannot support complex cryptographic operations. The tag can be set to a 32-bit access password and a 32-bit kill password, and the physical tag that is killed will no longer be available.
- *Anti-collision*: The standard uses a relatively simple anti-collision algorithm to avoid interference and collisions among multiple tags.

- *Three modulation modes*: The supported modes are double side band (DSB-ASK), single side band (SSB-ASK) and phase reverse-amplitude shift keying (PR-ASK).

The improvements of EPC G2 in security are analyzed as follows.

More memory as four banks in EPC G2 tag memory: EPC code bank, TID bank for tag identifier, user bank for data definition of users, and reserved bank for kill password and access password.

EPC Gen2 specifies four states that tags may implement: *open, ready, secure, and killed.*

Open is the initial state; ready is a holding state until the tag receives the next message from the reader; secure is a state into which a tag transitions on receiving an authenticator from the reader; killed is a state into which a secured tag transitions on receiving a kill mandate.

The killed tags should "cover" their history information without tracing and "keep silence" in a future unexpected conversation with malicious readers, which facilitate security and personal privacy protection. "Killed tags can't talk", that helps prevent unintentional or malicious "talking" to get private information.

Although application of anti-collision algorithm and simple authentication scheme are used in EPC G2, threats remain. In the EPC G2 protocol, the reader manages the tags through three kinds: select, inventory, and access. According to the operation of the reader, the tags correspond to

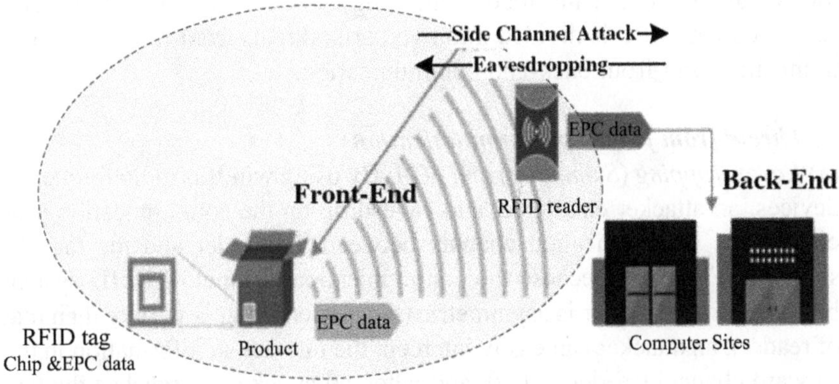

Figure 4.9 Threats from front-end and from back-end communications in a typical EPC application.

one of the seven states: *ready, arbitrate, reply, acknowledged, open, secured, and killed.*

- First, during the inventory state, the tag information is transmitted in plaintext. It is easily eavesdropped by attackers, and the private information of the tag is easily exposed. So long as the readers complying with the EPC G2 protocol inventory the tags, each time the tags are inventoried, the tags always transmit the same EPC, which will result in tracking of the tags.
- Second, when the reader sends an access password during the access state to make the tag enter a secured state, the random number RN16 and the access password are *XOR* calculated ($\otimes$), so that the plaintext transmission is avoided. But the attacker can easily eavesdrop or intercept the RN16. Therefore, the attacker can obtain the access password by *XOR*($\otimes$) calculating with the cipher text, and the illegal reader can arbitrarily tamper with the tag data if an access password is obtained.
- Third, in the EPC G2 protocol, the tag is not protected by dual-process authenticated with reader. Therefore, mutual authentication is required to ensure that both the reader and tag are legal.

2. Analysis of threat in RFID and EPC: As shown in Fig. 4.9, inside the dotted area is front-end communication between tags and readers, where information is transmitting by modulating an RF signal. The outside threat of dotted area is from back-end communication, where the security is guaranteed partly through the Internet protocol (IP network or Ethernet, locally or distributed in cloud computing). So, the analysis of security scenarios with EPC is divided into two parts: threats from front-end communication and from back-end communication.

(i) *Threat from front-end communication*

(a) *Eavesdropping* (*Skimming*) *and SCA*: By using wireless radio frequency devices, an attacker can detect and eavesdrop on the communication process in the communication channel between the reader and the tag. As shown in Fig. 4.10, because the communication channel of RFID system between tag and reader is asymmetric (the power of tag is weaker than that of reader), an attacker can easily intercept the interactive information in the forward channel (reader-to-tag), and when an attacker approaches the tag, he can also obtain the interactive information in the backward channel (tag-to-reader). Furthermore, radio signals transmitted from the tag or the reader

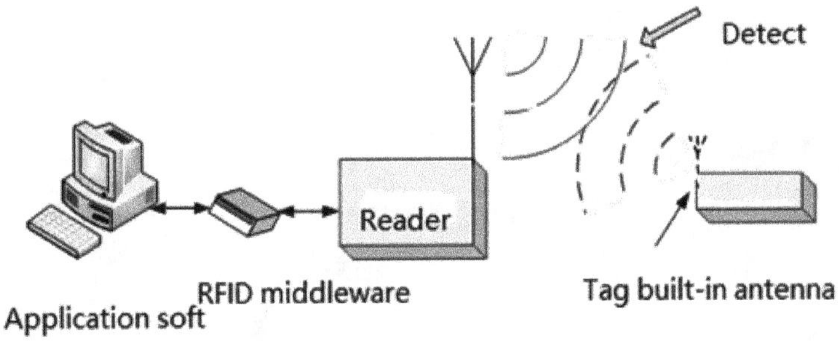

Figure 4.10 Typical scenarios when a RFID system is eavesdropped on or suffered SCA from front end (to be translated).

can be detected several meters away by other radio receivers. It is possible therefore for an unauthorized user to gain access to the data contained in RFID tags if legitimate transmissions are not properly protected.

Any person who owns a RFID reader may interrogate tags lacking adequate access controls and eavesdrop on tag contents. Researchers in the US have demonstrated a skimming attack on an RFID credit card, through which credit card information, such as the cardholder's name and account information, could be skimmed if not properly encrypted. As shown in Fig. 4.10, this kind of detection can not only launch eavesdropping attacks but also launch side channel attacks (SCAs). SCA can be understood by analogy or metaphor as, someone can tell the password of the device when you enter the key and release the sound of your keystrokes as "Di, Da. Du…".

If eavesdropping and SCA attacks are passive in RFID security threats, the following are "active attacks".

(b) *Counterfeiting*: There are two kinds of counterfeit attacks: one is the counterfeit reader, which sends a communication request to the legitimate tag to obtain tag data. The reason is radio signals transmitted from the tag and the reader can be detected several meters away by other radio receivers. It is possible therefore for an unauthorized reader or user to gain access to the data contained in RFID tags if legitimate transmissions are not properly protected.

The other is the attacker who imitates the eavesdropping tag signal and counterfeits the legitimate tag. As shown in Fig. 4.11, if the tag is counterfeited, a counterfeit product appears.

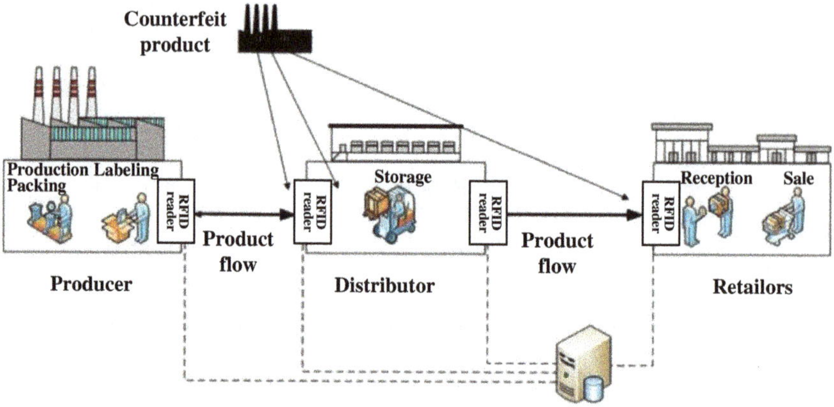

Figure 4.11 Counterfeit product attack on the supply chain in three locations.

(c) *Man in the middle*: When the attacker's position is in the middle between the reader and the tag, and the tag is outside the normal reading range of the reader, but the attacker connects them two separately, as a man in the middle.

All communication between the reader and the tag is possible to pass through the attacker. Under this situation, when a session is undergoing, an attacker can replace, exchange, and delay communication content synchronously.

Spoofing is another kind of man-in-the-middle attack, which is possible to perform tag spoofing asynchronously based on the data collected from eavesdropping or traffic analysis previously. For instance, a software package known as "RFDump", that runs on a notebook computer or personal digital assistant, allows a user to perform reading or writing tasks on most standard smart tags if they are not properly protected. The software permits intruders to overwrite existing RFID tag data with spoof data. By spoofing valid tags, the intruder could fool an RFID system and change the identity of tags to gain an unauthorized or undetected advantage. One example is trying to save money by buying expensive goods that have had their RFID price tags spoofed to display cheaper prices.

(d) *Replay attack*: Replay attacks do not require real-time attacks. During the operation of the protocol, the response from the attacked object (a tag) is monitored and stored by the attacker. When the next session is run and the reader accesses tag, the attacker can send the previously stored information to the reader as a response and coax the reader to authenticate the attacker as the attacked object.

In the scenarios of counterfeit, man-in-the-middle, and replay attacks, they can be illustrated by placing counterfeit reader, counterfeit tag, or both of them at different time points along the time axis of the detection, as shown in Fig. 4.11. These scenarios can be attributed to physical attacks based on node camouflage and concealment asynchronously or synchronously.

(e) *Denial of service* (*DoS in channel*): An attacker could use an illegal high-power radio frequency (RF) transmitter in an attempt to jam frequencies used by the RFID system, bringing the whole system to a halt. This means the attacker interferes with the communication channel between tag and reader by using electromagnetic interference, which makes the RFID system unable to communicate normally. Such attacks do not damage the reader and tags but interfere with the communication process of the system. Such attacks in public places cannot be carried out for a long time, and the system can recover quickly after attacked.

(f) *Desynchronization attack*: Attackers tamper with the information communicating between the tag and the reader or prevent the normal transmission of legitimate information, which results in the information in the database and tag not being updated synchronously. Then, the legitimate identity authentication cannot be achieved in the next session between the reader and the tag.

The kind of active threats to security has certain characteristics, and active threats are easier to find according to their characteristics. Moreover, the attacker manipulates the communication process between the reader and the tag by eavesdropping or tampering with communication data, but the attacker cannot crack the tag generally. If the tag was cracked, for example, an attacker can use the "kill" command, implemented in RFID tags, to make the tags permanently inoperative if they gain password access to the tags.

(ii) *Threat from back-end communication*: Back-end threats exist where information exist. We illustrate their four kinds, and a hierarchy analysis table of EPC is followed. First, trace and traceability are discussed.

In ordinary usage, a trace is defined as a mark, track, tag, etc. showing what has existed or happened. The mark may be a non-material indication or evidence of the presence or existence of something, or of a former event or condition. The existence of a former event or condition is stressed in the usual definitions of requirements traceability.

Gotel and Finkelstein express the concept of requirements traceability in a more complete way than the IEEE standard 830–1984[11]: Requirements traceability refers to the ability to describe and follow the life of a requirement, in both a forwards and backwards direction (i.e., from its origins, through its development and specification, to its subsequent deployment and use, and through all periods of on-going refinement and iteration in any of these phases).

On the one hand, in order to follow (i.e., to trace) a tag and its behavior, it has to be described explicitly. On the other hand, if you spoof the reader that you are the "true" tag, you can pretend to play it again and again. So, traceability can be misused maliciously both forwardly and backwardly.

(a) *Backward traceability threat*: Backward traceability threat[12] means that attackers use some means to obtain the current information of a tag, and hope to use deductive methods to infer the useful historical information of the tag from this information, which will threaten the security of the entire database.[13]

(b) *Forward traceability threat*: The attacker uses the current internal state of the tag to track future interactions between the server and the tag. That is to say, all internal states of the target tag given at time t can help the attacker identify the interaction of the target tag after time t.

---

[11]A software requirements specification is traceable if: (i) the origin of each of its requirements is clear and if (ii) it facilitates the referencing of each requirement in future development or enhancement documentation. In the natural world, the tracing of something amounts to look for, or to follow the course, development, or history of traces, or occurrences of traces left by whatever is being traced. Requirements traceability is the ability to trace requirements, and to this end, more than a traceable specification is necessary.

[12]Forward security can be guaranteed by eliminating backward traceability threat.

[13]Compared with the traditional digital signature, the forward secure signature scheme can ensure the security of the signature before the key disclosure and effectively reduce the loss caused by the key disclosure. However, there is a common defect in forward secure signature schemes. It is unable to guarantee the security of the signature in the future period after the key disclosure as well as the lack of the timely discovery mechanism after the key disclosure.

Threat problems surrounding backward traceability and forward traceability are greatly increased when large volumes of internal RFID data are shared among business partners.

(c) *Virus*: When a RFID reader reads the tag containing malicious code, or when unauthorized intruders set up hidden readers with malicious code to access the information being transmitted by the readers, even a virus can compromise the readers and tags, thus affecting their integrity.

The malicious code or unauthorized readers may also compromise privacy by accessing tags without adequate access controls. Furthermore, after they intruded the computer system of RFID, information collected by them and passed to the RFID application may have already been tampered with, changed or stolen by unauthorized persons. For instance, they may change the price and sales data of the product and create a login interface to allow external visitors to enter the database of the RFID back-end system. An RFID reader can also be a target for viruses.

In 2006, researchers demonstrated that an RFID virus was possible. A proof-of-concept self-replicating RFID virus was written to demonstrate that a virus could use RFID tags to compromise back-end RFID middleware systems via an SQL injection attack.

(d) *Server attack*: An attacker can simulate a legitimate server using the internal information of the tag. For example, if an attacker has the chance to update the status of a tag, the legitimate server may no longer communicate successfully with the cracked tag.

Attack from back end can also crack the tag to get its information.

The sever of RFID systems also suffers from back-end DoS attacks in the network of EPC system, where source address authentication, traffic (packet) filtering,[14] and other network security technologies are needed.

Either the back end or front end of the EPC system suffer from the security and privacy risks. In view of the physical protection of RFID and EPC devices, we can use electromagnetic shielding (such as "Faraday age") or other active anti-interference methods, such as changing the frequency of reader or tag dynamically, physical locking of tag memory, and so on. Physical protection methods are needed to prevent the malicious communication between readers and RFID tags.

[14]Packet cleaning, in another word.

In view of the technological and strategic protection, on the one hand, sleeping or killing the tag can be done, if necessary, and other functional designed strategies can be applied. On the other hand, encryption and authentication mechanisms can be applied to ensure the security of communication between tags and readers between the front end and back end. There are many RFID security protocols, such as logical "hash-lock", random hash-lock, hash-chain protocol, distributed RFID query-response authentication, LCAP protocol, and re-encryption mechanism. Table 4.5 gives an EPC security hierarchical analysis based on security threat scenarios.

3. Research Methods on Security as Extended to IoT Scenarios: From the security of the perception layer to the outside extension of network communication layer security of IoT, one of the key security threats is unauthorized network access. No company wants its information system to be open to malicious devices or programs and allows them access the network arbitrarily. Fortunately, network security is a highly developed and mature technology. RFID reader manufacturers can apply standard and mature security technologies, such as secure socket layer (SSL) and secure shell (SSH) in their IP networks, close unsafe ports (e.g., Telnet, Com, and JTAG port, shown in Table 4.5), and achieve a secure process, such as authentication mechanism to keep unauthorized persons (hackers, etc.) out of the door.

On the one hand, RFID manufacturers actively use powerful and standard tools to ensure data security. On the other hand, users should try their best to ensure that the RFID system they choose meets industry standards.

Security threats of RFID in IoT perception layer are challenging, complex, and changing and are the hot research topics in recent years. After all, the air interface between tags and readers is an open and weak "door". As mentioned above, most RFID security threats involve spoofing, manipulation, or malicious use of RF communication between tags and reader. A malicious reader can read a tag and record confidential information; it can also illegally access to rewrite or kill tags.

The skimming and malicious actions of man in the middle, counterfeiting of reader or tag, discovery of malicious behavior, and elimination of unauthorized behavior need to be considered. Table 4.6 lists some research ideas.

As shown in Table 4.6, personal location privacy protection research are originated from k-anonymity. k-anonymity model, which was

Table 4.5 A hierarchy analysis table of EPC according to threat category.

EPC Security analysis	Threat to security	Defense methods	Remark and discussion
Front-end security	Eavesdropping and SCA	Secure network coding[a]; Ultra-wide band modulation[b]; Anti-SCA, such as electromagnetic shielding with foil-lined[c], masking, leakage stopping.	Extended physical attack beyond SCA, includes: Tag chip packaging is removed by physical means, sensitive signals are acquired by microprobe, and even tags are reconstructed in a laboratory. Scanning tags and their response by the general interface of microprocessor with malicious software, and seeking for weaknesses of both security protocol/encryption algorithm and reader/tag, so as to delete or tamper contents
	Counterfeiting	Authentication	Extended defense methods for the three scenarios: Lightweight encryption; trusted network connect (TNC); trusted third-party authentication. Challenge-response system is a kind of zero-knowledge proofs (ZKPs), which will be discussed in the final chapter
	Man in the middle	Authentication; encryption	
	Replay attack	Encryption; timestamp; one-time password as challenge-response system	
	DoS (in channel) attack	Block radio signals of certain frequencies and thus protect tagged products and RFID communication between reader and tag from being detected	Active jamming of RF signals. Under some conditions, channels or radio signals protection is important EMI protection

(*Continued*)

Table 4.5 (*Continued*)

EPC Security analysis	Threat to security	Defense methods	Remark and discussion
	Desynchronization	timestamp	Two-factor authentication (2FA) at the cost of additional hardware, may be appropriate for the defense for desynchronization
Back-end Security	Backward traceability	*Hash-chain* of "forward security"; digital signature scheme of forward security; key management protocol	Other security technologies: Timestamp; trusted third-party authentication, including PKI/PKC
	Forward traceability	Key management protocol of "**backward security**"	
	Virus	Code signature; authentication; access control, etc.	End-to-end encryption, which will be discussed in the final chapter
	Server attacks (adaptive attacks, unauthorized access, vulnerability attacks, data tampering, etc.)	Encryption; authentication; secure connection, remote certification, quantity of service (QoS), etc.	In the network layer, network security technologies, such as traffic (packet) filtering (or cleaning), trusted computing, or secure network routing, source address authentication and protection, etc.
Extended to the network layer and application of IoT	Traffic analysis	Anti-traffic analysis schemes, such as the onion router (TOR) and invisible internet project (I2P), will be discussed in the final chapter	It is possible to use traffic analysis tools to track predictable tag responses over time. Correlating and analyzing the data could build a picture of movement, social interactions, and financial transactions. Abuse of the traffic analysis would have a direct impact on privacy

Other threats **of security in** network layer and application of IoT will be discussed in the final chapter of this book	Network security technologies, such as authentication, access control, encryption, IPsec, SSL, and TLS. Application layer security technologies, such as cloudy computing security and edge computing security architecture (E-Spion)	First, adaptive RFID security authentication and other kinds of RFID security authentication protocol. Second, cryptographic system on chip (SoC)-oriented secure JTAG (Joint Test Action Group) scheme and other schemes based on service-level agreement (SLA). Finally, from the security management insight, IoT regulations (GDPR and statement in Chapter 2) and legislation from the government are necessary

[a]Secure network coding was presented by Ahlswede *et al.* (2000). After linear network coding approach was presented in this direction subsequently in 2003, Cai and Yeung designed a specific secure network coding method based on the theory of information security, in order to prevent the eavesdropper from eavesdropping a certain number of channels. The theory of secure network coding is a promising way to deal with RFID eavesdropping issues in EPC system.

[b]UWB modulation method is based on the time slot of time-division transmission. Its security lies in that it is difficult for the illegal attacker to know which time slot the useful information is sent in. In this process, the phase modulator and the time hopping codes pseudo-random sequence generator are used.

[c]RFID Security.

[d]Anderson proposed the concept of forward security in 1997. He divided the validity time of a key pair into time periods; at the end of each period, the user updates the new secret key from the current time period in a one-way function and deletes the private key of the current time period securely. Meanwhile, the public key remains the same in all of the time periods. This general approach ensures validity of all documents signed or encrypted prior to the time period of compromise.

[e]Adaptive attack means that an attacker tries to pass the security authentication of the system by collecting a large number of normal authentication session information (or even acting as a legitimate RFID reader or tag) in order to intrude into the system.

[f]E-Spion is an anomaly-based system level intrusion detection system (IDS) for IoT devices, which is based on an edge computing architecture. E-Spion profiles IoT devices according to their "behavior" using system-level information, such as running process parameters and their system calls, in an autonomous, efficient, and scalable manner. E-Spion is presented by Dr. Elisa Bertino and her working group.

Table 4.6 Research methods on security extended to IoT scenarios.

Security scenarios of IoT	**EPC as perception layer of IoT**	**Network communication layer**
Security technologies	Lightweight encryption, signature and key management, etc.	End-to-end encryption, authentication and authorization (For instance: from reader to tag and from tag to reader authentication); SSL, SSH, and other network security technologies
Security strategies	Access control, mutual authentication, exception discovery (Section 4.6 of this chapter), identification (protection), proxy re-encryption[a], and other privacy protection proxy schemes in IoT cloud/frog; functional design based on securing scenarios; location privacy protection	Close insecure ports (e.g., Telnet, Com, and JTAG Port)
Security management	Industry alliance of IoT security (healthy, logistic, etc.); security regulations, such as GDPR of Europe; public feeling between IoT security threats and convenience	Trusted computing and trusted cloud computing (alliance of security cloud and/or edge computing); definition of security scenarios through human–machine and machine–machine interfaces. Security grid (just as security and privacy of SLA, details in the final chapter)

[a]In the proxy re-encryption (PRE), cloud server will play the roles of data storing and re-encrypting, which would reach the full potential of cloud computing and reduce the cost of nodes.

proposed by L. Sweeney and Samarrati at the end of the 20th century, can protect individual sensitive privacy. Marco Gruteser first paid attention to location privacy protection with location k-Anonymity; he indicated that the location identity (ID, such as telephone number) of a user should be anonymous if the user's accurate location information was replaced with a spatial area, where there are at least K different users. When the user requests location service, the service provider cannot distinguish the user from other k – 1 users in the spatial area. Thus, the purpose of k-Anonymity is to protect the user's identity privacy, such as coordinates, and possible quasi-identifier attributes, including time, location, query content, etc.

The remaining scenario-based privacy protection methods will be presented in the final chapter.

4. Further Discussion: EPC G2 and other standards facilitate the integration and development of the different manufacturers with RFID. As shown in Fig. 4.12, in the industry scenarios of EPCglobal, the more the connected things and the more complex the integration of EPC application, the more the concerned security problems.

As shown in Fig. 4.12, a logistic chain begins with a radio electrical characterization of the environment where the check points will be implemented, continues with the integration of a set of data acquisition and wireless communication devices, and ends with a logistics information system able to provide final user services. The **combination of security analysis with a top layer system view can aid the planning as well as operational phase of this type of EPC system within a logistic chain, which is bringing us a feeling of Industrial 4.0,**[15] especially accompanying with a smart factory.

- *Distributed security*: Distributed logistic chain from factory to production, from transportation to warehouse.
- *Consuming security*: Facing consumer, consumer-oriented retail stores and households, electronic payment.
- *EPCIS security*: Technology support of EPCIS.
- *Security services*: SLA, WMS, ERP, etc., which includes readers/tags, are shown in Fig. 4.12.

[15] Industrial 4.0 will be introduced in Chapter 6.

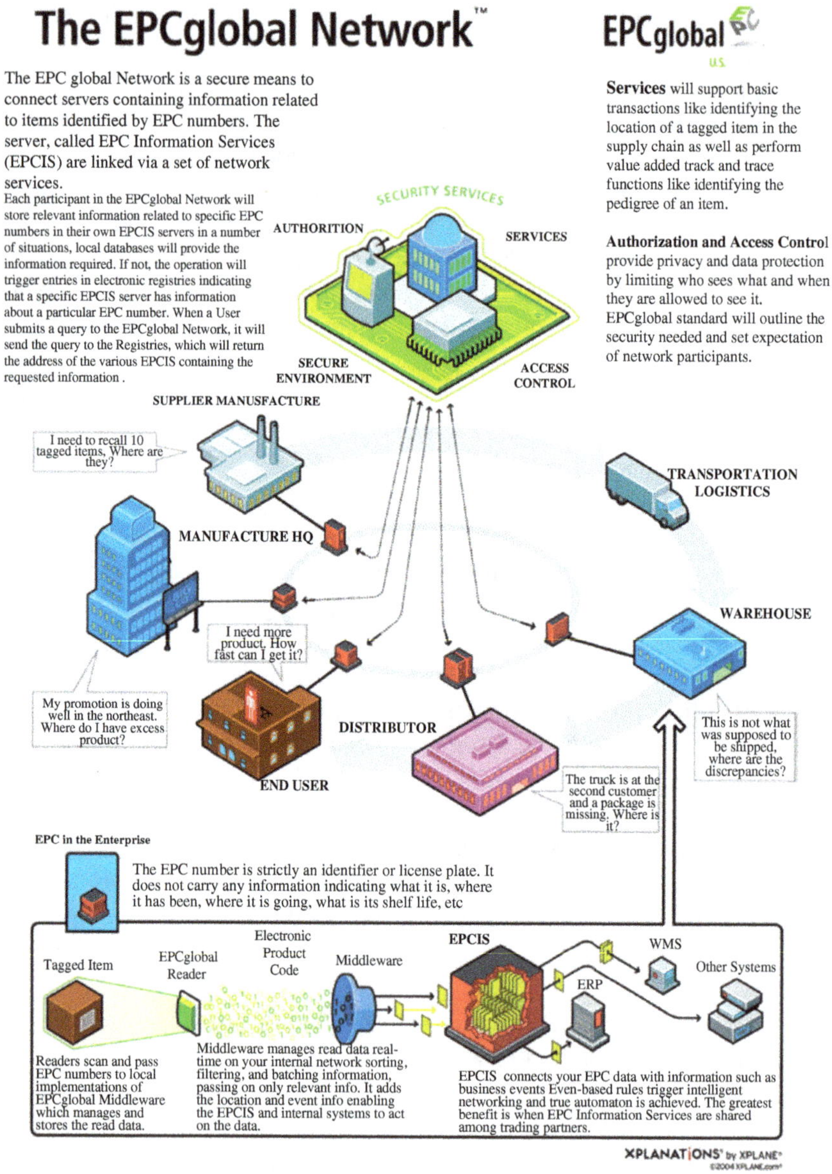

Figure 4.12 EPC industrial scenario as a smart factory, which is feeding the need of Industrial 4.0.

Source: XPLANATIONS/XPLANE.

The security problems covering the scenario in EPC application layers, which needs further research, integrates and connects with the security thoughts in the application layer of the whole IoT. With the expansion of EPC industry, more and more occasions require electronic tags/readers, whether on pallets, supermarket products, or on cars. Along with new applications, new security requirement dealing with new threats arise.

It is believed that the emerging security protocols and technologies of the IoT will realize not only the security assurance of EPCs but also of the perception layer, network layer, and application layer in connecting things to IoE.[16]

4.2. Sensors and WSN

Sensor technology and sensor networks (SNs) are the core technologies in the perception layer of the IoT. As multi-disciplines of modern science and engineering technology, they mainly study how to obtain data/information from natural sources, process (transform), and transmit it. Sensors, wireless sensor networks, or wireless sensor and actuator networks (WSANs) are important parts of information interaction between things and people in the IoT. From the view of the perception layer of IoT, WSN/WSAN technology not only includes sensors but also involves the processing and identification of sensor sensing information as well as the planning, design, development, networking, testing, and other activities in its application.

The formation and development of sensing technology is actually as difficult as the evolution of human eyes. Sensors try to obtain all kinds of physical, chemical, or biomass information from "things" in the IoT. Its function and quality determine the quantity and type of information obtained from natural targets. For example, the range, resolution, and other parameters determine the details of a camera vision can include.

Information processing includes signal pre-processing, post-processing, feature extraction, and selection. These are just like the eyes combined with the optic nerve, and the brain nerve can distinguish the color and outlook, then figure out things. So, smarter sensors will tell us more with artificial intelligence (AI) programs.

---

[16]The EPC application layer security needs further research, which also partially integrates the application layer security requirements of the entire IoT. The expansion of EPC industry and more occasions requiring electronic tags, more tags on pallets, supermarket products or cars means that new threats may occur. The following new security requirements need stronger security assurance.

The main task of sensing is to identify and classify the processed information, then tell the features set by using the correlation model between the identified (or diagnosed) object and the input information. In IoT, sensor technology itself contains many associated high-tech development directions, such as smart sensor, micro-electro-mechanical systems (MEMS), WSN/WSAN, biometric identifications, and IoT senses.

In recent years, with the development of biological science, information science, and material science, sensor technology has developed rapidly by realizing systematization, miniaturization, multi-function, intelligence, and networking. All these have greatly expanded the application field of sensor technology and also released the development of IoT sensing power. The sensor technologies applied in the IoT mainly include sensors, sensor systems, and sensor networks, and the latter are based on the networking of various distributed sensor nodes.

4.2.1 *Introduction of sensor*

What are the five senses of human beings? Vision, hearing, taste, smell, and touch respectively correspond to the functions of eyes, ears, mouth, nose, and body feeling parts (e.g., hands). Touch also covers the peripheral nervous system's perception of touching, feeling, and even falling. The five senses of human beings are five kinds of sensors or sensing systems, through which human beings can be aware of the world. What's more, babies can develop better under the touch of their mothers. This means that the human "sensor" is more precise, intelligent, and connected with the emotions in the mind.

As the realization of sensor technology, sensor is a necessary part of information interaction between things and people in the IoT. The sensor transforms the physical quantity, chemical quantity, and biomass in the physical world into digital signals for processing, so as to provide a source of information collection for perceiving the properties of objects in the physical world. No matter how accurate the measurement and control, it is a blind spot without the sensor to accurately acquire and transform the original information of the measured object.[17] At present, we can pursue its functionality and precision. In the long run, with the development of AI, an artificial brain may be inside a sensor for "thinking and action" by itself.

[17]As a famous Chinese saying, "A leaf blinded, not seeing Mount Tai".

Sensors can convert physical quantities into electrical signals, representing the data interface between the physical world and the IoT world, and these measured values includes temperature, pressure, flow, displacement, speed, and so on. In addition to sensor nodes, the perception layer of the IoT also includes actuators and controllers, and networking nodes, by which nodes in a WSN is connected with gateways through the built-in communication modules (and then be covered in LAN/WAN). Three aspects are discussed regarding sensors or WSNs:

- *Data acquisition in a given sensor and the added actuator*: A special sensor collects data from single technology, such as physics, chemistry, biology, etc. For example, pressure, flow, displacement, speed, vibration, temperature, humidity, pH, as well as various sensors, such as radiation value and odor concentration that can be detected by nuclear radiation sensors and biosensors, these are like "perceptrons" that are easy to think. After the combination of sensors and actuator, an action may be achieved according to the command from the application layer or when the accumulating data reach a preconfigured threshold. Whereas, a compound sensor and actuator system can be used to control the flight of a missile or aircraft by e.g., the inertial navigation system (INS), that respond to inertial forces.
- *Extension by networking*: Sensory information includes auditory, visual, tactile, vibration, and other information that can be sensed or collected but often in a limited range. WSNs extend the sensing coverage (e.g., from one node to a more sensing node) and provide an interwork mechanics for the communications and cooperation among sensors nodes.
- *Intelligent processing and mining of perceptual information*: Audio and video, vibration, and other original information collected can also be regarded as a perceptron by using intelligent technology to analyze and extract them (such as intelligent video analysis by computer vision (CV), vehicle license plate or electronic identification plate recognition, biometric recognition technology, etc.). The more information mined from video, audio, and image data, the easier for us to understand. AI algorithms can effectively improve the identification ability or resolution. For example, the application of artificial intelligence in semantic recognition needs the context covering voice, background, intonation, and even a training data set but can tell the name of each object in a picture or a movie.

In short, for the IoT, sensors and WSNs/WSANs are in the front end of the network to extract certain information by data collection and transmission, where they make up as an important data source for supporting the perception layer. With sensors, IoT adds the dimension of connecting to the real world of machines, things, and spaces, where beyond the existing Internet by embedding sensors to capture physical properties, beyond our human sensory of just five kinds, and beyond actuators controlling their states.

4.2.2 *Sensors and WSN*

Sensor is used to sense the environmental parameters of the information at the collection point. Sensors can sense heat, force, light, electricity, sound, displacement (position, acceleration, gesture, voice), and other signals, providing the original information for the processing. Then, it is transmitted to the sensor network and/or the background system.

There are various types of sensors, which can be classified according to the use, material, measurement method, output signal type, manufacturing process, etc. According to different measurement methods, sensors can be divided into contact measurement and non-contact measurement sensors; according to whether the output signal is analog or digital, it can be divided into analog sensor and digital sensor; according to the purpose, it can be divided into visible video sensor, infrared video sensor, temperature sensor, gas sensor, chemical sensor, acoustic transmission sensors, pressure sensors, acceleration sensors, vibration sensors, magnetic sensors, electrical sensors; according to the working principle, they can be divided into physical sensors, chemical sensors, biological sensors; according to the application occasion, they can be divided into military sensors and/or civil sensors.

The common sensor is just a device used to detect and monitor the state, the physical changes of things, or their surrounding environment. It converts the sensed information into the form of electronic signal output. Common sensors are as follows:

1. Temperature/Humidity Sensor: The temperature/humidity sensor measures the temperature/humidity of the surrounding environment and converts the result into an electronic signal. Temperature sensor (as shown in Fig. 4.13) uses thermistor, semiconductor temperature sensor, or thermocouple to realize temperature detection. Thermistor mainly uses

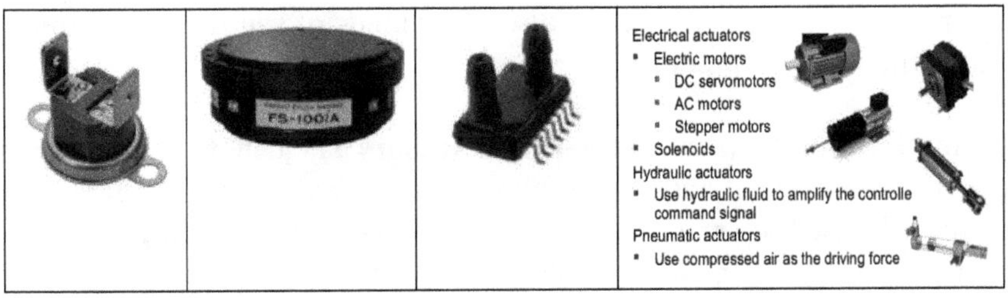

(a) (b) (c) (d)

Figure 4.13 Sensors and actuators: (a) temperature sensor — digital board mount, industrial, and thermostats in many temperature ranges; (b) force sensor-Fs-100iA of Shanghai-FANUC.inc; (c) pressure sensors, PCB mount or industrial sensors measuring absolute, differential, or vacuum pressure; (d) different types of actuators.

the temperature sensitivity of the resistivity of various materials to protect the equipment from overheating and alarm for temperature control. The semiconductor temperature sensor uses the temperature sensitivity of the semiconductor device to measure the temperature, which is low cost and has good linearity. Thermoelectric couple makes use of thermoelectric phenomenon to convert the temperature of the measured end into the change of voltage and current; thermoelectric couple, composed of different metal materials, can measure temperature in a relatively large range.

Humidity sensor mainly includes resistance type and capacitance type. The resistance humidity sensor also becomes the humidity sensitive resistor, which uses the humidity sensitivity of the resistivity of lithium chloride, carbon, ceramics, and other materials to detect the humidity. Capacitive humidity sensor, also known as humidity sensitive capacitance, uses the humidity sensitivity of the dielectric coefficient of the material to detect the humidity. Temperature/humidity sensor is widely used to measure indoor environment, such as home, factory, green house, and so on.

2. Force Sensor: The force sensor can calculate the force applied on the sensor and convert the result into an electronic signal. The common pressure sensors are flaky and switch type. When they are under external pressure, they will produce a certain deformation or displacement of internal structure, which will be converted into the change of electrical characteristics and generate corresponding electrical signals. As shown in Fig. 4.13(b), **force** sensor is widely used in intelligent robots. Figure 4.13(c) shows a kind of force sensor; it is pressure sensor that is from Honeywell. Inc. There are also other kinds of sensor that can measure altitude by air pressure.

3. Acceleration Sensor: Acceleration sensors calculate the acceleration applied to the sensor and convert the result into an electronic signal. It is commonly used in smart phones, fitness tracker for generating acceleration information by measuring the quantity of exercise according to user movement, and other smart terminals, e.g., for sensing the gravitational acceleration.

Force sensors and **acceleration sensors are two kinds of** sensors that are used in INS (Inertial Navigation System, including IMU[18]), which is important for AGV (automated-guided vehicle) and AVS (Autonomous Driving System), and also can be found in smartphones or fitting devices.

4. Optical Sensor: Optical sensor can mainly be divided into two categories: photoresist and photoelectric sensors. Photoresistors mainly use the light sensitivity of resistivity of various materials to detect light. Photoelectric sensors mainly include photodiodes and phototriodes, both of which make use of the sensitivity of semiconductor devices to light. The reverse saturation current of photodiode will increase significantly under the action of light, while the collector and emitter of phototriode will be on when it is illuminated. In addition, photodiode, phototriode and signal processing circuit can also be integrated in a chip of light sensor. Different kinds of light sensors can cover the sensing applications of visible light, infrared, ultraviolet, and other wavelength ranges. If optical sensors are divided more in detail from industrial view, there are fiber optic sensors, image sensors, light-to-digital converters, light to frequency and light to voltage, photoelectric sensors, safety light curtains, and so on.

5. Ranging Sensor: The distance measurement sensor measures the distance between the sensor and the obstacle. Generally, it collects the reflection results by irradiating infrared rays and ultrasonic waves, measures the distance according to the reflection, and converts the results into electronic signals. The irradiation means also include laser rangefinder which can scan two-dimensional plane. It is often used in vehicles such as

[18] There is a small difference between INS and inertial measurement unit (IMU). Generally, IMU is a sensor part of INS, and IMU belongs to a kind of MEMS sensors.

automobiles, e.g., reversing alarm. **Similarly, velocity sensor is another kind of sensor, such as a RADA for velocity detection.**

6. Magnetic Sensor: Magnetic sensor is a kind of magnetic sensor that makes use of Hall effect, so it is also called Hall sensor. Hall effect refers to that when a metal or semiconductor material sheet is placed in a magnetic field, when there is current flowing through it, the electrons that form the current receive the force of the magnetic field due to the movement of the electrons in the magnetic field, so that the material produces a voltage difference perpendicular to the direction of the current. The magnetic field strength can be calculated by measuring the voltage generated by the Hall sensor. Combined with different structures, it can indirectly measure current, vibration, displacement, speed, acceleration, speed, etc.

7. MEMS Sensor: MEMS is an integrated system made by the combination of micromachining technology and microelectronics technology. It includes micro electronic circuit (IC), micro actuator, and micro sensor. Most of them are processed by semiconductor technology. At present, the MEMS devices include pressure sensors, accelerometers, micro gyroscopes, and hard disk drive heads. The emergence of MEMS reflects the current trend of device miniaturization. The common ones are MEMS pressure sensor, MEMS acceleration sensor, and MEMS gas velocity sensor.

The application of nano technology and MEMS technology reduces the size of the sensor and greatly improves the accuracy. The goal of MEMS technology is to integrate information acquisition, processing, and execution into a real microelectronic system. These devices put the circuit and the running machine on a silicon chip. For the traditional electronic mechanical system, MEMS is not only the beginning of the real realization of mechatronics but also the opening of the door of the micro field of "IoT", such as the micro robot in the blood vessel. For example, MEMS-INS or MEMS-IMU is a common on-board device for vehicle localization.

8. Biosensor: The working principle of biosensor is that organisms can respond to various external stimuli. Biosensor is an instrument which is sensitive to biological substances and converts its concentration into electrical signal for detection. The electronic nose and electronic tongue in the intelligent interaction technology are the application of biosensor technology.

9. Smart sensor: Smart sensor is a kind of sensor with certain information processing ability or intelligent characteristics. For example, it has the functions of sensitivity adjustment, self-compensation and calculation, self-inspection, self-calibration, self-diagnosis, information storage, and transmission (two-way communication) and has the characteristics of composite integration.

It should be emphasized that there is a fundamental difference between "smart" and "intelligence" in artificial intelligence; the former focuses on the comparison with traditional sensors, and the latter emphasizes the trend of "anthropomorphic" thinking ability. Intelligent sensors originated from the requirements of space equipment for sensor processing ability. At present, they are mostly made by combining traditional sensors with microprocessors. Representative products are intelligent pressure sensor, and intelligent temperature and humidity sensor.

Because the embedded intelligent technology is an important means to realize the intelligent sensor, the intelligence of intelligent sensor is usually called "embedded intelligence", which is characterized by the microprocessor hardware. Embedded microprocessors have the advantages of low-power consumption, small size, high integration, and high efficiency and reliability of embedded software. Under the promotion of artificial intelligence technology, they jointly build the intelligent sensing environment of the IoT. With the development of embedded intelligent technology, cyber physical systems (CPS) is considered to be closer to the IoT in the field of automation and control. It uses computers to monitor and control physical equipment, integrates automation technology, information technology, control technology, and network technology, pays attention to feedback and control process, and realizes real-time and dynamic control and service of objects. Although CPS is the same as IoT in application and network, there are differences in information collection and control.

10. Sensor System and Sensor Network: Sensor system is a system for realizing single or compound sensing function, which usually has "front-end": original/raw data collection and "back-end": data analysis and processing unit (e.g., CPU); sometimes there is a "middleware" for communication transmission.

The difference between CPS and sensor systems is that CPS is embedded, tightly coupled, and highly integrated, while sensor systems are usually loosely coupled as front-end and back-end systems with clear division and more specific functionality. For example, the low-altitude detection system of the airport, grating access control system, and novel sensor system introduced in the next parts. When there are many distributed sensors or sensor nodes in a sensor system and their inter links are realized by networking, WSNs arise; see the following part.

11. WSN and WSAN: Sensor network (SN or WSN) is a network that realizes more functions through distributed in the front end of data collection nodes (or devices), which often interwork or network with others by wireless communication. WSANs are interconnected sensor nodes and actuators that collect data about the physical condition of an environment and are built by the networking of embedded systems, and the actuators react according to the changing of the physical condition.

Sensors and actuators are both essential elements of the embedded systems for "reaction" of things to the physical world. The sensor is used to monitor the changes in the environment by using physical measurand (typically from an electrical signal to be converted to a digital signal), while the actuator is used when along with monitoring the control is also applied such as to control the physical change.

A sensor is a device that changes a physical parameter to an electrical output. As against, an actuator is a device that converts an electrical signal to a physical output through producing force, heat, motion, etc.

Their integration acts as the mediator between the physical environment and the electronic system where the sensor and actuator are embedded. Take the stepper motor (as an actuator) in the arm of a robotic system as an example. After getting some input from the sensor (an electrical pulse given in the input accordingly motor rotates in a predefined amount), an electrical pulse drives the stepper motor. Additionally, other sensor system in the robotic system can transfer the position and direction of the object for better control precision. The loop of sensing–acting–sensing in controlling a stepper motor is suitable for robotic applications. For other types of actuators, see Fig. 4.13(d).

In a word, continuous application of new theories, new technologies, and new materials, research of all kinds of new sensors and embedded smart systems, and the development of the ability to perceive the physical world and communicate with the physical world are the foundation of realizing the perception link in the IoT world.

4.2.3 *Novel sensor system and smart applications*

Sensors and WSNs in IoT are in essence about enabling smart operations and applications involving real-world assets, machines, human, and even animals, whether they are in the consumer, enterprise, farm, or industry domains.

Now that we are in the beginning of the IoE, let's look at how smart the sensors and systems of IoE era are. Smart operations and applications are about using software to gather insights about the real world and to automate processes for transformational outcomes of different kinds.

This is a trend of perception with more functional system integration application. For example, the eye is not only a "camera" for perceiving the light but also a window for understanding, recognizing, and enjoying the feeling of super connections between humans and smart things.

1. Sensors Aided in the Farm: Before the arrival of the IoT, only listening to music can improve the output of cows. As shown in Fig. 4.14, the sensors are implanted in the ears of cattle. In the world of the IoT, not only humans need "hearing aids" (no malice) but also cattle will have "productivity" sensors. This allows farmers to monitor the health and movement of cows to ensure a healthier and more adequate meat supply for people to consume. Even the guide dog needs a sensing system to help the owner more attentively.

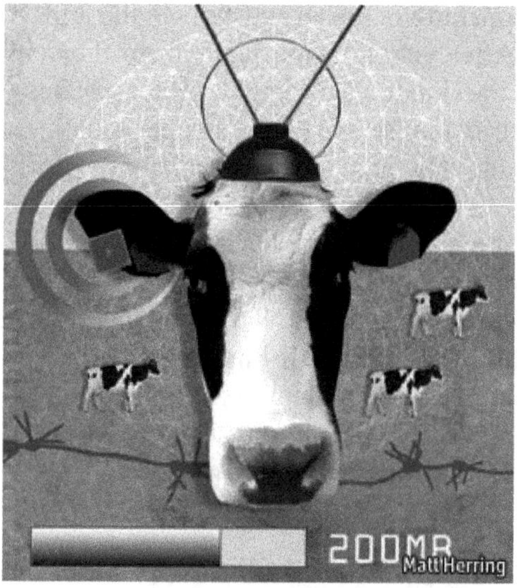

Figure 4.14 Sensors implanted in the ears of cattle.

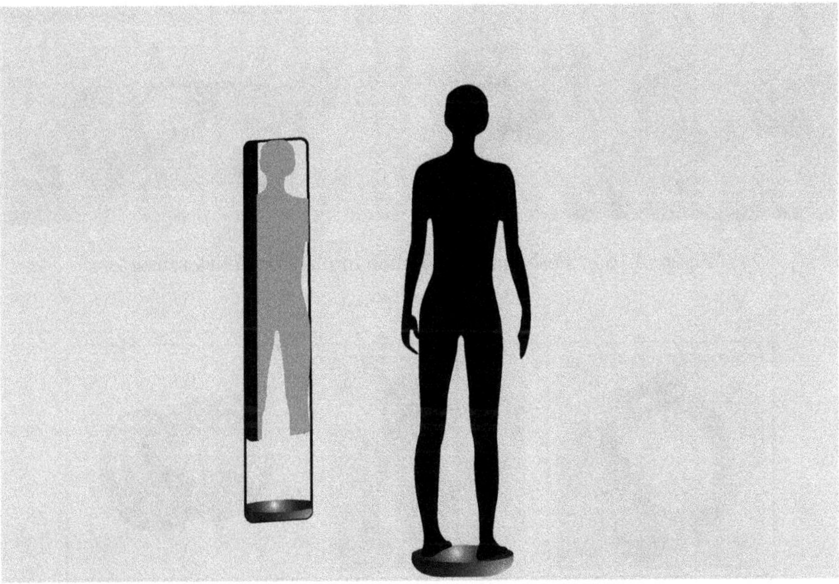

Figure 4.15 Fitness mirror launched by Naked Labs.
Source: nakedlabs.com

2. Mirror for Tracking Body Shape of Fitting: Figure 4.15 is the 3-D fitness mirror launched by Naked Labs. This intelligent system tracks the body shape change through 3-D scanning and sends data to the mobile phone synchronization app to analyze the fitness effect.

3. Push-and-Buy Button: The "push-and-buy" button is a plastic button that can be pasted at home, with a wireless connection to its back-end system. For example, if you paste one on the washing machine and find that the washing liquid is used up, press the button to place an order, and then wait for the express delivery, as shown in Fig. 4.16.

4. More Connecting "Buttons" to Our Life: The extensive set of applications for IoT devices is often divided into consumer, industrial, and infrastructure fields (Fig. 4.17), the following example belongs to industrial applications, such as "Chinese dragon" with multi-sensor systems (Fig. 4.18).

5. "Chinese Dragon": The acoustic sensor system of Jiaolong, which is independently developed in China, includes communication acoustic

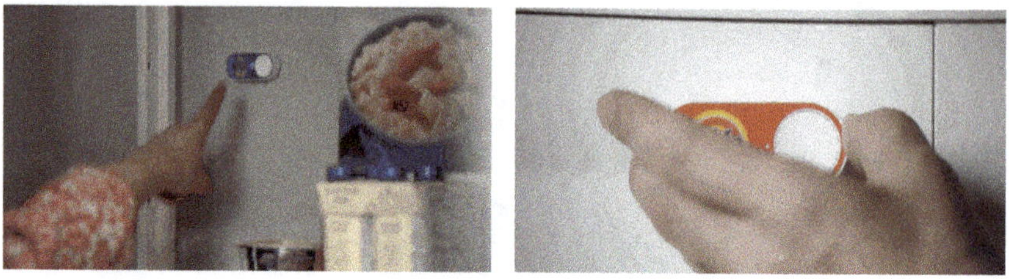

Figure 4.16 "Push-and-buy" button through one-click sensor.

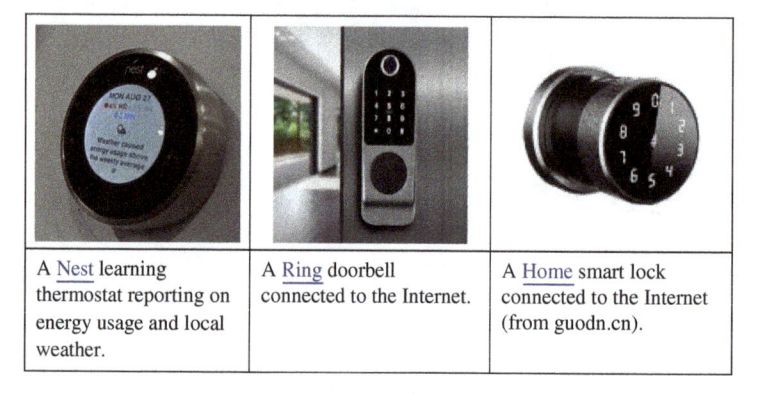

A Nest learning thermostat reporting on energy usage and local weather.	A Ring doorbell connected to the Internet.	A Home smart lock connected to the Internet (from guodn.cn).

Figure 4.17 More functional connecting devices.

system, sounding side scan sonar, collision avoidance sonar, imaging sonar, acoustic doppler velocimeter (ADV), etc. The "Jiaolong" manipulator also needs sensor and actuator technology for grasping and inserting, as shown in Fig. 4.18.

4.2.4 *Sensing technology and application*

IoT adds the sensing dimension to the real world, by machines, things, and the connection spaces for humans. IoT is in essence about enabling intelligent operations involving real-world assets and machines, whether they are in the consumer, enterprise, or industry domains. Intelligent operations are about using software to gather insights about the real world and to automate processes for transformational outcomes of different kinds

With extended "eyes, ears, and hands", the exploration sensing technology is helping people explore the mysteries of space and the deep

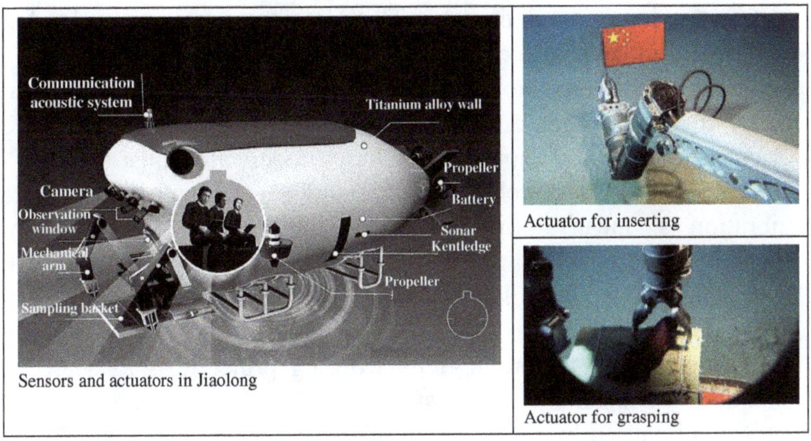

Sensors and actuators in Jiaolong

Actuator for inserting

Actuator for grasping

Figure 4.18 Sensing system of Jiaolong in China.

ocean: Kepler telescope and remote sensing system that can extend the function of eyes; acoustic sensing system that can extend the function of human ears[19]; mechanical arm that can extend the function of hands. When sensing technology and application are combing ICT with OT in IoT, this kind of combination not only can perform actions beyond human touch in remote space or deep ocean but also more firmly confirm the confidence of human exploration beyond our five kinds of "sensors".

In the past decade, driven by high technologies, such as microelectronics technology, MEMS, nanotechnology, and AI, modern sensors have also entered the new stage, and their typical characteristics are miniaturization, multifunction, digital, intelligence, systematization, and networking; the current sensor technology applied by them presents some trends in the following categories, according to different detection methods, application, and principles:

- **Imaging technology:** It can be divided into direct imaging and indirect imaging. Direct imaging technology is to directly transmit the image within the visible range of the equipment to the information processing center at the rear through the video equipment. Generally, it is realized by micro lens or CCD. Indirect imaging technology uses microwave, ultrasound and other methods to process image data in a certain range

[19]"千里眼, 顺风耳 (Clairvoyant, Omniscient)" in traditional Chinese saying.

to form an image, such as radar. The 360-degree imaging technology will be introduced as an example in Section 4.4.

- **Acoustic sensor technology:** The sound signals are amplified and transmitted to the back-end information processing center for detection or communication. Of course, it includes underwater sonar system.
- **Vibration sensor technology:** In order to detect the ground transmitted vibration as a means to find and identify the target, the military mainly focuses on the movement of detection personnel and vehicles, usually interested in detecting soldiers within 50 m and vehicles moving within 500 m.
- **Magnetic sensor technology:** Its working principle is to detect the change of geomagnetic field disturbance. The disturbance of geomagnetic field caused by the invasion of iron targets is exposed. The distance between the detector and the vehicle is about 4 m and 25 m. When it is used together with the vibration sensor, it can identify the nature of the target. **As a use case of magnetic sensor technology in AGV, magnetic strip navigation will be introduced in the following.**
- **Micro sensor:** Micro sensor refers to the general term of all kinds of sensors manufactured by microelectronic machining with the characteristic size of microchip, which is an important part of modern advanced MEMS. Now, the products and micro sensors under research are pressure, force, torque, acceleration, speed, position, flow, electricity, magnetic field, temperature, gas, humidity, pH, ion concentration, micro gyroscope, and wireless network sensors.
- **Smell, taste, and touch sensors:** It is a comprehensive technology that can realize anthropomorphic perception by combining biological sensing, chemical sensing, intelligent sensing, and other technologies in sensor technology. They are both the fusion recognition of chemical quantity and biomass. Compared with the recognition of physical quantity, the research methods are more complex. Now, some countries are developing tactile sensors that can recognize the shape of objects and olfactory and taste sensors that can distinguish different gases (liquids).
- **Infrared radiation sensor technology:** Infrared radiation sensor is a kind of passive infrared detection device, which can detect the temperature difference between the target and the thermal background and detect the target and its direction by detecting the temperature difference. Its outstanding advantage is to work in a passive way, which is conducive to anti-interference and concealment.

- **Location awareness technology:** The position of the object can be located by transmitting and receiving electromagnetic wave, so as to judge the movement of the object. Location awareness technology can be understood as the generalized sensing technology based on position sensing, including not only global navigation satellite system (GNSS) satellite positioning but also sensor network positioning technology, remote sensing/GPS/GIS, and other spatial positioning.

These sensors and technologies can not only be used in intelligent terminals but also extend the senses of machines to realize machine intelligence. These sensing technologies are used in the following specific equipment applications, which can be used in search and rescue, security and other fields:

(1) ***Portable multifunctional electronic equipment*****:** The device can be easily installed in all parts of human body, including all kinds of MEMS sensors and their measurement and control systems, mainly including intelligent helmets (including night vision apparatus, infrared/laser sights, etc.), which can effectively improve the field search-and-rescue ability.

(2) ***Robot applications*****:** There are more than 100 kinds of military robots equipped with many kinds of micro sensors, including robot tank, autonomous ground vehicle, mine sweeping robot, and underwater survey ship. During the Fukushima nuclear accident in Japan, the US was asked to provide the "magic grab" robot (see Fig. 4.19) for internal detection of the nuclear power plant; the throwbot robot (see Fig. 4.20) used in the reconnaissance was only 0.187 meters long.

(3) ***Unmanned technology*****:** Unmanned technology is the extension of robot technology, which is a collection of artificial equipment or systems that can interact with the environment. Unmanned technology can make machines imitate human senses to collect environmental information and even share information in groups, such as WSNs. The sensors collect the surrounding information and transmit the information to the processor for decision making. Robots, unmanned aerial vehicle (UAV), unmanned aerial system (UAS), and automated-guided vehicle (AGV) are common in our beginning of IoE era, as shown in Fig. 4.21. But which is not usually seen in our planet is the Mars rover. Hopefully, in the near future, we will

Figure 4.19 "Magic grab" robot in the US.

Figure 4.20 Throwbot reconnaissance robot.

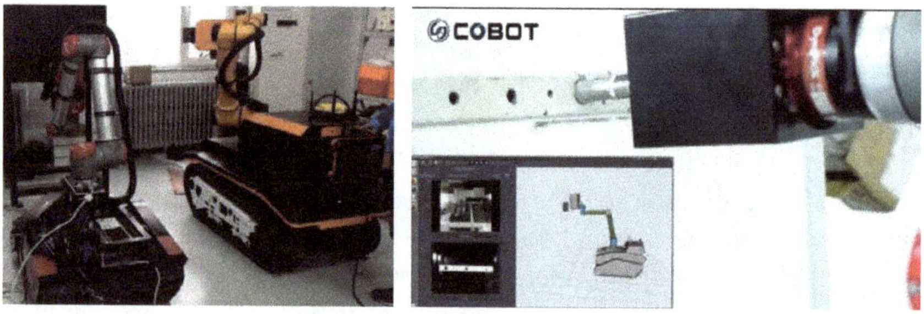

Figure 4.21 AGV and its working state. (a) Two AGVs and (b) the robotic arm of an AGV is screwing.

Photo credit: COBOT.

have the opportunity to "visit" Mars exploration vehicles through the sensors and actuators of Internet of satellites.[20]

Today, from the "Shenzhou" spacecraft to the "Jiaolong" in the sea, from satellites, aircraft carriers to wearable devices, sensor technology is widely used. And the military sensor technology has gradually opened the prelude of the military application of the IoT, especially the application of the sensor technology represented by intelligent dust in the second Gulf War.

4.2.5 *Sensing use case in AGV navigation*

AGV (as shown in Fig. 4.22) is described as one of hundreds of warehouse robots that have been employed to sort express parcels in modern automated warehouses and factory for sortation facilities. For example, one such automated sortation center has contributed to the delivery of over one billion express parcels throughout China within one week (Alizila, 2018).

Navigation of AGV is a semi-trackless mobile robot, and it has the advantages of high automation integration and high reliability. AGV needs more sensors and their combination of more than one, in its navigation controls which can help in providing the real-time feedback about the position for the purpose of position navigation of the vehicle. These sensors contain magnetic strip, visual, laser, and INS, as shown in Table 4.7,

Figure 4.22 AGV in a factory.

[20] Some ideas from Elon Musk and IoS will be introduced in the next chapter.

Table 4.7 AGV navigation methods.

Methods	Cost	Work	Applicability	Maintenance	Stability
Mag	Low	High	Middle	Low	High
Visual	High	Middle	Low	Middle	Middle
Laser	High	Low	Low	High	Middle
INS	Low	Middle	High	Middle	Middle

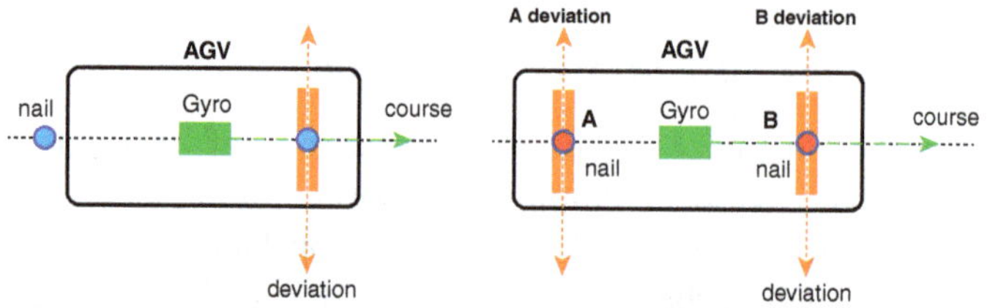

Figure 4.23 Single magnetic nail and double magnetic nails navigation magnetic strip.

which can help in determining that the position of the load is correct and the vehicle is going right. Some advantages and disadvantages of each navigation method are shown in Table 4.7.

Take magnetic navigation as an example; a magnetic navigation sensor is required to locate the left and right deviation of the AGV from the path, as shown in Fig. 4.23. In order to ensure that the heading angle provided by the angle sensor is always accurate, INS can be used to correct the real-time direction angle. If considering the drift error and noise due to the integrated gyroscope in the angle sensor, another line of magnetic strip can be used to assist inertial navigation by adding the function of error compensation for angle sensor, as shown in Fig. 4.23.

Two-dimensional (2-D) code-assisted navigation method is introduced in Fig. 4.24; the continuous scanning of the codes on the ground can help in determining whether the position of the load is correct and the vehicle is going right.

The 2-D barcode scanning module utilizes its own barcode recognition function. According to the 2-D code reading in the motion state, AGV needs to know the angle and other information when reading the code. In particular, the industrial 2-D code scanning module is introduced to achieve 2-D sensing on the assembly line.

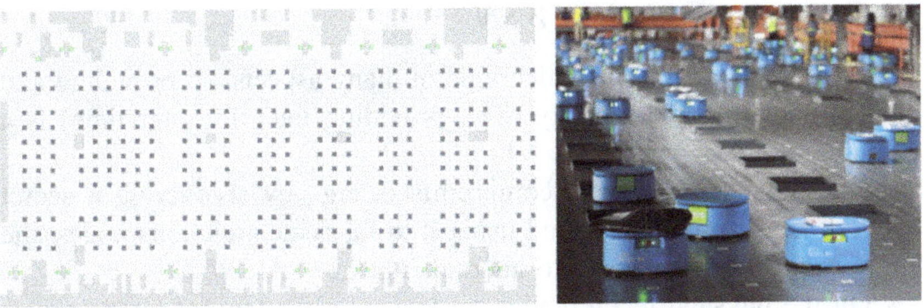

Figure 4.24 Navigation by 2-D barcode during the entire operating cycle of the vehicles.

Notes: The 2-D grid layout of an automated sortation center. Green cells represent sorting stations. Gray cells represent obstacles. Blue cells represent sorting bin.

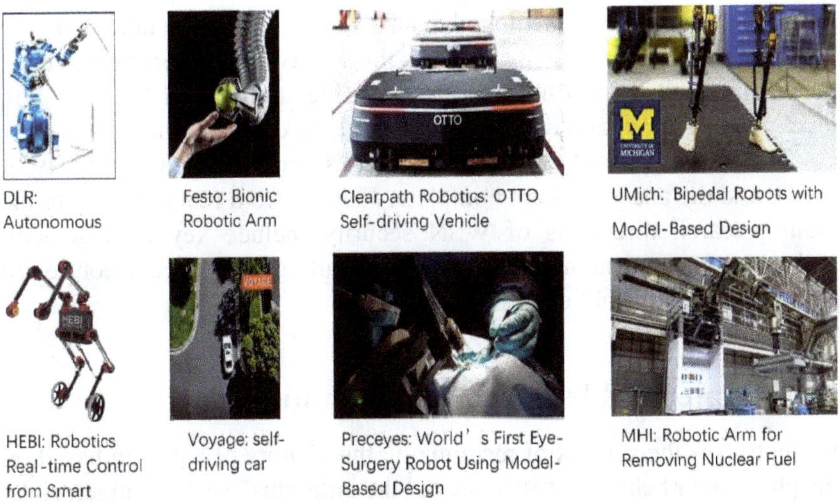

Figure 4.25 More robotic things are available in the markets.

The AGVs in Figure 4.23 are able to communicate with other systems by interface handshake sensors in their movement. Obstacle detection sensors are also being used which has the ability to bring the vehicle at a safe stop and can prevent the contact of the vehicle with any obstacle which may come in path accidently. The above AGV navigation and control can be extended into the following robotic things, as shown in Fig. 4.25.

4.2.6 *Security analysis of WSN*

Nodes in WSN or IoT are vulnerable in many aspects, so providing and maintaining trust and security (e.g., providing integrity over time) is a continuous endeavor.

Once token integrity is compromised, e.g., by recovering a secret network key from a device and using it to fabricate malicious nodes, the entire network is vulnerable to internal attacks.

On the physical level, device enclosures are often not tamperproof; devices can be opened and their hardware can be accessed by probes and pin headers. Low-cost device and its components often have no sophisticated means to protect their code, data, and tokens from external access. So, the test with its Joint Test Action Group (JTAG) method is necessary. This prevents an attacker to clone entire devices or manipulate software and data. If the device is deployed in an unsupervised environment, it may be attacked or accessed by a malicious third party without notice and even be manipulated or destructed. Other considerations from the data link level, routing level, and data transport level are discussed in Table 4.8.

The above lists only some of the attacks that threaten the security of WSN, and the analysis is not complete. Judging from recent research, the main research directions of WSN security include key management, authentication and authorization, secure routing, and access control in addition to lightweight encryption.

4.3 Biometric Identification Technology

Biometrics is the science of recognizing the identity of a person based on the physical or behavioral attributes of the individual, such as fingerprints, face, voice, and hand geometry, to establish the identity of an individual. The "innate" and "congenital" biometric identification (B-ID/BId or E-ID) is used to distinguish individuals in groups. For example, in 2017, the UK tested a facial recognition system that wanted to replace the purchase system of train tickets. From 2019, facial recognition had been used in the access control system of the metro station of Zhengzhou city, Henan Province of P.R.C.

What's more interesting is that if your pet doesn't recognize you and runs away with someone else, how embarrassing would be the wrong recognition. One day our robot pets or other IoT severs in our future families really need our IDs by nature. In the IoT world, not only

Table 4.8 Possible attack methods and main defense methods of WSN system.

Network level	Attack method	Defense method	Remarks and comments
Physical layer	Congestion attack	Frequency modulation, message priority, low duty cycle (switching periodically on and off)	Also need to consider EMC and malicious EMI
	Physical destruction	Destruction proof, node camouflage, and concealment	Also need to consider hardware damage; hardware destroyed and accessed by probe and pin header; middle-man attacks and man-in-the-middle attacks
Data link layer	Collision attack	Error correction code	Also need to consider the attack and defense of energy depletion; end-to-end security at the link layer
	Exhaustion attack	Set competition threshold	
	Unfair competition	Short frame and non-priority strategy	
Routing layer	Discard and greedy destruction	Redundant path, detection mechanism	Secure routing protocol
	Convergence node attack	Encryption, hop-by-hop authentication	
	Misdirected attack	Export filtering, certification, monitoring	
	Black hole attack	Authentication, monitoring, redundancy	
Transmission control layer	Replay attack	Timestamp, use challenge-response method, etc.	SSL and its successor, transport layer security (TSL) provide a security protocol for security and data integrity
	Flood attack	Client puzzle	
	Out-of-step attack	Certification	

you need to identify or recognize objects but also things need to identify "who are you". On the one hand, when it is necessary to identify an individual, the innate characteristics of the individual can be regarded as his unique "natural code", and the identity of the personal property protection is important, which belongs to the "property right"[21] of the object.

On the other hand, the object itself has some attributes or own individual information, which may contain privacy items. For example, the object should protect the privacy of its owner or user, which is sensitive and cannot be open to the public. "Responsibility of the object in IoT" requires determining the identity of the user and the authorities for usage.

At least two points are benefiting from recognition in IoT world: First, let things or other objects figure out "who am I" to gain the access right into the door of IoT world, and second, "which belongs to me" to gain clarification of real right of property, especially personal property and privacy.[22] The latter means that no one would share the IoT property without permission. Furthermore, "Unsuitable assignation of rights and duties of private actors could stifle innovation. Lack of accountability could jeopardize the functioning of the IoT system itself."[23]

In the applications, the basic methods of ID can be divided into three types: The first one depends on "what do you know". As long as you say or enter the key that only you know, such as passwords or graphics, you pass the identification. The second depends on "what do you have?" The individual shows what he has, such as keys, ID cards, or tokens, in order to prove his identification. The third depends on "who are you", which means that locking the identity of the individual according to his unique biometrics.

Obviously, the first two methods are easier to steal or replace, while the third is more secure. Driven by high tech, biometric-based identification technology has become a hotspot for identification in

[21] In the sharing economic era, ownership and the right of use are divided, such as "Car to Go" or short-time rental vehicle. How stakeholders are accountable for the sharing and security is a new issue; may be identification is good. But it may not be so good as to moral or human emotion.

[22] As an additional research on "Sharing economic", ownership (belonging to) and user ship (usage and controlling for a while) may be divided.

[23] Commission of the European Communities. Internet of Things — An action plan for Europe 2009.

Figure 4.26 Night vision system in a vehicle.

recent years due to its advantages of stability, convenience, and difficulty in forgery. At present, there are many research fields in feature recognition, including the recognition of physiological features, such as voice, face, fingerprint, palm print, iris, retina, body shape, behavioral feature recognition such as the style of typing on keyboard and signature, and composite biology identification based on physiological characteristics and behavioral characteristics. These feature-recognition technologies are one of the most important means of achieving electronic identification.

In the domain of authentication and estimation, biometric identification plays the role of "door" for an individual to enter into the IoT world, which is also open for individual healthcare. For instance, a deep learning framework (CorNET) to efficiently estimate heart rate (HR) information and perform BId using a wrist-worn is presented. Besides this, in some situations (at night or low-visible conditions), an on-board sensing system (e.g., ADAS in a partly automated vehicle) should find a human on the road, as shown in Fig. 4.26.

4.3.1 *Introduction to biometrics*

Biometrics (biometric identification technology) provides a profile of identifying information and technologies that measure human physiological or behavioral characteristics for authentication or identification purposes. Some of the most widely used characteristics or biometric factors are fingerprints, palm prints, irises, retina, auricle, blood pulse, voice patterns (or voice prints), and the spatial geometry of the face. Based on the different type of biometric factor, biometric solutions can be divided into three groups:

- Solutions based on a **physiological** factor; examples are fingerprint recognition and iris recognition.
- Solutions based on a **behavioral** factor; examples are voice pattern recognition and keystroke dynamics.
- Solutions based on the composite features of **physiological or behavioral** factor; examples are "cognitive fingerprint"[24] of active authentication program and MORIS of BI2 Technology Inc.

Theoretical basis of solutions lays two points: one is based on the fact that human biometrics is unique; the other is based on that these factors can be verified by measurement or automatic identification. For those factors to be suitable for *authentication* or *identification*, it must meet the following criteria:

- **Universality** — the biometric factor must be something each person has.
- **Uniqueness** — with the factor it must be possible to separate individuals from another, this must be possible and not be overly expensive with existing technical means.
- **Permanence** — how well the biometric factor resists the effect of time, generally speaking "aging".
- **Collectability** — it must be possible and not overly expensive or time consuming to measure the factor.
- **Acceptability** — biometrics is not always very well accepted. This is generally dependent on people's view and on how invasive a certain

[24]**Active** authentication program focuses on the behavioral traits that can be observed through how we interact with the world. Just as when you touch something, your finger leaves behind a fingerprint, when you interact with technology you do so in a pattern based on how your mind processes information, leaving behind a "cognitive fingerprint".

technique is. For example, retina scans have low acceptability with the general public because retina scans require direct contact with the reader and retina scans can demonstrate pregnancy and other medical conditions, such as high blood pressure.
- **Performance** — in general terms, the speed, accuracy, and robustness.

The technical basis of biometrics mainly includes computer technology and image-processing technology. Almost all biometric systems work as the following processes: acquisition, decoding, alignment, and matching. Biological image acquisition includes high-precision optical devices, such as scanners and cameras, as well as crystal sensor chips based on capacitance and electric field technology, ultrasonic scanning equipment, and infrared scanning equipment. In the aspect of comparison and matching technology, various advanced algorithms have been successfully developed, and the development of large-scale databases and distributed network technologies has enabled the application of biometric systems to be successfully implemented. In terms of applications, driven by the application of mobile phones, password (or graphic) locks, and fingerprint locks have been developed to iris locks.

In terms of development, there are already companies providing biometric-based technology development platforms, including highly accurate, scalable development kits: biometric device as SensorTile, multi-sensor module as Valencell[25] reference, and other kind of biosensor system integration.

Biometrics plays an important role in the access control of national defense, security, finance, insurance, healthcare, and computer management. In the market, in addition to the traditional automatic fingerprint identification system (AFIS), there are also fingerprint keyboard, fingerprint mouse, fingerprint mobile phone, iris access control in automatic teller machine (ATM), face recognition in check payment system, and so on. Especially, in the aspect of authentication, object recognition, and security of the IoT, biometrics has broad application prospects. The biometric identification systems, such as fingerprint, palm print, face, and iris are introduced below.

[25] Valencell also has accurate biometric sensors for wearable technology that continuously measures heart rate and activity in virtually any form factor.

4.3.2 *Fingerprint and palm print recognition*

Fingerprint recognition is one of the most well-known and widely used biometrics, and it is by far the most used biometric solution for the authentication of smart devices, such as mobile phones and notebooks. The reasons for fingerprint recognition being so popular are the ease of acquisition and acceptance when compared to other biometrics.

Fingerprints are the physical characteristics of human beings, and there are numerous (ten for hands) sources of this biometric on each individual.

Fingerprint recognition refers to the automated method of identifying or confirming the identity of an individual based on the comparison of fingerprints. Each individual fingerprint has been shaped, and it will not change as the individual ages after about the age of 14.

The fingerprint is unique, and two different people, even twins, will never share the same fingerprint. Fingerprint recognition has been developed with digitalization, as three basic patterns[26] of fingerprint ridges. They are the arch, loop, and whorl.

Through complex fingerprint recognition algorithms, the detected fingerprint is contrasted with the fingerprint data in the database, and the fingerprint identification process can be completed quickly. Today, identifying the fingerprints is widely used in access control, such as fingerprint keyboard, fingerprint mouse, fingerprint phone, and fingerprint lock.

Optical readers are the most common type of fingerprint readers, as shown in Fig. 4.27. The type of sensor has an optical reader that acquires a visual image of the fingerprint.

With the fingerprint collation optical module, the mouse can be used to legitimate users fingerprint identification.

Once the fingerprint is recognized, the user can boot the operating system of the computer. For security reasons, if you don't move the mouse for a long time, it will automatically start the screen saver until the user

[26]An arch is a pattern where the ridge enters one side of the finger, then rises in the center forming an arch, and exits on the other side of the finger. With a loop, the ridge enters one side of the finger, then forms a curve, and exits on the same side of the finger from which it entered. Loops are the most common pattern in fingerprints. Finally, a whorl is the pattern you have when ridges form circularly around a central point. Further, there are three major types of minutiae features: ridge ending, bifurcation, and dot (also called short ridge). The ridge ending is, as indicated by the name, the spot where a ridge ends. A bifurcation is the spot where a ridge splits into two ridges. Spots are those fingerprint ridges that are significantly shorter than other ridges.

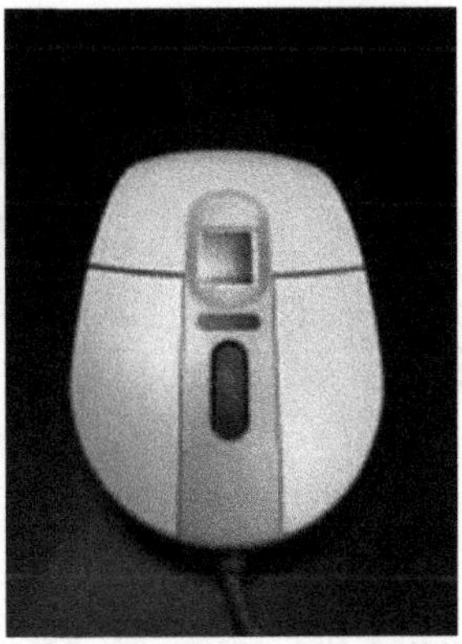

Figure 4.27 Fingerprint mouse.

Figure 4.28 Fingerprint phone.

touches the ID sensor again. The fingerprint keyboard is similar to the fingerprint mouse and is widely used in computer access identification.

As shown in Fig. 4.28, a fingerprint phone refers to fingerprint identification that can be used for legitimate user identification of mobile phones. Towards the era of IoE, a lot of new technology gives new issues to mobile: Internet application access when shopping, payment and even using a mobile phone as ID for authentication and access control.

But your personal information and credit card details may be stored in your mobile phone. Once the mobile phone is lost or stolen, the consequences will be very serious. Therefore, many mobile phone manufacturers are also making a fuss about the security of mobile phones, until fingerprint recognition replaces the traditional password.

Relying fingerprint payment does not infringe the privacy of fingerprint identification with individual.

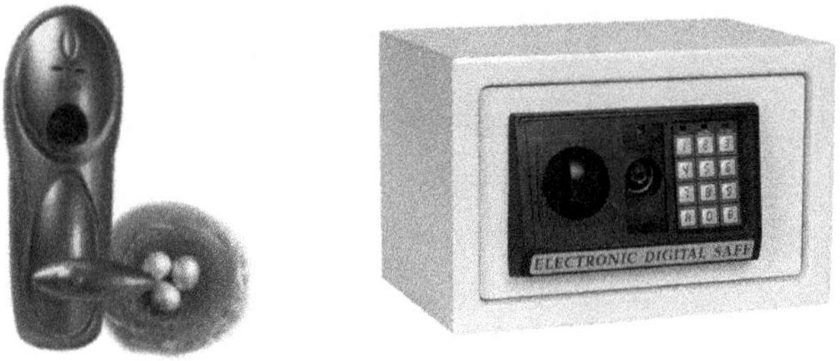

Figure 4.29 Fingerprint safe box.

When a customer makes the payment, he presses his finger on the fingerprint payment sensor, and the terminal device transmits the user's fingerprint data (non-image information) to the back-end system, which finds the payment account corresponding to the fingerprint information through the system authentication. Then, the consumption amount is automatically transferred from the customer's bank account to the merchant to complete the payment. At present, fingerprint payment is an ordinary technology in a mobile phone.

Fingerprint lock, shown in Fig. 4.29, can be applied to safe boxes, house locks, and other personal belongings or place for authentication. Smart settings can be implemented based on different users. As for a car, fingerprint lock enables the owner to start the vehicle without a key. Maybe one day of IoE era, key-lock devices are no longer needed, instead of which will be a fingerprint information pre-storage of personal information representative of the user, for the automatic adjustment of the height of the vehicle driver's seat, automatic connection to car phone, and other functions.

Fingerprint attendance systems is a system that uses fingerprint recognition instead of swiping, records employee attendance, and implements attendance registration and attendance management. Its technical basis of these fingerprint identification applications is the automated fingerprint identification system (AFIS), which refers to the computer processing the input fingerprint image to realize the classification, location, extraction form, and detail features of the fingerprint. Other examples are listed here:

- Logical access control; for example, there exist numerous fingerprint reader devices and software for access control to personal computers.

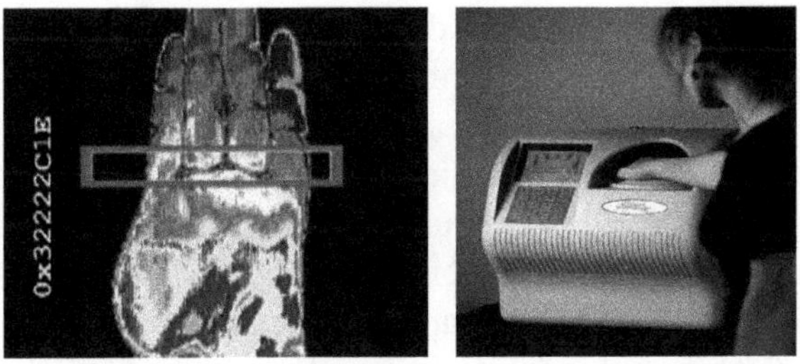

Figure 4.30 Palm print in recognition schematic.

- Physical access control; for example, locks with a fingerprint reader.
- Biometric alternative to loyalty card systems.

The fingerprints are compared and identified based on the extracted features. Because it is one of the cheapest biometric solutions, fingerprint recognition already focuses on situations where advanced security protection is required, such as banking, healthcare, legal companies, and military departments, and is expanding into many areas, such as the IoT, e-commerce, and insurance, such as fingerprint payments. Palm print recognition is very similar to fingerprint. As shown in Fig. 4.30, by using a palm print recognition with an infrared scanning hand, extracts of features from the basic structure of a human hand are saved, and these features will be used for personal authentication.

Palm print and its combination with fingerprint are also discussed. As for fingerprint and palm print, multispectral imaging can also quickly detect a fake by characterizing the subsurface data against the known characteristics of the human skin.

4.3.3 *Facial recognition*

Facial recognition uses the spatial geometry of distinguishing features of the *face*. It is a form of computer vision that uses the face to identify or to authenticate a person. An important difference with other biometric solutions is that faces can be captured from some distance away, with for example, surveillance cameras. Therefore, face recognition can be applied without the subject knowing that he is being observed. Facial recognition technology, which can identify people according to their facial features, is generally divided into standard video-based recognition, 3-D face recognition, and thermal imaging-based recognition.

The recognition based on standard video can record the facial features such as the shape and relative position of the eyes, nose, and mouth of the photographed individual through an ordinary camera and then convert it into a digital signal for identification. Or it is based on images and videos in a standard format for local feature extraction. Video face recognition is a common method of identification.

One of the hot spots of research in this aspect is the collection and application of structured video (image) information. The other hot spot is **Machine Learning**[27] (with heart rate example in the beginning part of this section). For example, researchers of the University of Southern California and the University of Germany had developed the software called "Mugshot" that scans and stores the face of the person you are looking for in a computer and then automatically finds and analyzes images to identify the faces in a crowd of people.

Scientists from the Commonwealth Scientific and Industrial Research Organization (CSIRO) of Australian have developed an automated face recognition system that recalls pre-stored face images from stored smart cards or computer databases and compares them with real faces. Within seconds, the identity of the person is identified. This system uses only a normal personal computer and a normal camera as hardware. Scientists point out that the system is accurate to 95%, and with a voice recognition system, the accuracy can be increased to a higher level.

In 3-D face recognition, the actual 3-D form of the face is evaluated; this is not affected by lighting and does not change with ageing. Also, different viewing angles can be compared better when using 3-D images. Of course, the hardware for 3-D face recognition is more expensive.

The identification based on thermal imaging technology belongs to the application of infrared technology, mainly by analyzing the thermal radiation generated by facial blood to generate a facial image. Unlike video recognition, thermal imaging technology does not require a good light source and can be used even in the dark. The advantage of facial recognition is its naturalness and characteristics that are not perceived by the individual being tested. However, facial recognition technology is very difficult and is considered to be one of the most difficult research topics in the field of biometric identification and even AI.

For example, the UK is testing a facial recognition system to replace the purchase of train tickets, which is developed by Bristol Robotics

[27]Maybe the next book will discuss ML.

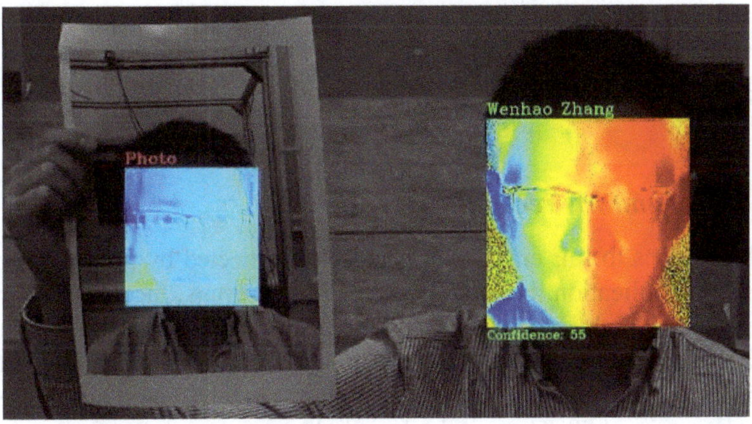

Figure 4.31 Facial recognition technology for railway safety.

Source: Bristol Robotics Laboratory.

Laboratory. The system uses two high-speed infrared cameras to capture facial information of passengers. Unlike existing feature point recognition cameras, infrared recognition can obtain more details, such as nose height, eye socket depth, binocular spacing, and even skin wrinkles. This may mean that even prints or photos of twins will be distinguished by this technology as shown in Figure 4.31.

In 2017, some banks in China, such as China Commercial Bank (CCB), implemented facial recognition by ATM machines. In 2019, some cities with intelligent transportation systems, such as Zhengzhou city of China, facial recognition was used in its metro stations as a kind of electronic ID (EID).

With the development of facial feature recognition technology, it is not only used for identification but can also infer people's psychological activities according to facial expressions and subtle changes. The American drama "Lie to me"[28] reveals the connection between facial expressions and mental activity. If this connection can be analyzed with intelligent pattern recognition, facial pattern recognition can be used to detect lies. We can conclude that face recognition is very interesting because the subject is not necessarily aware that his identity is being verified; this is very useful for surveillance applications.

[28]The play was inspired by the research and writing of behavioral expert Dr. Paul Ekman, Telling Lies.

Circumvention is an important factor to consider when choosing face recognition for authentication purposes. Furthermore, permanence and uniqueness of the face might remain a limiting factor of this biometric solution.

4.3.4 *Eye and iris recognition*

With the steps to IoE era, which is closely connected by perception, network and application, biometrics such as fingerprints, faces, DNA, irises and sclera, which are indispensable to the human body, are gradually replacing passwords and keys to protect personal and organizational information. "Precise identification" technology is to prevent "sin and evil" from accessing IoT. The eye is the window of the soul. As our unique visual organ, it hides a lot of high-tech secret that you don't know.

In the technique of using human eye features for recognition, eyeball and iris recognition are concepts that are relatively confusing. This has to be said from the human eye structure, the human eye is composed of the pupillary lens, iris, sclera, retina, and other parts. The pupil refers to the opening in the middle of the iris, which is the portal for light to enter the eye. The iris is located between the sclera and the pupil, and contains the most abundant texture information, occupying 65%.

The sclera is the white part of the periphery of the eyeball, accounting for about 30% of the total area. The eyeball recognition is usually divided by the recognition area. The recognition mode can be divided into two types: one is to identify the iris, which is what we often call the "black eye" to remove the annular part of the middle black pupil; the other is to identify the sclera, which is what we often say "eye white" section.

Because the accuracy of iris recognition is higher, the research of iris is hot. Generally speaking, the eyeball recognition with high accuracy refers to iris recognition.

The iris is a colored muscle annular tissue around the pupil and within the sclera (white part of the eye), as shown in Fig. 4.32.

There are many tiny bumps and strips on the iris, and the surface features are almost unique. The working process of iris recognition is somewhat similar to fingerprint recognition. The scanned high-definition iris feature image is first converted into a digital image feature code and stored in a database. When the identification is performed, the image feature code of the scanned iris image of the object to be detected is

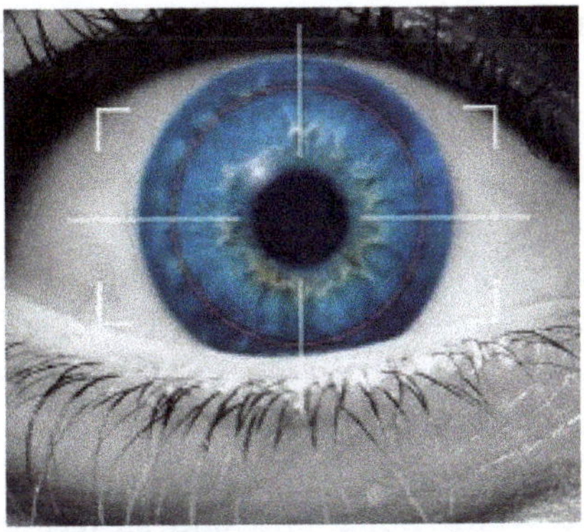

Figure 4.32 Position of the colored, circular iris, which is responsible for controlling the diameter and size of the pupil (picture in public domain).

compared with the previously stored image feature code, in order to determine the identity.

In 1991, the world's first iris feature extraction technology patent **IrisCode™** was obtained by Professor John Daugman in University of Cambridge.

Among all biometrics, Iris recognition is nowadays the most used recognition in commercial devices, thanks to its speed of matching with very low false match rates and ease of non-contact use.

With IrisCode, the visible characteristics of the iris are transformed into a **phase sequence**, which contains information on the orientation, spatial frequency, and position of segments in the iris. The phase is not affected by contrast, camera gain, or illumination levels.

The result of the algorithm is an IrisCode, 256 bytes of data which describe the phase characteristics of the iris in a polar coordinate system.

During recognition, the difference between iriscodes is determined; this difference is called the **Hamming distance**. If the Hamming distance indicates that less than one third of the iriscodes is different from each other, then it is concluded that there is no statistically significant difference between the IrisCodes and they are considered to come from the same iris.

Using 256-byte templates for all scanned irises allows matching up to 500,000 templates per second using IrisCode. Although iris recognition has more accuracy than other biometrics, iris recognition has some drawbacks. The user's eyes must be aimed at the camera, and if the camera scans the user's eyes at a close distance, this kind of intrusive recognition may cause discomfort to some users.

In commercial iris image sensors, based on CCD or CMOS technology, digital cameras capture iris features without direct physical contact between the collectors and collection apparatus.

Scleral recognition is also called eye pattern recognition, although its recognition accuracy is slightly lower than iris recognition.

Sclera or eye white recognition is to extract the blood vessel composition of the white part of the eye. When we look at our eyes in the mirror, we find some red blood vessels in our eyes. Usually, these small blood vessels will change with a long-term and slow process. Small blood vessels can be captured by high-pixel front cameras, so although the accuracy is not as high as iris recognition, white eye recognition is easier to achieve. After all, it's technically less difficult than iris recognition and costs less.

4.3.5 *Behavior recognition and secure consideration*

Take the "cognitive fingerprint" as a behavior feature recognition example, which contains two phases for authentication. The first phase of the program will focus on researching biometrics that do not require the installation of additional hardware sensors, rather the program will look for research on biometrics that can be captured through the technology we already use looking for aspects of this "cognitive fingerprint". These could include, e.g., how the user handles the mouse and how the user crafts written language in an e-mail or document. A heavy emphasis will be placed on validating any potential new biometrics with empirical tests to ensure they would be effective in large-scale deployments. The later phases of the program will focus on developing a solution that integrates any available biometrics using a new authentication platform suitable for deployment on a standard department-of-defense desktop or laptop. The combinatorial approach of using multiple modalities for continuous user identification and authentication is expected to deliver a system that is accurate, robust, and transparent to the user's normal computing experience. The authentication platform will be developed with open application programming interfaces (APIs) to allow the integration of other software or hardware biometrics available in the future from other sources.

The above-mentioned biometric technologies in this section do not need to be maintained like cryptography, and they are also more difficult to be stolen. However, due to this unique persistence, the damage of biometric data may have a risk or even devastating impact, as discussed in the following:

- **Moral hazard:** At present, organizations and even countries can lock, manipulate, and distinguish specific groups according to the collected biometric data.
- **Privacy:** Data and interfaces used to monitor individual health conditions (e.g., blood glucose levels in patients with diabetes) may be sold to health insurance companies to assess the long-term risks of insurance coverage and to set up premium.
- **Safety:** For the large amount of data collected by the intelligent interface and the interface itself, if the organization does not maintain these data and interfaces, it will bring significant security risks. Theft is not revocable.
- Personal identification marks (e.g., fingerprints) may have a lifelong impact on an individual's ability to protect his or her personal data.
- **Regulation:** With the rapid expansion of intelligent interface applications, it is difficult for regulators to match. The general data protection regulation (GDPR), which has an impact on enterprises operating in the European Union, contains the guarantee.

4.4 Interaction of H2M and IoT Senses (IoTS)

The IoT can be understood as a kind of "things connected and interacted" network which takes the intelligent interaction of machines to humans (M2H or H2M) as the links and realizes the networked applications and services. In fact, in the IoT, there is no natural boundary between the communication of machines (M2M) and the communication between humans and machines. The communication between machines is still controlled by human beings (e.g., a pre-design pattern or different levels of automation) and ultimately serves us. Therefore, human–machine interaction (HMI) is an essential part of the IoT.

The intelligent features of the IoT also require more smart senses and interaction methods. On the one hand, it emphasizes the intellectualization of the machine/device on endowing IoT with human-like perceptual abilities. In order to combine the IoT world with the human world, we need to enhance the ability of the things to collect and process information intelligently, even know the world by their "sensory systems", which leads the machines or things to have more sensory modalities. At the same time, the required intelligence of the IoT perception layer lays on not only things based but also the human sensory simulation. On the other hand, it emphasizes smart interaction because we never just stay in the interaction of mouse and keyboard. We need to use touch, voice, eyes, actions, and even psychological induction to communicate with machines in a more harmonious human–computer environment (HCE). Therefore, HCI is an important aspect of the connection among things and people in the IoT, and the smart interaction is also an important embodiment of the intelligence of the IoT.

Besides HMI, IoT senses (IoTS) is also part of the IoT concept involving new sensing technologies to reproduce them over the Internet, e.g., the senses of touch, sight, hearing, taste, smell, and some of them are enabled and extended by AI, such as VR/AR.

The IoTS developments are key for the IoT considering that the cognitive decision-making capabilities of the devices can be implemented by AI algorithms implemented into the intelligent IoT devices (e.g., robotic things). The IoTS complements and extends the capabilities of many IoT applications by including other senses (e.g., vision, hearing, touch, taste, smell, pain, balance, temperature, etc.) and providing new perceptions and experiences by integrating augmented intelligence and information across senses, time, and space. A list of human senses related IoT perceptions are presented in Song (2013). The IoTS is bringing the technological advances for developing new sensing solutions as part of the intelligent things to address the implementation over the Internet of the senses of touch, sight, smell, taste, hearing, and space.

Human–computer interaction (HCI) or HMI is an interdisciplinary field that studies the interaction between system and user. It is the integration of computer science, psychology, sociology, graphic design, industrial design, and other disciplines. In a broad sense, it can be understood as user experience (see micro interaction in the following in a narrow sense). In the early 1980s, the academic community summarized the latest research results of HCI, and the subject of HCI gradually formed its own theoretical system and practical category framework. In terms of theoretical system, it is independent from ergonomics and emphasizes the theoretical guidance of cognitive psychology, behavioral science, and sociology; in terms of practice, it is expanded from human–computer interface (HMI) and emphasizes the feedback interaction of computer for human. Human–computer interface is replaced by HCI. Since the late 1990s, with the rapid development and popularization of high-speed processing chip, multimedia technology, and Internet web technology, the research on HCI focuses on intelligent interaction, multi-mode (multi-channel), multimedia interaction, virtual interaction and human–computer collaborative interaction, i.e., HCI technology.

In the 21st century, with the rapid development of the IoT, HCI has entered the era of the IoT, and there are many wearable products based on micro interaction. Micro interaction is a series of operations that exist only to achieve a single task. Michal Levin divides the (micro) interaction model into three kinds: manual operation, semi-automatic operation, and full-automatic operation, which are the current mainstream micro interaction implementation methods. Although the IoT is a "network connected with things", it still needs human operation and control. However, the HCI here has gone far beyond the concept of HCI but generally refers to the interaction and feedback between various devices connected with applications and people. For example, Google AR glasses, 3-D gesture interaction, **somatosensory** interaction, and other concept products are subverting our traditional cognition. These multi-dimensional collaborative perception and interaction based on five senses (eyes, ears, mouth, nose, and tongue) and their comprehensive applications are the important embodiment of the IoT as a deep information technology, which will profoundly affect our daily life.

The "interaction" and IoTS discussed in this section, according to the technical analysis of "personification", divides the sensory organ function of human perception of the external world in the era of IoT into "six senses": touch, sight, smell hearing, taste, hearing, and space, as shown in Fig. 4.33.

4.4.1 *Touch*

Tactile perception is a new mode of HCI and information transmission. As the most important form of perception besides vision and hearing, touch is an information transmission channel that human body is born with but has not been fully utilized at present. How to make full use of a variety of perceptual capabilities, so that people can get a variety of information quickly and comprehensively has become a hot topic in the field of HCI. Touch screen, haptic reproduction, gesture interaction, and other

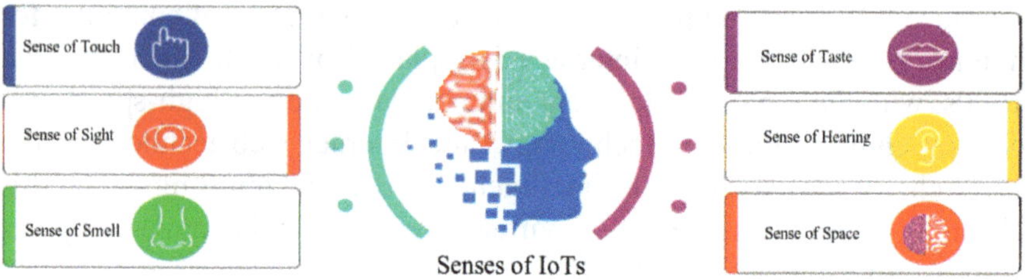

Figure 4.33 Six kinds of IoTS.

haptic HCI methods have been proposed and studied. In the next chapter, touch will be discussed as part of tactile IoT (TIoT)—a new modality, which consists of several distinctions.

1. Touch screen: With the rapid development of mobile devices, the technology of touch screen (or panel) has developed from single touch to multi touch. One of the most successful applications of multi-touch technology is Apple's iPhone series, though Apple OS, multi-touch technology can support users to use gestures to zoom and rotate pictures. Microsoft also launched the concept product Surface based on multi-touch technology. It allows users to interact with the computer on a horizontal table with their hands or other objects.

Traditional ways of interaction mainly use mouse, keyboard, and buttons for remote control to interact. These ways generally have the disadvantages of complicated operation and lack of humanization, which has become an obstacle to the popularization of intelligent interaction in the IoT. When you pick up a touch screen inside mobile phone or tablet computer, the display screen and touch panel with tactile effect can let you reflect the joy of touch. Multi-touch screen reduces the complexity of HCI, so that children and adults up to an age of 80 can use the touch screen freely in electronic products.

2. Touch device: One of the oldest touch devices was born in 1961 to predict the number of roulette wins in Russia. It was also a wearable device because the two parts of it was in a shoe (as shown in Fig. 4.34). Wearable touch devices can serve as intelligent interaction for touch, movement, and human blood pressure sensing.

Nowadays, more modern touch devices are in design for bridging the gap between buyers and sellers. For example, you can feel the cloth you

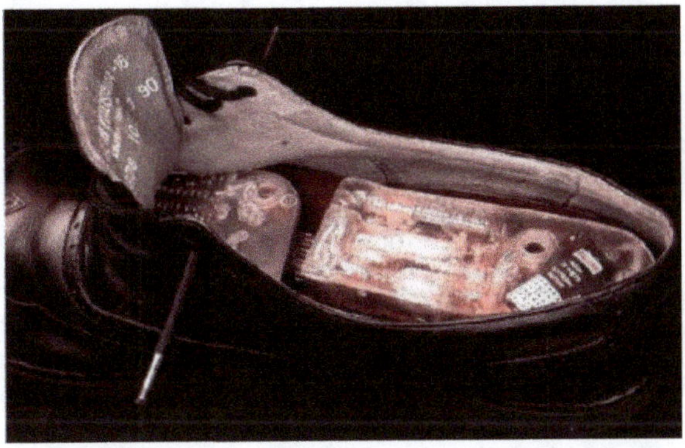

Figure 4.34 An in-shoe touch devices to predict the number of roulette wins in Russia.

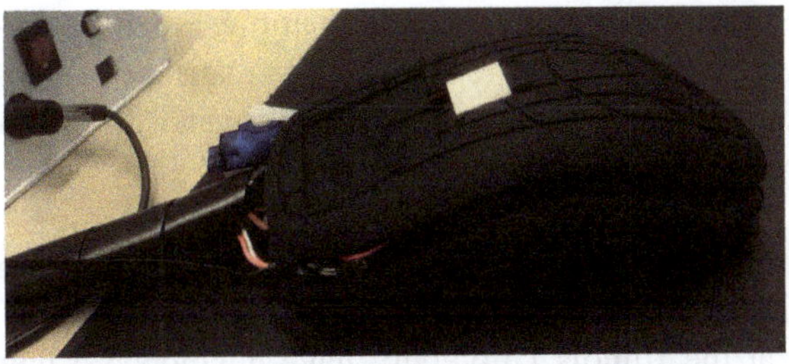

Figure 4.35 A computer mouse-like tactile display.

want before buying it in the Tactile IoT.[29] Another device for this kind of experience is an unordinary computer mouse described in. The tactile computer mouse (shown in Fig. 4.35) uses several actuators to display surface material properties. It has been shown that this device is able to represent the five major tactile dimensions (shown in Fig. 4.36) in a real–virtual material comparison test and that subjects were able to identify ten virtual surfaces (VS0 to VS9) using this device without visual and audible information (Steinbach *et al.*, 2018).

Senseg (a Finnish company) is oriented to a more realistic "three-dimensional touch feedback", which makes the touch feel like hands-on-a texture. The company owns the "SensegE-Sense" as its touch technology.

---

[29]Another sensor example, the fitness mirror, is shown in Section 4.2.

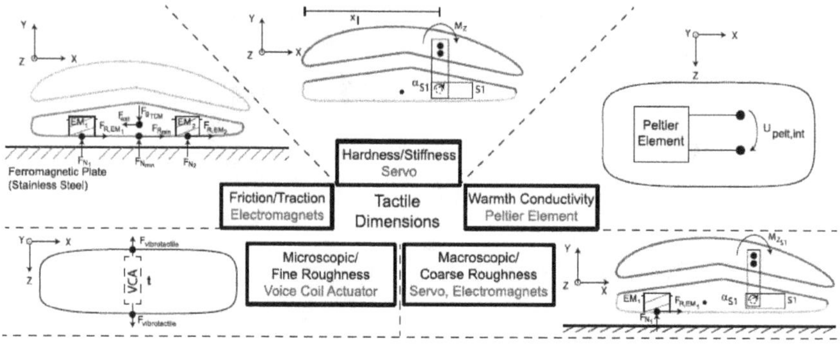

Figure 4.36 Elements of the mouse-like tactile device.

In short, when the user touches something on the touch panel, his fingers will feel the texture of the object. For example, when he touches a rock, his fingers will feel as if they really touch the surface of the stone. There are other tactile objects, such as silk, rubber, water drops, and paper, for different feeling dimensions.

3. Virtual haptic rendering: Virtual haptic rendering is being used to develop artificial tactile devices in the field of artificial simulation. Researchers at the Illinois University have developed a hair-like tactile sensor. Many animals and insects can use their hair to distinguish many different things, including direction, balance, speed, sound, and pressure. This kind of artificial hair is made of glass and polysilicon with good performance and etched from silicon substrate by photolithography. This large array of artificial hairs can be used in space probes, and its ability to detect the surrounding environment is far beyond any existing system. NASA is actively participating in this research. The following example (Fig. 4.37) shows the smart haptic applications which allow users to experience selected surface properties of offered products on websites using surface haptic displays.

For humans, touch consists of several distinct sensations (e.g., pressure, temperature, light touch, vibration, pain). The sensations are part of the touch sense and are attributed to different receptors in the skin. For robotic and other types of things, the sensations are generated by sensors that mimic the reaction to pressure, temperature, touch, vibration, etc. Touch sense transmits other different messages in the case of human interaction, which can be transferred as well to things. How to code the

Figure 4.37 Example applications which allow users to experience selected surface properties of offered products on websites using surface haptic displays (left: Tanvas Touch tablet, right: TPad phone).

different level of the diversity of distinct sensations in haptic codecs for the tactile internet or tactile IoT (TI/TIoT) and how the human operator–machine teleoperator address the interactions between human operator with a virtual object by touch feedback (e.g., multi-player, collaborative-VR gaming and telemedicine)? Answers will be found in the TIoT section of the next chapter.

4.4.2 *Sight of IoT*

1. Visual enhancement: Visual enhancement belongs to AR, as one aspect of mixed reality (MR). Visual enhancement is the use of computer technology, visualization technology, and others that can break through the limitations of human vision, such as night vision technology, 3-D technology, and so on, so as to produce some not-real objects but provide assistance to understand the real environment or extra information of the objects that cannot be found by human eyes. The virtual objects are accurately "placed" in the real environment through the sensing technology, and the virtual objects are often displayed in a visual device, where the image and its relative enhancement information are integrated with the real environment and presents users with a new environment with real visual and augmented visual from sensors.

In short, visual enhancement is a kind of AR technology that combines virtual world and real-world through human vision, which belongs to visual HCI technology. Visual enhancement will be one of the technologies that can break through the limits of human vision by visual fusion and information augmentation. Its emergence is closely related to the computer graphics and image processing technology, and optical (or infrared) sensor. The realization of visual enhancement can achieve the breadth and clarity that human eyes cannot achieve through the fusion of graphics and image processing technology. Through visual enhancement, we can see more than our eye sight. After the image is processed by a computer, we can see 360 degrees and more pixels. The augmented visual information can be virtual objects (or digital shadow aside) coexisting with them in real environment or non-geometric information of real objects, as called AR. These comparisons with VR are at the end of this section.

Figure 4.38 shows a thermal monitoring system from Colorado Industrial Zone in the US: The thermal radar system can provide 360-degree infrared coverage, which can make people, fire, and cars invisible. The core of the system is a continuously rotating thermal sensor on which the processor continuously stitches the images together, providing a continuous stream of images for a continuously refreshing panoramic video system, and the intelligent software of the system will find potential threats by the rotating camera which takes 16 thermal images per second, according to the infrared light from warm objects—people, car engines, tires, etc.

Infrared technology and (micro light level) night vision technology, as the mature technology in night vision sensing, which break through the vision limitation of eyesight in the dark environment and are widely used in searching for rescue and military purposes. The 360-degree round view is widely used to expand the perspective of automobile. Other applications of vision enhancement technology include electronic-aided sensing systems, such as Hubble telescope, electron microscope, penetration

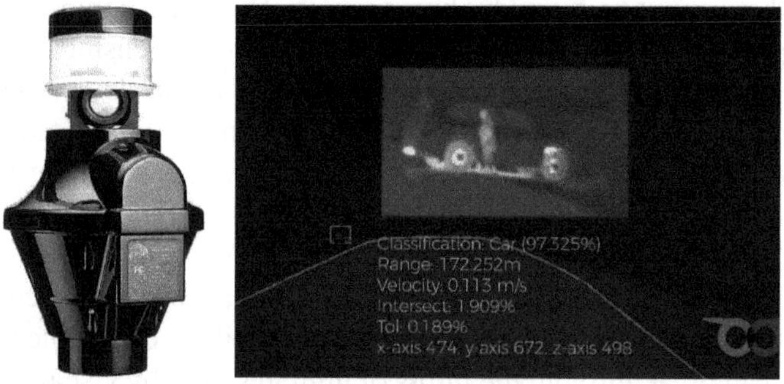

Figure 4.38 360-degree AR thermal monitoring system and another diagram for the explanation of infrared technology.

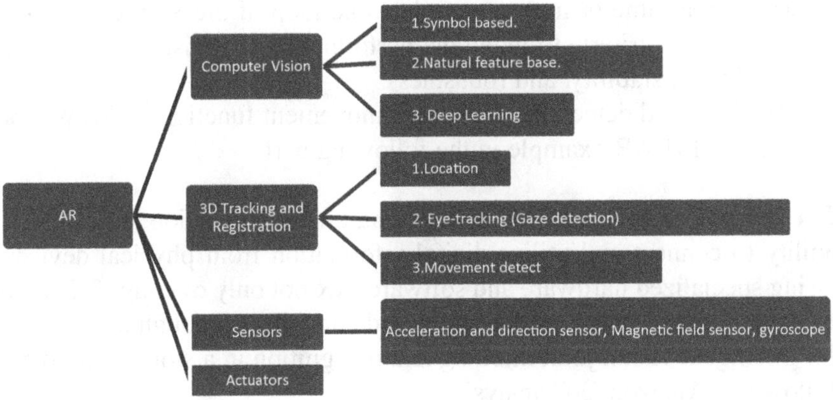

Figure 4.39 Technologies in AR.
Source: ARVRSchool.com.

vision radar, and remote sensing (RS) applications commonly used in satellite or high-attitude platforms (HAPS).

2. AR: The above analysis lays the foundation for multi-sensor fusion and representation and multi-scene fusion and representation. Visual enhancement provides information that is different from human perception. But how real scenes and augmented scenes are superimposed effectively? In addition to the location sensing and (indoor and outdoor) positioning that will be discussed in the next section, there are also real-time tracking and registration technologies, computer vision (CV), and sensors (e.g., acceleration, magnetic field sensor, and gyroscope), which are mainly used to establish the association and expression between virtual information and real scene, as shown in Fig. 4.39.

3-D tracking and registration of AR is not only the basic technology to realize visual enhancement applications but also the key to determine the performance of augmented reality application system.

Therefore, 3-D registration and tracking relative aspects (location and identification, movement detection) have always been the focus and difficulty of augmented reality system research. Its main tasks are to calculate the real-time pose of the camera relative to an object in the real scene (or *vice versa*), detect the object and track its movement, determine the position of the virtual information to be superimposed in the projection plane, and display the virtual information in the correct position on the screen (in real time or not) to complete one loop of the 3-D registration. There are three criteria to judge the performance of registration technology: real time, stability, and robustness.

Tracking and detection of a human movement function of AR will be taken as an IoT-AR example in the following part.

3. Use Case of IoT-AR: AR is acquiring a new dimension with the IoT ability to connect and utilize digital information from physical devices. Using specialized hardware and software, AR not only overlays 3-D digital content seamlessly onto the real world but collects enough information for intelligent vision joint marking and recognition in a store, such as the following "Amazon Go" analysis.

Enhanced by IoT, AR is no longer restricted to the media and entertainment and gaming industries. Through its unique user experience and the reduced contact between a customer and a cashier, buy and go will be popular in the near future. Furthermore, AR is enabling enterprises to modernize the entirety of business functions from R&D and customer and employee engagement to manufacturing, production, and field services.

In December 2016, the Amazon Go mode (demonstrated in Fig. 4.40) with "checkout free" was launched in the convenience stores by Amazon.

Figure 4.40 Cameras with the computer vision as the fixed position tags in the shelves for detecting customers and actions.

There is no need to queue up for checkout in the exit of the stores. When customers enter, they just need to open the two-dimensional code of Amazon Go apps on their mobile phone, brush it on the gate, then select and pick up the product item and leave directly. From some reports in the Internet, the highlights of "Amazon Go" include sensor fusion and CV algorithm. However, Amazon has not released any details. The following points are discussed on the Internet, based on some guesses about cameras, computers, and CV.

1. *Device*: Why does Amazon want to use smart phones instead of other IoT hardware? How can Amazon add item information about sales to the customer's shopping experience?

2. *Data and interactivity*: If the RFID sensor is just in the shopping cart, RFID will only tell you what goes into the shopping cart and what stays in it. If the RFID sensor is at the exit door, it will tell you what items a customer has bought when leaving the store. With the vision of fixed cameras, the recognition of CV, and RFID readers, Amazon knows what everyone is doing in the store.

3. *RFID*: Even if customers cannot be RFID tagged, cameras and computer vision can track them. Now, many stores have added cameras that can be reused. If products or items are labeled with RFID tags, such as those passive RFID tags, all items in the store will be with asset tags for location.

All items in the store will be with asset tags for location, and if a customer has been locked by the fixed position tag (by the CV system), the CV system can create a dynamic map of the items and the customer (as shown in Fig. 4.41). In addition, through the pressure sensor or the tracking sensor (e.g., distributed RFID readers), the system can determine whether the items are on the shelf or taken away or returned.

Brian Roemmele (a netizen) revealed that Amazon had submitted two patent documents, which may describe the mode of Amazon Go, namely "detecting item interaction and movement" and "transiting items from the materials handling facility". The general content of the former patent is: When customers pick up or put down items from the shelf, the system can detect this action and update the list in the customer's mobile device.

It can be learned from the patent that the system contains multiple cameras, which are respectively placed on the ceiling, on both sides of the

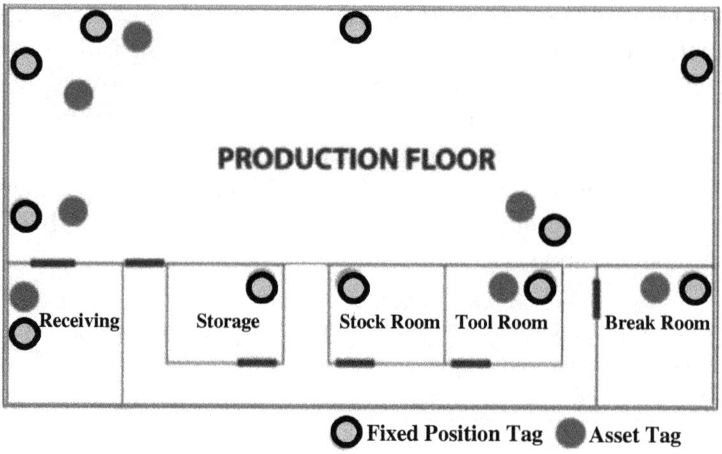

Figure 4.41 Asset tag associated with each item in the transition area.

shelf, or inside. Among them, the cameras on the ceiling are used to capture the location of customers and items, the cameras on both sides of the shelf are used to capture the images of customers and the surrounding environment, and the cameras in the shelf are used to determine the location of items or the movement of a customer's hands.

The latter patent "transfer of items from material handling facilities" mainly states that items are identified and automatically associated with customers when they are picking up items. When the customer enters or passes through the "transition area", the picked-up items will be automatically transferred to the user without the customer's "confirmation" input. Then, some details can be concluded as follows:

- *Customers and relative movement detection*: When a customer moves close to an items shelf, the **IoT–AR** system identifies the customer by either NFC (of one's smart phone) or camera (in Fig. 4.40, the camera also acts as the fixed position tag in a given product shelf, as shown in Fig. 4.41) and focuses on the movement of the customer. After the customer picks up an item from the shelf, the CV system locks the customer as a potential buyer and waits for his next action. If the customer does not put the item back, go to the next step.
- *Detection for items/products transitioning from shelves*: Each item with an RFID (asset) tag is located on the shelf, and its corresponding

tracking systems (as RFID readers distributed in the store and a RFID management system) is used to detect whether the item is taken away (e.g., out of the detecting range). If the item is taken away and the customer is found by the CV system that he is out of the "Transition Area", the item is associated with the customer. After all items are collected by the customer and he goes through the automated cashier point, the RFID reader there makes out bills for items at once and collects money from the electronic account ID associated with the customer (by the Amazon Go app, which identified the customer electronic ID when he opened his 2-D QR code by his smart phone before he came in the store).

- *Sensors and CV cameras*: CV cameras in the store can be of various types, which can be RGB cameras or depth sensing cameras. There can also other sensing devices, such as pressure sensor, infrared sensor, volume displacement sensor, light curtain, and so on. The pressure sensor can detect the time when the item moves out and (re-)enters, and the infrared sensor can be used to distinguish a hand on or away from the item (which linking to a customer by the back end of the system).

Through the analysis spreading on the Internet, the smart phone of a customer plays the role of AR device and the customer is like playing an AR game in the process of shopping experience, where the AR-IoT system can judge when the customer puts up/down or takes away the item from the shelves. After all the items marked as "taken away" by the same customer, he can go with automatically checking out at the exit. Intel has found some opportunities in the AR-IoT system and plans to invest the platform of "reactive retail platform" (RRP), which will connect all the hardware and software as the IoT in chain stores.

IoT-AR technology has been used in medical, military, industrial, and other fields. In healthcare, it can visualize the previous records and information invisible for doctors in guiding a surgery (MIT and Nanyang University of technology in Singapore are committed to enhancement systems to help surgeons observe the patient's internal conditions), and it can enable surgeons to perform complicated procedures better by rendering accurate 3-D reconstructions of the body part they are operating on while being connected in real time to devices that relay vital stats and information. According to a report from Software.org, adding the AR dimension to IoT expands its potential. Take the retails as an example, AR can bridge the gap between online and offline, providing the customer with the best of both worlds. For instance, IKEA is already harnessing the power of AR by helping customers visualize how their furniture will look in their house and how those pieces can be customized to fit the desired decor.

Furthermore, it can develop real-time interactive 3-D simulations by employing digital twins, which can be well matched with the physical environment and provide reference for the construction by a designer (e.g., in pre-design stage).

Finally, sight is the capability of perceiving things through the vision system that can be represented by different types of cameras, AR glasses that support the navigation, searching for routes, identify places, recognizing objects, persons, and sceneries. The sight will improve the capabilities of robotic things and enhance their functional abilities.

4.4.3 *Auditory sense*

According to the analysis of relevant researchers from Harvard Business School, the proportion of people's brain receiving external information through five senses every day is 1% for taste, 1.5% for touch, 3.5% for smell, 11% for hearing, and 83% for vision. Although hearing accounts for a small proportion, it belongs to another important "channel". If you don't believe it, you can turn off the sound while watching TV. It can be imagined that one morning in the era of IoT, when you wake up and don't want to open your eyes, you can control all the electrical appliances in your home by saying some voice commands in bed, connect the phone, brush your teeth, and listen to the news. Vision and hearing are also the first two fields of AI application.

Hearing-based HCI is the interaction between human voice and machine. This kind of interaction includes intelligent speech interaction functions, such as speech understanding, speech interaction, and speech synthesis. Early HCI based on hearing focused on controlling the machine through sound, such as voice-controlled lights, voice-controlled toy cars, and so on. At this time, the machine only needs to be able to hear. With the development of information technology, today's machines can not only hear, but also "understand" human voice. Thanks to artificial intelligence, the degree of understanding is also higher than before. At present, the research and application of intelligent hearing technology mainly focus on the following aspects:

1. Voice (Phonetic) Semantic Understanding: Voice semantic understanding is the process of studying the interaction of human speech simulated by computer. In order to make the computer understand and use the natural language in the society (such as Chinese, English, etc.), the communication between human and computer through natural language needs to be realized, which can help humans query information, answer questions, extract literature, compile information, and process all the information that natural language handle.

Voice in the IoT sense is to recognize the sound and decode the sound waves and vibrations. The detection of sound using different types of microphones, vibration sensors, etc. allows for enhancing the capabilities of the things/devices/machines by developing techniques for voice control, automatically translate languages, voice biometrics, etc.

Among these fields, the appearance of the automatic speech recognition (ASR) has significantly changed the way of HCI in IoT world.

2. Automatic Speech Recognition (ASR): In the research of speech recognition technology, Siri (voice interaction function of iPhone), which is in the leading position in this field, found that the ASR accounts for an increasing part of the speech interaction and understanding, and the really important thing is the "understanding" after speech recording and recognition.

In the process of speech understanding, in order to make the computer "understand" the human speech indeed, the context information contained in the speech is "extracted"; in the basic principle, it includes two stages: training and recognition. The former is based on the statistical language model (SLM), with a large amount of data is needed to make the agent improve the accuracy of understanding through "self-learning and self-training by the agent". In the training stage, the agent learns from the multiple inputs of training speech, obtains the feature vector parameters after the preprocessing and feature extraction, and then establishes the reference model library of training speech through feature modeling.

Whether it is training or recognition stage, it is necessary to preprocess the input speech first (e.g., figure out the word one by one) and then learn or extract the features. These are not enough; how to make the machine understand the "implication" of the context analysis? it involves linguistics, psychology, sociology, and other interdisciplinary subjects. This also leads to a branch of the application of artificial intelligence called natural language processing (NLP) for semantic understanding.

4.4.4 *Smell and taste*

Smell and taste are some mysterious powers of human beings. It does not only mean that when we see the wine taster's identification, and he says the years and origins of the wines as Lafite or MaoTai. It also recalls us that someone knows how to distinguish "fragrance or smell/taste good" and "delicious but smelly" even at birth.

When I write about this, I suddenly think of a movie, "Scent of a Woman" (by the director Martin), and the reason why my 3-year-old child didn't let me wash the quilt: there is a smell of her mother in the quilt, so don't wash it off. In addition, the inspiration of this section comes from an English book I read ten years ago. I only remember that the book sums up several major enjoyments of human beings: sunshine, music, food, and smell.

Human sense of smell comes from the sense of volatile gas molecules; human sense of taste comes from the sense of non-volatile ions and molecules in the liquid. They are all recognizable organs of chemical quantity and biomass. Compared with the visual, auditory, and tactile recognition of physical quantity, the research methods are more complex and the research progress is relatively slow. In the past decade, with the rapid development of life science and artificial intelligence, especially the joint promotion of life science and biochemical sensor research, the deep understanding and application of smell and taste presents a trend of intelligence. For example, in the IoT, intelligent sensors can be used to monitor the perception of air pollution (PM index), toxic gas and explosives monitoring, toxic substances detection; and similarly, taste sensors can be used for hydrological perception and water quality monitoring.

1. Smell and AOS: Olfaction originates from the stimulation of olfactory receptors by molecules. The recognition process is as follows: When gas molecules pass through the olfactory mucosa epithelium in the nasal cavity, the cilia of olfactory cells protrude out of the surface, and the cilia surface is like a nasal chemoreceptor, producing olfactory signals to the odorant molecules, and finally the olfactory signals generate corresponding judgment reactions through the brain.

The study of smell and taste began in the 1960s. On the one hand, biologists, neurophysiologists, and chemists have made a long-term

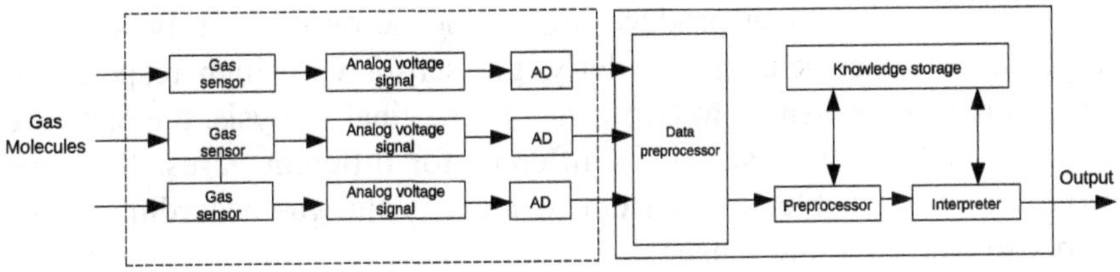

Figure 4.42 Principle of AOS.

exploration on the neural conduction mechanism of smell and taste and put forward many models and experimental analyses. For example, Professor Freeman, a neurophysiologist of MIT University in the US, has studied the olfactory model for several decades. On the other hand, scholars engaged in analytical chemistry, electronics, instrument science, and other engineering fields have carried out extensive research and instrument development on gas and ion sensors, and developed analytical instruments with olfactory and gustatory functions in many fields. For example, the artificial olfactory system (AOS) called the electronic nose and the artificial taste system (ATS) or the electronic tongue.

The working principle of electronic nose is similar to that of olfactory organ, as shown in Fig. 4.42. Odor molecules are absorbed by sensor array in electronic nose and generate signals. The generated signal is processed and transmitted by various methods, and the processed signal is judged by the pattern recognition system. The principle is shown in Fig. 4.42, which can be summarized as: sensor array signal preprocessing neural network and various algorithms computer identification (gas qualitative and quantitative analysis). In terms of function, gas sensor array is equivalent to a large number of olfactory receptor cells in biological olfactory system, neural network and computer recognition are equivalent to biological brain, and the rest are equivalent to olfactory nerve signal transmission system.

Electronic nose is an electronic system that uses the response pattern of gas sensor array to identify odor. It can continuously and in real-time monitor the odor status of a specific location for a few hours, days, or even months. Electronic nose is a kind of biosensor technology, which is mainly composed of odor sampling operator, gas sensor array, and signal processing system.

The main mechanism of electronic nose recognition is that each sensor in the array has different sensitivity to the gas to be measured. For example, No. 1 gas can produce high response on one sensor and low response on other sensors; similarly, the sensor with high response to No. 2 gas is not sensitive to No. 1 gas. In the final analysis, the response diagram of the whole sensor is different for different gases. It is this difference that enables the system to identify the gas according to the response pattern of the sensor.

As for the IoT smell, it is often described as the ability to detect the different odors/scents/aromas (up to 1 trillion scents) that can be represented by different sensors that are sensitive to various odors. The remote smell integrated as online experience for humans and things can improve the capabilities of the sensing things to smell scents in different remote environments, provide new services and improve the perception in these environments.

For instance, if we can put the odor of various objects into the odor library and then identify the odor objects through the olfactory interaction system, such as identifying medicinal materials through the odor, identifying family members through the odor, and learning something else through the odor. The olfactory interaction system can capture, analyze, and compare the odors that a user is interested in.

Maybe one day, according to a unique smell corresponding to each person or each meal, we can search him through the smell or find how a meal is cooked, no matter where she (or he) is or what the stuff is needed for a meal. The following is an example of "smell online".

The main way people perceive the Internet is through vision and hearing. In 2012, the R&D team of "Mint Digital Foundry" developed the sniffer "Olly", which enables users to sense the Internet through smelling. Olly is a small white cube device, which can be placed on the palm of the hand. There are many holes on it, and it is connected with the computer through the USB interface; see Fig. 4.43.

Olly's structure includes a fan, chip, shell, and stretch tray. The tray at the back of Olly is specially designed for placing odorous items, such as fruit, mint, essential oil, or any other spices that we love. The user can connect Olly with any network account in the computer and set the rules for Olly to emit odor. In this way, "Olly" can sniff when users update their microblog, enter their mailbox, or when someone mentions their name in the social network and inform users by sending out the smell. For example, when office workers go to work in the morning to check their e-mail, they can smell the mint fragrance of "Olly", which gives them a boost.

In addition, in the food safety application of the IoT, many promising sensor detection technologies are still in the experimental stage of

Figure 4.43 Olly's appearance.

development, such as biochemical sensors, electronic nose, and "lab on a chip". The latter conception broke the limitation that microbial quality analysis is measured in the traditional laboratory. However, with the electronic nose, the predictive analysis of quality monitoring can be increased, for example, to accurately determine the remaining shelf life of a good, basing on the taste of food spoilage.

2. Taste and artificial taste system: Taste originates from the stimulation of liquid molecules and ions in taste receptors. The recognition process is very similar to that of olfaction, except that the taste receptors are taste buds. In mammals, taste buds are mainly distributed on the surface of tongue epithelium, oral cavity, and pharyngeal mucosa. Their recognition process can be described as: the receptor generates signals — signal transmission and preprocessing — brain recognition.

Restricted by the research of biological sensing and biochemical sensors in early times, the electronic tongue system or ATS has been put forward for a short time. ATS has been produced and developed in the last 20 years. In 1995, it was proposed by Professor Yu. G. Vlasov of Russia and included in the international cooperation project of Professor Damico from Italy. In short, a non-selective taste sensor array and its digital signal processing method can be used as an ATS to simulate human and biological electronic tongue.

Limited by the previous research methods and means, the research of taste has been lagging behind the research of vision, hearing, touch, and smell. In recent years, with the use of microelectrode recording of taste receptor potential on animal single taste cells and with the development of semiconductor microfabrication technology, the miniaturization of analysis technology provides a powerful means for cell microenvironment analysis. As a **non-destructive** real-time sensing technology, taste cell chip will play an important role in the study of taste conduction mechanism. The working principle of the electronic tongue is very similar to that of the electronic nose, but the electronic tongue is a bionic process based on the simulation of biological taste formation process. What the artificial taste sensor measures is the whole information of the taste of the whole substance. The most studied is the multi-channel lipid membrane taste sensor array, which can partially reproduce the human taste response to taste substances.

At present, the application of ATS can easily distinguish several kinds of drinks, such as coffee, beer, and ionic drinks. One of the advantages of using ATS is that it doesn't need any pre-treatment of the food, and the taste can be detected quickly by pouring the drink into the test cup. Figure 4.44 shows the taste comparison of two kinds of coffee drinks heated and stored in the vending machine.

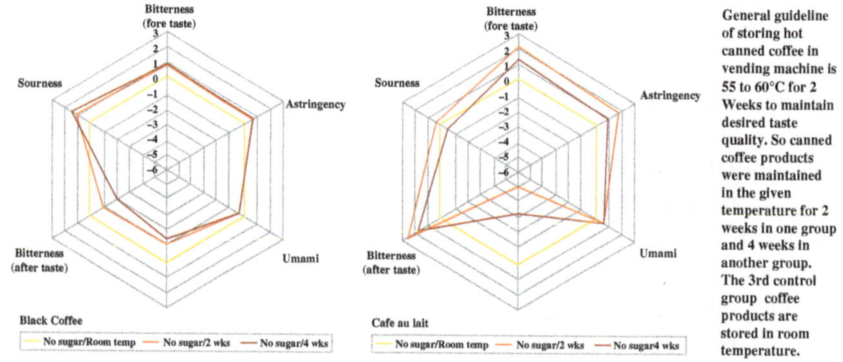

Figure 4.44 Taste comparison of two kinds of coffee heated in the vending machine and the taste changing with stored conditions.

Note: In the left picture, the sour, bitter, and astringent taste of black coffee increased, while the bitter aftertaste, salty, and delicious taste decreased. The drastic changes of taste were mainly concentrated in the first two weeks, and the changes were small in the second two weeks. Therefore, this storage standard is appropriate. The picture on the right shows the taste changes of canned coffee (milk). Compared with black coffee, the taste of Orey changes greatly, especially the base bitterness, which is easy to leave a bad aftertaste in the mouth.

The shelf life under normal temperature is reflected in the product label, but it is less for heated canned drinks because it is difficult to standardize the effective taste information. The data of taste sensor can provide reliable basis for storage standards under different conditions.

3. Food safety control as an use case: Biosensors can make food safer. The application of biosensors in food safety control includes the determination and analysis of food ingredients, food additives, and toxic substances and food freshness determination, discussed as follows:

- ***Food composition analysis***: In the food industry, glucose content is an important index to measure the maturity and storage life of fruits. Enzyme electrode biosensor has been developed for the analysis of glucose in wines, apple juice, jam, and honey. Nitrogen is often used to determine the content of protein in food.
- ***Analysis of food additives***: Sulfite is usually used as bleaching agent and preservative in food industry. The current type sulfur dioxide enzyme electrode made of sulfite oxidase as sensitive material can be used to determine the sulfite content in food. In addition, biosensors are also used for the determination of pigments and emulsifiers.
- ***Determination and analysis of toxic substances and food freshness***: The content control of melamine and other toxic substances; determination and analysis of harmful substances to human health in waste oil; determination of freshness of food within the shelf life and safety control of preservatives used for preservation; changes of harmful substances and taste within and outside the shelf life. In the IoT, food safety life cycle management is shown in Fig. 4.45.

4.4.5 *VR and AR*

1. A Taste-VR Example by Visual Simulation for Brain: Public interest research using taste can help blind people form images in their minds. Figure 4.46 is a high-tech VR device designed and produced by Wicab company in the US. The Brainport V100 device consists of three parts: sunglasses that capture video (images), a handheld joystick, and a lollipop like taste sensor (as shown in Fig. 4.46). The sunglasses are equipped with a micro camera for capturing video or images. The taste sensor has an area of about one inch and contains 400 electrical stimulation contacts array (as shown in the left part of Fig. 4.46).

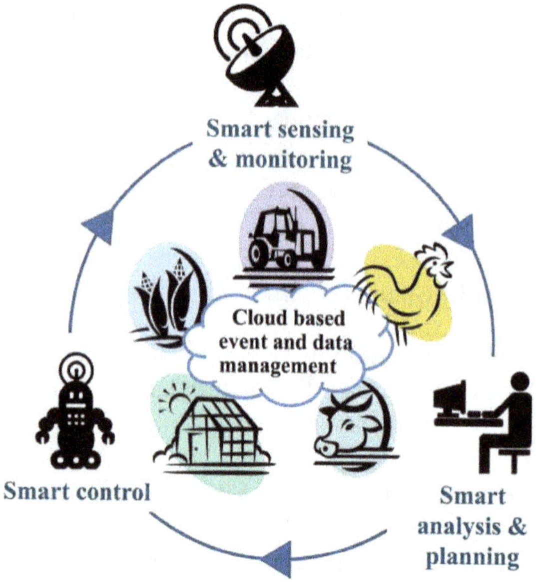

Figure 4.45 Life-cycle management of IoT in food safety: Smart control at the source of food production; monitoring at the supply chain; analysis before dinner table.

Note: The central part of the diagram is cloud-based event and data management for each stage. The core part of the figure is cloud-based event and data management; the remaining three parts are: intelligent perception and monitoring of the origin of agricultural products, intelligent analysis and planning in the process of processing and transportation, and control when entering the family table.

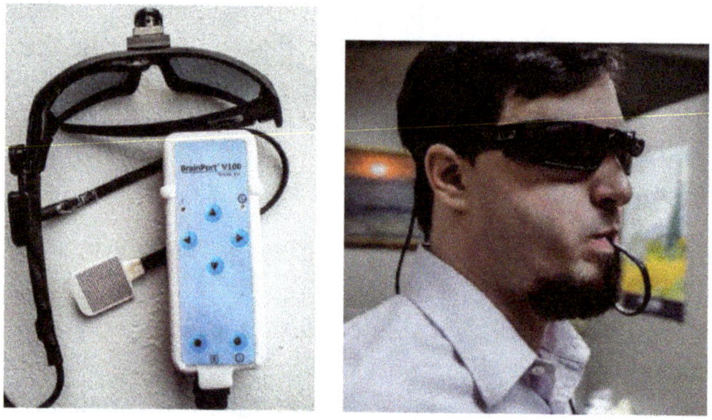

Figure 4.46 BrainPort V100 helping the blind travel with the process: Electric pulse — tongue — image generation.

Source: Stronks, H. C. *et al.* (2016). Visual task performance in the blind with the BrainPort V100 Vision Aid. *Expert review of Medical Devices*.

The user wears the sunglasses, and the sensor is placed in the user's mouth. The camera on the sunglasses will automatically capture the surrounding environment and generate images with low pixels as black, white, and gray. The built-in software will convert these images into electrical signals and send them to the (lollipop-like) sensor in the user's mouth. When the electrode on the sensor receives the signal, it will stimulate the user's tongue and transmit it to the brain through the tongue. The brain can take these signals as visual signals and locate them in the visual cortex so that people can "see" things through the tongue.

BrainPort V100 translates digital information from a wearable video camera into gentle electrical stimulation patterns on the surface of the tongue. Users feel moving bubble-like patterns on their tongue which they learn to interpret as the shape, size, location, and motion of objects in their environment. Some users have described it as being able to "see with your tongue" and say that the intensity of this stimulation is similar to eating pop sugar (or popping/leaping candy).

2. Design in AR/VRs: As mentioned above, visual enhancement is one of AR. AR and VR family is based on human's sense of enhancement experience. In addition to visual enhancement (the BrainPort V100 is a VR example), there are auditory and tactile enhancements. Of course, the complicated ones but with the most potential are olfactory and taste enhancements, which apply virtual information to the real world through computer and network **technology. In order to enhance the interactive experience, virtual environment and virtual objects are superimposed on the same picture or space in real time.**

Because AR is the combination of real scene and virtual scene, camera (as well as sensory sensors for listening, touching, smelling, and taste in the future) is basically needed. On the basis of images captured by the camera, virtual images are combined for display and interaction, such as the thermal radar (see Section 4.4.2). Using Hololens, and Meta's Pro (even with an interface for 3-D printing) with an AR glasses, using 3-D holographic imaging technology, users can operate and interact with these virtual images.

VR is another new technology which has appeared in recent years. VR is the use of computer simulation to produce a virtual world of 3-D space, providing users with visual, auditory, tactile, and other sensory simulation, so that users can observe virtual things in 3-D space in an unrestricted manner as if they were experiencing in a true environment.

VR is a pure virtual scene, and its equipment is mostly used for the interaction between users and virtual scene, such as: position tracker, data glove, motion capture, data helmet, etc.

Both AR and VR belong to the application of intelligent interaction technology in five senses: they are penetrating into existing and upcoming interaction modes at an amazing speed, occupying screens and glasses; bracelets, foot rings and belts; rings, necklaces, earrings, nose rings, tongue rings, and navel rings; suits, business bags, and buttons; movies, games, and fitness; and so on. Wearable technology will be discussed as one of the application layer technologies of IoT. A comprehensive analysis is shown in Table 4.9.

4.4.6 *Sense of space*

Sense of space is part of the proprioception which includes the sense of movement and position of the movable parts of the items, from human sense, as visual, hearing, feeling. When this sense is extended to IoT world, it has a new name in this book — location awareness, which is an important technology for the IoT to perceive the location and movement of people and objects and then to determine the geographic location, relative location, and spatial location relationship between people and objects or among objects (e.g., the locations of nodes in WSN) in a certain environment. The maturity and development of wireless communication technology has promoted the arrival of the IoT era. At the same time, more and more application fields need to realize location awareness in IoT, e.g., after the information fusion from multiple sensor types and cognition process to comprehend in a vehicle, it will find where the roads, obstacles, and other "things" are in space, as shown in Fig. 4.47.

Speaking about ourselves, we need to know where we are in a strange place; if we are driving, we need to know where to drive or where the nearest gas station is. For example, in order to protect the petrels on Big Duck Island off the coast of Maine by WSN, we at least need to know the location of the protected object. Another example is the networked dust (a project of WSN) deployed on the San Francisco Golden Gate bridge to detect the condition of the bridge. When the dust (nodes) are detected in the moving range beyond the normal, the sensor network plays the role of predicting the danger. For details, see the next section.

Besides GNSS, localization is another growing trend in our hyperconnected society with a large amount of research and industrial focus.

Table 4.9 Some considerations about intelligent interaction modes.

Intelligent interaction mode	Traditional	Present	Future	Extension in IoE era	The core of design
Visual	Screen, LED, and other graphics	Visual enhancement (including 3-D technology), visual understanding and communication	Auto-driving, 3-D holographic imaging.	What you see is what you get from 3-D printing (Additive manufacturing); remote sensing and presentation.	Easy to use and feel, expanding human visual ability; BCI* or brain–machine interface (BMI),such as Neuralink (a company founded by Elon Musk) or Avanda project
Auditory	Text to speech (TTS)	Audio structure analysis and reproduction, context understanding NLP, audio recognition	Audio structural analysis and reproduction,	Speech interaction with machine	Context awareness-based understanding; automatic lip recognition for the disabled
Tactile	Button	multi point touch, gesture recognition, somatosensory (action recognition)	"subcutaneous" tactile	machine imitates production — intelligent manufacturing	Immersion,Ergonomics, AmI (Ambient Intelligence)
Smell	Smoke alarm	Electronic nose	odor simulation, reproduction and sharing	(Contactless) environmental monitoring and Prevention (contactless)	smell simulation and experience
Taste	None	Electronic tongue	Taste simulation reproduction and sharing	Food safety control-contact in sampling	Taste simulation and experience
VR/AR	3-D movie with legacy glasses	VR interaction and AR audio, MR	"Mixed five senses" of VR and AR in fusion and expression	Perfect fusion of imagination, feeling and experience	Natural HCI guided by psychology and behavior, context agent

Notes: In the post-pandemic era, no-touch or contactless mode pushed the interaction technology toward the IoE, the next generation of IoT.

*Agent/robot acting as the person surrogate and dual-Brain Computer Interface (BCI), as an example (Avanda project) from the author's another book *Internet of Things Technology and Its Military Applications*, National Defense Industry Press, 2013, pp. 189--191.

Figure 4.47 Navigation of outdoor/indoor environment.

Moreover, the demand for location-based services (LBSs) has been rapidly expanding in many fields, such as goods/robot tracking in industry or indoor navigation for people with visual impairments and is supported by the emergence of several powerful commercially available localization solutions. Due to their diverse positioning techniques and technologies, each localization solution has unique capabilities, limitations, and also varying costs.[30]

4.5 Location Awareness

> *"According to statistics, 95% of users can be identified by analyzing the four locations that users have visited." The research report was published in the open-access journal "Scientific Reports" under "Nature". This shows how powerful* location awareness *is!*[31]

The concept of location awareness is often referred to as positioning, just as GNSS is often understood as GPS; in fact, the former has a wider range than the latter. Location awareness is widely used in navigation, geodetic surveying, photogrammetry, exploration, rescuing, and other fields of vehicles (cars, ships, airplanes, etc.), as well as people's daily life (tracking objects, travel, and entertainment). The positioning technology is more specific, including satellite positioning, radio wave positioning, sensor node positioning, RFID positioning, cellular network positioning, etc. In order to facilitate understanding, "positioning or localization" will

[30]By the introduction of the DPS i-series, KONGSBERG fuses decades of experience within GNSS and inertial technology in order to create a fully scalable and future-proof reference solution with emphasis on operational efficiency for DP applications.

[31]Big Data triggers personal privacy related location. How to solve the security problem. January 27, 2016. Source: http://www.boiots.com/news/show-14665.html.

Table 4.10 Categories of location awareness.

Category	Open space and outdoor	Indoor (indoor position system, IPS)	Sensors	Hybrid in IoT	Other
Technology	GNSS, INS(IMU), and radio frequency-based cellular positioning	Frequency-based beacon, fingerprinting, and nodes of WSN in WPAN/WLAN	Sonic, visual light, infrared, atmospheric pressure and magnetic sensor, RFID beacon	GNSS-INS, RSSI-INS, multi-sensor fusion, hybrid modals in smartphones, and LBS indoor or outdoor	Machine vision, SLAM (see the next section)

be used in this chapter instead of location awareness. Main topics of this section are listed in Table 4.10, and there is inter-cross among them.

4.5.1 *GNSS and INS*

Global navigation satellite system (GNSS) is a multi-system, multi-level, multi-mode complex combination system, which includes global constellations, regional constellations, satellite-based augmentation system,[32] and ground-based augmentation system.

Currently, there are GPS, GLONASS, Galileo, BeiDou (or BDS), and so on. Among these in-use GNSSs, global positioning system (GPS) is relatively mature and widely used. The GPS project began in 1973, under the leadership of the US Department of Defense. The launch of GPS satellites began in 1989, and the satellite constellation was completed in 1994, in which year GPS was put into use. In addition to the GPS, satellite navigation systems currently in use include Russian GLONASS, Chinese Beidou satellite navigation system, and the European Union's Galileo.

Table 4.11 shows the proportion of different GNSS systems among the 300 receiver models on the market before March 2015. All devices have GPS capabilities. GLONASS is second only to GPS. Galileo and Beidou are gradually being accepted by industry-leading manufacturers.

[32]Augmentation systems, such as Wide Area Augmentation System (WAAS) in the US, European Geo Navigation Overlapping System (EGNOS) in Europe, and Multi-Function Satellite Augmentation System (MSAS) in Japan.

Table 4.11 The proportion of the number of constellations for receivers.

Type	GPS only	Supported by two kinds of constellation receives	Supported by three kinds of constellation receives	Supported by four kinds of constellation receives
Constellations		E.g. "GPS+Galileo", "GPS+GLONASS" or "GPS+Beidou"	E.g. "GPS+Galileo+GLONASS", "GPS+Galileo+Beidou" or "GPS+GLONASS+Beidou"	GPS, Galileo, GLONASS, and Beidou
Percentage	40	27	11	22

Among commercially available receivers, more than 60% of products have the ability to receive at least two constellation signals.

GPS is composed of three parts: space constellation, ground control, and user equipment. GPS measurement technology can efficiently and accurately provide precise 3-D coordinates of point, line, and area elements and other related information. It has outstanding characteristics such as all-weather, high precision, automation, and high efficiency.

(1) GPS constellation: The space constellation part of the GPS system is composed of 24 working satellites (21 for formal operation, 3 as backup). In the initial design, 24 satellites were distributed evenly on 3 orbital planes, with eight satellites in each plane. Later, the design of the orbital plane was changed to four satellites per plane, which ensured that the four satellites can be seen at any time and place on the earth as a 3-D positioning.

(2) Ground monitoring system: Take the GPS positioning system in the US as an example. Its ground control system includes a master control station located in Colorado, US, with four dedicated ground antennas and six dedicated monitoring stations. In addition, there is a backup master control center in Gettysburg, Maryland. The monitored satellite data is immediately sent to the SPRINGS Master control station in Colorado. The high-speed computer calculates the orbital parameters and correction instructions of each satellite and connects the results to the orbiting satellites via the radar, which keeps the satellites in accurate state and as the basis for navigation carriers.

(3) GPS receiver: The user shall have a dedicated GPS receiver (e.g., in a vehicle, as the GNSS use in Fig. 4.48), which usually includes a dedicated

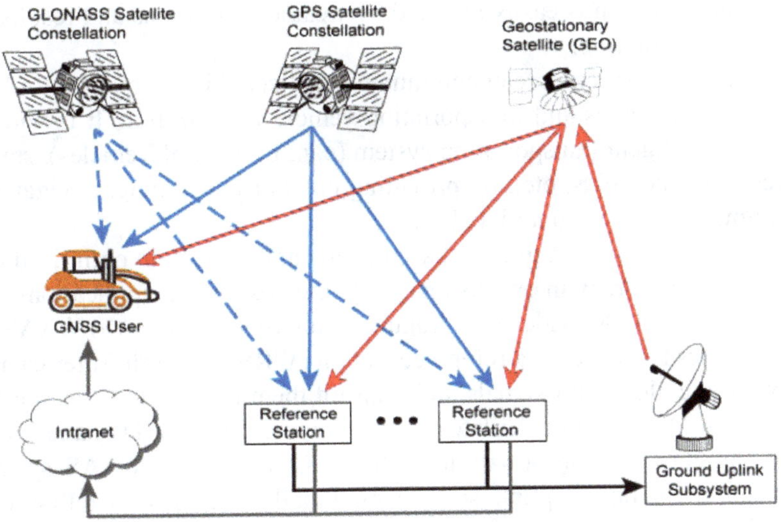

Figure 4.48 An example of ground-based augmentation system.

antenna for communicating with satellites, a processor for position calculation, and a high-precision clock. As long as the antenna is not disturbed or obscured and the signal from more than three satellites can be received at the same time, the coordinate position can be calculated and displayed.

Each satellite is constantly sending out information, and each message contains the time when the information was sent and the coordinates of the satellite at that time. The receiver will receive the information and record the time when the information is received according to its own clock. By subtracting the time when the information is sent from the time when the information is received, we get the propagated time in space. Combined with the speed of information propagation, the distance between the receiver and the satellite coordinates is obtained.

Satellite positioning requires extremely high clock accuracy, resulting in high costs, and the accuracy of the clock on the receiver is lower than that of the satellite clock, which affects the positioning accuracy. Theoretically, three satellites can be used for positioning, but in practice, at least four satellites are required for positioning. When indoors, it is often difficult to receive satellite signals. Therefore, the GPS positioning method mainly works outdoors. GPS signals must propagate through the atmosphere, which is easily affected by weather conditions and results in unstable positioning.

Satellite positioning can continuously collect object movement information for logistics and transportation vehicle visualization. It is widely used in intelligent transportation system (e.g., Internet of Vehicles), smart cities, military fields, etc., by providing outdoor positioning, navigation, and timing services on a global scale.

In recent years, the ground-based augmentation system optimized the positioning accuracy in expansion of satellite positioning applications. As shown in Fig. 4.48, Wide-Area Augmentation System (WAAS) WAAS in the US uses the wide-area reference station (WRS) in North America and Hawaii to collect GPS signals and transmit them to the wide area master station (WMS). WMS calculates the deviation correction (DC) and transmits the correction information to the GEO satellite of WAAS system through the ground uplink subsystem. Finally, the GEO satellite will broadcast the information to the GNSS/GPS users on the earth, so that the users can accurately calculate their position through the correction information. The DC information can also be broadcast through Intranet.

As to the Internet of Vehicles (IoVs), satellite positioning accuracy can be improved in many scenarios through multi-sensor fusion. For example, assisted GPS positioning based on cellular networks; Bluetooth and Wi-Fi-based positioning can be combined with GNSS to help improve indoor navigation capabilities.

From the outdoor views, inertial navigation systems (INS), as navigation sensors, have been widely used for estimating the positions and orientations (6DOF poses) of sensing platforms (e.g., autonomous vehicles) in GPS-denied environments, such as underwater, indoor, in the urban canyon, and on other planets. Most INS rely on a six-axis inertial measurement unit (IMU) that measures the local linear acceleration and angular velocity of the platform to which it is rigidly connected. With the recent advancements of hardware design and manufacturing in MEMS, IMUs enables high-accuracy localization for, among others, mobile devices and micro aerial vehicles (MAVs) or UAVs, holding a wide range of emerging applications from the above-mentioned AR and VR (see Section 4.4.5) in mobile devices to autonomous driving.

As a GNSS-INS sensor fusion example, MGC (a product of KONGSBERG) offers an optimal integration of multi GNSS and inertial sensors, in which the integration ensures a continuous position solution by bridging gaps in the GNSS reception and increasing position stability in periods with limited GNSS availability due to masking, scintillation and interference. GNSS and INS are perfectly matched as they overcome each other's limitations. Using both systems is superior to using either system alone. Receiver autonomous integrity monitoring (RAIM) extended by data from the INS provides ultimate reliability of the position and velocity data under difficult GNSS conditions. GNSS-INS sensor fusion in the multi-use of MGC sensor as the inertial sensor, a high-quality WheelMark gyro compass becomes a part of the solution. In addition, MGC can serve other on-board systems, such as navigation equipment and other systems that require attitude data.

4.5.2 *Positioning in cellular network and assisted GPS*

Cellular network positioning technology is widely used in cellular networks by MNOs. The E911 (Enhanced 911) system in North America is a relatively mature emergency phone positioning system based on cellular positioning technology. The demand for the E911 system originated from a kidnapping and murder case in the US in 1993. The victim girl used her mobile phone to call 911, but the 911 call center could not determine her location through the phone signal.

In 1996, the Federal Communications Commission issued an administrative order requiring mandatory construction of a public safety network, as the later E911 system. The E911 system can track the user's location through wireless signals and requires the operator to provide the location of the cell phone user with an accuracy of 50–300 m.

1. Cellular Positioning: When performing cellular communications, the mobile device is always connected with a cellular base station, and cellular base station positioning service is used to locate the mobile device. MNO operators provide cell positioning services, mainly based on the following methods.

The first is cell of origin (COO) positioning. COO positioning is the simplest and most primitive positioning method in base station positioning, that is, the coordinates of the base station in which the mobile device belongs are the same as the coordinates of the mobile device. The accuracy of this positioning method is extremely low, and its accuracy directly depends on the coverage of the base station. This technology was used when the aforementioned E-911 system was first built.

The second is time of arrival (ToA)/time difference of arrival (TDoA) positioning. In order to obtain more accurate positioning than the radius of the coverage area of the base station, it is necessary to use the data measured by multiple base stations at the same time. Among the multi-base station positioning methods, the most commonly used is ToA/TDoA positioning. ToA base station positioning is similar to GPS positioning; the difference is that satellites are replaced with base stations. This method requires high clock synchronization accuracy, and the base station clock accuracy is far less than that of GPS satellites; in addition, multipath effects can also cause errors in the measurement results. Based on the above reasons, people use the TDoA positioning method in practice, instead of directly using the signal transmission and arrival time to determine the position. The time difference between signals arriving at different base stations is used to establish the equations for the solution, and the error caused by clock asynchronous is eliminated by TDoA.

The third is angle of arrival (AoA) positioning. ToA and TDoA measurement methods both require at least three base stations to perform positioning. If the base stations are sparsely distributed and there are only two base station signals received around, the positioning cannot be performed. In this case, AoA positioning method can be used. As long as the antenna array is used to measure the azimuth of the line between the positioning target and the two base stations, the focus of the two rays can be used to determine the position of the target.

The positioning accuracy based on cellular is not high, and its advantage lies in the positioning process, which can be completed in a few seconds. A typical application of the cellular base station location method is emergency phone location. For example, the E-911 system is used in the prevention and detection of criminal cases. Technologies similar to cellular base station positioning include wireless access point (AP, access point)-based positioning technology, such as Wi-Fi positioning technology. It is similar to the COO positioning technology of cellular base stations which uses Wi-Fi access points to determine the location of the target. When various Wi-Fi devices looking for an access point, and each AP constantly broadcasts the address information, this information contains its own globally unique MAC address. If a database is used to record the MAC addresses of all wireless APs in the world and the location of the AP, the location of nearby APs can be obtained by querying the database, and then a more accurate location can be estimated by signal strength.

This positioning technology based on the combination of wireless access points and cellular base stations is also widely used, such as proximity detection in D2D communication or WSN.

Other examples as the WSN node in conjunction with satellite positioning or cellular, can be found in LoRa/LoRaWAN and other LPWAN, for the low-power consumption and low networking cost of the positioning module.

2. Assisted-Global Positioning System (A-GPS): A-GPS is widely used in mobile phones to compute position data. A-GPS technology includes high-sensitivity signal processing to acquire weak signals and external assistance of data, such as time, approximate position, and satellite orbit–related parameters. Provision of assistance data requires a communication link between the receiver and the data source, for example, the mobile phone network itself. Thus, A-GPS will not be possible if there is no communication link. Normally, A-GPS provides 2-D position data. The height data (if 3-D output is available) will be highly erroneous. The accuracy of such position data varies from 10 meters to few hundreds of meters. Also, the position data is heavily affected by signal multipath.

Assisted with the combined application of GPS positioning and mobile cellular access positioning technology, positioning can be achieved through mobile access positioning technology based on mobile communication operating base stations, which is widely used in mobile terminals with GPS functions.

When in poor signal conditions, such as in a city, these signals may be weakened by many irregular buildings, walls, or trees. Under such conditions, non-A-GPS navigation equipment may not be able to locate quickly. As shown in Fig. 4.49, the A-GPS system can first use the operator's base station information to perform a quick preliminary positioning, bypassing the problem of GPS coverage in the preliminary positioning. It can be used in almost all the cellular networks, as GSM/GPRS/CDMA2000/WCDMA/LTE (-A or -pro) and 5G.

Although this technology is the same as the GPS solution, it is necessary to add a GPS receiver module in the mobile terminal, modify or add the mobile terminal antenna, and a location server and LBS service deployment from the mobile cellular network; however, the use of A-GPS has technical advantages over GPS in the following two points.

On the one hand, the first positioning time can be reduced. With A-GPS, mobile terminal receivers no longer need to download and decode

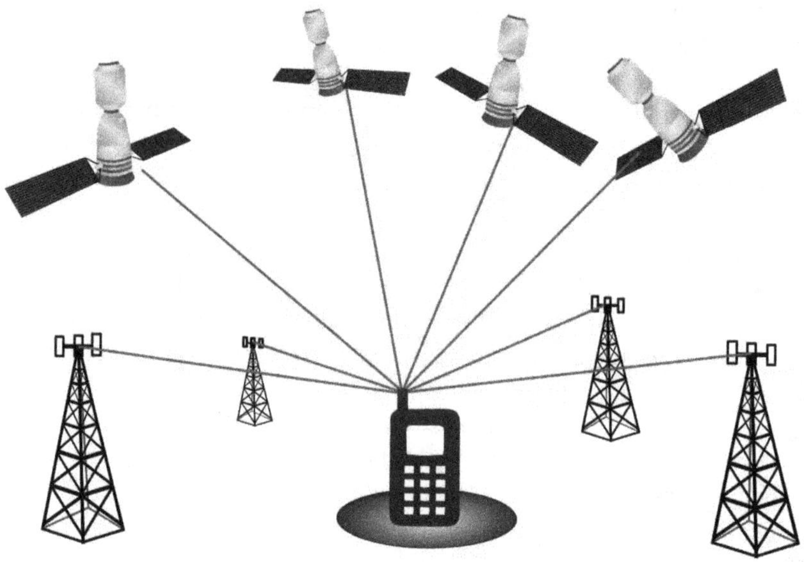

Figure 4.49 A-GPS with the cellular networks.

navigation data from GPS satellites first, so they can have more time and processing power to track GPS signals, which can reduce the first positioning time. The mobile terminal itself does not calculate the position information but transmits the GPS position information data to the mobile cellular network; the position calculation is performed by the network positioning server, which is based on the auxiliary data generated by the GPS reference network, such as differential correction data and satellite operating status.

Then, the approximate location of the mobile phone and the location information in the cell are found from the server database and transmitted to the mobile phone. At this time, the mobile phone can quickly capture the GPS signal. The process usually only takes a few seconds and better than the several minutes of the first acquisition time only with GPS.

On the other hand, the positioning accuracy can be improved. In open outdoors, its accuracy can reach about 10 m under a normal GPS working environment. Due to the high-rise buildings in the city or the weather, the received GPS signal is unstable, resulting in inevitable positioning deviation. Because A-GPS has base station–assisted positioning, the accuracy of positioning is greatly improved. Generally, the outdoor accuracy is higher than the measurement accuracy of GPS.

There are many positioning technologies based on GPS and cellular communication networks. In addition to technologies based on AP and cellular, GPS and cellular, and AP and GPS coordinated positioning, there is also differential GPS (D-GPS). D-GPS is a positioning system that improves positioning accuracy by improving GPS positioning methods. Its working method is based on the principle of relative positioning. First, a fixed GPS reference station (Reference Station) is set up and its geographic location has been precisely calibrated. Then, the GPS receiver compares the location with the position determined by the reference station to find out GPS positioning error and broadcast the error to the user. D-GPS accuracy can be increased to reach the meter level.

4.5.3 *Node localization*

Besides GNSS and above outdoor localization, indoor localization is another growing trend in our hyper-connected society, with a large amount of research and industrial focus. Moreover, the demand for LBSs has been rapidly expanding in many fields, such as goods/robot tracking in industry or indoor navigation for people with visual impairments, and is supported by the emergence of several powerful commercially available localization solutions. Due to their diverse positioning technologies, each localization solution has unique capabilities, limitations, and also varying costs. For instance, although GNSS is the de facto positioning solution for outdoor environments, Zigbee, ultra-wideband (UWB) and WPAN-based or LoRa-based technologies can be the first choice for applications that have high positioning accuracy or low accuracy but long-range and low-energy requirements, respectively. Despite this plethora of technologies and the remarkable interest in the localization domain, the service inter-operation and technical orchestration of IoT and their integration into other ecosystems is still an open issue that requires innovation.

When considering node positioning as determining the relative or absolute position of the node in a wireless network, the node location technology refers to the technology that determines and obtains the location information of nodes in a wireless network through certain methods or algorithms. The node may be a WSN node or not; e.g., the aforementioned GPS node, cellular network node, or sensor and actuator node in WSN/WSAN.

In order to distinguish from the GPS and cellular positioning mentioned above, the node positioning referred to in this section is the node of WSN and typically is an indoor node. As one of the key technologies of WSNs, node location is the basis for specific tasks. When monitoring an event in a certain area, the perceived data may lose application value and become meaningless without being associated with a specific location. Take the fire rescue for an example, after receiving the signal that the smoke sensor exceeds the fire alarm standard, we can start the rescue only if we know the exact location of the alarm sensor.

Node localization systems use various measurement types and positioning techniques in order to calculate the position of the target object.

Independent of their technology, their algorithms can be divided into range-based and range-free positioning algorithms according to whether it is necessary to measure the distance or angle information between neighboring nodes during the positioning process.

• **Range-based Algorithms:** Range-based algorithms need to measure distance or angle information and must be directly measured by sensor nodes.

ToA, AoA, TDoA, and received signal strength indicator (RSSI) are the most commonly used techniques for nodes to obtain information, and then trilateral calculations or triangulation calculations are used to obtain their own position. This type of algorithm requires the node to load a dedicated hardware in device or has a ranging function integration, in order to provide more accurate distance or angle information. Typical algorithms are AHLos algorithm, two-step LS algorithm, and so on.

• **Range-free Algorithms:** In recent years, related research has proposed range-free algorithms that are more suitable for WSN (for low cost). The range-free algorithm is obtained indirectly by relying on communication between nodes, and positioning can be achieved based on information such as network connectivity. Since there is no need to measure the distance or angle between nodes and other azimuth information, the hardware requirements of nodes are reduced, and it is more suitable for energy-limited WSNs. Although the accuracy of positioning is not as good as range-based algorithms, it can already meet most applications with cost-effectiveness. However, such algorithms rely on efficient routing algorithms and are restricted by the network structure and the location of reference nodes. Typical distance-independent algorithms include DV-Hop algorithm, centroid algorithm, APIT algorithm, etc.

Finally, we also see variation in the type of algorithms. Take AoA based acoustic positioning system (APS) algorithm as an example, it belongs to ultrasonic positioning based on the angel measurement. Another indirect ranging example is TBL, which uses sound waves (ultrasonic or other waves) and time difference of arrival (TDOA) based on electromagnetic waves to achieve WSN node ranging and positioning. The attenuation of sound waves in the air decreases as the frequency decreases. At a few kHz, the use of low-cost audio transceiver technology can achieve distance measurement within a range of tens of meters. It is an effective method suitable for outdoor and open conditions algorithm. TBL is based on the positioning research of different waves (which can propagate in different media) arrival time difference; it is very enlightening. For example, if seismic waves are used as a reference, based on the time difference between the arrival of seismic waves and electromagnetic waves (or other reference waves), it can be used for early warning of natural disasters, such as earthquakes. The realization of TBL algorithm is specifically divided into the ranging phase, the position calculation phase, and the loop iterative positioning phase.

Some of the technologies aforementioned use a self-positioning architecture, in which objects calculate their position themselves. There are also systems that include an infrastructure or back-end server that calculates the location of the targets. Self-oriented infrastructure-assisted architectures where a back-end system determines the position and then informs the tracked object in response to its request are introduced in the following parts.

4.5.4 *Indoor positioning and beacon*

Indoor position system (IPS) is actually a very relaxing topic. When you walk into the mall and buy what you want, you are tired or hungry. Even if you see the sign for marking yourself, it is difficult to go straight to the restaurant you want to go. All the billboards dazzle you. And all the road settings seem to be afraid that you will walk out of the shopping mall "accidentally".

Without the "bat" ability to locate by echo, you have to take out the mobile phone and find that the mobile phone is even more idiotic indoors. Even more embarrassed you become when you happen to be shy of asking other people where you are and where to go.

This is the importance of indoor positioning. When changing the viewpoints to that of business men, after providing you with free Wi-Fi, they also want to know which stores you went to and what you bought.

Then, they push the products you are most likely to buy next time, "accidentally".

In an indoor environment, it is difficult for the satellite based GNSS positioning system to receive signals due to shielding and indoor walls; and the signal for base station positioning is also affected by the multipath effect (generated by the principle of wave reflection and superposition), then the positioning effect will be greatly reduced. Most of the existing indoor positioning systems are based on signal strength (Radio Signal Strength, RSS). Its advantage is that it does not require special positioning equipment and uses existing laid-out networks such as Bluetooth (BLT), Wi-Fi, and ZigBee sensor networks for positioning. The current IPS methods mainly include infrared positioning,[33] ultrasonic positioning, Bluetooth positioning, RFID, ultra-wideband positioning (UWB), ZigBee positioning, etc. Due to space limitations, here are just a few popular positioning (or location awareness) technologies.

1. Positioning for ZigBee Nodes: ZigBee positioning is a typical WSN node positioning method. By deploying a large number of cheap reference nodes in the area to be located, these reference nodes form a large self-organizing network system through wireless communication. When it is necessary to locate the nodes in the WSN area, reference nodes within the communication distance can quickly collect the information of these nodes and at the same time use routing and broadcasting to transmit the information to other reference nodes.

In the finally formed information transmission chain between each node and the back-end system/server through multi-hops meshing, the position is determined, and then the server informs the tracked object in response to its request, so as to achieve long-term monitoring and positioning of a certain area. UWB indoor positioning works following the same principle.

In detail, the positioning engine calculates the node to be positioned based on the RSSI of nearby radio frequencies in the wireless network. In different environments, the RSSI signal between the two radios will change significantly. For example, when there is a pedestrian between two radios, the received signal will be reduced by 30 dBm. In order to compensate for this difference, and for the consideration of the accuracy of the

[33]As known in the dancing robotics bulls of the 2021 China Spring Festival, where the positioning in the robotics is by infrared positioning.

positioning results, the positioning engine will perform relevant positioning calculations based on RSSI values from up to 16 radio frequencies. It is based on the viewpoint that when a large number of nodes are used, the change of RSSI will eventually reach an average value.

The only information required to be transmitted between the reference node and the node under location is the X and Y coordinates of the reference node. The positioning engine calculates the positioning position based on the received X and Y coordinates, combined with the RSSI value measured from the reference node.

The coverage area of the positioning engine is 64 × 64 m, however, most applications require greater coverage. Enlarging the coverage of the positioning engine can be achieved by arranging reference nodes in a larger area, and using the strongest signal to perform positioning calculations for related reference nodes. The specific working principle is:

(i) The node under location in the WSN sends out broadcast information, collects data from each adjacent reference node, and selects the X and Y coordinates of the reference node with the strongest signal.
(ii) Calculate the coordinates of other nodes related to the reference node.
(iii) Process the data in the positioning engine and obtain the actual position of the node under location in the large network, with the consideration of the offset value of the nearest reference node.

The positioning engine uses RSSI measurements from nearby reference nodes to calculate the position of the node under location. RSSI will vary with changes in antenna design, surrounding environment, and other nearby RF sources, including several other factors. The positioning engine averages the position information of several reference nodes. Increasing the number of reference nodes can reduce the dependence on the specific test results of each node and improve the accuracy overall. No matter under what circumstances the reference node is set, it will affect the accuracy of positioning. This is mainly because when the reference node is set close to the relevant surface, it will cause the signal attraction of the ceiling or floor. Therefore, using omnidirectional antennas with the same transmitting capability in all directions is a better option. Accordingly, this marker-based positioning and its extended algorithm can achieve good positioning performance in the aforementioned indoor situation. For

Figure 4.50 Location requirements in shopping malls.

example, AT&T Laboratories Cambridge developed the indoor positioning system "Active Badge" in 1992.

The above-mentioned indoor 3-D position awareness technology uses wireless means for non-contact positioning. This technology has a short range, generally up to several tens of meters. However, it can obtain centimeter-level positioning accuracy information within a few milliseconds, with a large transmission range and low cost. Other indoor positioning methods based on distance or signal strength measurement include infrared indoor positioning technology, ultrasonic positioning technology, active RFID positioning, and Bluetooth beacons, for location requirements such as shopping malls shown Fig. 4.50.

2. Beacon and iBeacons: The Bluetooth beacon technology was first initiated by Nokia. In 2013, Apple released the iBeacon protocol based on Bluetooth 4.0 low-energy protocol (BLE), which is mainly used for retail applications and has attracted widespread attention. Subsequently, similar technology platforms appeared one after another: Qualcomm launched Gimble, Samsung launched Proximity, and Google launched Eddystone.

The normal operation of Bluetooth beacon technology requires beacon hardware, applications on smart terminals or mobile phone devices, and back-end application working together. The beacon broadcasts its own ID to the surroundings via BLT, and the application on the device will take corresponding actions after obtaining the ID of the nearby beacon, such as pulling the location information corresponding to the ID from the cloud or back-end system. The device can measure the received signal strength (RSSI) at its location to estimate the distance from the beacon.

Therefore, as long as there are three or more beacons near the device, the device location can be calculated using the trilateral positioning method.

The positioning accuracy of Bluetooth beacon technology can meet most consumer-grade indoor positioning applications: if a beacon is arranged every 30–50 square meters, a positioning accuracy of about 3 m can be achieved. Obviously, denser beacon arrangements can achieve higher (sub-meter) accuracy. Both the beacons and the software and hardware in the mobile device (e.g., a cell phone) that needs to be positioned shall support BLE.

As a device-based indoor localization, Bluetooth beacon positioning requires laying and maintenance of the beacons network, which is not so applicable in outdoor scenarios such as emergency rescue and asset management. The target beacon battery has a limited life and needs to be replaced manually. Some beacon products already support power monitoring and can also provide information other than ID (such as URL) sending. In addition to Apple's iBeacon, Google's Eddystone, and Radius Network's Alt Beacon are also based on Bluetooth beacon application specifications.

As another device-based indoor or outdoor localization, active RFID (see Section 4.1.2) beacons work under the same principle of BLE beacons. When outdoor, real-time locating system (RTLS) is usually used, by which the precise location of an object is tracked. In an RTLS, a beacon emits a signal with its unique identifier at pre-set intervals. The beacon's signal is picked up by at least three interrogator antennas (triangulation or trilateration) positioned around the perimeter of the area where assets are being tracked. RTLS is usually used outside in a container base or inside large facilities to track parts or personnel. Active tags can be read reliably because they broadcast a signal to the interrogator.

4.5.5 *Wi-Fi fingerprint and IMES*

Fingerprint positioning is a technology that uses radio feature comparison to achieve positioning in a fixed area. Wi-Fi (detailed in the next chapter) fingerprint technology is currently one of the most mature commercialized large-scale indoor positioning methods.

Wi-Fi fingerprint refers to the received signal strength (RSSI) of each Wi-Fi access point at different indoor locations. By matching the fingerprint currently detected by the terminal with the fingerprints of each reference point collected in advance, the position of the terminal can be calculated. Pre-collection of reference point fingerprints requires staff to carry a smartphone equipped with special software to traverse every empty place in the room.

The localization with a fingerprint positioning method for a specific area is with an accuracy of 3–5 m; when the improved algorithm is used, the accuracy reaches the meter level. For large-scale positioning, by using triangle (three-sided) positioning or proximity detection (proximity detection method, also known as COO, see the aforementioned cellular network positioning), the accuracy ranges from 10 to 30 m.

The fingerprint database requires a lot of manual labor; the signal is easily interfered by the crowd environment, and the signal environment may change rapidly, which results in reduced accuracy. However, the wide-area triangulation method needs to know the coordinates of the hot spot, which is not accurate enough for many indoor applications.

Representative companies of this technology include Cisco, Motorola, AeroScout, Ekahau, etc. The common practice of these companies is to first deploy their own dedicated Wi-Fi network and then collect fingerprints, mainly for industrial-level positioning, such as asset management and people flow statistics. Some companies, such as Wisdom Map and Wi-Fi SLAM, improved the algorithms for better positioning accuracy to meet consumer-level applications.

In addition to the above-mentioned positioning technology, there are also positioning based on computer vision and light tracking positioning, magnetic field, and positioning technology based on just one sensor (e.g., atmospheric pressure or magnetic), or the fusion of indoor and outdoor sensors.

From the device-based views, the indoor location awareness technologies are grouped into smartphone-based and tag-based localization. Smartphone-based ranges from the Wi-Fi fingerprint, BLT beacon, INS/light/atmospheric pressure/magnetic/acoustic sensor-based methods, and cellular-based localization (e.g., 5G indoor LBS enhancement) to the hybrid modals of these methods, as shown in Fig. 4.51.

As to those low-end IoT devices, tag-based localization ranges from ultrasonic/acoustic (e.g., APS/TDOA above mentioned), infrared, UWB, RFID to node localization in WSN, e.g., WPAN/WLA. Figure 4.51 gives a short summary of device-based indoor location awareness technologies.

At present, many technologies are still in the research and test stage, such as the positioning technology based on magnetic field pressure induction. There is also an indoor messaging system (IMES) technology

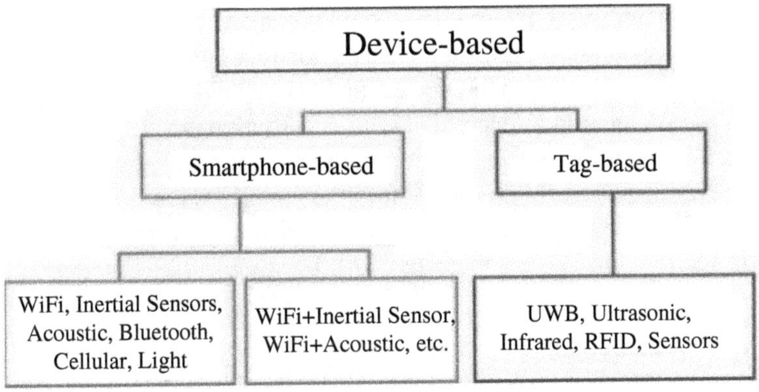

Figure 4.51 Summary of indoor device-based localization.

from Japan, and the main concept of IMES is to transmit position and floor ID of the transmitter with the same RF signal as GPS. IMES transmits latitude, longitude, height, and floor ID by replacing the ephemeris and clock data in the navigation message of GNSS/GPS.

IMES signal transmitter is installed on the indoor ceiling to transmit a positioning signal with the same structure as the GNSS signal, and the signal is received by the terminal, thereby achieving a seamless indoor and outdoor positioning effect.

The positioning accuracy of the IMES receiver depends on the interval setting of the signal transmitter and the intensity of the radio wave, which is generally 10 m. But windows may shield signals. IMES signals need line-of-sight propagation, with weak penetration, and there are gap areas that cannot be covered between transmitters.

4.6 AI-related Sensing and Location

The technology of perception and recognition originates from deep thinking about human visual intelligence: Why do humans have two eyes? At what stage of the baby's vision development? When did you begin to have a sense of space, knowing that "when near sight of an object, it is big but when see far away the same object, it become small"?[34] Why can a baby

[34]When human eyes look at objects near and far away, the angle between the two eyes (convergence angle) differs greatly. Far away, the angle is small; close, the angle is large.

classify cats and dogs accurately, even when he has not seen enough cats and dogs (especially when the samples for recognition training are seldom)? How does the human eye realize both perception and recognition? The sense of time and space, discernment, thinking ability, etc., may be unique human abilities. How are they inherited through genes?

These questions involve psychology, sociology, genetics and evolution, artificial intelligence, neurology, etc. However, after the discussion in this section, we believe that there will be some enlightenment.

4.6.1 *Machine vision*

If you want a machine to do a good job, you must first let the machine figure out the situation; e.g., the vision description from the samples how do humans figure out the situation. Vision occupies about 80% of the information acquired by human beings. With the acceleration of the process of computer vision (CV) or machine vision (MV) and intelligence control, robotics, and other applications in industrial automation have developed rapidly. MV and its application technology are gradually becoming a research hot spot. In the IoT, MV can not only sense the position of target objects in the environment, obtain 3-D coordinates of the target, and judge human body actions but also it can perform accurate object recognition and positioning.

The MV market is growing and is not set to slow down anytime soon as businesses are increasingly looking to automate business processes through the introduction of automation capabilities, such as MV and robotics. Due to COVID-19, businesses within logistics, healthcare, manufacturing, and food and beverage have been hit hard with the social distancing measures being brought in to stop the spread of the virus. Automation and robots for this reason are really showing their strengths and capabilities as businesses struggle to meet business and consumer demands with reduced labor.

1. MV and CV: The concept of MV is derived from CV. CV is the study of how to allow computers to obtain high-level and abstract information from images and videos. From an engineering perspective, CV can automate some tasks of human vision and can be organized into three

---

The brain uses the rotation information of the eyes and the image synthesis, so that we can feel the distance.

categories. First, image processing in the operation on pixels without much regard for what they represent, which tends to operate directly on the raw input data at the level of individual pixels or windows of pixels or shapes in an image. Second, geometric CV focusing on inferring shape or motion or both or on constructing models or maps, and understanding spatial relationships, on localization of objects in the scene, or on relative motion of the sensor and of objects. Finally, semantic CV recognizing or reasoning about the nature of objects or parts of the scene, and its algorithms try to understand or interpret the content of the scene including algorithms of AI or machine learning (ML).

MV mainly refers to the capture of information instead of human eyes, and the information will be translated into a form of data to make sense of it such as the identity, position, and orientation of the object(s) that are being captured by the MV system. And at the higher "understanding" stage, MV techniques tend to perform such actions as object recognition, measurement, judgment, and scene understanding.

The MV system converts the captured target information into an image signal through a MV product (i.e., image capture device, divided into CMOS and CCD) and transmits it to a dedicated image processing system to obtain the morphological information of the captured target. According to the pixel distribution and brightness, color, and other information are transformed into digital signals, the image system performs various operations on these signals to extract the characteristics of the target and then controls the on-site equipment actions according to the results of the discrimination. In short, as a combination of hardware and software, MV provides operational guidance to devices in the execution of their functions based on the capture and processing of images. Nowadays, more AI/ML algorithms are included in the guidance and execution.

A large number of MV applications have found good use in mobile robot, industrial automation, but they cannot all be presented in this text. Those that are presented here can be mainly included as detection and robot vision:

- ***Detection***: The MV system can significantly improve the flexibility and automation of production. In some dangerous working environments that are not suitable for manual operations or occasions where human vision is difficult to meet the requirements, MV is often used to replace human vision. At the same time, in the process of mass industrial

Table 4.12 Comparison of detection with AI/ML and traditional MV.

Detection scenario	Detection with AI/ML	Traditional MV
Unseen defects (similar but new)	Self-learning, adapts quickly	Reprogramming needed
Tiny defects	Auto fitted from learned patterns	Ineffective
Complex background texture	Automatically learns and filters background texture	Unable to reliably distinguish product feature from background
Change of targets for inspection	New models easily generated from samples	Ineffective
Samples required	Large amount of training data (online or offline)	Few shot feature design

production, humans are freed from tedious and repetitive work; MV inspection methods can also greatly improve the efficiency and automation of production.

Specific applications include facial recognition, text (texture of the surface) recognition, etc., and recognition applications that overlap with feature recognition technology; as well as industrial production for product quality classification, printed matter quality inspection, etc., e.g., high-precision inspection of mechanical parts, fruit sorting line according to size and shape, etc.

For example, if the MV system requires an inspection when a product comes onto the process line, then needs the different labels checked halfway through the system, and when the product comes to the final stage it might need closer detection for specific defects, more detail that needed to be checked by a standard camera including new or tiny defects, reliably distinguish product feature from background, adaptation to the changing of objects. With the introduction of AI/ML algorithms, some conditions can be improved as Table 4.12 shows.

Typically, MV components of an automatic inspection and sorting system will include some form of lighting to make the object clear and visible, a camera to see the object, a processor, software to understand the processor, and an output device or human interface (HMI) screen to visualize the data.

• ***Robot vision*:** Robot vision is used to guide the robot's operations and actions in a wide range. For subtle operations and actions, tactile sensing technology is also needed (see Section 4.4.1). The technology can be applied to a robot for it to spot where to put things or where to pick things up, also known as pick and place, while it can also be applied to be part of an end-to-end solution at multiple points of the system to spot, inspect, and moving around, even for automated driving cars. Robots are increasingly having MV built into them to improve efficiency and accuracy, which also enables intelligent robots to carry out more complex tasks.

Intelligent robots, whether in the air, on the ground (including unmanned vehicles), or in the water, need to interact well with the external environment in real time and can obtain a lot of effective information from the external environment to complete a series of tasks. To obtain effective information such as real-time images, force, distance, position, etc., highly intelligent robots must have corresponding sensors, such as vision, space, position, touch, and force, among which the robot vision sensor can make it more comprehensive and accurate external environment. Therefore, intelligent robots with real-time high-precision image sensors can feel the local environment where they are located, obtain information about the local environment, and process the external environment information captured by the vision system, as well as a series of algorithms. It can complete tasks such as obstacle avoidance, navigation, and detection of mobile robots.

The key technologies in robot vision include image processing, vision detection and tracking technology, vision understanding and prediction technology, and intelligent control technology. For example, in intelligent control technology, image sensors, such as 2-D color CCD cameras and 3-D laser radars, are used to control the movement of the robot using the collected 2-Dl or 3-D image information. Whether the robot's visual information can be processed accurately and in real time, and correctly understood and judged, directly affects the accuracy of the robot's driving speed, path tracking, and obstacle avoidance functions. Some instances can be found in the automated-guided vehicle (AGV) or autonomous mobile robot (AMR), for the location and autonomous (self-) driving (by the assistance of GNSS outdoor or beacon indoor).

Take robotic guidance with MV as an example. MV gives robotic things (from IoT views) much greater accuracy, orientation, and understanding. It allows them to more accurately grasp an item, place an item with increased precision, and carry out more complex tasks, such as inspection in quicker time. This capability allows operators to move robots in a simpler manner by using a one- or two-axis motion controllers.

2. Deep learning and Visual Understanding: AI is the study of how to imitate principals, patterns, and models of human intelligence activities in the construction of artificial systems with certain intelligence, and the process of how to allow computers to complete tasks that required human intelligence in the past, that is, the automation of how to use computer software and hardware to simulate human intelligent behaviors in some degree.

Deep learning is a field of ML research, which promotes the theory, method, and algorithms of AI these years. Its motivation is to establish and simulate a neural network that simulates the human brain for analysis and learning, e.g., it mimics the mechanism of the human brain and visual neural to classify and interpret data, such as images, sounds, and text.

AlphaGo uses deep learning from the past experience and the current situation existing in Go games to construct its software-defined policy in Go games (e.g., algorithm of reinforcement learning). It uses computational experiments, i.e., self-play games, for further exercising on possible situations of the games. In the match vs. Lee, AlphaGo searches its strategy space in the virtual games and defeats Lee in March 2016. The defeat over humanity by a machine has also generated huge public interests in AI techniques around the world.

Before the deep learning algorithm came out, the understanding of the five senses of sight, hearing, touch, smell, and taste discussed in Section 4.4 roughly consisted of the following five steps: feature perception, preprocessing, feature extraction, feature selection, and the last classifier design step for reasoning, prediction, and recognition. The olfactory understanding of the electronic nose follows these five steps. For MV algorithms, the second and third steps are replaced by image preprocessing and image feature extraction. In the early MV, statistical learning was dominant.

For MV, the traditional method is to separate feature extraction from classifier design, and then combine them together during application. For example, we take two piles of pictures, one of which are cats (with their cat label) and other piles are dogs (with their dog label); after extracting their respective feature expressions (as cat feature, and dog feature, the expressed features are put into the learning algorithm for classification learning (e.g., the classic support vector machine (SVM) of supervised learning). Artificially designing features requires a lot of brainpower and energy, and it requires a special understanding of the relative fields, without mentioning the generalization ability from the designed features into a high-level extension. What enlightens us mostly is, when humans did not come into contact with enough cats and dogs in their childhood, they can distinguish cats and dogs well. This is not consistent with the "classifier design" step.

Neurobiologist David Hubel and Torsten Wiesel discovered that the visual cortex (part of cerebral cortex) of the brain is hierarchical analyzed in sequence by cells with the specific tasks of interpreting contrasts, patterns, and movements, after the light of an object is converted into signals that are sent to the brain and there converted into visual impressions. Two functions of the human vision then explained as abstraction and iteration, from the views of MV, and the supervised learning (Deep Learning is a branch of supervised learning). Abstraction is to abstract very specific image elements, that is, primitive light pixels, shape, and other information, to form meaningful concepts. These meaningful concepts will iterate upward and become more abstract, until people can perceive. These two functions upgrade the action of "seeing" to "understanding" in the process of visual understanding.

In supervised learning, large sets of images are collected first, and each image is labeled with its category. The known borders are set between each other with assumption and images classifying is needed, the machine is made to find the parameters for the set division. The methods include several steps in multilayer neural networks and back-propagation, in which the convolution and pooling layers of ConvNets (or convolution neural network (CNNs)) are directly inspired by the above notions in visual neuroscience. A deep learning architecture with multiple nonlinear layers can implement extremely intricate functions of its inputs that are simultaneously sensitive to minute details and insensitive to large irrelevant variations, such as the background. The "migration" of these two visual functions (abstraction and iteration) to the formation of simultaneous learning features and designing classifiers forms the "deep learning" method. The specific content is more complicated and beyond the scope of this book, and for details see "deep learning".

Based on the discussion above, the deep rule-based network is introduced in Fig. 4.52, as an action vector generator example, where classification network classifies input vector x, and generates M patterns; the

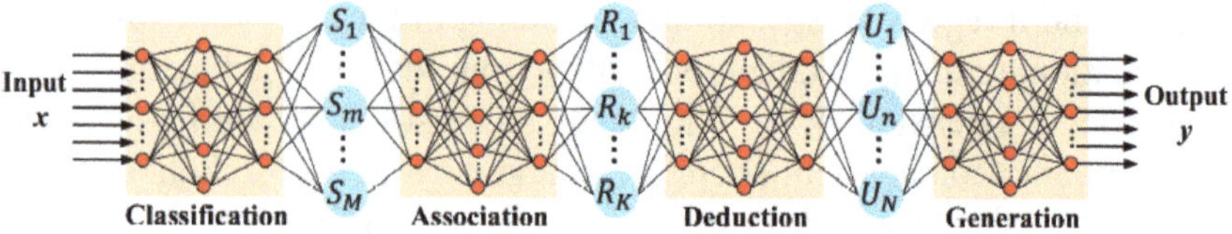

Figure 4.52 Deep rule-based networks: building an understandable decision for deep networks.

Note: This is similar to the adaptive dynamic programming (ADP) developed in control, except that normal neural networks instead of DNN are used in ADP.

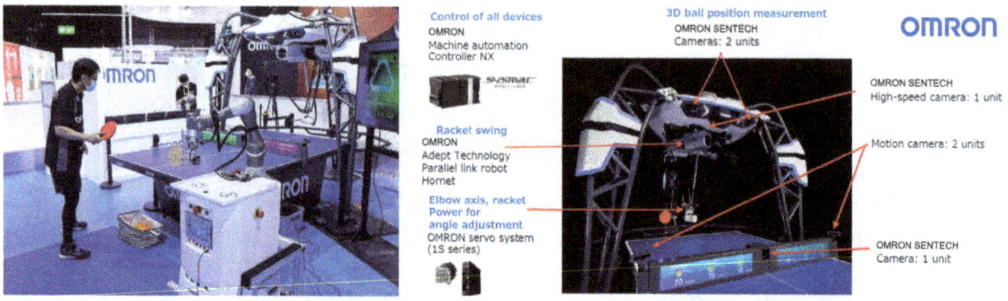

Figure 4.53 Ping Pang robot — FORPHEUS.

Source: Omron.

association network associates the patterns with K decision rules; through the deduction network, N patterns are designated as the input to the next stage; finally, the generation network generates output vector y. In this way, we do not have to specify how to implement the classification, association, deduction, and generation networks, and they might be CNN, deep belief network (DBN), stack auto-encoder (SAE), recursive neural network (RNN), or other forms of networks.

As to visual understanding or voice recognition (e.g., NLP in Section 4.4), deep learning algorithms in recognition and complex scenario understanding is a carefully designed and stable structure that has been studied for many years. From an end-to-end MV views, after the action vector generator is merge into the deep learning structure, the following example in Fig. 4.53 will demonstrate how sensing and control technology can be used for robots to cooperate with humans.

4.6.2 *SLAM*

When neither the robot nor any objects are known with respect to the world frame, then it is still possible to build a map with simultaneous localization and mapping, synchronous positioning and map construction (SLAM), which is mainly used to solve the problem of robot positioning and environmental map construction when moving in an unknown environment.

In terms of robot navigation, SLAM can be used to generate a map of the environment, so that it can perform tasks such as path planning, autonomous exploration, and navigation. From the research on the spatial representation of mobile robot navigation in the 1980s, the development of SLAM technology has a history of more than 30 years, involving many technical fields. Since it contains many steps, each step can be implemented using different algorithms; SLAM technology is also a popular research direction in the field of robotics and computer vision. SLAM tries to solve the problem: A robot is moving in an unknown environment, how to determine its own trajectory by observing the environment and at the same time construct a map of the environment.

To ensure real-time performances and accurate map construction, in practical use case, SLAM algorithms are an interesting topic especially when it comes to explore extremely difficult situations for the robot without high-performance computer, e.g., an AGV or just a low-end mobile device. Therefore, embedded SLAM is a general need, in case of embedded device in IoT world, in order to have an architecture that allows efficient implementation and to ensure real-time constraints of the SLAM algorithms.

1. Framework of SLAM: SLAM technology covers a very wide range and many classification methods according to different sensors, application scenarios, and algorithms, so as to the different sensors, it can be divided into 2-D/3-D SLAM based on laser or LIDAR, RGB-D SLAM based on depth camera, visual inertial odometry based on visual sensor and inertial unit system (INS)[35] and visual semantic odometry SLAM.

The classic SLAM has the following five steps, as shown in the followed visual SLAM example of camera sensors:

---

[35] The inertial measurement unit (IMU) can measure the angular velocity and acceleration through the built-in gyroscope and accelerometer, and then calculate the attitude of the camera, but there is a cumulative error in the estimated attitude.

(i) Reading of sensor data. In visual SLAM, it is mainly the camera's reading and preprocessing of scene image information. The data reading by sensors such as RGB-D cameras, includes image information and depth information.

(ii) Visual odometry (VO), which estimates the movement of the camera between neighbors, and the local map, is also called front end. The simplest case is that the camera obtains two adjacent frames through rotation, and VO estimates the camera's motion from the images between the adjacent frames and the structure restores of the scene.

(iii) Back-end optimization. The back end optimizes the camera pose measured by the VO at each time and the loop closure detection information, to obtain a global motion trajectory and a large scene map. In order to solve the subject's estimation of the spatial uncertainty of itself and the surrounding environment in the SLAM process, the uncertainty of positioning and mapping needs to be expressed through the state estimation theory and then filters (e.g., Kalman filter/extended Kalman filter) or nonlinear optimization are used to estimate the mean and variance of the state. The VO is responsible for providing the data to be optimized for the back end, and the back end is responsible for filtering and linear optimization algorithms.

(iv) Loop closing, also known as loop closure detection, performs loop detection to know whether the sensor has reached the previously passed position and provides the information to the back-end processing. The back end optimizes the camera pose measured by the VO at different times. During the movement of the robot, due to on-board equipment error or model inaccuracy, the position estimation drifts over time. Loop detection means that the robot detects the scene it has visited through algorithms and eliminates the problem of position drift. By comparing the similarity of the scene pictures, it is judged whether the robot enters the loop, and the pose constraint is added for improving the convergence of the SLAM algorithm.

(v) Mapping, refers to the process of building a map, which constructs a scene map based on the estimated trajectory. A map is a description of the environment with diversities. For example, a sweeping robot only needs a 2-D map to navigate within a certain range. The form of the map is determined by the application scenarios of SLAM and can generally be divided into two types: metric map and topological

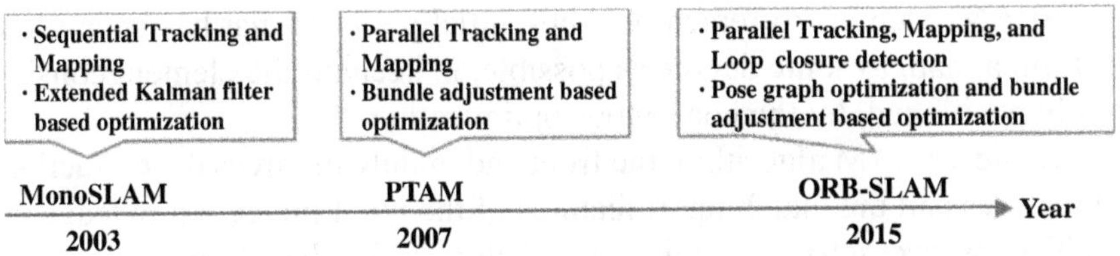

Figure 4.54 VSLAM development.

map. The metric map emphasizes accurately representing the positional relationship of objects in the map. Usually, we use dense map and sparse map for classification. Sparse maps generally do not need to express very detailed map details and mainly select objects in the map, which are called landmarks. A dense map is similar to a 2-D map. A 2-D map is composed of pixels, while a dense map is 3-D, composed of small squares, which express the information of objects in space detailed enough for meeting various map-based navigation algorithms.

Visual SLAM (VSLAM) method uses a camera as the sensor and has advantages, such as small size and low price. Early VSLAM, such as MonoSLAM, adopted the filtering methods from the field of robotics. Nowadays, more optimization methods in the field of computer vision are used, specifically, the bundle adjustment in the structure-from-motion (SfM). In VSLAM, according to the extraction method of visual features, it can be divided into feature method and direct method. The current representative algorithms of VSLAM include MonoSLAM, ORB-SLAM, SVO, DSO, etc.

2. VSLAM Algorithm: Since the algorithm of parallel tracking and mapping (PTAM)[36], the framework of VSLAM has basically tended to be fixed, as shown in Fig. 4.54.

---

[36]PTAM was proposed by Klein et al. (2007) and is a technology for augmented reality. PTAM proposed and realized the parallelization of the tracking and mapping process; it was the first solution to use nonlinear optimization instead of using traditional filters as the backend. It introduces a key frame mechanism: Instead of processing each image carefully, it strings together several key images and then optimizes its trajectory and map.

SLAM attempts to remember substantially all of what has been seen to form a map, to some degree as possible, in keeping the element consistently positioned, by the continuous optimization.

In the VSLAM algorithm, the front end mainly involves the extraction of features and the matching of features of the input image; knowledge of multi-view geometry is required for feature point detection and feature descriptor calculation.

The feature of the image is matched to obtain a 2-D–2-D feature matching point set; then, according to the depth information of the depth image, the spatial 3-D coordinates of the 2-D–2-D feature matching point pair are calculated to obtain a 3-D–3-D matching point set. From the matched 3-D–3-D points, the rotation and translation matrix between two adjacent frames can be calculated, and finally the motion estimation error is optimized to obtain the pose estimation result with the smallest error. In this way, the incremental change of the camera pose can be continuously obtained according to the input video stream.

Optimization techniques, such as key frames widely used in matching, are to control the scale of the matching problem and maintain the sparsity of the problem.

The back end of the algorithm is mainly to optimize the noise problem in the SLAM process. The maximum posterior probability involved belongs to the content of numerical optimization. After obtaining the motion estimation between two adjacent frames of images through the front end, we should also care about how much noise this estimation carries. Back-end optimization is to estimate the state of the entire system from these noisy data and give the maximum posterior probability (maximum a posteriori, MAP) of this state. Specifically, the back end receives the camera pose measured by the visual odometer at different times and the loop detection constraint information and uses nonlinear optimization to obtain the global optimal pose. In VSLAM, the front end and computer vision research fields are more related, such as image feature point detection and matching, while the back end is mainly filtering and nonlinear optimization algorithms.

Loop detection involves location recognition, which is essentially an image retrieval problem. It mainly solves the problem of robot position drifting over time. Visual closed-loop detection is to compare the similarity of two image data. If the loop detection is successful, it is considered that the robot has been to the same location point, and the comparison information is sent to the back-end optimization algorithm. The back end adjusts the robot's trajectory and map based on the information of the closed-loop detection. For example, ORB-SLAM's loop closure detection algorithm effectively prevents accumulated errors.

Although the original intention of SLAM only focuses on the geometric information of the environment, there should be more integration with semantic information in the future. With the help of deep learning, current object detection and semantic segmentation technologies have developed rapidly, and rich semantic information can be obtained from images. This semantic information can assist in inferring geometric information. For example, the size of a known object is an important geometric clue.

Finally, some low-cost SLAMs, such as Visual-INS (VINS) technologies are emerging, largely due to the demanding mobile perception/navigation in light-weight and energy-efficient applications. By jointly estimating the location of the sensor platform (INS, visual) and the features in the surrounding environment, SLAM estimators are able to easily incorporate loop-closure constraints, thus enabling bounded localization errors.

4.7 Anomaly Detection Technology

At the perception layer of the IoT, the technology that obtains the required information through the perception (device) of the physical world is advancing with the times. However, in the wave of IoT devices brought about by the great development of IoT applications, IoT security threats have appeared, and it is time for us to face up to "IoT devices will also get sick or violation". Reflections on the hidden dangers of the IoTs is simple as the question of "to be" or "not to be". Just imagine, what should we do if our child is sick? Insecurity clues finding in the perception layer for vulnerabilities is as important as finding out early and get treatment as soon as possible for our child. The vulnerabilities come from insecure network connections (internal and external), utilization of technologies with known vulnerabilities, unknown risks into the OT environment, and insufficient understanding of requirements for secure environments.

This section attempts to introduce security for perception devices from the source; that is, from the perception layer that can perform functions normally, leading to the diagnosis of the "health" of the perception devices; it is about thinking about the "early and outlier detection" in the IoT. As for the "treatment" of the illness, see the final chapter of this book.

The reason why anomaly discovery technology is placed on the perception layer is because it is hoped that the thriving IoT can put "risk discovery" in front of the perception layer, so that "things" have the ability to "sense and finding abnormalities" and can prevent them at the perception layer. Take precautions before suffering happens.

From the view of data governance and privacy protection, especially in healthcare and insurance domain, MDM Event Management Services (an example of data governance service @ https://www.softwareadvice.com/mobile-device-management/) are called to detect any actions that should be triggered based upon business rules or data governance policies. Work is now going on in the SAE to automate the end-user feedback collection and support a level of community moderation compliant with enterprise data governance and security policies.

1. Natural limitations of IoT devices: Compared with computers and smartphones, due to the lack of robust operating systems, infrastructure required to support related applications and necessary security technical support for IoT devices, a considerable proportion of IoT devices cannot run anti-malware software. Moreover, some hardware solidifies the user name and password in the device hardware, which is very convenient for intrusion. This is the problem of limited security capabilities caused by limited resource costs and limited resources. Because IoT devices cannot withstand malicious intrusions, they lack the necessary technology to maintain their own healthy operation, and at the same time, they do not have enough storage space in the face of ever-expanding malicious behaviors; therefore, they are powerless to deal with increasingly complex attacks.

In case of light weight, the constrained capabilities of IoT devices therefore include security or protection capabilities from others. This is why the IoT perception layer device was compared to a growing child. But the enabling edge computing will give a hand, and maybe it will work as a safe-guard device on the edge.

2. Find abnormalities and locate them as soon as possible: "When my smart TV (controlled by hackers) attacked the robots on the other side of the earth (the more terrifying is the pacemaker in the body), what does it matter to me?!" This is when the large-scale IoT security event happened in 2016, a sentence that the author remembered deeply among many online reviews. If no one is bothering about the security responsibility of his IoT device to other IoT devices, then, sooner or later, he will also suffer for the insecurity of his device.

Anomalies are discovered and located in the perception layer as much as possible to prevent malicious behavior from spreading to the network layer. "This feature is designed to prevent IoT devices from becoming bridgeheads that bring greater vulnerabilities to the network." For real-time data transition to all devices, collecting data related to represent the device status and analyzing or diagnosing malicious behaviors for each other, it is a good idea to protect IoT devices from threats. Compared with computers and smart phones, IoT devices are built for a specific purpose and with limited functions. This requires us to solve security issue from a completely different perspective. By analyzing the output data of the device and its own state data, defining abnormal patterns and behavior characteristics, activities that exceed the expected behavior being detected, which indicates that the device may be maliciously attacked. This will help to find abnormalities in IoT devices as soon as possible.

In addition to establishing a baseline of normal behavior for "resource-limited" IoT devices, abnormal behavior can be found though abnormal behavior detection[37] or outlier detection. One can also use attack detection and defense, logs, and audits, such as summarizing and analyzing log files, to find abnormal behavior. It is not always possible to completely rely on abnormal behavior detection in the network layer or cloud security. If devices with limited resources at the perception layer cannot withstand the resources required for abnormal behavior detection, the consideration of placing them in a secure gateway/edge devices is an option or similarly as services from an edge middleware (e.g., data desensitization/data outlier detection). In short, how did we discover that the child was sick? Anomaly recognition is the same for IoT devices. Apart from seeing a doctor (metaphor for the cloud), who can find out that a child is sick as soon as possible? Parents at the edge side.

---

[37]In the article from "http://smart.huanqiu.com/roll/2016-12/9819566.html", the IoT abnormal behavior detection technology are introduced as using big data analysis technology to perform analysis and abnormal behavior detection. In the Internet environment, this method is mainly to detect TCP/IP protocol traffic. In the IoT environment, it is also necessary to analyze other protocol traffic (such as Modbus and PROFIBUS), such as industrial control environments. In addition, the abnormal behavior detection will also be applied to the abnormal behavior detection of cars in the Internet of Vehicles. 360 researcher Li Jun used ML methods to establish a model for the correlation between different data of cars. Relying on the analysis of behavior patterns, it is able to detect hacker intrusion by data relevance.

3. Bionics for system-level discovery and defense-learning from biological intelligence: An article analyzing the security of the IoT from a biological perspective has caused system-level discovery and defensive thinking:

The number of potential edge nodes of the IoT may be as high as 1 trillion. In other words, such a system may increase the current number of Internet devices by more than a thousand times, and it is currently in the initial stage of this growth period.

"One trillion" is an ordinary order of magnitude in biology. For example, a newborn baby has about 1 trillion cells and has a very strong ability to prevent the attack of infectious bacteria, which can be achieved through a complex immune system. Detect, counterattack, and isolate these harmful germs; at the same time, the human body can automatically recover the local defects caused by the attack. Perhaps, people can learn something from how nature forms such a powerful defense system. More specifically, borrowing from biology can help humans think in a different way and implement defense measures at the system level. But it needs to be pointed out that the construction of the security system mentioned here is based on the existing strategy, not to replace the existing defense measures but to further enhance and improve.

The normal operation of the system is classified as "self-behavior", and any action other than self-behavior will be regarded as an attempted intrusion signal. The most interesting thing about this approach is that it is partial, may be very cheap (behavior detection is usually much simpler than matching many features), and can automatically detect new "non-self" threats, so it can be at the lowest cost, respond quickly, and automatically detect new threats (the method based on signature recognition cannot do this). Of course, behavior detection also has a weakness: When a virus is detected, the node may have been infected; similar problems also exist in cell biology, and defense methods need to be considered at the system level.

—— "Discussion on the Construction of Security Mechanism of the IoT from a Biological Perspective"

The above-mentioned method is applicable to the IoT security threat discovery technology, which is also summarized here as the abnormal detection technology of the IoT perception layer device, which belongs to the prevention technology of the perception layer security threat.

There have been solutions to this problem in smart routers or "cloud security" (detailed in Chapter 8 of this book), which may lead to continuous research on the problem of abnormal detection technology in the IoT. For example, if the "problem" is the condition of the "node" in the network layer of the IoT, the identification of "abnormal nodes" "Diagnostics in the network layer should also receive attention. In the perception layer of the ultra-large-scale IoT in the future, the abnormal discovery of a single or partial sensor requires the above-mentioned bionics point of view to find anomalies and maintain the "health" of the perception layer.

The "cloud abnormality judgment" based on cloud security can not only lock the object to the abnormal IoT device from the source (or the exploited vulnerability) but also be able to analyze other devices that can communicate with it; just as it is impossible to attribute illness solely to "immunity system decline", we should also pay attention to possible sources of infection and transmission channels.[38]

Smart routers/gateway or "cloud/edge security device" countermeasures to transfer the inspection work required for abnormal discovery to host nodes with less power restrictions. Compared with these, more importantly, a system perspective is needed to look at "IoT security" with holistic view, which not only extends the exploration of IoT security issues to the IoT network and application layers but also needs a scalable and biologically intelligent viewpoint. Collective defense in an IoT sector or domain, with an IoT grids view points to the work done in Chapter 8 of the book. For the discussion of security in the cloud, also sees Chapter 8. Before that, in the discussion of security middleware in Section 6.1, attack detection technique based on the biologic dendritic cells of the innate immune system is furthered.

---

[38]The author believes that there is a similar connection between system theory and cloud computing and tries to use this connection to analyze the relationship between IoT systems and cloud security. This will be used to guide the security based on swarm intelligence of the large-scale IoTs (the third level of security intelligence), which is similar to herd immunity; the security of "sources and transmission routes" is similar to the security of cluster intelligence (the second level) security wisdom), you can avoid the specified type of virus attack. The single security of "things" is the first level of security wisdom. The first, second, and third levels of security intelligence correspond to the perception layer, network layer, and application layer security of the IoT.

In short, IoT security is a systematic project that runs through all links of the entire IoT industry chain. It is difficult to fundamentally eliminate potential safety hazards, especially when it comes to national economy and people's life or work, and other major IoT projects, the need for closed-loop security ecology has become more urgent. Large-scale system security should be viewed from the perspective of the closed-loop application of the IoT: perception security from the underlying chip and data collection; network security from network transmission to upper-layer applications; application security and privacy protection from data storage and analysis. Looking at the IoT security ecological chain from the perspective of big IoT security, it will become more and more important.

Chapter 5

Communication Technologies Layer of IoT

"Universal connection and eternal changing/development are the two basic principles of materialist dialectics."

Ubiquitous network (UN) has always been our pursuit and goal, whether for us, or for digital and physical things or devices (e.g., smartphones, TVs, vehicles, and sensors). The communication and network layer of Internet of things (IoT) envisages a future in which everything can be connected by means of suitable information and communication technologies to enable a range of applications and services.

Chapter 5 provides an overview of the communication and network technology in vision and market conditions for the perception layer of IoT. In this chapter, interworking and coverage supported short-/long-range communications, diversity as M2M and LPWA, mobility as cellular and SatCom in different bandwidth, delay demands, and TSN are discussed.

In the following chapters, we focus on the technology building blocks (e.g., middleware, platforms, services and their integration/disassembling, industrial user cases and standards, primitive IoT, etc.) that form the basis of IoT solutions. During the last few years, the technical building blocks, such as different platforms and service, have grown exponentially and entwined with communication and network in breadth and depth. We also emphasize on an overview of the architectural foundations of IoT, from many technical views (e.g., architectural view, M2M/platform view, networking view, edge/cloud view, IIoT/TIoT view, and SatCom view) relative to the above-mentioned IoT architecture (IoT-A) and the Industrial Internet Consortium (IIC) standard are discussed in Chapters 5 and 6. In Chapter 7, we outline the applications of these technologies within real-world use case contexts, illustrating how the IoT perception, communication and network, platform and service, and applications combine with the reference architectures to create real-world value.

The growth in mobile device market is pushing the deployment of IoT applications where these mobile devices (smart phones, tablets, etc.) are seen as gateways for wireless sensors and actuators. Communications technologies for the future Internet and the IoT/IoE will have to avoid such bottlenecks by construction/creation not only for a given status of development but also for the whole path to fully developed and still growing nets.

In this chapter, common communications will be introduced according to their covering range or area. Short-range communications for sensor networks (SNs) including WSNs and wireless sensor and actuator networks (WSANs), RFID, and local SCADA are the essential components of IoT. These wireless or wired short-range communication technologies are summarized in a comprehensive view, such as WLAN/IEEE 802.11, Zigbee//IEEE 802.15.4 following the IEEE definition in Sections 5.3–5.5, and these are called Group 1 — short-range group.

Group 2–long-range group is involved with range communications for 6LoWPAN, M2M communications, and LPWA, including some intersecting point-to-cloud communications and network technologies (e.g., in wide-area SCADA, in cellular IoT (CIoT), or in 5G slicing for IoT usages), which is described as Group 2, in more detail in Sections 5.6–5.8 of this chapter.

Satellite IoT communications, tactile IoT, and other overlapping communications (e.g., 5G/B5G satellite architecture and time sensitive networking (TSN)) are introduced as Group 3. In the Group 3, this promising group is also the essential components of IoT when the Internet of everything (IoE) era approaches because the provisions for point-to-gateways or point-to-cloud communications in a transparent (between relay nodes/gateways) but integrated way in covering a far and sparse area (seamless connection is an important characteristic for both IoE and 6G).

5.1 Introduction

The expected number of connected devices that are in use worldwide will exceed 23 billion at the end of the year 2021, as shown in Fig. 5.1. Global

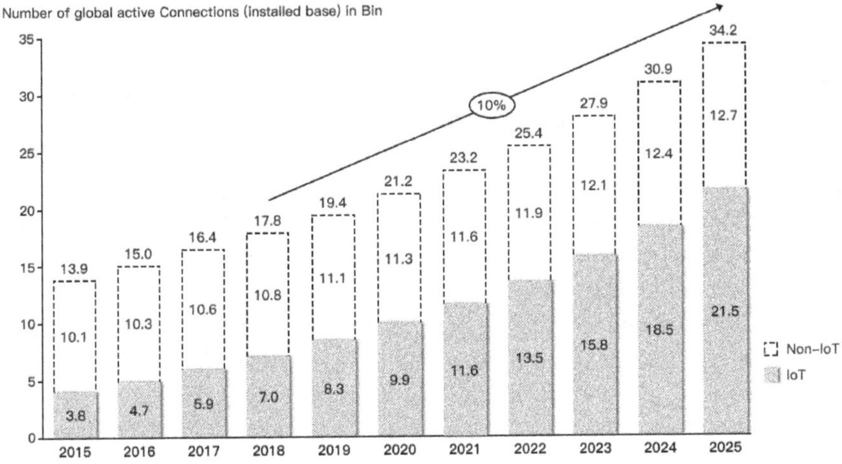

Figure 5.1 Total number of active device connections worldwide.
Source: IoT Analytics Research 2020.

connection growth is mainly driven by IoT devices — both from the consumer side (e.g., smart home) and from the enterprise/B2B side (e.g., connected machinery). The number of IoT devices (excluding smartphones, tablets, laptops, or fixed-line phones) that are active is expected to grow at the same speed as that of non-IoT to 11.6 billion by 2021. And the growing rate of global market for IoT (end-user spending on IoT solutions) is expected to be more than 10% annually from 2018 to 2025. Due to the market acceleration in the IoT, those estimates have been revised upwards and it is now expected that the total global market will reach USD 1,567 billion by 2025. Software and platforms are expected to continue to drive the market as more data are moved to the cloud and edge, and new IoT communication and networking technologies are brought to market. Meanwhile, the analytics towards IoE connections continue to gain importance.

Communication and networking technologies of IoT are a series of comprehensive academic and technical layout which focus on communication and network systems. To make IoT/IoE inter-connection easy to follow, topics under this chapter range from the theory and use of systems involving communication, networking, and information processors to wired and wireless networks and network layouts, protocols, and implementations. The developments stemming from new trends and demands in connection systems, products, and technologies, such as personal or things communications services, PAN, LPWAN, enterprise networks, and optical communications are also covered.

In the above-mentioned Group 1, there are a number of the IoT characteristics that are inherited from one or more of these components in the perception layer. For instance, "resource-constrained" is inherited from RFID and SNs, the communication they need are rich enough in diversity of communications/networks.

In Groups 1 and 2, "intelligence" and light weight are inherited from WSNs, M2M. As to wide spread, wireless LAN/WAN/PAN and other characteristics (e.g., ultra-large-scale network, spontaneous interactions) specific to the IoT, communications interfaces and networking in wireless or wired technologies are used to connect devices to one another, such as gateways, the Internet, and remote servers. When the characteristics of the IoT are presented from infrastructure and application perspectives, ETSI M2M, LwM2M or cellular M2M, and proprietary LPWA are introduced from platform views. From 5G (5th generation of mobile tech.) perspectives (Sections 5.7/5.8), M2M/WANs can also be provided by different actors, where some networks can be regarded as public (i.e., offered as commercial services for the general public) or as private (i.e., dedicated networks that provide services in a more closed business or entirely company internal environment). Particularly in the mobile network industry, there are different models for how the communications services are provided that include wholesale of access and dedicated virtual network operators that focus on managed M2M connectivity offerings without owning licensed mobile spectrum (e.g., cellular LPWAs) or actual network resources.

In IoE era, 5G accelerating our experience of IoT interworks with M2M, CIoT, satellite IoT, and new trends of network function virtualization (NFV) (providing abstraction) and software-defined networking (SDN) (providing flexibility). NFV provides the separation of network functions from the hardware infrastructure; the network function can be managed as a software module that can be deployed in any standard cloud computing infrastructure. On the other hand, SDN provides an architectural framework wherein control and data planes are decoupled and enables direct programmability of network control through software-based controllers.

Both NFV/SDN and edge computing are critical in shaping such an envisioned architecture in the satellite IoT, which will be detailed in

Group 3, together with an edge framework from IIRA and satellite IoT use cases. A new modality of tactile IoT is also covered in the last of Group 3.

The evolution and pervasiveness of present communication technologies have the potential to grow to unprecedented levels in the near future by including the Web of Things (WoT) into the developing IoT. Network users will be extended from humans to machines and things, and their groups, in a refreshing IoE world.

5.2 Wired and Wireless Access of IoT

In a ubiquitous computing environment like IoT, it is impractical to impose a single set of communication or networking standards and make everyone/everything comply. An ultra-large-scale network of things and the large number of events that can be generated spontaneously by these things, along with heterogeneous devices/technologies/applications of IoT, bring new challenges in developing applications and make the existing challenges in IoT world considerably difficult.

In this section, from a typical communication perspective, the heterogeneous accesses of IoT are divided into two main groups, the wired and wireless communication technologies.

5.2.1 *Wired access*

In many scenarios, a wired device connection is still the most reliable option that provides high data rates at very low cost but with less mobility. Particularly in industrial settings, fieldbus and Ethernet technologies use wired connections to a large extent. It is expected that the wired device connection will continue being the domain in the near future, such as Ethernet in a wired industrial communication networks (e.g., Fieldbus or TSN), an automobiles intranet in a vehicle (e.g., CAN/LIN, which is challenged by Ethernet-on-board and software-defined vehicle, on its upgradation to support intelligence and connected vehicle or automated/autonomous vehicle), and the complex wired connection in a robot (e.g., from head to feet) or machine.

- **PLC:** Sensor/actuator units that are installed within a building automation system or public utilities can use wired networking technologies such as Ethernet over the electrical lines. Power line communication (PLC) is a hard-wired solution that uses existing electrical wiring instead of dedicated network cables and for industrial applications (including controlling energy use/smart grid and building/factory controls), has significant advances.

At low frequencies (tens to hundreds of Hertz) it is possible to communicate over kilometers with low bit rates (hundreds of bits per second). Typically, this type of communication was used for remote metering and was seen as potentially useful for the smart grid. Enhancements to allow higher bit rates have led to the possibility of delivering broadband connectivity over power lines. The standardizing PLC includes IEEE 1901 (in 2011) and ITU-T G.hn (G.9960-PHY in 2009 and G.9961-Data Link Layer in 2010). In 2011, the ITU referenced G.9903 that specifies the use of IPv6 over PLC.

According to the frequency bands allocated for operation, PLC systems can be divided into narrowband PLC (NBPLC) and broadband PLC (BPLC). NBPLC refers to low-bandwidth communication, utilizing the frequency band below 500 kHz and providing low-speed approach (data rates of tens of kbps), while BPLC utilizes a wider frequency band, typically between 2 and 30 MHz, and allows for data rates of hundreds of Mbps.

BPLC is recommended for smart home applications requiring high-speed data transfer applications, such as Internet, HDTV, and audio, while the use of NBPLC systems is more appropriate for remote data acquisition, automatic measuring systems, renewable energy generation, advanced metering, street lighting, plug-in electric vehicles, etc. BPLC has higher speed that reduces the data collection period and ensures a real-time remote-control command, but its stability and reliability are still determined by the quality of power lines.

Another way to classify PLC is as PLC over AC lines or PLC over DC lines. Most companies are currently providing AC-PLC solutions, and PLC in DC lines also has applications for distributed energy generation and transportation (electronic controls in airplanes, automobiles, and trains). Among these, HPLC is a BPL approach based on IEEE 1901.1, developed by Huawei, and utilizes the frequency band between 0.7 and 12 MHz. An HPLC-IoT(RF) solution is described in Fig. 5.2, in which the under layers conform to 6LoWPAN (introduced in Section 5.5), and its data rate in applications ranges from 100 kbps to 2 Mbps. The solution is promoted by Huawei and VertexCom companies.

- **Fieldbus:** Fieldbus belongs to wired short-range communication in industrial, building, instrumentation, in-vehicle or mobile, and commercial areas. It includes RS232/RS422/RS485 (or twisted pair-based), CAN/

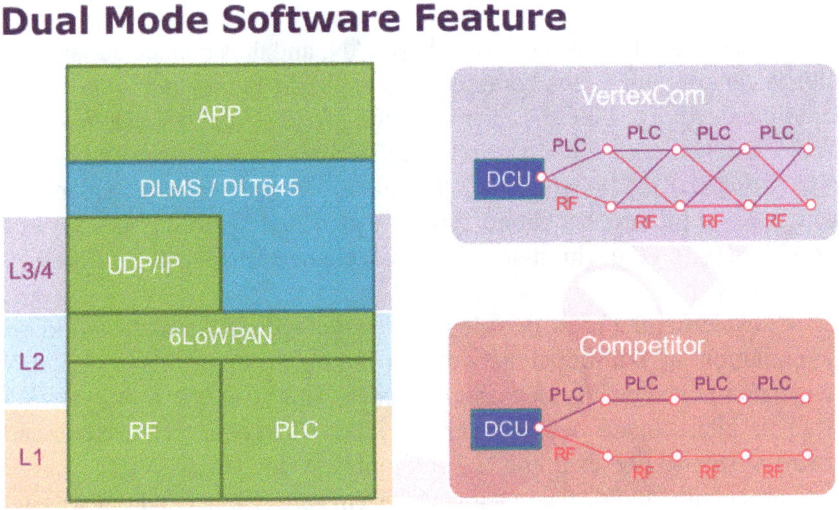

Figure 5.2 System topology for HPLC-IoT access solution.

Source: VertexCom.

LIN/Flexray (including CAN-based DeviceNet), Ethernet/IP (supported by common industrial protocol (CIP)), shared by ControlNet and DeviceNet), ControlNet,[1] Lonworks, European installation bus (EIB), Interbus, Profibus/Profinet, FF HSE (Fieldbus Foundation, High-Speed Ethernet), CC-Link, etc. Some of them are used in wired LAN or TSN supported, and most of them are popular in M2M wired connection. They will be discussed in the following sections and the next chapter (such as M2M, industrial 4.0, vehicle).

• **xDSL and fiber:** Digital subscriber line (DSL) broadband connectivity traditionally arrives over telephone lines. "xDSL" refers to Internet access carried over legacy (wired) telephone networks and encompasses numerous standards and variants, such as ADSL, RADSL, VDSL, SDSL, IDSL, and HDSL. "xDSL", or fiber, often works as a fixed point to the wireless router for the wireless access point commonly found in homes and

[1]ControlNet is one of three open network standards (DeviceNet, ControlNet, and EtherNet/IP), all of which use a common application layer, the "Common Industrial Protocol" (CIP). The Family of CIP Networks is specified and published by ODVA (Open DeviceNet Vendor Association — http://www.odva.org) and CI (ControlNet International — http://www.controlnet.org).

buildings. For example, in the home, the "wireless router" typically behaves as a link between the Wi-Fi (WLAN, and thus connected laptops, tablets, smartphones, etc., commonly found in the home) and DSL broadband connectivity. Take the factory or the office as another example, the Wi-Fi wireless access points are typically connected to the wired corporate (Ethernet) LAN, which is subsequently connected to a wider-area network and Internet backbone, typically provided by an Internet Service Provider (ISP). Fiber (high-speed optical) connections are also offered by many ISPs.

Considering the breadth of IoT applications, there are likely to exist a combination of traditional networking approaches, including not only above mentioned but also legacy cable/coax. This attributes to the existing need to interconnect devices and the inner interconnect for integrated micro systems. For example, in automobiles, connections with central data processing and decision support systems are still needed but waiting for an E/E revolution towards the IoE era (see Internet of vehicle, IoV relative section in Chapter 6).

In addition to these wired solutions, Li-Fi and satellite communication (SatCom) give new business logic and requirements beyond embodiments covered in the wired/wireless solutions. The SatCom will be arranged as a single section at the end of this chapter.

5.2.2 *Wireless communications*

The diversity of wireless demand in the communications and networks layer plays the role of a dynamic channel for transferring/exchanging information from the perception layer to processing, storage and service functions of upper layers and beyond base almost 50 wireless and cellular communication protocols. They range from wireless personal area network (WPAN), wireless local area network (WLAN), wireless neighborhood area network (WNAN), and wireless wide area network (WWAN).

But from IoT connections view, they differ with the coverage, e.g., short range referring to a coverage typically below 100 m. CIoT covers more than 50 km, and it is included in the wide-area IoT. Another branch of wide-area IoT or WWAN for IoT is LPWA networking (LPWAN), with the coverage below 50 km and most of the LPWAs limited to 5 km. The three kinds of connections can be seen in Table 5.1, together with a forecast from Ericsson Mobility Report, which shows the respective trends of wide-area IoT, CIoT, and short-range IoT.

Table 5.1 IoT connections (in billions).

IoT	2019	2025	CAGR (%)
Wide-area IoT	1.6	5.5	23
Celluar IoT	1.5	5.2	23
Short-range IoT	9.1	19.1	13
Total	10.7	24.6	15

Note: The figures for CIoT are also included in the figures for wide-area IoT.

- **Short-range:** Typically, short-range communication for IoT includes LAN/WLAN and WPAN. As the forecast in Table 5.2 shows, the highest number of IoT devices is connected through WPAN/WLAN, which does not exceed 100 m in the maximum range. WPAN includes Bluetooth or Bluetooth low energy (BLE)–connected devices, such as headsets and speakers, as well as ZigBee series and Z-Wave–connected devices, which can mostly be found in smart homes, e.g., for connecting smoke alarms, thermostats, or fitness monitors.

BLE/Bluetooth is designed for point-to-point or point-to-multipoint, star (up to seven slave nodes) network configurations and data exchange among devices and mainly regulated by IEEE 802.15.1. The connection of BLE is designed as an open wireless protocol that targets typical IoT applications in the unlicensed industrial, scientific, and medical (ISM) 2.4 to 2.483 GHz short-range radio frequency bandwidth. BLE is utilized for exchanging data over short distances from fixed and mobile devices, creating personal area networks (PANs). Bluetooth uses frequency-hopping spread spectrum, which chops up the data being sent and transmits chunks of it on up to 79 frequencies. The Bluetooth modulation used in the basic mode is GFSK. Bluetooth devices must operate in one of four available modes from mode 1 (insecure mode) to mode 4 where security procedures are initiated after link setup. Secure simple pairing uses elliptic curve Diffie–Hellman (ECDH) techniques for key management and link key generation in mode 4.

Zigbee 3.0 is a networking solution used on top of IEEE 802.15.4 radio technology, which includes IP Internet capability. Zigbee 3.0 has meshing capability and is used as an IoT connectivity solution for a range of smart home and industrial applications, including lighting, security, thermostats, and remote controls. It is secure and supports battery-free devices, meshing, low latency, and energy harvesting (e.g., motion, light). Zigbee 3.0 also includes Zigbee Green Power, which was developed as an ultra-low-power wireless standard to support energy-harvesting IoT devices and is effective for IoT devices that are only sometimes on the network (i.e., when they have power), enabling them to go on and off the network securely, so they can be off most of the time. The technical details of Zigbee will be discussed in the following section.

Z-Wave is a mesh (*ad hoc*) network low-energy wireless communications protocol used mainly for wireless control of home appliances, such as lighting control, security systems, thermostats, windows, doors, and locks. Z-Wave systems can be controlled via the Internet and locally through devices or using a Z-Wave gateway or central control device serving as hub controller. Z-Wave uses the unlicensed ISM band and operates at 868.42 MHz in Europe and 908.42 MHz in the US. Z-Wave provides data rates of 9600 bps and 40 kbps, with output power at 1 mW. The Z-Wave range between two nodes is up to 100 m in an outdoor, unobstructed setting. For in-home applications, the range is 30 m for no obstructions and 15 m with walls in between. Z-Wave Alliance requires the mandatory implementation of Security 2 (S2) framework on all devices receiving certification. Z-wave provides packet encryption, integrity protection, and device authentication services. End-to-end security is provided on application level (communication using command classes). It has in-band network key exchange and AES symmetric block cipher algorithm using 128-bit key.

6LoWPAN is a network protocol that defines encapsulation and header compression mechanisms. The standard has the freedom of a frequency band and a physical layer and can also be used across multiple communications platforms, including Ethernet, Wi-Fi, 802.15.4, and sub-1 GHz ISM. The protocol is implementing open IP standards, including TCP, UDP, HTTP, constrained application protocol (CoAP), message queue telemetry transport (MQTT) and web sockets, and offers end-to-end addressable nodes, allowing a router to connect the network to IPs. 6LoWPAN is a mesh network and mesh router devices can route data destined for other IoT devices, while hosts are able to sleep for long periods of time.

Near-field communication (NFC) is a short-range technology that operates at high frequency band at 13.56 MHz and supports data rate up to 424 kbps. The applicable range is up to 10 cm where communication between active readers and passive tags or two active readers can occur. NFC protocol allows two devices to communicate when they are placed within touching distance. NFC enables sharing power and data using magnetic field induction at 13.56 MHz (HF band), at short range, supporting varying data rates from 106 kbps, 212 kbps to 424 kbps.

A key feature of NFC is that it allows two devices to interconnect. In reader/writer mode, an NFC tag is a passive device that stores data, which can be read by an NFC-enabled device (e.g., smart poster, for which a technical specification was developed). NFC devices are designed to exchange data in peer-to-peer mode. Bluetooth or Wi-Fi link set up parameters can be shared using NFC and data like digital photos, and virtual business cards can be transferred. The NFC device itself acts as an NFC tag in card emulation mode, resembling an external interrogator as a traditional contactless smart card. This facilitates contactless payments and e-ticketing. NFC standards are acknowledged by major standardization bodies, such as ISO (e.g., ISO/IEC 18092). Security is implemented in the NFC using mechanisms such as digital signature and trusted tag. The digital signature (defined in the NFC Forum Signature RTD 2.0) uses asymmetric key exchange and it is a part of the NFC data exchange format (NDEF) message, which includes a certificate chain and a root certificate. Each NFC device has a private and a public key. The trusted tag method is fully compliant with NFC Forum Tag Type 4 and works with any NFC forum–compatible devices. The trusted tag is protected from cloning and embedded with cryptographic code that is generated by every "tap" or click on NFC button. This cryptographic code protects the transmitted information.

WLAN/LAN continues to be important technology for IoT communications. This is due to the high bandwidth, reliability, and legacy of these technologies. Where power is not a limiting factor, and high bandwidth is required, devices may connect seamlessly to the Internet via Ethernet (IEEE 802.3) or Wi-Fi (IEEE 802.11). The utility of existing WLAN infrastructure is evident in a number of early IoT applications targeted at the consumer market, particularly where integration and control with smartphones are required (irrespective of the actual technical architecture or optimality of the solution).

Wi-Fi/IEEE 802.11 is the most common standard in WLAN category and experiencing significant growth, mostly through the use of home assistants (e.g., connected home camera, smart TVs, and smart speakers) as well as through use in industrial settings, such as factories (although it continues to play a minor role in those settings compared to other technologies).

The IEEE 802.11/Wi-Fi standards continue to evolve in various directions to improve certain operational characteristics depending on usage scenario. Widely adopted release as IEEE 802.11n/Wi-Fi 4 was specifically designed to enhance throughput (typically useful for streaming multimedia). IEEE 802.11ac/Wi-Fi 5 (adopted in 2013) aims at a higher throughput version to replace the focusing efforts in the 5 GHz band. Moreover, IEEE 802.11p/DSRC communication can also be used in more *ad hoc* scenarios. Vehicle-to-vehicle (V2V) is one example that can target safety applications, such as collision avoidance or car platooning. As opposed to the situation for WANs, the interface technologies used within LANs are characterized by being very industry segment-specific, being supported by a plethora of different standards, or even being proprietary or at best de facto standards. LANs use both wired and wireless technologies. General examples of wired LANs include Ethernet, PLC, and the family of different fieldbus technologies used in industrial real-time control applications.

At last, Li-Fi (light fidelity), together with visible light communication (VLC), is used in different IoT applications as mentioned above. As shown in Fig. 5.3, they are a wireless communication technology that uses light to transmit data and position between devices. The technology addresses some of the shortcomings of radio-based wireless communications and has applications for industrial IoT (IIoT) connectivity by improved solutions for security, scalability, bandwidth, interference, latency. Li-Fi uses the modulation of light intensity to transmit data at high speeds over the visible light (e.g., LED devices), ultraviolet, and infrared spectrums. Li-Fi can transmit at speeds of up to 100 Gbit/s. A unique feature of Li-Fi is that it combines illumination and data communication by using the same device to transmit data and provide lighting.

Typically, a Li-Fi modem in a room serves as an optical base station or access point (AP). According to the standardization of IEEE 802.15.7, it supports high-data-rate visible light communication up to 96 Mb/s by fast modulation of optical light sources which may be dimmed during their operation.

- **Long Range:** Long-range communication links that cover longer distances, such as across metropolitan, regional, or even global

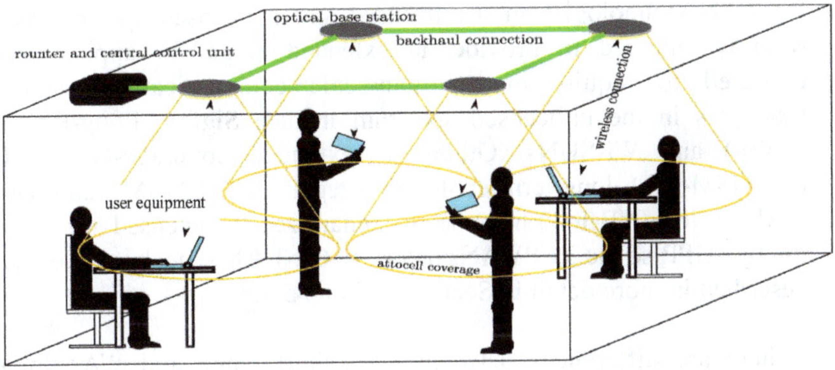

Figure 5.3 Li-Fi concept in attocell networks applied to indoor wireless networking.
Source: H. Haas. LiFi is a paradigm-shifting 5G technology. *Reviews in Physics* 3: 26–31, 2018.

geographic areas, in terms of communication range. Besides SatCom, WWANs provide group technologies used to link LANs and metropolitan area networks (MANs) — where LAN technologies cannot provide the communications ranges to otherwise interconnect — and commonly to link LANs and devices (including smartphones, Wi-Fi routers that support LANs, tablets, and IoT devices) to the Internet. Quantitatively, LANs tended to cover distances of tens to hundreds of meters, whereas WAN links spanned tens to hundreds of kilometers. The current generation of long-range/WWAN technology for IoT includes cellular WWAN/CIoT, LPWAN, etc.

- **CIoT:** Cellular mobile communications cover cellular mobile telecommunication networks from 2G to 5G by now, and it is a typical WWAN infrastructure with a significant departure from WLAN in terms of technology, coverage, network infrastructure, and architecture. Acting as a link between LANs and WPANs. Gateway devices (Section 5.6) typically include cellular transceivers and allow seamless IP connectivity over heterogeneous physical media. Gateway, such as M2M/MTC or IoT gateway, and an example of its logical functionality is presented in Fig. 5.23 in Section 5.6, which shows how NB-IoT or wireless smart ubiquitous network (Wi-SUN) bridging to WAN through a 6LoWPAN (conforms to IETF CoAP and HTTP proxy) gateway and communication stacks.

- LP-WAN technologies in the licensed and unlicensed spectra have recently emerged to provide an extended range for applications expected to require metropolitan-scale communication ranges. Examples in the unlicensed spectrum include Sigfox, Long-Range (LoRa) and Wi-SUNs. Others as extended coverage-GSM-IoT (EC-GSM-IoT), long-term evolution category M1 (LTE-M), and narrowband IoT (NB-IoT) have been standardized for licensed-spectrum use by 3GPP, so the 3 LPWANs belong to CIoT. These technologies are described in more detail in Sections 5.6 and 5.7.

There are differences between LAN/short range and WAN/long range with respect to IoT communications. WANs can be provided by different service suppliers. From human-centered view, some networks can be regarded as public (i.e., offered as commercial services for the general public) or as private (i.e., dedicated networks that provide services in a more closed business or entirely company internal environment).

From things/devices-centered view, when it comes to LANs/WANs according to networking technologies, there are many examples of different types, and there is also no stringent definition of what might be considered a LAN or a WAN, but either of them provides a fix or mobile access point for things/devices.

Prime examples of LANs include WPANs (also known as body area networks, BANs) for fitness or healthcare applications, home or building area networks (HANs and BANs, respectively) used in automation and control applications, and neighborhood area networks (NANs) or field area networks (FANs) which are used in the distribution grid of a smart electricity grid. Communication can also be used in more *ad hoc* (mesh) scenarios (see Section 5.3.3).

Particularly in the mobile network industry, there are different models for how the communications services are provided that include varieties of access and dedicated virtual network operators that focus on managed M2M (MTC) connectivity offerings without owning licensed mobile spectrum or actual network resources.

From data centered view, LoRaWAN, 6LoWPAN, and other LPWA (or LP-M2M) provide dedicated communication platform for the data acquiring, processing, and controlling (sometimes with feedback, then providing dual direction information loop), locally or widely (or cloudy). If the IoT data is private and the corresponding networks are private (or non-public from 3GPP views), the communications can be referred as IoT native (short- or long-range communications, which is simple as "point to point" or *ad hoc* by points self-organizing).

On the conditions that cellular and satellite networks only provide communication "pipelines" (or tubes) for the connections of things, (publicly and usually declaring the protection of privacy IoT data), the communications can be referred as M2M(type)-IoT, and at this stage, this means a "point-to-cloud" connection for things/devices. The integrated examples of cellular and satellite networks will be given in the last part of this chapter. V2X communications are discussed in Sections 5.8 and 6.5. When the vehicles communicate to the public transport infrastructure, or they are just mobile points in IoV and in which communications to each other directly, originally belonging to "point-to-point" example that can target safety applications, such as collision avoidance or car platooning.

5.2.3 *Three basic prototypes of IoT communications*

The communication function means that different sensors, actuators, and support infrastructure (gateways, controllers, routers, etc.) connect to each other for the purpose of exchanging messages. The communication function can be an abstraction of different types of physical/link layer/networking technologies which include a variety of topologies as well (e.g., bus, *ad hoc* network, point to point). An *ad hoc*/mesh for WLAN network will be discussed as an example of an implementation of the communication function. Since interoperability and automatic control is an essential functional domain from the IIRA (see Section 5.9) view, communication characteristics in networking such as how to formulate linking which affect the delay, bandwidth, and controllability of a system are important in the communication function.

Topology of communications for IoT nodes/device networking in IoT environments are complex with heterogeneous physical devices supporting various communication protocols, while they are possibly connected to an intermediary gateway and then to their virtual representations (i.e., services) running on different platforms. Thus, it is possible to interact with a single IoT device in many interoperable ways using its varied interfaces and representations.

IoT communication and network require interoperability by defining multiple topologies and then find the characteristic functionalities and define meta-protocols that can be mapped on the ones used in the platforms (i.e., on the level of syntactic interoperability, the characteristic functionality is resource access). A lot of work has been done in this field. For example, the INTER-IoT project has defined an IoT multi-layer approach to provide semantic interoperability. In order to promote the interoperability for the devices in various forms of communication models that will coexist in heterogeneous environments, the topology models will range from device to device, device to cloud, and device to gateway communications that will bring various requirements to the development of electronic components and systems for IoT applications.

5.2.3.1 *Point to point approach*

The first approach considers the case of devices that directly connect and communicate between each other (i.e., using a twisted pair, Bluetooth, NFC, ZigBee, etc.) not necessarily using an intermediary application server to establish direct device-to-device communications.

The simplest communication for this typical IoT device is known as "Point to Point", and the topological extension for multi-nodes formulates the network, where each point/node communicates over links. From two links (Fig. 5.4(a)) to more links in one plane, and to 12 links in two layers point-to-multipoint communication are shown respectively in Fig. 5.4(a)–(c).

Point-to-point or point-to-multipoint communication in the selected physical medium (wired or wireless) is determined by a number of technical and economic considerations. Technically, the connectivity of any two nodes is fundamental for forming a network in the technological solution designed and implemented to communicate over that medium links. In order to provide some degree of accurate and feasible connections, the primary enabler of bandwidth is also necessary.

RFID communication belongs to this topology. An example of RF bandwidth management is introduced by an RF front-end calibration

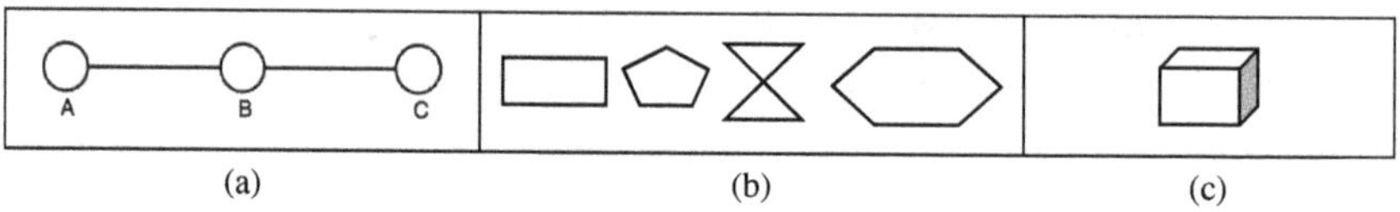

Figure 5.4 Topology of point to point and its extension. (a) 3 links, (b) 4, 5, 6, 6 links in point-to-point combinations and (c) two layers point-to-multipoint.

scheme using signals from a fractional-*N* frequency synthesized and received signal strength indicator (RSSI) are provided. Another example can be found in the Texas Instruments Sensor Tag.

When direct communication between two nodes over a physical medium is not possible, networking can allow these devices to communicate over a number of hops. To achieve this, nodes of the networking are organized either in an infrastructure (with a center node) or in an *ad hoc* network (with multi-hops).

Simultaneously, different technological solutions require certain economic considerations, such as the cost of deployment and maintenance of the networking infrastructure. When the cost of point-to-point/point-to-multipoint is too expensive in certain application, alternative methods are considered, such as point to gateway and point to the cloud. For example, consider the cost of embedding wires across a metropolitan or larger, geographic region (e.g., electricity and legacy telephone networks). To achieve this, diversity of sets of communications and protocols are designed and deployed, which is one of the targets of this chapter.

5.2.3.2 *Point to gateway*

The second approach considers that the IoT device connect to a gateway, where the connection between the devices and the IoT Gateway is generally wireless (Wi-Fi, Z-wave, Zigbee, etc.). And the connection between the IoT-gateway and the cloud can be an Internet connection.

In a typical scenario, the IoT-gateway is connected via Wi-Fi/Ethernet to a second gateway that performs the Internet connection via 2G/3G/4G/5G or a wired connection (xDSL, cable, fiber) or satellite gateway. On the application end, the connection between the user and the cloud can be wired or wireless. The wired connection can be through the twist pairs, LAN (Ethernet), gateway.

The gateway allows connecting the user with the Internet network and this one to the cloud. Take another scenario from Fig. 5.4(a), as an example for RFID linking to EPC system (by EPCIS): Point A is an RFID tag and B represents an RFID reader; C can be a gateway of LAN or a local server. The scenario also can be extended to WSN: Point A is a sensor or actuator; B is another sensor node (if with routing functions, it is also called as sink node); C can be a gateway of LAN or a local server.

As a review of Section 4.1, when a tag ID is responding by a RFID reader or scanning a barcode from a product at a point of sales (POS), an event that could be used either by the logic processing a purchase or by the logic processing a product return is generated. As to EPC (conforms to GS1 in the regulation of interface and functionality), the electronic product code information services (EPCISs) interfaces and the EPCIS repository (see Section 4.1.3). The point A to point B to the gateway of the EPCIS capture interface is exposed by the capture layer while the EPCIS query interface and the EPCIS repository belong to the share layer. The EPCIS functionality and interfaces are presented as middleware in Section 6.2.

In the LAN, information is transmitted from endpoints to a gateway, where it is then transmitted to sources for processing and return transmission. The wireless connection (e.g., the cellular 2G/3G/4G/5G, or Wi-MAX/IEEE 802.16 or satellite) is done either by connecting the smart phones and tablets directly to Internet having access to web applications and web service (the followed point to cloud) or by the gateway of LAN/PAN. By using wired Ethernet or Wi-Fi gateway connections (often called as capillary networking) to Internet, cloud/edge service of various service providers support to exchange data and control message traffic.

5.2.3.3 *Point to cloud*

As the third approach, the point-to-cloud communication is a good option when a sensor with less nodes around it. In this approach, the IoT devices connect to an application layer gateway (or M2M gateway for WAN) running an application software operating on the gateway device, serving as a "bridge" between the device and the cloud service to provide secure data protocol translation and other functionalities. Many examples of this typical "Point-to-Cloud" approach will be introduced as cellular LPWA networks (LPWANs), including narrow band IoT (NB IoT) and LTE-M, and other non-cellular LPWA communications as LoRa, Sigfox, Weightless, etc.

The deployment of billions of devices requires network agnostic solutions that integrate mobile/CIoT, LPWA networks, and high-speed wireless networks (Wi-Fi) or low-power Wi-Fi (HaLow), specifically for applications spanning multiple jurisdictions. And at least two features of LPWA networks for IoT devices are worth mentioning despite the low levels of mobility and data transfer:

- Low-power consumption that enable devices to last up to 10 years on a single charge (e.g., battery).
- Optimized data transfer that supports small, intermittent blocks of data.

All the three-topologies of IoT communication are unfolded in to the heterogeneous networks, as shown in Fig. 5.5.

Figure 5.5 presents the global number of connected IoT devices categorized by the communication/protocol technology.Technically, the different hybrid methods of the three communication prototypes are contained in different IoT connections scenarios, as wirelessly or wired, in LAN or WAN, by the access of Cellular, M2M or LPWA, or others.

5.3 WLAN and Wi-Fi 6

LANs use both wired and wireless technologies. General examples of wired LANs as mentioned above, include Ethernet, PLC, and the family of different fieldbus technologies used in industrial real-time control applications. Prominent examples of WLAN networking technologies include the IEEE 802.11 and IEEE 802.15.4 families, as introduced in this and the later section. As for WLAN, the number of IoT devices in it is

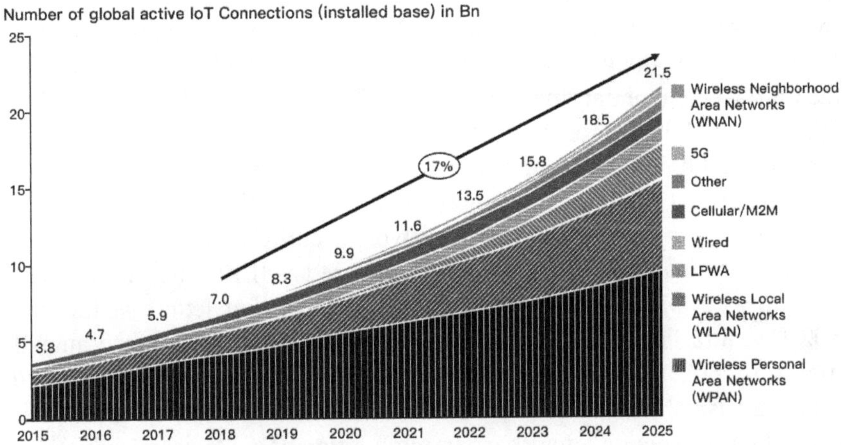

Figure 5.5 Trends of connected devices in diversities from 2015 to 2025.

Note: IoT connections do not include any computers, laptops, fixed phones, cellphones or tablets. Counted are active nodes/devices or gateways that concentrate the end-sensors, not every sensor/actuator. Simple one-directional communications technology not considered (e.g., RFID, NFC). Wired includes Ethernet and Fieldbuses (e.g., connected industrial PLCs or I/O modules): Cellular includes 2G, 3G, 4G; LPWAN includes unlicensed and licensed low-power networks; WPAN includes Bluetooth, Zigbee, Z-Wave or similar; WLAN includes Wi-fi and related protocols; WNAN includes non-short range mesh; Other includes satellite and unclassified proprietary networks with any range.
Source: IoT Analytics Research 2018.

expected to grow to occupy almost one third of the total IoT connections by 2025 (see Fig. 5.5).

5.3.1 *Wi-Fi and IEEE 802.11 standards*

WLAN belongs to short-range IoT wireless technologies. In the case of the LAN or WLAN, a smaller geographic region is covered in a typical range of connectivity to 100 m (and up to 1 km, as Wi-Fi HaLow), and the most popular wired LAN technology is Ethernet. Wi-Fi as one of WLAN commercial solutions, often covers a building, an office block, or a home, and even does not require any leased communications infrastructure, just by a point-to-point link.

As the most prevalent WLAN technology, Wi-Fi/IEEE 802.11 series standards define the physical (PHY) layer and media access control (MAC) layer of wireless communication. The first protocol as IEEE 802.11 was released in 1997, which was a milestone in the history of wireless network technology. Later, Wi-Fi became a trademark of Wi-Fi Alliance in 1999. Now, it has been widely used in daily production and life because of its strong mobility, flexible networking, low-cost (low equipment price, license-free frequency band), and other advantages. With the increasing demand of users, IEEE 802.11 working groups have improved the protocols, mainly including the improvement of transmission rate and distance, such as 802.11a, 802.11b, 802.11g, and 802.11n (or Wi-Fi 4 in Table 5.2). Other improvements such as service quality (QoS) guarantee and security in its series protocols are 802.11e, 802.11i (defined strict encryption format and authentication mechanism, as the supplement of wireless network security), etc.

The original Wi-Fi standard was numbered as IEEE 802.11 (with data rate up to 2 Mb/s) with speedier extensions getting letters at the end: 802.11a, 802.11b, 802.11g, and 802.11n. Eventually, with more amendments to 802.11 than letters, the engineers started wrapping around: 802.11ad isn't the fourth addition to 802.11a but an amendment of its own; in this version, dual carrier modulation (DCM) is introduced in Wi-Fi. The mainstream Wi-Fi versions are introduced in Fig. 5.6.

In order to improve the transmission rate, IEEE 802.11n (Wi-Fi4) supported multi input multi output (MIMO). And the dual band combined the benefits of Wi-Fi 2 and 3 (as shown in Table 5.2). Increasing the basic rate of Wi-Fi 4 to 72.2 Mb/s and doubling the bandwidth (i.e., dual-band routers with 2.4 GHz and 5 GHz radios) of 40 MHz could achieve the rate of up to 150Mb/s. If a Wi-Fi 4 device had a multiple stream radio built-in,

Table 5.2 Comparison of the seven current Wi-Fi standards.

Name in Wi-Fi standards	IEEE 802.11	IEEE 802.11a (unofficial Wi-Fi 2)	IEEE 802.11b (unofficial Wi-Fi 1)	IEEE 802.11g (unofficial Wi-Fi 3)	802.11n Wi-Fi 4	802.11ac Wi-Fi 5	802.11ax Wi-Fi 6
Bands	2.4 GHz	2.4 GHz	5 GHz	2.4 GHz	2.4 GHz and 5 GHz	5 GHz	2.4 GHz and 5 GHz
Max. Speed	2 Mbps	54 Mbps	11 Mbps	54 Mbps	150 Mbps (40 MHz, 1SS); 600 Mbps (40 MHz,4SS)	433 Mbps (80 MHz, 1SS); 6933.3 Mbps (160 MHz, 8SS)	600.4 Mbps (80 MHz, 2SS); 9607.8 Mbps (160 MHz, 8SS)
Modulating in PHY.	DSSS/FHSS/IR	OFDM	DSSS(CCK)	PBCC/ CCK-OFDM	MIMO-OFDM(QAM); DSSS(CCK); BPSK/ QPSK;16/64-QAM	OFDM; BPSK/QPSK; 16/64/256-QAM	OFDM/OFDMA; BPSK/QPSK; 16/64/256/1024-QAM
Topology	*Ad Hoc*; Infrastructure						
LLC	IEEE 802.11 LLC						
MAC	IEEE 802.11 MAC(CSMA/CA)						
Bandwidth (MHz)	20 MHz (for each DSSS channel of total 14 channels; and 1 MHz for each FHSS of total 75 channels)	20 MHz	20 MHz	20 MHz	20 MHz, 40 MHz	20 MHz, 40 MHz, 60 MHz, 80 MHz, 160 MHz; 80 MHz + 80 MHz	20 MHz, 40 MHz, 60 MHz, 80 MHz, 160 MHz; 80 MHz + 80 MHz
Characteristics	The originally released WLAN by IEEE (and Wi-Fi Alliance), low data rate	Signals were easily absorbed by solid obstacles, reducing range.	Interference from other ISM band devices slowed internet speeds.	Backwards compatibility	MIMO signaling boosted data speed, but Wi-Fi 4 could handle just one device's signal at a time (i.e., without Multi-user MIMO/ MU-MIMO)	Multi-user MIMO supports up to four simultaneous streams to communicate with more devices (download links only). Speed is increased by reducing lag time in networks with many devices.	Routers with more spatial streams — better capacity & efficiency; MU-MIMO for down and up links

Notes: There is no Wi-Fi 1, 2, or 3 versions formally, although they are referred as 802.11b, 802.11a, or 802.11g, respectively. When the IEEE 802.11ax (Wi-Fi 6) standard was first announced, it was limited by law to a wireless spectrum that only covered the 2.4 GHz and 5 GHz bands.

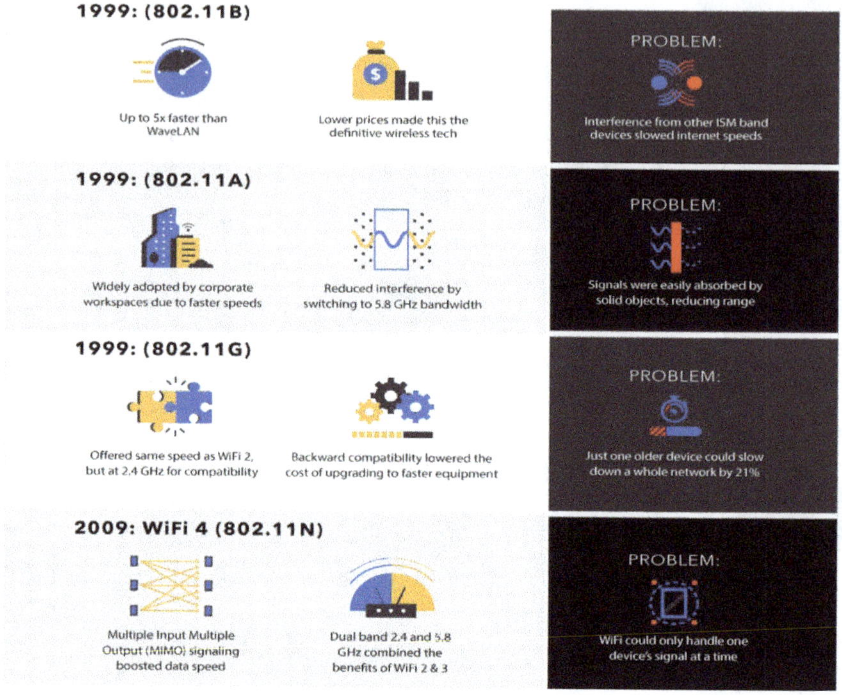

Figure 5.6 History of mainstream Wi-Fi versions.

e.g., four-stream radio onboard, the maximum speed would go up to 600 Mbps.

In 802.11ac (Wi-Fi 5), the max speed of 150 Mbps per stream was raised to 433 Mbps (Wave 1 and 256QAM in 2013) and 867 Mbps (Wave 2 and 256QAM in 2016) in the 5 GHz band only. When Wi-Fi 5 followed path N, with up to 8 streams per radio band, the max speed was raised to 6933.3 Mbps (3.46 Gbps under the condition of $N = 4$.). Take NETGEAR Wi-Fi 5 router (Nighthawk R7000) as an example, a total combined speed of 1900 Mbps was given by the combination of the comprised of three ($N = 3$) streams for a total speed of 1300 Mbps (3×433), plus the total speed of 600 Mbps (4×150) of 4N-based 150 Mbps streams in the 2.4 GHz range.

Today, higher wireless bandwidth (80–160 MHz), more MIMO streams (up to eight streams), better modulation mode (QAM256/QAM1024) are used in the new generation Wi-Fi 6 (802.11ax). Table 5.2 shows the seven current consumer standards.

With the introduction of Wi-Fi 6 (802.11ax standard, taking hold in 2019) and its wide spreading in 2020, the connectivity performance is enhanced for the use of IoT devices and businesses and operators running large-scale deployments. The Wi-Fi Alliance improves Wi-Fi 6/802.11ax performance in crowded Wi-Fi areas, where there are a lot of new numbering on routers, laptops, and other devices going forward in different networks or a lot of people.

More capabilities are brought Wi-Fi 6 to support next generation connectivity uses. For example, Wi-Fi 6 offers faster speeds for all devices on the 2.4 GHz and 5 GHz spectra, with adding more spatial streams (up to four/eight streams) and QAM (up to 1024) to vastly increase overall network capacity and efficiency.

5.3.2 *Wi-Fi 6 and IEEE 802.11ah*

The new standard of Wi-Fi 6 uses orthogonal frequency-division multiple access (OFDMA) to improve the efficiency of multi-user multiple-input, multiple-output (MIMO) streams. MIMO works both on the uplink and on the downlink and can simultaneously receive data from different devices on different channels (maximum of eight in Wi-Fi 6) at once. Some supplementary versions of IEEE 802.11 are introduced in Table 5.3.

Wi-Fi 6 also delivers significant improvements for the devices of the coming IoE generations. IoT devices can shut down Wi-Fi connections most of the time using the target wake time feature and connect only briefly as scheduled to transmit data they have gathered since the last time this was performed, thus extending battery life.

The target wake time feature improves sleep and wake efficiency, reduces power consumption, and decreases congestion on crowded networks. In Wi-Fi 6, the theoretical maximum bandwidth of a single stream is 3.5 Gbit/s, and up to four streams can be delivered to a single device, which means a maximum of up to 14 Gbit/s.

In Table 5.3, if Wi-Gig seemed as (in) home-centric progress for better quality and fast consumer (including the emerging immersive experience represented by VR/AR, 4K video, the projection of mobile/laptop screen content for displays somewhere indoor, and other high data rate indoor mobile applications, such as new routers or game devices.), Wi-Fi HaLow/802.11ah is things-centric progress for low-power, low-speed, extended range data transmission. Furthermore, the announced Wi-Fi 6E (designation in 2020) for Wi-Fi 6 products mean that support 6 GHz

Table 5.3 Some supplementary versions of IEEE 802.11.

Versions of IEEE 802.11	Characteristics	Year
n	MIMO (Multi)	2009
ac	Speedier Wi-Fi standard, now called Wi-Fi 5.	2013
ad	"Wi Gig" (Wireless Gigabit) for transmitting data very short distances on the **60 GHz** band. As an unlicensed band technology, Wi-Gig or 802.11ad, is mature enough for massive deployment and can be used for cellular networking backhaul.	2012
af	"White Spaces" standard for transmitting Wi-Fi over empty TV channels.	2013
ah	Low-power, low speed, extended range data transmission, as "Wi-Fi HaLow" for light-weight IoT devices.	2017
ak	Lets Wi-Fi be used to bridge other networks more efficiently.	2018
ai	A standard that lets Wi-Fi devices connect to a network in 100 ms.	2016
aj	Wi-Gig for China using the 45 GHz band.	2018
aq	A standard to help devices negotiate connections.	2018
ax	Wi-Fi 6	2019
ay	A proposed enhancement to Wi-Gig to make it faster.	2019
az	A way for Wi-Fi devices to better determine their physical location.	2021
ba	"Wake up radios" that use very little power to wake up the main radio.	2020
bb	Networking using visible light.	2021

wireless spectrum. Essentially, Wi-Fi 6E enables faster speeds and lower latencies than Wi-Fi 6. Features and IoT applications of Wi-Fi 6 are described in Fig. 5.7.

IEEE 802.11ah was adopted in 2017 targeting an evolution of the 2007 standard that will allow many networked devices to cooperate in longer range and lower power connectivity, in the spectrum below one gigahertz (<1 GHz, or sub1 GHz) ISM band. IEEE 802.11ah is designed to exploit collaboration (relaying or networking in other words) to extend the range and improve energy efficiency (by cycling the active periods of the radio transceiver). The standard aims to facilitate the rapid development of IoT applications that could exploit burst-like transmissions, such as in metering applications. This type of thinking is very similar to traditional WSN theory and practice, which push the development of technologies such as 6LoWPAN, RPL, and CoAP mentioned below.

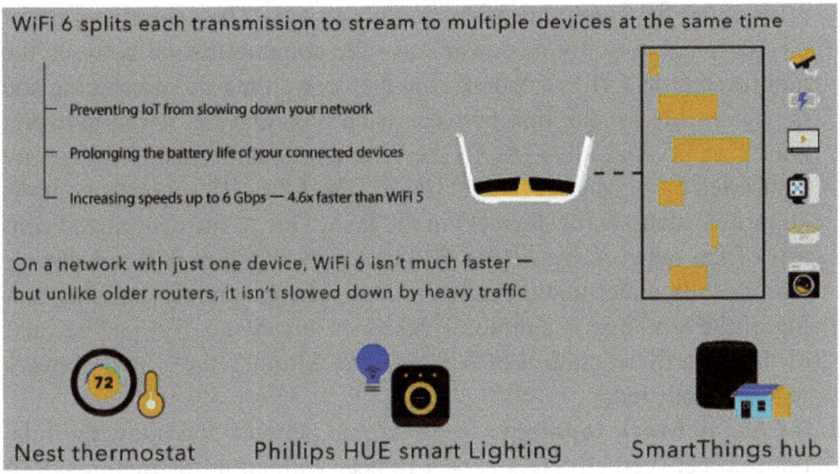

Figure 5.7 Features and applications of Wi-Fi 6.

Wi-Fi HaLow wireless technology is based on the IEEE 802.11ah protocol standard. The technology augments Wi-Fi by meeting the requirements for the IoT to enable a variety of use cases in industrial, energy (e.g., smart metering), smart home/building, agricultural, and smart city environments. The Wi-Fi Alliance, a group of Wi-Fi platform vendors that work with the FCC and electronics manufacturers, is improving the series standards for Wi-Fi technology and for the supporting of IoT devices (as shown in Fig. 5.7).

With the introduction of 5G (the fifth Generation of mobile communication technologies) and the mMTC slicing, other low-power applications in WLAN or low-power wide area (LPWA) for IoT are improved in licensed/unlicensed spectra. And there is a trend to develop new standards with low-power consumption and low speed in recent years, including Wi-Fi HaLow, Zigbee, BLE, and 6LoWPAN in their respective things-centered directions.

The following part introduces two kinds of WLAN/Wi-Fi topologies (as an introduction of the following part): centralized topology and distributed peer-to-peer (point-to-point) topology, corresponding to the infrastructure network and the *ad hoc* network (in Table 5.2).

- **Infrastructure network topology:** In an infrastructure network, at least one access point (AP) or base station (BS) is responsible for relaying all the communications in the network. The centralized BS or AP station is not only responsible for the communication between the mobile stations (STAs, stations) but also plays the role of bridging and is responsible for the link between each STA and the wired network. An P or BS and all STAs in the wireless communication range are controlled by a basic service set (BSS). The AP or BS centrally controls all mobile stations (or devices) in the BSS. Due to the centralized control of the network by AP (or BS), the network QoS will not change dramatically under that the network loads change greatly, and the routing of the topology is simple, which is its advantage. But just because of the centralized control of AP, once the AP fails, the whole network will be paralyzed.

- ***Ad hoc* network topology:** In an *ad hoc* network topology, the relationship between all STAs is peer to peer without infrastructures. STA can communicate with each other directly or indirectly, without the relay of a centralized node (e.g., AP or BS). Peer-to-peer topology has the characteristics of no central node, convenient networking, and flexible topology, which is widely used in temporary networking and emergency networking. So, it is also named as multi-hop network, infrastructure-less network or self-organizing network.

Mesh networking is typically implemented by the hybrid of the two basic topology modes: infrastructure and/or *ad hoc* network meshing (Fig. 5.8). To gain the maximum benefit that meshing can offer, both need to be supported simultaneously and seamlessly in a single network. Infrastructure meshing creates wireless backhaul mesh among wired APs

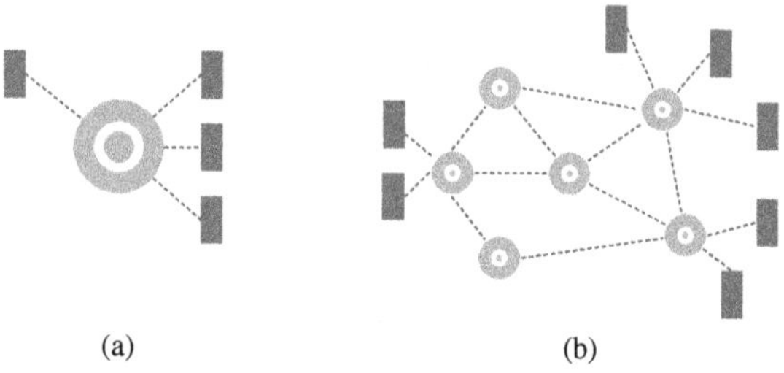

Figure 5.8 Infrastructure and *ad hoc* topology, where the bigger circle node means an AP with router function as sink node or coordinator in WSN/Zigbee and the other means a mobile station (or device). (a) Infrastructure (one centralized AP) and (b) *ad hoc* (peer-to-peer STAs).

and wireless routers. This reduces system backhaul costs while increasing network coverage and reliability.

5.3.3 *Ad hoc networks for WLAN*

Ad hoc network is a special network regulated by IEEE 802.11 standard groups. The term *ad hoc* means "for this" in Latin, which denotes this special self-organizing, peer-to-peer, multi-hop mobile network and nowadays with characteristics as robust, scalable, and self-healing. One of the most practical applications for *ad hoc* sensors networks is environmental monitoring, where wireless nodes are scattered over a geographical area. The structure of *ad hoc* network generally has two kinds: plane structure and hierarchical structure.

• **Plane structure:** In *ad hoc* network structure, all nodes are equal. Networking relies on the *ad hoc* interconnection between WSN nodes to form a "centerless, self-organizing, multi-hop routing, dynamic topology" network, which is related to the initial use of sensor networks for military purposes (battlefield monitoring). Four steps in the *ad hoc* networking are listed as follows:

Step (1): Deployment: WSN nodes can be placed flexibly according to the needs of the monitored environment;
Step (2): Wake up and self-detection: WSN nodes wake up and configure automatically;
Step (3) Automatic identification and organizing: WSN nodes identify each other automatically and form WSN automatically by learning/awarding of their location relationship;
Step (4) Establish routing and start communication: Based on the automatic formation of WSN network topology and channel conditions, automatically establish routing and data flow and start to transmit information.

The steps in an *ad hoc* WSN are designed for the most primitive and worst deployment environment. In other words, there is no other communication network to rely on in the deployed area and no network planning or infrastructure. Assuming that WSN is completely in an "isolated" and unfamiliar environment, it has to be complete "self-configuration, self-identification, self-networking, self-routing". This is a feasible networking method in some special application scenarios (such as field operation environment or agriculture land or forest), but in conventional application scenarios, this kind of "no center" *ad hoc* network is bound to be inefficient. Therefore, the concept of central control partly in different levels, namely hierarchical structure, is introduced into the *ad hoc* WSN.

- **Hierarchical structure (multi levels):** In a hierarchical structure, a cluster head node is responsible for forwarding information between clusters. Several nearby WSN nodes form a "cluster" (shown as the dotted circle in Fig. 5.9(a)). The information of each node in the cluster is gathered to the cluster head node, and then the information collected in the cluster is transmitted upward through the cluster head, to an upper-level cluster (shown as the solid line circle in Fig. 5.9(a)). Due to the short transmission distance of WSN nodes, the size of a cluster cannot be too large.

The coverage of wired IP network is very limited. It is difficult to guarantee that the interface of wired IP network can always be found within the coverage of a cluster. Therefore, in order to form a larger WSN, it is necessary to conduct *ad hoc* networking among multiple cluster heads, thus forming a hierarchical WSN (see Fig. 5.9). This dual-band hierarchical structure is used by the US military in its tactical Internet in the near-term digital radio (NTDR) networking. After the cluster heads of the upper level are interconnected, the information is gathered to the cluster heads of the higher level and transmitted upward, and so on. Until a cluster head enters the coverage of the WLAN or wired IP network, the cluster head can become a "WSN gateway" (sink node as a router) and transmit all the information collected in the WSN back to the IP network. Figure 5.9(b) gives the three-level topology of hierarchical structure as an example.

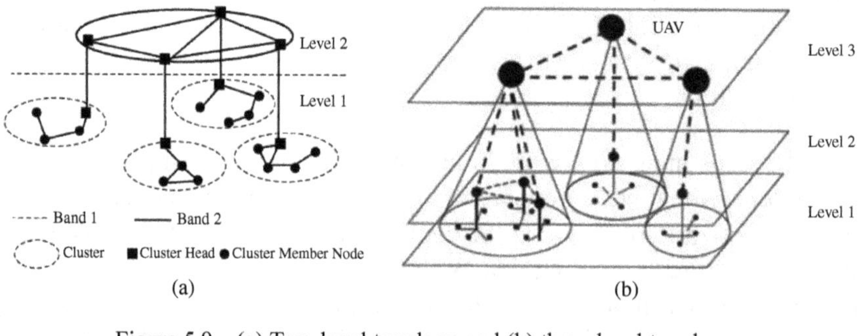

Figure 5.9 (a) Two-level topology and (b) three-level topology.

Several aspects are worth our attention when considering the management and security, in forming a dynamic, infrastructure-less *ad hoc* network; they are as follows:

- Requirements of security and privacy protection include availability, authentication, confidentiality, integrity, non-repudiation, anonymity, location privacy, trust, etc.
- System requirements, including timeliness, isolation, lightweight computation, self-stability, reliability/robustness, etc. As an example of reliability, Z-Wave *ad hoc*/mesh networks become more reliable as more devices are added in (e.g., a Z-Wave network with 50 devices is more reliable than a Z-Wave network of 25 devices).
- Security requirements of perception environment, including key management, authorization, strategies of routing security, access control, etc.

According to the strategy and mechanism of *ad hoc* network security requirements, the current research contents include lightweight encryption, routing security, key management, identity and authentication, access control (sub-roles in groups, hierarchical management, and according sub policies), intrusion detection, etc.

5.3.4 *Access for WSN*

In the above leveled WSN structure of *ad hoc* network, the continuous level-by-level expansion can form an unlimited scale of WSN theoretically; however, due to the limitations of software and hardware in WSN, it is difficult to form an "ubiquitous" coverage only by WSN itself. These limitations are discussed as follows:

(1) The increase of transmission delay caused by the increase of the number of WSN level is not only the introduction of a certain processing delay for each cluster head but also the use of time division multiplexing (TDM) in many cases due to the sharing of the same air interface resources between levels.
(2) With the increase of the number of levels, more and more information converges to the cluster head, the power consumption and transmission load of the high-level cluster head increase sharply, and the battery life shortens.

(3) In some areas, the coverage capacity of wired IP network/WLAN is limited, so it is unrealistic to only rely on wireless multi-hop and mesh to reach the boundary of wired/wireless IP network.
(4) If multi hop and mesh networks are widely used, the routing algorithm is complex.

In order to reduce the delay, balance the load, reduce the cost, and simplify the routing, we must realize the flat network architecture as far as possible, reduce the number of layers, increase the number of WSN gateways (sinks), and reduce the scope of each sink's burden. This contradicts the efficient coverage of WSN. Therefore, it is difficult to bridge the coverage gap between WSN and IP network only relying on WSN itself.

According to the differences in application scenarios, here we discuss two solutions:

- **Mesh access by gateway:** Client meshing enables wireless peer-to-peer networks to form between and among client devices (i.e., WSN nodes/end users) and does not require any network infrastructure to be present. In this case, clients can hop through each other to reach other clients in the network. Mesh network supports both infrastructure and *ad hoc* meshing. Infrastructure meshing creates a robust and scalable network, while *ad hoc* nodes meshing enables end nodes/devices to instantly form a wireless network among themselves — with or without the inclusion of network infrastructure. Enabling multiple hops can even turn every device/node into a router/repeater. As they join the network, they improve network coverage and increase network throughput. Continuous mesh routing in which the simultaneous operation of infrastructure and *ad hoc* meshing is also possible.

In this scenario, nodes/devices can move seamlessly between infrastructure-based and *ad hoc*-based peer-to-peer networks. So, mesh network topology is very suitable for wide area coverage and low data rate applications in industrial automation applications, as well as business, medical monitoring, agriculture, and so on. In the application, Ethernet (IP network) can be accessed through a gateway node (which plays the role of uppermost cluster head node in its own leveled *ad hoc* networks), as shown in Fig. 5.10. There are three kinds of nodes: sensor node, sensor node with routing function (sink node), and gateway node. WSN is connected to an IP network or another mesh network through the gateway node.

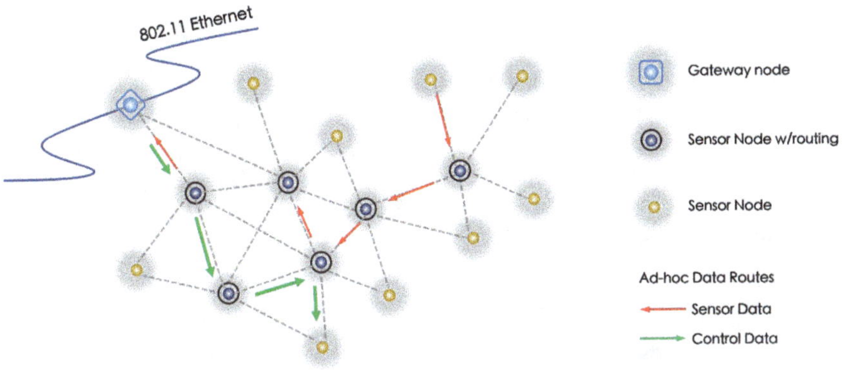

Figure 5.10 Gateways as AP of mesh WSN network.

If the WSN is based on 802.11 Ethernet, the administrator can read the data remotely, and the direction of the control data is shown as the green arrow in Fig. 5.10. The sensor data from nodes is collected through an *ad hoc* way (shown as the red arrow in Fig. 5.10) and finally aggregated to the gateway. Most WSNs or WSANs support dual-direction communication, and control data can be sent from the gateway to the sensor/actuator node, as shown by the green arrow in Fig. 5.10. ZigBee and Z-Wave protocols in the following section also support this mesh access mode.

- **Hybrid Access for Point to Cloud:** This and the next section detail a number of the standards and technologies currently in use and under development that enable *ad hoc* connectivity between the devices that will form the basis of the IoT. These are the communication technologies and their hybrid (in heterogeneous networking) that are considered to be critical to the realization of massively distributed M2M applications and the IoT at large. The combination of the advantages of each hybrid communication technology pushes IoT from LAN to WAN use cases. As shown in the right side of Fig. 5.11, an intermediate layer (sometimes working as middleware of heterogeneous communication, detailed in Chapter 6) is inserted between WSN and wired IP network. This layer is composed of dual-mode WSN gateways (dual-mode sink). These dual-mode sinks can act as the cluster head of the top level of WSN downward to collect the information/data gathered by WSN nodes. Upwardly, it can be equivalent to the gateway of WSN wireless access system and transmit WSN information back to wired IP network (or wireless WAN, cloud/edge) through

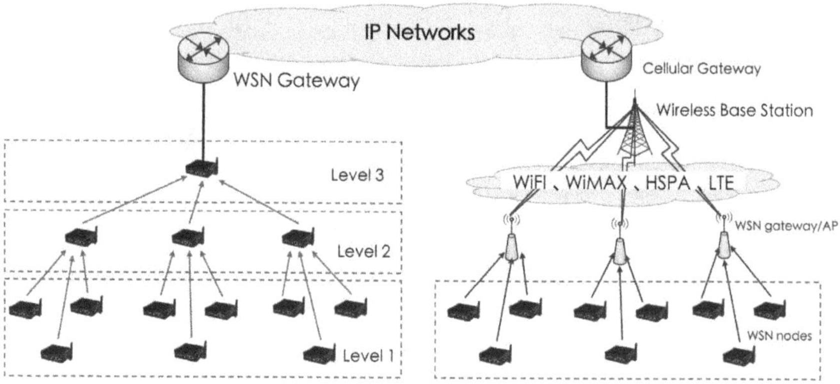

Figure 5.11 Comparison between traditional WSN and heterogeneous fusion WSN.

wireless communication system (including but not limited to Wi-MAX/802.16, 802.15.4, cellular communications such as GPRS/HSPA/LTE or 3G/4G/5G, and SatCom). In fact, the vast majority of WSN application scenarios can always find wireless communication systems such as cellular systems and broadband wireless access systems, so it is not necessary to rely on WSN itself to complete the backhaul (as shown in the right part of Fig. 5.11).

Traditional WSN relies on the *ad hoc* interconnection of WSN nodes to form a multi-level converging WSN network. As shown in the left part of Fig. 5.11, WSN can also access the network in the sink node by wireless way. In recent years, the development of broadband wireless/wired access, broadband SatCom and cellular mobile communication technology has created conditions for the combination of WSN and wireless communication network. Wi-MAX, LTE/3G, 4G or 5G, and other communication systems can provide the backhaul and access of WSN gateway. Compared with the traditional multi-level WSN architecture, this heterogeneous access in the communication and network layer of IoT has the following advantages:

(1) Reduce the number of WSN levels, build a flat network, and realize low delay monitoring/controlling in the multi-mode heterogeneous access.
(2) Increase in the number of WSN gateways can disperse the load of the AP gateway and achieve load balancing.

(3) By using the backhaul capability of broadband wireless or cellular network, multiple access modes can backup each other.
(4) Control the number of multi hops and simplify routing algorithm.
(5) It creates conditions for LPWAN access of WSN, and it provides cellular options for point-to-gateway and point-to-cloud connectivity, in distributed M2M or WAN applications.

As shown in Fig. 5.12, WSN nodes can form a certain scale-leveled network through limited hierarchical aggregation and then backhaul to the mobile communication system through the WSN gateway with the function of mobile terminal (with the dual modes as gateway, and UE from the view of 3GPP). The mobile base station can also directly connect each sensor with the mobile terminal (UE accessing directly), at this time, these sensors are not only WSN nodes, but also WSN gateways.

The former belongs to the "point to gateway" of the three communication prototypes in IoT, as previously mentioned in Section 5.2; the latter belongs to the "point-to-cloud" prototype. The latter structure can ignore the *ad hoc* meshing between WSN nodes and support high real-time monitoring (data traffic in video level) applications.

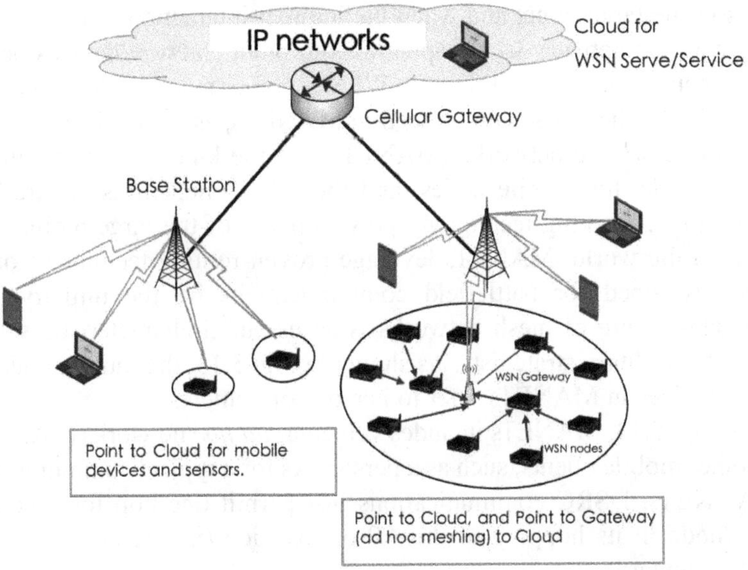

Figure 5.12 Point-to-gateway/M2M and mesh access with AP.

In order to meet the ubiquitous mobile access, there are other solutions. For example, Wi-Fi can be integrated with 6LoWPAN access. Many CIoT standards (e.g., NB-IoT, LTE-M, EC-GSM) and IoT UE (e.g., cat.0, cat.m1, Cat.m2, or on-board unit of vehicles) support point-to-cloud approach (see Section 5.8), including mMTC in 5G and IoE era. Now, an option that is compatible with WSN access module or dual-mode (for both point to gateway and point to cloud) has occurred. Various technologies and products conducive to network integration will appear with the growth of IoT.

Finally, as an extension of Section 4.5, some location awareness features in WSN are discussed in an intelligent model for developing localization pattern in WSN with a group of anchor nodes, rest nodes, and target nodes, in a new book. Readers of special interest in node localization model and the optimization algorithm can read the referred book.

5.4 IEEE 802.11p(DSRC) and VANETs

5.4.1 *DSRC in VANETs*

As mentioned in Chapter 4, wireless sensor network is a self-organization and multi-hop network system which deploys a large number of sensor nodes in the target area, and when the indirect interaction of each sensor node with the network layer capabilities through gateway devices or any *ad hoc* networking capabilities, the WSN becomes a part of the perception layer of IoT. These also can be seen in MANETs, as shown in Fig. 5.13.

Mobile *ad hoc* networks (MANETs) are the kind of wireless multi-hop networks for mobile nodes, and their dynamic, infrastructure-less, and mesh networking technology powers many of the large mobile networks in the world. MANETs leverage proven routing techniques originally developed for battlefield communications by the military. The redundant nature of mesh networks is an essential characteristic sought out by for military strategists. As shown in Fig. 5.13, the mobile nodes as client devices in MANETs refer to persons or vehicles.

In Fig. 5.13, MANETs includes vehicular *ad hoc* networks (VANETs) and other mobile clients, such as a person. As for a typical communication for VANETs, DSRC communications just permit one hop for a vehicle client/node in its hopping to the AP of roadside (i.e., road side unit in DSRC standard).

VANETs belong to a kind of MANETs where the mobile nodes are only referred as vehicles. In VANETs, self-forming, self-healing routing

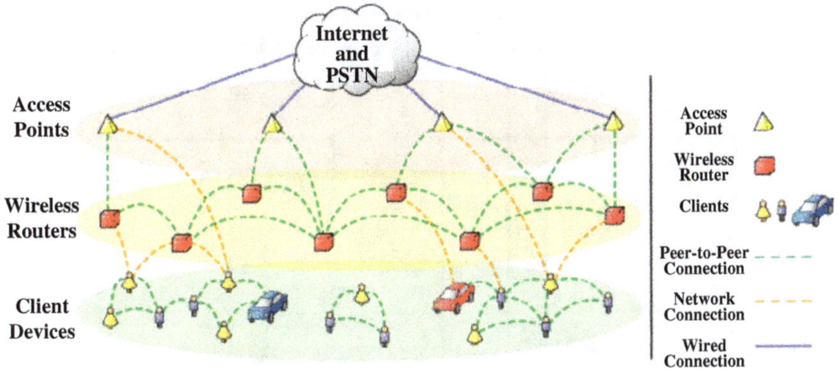

Figure 5.13 MANETs including VANETs and person client devices.

intelligence distributes vehicular clients between APs, eliminating bottlenecks and improving overall network performance. Mesh technology also improves VANETs robustness, as clients/nodes can hop to alternate APs if their current AP is congested or fails. It also lets clients form large, *ad hoc* peer-to-peer networks anywhere, anytime. Peer-to-peer networking reduces the demand on network APs, freeing up capacity for other users.

As a networking prototype of Internet of vehicles (IoVs), VANETs and these capabilities create low-cost, seamless, and simple to deploy wireless PAN/LAN solutions. Even cellular based solutions for wireless WAN in vehicular communications can be found as clues in VANETs, and they are named as "cellular-based vehicle-to-everything (V2X)" communication in the next chapter, in contrast to dedicated short-range communications (DSRC).

Some underlying communication technologies that can be used to support VANETs are regulated as DSRC in the 1990s, and DSRC is an extended version of IEEE 802.11 series for automobile communication.

By using DSRC, the short-distance communication service of public safety and private communication from Road Side Unit (RSU) to vehicle, and from vehicle to vehicle (by on-board unit, OBU) can be realized. DSRC was originally set to have a transmission speed of 6 Mbps over a distance of 300 m. DSRC was widely used in ETC charging and intelligent transportation system (ITS) in many countries.[2]

[2]For example, in Japanese ETC systems, the microwave linking is established between OBU and RSU, by DSRC.

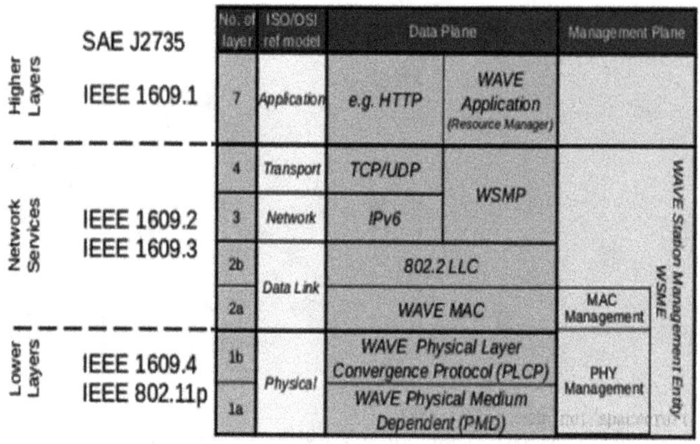

Figure 5.14 DSRC standard stacks.

Before one vehicle establishes communication with another vehicle on the road, it can't tolerate the delay caused by the long-time establishment of the connection considering the fast-moving and complex road conditions; this brings great challenges to the physical layer (PHY, as the OSI model layer1 in Fig. 5.14).

DSRC is considered as IEEE 802.11p (also known as WAVE, wireless access in the vehicular environment), but it is not an independent protocol because it shares the same underlying technical standards with IEEE 1609 series.[3] IEEE 802.11p/WAVE and the layered structure in DSRC stacks are introduced in Fig. 5.14. In the application layer (as the OSI model layer7), IEEE 1609.1 and SAE J2735 defined the relevant applications' standard of the ITS. The application layer includes data exchange between high-speed vehicles and between vehicles and its roadside RSU infrastructure (in 5.9 GHz band).

IEEE 802.11p/WAVE standard is mainly to solve the problem of fast connection, high-frequency switching, and security issues. Some improvements from IEEE 802.11 are as follows:

(1) By designing the functions and services required by the workstation that is consistent with WAVE, i.e., exchanging information in the rapidly changing environment, WAVE BSS as a new type of basic service set (BSS) is introduced to the traditional IEEE 802.11, and others include WAVE short message protocol (WSMP) and WAVE station management entity (WSME).

[3] IEEE 1609.3-2007, WAVE Networking Services.

(2) The definition of WAVE signaling technology, including WAVE physical medium dependent (PMD), physical layer convergence protocol (PLCP) in PHY, multichannel operation, MAC layer management entity (MLME), and physical layer management entity (PLME).
(3) From a technical point of view, IEEE 802.11p/DSRC has made improvements to IEEE 802.11 for special automobiles environments, such as more advanced handover between hot spots, more support for mobile environment, enhanced security, enhanced identity authentication, and so on. DSRC based V2X networking scenarios in 3G era are shown in Fig. 5.15 (in the next section).

5.4.2 *DSRC based V2X*

DSRC is an *ad hoc* technology for V2V and V2I applications. In about 2009, based on cost analysis and technology readiness level, DSRC is expected to be suitable primary communication technology for V2X

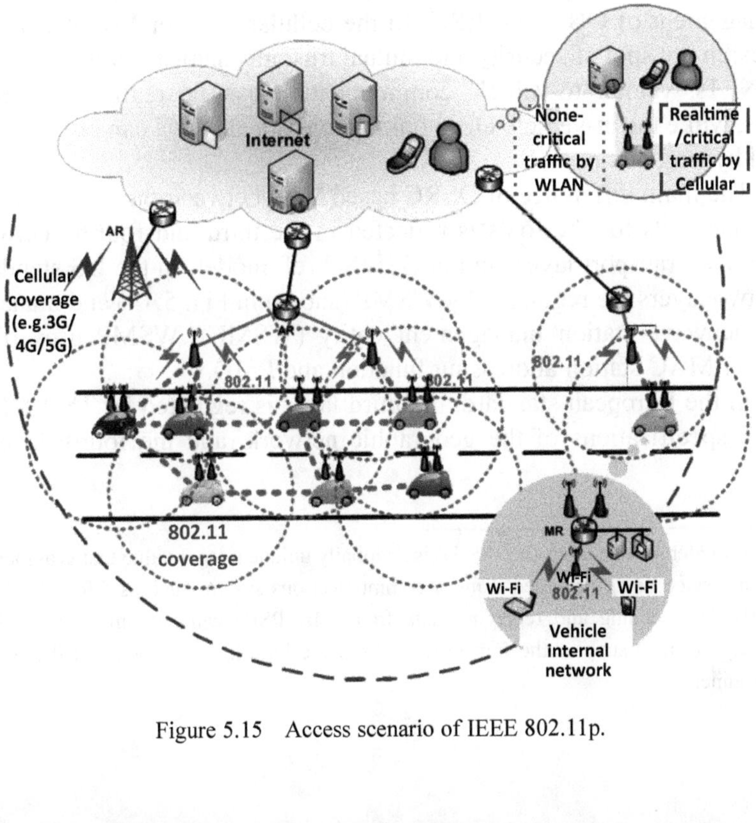

Figure 5.15 Access scenario of IEEE 802.11p.

communication and to be tentatively adopted by the National Highway Traffic Safety Administration (NHTSA), US, for vehicular communication, as shown in Fig. 5.15.

In 2010, DSRC standard was officially released in the US. Under the concept of ITS, four subsystems are proposed as a whole: center subsystem, vehicle subsystem, road subsystem, and pedestrian (passenger) subsystem; for details see the next chapter. Constrained by the cost estimation of the central subsystem, the early development of the central subsystem is not smooth, in contrast with the ITS system of the European Union.

The vehicle subsystem includes the communication among emergency vehicles, commercial vehicles, convenience vehicles, maintenance, and infrastructure; the designed cooperation between the vehicle subsystem and pedestrian subsystem is realized through WWAN/cellular mobile communication; DSRC between the vehicle subsystem and road subsystem are realized through linking OBU with road side unit (RSU) to achieve safety monitoring, roadside payment, parking management, commercial vehicle inspection, etc. Generally, there is a trusted key generation center (KGC), which is responsible for the registration and management of OBU and RSU. In the cellular V2X or IoV, it is also a research hot spot of security and mutual trust mechanism. In the design of VANETs, vehicle-to-vehicle communication can be realized by multi hops, while the in-vehicle OBU linking to roadside RSU can only be realized by single hop.

The main difference of DSRC based V2X between the European and US standards for the IoVs is reflected in the third and fourth "network layer and transport layer" in the OSI/ISO ref. model: In the US standard, the two layers are regulated by WSMP (shown in Fig. 5.14) and managed by the wave station management entity (WSME). WSMP uses IEEE 802.11 MAC station addressing function and PSID.[4]

In the European standard, the third layer is regulated by TS 102636-4-1/2 specifications of the geographic network, and the fourth layer is

[4] The provider service identifier (PSID) is a globally unique integer value that is associated with a service being provided using a communications system such as 5.9 GHz DSRC WAVE. The sending and receiving data frames by PSID can not only communicate securely but also support the transmission from the high-level protocols in the *ad hoc* environment.

regulated by basic transport protocol (BTP). BTP is a transport protocol over a geographic network.[5]

Another major difference is reflected in the application layer of the seven-layer OSI/IOS ref. In the application layer, the European standard defines CAM, DENM,[6] and other application support for local dynamic maps. In addition, the application layer is enriched by application facility layer, which supports more for the information and communication.

Corresponding to VANETs, the academic term for the vehicles in IoVs are connected vehicles (CVs), and the concept of CVs is now extended to connected and intelligent vehicle (CIV), intelligent connected vehicle (ICV), connected and automated vehicle (CAV), and so on.

Furthermore, DSRC and cellular V2X (mentioned later) both belong to the hybrid of point-to-point meshing and point to cloud, from the communication views. They provide the indirect interaction with the network layer capabilities through gateway devices, and *ad hoc* networking capabilities (for V2V and P2P), as well as low-power operation capabilities (e.g., capability to sleep and wakeup) that affect communications. By pushing intelligence and decision making to the edge (e.g., RSU or user function plane in cellular network) of the network, high performance and scalable broadband networks can be built at very low cost using an *ad hoc* or mesh network.

5.5 WPAN/IEEE 802.15.4 and ZigBee

IEEE standards committee, whose task is to develop a low rate WPAN (or LR_PAN) standard, formally approved and established 802.15.4 working group in December 2000, which has the characteristics of low complexity

---

[5]In intelligent transport systems (ITSs) standard by ETSI TS 103 248 V1.2.1, GeoNetworking is for the networking based on the geographic in the network layer. In the transport layer, BTP, port numbers for the BTP and fast networking & transport layer protocol (FNTP) are regulated for upper layer. For details see "SAE J 2945: 2017, Dedicated Short Range Communication (DSRC) Systems Engineering Process Guidance for SAE J2945/X Documents and Common Design Concept", or http://www.ptsn.net.cn/ and https://infostore.saiglobal.com/en-us/Standards/ISO-TS-16460-2016-606707_SAIG_ISO_ISO_1390654/.

[6]Cooperative Awareness Message (CAM, ETSI EN 302 637-2) and Decentralized Environment Notification Message (DENM, ETSI EN 302 637-3). CAM and DENM are built on top of Common Data Dictionary (CDD, ETSI TS 102 894-2).

and low-power consumption and can carry out low data rate transmission between low-cost (or light-weight) devices. IEEE 802.15.4 mainly works at 2.4 GHz and 868/915 MHz with an economical, efficient, and low data rate (<250 kbps) wireless technology. As an important representative of WSN implementation, ZigBee (IEEE 802.15.4) technology is widely used in monitoring and control. IEEE 802.15.4 focuses on 802.15.4e (MAC layer improvement), 802.15.4f (active RFID improvement), 802.15.4g (power application physical layer improvement), etc.

IEEE 802.15.4 is the basis for protocol stacks that target different IoT applications in different sectors; besides ZigBee specifications, others include the proprietary Z-Wave protocol stack for home automation, Wi-SUN Alliance, and ISA100.11a. There is a growing number of examples in industry-specific LAN/PAN protocol stacks where the so-called legacy protocol stacks are needed for legacy device connections.

5.5.1 *Introduction of IEEE 802.15.4*

The IEEE 802.15.4 standard architecture is shown in Fig. 5.16. IEEE 802.15.4 defines PHY and MAC layer, and PHY layer regulation includes

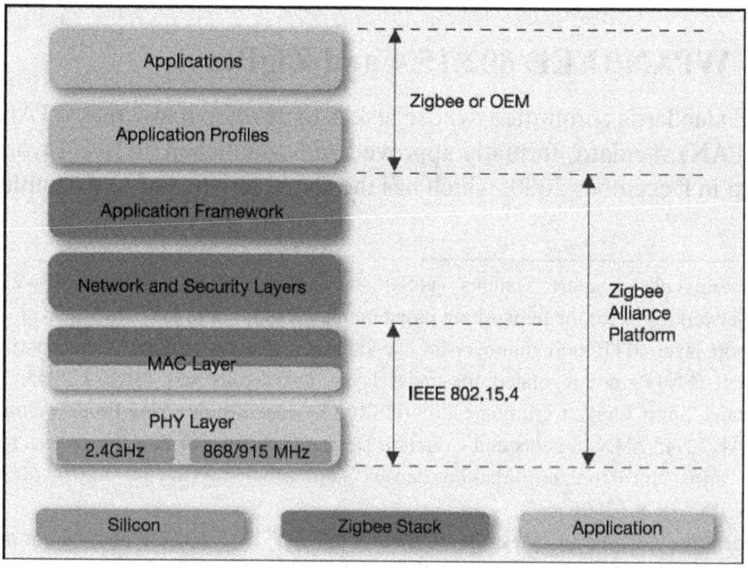

Figure 5.16 IEEE 802.15.4 standard and Zigbee stack architecture.

RF module and physical layer control mechanism; MAC layer provides access control mode and encapsulation of physical channel. On the MAC layer, it provides the interface with the upper layer, which can be directly connected with the network layer (i.e., Lay3 of OSI/ISO ref. model) or through the middle sub-layers (e.g., service specific convergence sub-layer (SSCS) and LLC sub-layer regulated by IEEE 802.2). The relationship between ZigBee and IEEE 802.15.4 is shown in Fig. 5.16.

IEEE 802.15.4 defines two physical layer standards: 2.4 GHz physical layer and 868/915 MHz physical layer. Both physical layers are based on direct sequence spread spectrum (DSSS) and use the same physical layer packet format. The difference lies in the silicon-based RF modulation with working frequency, spread spectrum chip length, and transmission rate. The 2.4 GHz band is a globally unified unlicensed ISM band, which is conducive to the promotion of low-power wireless devices and the reduction of production costs in ISM areas. There are 16 channels in the 2.4 GHz band, which can provide 250 kbit/s transmission rate; 868 MHz is the ISM band in Europe, and 915 MH is the ISM band in the US. The introduction of these two bands avoids the mutual interference of various wireless communication devices near 2.4 GHz. There is only one channel in 868 MHz band and the transmission rate is 20 kbit/s; there are 10 channels in 915 MHz band and the transmission rate is 40 kbit/s. Because the transmission loss of wireless signal in these two bands is small, the requirement of receiver sensitivity can be reduced, and a longer effective communication distance can be obtained, so that a given area can be covered with fewer devices.

The physical layer of 2.4 GHz band adopts O-QPSK modulation, and the 868/915 MHz band adopts BPSK modulation. In addition, carrier sense multiple access with collision avoidance (CSMA-CA) mechanism is adopted in MAC layer, and special time slot (i.e., GTS) is reserved for communication services that need fixed bandwidth to avoid competition and conflict when sending data. These effectively improve the reliability of transmission.

The main features of IEEE 802.15.4 standard are as follows:

(1) Low-power consumption. Generally, the nodes running IEEE 802.15.4 just require the use of low-weight (low-cost) hardware devices (including low-power and computation consuming, e.g., battery powered). Nodes usually have sleep mode and the embedded devices in it are even tiny devices.

(2) Low speed rate. The data transmission rate is low in the bands of 2.4 GHz, 868 MHz, and 915 MHz; the corresponding three rates are 250 kbit/s (2.4 GHz), 20 kbit/s (868 MHz), and 40 kbit/s (915 MHz).
(3) The length of message allowed to be transmitted is short. The maximum message length allowed by MAC layer is 127 bytes. After removing 25 bytes of MAC header, only 102 bytes of MAC data are left. If a security mechanism is added to the MAC, a maximum of 21 bytes of security related fields are needed, so the length of the message provided to the upper layer will be only 81 bytes.
(4) Two addresses are supported. The standard EUI-64 MAC address with the length of 64 bit and the short MAC address with the length of 16 bit can be selected according to the protocol implementation.
(5) Low cost. Usually, some sensors (such as temperature sensors and humidity sensors) are attached to wireless nodes, and the MCU (wireless microcontroller) used to control these sensors is usually low speed, with limited memory inside.
(6) Multi mode: MAC layer defines two transmission modes, one is synchronous mode (beacon-enabled mode), the other is asynchronous mode (beacon-not-enabled mode). In asynchronous mode, CSMA-CA mechanism is directly used to avoid transmission collision, while in synchronous mode, CSMA-CA mechanism based on time slot is used to make the device enter the sleep state when necessary, effectively saving power.

5.5.2 *Zigbee*

By the continuous promotion of Zigbee Alliance, ZigBee standard (including the PHY/MAC regulations of IEEE 802.15.4 in WSNs) has been one of the earliest sensor network standards in the world. ZigBee alliance defines wireless sensor network, from PHY (Physical), link (MAC and LLC), network to application (including transport, session, representation, and application) layers in the OSI/ISO model view. The latter two layers of network and application are shown in the Zigbee stack of Fig. 5.16 as network/security layer and application framework layer, respectively. Other details of Zigbee Alliance working group include protocol stack specification (stack profile), ZigBee cluster library, application profile, test specification, gateway specification, etc., as shown in Fig. 5.17.

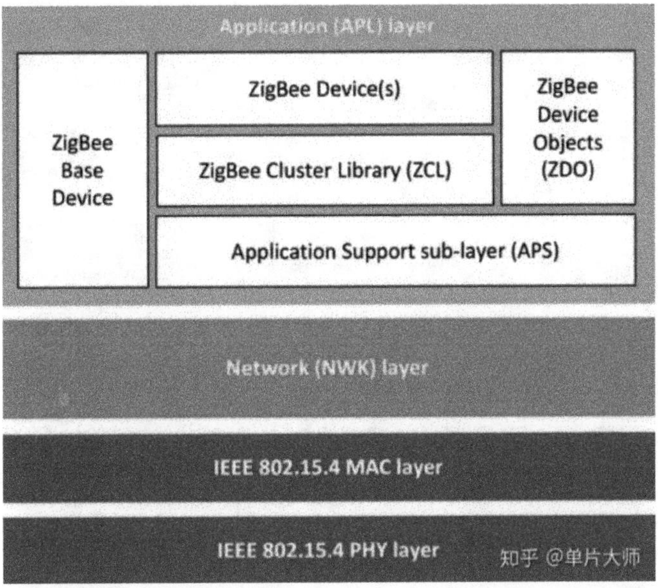

Figure 5.17 Network/Security layer and application framework layer in ZigBee stack.

Notes: ZDO is Zigbee device object; NWK is Network layer including net layer data entity (NLDE) and net layer management entity (NLME); APL/AFL: Application framework layer; APS: Application sub-layer; APSDE: APS data entity.

The underlying PHY (Physical) and link (MAC and LLC) layers of Zigbee stack are regulated by IEEE 802.15.4. MAC layers are in charge of data entity (MLDE) and management entity (MLME), the former service ensures the correct sending and receiving of MAC protocol data unit in the physical layer, and the latter service is engaged in the management activities of MAC layer and the maintenance of information database.

Network layer (NWK) logically includes two parts: data entity (NLDE) service and management entity (NLME) service, as shown in Fig. 5.17. It provides some necessary functions to ensure the correct operation of MAC layer and provides an appropriate service interface for application layer (APL). APL mainly includes application sub-layer (APS), and application framework sub-layer (AFS), where ZigBee device object (ZDO) and application objects (including APS data entity and APS management entity) are defined by SAPs (Service Access Points).

In the ZDO panel (in Fig. 5.17), IEEE 802.15.4/Zigbee defines two types of device objects: reduced function device (RFD) and full function

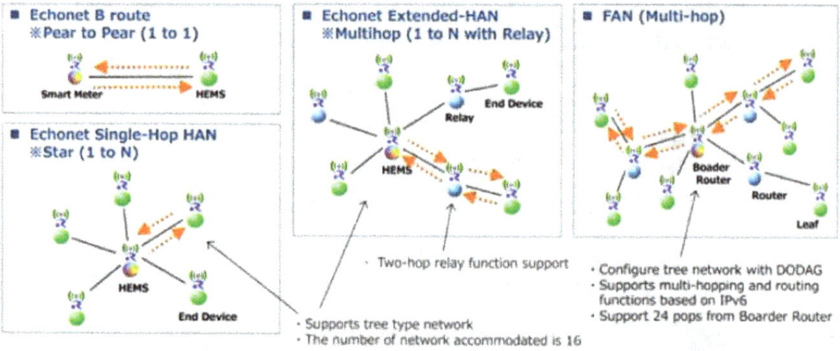

Figure 5.18 *Ad hoc*, star, and their hybrid into tree topologies.

Notes: Star (single-hop), tree, and their meshing in the Echonet HAN extended Echonet HAN, and field area network, respectively. In essence, they are "point to point (*ad hoc* or pear to pear)" and "point to gateway" combined topologies, e.g., DODAG (see Section 5.6.3).
Source: http://www.superfly.com.cn/content/?178.html.

device (FFD). Multiple devices on the same channel form a WPAN, in which one WPAN needs at least one FFD to act as the PAN coordinator. Coordinator refers to a specially configured FFD (typically the cluster head node of a cluster network, as referred in Section 5.3), which provides synchronization services to other nodes/devices (such as relay/end device in Fig. 5.18) by sending beacon frames periodically. If the coordinator is the main controller in a PAN, the coordinator is called PAN coordinator (similar to the sink node or gateway/server in the mesh LAN, in Section 5.2.3.2). The device in the network can use a unique 64-bits long address or a 16-bits short address assigned by the PAN coordinator.

According to different applications, Zigbee networking supports two topologies: single-hop star topology (the same as infrastructure network in Section 5.3.2) and multi-hop (peer-to-peer) topology (the same as *ad hoc* network topology in Section 5.3.2). The star topology consists of a PAN coordinator acting as the central controller and a series of FFDs and RFDs. The relatively simple star topology is shown in the left part of Fig. 5.18.

In the hybrid of the two topologies, tree type network is shown in the center part of Fig. 5.18, as an Echonet[7] use case of the extended

[7]Energy Conservation and HOmecare NETwork (Echonet) established in 1997, is an alliance providing technology for Smart Home/Houses/ Communities/Healthcare, and has ECHONET Specification versions.

PAN/HAN (home area network). The right part of Fig. 5.18 is a hybrid of multi-hopping use case in field area network (in this case, the boarder router as a PAN coordinator supports routing functions based on IPv6).

P2P topology (also known as peer-to-peer, or pear to pear topology) also needs a PAN coordinator but different from star topology; each device in this topology can communicate with other devices directly. Peer-to-peer topology allows more complex network extensions, such as tree topology, mesh topology by multi-hops routing among devices. Other characteristics of Zigbee are shown below:

- **Security management:** ZigBee security management is reflected in the security service provider, e.g., using the optional AES-128 to encrypt the communication, for ensuring the integrity of the data. The security management provided by ZigBee security system mainly relies on symmetric key protection, application protection mechanism, appropriate password mechanism, and relevant security measures. The implementation of security protocol (such as the establishment of key) should be based on the correct operation of ZigBee protocol stack without missing any step. MAC layer, NWK layer, and APS layer all have reliable security transmission mechanism for their own data frames. APS layer provides the service of establishing and maintaining security contact, and ZDO manages the security policy and security configuration of devices.
- **Networking:** Zigbee 3.0 (or Zigbee IP) by ZigBee Alliance is a networking solution used on top of IEEE 802.15.4 radio technology, which includes Wi-Fi and IP Internet capability. Zigbee 3.0 has meshing capability and is used as an IoT connectivity solution for a range of smart home and industrial applications, including lighting, security, thermostats, and remote controls. It is secure and supports battery-free devices, meshing, low latency, and energy harvesting. Zigbee 3.0 also includes Zigbee Green Power, which was developed as an ultra-low-power wireless standard to support energy-harvesting IoT devices and is effective for IoT devices that are only sometimes on the network (i.e., when they have power), enabling them to go on and off the network securely, so they can be off most of the time. As for Zigbee Smart Energy, it provides the applications of XML/HTTP/EXI for web services, by using URL structure, data handling, and event handling.
- **Simple topology:** The network topology is rich, supporting star topology and point-to-point topology, and supporting the hybrid networking of the

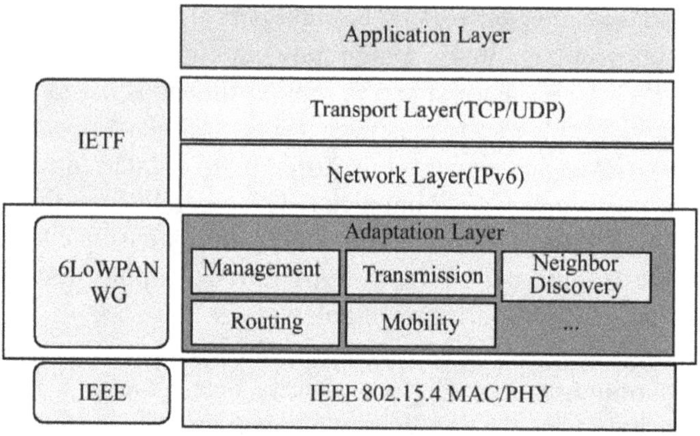

Figure 5.19 6LoWPAN stacks.

two basic topologies as meshing. For example, star network, tree network, and mesh network can operate multi-hop routing in topology.

- **Multi-device type:** Generally, it is divided into full function device (FFD) and reduced function device (RFD). FDF is powerful, suitable for star topology and point-to-point topology, and can communicate directly with RFD and FDF; RFD is used for star topology and can only communicate directly with FDF, so it has a simple function and requires little computing and storage resources.

5.5.3 *6LoWPAN*

IPv6 over low-power wireless personal area networks (6LoWPAN) is a network protocol that was developed initially by the 6LoWPAN WG of the IETF as a mechanism to transport IPv6 over IEEE 802.15.4-2003 networks. The standard defines encapsulation and header compression mechanisms, considering the fragmentation reassembling in the large size of IPv6 packets and the limited space in the protocol data unit.

IoT on the Internet layer is the adaptation of the layer's functions to link layer technologies with restricted frame size. The base maximum frame size for 802.15.4 is 127 bytes, out of which 25 bytes need to be reserved for the frame header and another 21 bytes for link layer security. IEEE 802.15.4 g increased the maximum frame size to 2047 bytes, which make it possible to compress IPv6 packet headers over the link layer.

The standard has the freedom of a frequency band and a physical layer and can also be used across multiple communications platforms, including Ethernet, Wi-Fi, IEEE 802.15.4, and sub-1 GHz ISM.

As shown in Fig. 5.19, the IETF WG also developed methods to handle address auto configuration, the hooks for mesh networking, network management, and neighbor discovery; in IETF RFCs including RFC 4919 (problem statement), RFC 6282 (header compression), and RFC 6775 (neighbor discovery).

In the adaptation layer of 6LoWPAN, the IETF routing over low-power and lossy networks (RoLL) WG defined RPL (IPv6 routing protocol for low-power and lossy networks) for the low-power lossy networks (typically characterized by high data loss rates, low data rates, and general instability). 6LoWPAN provides three main functions, IPv6 header compression, IPv6 packet segmentation and reassembly, and layer 2 forwarding. 6LoWPAN allows compressing the IPv6 header into two bytes, as most of the information is already encoded into the link layer header.

6LoWPAN operates in the 2.4 GHz frequency band providing a data rate of 250 kbps with a coverage range of 100 m. The security implemented is AES-128 link layer security defined in IEEE 802.15.4 protocol providing link authentication and encryption. Security features defined in (IETF) RFC 5246 standard are enabled by the transport layer security mechanisms over TCP. The RFC 6347 standard defines the transport layer security mechanisms over UDP.

The protocol is implementing open IP standards including TCP, UDP, HTTP, COAP, MQTT, and web sockets, and offers end-to-end addressable nodes, allowing a router to connect the network to IPs. 6LoWPAN is a mesh network that is robust, scalable, and self-healing. Mesh router devices can route data destined for other IoT devices, while hosts are able to sleep for periods.

For capillary networks (short-range IoT communications, compared to WAN and typical cellular networks) that expose devices to the cloud/Internet, IP is envisioned to be the common protocol waist. IPv6 is to be the protocol of choice for IoT devices that operate a 6LoWPAN-based stack. IPv4 is used for capillary networks operating in non-6LoWPAN IP stacks (e.g., Wi-Fi capillary networks). The protocols from capillary to cellular (or WAN) will be introduced in the next section, where the LPWA stacks will be taken as an example, when considering the links over PLC, IEEE 802.15.4, low-power Wi-Fi and Wi-SUN.

5.5.3.1 *Wi-SUN and SUN*

Wireless smart ubiquitous network (Wi-SUN) is an open standards-based field area network (FAN) used for the IoT and can support applications such as advanced metering infrastructure, distribution automation, intelligent transport and traffic systems, street lighting, and smart home automation. The suite of IoT technologies is based on IEEE 802.15.4g (in PHY/MAC layer), TCP/IP, and related standard protocols with a bandwidth of up to 300 kbps, a low latency of 20 ms, power efficiency (less than 2 mA when resting; 8 mA when listening), resilience, scalability (networks up to 5,000 devices; 10 million end points worldwide), and using security mechanisms based on public key certificates, AES, HMAC, dynamic key refresh, and hardened crypto. The network layer is IPv6 with 6LoWPAN adaptation supporting star and mesh (multi-hops) topologies as well as hybrid star/mesh deployments.

IEEE 802.15.4g seeks to extend the operational coverage of these networks up to tens of kilometers in order to provide extremely wide geographic coverage with minimal infrastructure. As for *smart utility* network (**SUN**) devices, in IEEE wireless personal area networks (LR-WPANs) standard *for* Low-Rate Wireless *Networks Amendment 3* (*in 2012*), LR-WPANs defined some enhancements to the SUN including PHYs specifications to support SUN (smart grid in particular).

So, SUN is an overlapping word of Wi-SUN, and **SUNs** conform at least to the IEEE 802.15.4g standard. The *latest Amendment 7* (*in 2019*) of IEEE 802.15.4g towards SUN was the defining enhancements for PHYs to support up to 2.4 Mb/s data rates.

IETF (LwM2M WG) defines a framework for device and service enablement of Wi-SUN, and Wi-SUN Alliance defines conformance and interoperability test specifications for wireless IoT mesh networks based on the IEEE 802.15.4g standard for utility networks. Other alliances can work on identifying, agreeing on, and defining best practices on how to build IoT solutions.

With IPv6 networking, IETF attention is paid to the ongoing work to facilitate the use of IP to enable interoperability irrespective of the physical and link layers (i.e., making the fact that devices are networked, with or without wires, with various capabilities in terms of range and bandwidth, essentially seamless). It is foreseeable that the only hard requirement for an embedded device will be that it can somehow connect with a compatible gateway device (assuming it is a capillary device without an in-built WAN connectivity, i.e., a cellular modem). The advances in this space have been driven by the IETF in request for comments (RFC) specifications and documents, in a continuous standardization perspective.

5.5.3.2 *Comparison with IEEE 802.11ah and BLE*

As introduced before, IEEE 802.11ah (low-power Wi-Fi/Wi-Fi HaLow) and BLE are also low-power short-range communications for IoT. Wi-Fi HaLow was extended up to a 1,000 m range and improved energy efficiency for IoT applications that could exploit burst-like transmissions, such as in metering applications. BLE was originally developed and maintained as IEEE 802.15.1 and Bluetooth SIG. It is designed for short-range (<50 m) applications in healthcare, fitness, security, etc., where high data rates (millions of bits per second) are required to enable application functionality. Table 5.4 gives the comparison of BLE, IEEE 802.11ah, Wi-SUN, ZigBee, and 6LoWPAN.

Low-rate, low-power networks are among the key technologies that form the basis of the IoT. And many of them are regulated by "IEEE 802.15.4 — Wireless Medium Access Control (MAC) and Physical Layer (PHY) Specifications for Low-Rate Wireless Personal Area Networks (LR-WPANs)", as mentioned before. The IEEE 802.15.4 family of standards supports data rates from 20 Kbps up to 256 Kbps, depending on the selected band, over distances ranging from tens of meters to kilometers (also depending on transmission power level). Typically, radio transceivers developed in compliance with this standard consume power in the tens of milli-Watts range in active modes. "Low-Power" of IEEE 802.15.4 often means long-lasting battery life (i.e., >5 years) for continuous operation or energy harvested operation, without aggressively duty cycling the active period of the transceiver. Radio duty cycling refers to managing the active periods of the radio frequency integrated circuit (RFIC) during transmission and listening to the medium. It is typically quantified as a percentage with respect to active time.

When considering the internetworking between Zigbee/802.15.4 and IPv6/802.3, how to network ZigBee device over the TCP/IP is a problem. Since the TCP/IP has become the dominant protocol on the Internet due to its widespread use and reliability, the wired 802.3 Ethernet meets the demand for internetworking between ZigBee/802.15.4 and

Table 5.4 Comparison of BLE, IEEE 802.11ah, Wi-SUN, ZigBee, and 6LoWPAN.

Specifications	**BLE (Bluetooth)**	**IEEE 802.11ah (Wi-Fi HaLow)**	**Wi-SUN**	**ZigBee**	**6LoWPAN**
Modulation	GFSK/DQPSK/DPSK	OFDM	Multi-Rate FSK (MR-FSK), with 2-FSK or 4-FSK,etc.	BPSK/O-QPSK	BPSK/O-QPSK
MAC	802.15.1 (FDMA/TDMA)	802.11 (CSMA/CA)	802.15.4g (CSMA/CA)	802.15.4 (CSMA/CA)	802.15.4 (CSMA/CA)
Data rate	3 Mbps	100 Kb/s	Up to 2.4 Mb/s	250 kbps	250 kbps
Battery power for device (/days)	1–5 (use case dependent)	300–1000	1000	100–1000	1000
Coverage	Up to 50 m	Up to 1000 m	Up to 100 00 m	Up to 100 m	Up to 100 m
Topology of networking	Mesh	Mesh	Mesh	Mesh	Mesh

TCP/IP/802.3 by providing fixed AP. However, when a legacy ZigBee device itself is not compatible with the IP-based network, sensor networks and IP can play together by means of three approaches:

(1) The straightforward method to make IPv6 work over ZigBee is to put the IPv6 stack on the top of ZigBee NWK layer. All the ZigBee nodes are assigned with an IPv6 address in the application layer gateways (ALGs). ZigBee gateway device is taken as an example of ALGs, which translates from ZigBee to simple object access protocol (SOAP) and IPv6 or gateways that translate from constrained application protocol (CoAP) to hypertext transfer protocol/representational state transfer (HTTP/REST).
(2) Another approach is IP-Net. It is a dual-stack approach. Both the 6LoWPAN design and ZigBee stack are working on the same 802.15.4 MAC.
(3) A gateway that allows both a 6LoWPAN and Zigbee device indifferently to be converted to IPv6 would be desirable. An interoperable gateway will be introduced in the next section.

5.6 Gateways and Protocols

A gateway typically includes multiple networking technologies and serves as a translator between different physical interfaces and protocols, e.g., IEEE 802.15.4 or IEEE 802.11 to Ethernet or cellular (i.e., point to cloud or WAN by means of cellular gateway and its protocols translator, or from "point-to-point" meshing to an AP/gateway).

5.6.1 *Gateways*

Gateways also often include a local or capillary networking technology and a WAN interface. A gateway refers to a device that performs translation or conversion on different levels of the stack (physical, link, network, transport layers of OSI/ISO model) between different network interfaces.

Gateways are used to provide an end-to-end communication service that bridges a LAN (for legacy devices, such as non-IP industry-specific LAN protocol stacks) and a WAN in physical and link layers, traditionally.

From a communication layer and interworking perspective, gateways are primarily used to do protocol translation at different levels of the protocol stack. But when gateways involved in the network layers (third layer in ISO/OSI model), the interworking on the communications or messaging level, e.g., between a legacy protocol like ZigBee to exchanging service operations using HTTP/REST as the means for communication; the various LAN and WAN aspects with their stack are discussed by IETF, and zigbee/6LoWPAN protocols translation as the example introduced in the following part after the discussion of gateways in details.

5.6.1.1 *Basic gateways*

From the basic view of gateways, the hardware, software, and protocols are typically focused on simplicity and low cost, but frequently the gateway devices are also used for many other tasks, such as data management (DM) and local applications, in the perception layer or up to the communication layer when necessary. In these cases, typical DM functions include sensor data collection, data visualization, local storage and synchronization with remote storage (e.g., cloud), processing of sensor readings, and caching of processed data, as well as filtering, concentrating, and aggregating the data before transmitting it to the communication layer, and then to backend or cloud/edge servers for the diversity of applications.

In the local applications, some basic devices (as IoT modular integrated connectivity) enabled by high-speed data and voice and various onboard selected 802.11 Wi-Fi/HaLow, Bluetooth, ZigBee, 6LoWPAN, Z-Wave protocols with the simultaneous use of multiple ISM radio bands (i.e., 169/433/868/902 MHz, 2.4 GHz, and 5 GHz). The basic connectivity modules are based on integrated circuits (ICs), reference designs, and feature-rich software stacks created according to a flexible modular concept, which properly addresses various applications (by their inter link gateway) in a local domain (PAN/LAN).

In short, basically the IoT gateway device is an integrated microsystem with multiple communication interfaces and computational capabilities as before. Now, it is a more and more critical component in the functional architecture, either allowing local usage to LAN, then to WAN or cloud (an example is the central gateway in Fig. 5.20), or being capable of handling all of the necessary interfacing to the cloud-based IoT services (a point/device to cloud or wireless WAN example as the right gateway in Fig. 5.20).

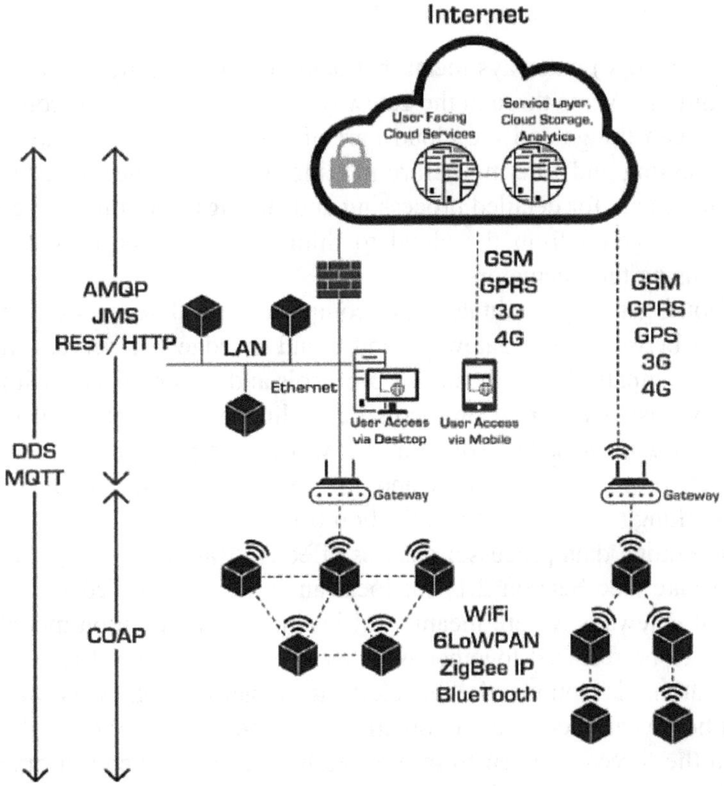

Figure 5.20 Gateways and protocols in IoT (without LPWA/LPWAN).

As to the build-in IoT gateway modular, the integrated connectivity creates a scalable mobile platform (modems for 2G/3G/4G/5G), enabling data transmission by M2M gateways which integrated in the same cellular device (UE, as cell phone from 3GPP view). It also works as a fixed or mobile AP for various onboard devices mentioned above.

When the created feature-rich software stacks for the across application domains and the interworking of different level (e.g., data/service level and management/security level) is required for flexible interoperability, cloud gateways appear, which often share some capabilities with middleware properly (see Section 6.1).

5.6.1.2 *Cloud gateway*

Cloud (or Edge) gateways mean that data goes from things to the cloud/edge and vice versa through the gateways. A gateway provides connectivity between things and the cloud part of the IoT solution, enables data preprocessing and filtering before moving it to the cloud (to reduce the volume of data for detailed processing and storing), and transmits control commands going from the cloud to things. Things then execute commands using their actuators.

Cloud gateway facilitates data compression and secures data transmission between field gateways and cloud or edge IoT servers. It also ensures compatibility with various protocols and communicates with field gateways using different protocols depending on what protocol is supported by gateways. And sometimes it works as a platform, both for feature-rich protocols translation and for services or information models interworking (e.g., OPC-UA in Section 6.1).

Streaming data processor ensures effective transition of input data to a data lake (see Section 2.1) for local analytics or cloud/edge analytics through gateways, where meaningful insights or information models are needed to be released together with services. Then, control applications send automatic commands and alerts to actuators, e.g., windows of a smart home can receive an automatic command to open or close depending on the forecasts taken from the weather service. When sensors show that the soil is dry, watering systems get an automatic command to water plants. Sensors help monitor the state of industrial equipment, and in case of a pre-failure situation, an IoT system generates and sends automatic notifications to field gateway or cloud gateway.

The commands sent by control apps to actuators can be also additionally stored in a big data warehouse. This may help investigate problematic cases (e.g., a control app sends commands, but they are not performed by actuators — then, connectivity, gateways, and actuators need to be checked). On the other side, storing commands from control apps may contribute to security, as an IoT system can identify that some commands are too strange or come in too big amounts which may evidence security breaches (as well as other problems which need investigation and corrective measures).

Control applications can be either rule-based or machine-learning based. In the first case, control apps work according to the rules stated by specialists. In the second case, control apps are using models which are regularly updated (once a week or once in a month depending on the specifics of an IoT system) with the historical data stored in a big data warehouse.

Although control applications ensure better automation of an IoT system, there should be always an option for users to influence the behavior of such applications (e.g., in cases of emergency or when it turns out that an IoT system is badly tuned to perform certain actions).

User applications are a software component of an IoT system that enables the connection of users to an IoT system and gives the options to monitor and control their smart things (while they are connected to a network of similar things, e.g., homes or cars and controlled by a central system). With a mobile or web app, users can monitor the state of their things, send commands to control applications, and set the options of automatic behavior (automatic notifications and actions when certain data comes from sensors), and data/services/devices management are often included in cloud/edge gateways or together with a server.

As to **device management** for sufficient functioning of IoT devices, some procedures are required to manage the performance of connected devices, e.g., facilitate the interaction between devices and ensure secure data transmission in a secure cloud infrastructure including the cloud gateways, edge devices, and more. Device identification to establish the identity of the device to be sure that it's a genuine device with trusted software transmitting reliable data. In the configuration and control to tune devices according to the purposes of an IoT system, some parameters need to be written once a device is installed (e.g., unique device ID). Other settings might need updates (e.g., the time between sending messages with data). Monitoring and diagnostics ensure smooth and secure performance of every device in a network and reduce the risk of breakdowns. Software updates and maintenance are required to add functionality, fix bugs, address security vulnerabilities. Some of them can be attributed to basic IoT gateways or edge devices with basic translating protocols function and limited device management. When considering beneficial knowledge and constructive control, **advance managements**, such as user management or security monitoring, should attribute to the cloud/edge gateways. Alongside device management, user management is also important to provide control over the users having access to an IoT system.

User management involves identifying users, their roles, access levels, and ownership in a system. It includes such options as adding and removing users, managing user settings, access controlling of various users to certain information, as well as the permission to perform certain operations within a system, controlling and recording user activities, and more. **Security management** is one of the top concerns in the IoT. Connected things produce huge volumes of data, which need to be securely transmitted and protected from cyber-criminals. Another side is that the things connected to the Internet can be entry points for villains. What is more, cyber-criminals can get access to the "brain" of the whole IoT system and take control of it. To prevent such problems, it makes sense to log and analyze the commands sent by control applications to things, monitor the actions of users, and store all these data in the cloud. With such an approach, it's possible to address security breaches at the earliest stages and take measures to reduce their influence on an IoT system (e.g., block certain commands coming from control applications and further use cases in a safety zone will be discussed in the last chapter). Some of these advance managements, such as access control and secure communication, can be shared with either the underlying communication protocols or an IoT platform which will be under focus in the following chapter.

Also, the knowledge relative management makes it possible to identify the patterns of suspicious behavior (see Sections 4.3 or 4.7), store these malicious samples, and compare them with the logs generated by an IoT system to prevent potential penetrations and minimize their impact on an IoT system. These issues will be discussed in secure middleware relative section as a collective bionics defense and be furthered in the discussion of federal learning in the last chapter.

Figure 5.20 shows the functional view of IoT gateways, where protocols and service are typically focused on the power releasing from local (proximity network, such as PAN/WPAN) to anywhere needed. Simply, in some WSN technologies, such as Wi-Fi and Z-Wave, the gateway is used for the inclusion and exclusion of devices. When considering the extending of WSN in LAN/PAN to encompass the idea of WPANs, IoT gateways and protocols include the description used for the series standards that govern low-power, low-rate networks suitable for IoT applications (among the so-called light-weight devices, such as the above-mentioned IoT modular). The standards and protocols not only include the IEEE 802.15.4-based series (MAC/PHY specifications) for low-rate WPANs (LR-WPANs), such as ZigBee, wireless HART, and other IETF initiatives 6TiSCH, 6LoWPAN, RPL, and CoAP, but also some penetrating protocols (including DDS and MQTT/AMQP) and REST/HTTP (for the better usage of IP-based web services). Some of them are described in Fig. 5.20.

With the introduction of IPv6 into 6LoWPAN, ALGs may provide a dual-stack gateway for the translation of IPv4/IPv6 and the translation to SOAP, and another option is the adaptation layer inserted between the network layer and underlying PHY/link layer (see the next section). Typically, IoT gateways that translate from CoAP to HTTP/REST are shown in the center of Fig. 5.20.

LR-WPAN, as described in IEEE 802.15.4 technology, is still undergoing amendments and upgradation (e.g., modifying and/or extending PHY parameters to ensure global utility concerning licensing, application suitability, and modifications to the MAC layer), along with a similar stepping of Wi-Fi/WLAN technology (e.g., from Wi-Fi 3 to Wi-Fi 6, etc.) and the evolution of contemporary related IoT technologies and protocols.

5.6.1.3 *M2M gateways*

From the view of a device to cloud directly, a gateway function integrated inside device is taken as an M2M example. The device incorporates both an IEEE 802.15.4–compliant transceiver (such as the Texas Instruments CC2520), capable of communicating with a LAN (or meshing capillary) network of similarly equipped devices and a cellular transceiver (a popular example of which is a Telit LN940A9) that connects to the Internet using the LTE/4G (or 5G) mobile network. This assumes the handover to the backbone IP network is handled according to the 3GPP specifications.

Transceivers sometimes referred to as modems or modules are typically available as hardware modules with which the central intelligence of the device (gateway or cell phone) interacts by means of standardized (sometimes vendor-specific) AT Commands. This device is now capable of acting as a physical proxy between the LR-WPAN and the cloud (or WWAN) in dual modes of both coordinator and gateway.

In this case, gateways and M2M communications in the ETSI M2M functional architecture, and 3GPP machine type communication (MTC) are to be described in the next two sections.

5.6.1.4 *Smart gateways*

Smart gateway is a broad concept, which can be referred as an extension of cloud/edge gateway. First is the compatibility for heterogeneous devices. At the lowest level, there are sensors and actuators. These are connected to the different input modules. These modules take care of connectivity with wireless smart objects. This smart gateway provides interoperability among very different network technologies and protocols for devices/services and even across platform interoperability. In addition to Wi-Fi and Bluetooth, INTER-IoT gateway supports network protocols and technologies specifically designed for IoT, such as CoAP, MQTT, and LoRa, as well as advanced techniques for offloading. The gateway in a middleware platform for multi protocols translation will be discussed in Section 6.1.3.

Second, the security and availability in certain industries are required in wide-area collaboration. Therefore, different types of networks are needed to address IoT products, services, and techniques providing at the edge/cloud to improve the grade of service (GoS), QoS, and quality of experience (QoE) for end users. Customization-based solutions are addressing the IIoT while moving to a managed wide-area communications system and ecosystem collaboration.

Finally, smart gateways will be needed at a lower cost to simplify the infrastructure complexity for end consumers, enterprises, and industrial environments. Multifunctional, multiprotocol processing gateways are likely to be deployed for IoT devices and combined with Internet protocols and different communication protocols. Some of the protocols are introduced below, according to Fig. 5.20.

5.6.2 *Protocols*

Protocols ensure effective communication between different objects or networks, and guaranteeing a continuous bond among them, which is a critical goal pursued by IoT. They also improve the interoperability of devices, approaches, and design for interworked IoT/WSN systems.

In the communication and networks layer of IoT, some common sets of protocols for end-to-end message exchange are listed below. Almost all of them support the publish–subscribe (pub–sub) model, which is a messaging pattern where message senders (publishers) categorize messages into classes without the receiver's (subscriber) knowledge, and in turn, the subscriber shows interest in one or more message classes to receive their messages. Another important IoT service model called DDS, together with pub-sub model, will be introduced in Section 6.1, as a type of middlewares example. Their underlying communication protocols from different standardization bodies and special interest groups are summarized as follows:

1. CoAP: Constrained Application Protocol for IoT applications, created by the IETF Constrained Restful Environment (CoRE) working group (WG), was developed as a specialized web transfer protocol for use with severe computational and communication constraints typically characteristic of IoT applications. Essentially, CoAP elaborates a simple request/response interaction model between application endpoints (e.g., from an IoT application to an IoT device). REST is essentially a simplification of the ubiquitous HTTP and thus allows for simple integration between them. This is especially powerful for integrating typical Internet computing applications with constrained devices.

CoAP is REST-centric (supports GET, POST, PUT, DELETE) and UDP-based. Although it can be used to compress HTTP interfaces, it offers additional functionalities, such as built-in discovery, multicast support, and asynchronous message exchanges. From the security point of view, several approaches are supported ranging from no-security up to certificate-based using DTLS. For other relative protocols in IETF RFCs and IETF WGs, see the next section.

2. XMPP: eXtensible Messaging and Presence Protocol is a relatively simple protocol that occurs over TCP sockets using XML messages. XMPP is an IETF (RFC 3920) instant messaging (IM) standard for asynchronous communication that occurs within XML streams and by which an IM communication occurs using XMPP between two clients.

As an example in IEC 61850, by providing a communication stack for interconnection in WAN based on applying XMPP for mapping information, this standard is appropriate for use in the smart grid communication.

XMPP is not alone as a general-purpose messaging transport. Other popular protocols, such as XML-RPC and SOAP, can provide this capability with function call–like semantics. Newer methods such as representational state transfer (ReST/Restful) provide managed file access using URLs to specify the location, object, and methods (e.g., the Restful as GET, PUT, POST, DELETE).

3. MQTT: Message Queue Telemetry Transport linking embedded devices and networks with applications and middleware. As previously mentioned, MQTT is a reliable low-bandwidth lightweight protocol developed for satellite monitoring of pipelines (originally). To provide simplicity and flexibility, asynchronous publish/subscribe model is used in MQTT. Moreover, MQTT has three levels of QoS (QoS0, QoS1, QoS2). And the TLS/SSL protocol provides secure MQTT transactions, including small code footprints (e.g., eight bit, 256 kb ram) and running on light-weight devices (e.g., with less than 65kb RAM).

4. AMQP: Advanced Message Queuing Protocol is largely used in the financial sector applications and applied to other types of applications. The protocol is standardized by Organization for the Advancement of Structured Information Standards (OASIS). AMQP is based on asynchronous publish/subscribe model and runs over TCP and is a binary message-oriented that provides message delivery guarantees for reliability, including at least once, at most once, and exactly once. The protocol offers flow control through a token-based mechanism to ensure that a receiving endpoint is not overburdened with more messages than it is capable of handling. AMQP is an interoperable and cross platform messaging standard. Different open-source implementations of the AMQP protocol are available.

5. DDS: Data Distributed Service, developed by the Object Management Group (OMG), was designed for low-latency data transmission (details in Section 6.1).

6. JMS: Java Message Service was designed to develop applications that asynchronously send and receive business data and events by defining a common messaging API that is supported by a wide range of enterprise messaging products. JMS supports both messaging models: point-to-point (queuing) and pub-sub. JMS falls under message-oriented middleware (MOM), which is a relatively low level of abstraction that runs underneath complementary layers such as database and application adapters, event processing, and business process automation. MOM is becoming an essential component for integrating intra-company operations, along with other middlewares, which allows separate business components to be combined into a heterogeneous IoT system (see Section 6.1).

The above short introduction of protocols is usually referred as application protocols, which are based on different communication technologies and protocols. Table 5.5 gives their technical description. Some of the above protocols will be introduced again in Chapter 6, where the focus is on the services of IoT and the internetworked service capabilities, including soft supporting for heterogeneous IoT (e.g., SOA and middlewares).

As seen in Table 5.5, DASH7 (D7A) protocol complies with the ISO/IEC 18000-7 standard, which is an open standard for the license-free 433 MHz ISM band air-interface for wireless communications. Using 433 MHz frequency provides D7A devices with long propagation distance and better penetration in objects (e.g., buildings). The protocol defines four different device classes, namely blinker that only transmits and does not use a receiver, endpoint that can transmit and receive the data and supports wake-up events, sub controller that is a full-featured device using wake on scan cycles similar to end points, and gateway that connects D7A network with the other networks and is always online and always listens unless it is transmitting. DASH7 uses AES-CBC for authentication and AES-CCM for authentication and encryption.

For weightless-SIG protocols and Telensa as the proprietary LPWAs, see the last part of this section, and for 3GPP related as cellular LPWAs see the next section.

5.6.3 *Protocols of IETF IoT-Related WPAN*

Some contributions of the IETF WGs, such as 6LoWPAN, 6Lo, LPWAN, and ipwave WGs, are introduced shortly, and the main theme is the defining adaptation layers for IPv6 for different PHY/MAC technologies. The 6LoWPAN WG defined the **adaptation** layer between IEEE 802.15.4 to IPv6 and also 6LoWPAN neighborhood discovery (6LoWPAN ND) on top of ICMP. The 6Lo WG has defined adaptation layers for IPv6 over G.9959, MS/TPBLE, DECT ULE, BTMesh, and NFC. The LPWAN WG defined adaptation layers of IPv6 over LoRaWAN, NB-IoT, Sigfox, and Wi-SUN, and the recommended layers on top of IPv6 are UDP and CoAP. The ipwave WG defines an adaptation layer of IPv6 over IEEE 802.11-OCB.

5.6.3.1 *IETF LR-WPAN protocols and security aspects*

In IETF-related WG, RoLL WG defined a new ICMP v6 message, with three possible types, specific for RPL networks (see Section 5.5.3). These

Table 5.5 Technical specifications for standardization bodies and special interest groups for IoT communication solutions.

Standardization Bodies and Special Interest Groups	Name	Modulation	Band	MAC	Data Rate	Coverage	Number of Channels
IEEE	IEEE 802.15.4 k (**Ingenu**)	DSSS, FSK	ISM SUB-GHz and 2.4 GHz	CSMA/CA, ALOHA with PCA	1.5–128 kbps	5 km (urban)	Multiple (depends on channel and modulation)
	IEEE 802.15.4 g	**FSK, OFDMA, OQPSK**	**ISM SUB-GHz and 2.4 GHz**	**CSMA/CA**	**4.8–800 kbps**	**Up to several km**	Multiple (depends on channel and modulation)
Weightless-SIG	Weightless-SIG-W	16QAM, DBPSK	TV white spaces (470–790 MHz)	TDMA/FDMA	1 kbps–10 Mbps	5 km (urban)	16 or 24
	Weightless-SIG-N	DBPSK	**ISM SUB-GHz**	ALOHA	30–100 kbps	Up to 3 km (urban)	Multiple, 200 Hz each
	Weightless-SIG-P	GPSK, QPSK	ISM SUB-GHz or licensed	TDMA/FDMA	200 bps–100 kbps	Up to 2 km(urban)	**Multiple, 12.5 kHz each**
DASH Alliance	DASH7(D7A)	GFSK	SUB-GH	CSMA/CA	9.6, 55.6, or 166.7 kbps	Up to 5 km (urban)	Multiple, 25 or 200 kHz each
3GPP	EC-GSM	8PSK, GMSK	Licensed GSM	TDMA/FDMA	74–240 kbps	Up to 15 km	124 channels, 200 kHz each
	NB-IoT	QPSK, 16QAM, 64QAM,	Licensed LTE	SC-FDMA (UL) OFDMA (DL)	20 kbps (UL) 200 kbps (DL)	35 km	Multiple, 180 kHz each
	eMTC (LTE-M)	QPSK, 16QAM, 64QAM,	Licensed LTE	OFDMA/SC-FDMA	1 Mbps	Up to 15 km	Multiple, 200 kHz each
ESTI	Telensa (LTN)	BPSK(UL) GFSK(DL) or OSSS	ISM SUB-GHz (433,868 and 915 MHz)	BPSK(UL) GFSK(DL)	10–100 bps	Up to 60 km	Multiple, 200 Hz each

Note: ETSI, European Telecommunications Standards Institute.

include a directed acyclic graph (DAG) information object (DIO) that allows a node to discover an RPL instance (e.g., through ICMPv4/v6 message defined by RoLL WG), configuration parameters and parents; a DAG information solicitation (DIS) to allow requests for DIOs from RPL nodes and a destination advertisement object (DAO) used to propagate destination information upwards (i.e., towards the root) along the DODAG[8] (specific RPL details are available in RFC 6550). The trickle algorithm, standardized in 2011 (RFC 6206) and well known in the WSN community, is an important enabler of RPL message exchange.

RPL was developed by the IETF RoLL WG. The WG defined low-power lossy networks as those typically characterized by high data loss rates, low data rates, and general instability. Typical links considered include PLC, IEEE 802.15.4, and low-power Wi-Fi. The message exchange of the RPL is based on the internet control message protocol (ICMP) v4, and ICMP v6 messages.

The CoRE WG defined an UDP with DTLS supporting the secure version of the protocol in the transport and transfer Layers (fourth layer of OSI/ISO ref.). It included the transport packet formats, reliability support on top of UDP, a RESTful application protocol similar to HTTP with CoAP clients operating on CoAP server resources, and the secure version of the protocol. As a logical protocol entity, a CoAP server can be hosted on a constrained device. CoAP over TCP and the use of TLS to secure the underlying TCP transport as well as transporting CoAP within WebSockets (transported over TCP) is also considered in additional transfer and application layers (Transfer' and Application', respectively) in order to show this encapsulation of CoAP in WebSockets which in turn is transported in TCP frames.

As shown in Fig. 5.21, a CoAP server resource, as a CoAP pub-sub broker, serves as the endpoint for CoAP clients to publish their resource representations and other CoAP clients to receive these representations if they have previously subscribed to them. In the resource directory (RD) for CoAP server resource descriptions, CoAP server resource maintains a list of resources, their corresponding server contact information (e.g., IP addresses or fully qualified domain name (FQDN)), their type, the interface, etc.

---

[8]Destination-oriented DAG (DODAG), including DAG structure, was concentrated to the initial development, on the traffic flow characteristics of such networks, where typical use cases involve the collection of data from many (for example) sensing points, nodes towards a sink, or alternatively, flooding information from a sink to many nodes in the network.

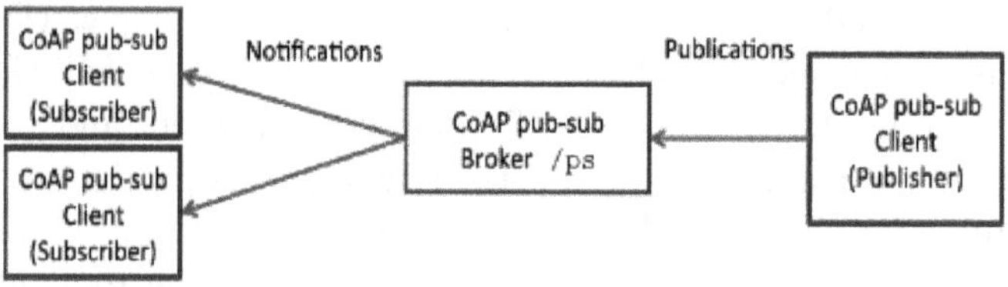

Figure 5.21 Pub–sub mode in CoAP server and client.

The specifications for CoAP management interface (CoMI) and SenML (as resource representation data models in the CoAP endpoints) in CoRE WG do not strictly define protocols or protocol behavior but define interfaces and architectural fragments, for the information generated by them or required by them.

As a complement to transport security based on DTLS or TLS, object security for constrained RESTful environments (OSCORE) WG provides authentication, encryption, integrity, and replay protection for CoAP by providing an object security solution based on CBOR and COSE. The security solution is designed for message traversal over multiple different underlying protocols (such as HTTP and CoAP in case of the message traversing an HTTP/CoAP proxy) and can secure both unicast and multicast communication requests with unicast responses.

Additionally, from the IETF views, a client as the resource server (RS), is granted access to a resource hosted on a device, and this exchange is mediated by one or multiple authorization servers (ASs). As shown in Fig. 5.22, a fully specified authorization solution includes this framework and a set of profiles. The framework of RS and AS described in an authentication and authorization for constrained environments (ACE)[9] interactions in generic terms while the profiles of this framework are additional specifications that define the use of the framework with concrete transport and communication security protocols (e.g., CoAP over DTLS). ACE is based on four building blocks: OAuth 2.0 (RFC6749 of IETF), CoAP (but not excluding other underlying protocols such as MQTT, BLE, HTTP/2, QUIC), CBOR, and COSE. When a client (C) intends to access a resource representation on an RS, the client contacts an AS to obtain a token. A token can be either an access token or a proof of possession token.

[9]Authentication and Authorization for Constrained Environments (ACE) using the OAuth 2.0 Framework (ACE-OAuth) (Internet-Draft, 2020).

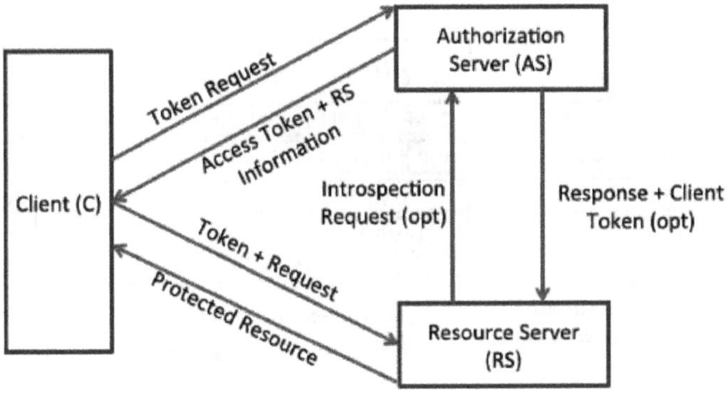

Figure 5.22 ACE architecture and the basic interactions.

5.6.3.2 *6LoWPAN as an example of interworking*

Based on the protocols introduced above and the design for point/device-to-cloud/WAN connectivity (as one of the three IoT communication topologies or prototypes), by IETF related WGs, IETF 6LoWPAN communication stacks are shown in Fig. 5.23(a). In Fig. 5.23(a), the recommended stack on top of IPv6 includes UDP/CoAP/RPL/ICMP v6/ 6LoWPAN ND (neighbor discovery in IETF RFC).

The gateway device connects to the Internet by an Ethernet cable using a LAN, and on the CoAP side, the CoAP server resides on a sensor/ actuator network (SAN) based on the IEEE 802.15.4 PHY/MAC. In the gateway device, dual stacks of IPv4 and IPv6 are designed for the IP address translation.

When the stack in Fig. 5.23(b) as IETF defined protocols that could be mapped on a communication stack similar to the ISO/OSI ref. model, the figure describes these protocols in the context of a modified OSI stack with two more layers: (i) an adaptation layer inserted between the network layer and each underlying PHY/link layer; (ii) a transfer layer, which includes protocols whose functionality lies in between the transport and application layers.

Considering that the adaptation and transfer layers are not strictly defined by IETF, in the example as Fig. 5.23(a), an adaptation layer protocol is 6LoWPAN layer and examples of transfer layer protocols are HTTP and CoAP (Fig. 5.23(b)), where proprietary technologies (such as

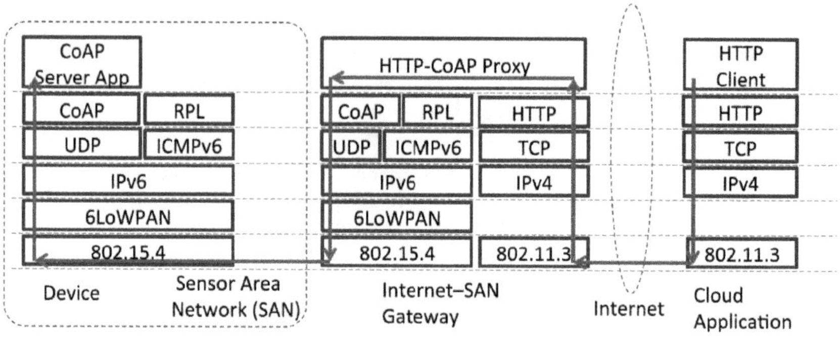

(a)

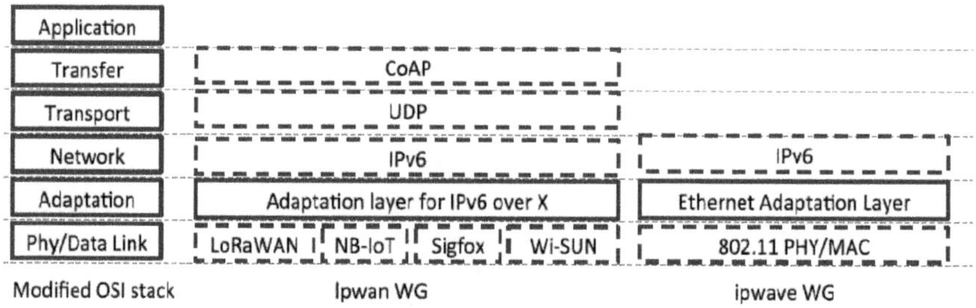

(b)

Figure 5.23 Stacks for WAN by a HTTP proxy and an adaption layer for IPv6. (a) IETF 6LoWPAN example stacks of interaction upon a request from a HTTP client to a CoAP server via an HTTP Proxy and (b) inserted adaption layer for IPv6 over LoRaWAN, NB-IoT, Sigfox, and Wi-SUN.

LoRa and Sigfox, to be introduced later), as well as Wi-SUN and cellular NB-IoT may have their adaptation layers respectively over them.

5.6.4 *Proprietary LPWA*

LPWA wireless communications and networking technologies are grouped into cellular LPWAs that operate in licensed spectrum and non-cellular LPWAs that typically operate in unlicensed spectrum, sometimes have proprietary technologies standards, such as Lora, Sigfox, Weightless (details in the next section). LPWANs have the potential to serve a range of scattered and unconnected devices. These devices are typically embedded sensors and actuators requiring long-range, low-data rate communication and extreme operational energy efficiency and are deployed at the metropolitan scale within various vertical industries' applications.

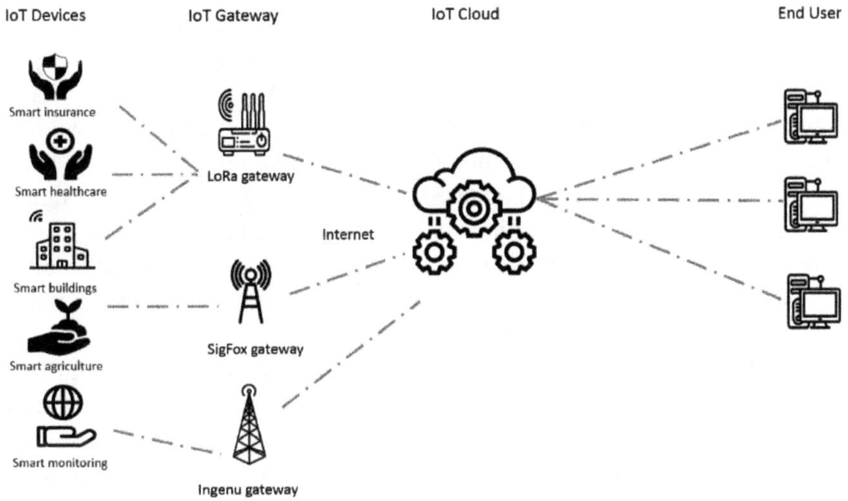

Figure 5.24 LPWA networking (long-range IoT), Sigfox, and Ingenu in commercial and proprietary solutions architecture.

Source: Noun project website.

A number of standards bodies, industrial consortia, and special interest groups (SIGs) are developing competing LPWA technologies, including 3GPP, IEEE, IETF, ETSI, LoRa alliance, Wi-Fi, Weightless SIG, and Wi-SUN alliance.

With regard to those standardized by the 3GPP for use in licensed spectrum, proprietary LPWA technologies with additional standards-driven LPWA technologies that are currently available are discussed here.

From the views of IoT wireless communication technologies, the proprietary LPWAs introduced here (in contrast to open standards-based Wi-SUN/6LoWPAN and cellular LPWA) belongs to the long-range categories of the two long-/short-range coverage, and their competing application scenario over WPAN (including low-rate, Wi-Fi, 6LoWPAN, and other short-range communications introduced above) is shown in Fig. 5.24. LoRa, Sigfox, and Ingenu are available on the market and also identified as commercial solutions.

As heterogeneous solutions of the communication and network layer in IoT, they are typical proponents of mesh networks or multi-hops *ad hoc* networks. In some cases, the technology is used as an alternative to cellular LPWA IoT (e.g., in utilities' field area networks) and in other cases such as a complementary element (e.g., for deep indoor metering where nothing else reaches or somewhere without cellular networks).

• LoRa is the standard protocol of the LoRa alliance (open, non-profit association established in 2015). LoRa has a bandwidth of 250 kHz and 125 kHz and a maximum data rate of 50 kbps (from 0.3 kbps to 37.5 kbps, typically, and depending on the spreading factor and channel bandwidth), enabling bidirectional communication albeit not simultaneously by chirp spread spectrum (CSS) techniques, spreading a narrowband input signal over a wide channel bandwidth, and has a maximum payload of 243 bytes. The range is up to 5 km in urban areas and 20 km in rural areas depending on the application. LoRa networks use gateway devices to work and manage the network for connecting IoT devices.

Its physical layer technology (published by LoRa alliance) that modulates signals in sub-GHz ISM bands using a proprietary spread spectrum technique developed by Semtech Corp. The resulting signal has noise-like properties, making it harder to jam. Processing gain allows resilience to interference and noise. Multiple transmissions using different spreading factors (for data rates) can be received simultaneously by a LoRa base station or gateway in the LoRaWAN (defined the upper layers and system architecture by LoRa alliance specification, which was released in July 2015).

• SigFox offers end-to-end LPWA connectivity based on its patented technologies and operates its own proprietary communications technology, which is an ultra-narrowband (100 Hz) with a maximum data rate of 100 bps, in sub-GHz unlicensed ISM spectrum. SigFox network operators (SNOs) deploy base stations with software-defined radios that connect to backend systems over IP networks. End-IoT devices connect to these base stations using binary phase shift keying (BPSK) modulation in the ultra-narrow band (UNB), by which SigFox uses the bandwidth efficiently and experiences low noise levels that result in high receiver sensitivity, ultra-low power consumption, and inexpensive antenna design (at the compromise of a throughput limited to 100 bps).

In the covering range of Sigfox, a small payload (maximum 12 bytes) means it can offer greater coverage geographically, reaching up to 10 km in urban areas and 40 km in rural areas. Sigfox offers bidirectional connections, with the downlink from base stations to end IoT devices occurring following uplink communication.

• Ingenu RPMA uses proprietary LPWA that is owned by Ingenu (previously On-RampWireless) company, which operates in the 2.4 GHz ISM band. In its patented physical access scheme, random phase multiple

Table 5.6 Comparison between long-range LPWA technologies.

Specifications	LoRaWAN	SigFox	Ingenu RPMA
Modulation	Chirp spread spectrum (CSS)	DBPSK (UL); GFSK (DL)	RPMA-DSSS (UL); CDMA (DL)
MAC	Unslotted MAC	Unslotted ALOHA	CDMA-like
Data rate	0.3 kbps–50 kbps	100 bps(UL) 600 bps(DL)	78 kbps(UL) 19 kbps(DL)
Coverage	Up to 5 km (urban) 15 km (rural)	10 km (urban) 50 km (rural)	up to 15 km (urban)

access (RPMA) direct sequence spread spectrum (DSSS) is used for uplink communication only. This technology can not only build a public machine communication network but also serve a variety of vertical machine communication markets through a private network. Ingenu RPMA is heavily involved in efforts to make RPMA compliant with the IEEE specifications.

Table 5.6 contains a summary of them in brand-defined approaches.

Long-range LPWA solutions share the common network architecture in Fig. 5.24. IoT devices transmit their data to a brand-defined gateway through a given technology including not only the proprietary communications but all underlying communications (e.g., Wi-Fi, Zigbee, Wi-SUN, BLE etc.) in this chapter. The gateway acts at the data link and physical layers where IoT application data are directly encapsulated. All involved protocols are strictly brand defined. Each gateway in Fig. 5.24 may also be included in IoT gateways of above section, and it is a protocol converter encapsulating the private IoT application into an Internet protocol stack to be conveyed to the IoT cloud where a brand-defined server will apply an application layer conversion from the IoT application to an Internet application protocol (such as HTTP/Rest/XMPP) suitable for end users. There are around 50 million LoRa-based end nodes and 70,000 LoRa gateways that have already been in use. In China, smart metering LoRa products account for 70% of all LoRa products and smart utilities (parking, smoke sensing, and utility management) and smart buildings occupancy account for 10% and 5%, respectively.

• **Weightless** (Weightless-N, Weightless-W, and Weightless-P) operates in the unlicensed spectrum (sub-GHz ISM bands) or licensed spectrum and is an open standard (Weightless SIG) designed to operate in a variety of bands, while featuring a 100 kbps maximum data rate on uplink and downlink. Weightless can handle 2,769 end points per base station on standard smart meter setups (200 bytes uploaded every 15 min).

Weightless-W leverages TV white spaces and supports several modulation schemes and a range of spreading factors. Depending on the link budget, packets with sizes upwards of 10 bytes can be transmitted at a rate between 1 kbps and 10 Mbps. End devices transmit to base stations in a narrow band but at a lower power level than the base stations to save energy. Weightless-W has one drawback in that shared access to TV white spaces is permitted only in a few regions; therefore, the Weightless SIG defines the other two standards in globally available ISM bands.

Weightless-N is a UNB standard for one-way communication from end devices to a base station and achieves significant energy efficiency and lower cost than the other Weightless standards. **NWave**, the company owns the technology as its patent, which is the basis of the Weightless-N protocol. NWave realizes multi-data stream transmission in the way of virtual hub, and the CPU classifies the data to ensure the data attribute. In July 2015, NWave and Acceleratace (an enterprise accelerator organization), in cooperation with Next Step City (another organization), deployed Weightless-N network in Denmark, covering Copenhagen, the capital, and other cities in Denmark.

Weightless-P blends two-way connectivity with two non-proprietary physical layers (FDMA + TDMA), which is introduced by M2COMM company. Single 12.5 kHz narrow channels in the <GHz band allow data rates between 0.2 kbps and 100 kbps.

- **Telensa** (formerly Senaptic) provides end-to-end LPWA solutions for applications incorporating fully designed vertical network stacks with support for integration with third-party software. It uses proprietary UNB modulation techniques operating in license-free <GHz ISM bands at low data rates. Telensa is aiming to standardize its technology using ETSI low-throughput networks (LTNs) specifications for easy application integration.

5.7 Cellular LPWAN and M2M in 5G Era

A large chunk of the future growth in the number of long-range IoT devices is expected to come from LPWANs. By 2025, it is expected that more than two billion devices will be connected through LPWANs. The technology, which promises extremely high battery life and a maximum communication range of over 20 kilometers, is used by the majority of which are smart meters, monitoring and building around us. A research report predicts that there will be 2.7 billion LPWAN IoT connections by 2029. LPWANs operating in the licensed spectrum are regulated by ITU, 3GPP and available from 2G to 5G (the fifth generation wireless mobile systems). As for light weight Sat-IoT device supported communications, they are expected in the near B5G/6G era.

From the CIoT views (standardized by 3GPP and ITU), cellular 2G-5G (for WAN accessing of things) and the IoT promise new capabilities and use cases, which are set to impact not only consumer services but also many industries embarking on their digital transformations. As a new branch of CIoT, massive cellular LPWAs technologies, such as NB-IoT, Cat-M1(LTE-M), and EC-GSM-IoT, are taking off and driving growth in the number of CIoT connections, with a CAGR of 30% expected between 2017 and 2023. These complementary technologies support diverse LPWAN use cases over the same underlying LTE/5G network.

5.7.1 *Cellular LPWAN*

CIoT is a new word referring to IoT whose networks can be built on cellular communications standards, such as 2G/GPRS, 3G/LTE, and 5G, wireless mobile systems by now. 5G and the IoT promise new capabilities and use cases, which are set to impact not only consumer services but also many industries embarking on their digital transformations. Originally, CIoT are known as cellular LPWAN (or mobile IoT) in three categories of NB-IoT, LTE-M, and EC-GSM-IoT, as GSMA terms which refers to the 3GPP standardized low-power wide area technologies using licensed spectrum bands. From 3GPP release 13 (R13) and the following releases, the category of user equipment (UE) that supports power consumption optimizations, extended coverage, and lower complexity (e.g., EC-GSM-IoT) is part of mobile IoT (also including Category M1, Category NB1 from GSM Association Non-confidential Official Document CLP.28).

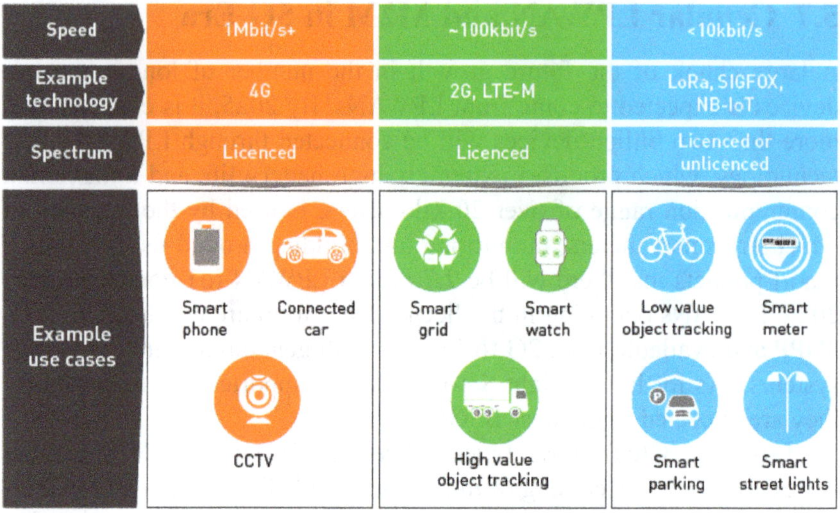

Figure 5.25 Diversity of rate and coverage in LPWANs of sharing (cellular and proprietary) markets.

Source: Analysys MASON, 2016.

By now, the term "Mobile IoT" is upgraded into "CIoT", which is including new emerging IoT cellular technologies and applications. Figure 5.25 shows some of them as use cases from the cellular LPWAN to proprietary LPWAN in the 4G era.

As shown in Fig. 5.25, Video Surveillance or closed-circuit television (CCTV) represents the largest segment of security technology in a city block/street. Video cameras are used to observe an area or a block. This type, together with the similar function devices of, Cat.1 and Cat.4 UE (category in different releases of 3GPP) as IoT UE (shows some low mobility characteristics, low data rate but higher than LPWAs) are contributed as MTC or M2M. In comparison to this type, V2X communications based on cellular/DSRC shows high mobility characteristics. Others in the figure (whose data rate is below 1 Mbps) are introduced as follows.

- **NB-IoT:** Narrow-band IoT (NB-IoT), as a 3GPP radio technology (3GPP R13 in 2016), coexists with EC-GSM-IoT and LTE-M standard in the 4G era. It is based on licensed cellular networks providing a 200 kHz bandwidth and a 200 kbps maximum data rate, which offers bidirectional communication, but not simultaneously, and has unlimited messages with a maximum payload of 1,600 bytes.

NB-IoT provides improved indoor coverage and supports a massive number of low-throughput devices, low delay sensitivity, ultra-low device cost, low device power consumption, and optimized network architecture. The technology can be deployed "in-band", utilizing resource blocks within a normal LTE carrier or in the unused resource blocks within an LTE carrier's guard-band or "standalone" for deployments in dedicated spectrum. NB-IoT aims to enable deployment flexibility, long battery life, low device cost and complexity, and signal coverage extension. NB-IoT is not compatible with 3G (before R12 of 3GPP) but can coexist with GSM/GPRS and LTE/5G (e.g., it is supported with a software upgrade on top of existing LTE infrastructure).

It can be deployed inside a single GSM carrier of 200 kHz, inside a single LTE physical resource block (PRB) of 180 kHz, or inside an LTE guard band. Compared to LTE-M (Cat.m1), NB-IoT cuts cost and energy consumption further by reducing data rates and bandwidth requirements and simplifying protocol design and mobility support. Standalone deployment in a dedicated licensed spectrum is supported. NB-IoT aims for coverage that can serve up to 50k devices per cell, with the potential to scale up by adding more NB-IoT carriers. The global shipments of NB-IoT devices will have a compound annual growth rate of 41.8% from 106.9 million units in 2018 to 613.2 million in 2023.

• **LTE-M:** LTE-M is another 3GPP LPWA standard that evolved from the low-cost MTC of R12, also named as enhanced MTC (eMTC). LTE-M provides extended coverage by using an installed LTE base with the same spectrum, radios, and base stations. It is implemented as a 4G technology with an important role in 5G. The uplink/downlink transfers 1 Mbps and, due to low latency and full duplex operation, can carry voice traffic. LTE-M supports more demanding IoT mobile devices, which require real-time data transfer (e.g., transport, wearable), while NB-IoT supports more IoT static sensors and devices.

LTE-M end devices (UEs) offer higher data rate services at cost and power consumption levels unsuitable for IoT-type use cases. To reduce the cost while being compliant with LTE system requirements, 3GPP reduces the peak data rate from LTE Category 1 to LTE Category 0 and then to LTE Category M (LTE-M, also as Cat. LTE-m1 when compared to

NB-IoT), the different stages in the LTE evolution process. To extend the battery lifetime for MTC, 3GPP implements "power saving mode (PSM)" and "extended discontinuous reception (eDRX)". These techniques enable devices to enter deep sleep modes for hours or days without losing network registration. End devices thus avoid monitoring downlink control channels for prolonged periods of time to save energy. The same power saving features are exploited in EC-GSM-IoT.

- **EC-GSM-IoT:** Extended coverage GSM IoT was proposed as part of the 3GPP R13 specification that aims to extend the GSM coverage by +20 dB using sub-GHz bands for better signal penetration in indoor environments while not being so demanding of the bandwidth. With a software upgrade to GSM networks, the legacy GPRS spectrum can use new channels to accommodate EC-GSM-IoT devices. It exploits repetitive transmissions and signal processing techniques to improve coverage and capacity of legacy GPRS. It can provide variable data rates up to 240 kbps (depending on the actual modulation, either via Gaussian minimum shift keying (GSMK, the original modulation of GSM) or 8PSK modulation) and aims to support 50k devices per base station with enhanced security features compared to existing GSM/GPRS-based solutions (e.g., integrity protection, mutual authentication and requires stronger ciphering algorithms). The latency is in the range of medium to high, as it could be derived from the known latency values of existing GSM/GPRS networks. Latency, while an important aspect of the technology choice for IoT, should not be an obstacle for certain applications.

3GPP wanted to leverage on the presence of GSM/GPRS without the need for a new network infrastructure. For a mobile network operator (MNO), the deployment of EC-GSM-IoT is as simple as dedicating one GSM carrier to the service, as it is an in-band technology. The standard mentioned backwards compatibility with GSM/GPRS, coexistence, and design re-use.

EC-GSM-IoT can be deployed easily on existing 2G infrastructures and the standard foresees that the enhancements in the air interface will have a minimal impact on the hardware requirements for the base station hardware. The receiver models proposed in the EC-GSM-IoT standard do fulfill the battery life expectation of 10 years in most of the use-cases.

As shown in the Table 5.7, the peak rate of LTE-M (CAT-m1) is relatively high. Whether it is advantageous or disadvantageous depends on the application scenario. Generally speaking, higher transmission rate will

Table 5.7 Parameters in CAT-m1, CAT-m2 (NB-IoT), and EC-GSM.

Parameters	**LTE-M (CAT-m1)**	**NB-IoT (CAT-m2)**	**EC-GSM**
Bands (Bandwidth)	1.4 MHz	200 kHz	2.4 MHz
Deployment	In-band	In-band, Guard-band, Standalone (GSM bands)	GSM bands
Duplex Mode	HD-FDD/FDD/TDD	HD-FDD (TDD in R15)	TDD
Peak rate	375 kbps (HD-FDD), 1 Mbps (FDD)	~200 kbps for HD-FDD	10 kbps
Emission power	23 dBm 20 dBm	23 dBm	23 dBm
VoLTE supported	Y (in R14)	N	N
Mobility	<120 km/h (switching in connection state)	<30km/h (switching in connection state)	<50 km/h (switching in connection state
Battery Life	>10 years	>10 years	>10 years

have more application scenarios. In terms of mobility support, LTE-M (CAT-m1) is better than NB-IoT.

The comparisons among the three categories cellular LPWANs and others latest details can be found in the book "Cellular Internet of Things: From Massive Deployments to Critical 5G Applications — 2nd Edition" (Academic Press, 2020).

5.7.2 *M2M in 5G era*

There has been an evolution of the concept of the IoT, which is transformed into a network of interconnected objects, collecting information from the environment and interactions with the real world (actuators/actuators/controllers or other devices). Among the heterogeneous connections of IoT communications and networking layer, a new form of communication is generally called M2M or MTC, where the connecting devices include biomedical sensors, actuators, smartphones and tablets, vehicles, cameras, and many others. M2M/MTC provides solutions to current and likely future demands for services, such as industrial automation, smart energy management and smart grid, automotive and traffic management.

It is possible to reach the capability of M2M where there is a cellular coverage (as 2G–5G), even with less configuration and without the additional devices such as gateways. This new type was called place-&-play (an option of point-to-cloud topology as for IoT), which pushes other new words to us, namely business to business to consumer (B2B2C). In B2B2C market, the services such as "live broadcasting" high-definition video service are offered to businesses like broadcasting operators, and they in turn offer the service to their premium customers.[10] In the IoT market, operators can leverage the low latency, high reliability, high bandwidth, and massive connections capabilities to offer several vertical industry use cases, such as connected vehicles, smart utilities, healthcare providers, and remote surgery types of applications, by participating in the industry-specific ecosystems and innovating new business models. Figure 5.26 illustrates the B2B2C applications market potential and readiness matrix presenting the connectivity and value-added services opportunities in different sectors.

From the view of M2M platforms which provide M2M service and data management, several aspects are important:

- **Service capabilities:** Service capabilities comprise the service that the end customer pays for that relies on the underlying connectivity, and operators are investing in building new capabilities that improve their offering to IoT service propositions. Examples include horizontal capabilities, such as remote provisioning of IoT devices, building platforms that allow for management of business rules, reporting, support for application programming interfaces (APIs) and the management and presentation of data.
- **Data analytics:** Furthermore, "Big Data" analytics is set to become a key part of IoT services in the future, with operators increasingly looking at ways to analyze data from various sources and create new service lines. An area in which there has been recent innovation is the capability for the remote provisioning of IoT devices.
- **Connected devices security:** In some connected devices or user equipment (UE), the module with the SIM card needs to be inserted in the machine and hermetically sealed during the production process. Examples include tamper-proof security or alarm systems. Other pieces

[10] In China, live show or live broadcasting at homes, emerging in recent years, gives a new sense of entertainment.

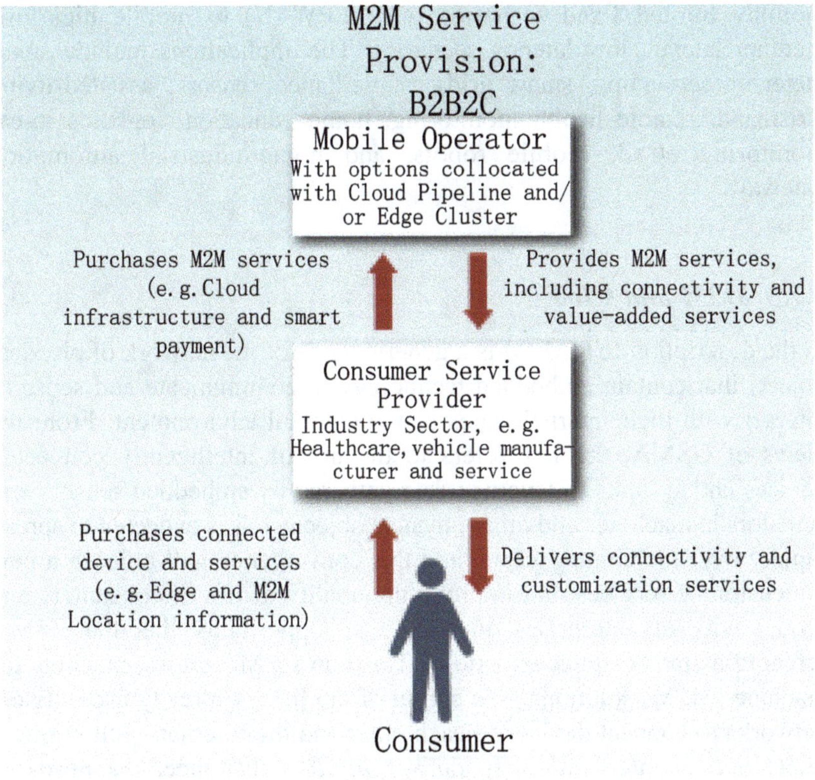

Figure 5.26 M2M connectivity service in B2B2C.

of connected equipment are located in remote or hazardous locations, such as weather, pipeline, or geology sensors, or equipment in chemical plants, meaning it is difficult or impossible to access the module after deployment. To address these specific market segments, the mobile industry through the GSMA has produced an "Embedded SIM" specification to enable the remote "over the air" provisioning and management of embedded SIMs in such devices.

In the 5G era, M2M markets supported by mobile operators, M2M connectivity (physically access the module, with or without a SIM card) and connectivity support platform are ranging from bandwidth and mobility limited fixed scenarios (e.g., LPWAN) to mobile high/low/medium latency low latency scenarios. The applications include smart meter, street lamps, smart grids, surveillance sensors, assisted-living wristband, remote health monitoring, home education, logistics in-car monitoring eCall, mobile robots, and home/industrial automation gateways.

5.7.3 *M2M and CIoT*

In the description IoT, M2M is a generic term for the network of physical objects that contain embedded technology to communicate and sense or interact with their internal states or the external environment. From the views of GSMA, the IoT refers to the use of intelligently connected devices and systems to leverage data gathered by embedded sensors and actuators in machines and other physical objects. IoT is expected to spread rapidly over the coming years, and this convergence will unleash a new dimension of services that improve the quality of life of consumers and productivity of enterprises, unlocking an opportunity that the GSMA refers to as the “Connected Life”. Also from GSMA views, machine-to-machine (M2M) solutions — a subset of the IoT — already use wireless networks to connect devices to each other and the Internet, with minimal direct human intervention, to deliver services that meet the needs of a wide range of industries. The relationship of the relative terms is described in Fig. 5.27.

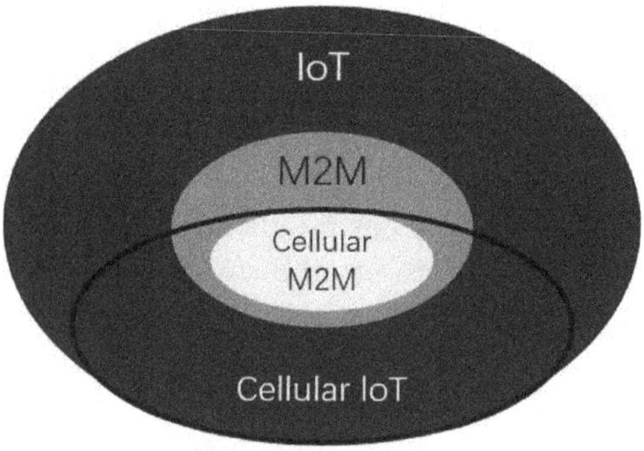

Figure 5.27 M2M, cellular M2M, CIoT, and IoT.

Cellular M2M using mobile technology, usually with a dedicated SIM and a connection to a cellular network, is typical for M2M solutions. Whereas, CIoT offers functions and services which go beyond the scope of the cellular, and it is generalized to the IoT scope where it takes advantage of cellular networks. For example, a group of sensors/machines connected together via Wi-Fi or Zigbee or Bluetooth are part of IoT, and they are connected to the cloud/WAN by cellular gateways.

Either M2M, cellular M2M, or CIoT is a subset of the broader IoT concept, and M2M attempts to refer to the connected machines that after they have been placed somewhere, and they seldom need moving.

As this particular term, M2M is widely used throughout the GSMA and ETSI, and machine-type communications (MTCs) are heavily referred to in the ETSI documentation. MTC, also widely used in the 3rd generation partnership project (3GPP) and a series of ETSI/OneM2M/GSMA use cases, such as eMTC in R12, LTE-MTC (LTE-M) in R13, massive MTC in R15, and critical MTC in R16/R17. However, in this book, it is considered that the two words "M2M and MTC" are interchangeable terms, especially in 3GPP view. Also from the 3GPP views, mMTC refers to the three categories cellular LPWAN and they are developed by 3GPP (see the next section).

5.7.3.1 *MTC in R11 and R12 of 3GPP*

In the early M2M stage, from 3GPP view, R11 (Release 11 of 3GPP) corresponded to the stage in which a certain number of M2M arose and the network needs to be upgraded to adapt to M2M applications; R12 corresponded to the surge in the number of M2M, and the network is mainly designed around the characteristics of M2M (see Table 5.8), considering the new physical layer design, and the M2M service at that time is low-cost MTC; R13 corresponded to the era of dramatic increase in the number of M2M, and the M2M network was smoothly upgraded or redesigned, then the service name changed to e(enhanced)-MTC, also known as LTE-M service in R13.

The requirements of M2M services are very different from those of mobile or cellular networks designed for human-to-human communication, and the characteristics of M2M services are very different among types. In the early days, the M2M service was called MTC (before R11, and as low-cost MTC in R12) by 3GPP. At that time, MTC requirements were divided into general service requirements and specific service

Table 5.8 MTC characteristics.

No.	Specific requirements	Description of characteristics
1	Low mobility	Low mobility, that is, the device doesn't move often or only moves in a specific area (e.g., health monitoring at home, mobile sales). Low mobility management can prolong the mobility management cycle and reduce the occupation of system resources by devices. It is necessary to enhance packet data serving node (PDSN)/mobile switch center (MSC) in the management of group domain and AAA/HSS/HLR (HLR: home location register) in the user database[a].
2	Time controlled	When time dependent, that is, to receive and send data within a specified period of time and to avoid unnecessary signaling outside the specified period of time. For example, meter reading. The network shall be able to control the time of terminal access to the network and also control the access of different terminals under the same user in different time periods or the random access of M2M equipment under one user in the same time period, so as to avoid the congestion caused by simultaneous access. If the access time exceeds, the network side can refuse the access request of the terminal. Separate the M2M device from the network side or reject any data or signaling request from the M2M device. It is necessary to enhance PDSN/AAA and user database (HSS/HLR) to allow the device access time period to be stored in AAA as contract data.
3	Time tolerant	Not sensitive to time and allow appropriate delay. The network shall be capable of time control or access rate control. If the access rate exceeds the configured rate, the access request is rejected. It is necessary to enhance the user plane device and user database.
4	Packet switched (PS) only	Services are provided only through PS domain, without the impact on the core network.
5	Online small data transmission	A small amount of data transmission that is always online. In order to reduce the impact of signaling on the network, the terminal devices that often send data should be registered in the network. It may affect the core network equipment of control plane and user plane.
6	Offline small data transmission	For the terminal equipment that only sends data once for a long time, the network side should separate the terminal equipment from the network side after the data is sent. For small traffic services, it is not appropriate to charge based on connection duration or traffic. It is necessary to consider charging based on connection number, signaling number, and group (e.g., charging based on traffic and access duration of all M2M devices under the same M2M users).

(*Continued*)

Table 5.8 (*Continued*)

No.	Specific requirements	Description of characteristics
7	Mobile originated (MO) only	When only MO terminal initiates services, it can remove the paging, even the location updating or even be disconnected. Mobility management is performed only when users access.
8	Infrequent mobile terminated (MT)	The MO terminal initiates the service (push) infrequently.
9	MTC monitoring	It is necessary for the network side to detect the status of the monitoring terminal (abnormal behavior, location change, connection loss, etc.) and take corresponding measures (alarm to users and servers or limit terminal services).
10	Offline indication	When MTC server perceives that the terminal is offline, the network side needs to send an alarm to the user and the server.
11	Jamming indication	When the terminal has been interfered or is being interfered, the network should send an alarm to the server.
12	Priority alarm message (PAM)	The network needs to ensure the priority of PAM message transmission in the priority configuration of different messages. To achieve this function, there are corresponding requirements for terminal equipment, such as fire alarm, which needs to transmit information to the fire alarm and control system in time.
13	Low-power consumption	Reducing the power consumption of the terminal can be achieved by simplifying the mobility management, timing mechanics for the wake-up and other measures.
14	Secure connection	The secure connection between terminal and server can be completed through data encryption, authentication and other mechanisms.
15	Location specific trigger	The network triggers the terminal to initiate service (e.g., report status) according to the location. Core network devices need to configure trigger information of specific location to trigger terminal services or notify serve of location information
16	Group based MTC features	According to the characteristics of group management, such as group QoS, group billing, group addressing, new capabilities of billing and addressing need to be considered. Group features are applied to a group of MTC terminals, including group-based policing and group-based addressing. The former implements a joint group QoS policy for a group of terminals; the latter addresses a group of terminals to optimize the amount of data transmitted by the network.

[a]The authentication, authorization, and accounting (AAA) server provides access authentication services for MTC devices on behalf of the 3GPP core network. The home subscriber server (HSS) locates in 3GPP core network and provides authentication and management services for MTC devices on behalf of 3GPP core network. In this relative research, group authentication and key agreement protocol are hot points for M2M (Rong *et al.*, 2013).

requirements. The general service requirements are independent of MTC application, and the specific features of the mobile communication network are summarized and defined from a macro perspective to support the basic functions of MTC services, including MTC device trigger, addressing, identification, billing, security, and MTC device remote management. Among the specific features, MTC device triggering and remote management are unique to M2M, while other requirements already exist in H2H communication.

MTC services, presented in the new features are different from H2H communication. For example, in terms of address, we need to consider the limited address space, which involves IMSI, MSISDN, and IPv4 addresses; the number (No.) of address should be able to uniquely identify an MTC device and an MTC device group; in terms of charging an MTC group, implement special rates for a specific period of time, and charge for specific events; in terms of security, it can at least provide the same security level as H2H.

5.7.3.2 *MTC service*

Some common services for the network include an MTC subscribe for MNOs identifying, addition/removing of an individual feature, mechanics to reduce peaks when great number of devices simultaneously attempting data and/or signal interactions, etc. As for MTC specific service requirements, 16 types of MTC service features are defined. See Table 5.8 for details of service features and their descriptions. These are the basis of 3GPP's research in 4G (R8–R11) MTC services. Even for non-cellular network M2M application scenario, the analysis of M2M specific service requirements also provide a good guidance.

According to the specific service requirements and the specific application characteristics of MTC, several MTC features are defined from different perspectives, and the functional requirements of a mobile communication network (e.g., by a certain mobile network operator, MNO) are described for each feature. The advantage of this is based on realizing the general service requirements of MTC, the system only needs to call one or more MTC features to support a variety of MTC applications. The above characteristics are specific data service characteristics for M2M. In order to control these characteristics, the network must have two conditions: knowing the service characteristics required by MTC terminal and having the ability to control different characteristics. So, we can optimize the network according to the service characteristics.[11]

From the above analysis, we can conclude that MTC/M2M refers to small amounts of data that are communicated between machines (devices to backend services and vice versa) with less mobility, less power consumption and less human intervention, typical over a cellular network. From the network side, the following are MTC-specific considerations mainly by 3GPP:

- An M2M/IoT identification module such as the concept of the machine communications identity module (MCIM) in the 3GPP SA3 work.
- User data management (e.g., subscription management).
- Network optimizations (e.g., 3GPP SA2 work).

There may be many suppliers of WAN functionality in a complete M2M solution. It follows that an important function in the M2M service enabling domain will be to manage business-to-business (B2B) relations between numbers of WAN service providers, in order to keep the competing position of cellular LPWAN, as compared to the proprietary LPWAN, as shown in Fig. 5.28. The cellular advantages for IoT include not only the coverage as ubiquitous perceptions and connections but the above-mentioned "place & play" and some kinds of mobility. 5G gives another competing road as critical services in which a high- or ultra-reliability and low latency (URLLC) is required in an IIoT, e.g., automotive and automation sector industrial, where better QoS in terms of reactivity, latency, and scalability compared to current cellular standards is needed. The next section mentions this.

5.7.4 *ETSI M2M and OMA LwM2M*

As for the data and connection management, service platforms, some leading works have been done by ETSI, which established the M2M

[11]Network enhancements for LTE MTC services in R11 were categorized into three models: (i) Indirect model that the MTC service isn't in the MNO domain; (ii) direct model that MTC applications lined to the MNO domain directly, without an MTC server; (iii) hybrid model where MTC-interwork function (MTC-IWF) is defined. Details and MTC user plane stack can be found in Song (2019).

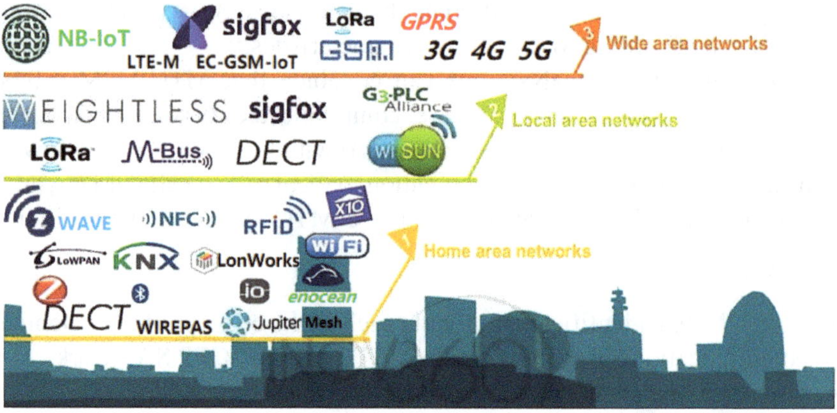

Figure 5.28 IoT communication standards and markets.

technical committee (TC) in November 2008. Its main responsibility is to collect and define the requirements of M2M and then develop an end-to-end (M2M overall high level) architecture for M2M applications. It also cooperates with the research of NGN in ETSI and the research of 3GPP. The main work areas include M2M device identification, name address system, QoS and security privacy, billing, management, application interface, hardware interface, interoperability, etc. M2M TC related projects have done research on all kinds of M2M applications, such as smart metering/instruments, smart health, electronic consumption, etc. These detailed documents for demand research are the basis for the study of M2M business application and network technology optimization, including:

- **Requirements of M2M:** As an important component of ETSI-3GPP interworking, ETSI also did in-depth research on various requirements, as above-mentioned common requirements, MTC services, and application use cases (in Table 5.8).
- **Solutions of business requirements:** Figure 5.29 gives the ETSI M2M structure (2012, in ETSI M2M standard Release 1), where describes the network architecture, data model, interface gateway, M2M device access/service, and management platform including security, traffic management, device discovery, and life cycle management features.
- **Components of ETSI M2M:** The M2M gateway device provides connectivity for M2M Devices in an M2M area network towards the

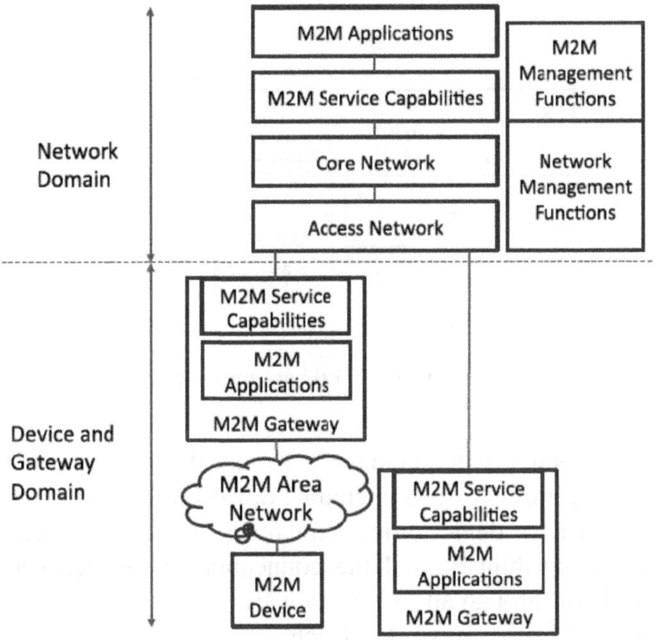

Figure 5.29 ETSI M2M structure.

network domain. The M2M gateway (functionally as a device gateway or server in Fig. 5.29) contains M2M applications and M2M service capabilities. The M2M gateway may also provide services to other legacy devices (e.g., non-IP devices) that are not visible to the network domain. The network domain contains the following functional/ topological entities:

Access network allows the devices in the device and gateway domain to communicate with the core network. Examples of access network technologies are fixed (xDSL, HFC) and wireless (satellite, GERAN, UTRAN, E-UTRAN WLAN, WiMAX). Core networks are those cellular 3GPP and ETSI TISPAN core networks, which provide the IP connectivity, service and network control, interconnection with other networks and roaming.

In ETSI M2M, the function of the network domain is similar to that of LwM2M (OMA light-weight M2M v1.1) platform layer (the top layer of Fig. 5.30), which is composed of M2M application, M2M service capability, core network, access network, M2M management function, and

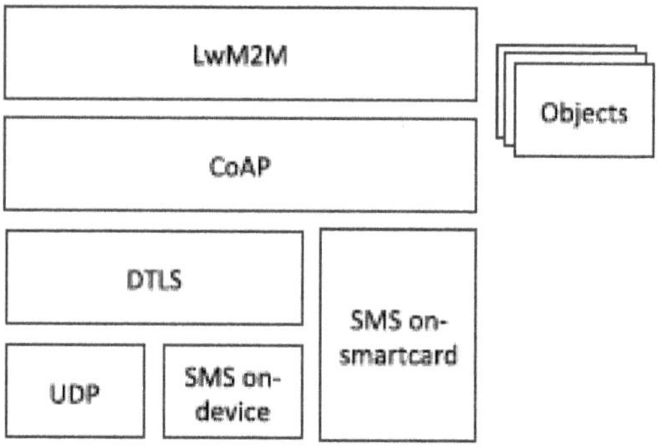

Figure 5.30 OMA LwM2M v1.0 implementation protocol stack.

network management function module. Device domain is also folded into the platform layer of LwM2M, including device/object and gateway management, such as a device/object contained in M2M applications and M2M service capabilities, and the connection to the network domain either directly or through an M2M gateway.

In the M2M area network, which is functionally included in the platform layer of LwM2M, a short-range network is built by LAN/WPAN and provides connectivity between M2M devices and M2M gateways.

For the **network domain** of ETSI views as well as the network function in the LwM2M platform layer, the **network domain** contains **access network**, as mentioned above, which is beside the 3GPP access and includes wired and wireless LAN/PAN, and **core network** (3GPP core network and ETSI core network). Other functions folded in the LwM2M platform layer but detailed from an ETSI view as follows:

- **M2M applications and API interface:** These are the specific M2M applications (e.g., smart metering) that utilize the M2M service capabilities through the open interfaces.
- **Network management functions:** These are all the necessary functions to manage the access and core Network (e.g., provisioning, fault management, etc.).
- **M2M management functions:** These are the necessary functions required to manage the M2M service capabilities on the network domain while the management of an M2M device or gateway is performed by specific M2M service capabilities. There are two M2M management functions: MSBF and MAS. M2M service bootstrap

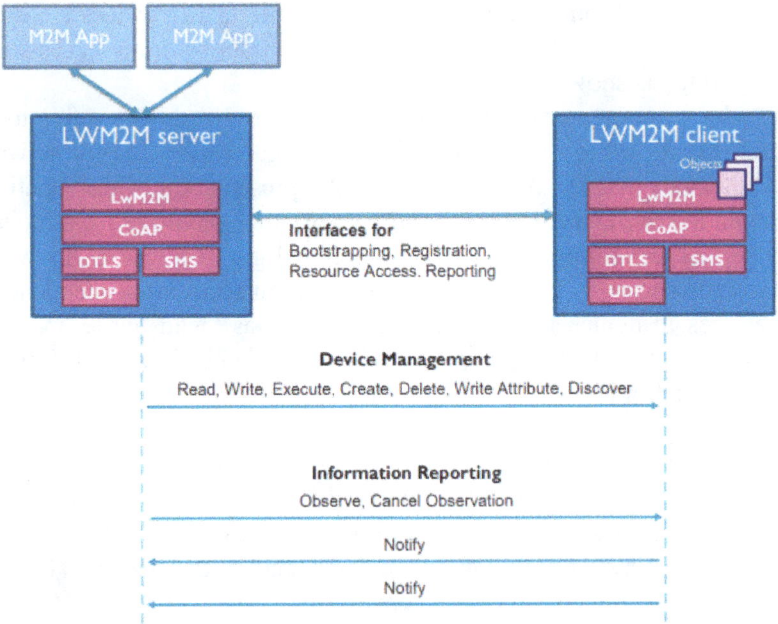

Figure 5.31 Open mobile alliance (OMA) LwM2M interaction model.

function (MSBF) facilitates the bootstrapping of permanent M2M service layer security credentials in the M2M device or gateway and the M2M service capabilities in the network domain. In the network service capabilities layer of ETSI structure, the bootstrap procedures perform, among other procedures, provisioning of an M2M root key (secret key) to the M2M device or gateway and the M2M authentication server (MAS). MAS is the safe execution environment where permanent security credentials such as the M2M Root Key are stored. Any security credentials established on the M2M device or gateway are stored in a secure environment such as a trusted platform module.

Management functions are also included in Fig. 5.31, illustrated as interfaces management and device management:

- **Interfaces management:** From an ETSI view, the interfaces are specified in different levels of detail, from abstract to a specific mapping of an interface to a specific protocol (e.g., HTTP or IETF CoAP). The most relevant entities in the ETSI M2M architecture are the M2M applications. From an LwM2M view, the interfaces services are operated by functions as bootstrapping, registration, resource access, and reporting, as shown in Fig. 5.31.

- **Device management:** From an ETSI view, M2M device refers to an M2M node, which can be a device M2M, gateway M2M, or network M2M node. An M2M node is a logical representation of the functions on an M2M device, gateway, and network that should at least include a service capability layer (SCL) functional group. From an LwM2M view, as shown in Fig. 5.31, a set of common application-independent services in device management are defined as "read, write, execute, discover, etc." And further services are extended by LwM2M (interaction model in Fig. 5.31) into interfaces services mentioned above.

There are three types of servers in the LwM2M architecture as follows: (a) an LwM2M server; (b) a bootstrap server; (c) a firmware repository server. These servers could be collocated on a single machine, but the specification leaves this choice to the developers of the system. The bulk of the specification covers the interactions between an LwM2M server and an LwM2M client. An LwM2M server and a bootstrap server operate through the specified interfaces on LwM2M client objects while the firmware repository server implements a firmware update protocol which is left open for OMA LwM2M. Firmware update procedures can also be implemented by the LwM2M server through the device management and service enablement interface.

As shown in Fig. 5.31, LwM2M core specification is called a "Transport" specification, the current assumed protocol is CoAP which is not technically a transport layer (as in the ISO/OSI ref. stack model) protocol but a transfer layer protocol. The supported underlying transport layer protocols are UDP and SMS (either on the device or on a smartcard if the device actually has such hardware). If the device contains a universal integrated circuit card (UICC)/subscriber identity module (SIM) that can send and receive SMS messages, then this system is considered secure in the protection of 3GPP/ETSI cellular capabilities.

Datagram transport layer security (DTLS) also can be used as a transfer layer on top of UDP, as a secure messaging/transport layer, for the upper CoAP.

As shown in Fig. 5.31, in the interaction between an LwM2M server and an LwM2M client, information reporting is part of the data model of the LwM2M protocol, and the specification responsibility falls in both the CoAP and LwM2M layers.

Next to OMA, the IPSO alliance performs a similar and adherent effort in order to provide a common design pattern and an object model based on the OMA LwM2M specification. By using reusable object and resource design, IPSO targets high-level interoperability between smart object devices and connected software applications on other devices and services. From the Azure view, some engineering details of LwM2M can be found in Chapter 3 Functional Description of LWM2M Client. On-line available https://docs.microsoft.com/en-us/azure/rtos/netx-duo/netx-duo-lwm2m/chapter3.

At last, let's take a glance at OneM2M, which was launched by seven of the world's leading ICT standard organizations on July 24, 2012, as a global organization to ensure the most efficient deployment of M2M communication systems. The OneM2M organizations include CCSA, ARIB and TTC, ATIS and TIA, ETSI and TTA. OneM2M released the first version (Release 1) series of specifications in early 2015. The series of specifications provides basic technical standards for building a unified horizontal IoT platform. From the perspective of end-to-end services independent of access, it defines the business architecture supporting device management, data model and connection control, as well as the open interface and protocol based on the architecture. On this basis, OneM2M in the series of release 2 specifications adds features such as enabling smart home and industrial fields, interoperability support for different systems such as lwM2M, and semantic-based interoperability. At the 23rd technical plenary session of oneM2M in May 2016, the standardization work of Release 3 started, and the specification was positioned at the key stage of the industrialization application of standards. Finally, from the view of an ICT Corp., Fig. 5.32 describes an M2M architecture with functional common service layer and extra-functional. And in the architecture, a cross-domain middleware is illustrated as the composition of computation models, data models, communication models, and SLA/Secure LA at the M2M Cloud. The given figure here is for readers to simply compare and deepen the impression of M2M from other views.

5.7.5 *3GPP network enhancement for LPWANs*

3GPP started the feasibility study of mobile communication system supporting machine communication as early as in 2005 and then formulated the optimization scheme of MTC communication structure based on GSM and UMTS. The formal study of MTC was launched in R10 phase in

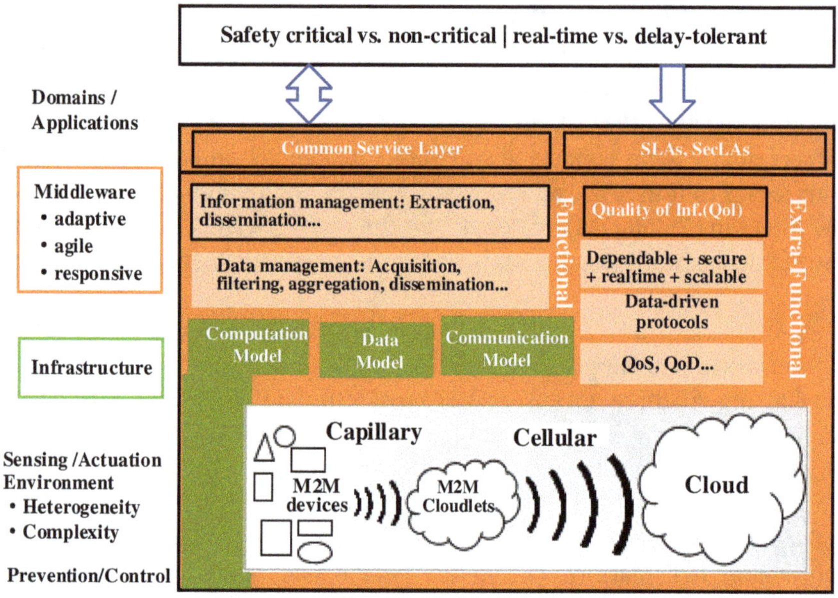

Figure 5.32 An ICT company view of M2M architecture with common service layer and extra-functional.

2008. 3GPP specification is constantly adding new features to meet the needs of the developing market. On the early stage, due to the particularity of MTC communication, it is necessary to send small amount of data discontinuously or continuously. Therefore, in 2013, MTC standardization of 3GPP began to study the MTC power optimization, which was included in the R12 version of standardization. 3GPP uses a parallel version system, and the system versions of its technical specifications include release 1–release 18 up to now.

3GPP only studies the machine communication with cellular communication module and data transmission through cellular network, namely MTC. In the R12 stage, in order to meet the surge of M2M, LTE-M (low-cost MTC) service provides a small bandwidth to meet the potential number of more than 30 billion IoT access users. 3GPP defines UE Cat-0 for the IoT, and its uplink and downlink rates are both 1 Mbps, and it optimizes the LTE network about M2M. After that, the subdivision of MTC related working group by 3GPP lays the foundation for MTC network enhancement architecture in R13 stage. For a kind of service that do not need mobility, small amount of data, and are insensitive to delay, such as smart meter reading, the proposed CIoT structure is shown in Fig. 5.33.

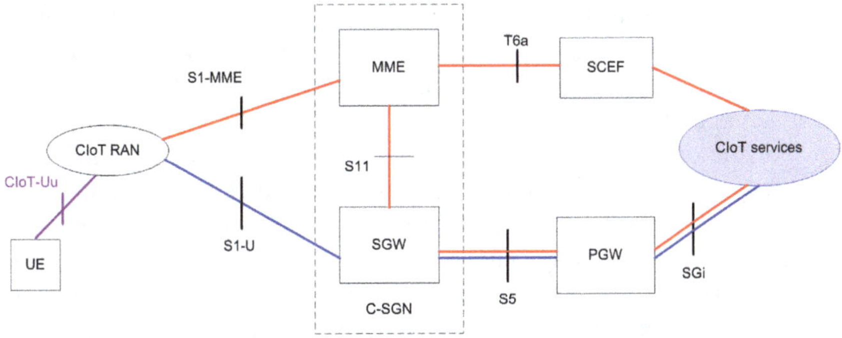

Figure 5.33 CIoT network enhancement of 3GPP in R13 phase.

In R13, a dedicated core network (DCN, or DECOR) provides specific characteristics and functions dedicated for specific types of LPWAN UEs (such as IoT subscribers). The main architecture enhancements are to route and maintain the UEs in their respective DCN. An operator may choose to deploy one or more DCNs within a PLMN with each DCN for specific types of subscribers.

In terms of DCN core network, the CIoT by R13 of 3GPP defines two optimization schemes in evolved packet system (EPS):

- User plane CIoT EPS optimization.
- Control plane CIoT EPS optimization.

As shown in Fig. 5.33, the red line represents the function optimization scheme of the CIoT EPS control plane and the blue line represents the function optimization scheme of the CIoT EPS user plane.

For the function optimization of CIoT EPS control plane, the uplink data is transmitted from eNB (RAN) to mobility management entity (MME), where the transmission path is divided into two branches: either serving GW (SGW) to PDN gateway (PGW) and then to the application server, or service capability exposure function (SCEF) to the application server (CIoT services), which only supports non-IP data transmission. The downlink data transmission path is the same but in the opposite direction. The two schemes do not need to establish a data wireless bearer, and the data packets are sent directly on the signaling wireless bearer. Therefore, they are very suitable for non-frequent small packet transmission.

SCEF, shown in Fig. 5.33, was newly (as compared to R12) introduced for NB IoT design. It was used to transmit non-IP packets on the control plane and provided an abstract interface for network services, such as authentication.

For the optimization of CIoT EPS user plane function, the IoT data transmission mode is the same as the traditional data flow, sending data on the wireless bearer, from SGW to PGW, and then to the application server. Therefore, this way generates additional overhead when establishing a connection, but its advantage is that the packet data sequence is transmitted faster. This scheme supports IP data and non-IP data transmission.

Taking the network enhancement architecture of one MNO in China supporting the CIoT as an example (in R13 stage), for the support of NB IoT (Cat.m2) and Cat.m (m1), the control plane and the user plane are transmitted to PGW through SGW and then to the application server, as shown in Fig. 5.34. The IoT platform based on the DCN was designed by the same MNO shown in Fig. 5.35.

Based on the original independent access (dedicated home subscriber server (HSS) and PGW), the dedicated CIoT (DCN) can be constructed by the deployment of core network elements such as MME and SGW, for the next step virtualization (e.g., network function virtualization, NFV,) promoted.

As shown in Fig. 5.35, the upper applications are based on the cloud of MNO cellular enabling infrastructures, including DCN and radio access network (RAN), such as the access for cellular NB-IoT/LTE-M.

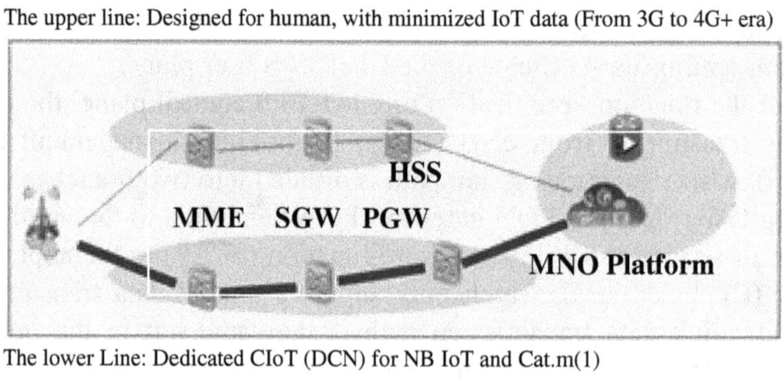

Figure 5.34 R13 and R14 network enhancement evolution architecture by a certain MNO in China.

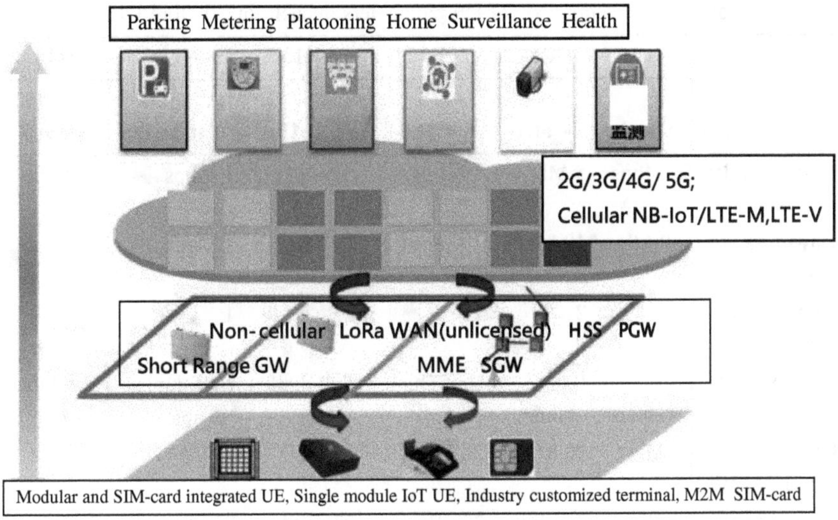

Figure 5.35 IoT platform from an MNO.

The MNO cloud platform also provides GW for non-cellular accesses as short-range WPANs and non-cellular LPWANs (e.g., LoRa WAN). In the lowest perception layer, diverse UE devices are incorporated, and they range from modular and SIM-card integrated UE, single module IoT UE, customized terminals to M2M SIM-card.

The devices type conforms to 3GPP standard as different Categories (Cat.) for IoT UE (user equipment, defined by 3GPP, i.e., terminal device as for IoT), which has been systematically described in the previous part of this section. For example, in order to adapt to the application scenario of tracking management (strong mobility with the performing frequent handoff but having a small amount of data) and monitoring (that do not need mobility and need a wider band for a large amount of uplink data), UE Cat.1 (its uplink rate is 5 Mbps and downlink rate is 10 Mbps.) and Cat.4 (see Table 5.9 for details) were defined in R8, for different IoT data rate of UE devices.

In order to further adapt to the low-power consumption and low-rate requirements of IoT devices (or sensors), the definition of IoT UE was first carried out in R12, that is UE Cat.0 (with lower cost). Table 5.9 shows the comparison of UE parameters in each stage (including R13).

Table 5.9 Comparison of UE parameters in each stage before R13.

UE	R8	R8	R12	R13	R13	R13
	Cat.4	**Cat.1**	**Cat.0**	**Cat.1bis**	**Cat.M(1)**	**Cat. M2 (NB-IoT)**
Uplink peak rate	50 Mbps	5 Mbps	1 Mbps	5 Mbps	1 Mbps	144 kbps
Downlink peak rate	150 Mbps	10 Mbps	1 Mbps	10 Mbps	1 Mbps	200 kbps
Number of antennas	2	2	1	1	1	1
Duplex mode	Full duplex	Full duplex	Half Duplex (opt)	Full duplex	Half duplex (opt)	Half duplex (opt)
UE receive bandwidth	20 MHz	20 MHz	20 MHz	20 MHz	1.4 MHz	200 kHz
UE transmit power	23 dBm	23 dBm	23 dBm	23 dBm	23 dBm, 20 dBm	23 dBm

3GPP is responsible for three categories of LPWAN technology that leverages cellular connectivity in R13. These are LTE-M, NB-IoT, and EC-GSM-IoT (Section 5.7.1) which are comparable with LoRa and Sigfox, among LPWAs. These technologies are all similarly constrained to those most considered by the IETF and may or may not leverage IP networking capabilities (e.g., it is optional for LTE-M and NB-IoT). Additionally, Cat.1bis[12] is a revised IoT UE category with just one antenna for lower cost (as 24–29% decreased).

There are always diverse demands in IoT; cellular LPWAN (such as smart meter reading) is just a branch of cellular-enabled IoT (including MTC/M2M business analysis of Fig. 5.35). However, considering the new demands of IoT, the cellular network enhancement and UE design for new emerging IoT scenarios appears in the 4G era, including video surveillance (such as monitoring), CCTV/LS (closed circuit television or live streaming in mobile Internet) and the connected vehicles, which may stimulate 3GPP to upgrade continuously for embracing the IoE era. In the 5G era, a new term — CIoT arises, and before the introduction of CIoT, the contemporary LPWAN technologies are summarized in the next part.

[12] 3GPP WI "LTE_UE_cat_1RX-UEConTest" defined the use cases set of Cat.1bis, in 3GPP TR36.888.

Table 5.10 Comparison of the three categories of cellular LPWAN and LoRA, SigFox.

	NB-IoT(LTE-M2)	eMTC(LTE-M1)	EC-GSM	LoRa(SemTech)	UNB(SigFox)
Bands	LTE and 2G	LTE bands	2G bands	Unlicensed 433/868 MHz	Unlicensed 902 MHz
Moduling	pi/4 QPSK pi/2 BPSK	QPSK QAM	GMSK	Chirp Spread Spectrum	FSK
Data rate	65 kb/s	375 kb/s	70 kb/s	100 kb/s	100 kb/s
RF	200 kHz	1.08 MHz	200 kHz	125–500 kHz	100 kHz
Emission power	23 dBm	20 dBm or 23 dBm	23 dBm or 33d Bm	14 dBm	14 dBm
construction	Mostly software update	Software update	Mostly software update	Green field	Green field
Coverage	164 dB, 15 km	163 dB, 15 km	164 dB,15 km	157 dB, 10 km	16dB (EU), 12 km

5.7.6 *Summary of LPWAN standards*

For MNO operators, operators with existing LTE network infrastructure (a lot of capital investment) are more inclined to use LTE-M1 (eMTC), such as Verizon and AT&T in the US, while for those regions with a large number of GSM network infrastructure and less LTE network, operators are more inclined to use NB IoT, such as T-Mobile and Sprint in the US, they are more willing to deploy NB IoT on the existing GSM network. The technical parameters of EC-GSM, NB-IoT, and LTE-M (eMTC) are shown in Table 5.10, which also gives comparations to aforementioned LoRA, SigFox (UNB).

In the network deployment, as shown in Table 5.7, in the previous section, NB IoT is not a part of LTE originally, so it needs to use different software (mostly software updates, as shown in Table 5.7 but not all) and make it run in LTE frequency band, which will increase the cost of operators because most operators supporting LTE do not intend to reduce the resource allocated to LTE mobile phones. Fortunately, there is also an optional deployed in the GSM band (GSM spectrum recultivation).

The low data transmission rate of LPWAN makes the power consumption of its device extremely low, and the battery power supply can last for several years or even more than 10 years. From the views of the communication and network layer of IoT, cellular or proprietarily,

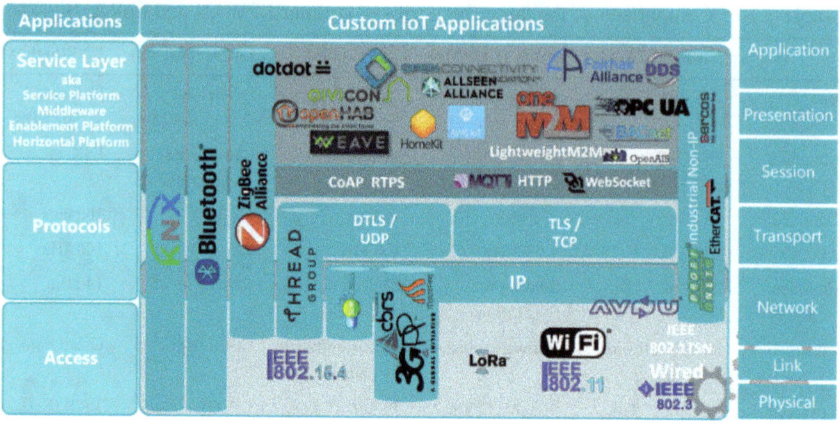

Figure 5.36 Protocols, standards, and stakeholders in the communications and networks layer of IoT.

Note: The right side is an "OSI/ISO equivalent".

LPWANs are making up for the major weakness of IoT network over WLAN/WPAN, not only for cost but also for coverage and complementarity (e.g., in heterogeneity of devices and networking). Although without the description of the LPWANs, Fig. 5.36 gives most protocols, standards, and stakeholders in the communications and networks layer of IoT. From the access views in the figure, KNX (wired or wireless bus connections improved by EIB and EHSA) and BLT are categorized into end-to-end solutions. And WLAN/WPAN/wired LAN and LoRa (not LoRaWAN) are included as capillary accesses for most short-range IoT communications. Some of the protocols in Fig. 5.36 from IETF or other organizations are introduced in Section 5.6. From the platform view, a lot of organizations, alliances, and interest groups are working collaboratively, such as LwM2M, OneM2M mentioned above, and OPC-UA, as a middleware platform, to be introduced in Section 6.1.

In the last part of this section, a summary is given as a conclusion in Table 5.11, where LTE-M(1) as a representative of cellular LPWAN, is compared to other LPWA networking technologies in parameters before the dead line year of 2016.

In Table 5.11, LoRaWAN, SigFox, Ingenu RPMA, and Weightless have been discussed in Section 5.7.4. as for the chip manufacturers, hardware providers and network service providers (including MNOs) in

Table 5.11 LPWAN Protocols.

Name of standard	Weightless –W	Weightless –N	Weightless –P	SigFox	LoRaWAN	LTE-Cat M1	IEEE P802.11ah (LP-Wi-Fi)	Dash7 Alliance Protocol 1.0	Ingenu RPMA	nWave
Frequency band	TVwhite space (400–800 MHz)	Sub-GHZ	Sub-GHZ ISM	868 MHz/ 902 MHz ISM	433/868/780/ 915 MHz ISM	Cellular	License-exempt bands below1 GHz, excluding the TV white spaces	433/868/915 MHz ISM/SRD	2.4 GHz ISM	Sub-GHz ISM
Channel width	5 MHz	Ultra-narrow band (200 Hz)	12.5 kHz	Ultra-narrow band	EU: 8 × 125 kHz, US: 64 × 125 kHz/ 8 × 125 kHz, Modulation: Chirp spread spectrum	1.4 MHz	1/2/4/8/16 MHz	25 kHz or 200 kHz	1 MHz (40 channels available)	Ultra-narrow band
Range	5 km (urban)	3 km (urban)	2 km (urban)	30–50 km (rural), 3–10 km (urban), 1000 km LoS	2–5 km (urban), 15 k m (rural)	2.5–5 km	Up to 1 km (outdoor)	0–5 km	>5 km LoS	10 km (urban), 20–30 km(rural)
End Node Transmit Power	17 dBm	17 dBm	17 dBm	10 µW to 100 mW	EU: < + 14 dBm, US: < + 27 dBm	100 mW	Dependent on regional regulations (from1 mW to1 W)	Depending on FCC/ETSI regulations	Up to 20 dBm	25–100 mW
Packet size	10 byte min.	Up to 20 bytes	10 byte min.	12 bytes	Defined by user	~100–1000 bytes typical	Up to 7,991 bytes (w/o aggregation), up to 65,535 bytes(with aggregation)	256 bytes max/ packet	Flexible (6 bytes to 10 kb)	12 bytes header, 2–20 bytes payload

Table 5.11 (*Continued*)

Name of Standard	Weightless –W	Weightless –N	Weightless –P	SigFox	LoRaWAN	LTE-Cat M1	IEEE P802.11ah (LP-Wi-Fi)	Dash7 Alliance Protocol 1.0	Ingenu RPMA	nWave
Uplink data rate	1 kbps to 10 Mbps	100 bps	200 bps to 100 kbps	100 bps to 140 messages/day	EU: 300 bps to 50 kbps, US: 900–100 kbps	~200 kbps	150 kbps–346.666 Mbps	9.6 kbps, 55.55 kbps or 166.667 kb/s	AP aggregates to 624 kbps per sector (Assumes eight channel access point)	100 bps
Downlink data rate	1 kbps to 10 Mbps	**No Downlink**	200 bps to 100 kbps	Max. 4 messages of 8 bytes/day	EU: 300 bps to 50 kbps, US: 900–100 kbps	~200 kbps	150 kbps–346.666 Mbps	9.6 kb/s, 55.55 kbps or 166.667 kb/s	AP aggregates to 156 kbps per sector (assumes eight channel Access Point)	—
Devices per access point	Unlimited	Unlimited	Unlimited	1M	Uplink: >1, Downlink: <100 k	20k+	8191	NA (connectionless communication)	Up to 384,000 per sector	1M
Topology	Star	Star	Star	Star	Star on Star	Star	Star, Tree	Node-to-node, Star, Tree	Typically Star. Tree supported with an RPMA extender	Star
End node roaming allowed	Yes	Yes	Yes	Yes	Yes	Yes	Allowed by IEEE 802.11 amendments (e.g., IEEE 802.11r)	Yes	Yes	Yes
Governing body	Weightless SIG			Sigfox	LoRa Alliance	3GPP	IEEE 802.11 working group	Dash7 Alliance	Ingenu (OnRamp)	Weightless SIG
Frequency band	TV white-space (400–800 MHz)	Sub-GHZ ISM	Sub-GHZ ISM	868 MHz/902 MHz ISM	433/868/780/915 MHz ISM	Cellular	License-exempt bands below 1 GHz, excluding the TV white spaces	433, 868, 915 MHz ISM/SRD	2.4 GHz ISM	Sub-GHz ISM

(*Continued*)

Channel width	5 MHz	Ultra-narrow band (200 Hz)	12.5 kHz	Ultra-narrow band	EU: 8 × 125 kHz, US: 64 × 125 kHz/ 8 × 125 kHz, Modulation: Chirp spread spectrum	1.4 MHz	1/2/4/8/16 MHz	25 kHz or 200 kHz	1 MHz (40 channels available)	Ultra-narrow band
Range	5 km (urban)	3 km (urban)	2 km (urban)	30–50 km (rural), 3–10 km (urban), 1000 km LoS	2–5 k (urban), 15 k (rural)	2.5–5 km	Up to 1 km (outdoor)	0–5 km	>500 km LoS	10 km (urban), 20–30 km (rural)
Typology	Star	Star	Star	Star	Star on Star	Star	Star, Tree	Node-to-node, Star, Tree	Typically Star. Tree supported with an RPMA extender	Star
End node roaming allowed	Yes	Yes	Yes	Yes	Yes	Yes	Allowed by IEEE 802.11 amendments (e.g., IEEE 802.11r)	Yes	Yes	Yes
Governing Body	Weightless SIG			Sigfox	LoRa Alliance	3GPP	IEEE 802.11 working group	Dash7 Alliance	Ingenu (OnRamp)	Weightless SIG

LPWAN/M2M markets are very cautious when deciding which standard to choose because many wireless standardization organizations have proposed corresponding technologies, such as 802.11ah (low-power Wi-Fi protocol) in Table 5.11, and massive MTC (a uniform name for the three-categories of cellular LPWAMs in 5G), which will be discussed in the next section.

According to the research of Analysis Mason, LPWAN technology alone can increase the number of the connected devices in the world to up to 3 billion by 2023. In the process of commercialization, these technologies can collaborate with each other's advantages to make up for each other's weak points, which can avoid comparing the advantages of one protocol with the disadvantages of other protocols. For example, compared with the cellular M2M, the transmission distance of Sigfox can reach more than 3 km in the complex urban environment, even more than 15 km in the open area, and the penetration is strong (with narrowband data transmission) in many harsh environments. But SigFox needs the combination of cellular networks as its public or private (data sharing) infrastructure for the device in SigFox network to the connection to cloud/WAN (typically, by SigFox gateways), when considering the combination of capillary network (either long range or short range) and cellular network.

With the development of science and technology, more and more devices have the ability of communication and networking, and the concept of "Networking Everything" has gradually become a reality when IoE era is stepping in to our daily lives. In the next section, CIoT in 5G will be introduced.

5.8 5G CIoT and Beyond

5G, the 5th generation wireless system, is being developed and enhanced to provide unparalleled connectivity to connect everyone and everything, everywhere. 5G got its start when the International Telecommunications Union (ITU) identified minimum recommendations for a new technology that was further defined and standardized by the 3GPP. The first version of the 5G System, based on the Release 15 ("R15") version of the specifications developed by 3GPP, comprising the 5G core (5GC) and 5G new radio (NR) with 5G user equipment (UE), is currently being deployed commercially throughout the world both at sub-6 GHz (FR1) and at mmWave frequencies (FR2: from 24 GHz to 52 GHz). R15 focused on the

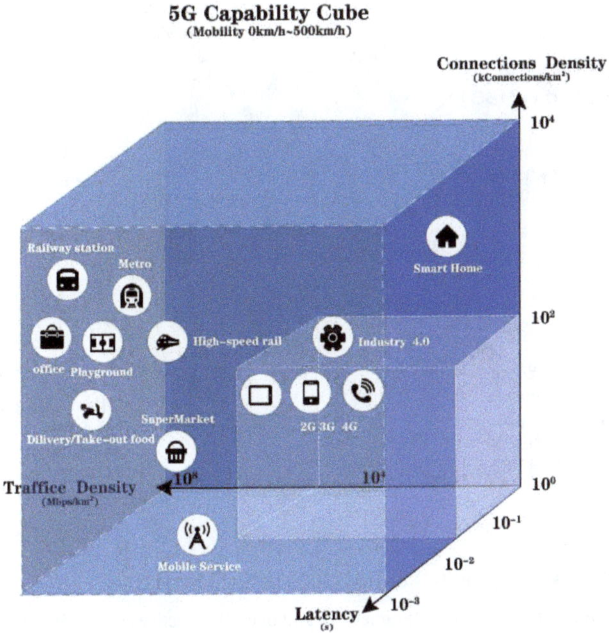

Figure 5.37 5G scopes.

enhanced mobile broadband (eMBB) services. And the released capabilities from R15 and later 5G phases (expected from R15 to R18) over 4G are shown in Fig. 5.37.

The second version of 5G standardized by 3GPP as the specifications of Release 16 (R16) stage focuses on new features for ultra-reliable low latency communication (URLLC) and IIoT, including time-sensitive communication (TSC), enhanced location services, and support for **non-public networks** (NPNs). Concurrently, R17 is on the way.

URLLC for critical M2M/MTC communication capabilities is an essential enabler for the development of the IoT. It will enable IoT use cases to go beyond data collection and respond to complex scenarios requiring precise actuation, automation, and mission critical communications.

The technological enhancements to telecommunication networks, brought about by 5G, will allow new connectivity to become the catalyst

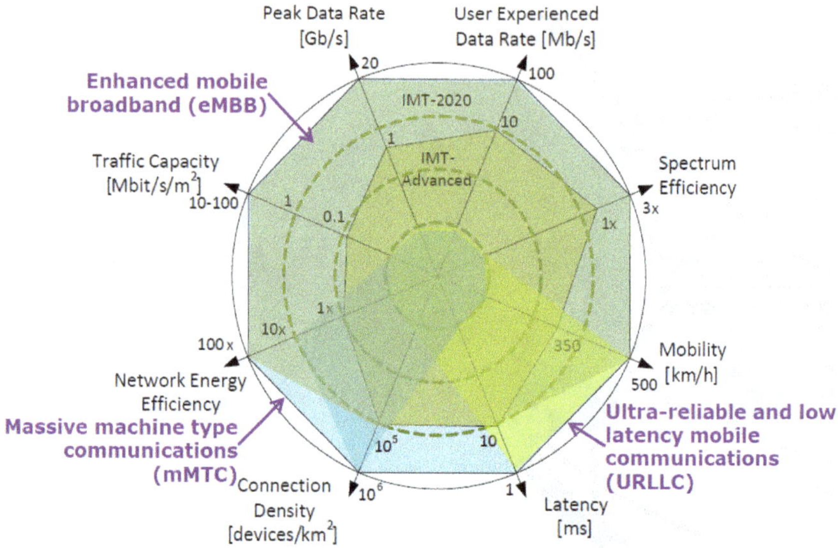

Figure 5.38 5G key capabilities of IMT-2020 defined by ITU.

Source: ITU Report (IMT Vision — "Framework and overall objectives of the future development of IMT for 2020 and beyond", ITU-R Recommendation M.2083-0, September 2015).

for new-generation IoT services by creating innovations such as advanced modulation schemes for wireless access, network slicing capabilities, automated network application lifecycle management, SDN, and NFV, as well as providing support for edge- and cloud-optimized distributed network applications. The requirements of critical IoT communications are numerous and diverse, ranging from the increased reliability and resilience of the communication network to ultra-low latencies and high capacities while also integrating the context of the mission with the ability to respond to strict energy efficiency constraints or to cover large outdoor areas, deep indoor environments, or vehicles moving at high speeds. Bandwidth and delay for services enabled by legacy networks (2G/3G/4G) and 5G are presented in Fig. 5.37.

The ITU-R M.2083-0 define the capabilities of 5G to use cases such as enhanced mobile broadband (eMBB), massive machine-type communications (mMTC), and ultra-reliable and low-latency communications (URLLC) that include the full deployment of IoT solutions, as shown in Fig. 5.38.

Instead of viewing 5G as a single technology, an important thing to understand is there are three different "flavors" of 5G (eMBB, mMTC, URLLC), each meeting different wireless technology needs and each meeting different IoT requirements and according functional specifications.

5.8.1 *5G CIoT*

The development of a critical IoT is mainly a business-to-business (B2B) and business-to-business-to-consumer (B2B2C) demand and strongly driven by the digital transformation of vertical industries and expanding the traditional cellular technology development (which relies heavily on "C" brands). As market estimating from IDATE, there will be about 60 million 5G units by 2030, from the views of B2B and B2B2C markets. The expected high average revenue per units (ARPUs) of the 5G technology will respond to a critical demand in many industries in terms of generating important cost reductions and new revenue opportunities. Some of the industry scenarios are classified according to the bandwidth and delay for 5G IoT services, as shown in Fig. 5.39.

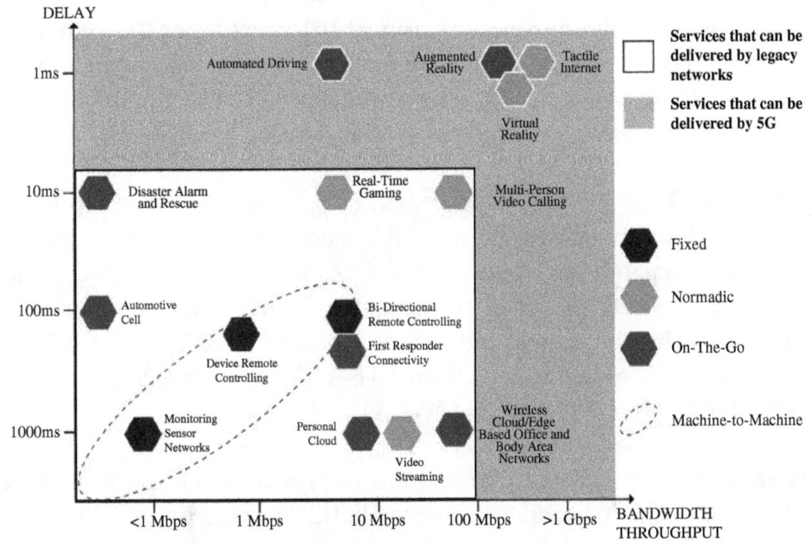

Figure 5.39 Bandwidth and delay for services enabled by legacy networks and 5G.

Note: mMTC in the dotted circle.

Compared with LTE advanced/4G, cellular communication standards have begun responding to these requirements by developing new technologies in 5G, especially for public safety operations (multi-person call), AR/VR, autonomous driving, etc., which are still limited in 4G scope and less ability to provide the ultra-low latencies required in many critical or IIoT use cases.

Accordingly, 5G networks are expected to support the new IoT technologies, enabling IoT/IIoT device producers to develop and deploy new IoT devices and systems across multiple industries and provide IoT/IIoT applications globally. Several aspects from 5G views are introduced below.

Massive MTC is an important IoT marked as mentioned above, which includes the monitoring sensor networks or other kinds of WSAN in low-latency, low-data-rate but low-mobility LPWAN use cases (mMTC), it is an enhancement in the 5G era and still popular, shown by the dotted circle in Fig. 5.39.

URLLC, which is beyond the dotted circle of Fig. 5.39, as mission-critical communication with ultra-low latency in verticals of importance includes connected health, in which critical IoT capabilities promise the generalization of teleoperations and robotics surgeries. Manufacturing will also be strongly impacted, as critical IoT capabilities are among the building blocks of the smart factory (enabling advanced automation and remote control). The key requirements for critical IoT communications in different industrial sectors are presented in Section 5.9.4.

Cellular V2X is another leading market for the automotive sector, in which the development of the most advanced autonomous cars will use critical IoT capabilities to perform tasks, such as complex intersection control, dynamic area management, and cooperative cruise control and platooning. The automotive industry is already strongly involved in the standardization process of 5G, from LTE V2X to 5G NR V2X, forming the 5G Automotive Association (5GAA).

eMBB in 5G use cases can be realized to provide solutions in the B2C, B2B, B2B2C, and IoT market segments. In B2C market, operators offer the services such as high-definition video (TV, movies, streaming live sports, and city/security video surveillance) or home/office automation solutions by eMBB. In the B2B market, operators offer the services such as mobility

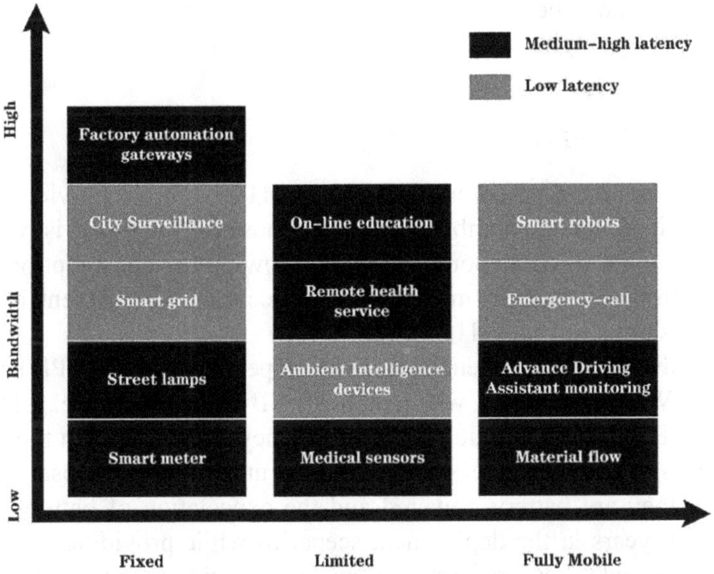

Figure 5.40 IoT service segmentation.

solutions and cloud services to businesses (SMEs, large corporations), where the services are typically consumed by high throughput.

Some of the 5G IoT scenarios are classified according to the bandwidth and mobility demands for 5G IoT services, as shown in Fig. 5.40.

5G is enabling faster, more stable, and more secure connectivity that's advancing everything from self-driving vehicles, to smart grids/smart sensors or multi person eCall (video call) for rescue, to AI-enabled robots on factory floors (e.g., AGVs). It's unleashing a massive IoT ecosystem where networks can serve billions of connected devices, with the right trade-offs between speed, latency, and cost.

As shown in Fig. 5.40, for the medium–high latency fixed use cases of smart meters, lamps home/office automations, and industrial WSN/WSAN, the latency of end to end is typically within 100 ms and with a communication reliability of 99.99% (3GPP TR 22.832 and TS 22.104 specifications). As for safety critical use cases in ultra-low latency, e.g., surveillance, the latency demands from 5 ms to 10 ms, with a typical bandwidth below 2 Mbps.

As for the medium–high latency limited or fully mobile use cases, e.g., home education, remote health monitoring, and logistics, their latency demand is below 500 ms, with the reliability of 99–99.9% (3GPP TR22.804) and higher bandwidth (e.g., 7.5–25 Mbps).

5.8.2 *Massive MTC*

Massive machine-type communication (mMTC) aims to provide spread connectivity to a huge number of devices whose traffic profile is typically a small amount of data sporadically, with low-power consumption (long battery lifetime). It is an important 5G directions for different IoT use cases, as shown in Fig. 5.41.

Massive MTC has been already developed as part of 3GPP Release 13/14 LPWA technologies, which includes NB-IoT, LTE-M (i.e., LTE Cat. m1), and EC-GSM, without concerning latency and throughput too much. The main concern is the optimal power utilization of those devices because they are battery powered and the expectation of battery life is around 10 years in the deployment scenarios while providing unrivalled low-power wide-area performance covering a wide range of data rates.

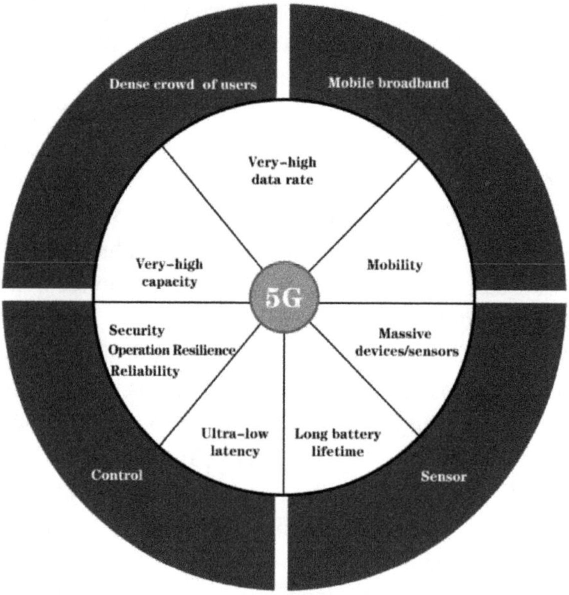

Figure 5.41 Several verticals of importance in 5G key capabilities.

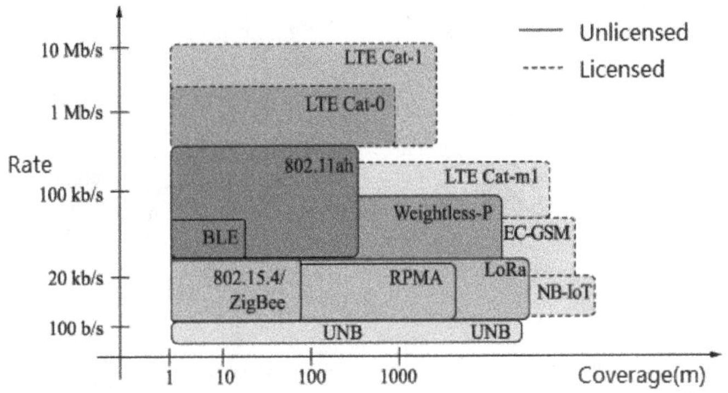

Figure 5.42 Comparison of the three categories mMTC (NB-IoT,LTE-M and EC-GSM in licensed cellular spectrum), unlicensed LPWAs (e.g., LoRa and SigFox/UNB), and other technologies.

They are compared in Fig. 5.42, where NB-IoT has some advantage in the coverage, and LTE-M (Cat.m1) performs a little better than other unlicensed LPWA technologies in the combination of coverage and data rate. These are expected to meet most 5G mMTC requirements (in 5G NR), while others that require more bandwidth with ultra-reliable low latency (full URLLC) will require the 5G core deployment for full end-to-end latency reduction, such as NR-V2X and IIoT.

Both LTE-M (eMTC) and NB-IoT cater to scalable connectivity for a huge number of devices and latency agnostic applications in mMTC. As for NB-IoT, it should be optimized for small packets, sporadic transmissions, and uplink centric activity. In terms of mobility, LTE-M (<120 km/h) is better than NB-IoT (<30 km/h). As shown in Fig. 5.43, typical use cases for LTE-M (eMTC) are energy management, connected home appliances, object tracking, smart watches, and so on. Typical use cases for NB-IoT are utility meters, city infrastructure, smart buildings appliances, and environment monitoring (more coverage and less data rate than LTE-M).

With the vision of 5G mMTC technology, LTE-M and NB-IoT are leading LPWANs to power a wide range of IoT devices, including smart parking, utilities, wearables, and industrial solutions. And they will continue evolving with the 5G specification.

As seen in Fig. 5.37, the number of connections in the 5G era will reach 10^7 per square kilometer. Of course, the connection needs

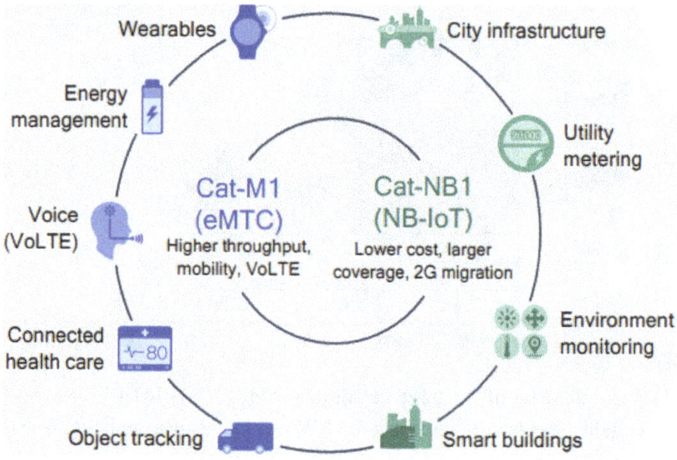

Figure 5.43 Comparison of LTE-M and NB-IoT.
Source: GSA NB-IoT and LTE-M: Global Market Status, March 2018.

of "things" are considered as mMTC developed for a history from R8 stage to now, from the continuous working of 3GPP. Table 5.12 introduces the MTC services developments in each release of 3GPP.

As previously mentioned, LTE-M is a LPWAN technology based on LTE evolution, with the older names being low-cost MTC in R12 and enhanced MTC (eMTC) in R13. In order to distinguish from NB-IoT, it was also called LTE-M1 or LTE cat-m1 in R13, and two low-power saving schemes were introduced: LTE extended discontinuous reception (eDRX) and LTE power-saving mode (PSM). The transmission of LTE-M can reach 1 Mbps, and eMTC has some advantages in price, coverage, automatic operation period, and compatibility with existing LTE mobile infrastructure. LTE-M (eMTC) network can be built on the basis of existing LTE network by updating software.

The low complexity optimization of eMTC includes narrowband operation and physical channel simplification. For example, MTC physical downlink control channel (MPDCCH) was introduced to reduce the cost, bandwidth, and transmit power based on Cat.0 (in R12), instead of LTE PCHICH and PHICH.

Table 5.12 M2M developments in 3GPP stages.

Year	Release	Name	M2M services	Notes
2009/2010	R8/R9	LTE	MTC services characteristics supporting (see Table 5.8).	In R8, Category4 (Cat.4) is defined as 50 Mbps uplinks and 150 Mbps downlinks.
2011	R10	LTE-Advance/ LTE-A(4G)	Overload control for a large number of MTC equipment access to the network. Low priority and other functions such as low power, low mobility, and other MTC features support.	R10 was issued in June 2011, and then LTE-Advance/LTE-A came.
2013	R11	LTE-Advance/ LTE-A(4G)	MTC network enhancement (see Figs. 5.33 and 5.34), access control to avoid congestion, random access analysis of smart metering, fleet management, and earthquake monitoring MTC applications. The corresponding M2M features improved.	In this phase, a certain number MTC increased, coordinated multi-point operation (CoMP) and other functions were proposed for MTC network enhancement.
2015	R12	LTE-Advanced pro (4.5G)	Cat. 0 of UE is defined for the first time, with 20 MHz bandwidth, half duplex support, and 23 dBm maximum transmit power; when the number of M2M surges, LTE-M (called low-cost MTC in R12) provides a small bandwidth to meet the potential access number of more than 30 billion in the IoT. D2D technology of R12 and R13 started the standardization of vehicle-to-vehicle communication (V2V).	LTE-Hi (hot spot indoor); TD-LTE and dynamic TDD for the improving of spectrum resources; massive MIMO; cloud EPC and shorter TTI for the delay reduced.
2016	R13	LTE-Advanced pro (4.5G)	LTE extended discontinuous reception (eDRX) and LTE power saving mode (PSM). In contrast to LTE-M (enhanced MTC), NB IoT is newly designed. EC-GSM see Section 5.7.1.	Licensed-assisted access (LAA); 3D/FD-MIMO (FD, full dimension), massive carrier aggregation; latency reduction; downlink multiuser superposition transmission. LTE-unlicensed (LTE-U); communication required by public services (critical mission).

Table 5.12 (*Continued*)

Year	Release	Name	M2M services	Notes
2017	R14	LTE-Advanced pro(4.5G)	enhancement NB-IoT (eNB-IoT): non-anchor carrier; release assistance indicator; re-connection with radio link failure (RLF); maximum TX power 14 dBm. Further enhanced MTC (FeMTC):VoLTE improvement; 5 MHz bandwidth.	Both of eNB-IoT and FeMTC: universal integrated circuit card (UICC) for MTC power optimization; enhance TBS/HARQ; single-cell multicast (SC-PTM); positioning (R13 does not support base station location, but the operator network can do private solutions, such as location based on cell ID, by increasing the location server for the contact with the base station. R14 positioning enhancement supports E-CID, UTDOA or OTDOA, and the desired positioning accuracy is within 50 m). Vehicle-to-everything (V2X) communication: V2V;V2I/N; V2P
2018	R15	5G phrase1	Early data transmission (EDT), wake-up signal, and other network-side enhancement for mMTC. As for eLTE-V2X, carrier aggregation (CA) and higher QAM support details, see the next sub-section	5G IoT evolution focuses on the following three main areas: (i) enhancements to features introduced in R13 and R14; (ii) features that are needed for operational enhancements; (iii) new features to further expand the applicability of the 5G system to new IoT markets and use cases, such as new vertical IIoT, smart home, smart city, public utilities, e-health, and smart wearable devices; see Fig. 5.43.
2020	R16	5G phrase2	New features for URLLC and Industrial IoT (i.e., critical MTC), including time-sensitive communication (TSC), enhanced location services, and support for **non-public networks** (NPNs)	Crucial new features, such as NR on unlicensed bands (NR-U) with the same flexible frame and slot structure and fundamental physical layer design and protocol stack as NR R15 (e.g., for eMBB services, for additional spectrum and for the offloading traffic in hot spots), integrated access and backhaul (IAB) and NR vehicle-to-x (V2X) are also being introduced as part of R16, as well as enhancements for massive MIMO, wireless and wireline convergence, the service-based architecture (SBA) and network slicing.

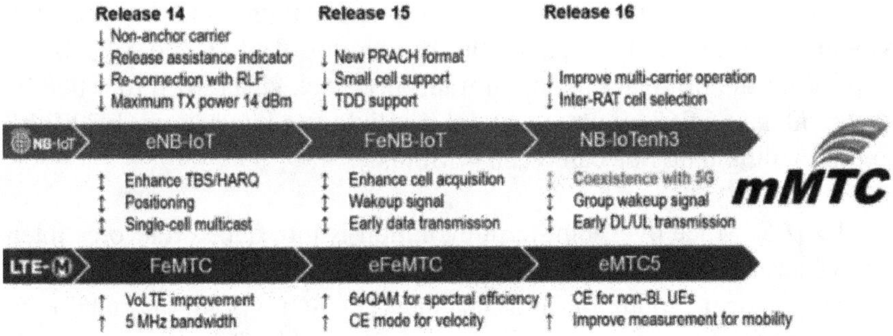

Figure 5.44 Importance of NB-IoT and LTE-M in R14, R15, and R16 for mMTC.

As shown in Fig. 5.44, some features are listed according to each direction of NB-IoT and LTE-M, ranging from R14 to R16 by now.

• **Enhancement for LTE-M in R14 (as FeMTC):** The R14 version of eMTC standard has further enhanced eMTC in positioning, multicast, mobility, and VoLTE and completed the standardization work in June 2017.

(1) *Positioning*: Positioning and tracking are important to mMTC, but the positioning method based on global navigation satellite has high cost and poor accuracy. Therefore, eMTC in R14 uses the time difference of arrival (TDOA) algorithm to calculate and determine the location information through the time difference of arrival of the received reference signals from multiple transmission points, providing positioning services, which can be widely used in asset tracking, emergency call.

(2) *SC-PTM*: When transmitting the same information for a group of specific devices, the traditional unicast will cause a lot of waste of resources. Single-cell point to multipoint, or single-cell multicast (SC-PTM) in R14, using single-cell multicast control channel and single-cell multicast transmission channel, supports downlink multicast, realizes group information transmission for mass devices, and effectively reduces the cost of terminal.

(3) *5 MHz bandwidth*: eMTC in R13 mainly focuses on sensors, smart meters, and other applications, and the data rate is relatively low. In order to cope with more high data rate services/applications, such as video surveillance, 3GPP rel-14 expands the bandwidth of eMTC to 5 MHz, by expanding the original maximum transport block size (TBS) to 4 008 bit downlink and 6 968 bit uplink, and the uplink data rate can reach 7 Mbit/s and downlink data rate can reach 4 Mbit/s.

(4) ***VoLTE*****:** Voice over long-term evolution is introduced for voice interaction services in wearable devices, smart home, and so on. eMTC introduces physical uplink shared channel (PUSCH) with asynchronous HARQ[13] and a new scheduling timing relationship. The latter is mainly aimed at the optimization of the interval time between the downlink and uplink feedback of half duplex users, which can increase the size of transmission data in VoLTE and improve the communication quality

- **Enhancement for NB IoT in R14 (as eNB-IoT):** R14 specification enhances the NB-IoT protocol. For example, R14 non-anchor carriers (or non-anchor NB-IoT carriers) may be configured only for data communication, by which narrowband reference signal (NRS) transmission is sent by a base station (e.g., eNB) only when data or signaling is sent, thereby minimizing NRS interference on other cells.

R14 introduces a new device category, NB2 (LTE Cat NB2), as the new NB-IoT protocol features in R14 refers to devices that are based on the enhanced NB-IoT protocol as standardized in the 3GPP Release 14. LTE Cat NB1 refers to IoT devices based on the NB-IoT protocol standardized in the 3GPP Release 13 specification. They, with Cat M1, all belong to wireless cellular LPWA connectivity protocols for IoT mMTC.

Here is a short introduction on how the 3GPP R14 specification enhances the NB-IoT protocol for NB2:

(1) ***NB2 positioning*****:** The 3GPP Release 14 introduces OTDOA and E-CID positioning methods into NB2 for higher location accuracy. Then, Cat-NB2 modem IP solution for positioning arises.

(2) ***Multicast in NB2*****:** The NB2 devices contain multicast transmission mode, which the NB1 device does not have.

---

[13] Uplink control information (UCI) can be carried on the PUSCH and may contain hybrid automatic repeat request ACK (HARQ-ACK) information. Formerly, PUSCH only supported synchronous HARQ.

(3) ***Enhanced NB2 mobility*:** NB2 devices provide better mobility — reconnection is now supported also in the device connected mode as opposed to idle mode only in NB1.

(4) ***LTE CAT NB2 peak data rates*:** The NB-IoT 3GPP Release 14 specification introduces higher data rates — NB2 devices can have maximum data speeds of ~127 kbps downlink and ~159 kbps uplink.

(5) ***NB-IoT multi-carrier operation*:** NB2 supports a multi-carrier mode with up to 15 non-anchor carriers, which can support up to 1,000,000 connected NB-IoT devices per square kilometer.

(6) ***NB2 frequency bands*:** Five new FDD frequency bands are introduced for NB-IoT: 11, 21, 25, 31, and 70.

(7) ***New NB2 device power class*:** 3GPP R14 enhances NB2 devices with a new 14 dBm power class to allow the use of smaller batteries and small form factors.

The comprehensive comparison, shown in Table 5.13, gives the differences between the NB-IoT 3GPP R13 and R14 specifications, as NB1 vs. NB2 devices.

- **Enhancement for mMTC in R15:** R15 further enhances the functions of LTE-M and NB-IoT mainly by adding TDD support (only support FDD mode in R13 and R14) and low-power consumption.

(1) ***Wake-up signal*:** In the idle mode power saving technology, R15 defines a new wake-up signal (or radio) to reduce the power consumption. Usually, the UE (LTE-M/NB-IoT) in idle mode will periodically decode the downlink control channel to obtain paging information. Because the UE does not know whether there is paging message before channel decoding, this process must be performed regularly, which will increase power consumption. Therefore, R15 defines a simple process to detect wake-up signal, so that the UE can directly determine whether there is paging message avoiding the periodical decoding, and the power consumption is further reduced.

(2) ***Early data transmission (EDT)*:** Many IoT applications only transmit tiny packets, such as smart meter reading. For these applications, EDT,

Table 5.13 NB1 vs. NB2 comparison.

Features	LTE Cat NB1	LTE Cat NB2
Channel bandwidth	180 kHz	180 kHz
Transmission duplexity	Half	Half
Max downlink TBS	680 bits	2536 bits
Max downlink data rate	~26 kbps	~80/127 kbps (1HARQ/2HARQ)
Max uplink TBS	1000 bits	2536 bits
Max uplink data rate	~62 kbps	~105/159 kbps (1HARQ/2HARQ)
Quantity of HARQ processes	1	1 or 2
Number of antennae	1	1
Latency range	<10 sec	TBD
Data limit	Not defined	Not defined
Size of payload in a data packet	Not defined	Not defined
Duty cycle	Not defined	Not defined
Data encryption	EPS-AKA	EPS-AKA
Device authentication	SIM	SIM
Voice communication support	No	No
Positioning	Cell ID	OTDOA, E-CID
Standardization organization	3GPP Release 13	3GPP Release-14
UE bandwidth	200 kHz	200 kHz
Maximum transmission power	20, 23 dBm	14, 20, 23 dBm

standardized in 3GPP R15, aims to improve the battery life of the user and reduce message latency by transmitting small data packets during random access (RA) procedure.

In a long run, R17 and beyond is expected to include (but not limited to) enhanced support of IIoT and enhanced support of NPN, enhanced support of wireless and wireline convergence, support for multicast and broadcast architecture, proximity services, enhanced support of multi-access edge computing, and enhanced support of network automation.

From an IIoT view and beyond, 3GPP community identified the major topics of interest for consideration for R17, including NR-Light which aims to enable lightweight communications for industrial sensors and similar applications in IIoT, MIMO enhancements, side-link enhancements for both V2X and public safety, support for non-terrestrial networks

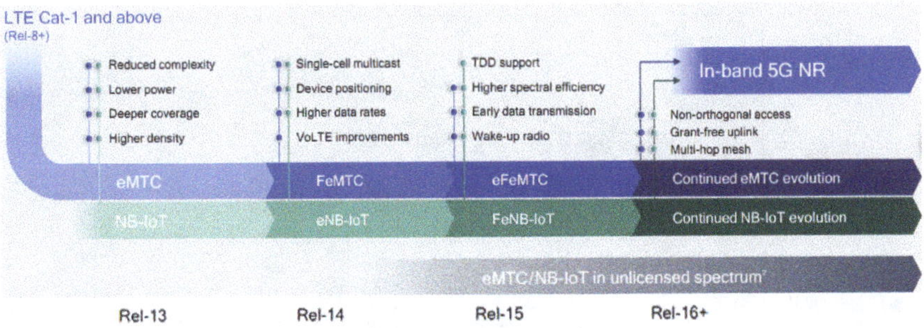

Figure 5.45 mMTC enhancements and evolution path in the 5G system and beyond.

(NTNs) and coverage enhancement techniques, as well as beginning the work to extend 5G NR to operate in frequencies beyond 52 GHz, which is expected to culminate in specifications in R18.

As shown in Fig. 5.45, the improvements to broaden and optimize the massive IoT service capabilities will continue, which is fueled by the commercial deployments of LTE M and NB IoT across the world.

As shown in Fig. 5.45, the improvements of eMTC and NB-IoT for support of 5G mMTC scenarios were summarized. Key technologies were discussed and analyzed above in this section. In terms of system cost and complexity, coverage (e.g., mesh) and power consumption, the standards are still on the way. Adaptations of the technologies to support satellite communications (e.g., Sat-IoT) to truly cover the uncovered area are also discussed in 3GPP (see the next section). In terms of **critical IoT**, the cellular industry has a strong focus on creating a new market for IIoT. To make 5G relevant, industrial use cases need to be addressed as well as the integration of 5G within larger industrial systems. New important features in this direction are, for example, the 5G support for time-sensitive networking (TSN) and non-public networks (NPN). Among these, one enabling technology is of great importance, network slicing (NS), which is based on new ideas as SDN/NFV, and the service-based architecture (SBA). See the following.

5.8.3 *Slices for critical IoT/M2M*

5G provides a resilient cloud-native core network with end-to-end support for network-slicing. Its continuous evolution (including the physical infrastructure and the cloud native foundation by means of the SBA enables

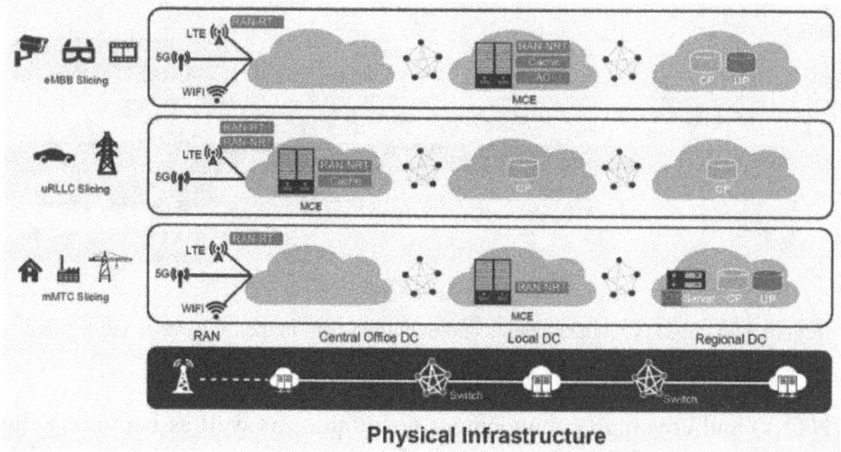

Figure 5.46 5G end-to-end network slicing for multiple industries based on one physical infrastructure.

new value creation through support for new services based on three major use case domains, namely enhanced mobile broadband (eMBB), URLLC, and mMTC. As shown in Fig. 5.46, network slices feature a logical arrangement and are separated as individual structures (just flavors as individual IoT wishes), which allows for heavily customizable service functions and independent operation and management.

R15, as the first version of 5G system (mainly include RAN and 5G core (5GC)), focuses on eMBB using the Release 15 (R15 or Rel-15) version of the 3GPP specifications, as shown in Fig. 5.46, as the eMBB slicing. For the mMTC component, LTE-M and NB-IoT, already developed and enhanced by 3GPP in and before R15 (discussed in the previous section), are folded in the mMTC slicing by LTE RAN, which provides the access for unrivalled LPWA performance covering a wide range of data rates and deployment scenarios. Furthermore, the evolving RANs still allow the coexistence with other IoT systems, such as IEEE 802.11 variants (such as Wi-Fi) or LTE licensed-assisted access (LAA), such as LTE-U or NR-U, because of the objective to provide universal connectivity via all access technologies.[14]

---

[14]The relative LTE-M-U and NB-IoT-U have been developed by 3GPP to support operation in unlicensed frequency bands (Liberg *et al.*, 2019).

Table 5.14 Vertical industrial sectors — key requirements for critical IoT communications.

Verticals	Critical IoT scenarios	Demand strength	Key requirements
Automotive	Automated vehicles (connected and automated vehicles, CAV)	+++	Latency, reliability, coverage (large-scale and mobility), point-to-point communication (V2V, V2I)
Health	Robotics	++	Latency, reliability, energy efficiency
Industrial IoT	Automation, time-critical automation, remote control	++	Latency, reliability, coverage (deep indoor) point-to-point communication, energy efficiency, and local (private) deployments
Energy	Fault prevention and alert, grid backhaul network	++	Latency, reliability, point-to-point communication, large-scale coverage
Public safety	Mission-critical communications	++	Reliability, coverage, resilience, energy efficiency
Agriculture, forestry, environment	Automation	+	Latency, reliability, energy efficiency, coverage of rural areas

Source: IDATE.

The commercial deployments of R15 are already under way and the eMBB characteristic (or eMBB slicing) for IoT applications, includes AR- and VR-based scenarios, and those revolutionizing customer experience in gaming, retail shopping and other customer-centric applications. By eMBB slicing, consumer experience will be enhanced by high data rates, while extremely (or some degree scenarios-depended) low latencies will be achieved (e.g., in BSN usages on bodies when the other side linking to the surveillance of a hospital IoT).

For uRLLC slicing, these developments are of interest to many industries, including the automotive, manufacturing, health, energy, and public service sectors. Among these vertical industrial sectors, key requirements for critical IoT communications are analyzed in Table 5.14.

Among these verticals, uRLLC slicing has strict latency requirements in different industrial sectors. For automated vehicles or connected and

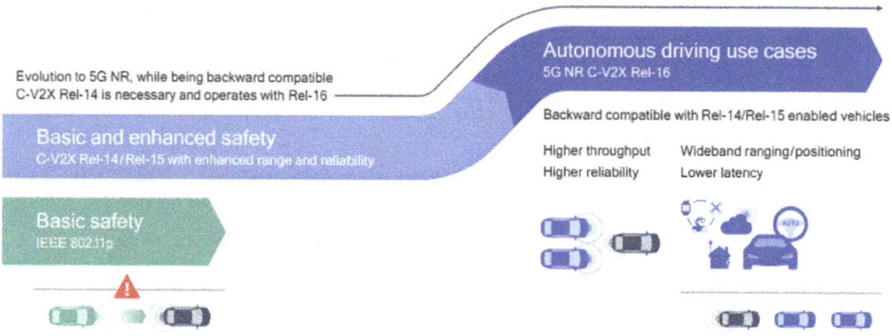

Figure 5.47 Scenarios from LTE-V2X to 5G NR C-V2X, including some enabling characteristics for CAVs and autonomous driving.

automated vehicles (CAV, as a revised name in China), the networks and application scenarios include self-driving, assistant driving (e.g., ADAS), remote management, and V2X.

V2X is a set of communication technologies, which includes cellular V2X (C-V2X) and DSRC/IEEE 802.11p based V2X (see Section 5.4). C-V2X server and service gateways should be deployed in the mobile cloud engine of the central office DC, with the distributed mobile edge computing (MEC, later as multi-access edge computing by ETSI revised). MEC and V2X will be introduced in the next chapter.

The enhanced (cellular) V2X in R15 extends the V2X (LTE-V2X) communication function released by R14, in improving the data rate and bandwidth of V2X communication, e.g., carrier aggregation (CA, up to eight for PC5 carriers) is introduced into mode 4,[15] which reduces the maximum time between packet arrival (at layer 1 of OSI/ISO ref. model) and resource selected for transmission. At the same time, the support for 64QAM modulation and radio resource pool sharing between UEs using mode 3 and UEs using mode 4, and some new UE performance specifications are added, to meet the requirement of low delay. Figure 5.47 gives

[15]R14 introduces two new modes (mode 3, base-station-scheduled and mode 4, autonomously-scheduled) specifically designed for V2V communications. In mode 3, two vehicles directly communicate with each other, but the communications are managed by the cellular infrastructure that selects the sub-channels or radio resources for each V2V transmission. Mode 4 does not require the support of the cellular infrastructure, and vehicles can autonomously select their sub-channels for their V2V transmission (using LTE PC5 interface).

some analysis from LTE-V2X to 5G NR C-V2X, including some enabling characteristics for CAVs and autonomous driving.

Subsequent releases of the 3GPP specifications will build in a backward-compatible manner on the foundation provided by R15 and R16, and R16, as the second phase of 5G has been standardized in 2020. In order to cover the requirements of vertical industrial sectors, R16 focuses on enabling full support for the IIoT for Industry 4.0, including enhanced URLLC and TSC, introducing support for NPNs (also referred to as private networks), operation in unlicensed spectrum, deployment enhancements utilizing IAB operation mainly geared towards mmWave networks, and full system resiliency. Some of them will be introduced as follows.

Generally, toward the advanced IoT expansions, in terms of mobility, V2X, edge, and URLLC slicing enhancements, the R17 architecture will provide:

- Further enhancements for analytics-powered networks and enablers for network automation (eNA),
- support for proximity services,
- a multicast and broadcast architecture,
- enhancements to support edge computing,
- enhancements to support the IIoT framework,
- support for NTNs and drones (also referred to as unmanned aerial system or vehicle (UAS/UAV), as a type of high-altitude platform station (HAPS). There will be a 5G-HAPS (including UAS) example in Section 5.9).

Network slices of 5G for the IoT applications give the selection of connectivity solutions. In this context, industry activities to standardize network slicing should focus on minimizing the complexity of the technical solution so that adoption can be made relatively easy, the IoT use cases need to be defined to drive economies of scale and reduce unitary cost of deployment.

5.8.4 *URLLC for critical IoT*

Generally, in R15, URLLC slicing improved latency, time synchronization, reliability, and resource management (as shown in Fig. 5.48), and details

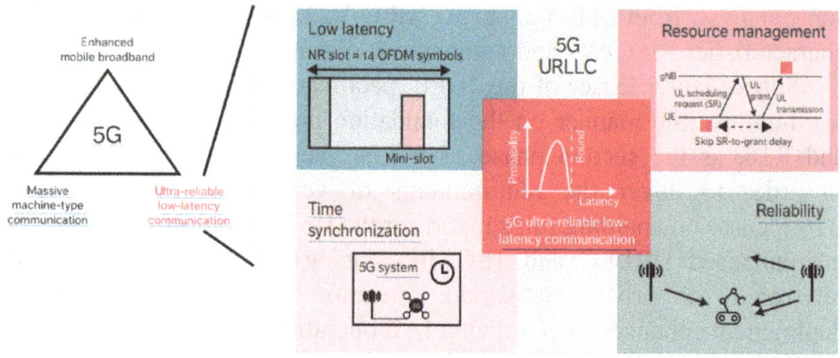

Figure 5.48 5G NR URLLC.

Note: Low latency NR slot = 14 OFDM symbols.

included wider subcarrier spacing of NR slots, reducing the number of OFDM symbols and R15 also defines new channel quality indicator (CQI) and modulation and coding scheme (MCS) for URLLC high reliability.

For the views of IIoT, as the basis for URLLC is inherent in the R15 version of the 5G System, especially in respect to support of low-latency, critical, or ultra-reliable machine-type communication (cMTC, or uMTC) emerges as new words in R16, together with 5G NR URLLC, in still focusing on reliability and low latency.

Typical NR URLLC use cases (i.e., E2E IIoT scenarios) are automated industries (e.g., smart grid and factory automation), AR/VR (e.g., remote surgeries, games), connected vehicles or V2X, and so on, as shown in Table 5.15.

To support URLLC services, the 5G system shall support the transmission over NR interface of a packet of 32 bytes with a reliability of 99.999%[16] (in a typical remote control use case) and a user plane latency of 1 ms.

5.8.4.1 *IIoT enhancement*

IIoT enhancement is to extend the applicability of NR to various verticals, such as further improvements for AR/VR, and new uses cases, such as factory automation, transport industry, and electrical power distribution. R16 focuses on IIoT-related enhancements (URLLC, TSC, and Uu interface), NPNs, operation in unlicensed spectrum, increasing resource

[16]As compared to the R16 of 3GPP in 5G stage-2, reliability of up to 99.999% in URLLC scenarios and even 99.9999% in a smart factory.

Table 5.15 Presentation of the performance requirements of NR URLLC technologies.

Scenario	End-to-end latency (note 2)	Jitter	Survival time	Communication service availability (note 3)	Reliability (note 3)	User experienced data rate	Payload size (note 4)	Traffic density (note 5)	Connection density (note 6)	Service area dimension (note 7)
Discrete automation	10 ms	100 μs	0 ms	99.99%	99.99%	10 Mbps	Small to big	1 Tbps/km²	100 000/km²	1000 × 1000 × 30 m
Process automation-remote control (note 1)	50 ms	20 ms	100 ms	99.9999%	99.999%	1 Mbps up to 100 Mbps	Small to big	100 Gbps/km²	1 000/km²	300 × 300 × 50 m
Process automation-monitoring	50 ms	20 ms	100 ms	99.9%	99.9%	1 Mbps	Small	10 Gbps/km²	10 000/km²	300 × 300 × 50 m
Electricity distribution — medium voltage	25 ms	25 ms	25 ms	99.9%	99.9%	10 Mbps	Small to big	10 Gbps/km²	1 000/km²	100 km along power line
Electricity distribution — high voltage (note 2)	5 ms	1 ms	10 ms	99.9999%	99.999%	10 Mbps	Small	100 Gbps/km²	1 000/km² (note 8)	200 km along power line
Intelligent transport systems–infrastructure backhaul	10 ms	20 ms	100 ms	99.9999%	99.999%	10 Mbps	Small to big	10 Gbps/km²	1 000/km²	2 km along a road
Remote control	[5 ms]	TBC	TBC	[99.999%]	[99.999%]	[From low to 10 Mbps]	[Small to big]	[Low]	[Low]	TBC

NOTE 1: Currently released via wired communication lines.
NOTE 2: This is the end-to-end latency required for the 5G system to deliver the service in case the end-to-end latency is completely allocated to the 5G system from the UE to the interface to data network.
NOTE 3: Communication service availability relates to the service interfaces, reliability relates to a given node. One or more retransmission over the radio interface may take place in order to satisfy the reliability requirement.
NOTE 4: Small: payload typically ≤256 bytes.
NOTE 5: Based on the assumption that all connected applications within the service volume require the user experienced data rate.
NOTE 6: Under the assumption of 100% 5G penetration.
NOTE 7: Estimates of maximum dimensions; the last figure is the vertical dimension.
NOTE 8: In dense urban areas.
NOTE 9: All the values in this table are targeted values and not strict requirements.
Source: 3GPP.

efficiency with duplication, and deployment enhancements by means of IAB operation (mainly geared towards mmWave networks). New use cases with more stringent reliability requirements (e.g., factory automation requiring reliabilities as good as $\mathbf{10^{-6}}$ packet error rate in Table 5.15). Key components of the R16 for enhanced URLLC feature include:

- Control channel enhancements including new compact downlink control information formats with improved reliability, increased downlink control information monitoring capability to minimize delay and service blocking due to the inability to schedule a user, and support for more than one uplink HARQ-ACK within a slot to reduce latency and provide separate feedback for different services.
- Scheduling and HARQ enhancements. This allows for out-of-order uplink scheduling and HARQ-ACK, and reduces latency by allowing a UE to be scheduled with a second uplink packet while still receiving the first uplink packet.
- Support for multiplexing and pre-empting different traffic types in the uplink as illustrated in Fig. 5.49. This allows the gNB to interrupt (i.e., pre-empt) data transmission from one user to accommodate higher-priority data from another user.
- Support for multiple active grant-free uplink transmission configurations to accommodate different service flows (e.g., one configuration for a robot arm/leg and one configuration for a pressure sensor).
- Support for the ability to schedule two or more uplink data repetitions that can be in one slot or across a slot boundary for improved reliability.

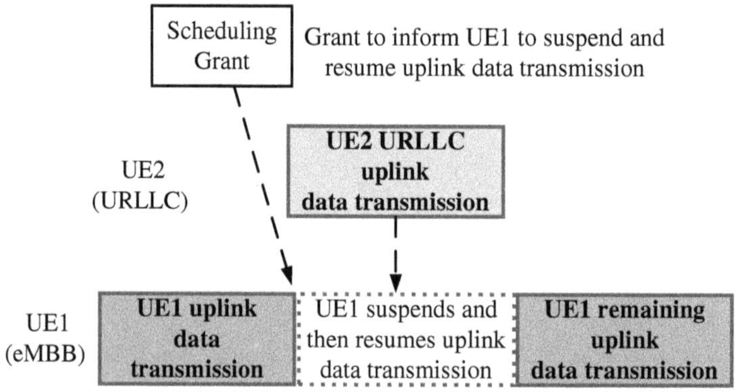

Figure 5.49 Uplink traffic type pre-emption in Rel-16 URLLC.

5.8.4.2 *Integrated access and backhaul for coverage enhancement*

IAB is introduced in R16 as a key enabler for fast and cost-efficient deployments, mainly targeting dense mmWave deployments outdoors. IAB nodes may be deployed for the following four fundamental purposes: (i) to remediate isolated coverage gaps; (ii) to provide backhaul where fiber deployment is sparse; (iii) to enhance system capacity; (iv) to bridge coverage from outdoor to indoor. IAB nodes use the same spectrum and air interface for access and backhaul and create a hierarchical wireless multi-hop network between sites. The hops eventually terminate at a donor node which is connected through a conventional fixed backhaul to the core network.

In the architecture of IAB (shown in Fig. 5.50), a central IAB donor node connects to the core network, parent links to the next node, child links to the node downstream from the core network, and access links to devices served directly by the IAB node. The IAB architecture leverages the gNB logical split architecture with a centralized unit (CU) at the IAB donor node and distributed units (DUs) at IAB nodes.

Further enhancements of IIoT in R17 are expected to focus primarily on enhanced support for TSC; Along with including aspects for IIoT and Industry 4.0, another important aspect is introducing support for NPNs.

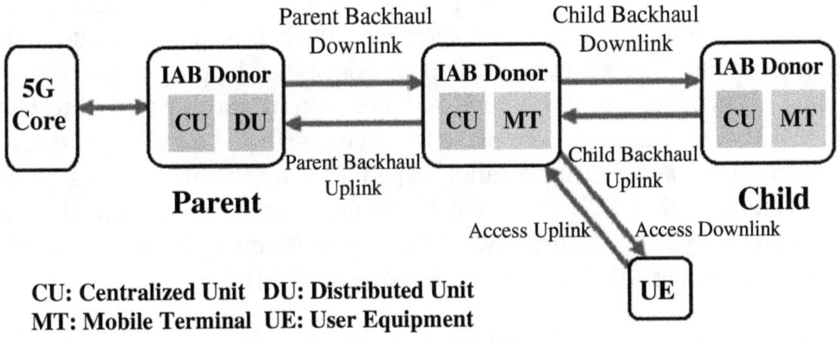

Figure 5.50 IAB architecture for multi-hops mesh by providing coverage to isolated coverage gaps.

5.8.4.3 *NR TSC*

After describing NR URLLC above (without too many details), a brief technology description as well as a presentation of the performance potential of these technologies are introduced in this section to show how the performance fulfills the 5G IIoT targets. In R16, support for E2E IIoT in the 5GS is based on a set of enabling features for IIoT and other vertical IoT (see Table 5.15), which includes the above URLLC and support for TSC. Besides, non-public (i.e., private) networks, 5G LAN-type services, and enhanced location services are specified in R16. Furthermore, the enabling integration with the IEEE TSN set of standards that developed by the IEEE 802.1 TSN task group, gives the foundation for TSC supporting in R16. For details of TSN, see Section 5.10.3.

TSC is a communication service that supports deterministic communication and/or isochronous communication with high reliability and availability. This is achieved by hard guarantees for QoS characteristics, such as latency bounds, packet loss and reliability, and synchronization down to the nanosecond level (10^{-9} second). The architectural model considers the 5G system as a bridge for integration of a 5G system within a TSN operating network, as illustrated in Fig. 5.51, a TSN translator function provides interoperation capability on both the device and the network sides, including support for time synchronization, hold and forward for de-jittering, and link layer discovery and reporting. Furthermore, QoS enhancements were introduced to support efficient scheduling in the RAN and 5G system for deterministic traffic.

Further support for IIoT and TSC without relying on IEEE TSN in the network is proposed, thus enabling private WAN type deployments. Use cases for this type of network include logistics, shipping harbors, and mine trucks. Feature-wise, this includes optimizations for UE-to-UE (E2E) TSC over a single user plane function (UPF) and exposure of deterministic QoS and synchronization capabilities to external entities. 5GS integration with IEEE TSN will be further improved specifically for uplink time synchronization, including support for multiple working clock domains and the collaboration on the edge (e.g., MEC).

- **NPN:** R16 support for **NPNs** includes enhancements for network deployments that are dedicated to specific use cases, such as IIoT, and are fully isolated to allow only authorized subscribers to camp in the network. As for security, it provides enhanced user privacy by also

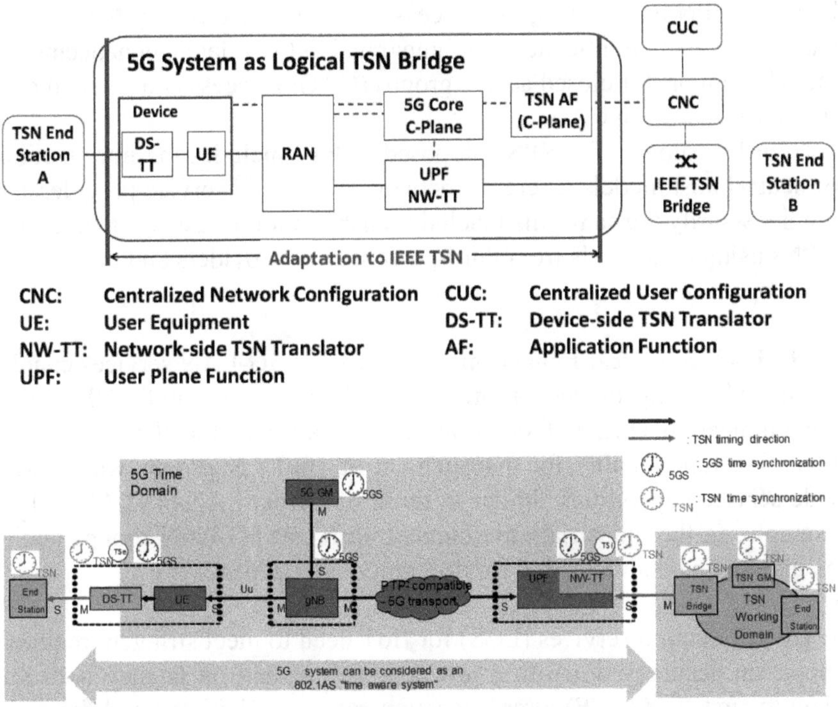

(either of the above)

Figure 5.51 R16 architecture support for integration with IEEE TSN.

Source: R16 3GPP TS 23.501.

protecting the subscription permanent identifier (SUPI) over the air using a privacy-preserving identifier that contains the concealed SUPI, called subscription concealed identifier (SUCI). Two types of deployments are envisioned with NPN: stand-alone NPN and public network integrated NPN.

Stand-alone NPN related enhancements include the introduction of a network identifier (NID) for unique network identification when a shared public land mobile network identifier (PLMN ID)[17] is used, enabling network/cell discovery, network (re-)selection using NID, access control and barring to prevent unauthorized users, NPN-specific authentication mechanism (allowing support for UE(s) without USIM), RAN sharing

[17]PLMN ID used for SNPN does not need to be unique.

between NPN and PLMN, and access to PLMN services by NPN RAN and vice versa. Public network integrated NPN-related enhancements include support for closed access groups (CAGs), access control, and cell (re-)selection using CAG.

Further support for NPN, proposed in R17 includes the introduction of neutral host models where the network owner and service provider are not necessarily the same, also includes enablers for accessing stand-alone NPNs using credentials from third-party service providers and public network operators.

- **5G-LAN Services:** Enhancements to support 5G-LAN services enable optimized routing and local switching within the 5G system for UE-to-UE communication (i.e., without routing the traffic to the data network), including functionality for management of 5G-LAN groups which provide service capabilities similar to those of virtual LANs (VLANs). For example, in the industrial environment, different 5G-LAN groups could be maintained and managed for different device types.

- **LCS:** Location services (LCS) for IIoT need to meet stringent requirements on accuracy down to a few centimeters, and on latency both for time-to-first-fix (TTFF) after a location request is initiated and for continuous localization of the device. This will impact the location and positioning architecture by introducing a RAN-based location management component (LMC) which reduces the latency incurred due to signaling with the access and mobility management function (AMF), thus being able to process measurement data faster. Further enhancements are proposed to be specified as part of the enhanced LCS architecture and 5G system procedures in R17.

5.8.5 *ML as a service in NWDAF*

R15 and R16 specify the framework for data collection and data analytics in the 5GS by introducing the network data analytics function (NWDAF), as illustrated in Fig. 5.52.

The NWDAF is responsible for providing network analysis information upon request from network functions, towards utilizing the potential of artificial intelligence (AI) and machine learning (ML) techniques to realize network automation with less human interaction. It is expected to

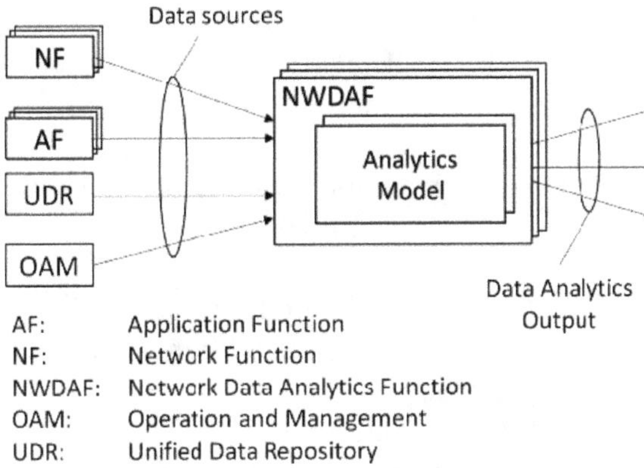

Figure 5.52 NWDAF as network data analytics function in the 5G system.

have a distributed architecture providing analytics at the edge in real time and a central function for analytics which need central aggregation (e.g., service experience).

On the one hand, more localized automated management by edge cognition for every radio access point and edge cloud entity is required, i.e., all the communication relationships and operational requirements are learned. On the other hand, in analytics-powered networks, the network management moves to higher-level abstractions for clusters of nodes, governed by a continuous of intent- and policy-based management interfaces, thus allowing a tight alignment with service management procedures.

As shown in Fig. 5.52, the collection and analysis of OAM data provides a broad range of management capabilities, including automated management, and the NWDAF service allows NF consumers to request and get load-level information of network slice instance.[18]

Advanced AI/ML algorithms are used in predictive analytics, anomaly detection, trend analysis, and clustering have become a top choice for use cases such as customer experience management, personalized marketing, or data monetization from the 4G era. New demands for 5G NWDAF, such as advanced prescriptive analytics to drive closed-loop automation and self-healing networks, calls for this kind of service not only for integrators (e.g., ISPs and communications service providers (CSPs)) but in dealing with non-standardized interfaces and inconsistent data collection

[18]ETSI TS 129 520 V15.0.0 (2018-07).

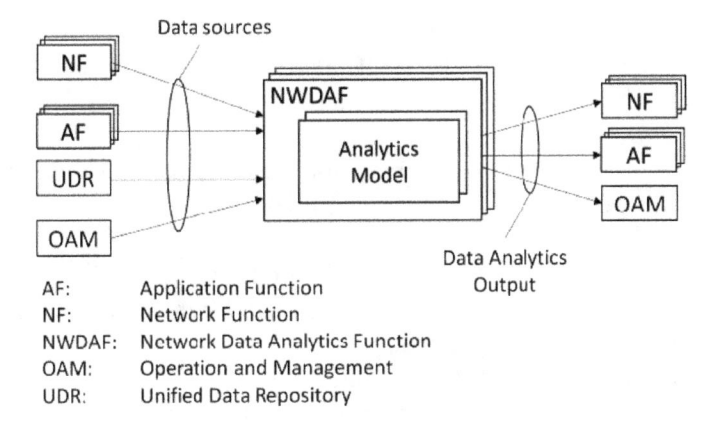

techniques across network vendors. 3GPP TR 23.791 has currently listed the following formula-based/AI–ML analytics use cases for 5G using NWDAF:

- Load-level computation and prediction for a network slice instance.
- Service experience computation and prediction for an application/UE group.
- Load analytics information and prediction for a specific NF.
- Network load performance computation and future load prediction.
- UE expected behavior prediction.
- UE abnormal behavior/anomaly detection.
- UE mobility-related information and prediction.
- UE communication pattern prediction.
- Congestion information — current and predicted for a specific location
- QoS sustainability, which involves reporting and predicting QoS change.

The NWDAF in the 5GC plays a key role as a functional entity which collects key performance indicators (KPIs) and other information about different network domains and uses them to provide analytics-based statistics and predictive insights to 5GC network functions, e.g., to the policy control function (PCF). Advanced ML algorithms can utilize the information collected by the NWDAF for tasks such as mobility prediction and optimization, predictive QoS, and data correlation. In the Tactile IoT relative section, support engine on the edge will be introduced as another ML as a service provision, for the Tactile and VR/AR IoT visions. The following are some of the objectives for the R17 work on enhanced network automation:

- NWDAF-assisted predictable network performance;
- UE driven analytics;
- NWDAF analytics exposure to applications, e. g., in smart city applications such as alleviating urban traffic congestion.

Other AI/ML aspects worth mentioned are included in Fig. 5.53. From the network-side view, digital value platforms and programmable/accelerated platforms are expected. From the CN views, SDN/NFV and smart network are expected. From the edge side view, AI enabling edge and integration of edge and cloud smart collaboration are expected. From the

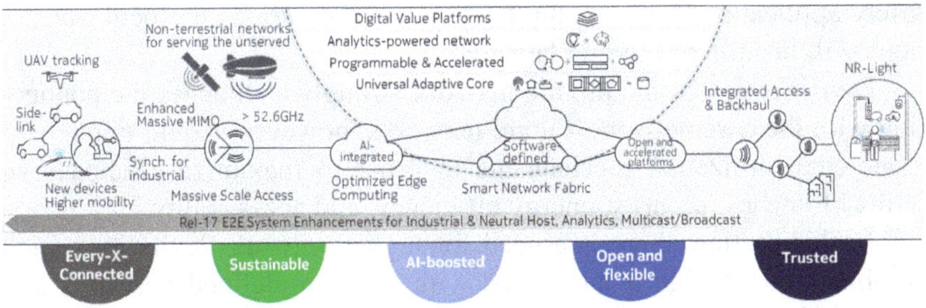

Figure 5.53 E2E architecture for 5G evolution.

Source: A. Ghosh, A. Maeder, M. Baker and D. Chandramouli. 5G Evolution: A view on 5G cellular technology beyond 3GPP Release 15. *IEEE Access* 7: 127639–127651, 2019. doi: 10.1109/ACCESS.2019.2939938.

IoE view, side link for CAVs, new IIoT devices of higher mobility are expected. NTN/Sat. IoT will be introduced in the next section.

5.9 Satellite IoT

5G communications could be considered a disruptive element enabling the vision of a global IoT, given that one of the key features of 5G is the focus on the integration of heterogeneous access technologies, including satellite communication (SatCom) systems. Satellites could play an important role in providing ubiquitous coverage and reliability in remote areas and enabling new IoT services to come out. Normally, IoT devices are not equipped with satellite connectivity, while IoT protocols are not designed with satellite requirements in mind. Thus, cross-layer study and optimization are required to allow the collection of IoT data from satellites, load balance, offloading of terrestrial networks, and cooperation with NTNs, in turn enabling smooth integration of IoT and satellite networks.

5G offers a more reliable network and will deliver a secure network for the IIoT by integrating security into the core network architecture. Industrial facilities are among the major users of private 5G (e.g., NPN) networks.

Future networks have to address the interference and collaboration between different radio access and develop new management models to control roaming while exploiting the coexistence of different cellular and radio access technologies is a beyond 5G (B5G) object.

Satellite communications need to be considered as a potential radio access technology, especially in remote areas. With the emergence of safety applications, minimizing latency and the various protocol translations will benefit end-to-end latency.

Densification of the mobile network strongly challenges the connection with the core network. Future networks, however, should implement cloud/edge utilization mechanisms in order to maximize efficiency in terms of latency, security, energy efficiency, and accessibility.

In this section, there is a need for higher network flexibility, which combines cloud/edge technologies with software-defined networks and network function virtualization in 5G, which will enable network flexibility to integrate satellite communications and configure network resources to an adequate degree (e.g., an edge-sharing computing resources, splitting data traffic, security rules, QoS parameters, mobility, etc.) for tomorrow's satellite IoT.

5.9.1 *Preparations for the edge and 5G*

As the evolution of heterogeneous IoT communications and IoT platforms for achieving a number of main objectives, such as flexibility (being able to deploy things in different contexts), usability (being able to make the user experience easy), and enabling service (creation to improve efficiency but also enabling new service development for productivity). An edge tier (as shown in Figs. 5.54 and 5.55) based on the edge computing (details to be provided in the next chapter) was forming gradually, in the access network (from the views of IoT communication), or the RAN as MEC (from the views of 3GPP).

In some cases, in order to facilitate communication, data flow, device management, and the sharing part functionality of applications-oriented data processing (Fig. 5.54), the edge tier in an IoT communication and networking layer (one of the typical four-layers architecture) provides the computational and analytics AI-based capabilities[19] close to the edge devices where data is generated.

IoT/IIoT edge tier delivers the management capabilities required to provide data from IoT devices to applications while ensuring the availability of management services for the devices over their lifetimes. Several IoT edge tiers are used for supporting developers to create, test,

[19] One of the two examples in the book is a Support Engine in the next section. And another is NWDAF in 5G Core, i.e. is the network data analytics function of 5GS, which can be deployment on the edge.

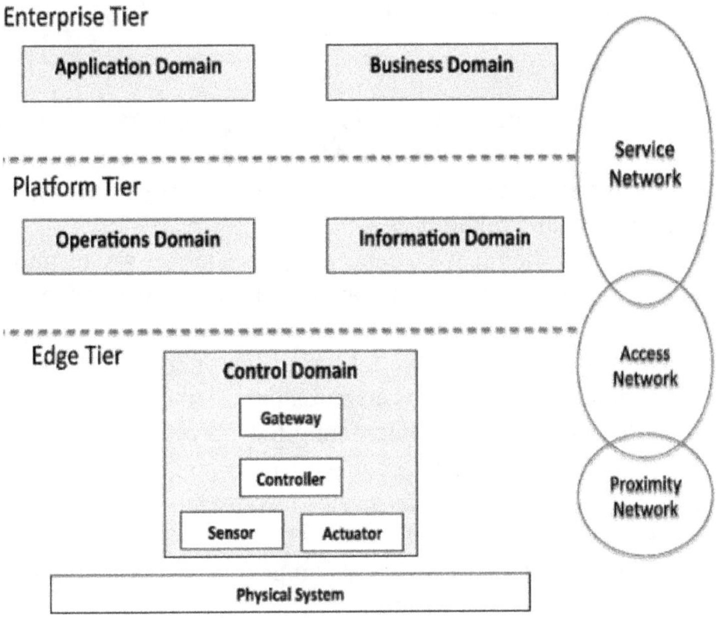

Figure 5.54 IIRA three-architectural pattern of IoT.

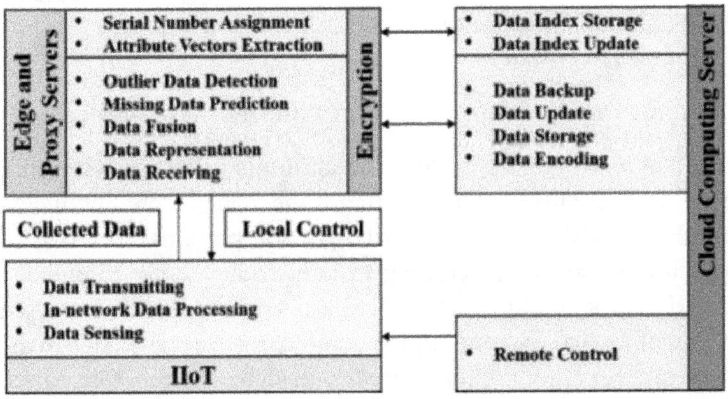

Figure 5.55 Framework of data collection, storage, retrieval, and mining on the edge tier.

and deploy IoT applications or services. The edge IoT tiers need to use hardware-agnostic scalable architectures to support the deployment of sets of functionalities across various types of IoT hardware without modifications.

Thus, below is a list of the main open research challenges for the edge of IoT:

- New IoT architectures that consider the requirements of distributed intelligence at the edge, cognition, AI, context awareness, tactile applications, heterogeneous devices, end-to-end security, privacy, proven trustworthiness, and reliability.
- Development of digital twin concepts (see Chapter 8), technologies, and standards that enable cross-domain collaboration and deployment.
- AR and VR IoT applications.
- Autonomics in IoT towards the Internet of autonomous things.
- Inclusion of robotics in the IoT towards the Internet of robotic things.
- AI and ML mechanisms for automating IoT processes.
- IoT service indexing patterns and structures that needed to be constructed on the edge for device/service discovery.

At last, the integration of AI-based components at all IoT architectural layers through a set of key capabilities, (e.g., data ingestion, processing, and transmission) that optimize edge analytics by placing data and secure computing infrastructure closer to the factory floor that leads to improved industrial product quality, operational performance, prediction of downtime, and automated operational flows.

5.9.1.1 *IIRA implementation viewpoint three-tier topology*

Because it is not realistic to describe an implementation viewpoint in a reference architecture document (e.g., the four-layers architecture in Chapter 2), IIC IIRA tries to describe generic patterns that IIoT systems are expected to exhibit. According to industrial internet reference architecture (IIRA), "an architecture pattern is a simplified and abstracted view of a subset of an IIoT system implementation that is recurrent across many IIoT systems, yet allowing for variants". In short, architecture patterns are common and recurring implementation mechanisms across industries, verticals, and applications.

As shown in Fig. 5.54, the IIRA[20] three-architectural patterns are discussed for the introduction of an edge tier (partly in and below the access

[20] IIRA developed by the Industrial Internet Consortium (IIC), see http:// www.iiconsortium.org/. IIRA provides guidelines about industrial IoT project management, solution

network of Fig. 5.54), the first two tiers of IIRA viewpoints are also identified in the IoT-A and in the reference architectural four layers introduced at the beginning of the book:

• First: Proximity networks (in IIRA control domain), as the network bearer of the perception layer, link the physical things (sensors or actuators) to a local controller/gateway for data collection and local control (partly as an aggregator and analyzer for information/service).

• Second: Access networks (between IIRA control domain and operations/information domain), as a part of the communication and network layers, where an edge tier may be "inserted in" around the edge (including the gateway, controller, or the edge and proxy server in Fig. 4.10-2). A satellite–5G integration use case will be followed in the next section.

The gateway for **edge connectivity and management** plays the following roles: (a) the gateway bridges physical and link layers, networking, and in some cases, application layers between the edge and the WAN; (b) the gateway plays the role of local sensor data processing and feedback control loop host; (c) the gateway is a host of a local device management functionality; (d) the gateway hosts application-specific logic which is needed to be located close to the edges; (e) the gateway acts as a security boundary protecting the edge nodes from security attacks from the WAN (e.g., from the cellular/satellite communication interface).

• Third: Service networks (including IIRA application domain and business domain), as the network bearer of the combination of the platform/services layer and the application layer (the top two layers in four-layers architecture), for (a) the service **provisioning and deployment**, (b) the devices/data/service **management**, and the commands/control to or from the edge tier, such as functions of the devices/assets and their respective control systems to respond to the control commands from an asset/device management centers (either located on the cloud, or the edge), and (c) the network management (e.g., NFV).

The **edge tier** functions (see Fig. 5.55) consist of the functionality for the **monitoring, diagnostics/prognostics, and optimization** for devices/

---

evaluation, and contractual issues mainly OT orientedly, and follows the standard ISO/IEC/IEEE 42010:2011.

assets management and the communications to/from the edge tier (e.g., sharing the data management locally with data centers on the cloud). A data-oriented framework on the edge tier is also included in Fig. 5.55. Some details of the function and capability are as follows:

- The **monitoring and diagnostics** function includes the collection of asset/device KPI data for the purpose of detection and diagnosis of potential problems and interfaces for upper application domain (such as commands from the application domain for actuator control or the aggregated/fusion data to the application domain, sometimes for prediction).

- The **prognostics** function refers to the predictive analytics functionality of a system. It uses historical performance data, asset properties, and models in order to predict a problematic situation before it manifests itself.

- The **optimization** function includes functionality that aims at optimizing asset performance in terms of reliability, availability, energy, output, and optimization for indexing or searching, functional safety, low cost, etc.

The edge data framework consists of several groups of functions for collecting, transforming, storing, and analyzing data from several domains, mainly the control domain.

- The **control domain** function is responsible for collecting data and local control in data transmission, in-(proximity) network data processing, data sensing and command acting (as shown in the left-bottom corner sub-frame of Fig. 5.55).

- The **edge server domain** consists of three main functional groups. First is edge analytics (as the modeling function in IIRA views), i.e., for collecting and analyzing data for implementing the local control loops in the edges, the data analytics to serve the purpose of system-wide operation optimization and control (system-wide analytics vs. edge analytics), together with web service or IP enabling integrated by proxy translation. At this point, AI and ML mechanisms for automating IoT processes modeling may be included (an example of support engine in the next section, as a part of TIoT, will be introduced), such as prediction and procession of false and missing data after data collected/aggregated/fused (from IIoT devices or assets) at the data level and delivered to the edge server; search efficiency improvement by supporting multiple search patterns, and optimization for indexing structures (according to the history index patterns), and device/service discovery.

Semantically, the edge server also transforms the data into a unified representation framework and fuse the information at the feature level for convenient storage, after data collection, aggregating into information (usually in a semantic model).

Second, the edge server acts as the "pipelines" to the cloud for the collaboration (if necessary, by which the data users and IIoT can communicate with the cloud server to execute specific instructions.) Due to the amount of IIoT data, the data users are likely to employ the cloud server to mine the data. The cloud is used for its parallel computing capabilities. In some situations, the data can be compressed semantically or by compressed sensing/compressive sampling according to the sensing patterns.

Third, the security safeguard function of the edge tier is a real demand for the server. The complexity of the data security sharing problem is increased in IIoT applications, especially when the integration of the edge device or the edge tier with other platforms in the industrial domains is required.

Opening data islands and sharing the same real-time data securely with any type and number of special applications and stakeholders are required in most of the edge-computing-based IIoT systems. Two challenges have to be addressed in edge data sharing: the inevitable increase of data interfaces that can lead to critical consequences (e.g., intrusion and destruction) and the limited performance of IIoT edge devices (e.g., strong/robust security algorithms are difficult to run on resource-constrained IIoT edge devices). The introduction of blockchain in edge computing in IIoT brings new challenges and opportunities for the secure sharing of data (for details, see Section 8.4).

5.9.1.2 *5G edge computing enhancements*

From the view of 5G architecture and functional deployment, the 5G system in R15 introduces a strong foundation to enable edge computing by means of the support for local UPF (re-)selection, concurrent access to local and central data networks, application influence for traffic routing, etc.

R16 provides further enhancements to improve coordination of mobility procedures with the application. Further enhancements are introduced in the R16 release to support edge computing for an extended set of vertical use cases, such as URLLC, V2X, and augmented/extended reality (AR/XR). This includes improvements to support discovery and seamless change of application server, and traffic steering from local (or edge) to central data (cloud as a data center) networks after processing. In a complementary manner, application enablers will be studied for interactions between UE, application server and network (e.g., for edge discovery at the application layer or the edge server, and the discovery in 5GS for TSN, see the next section).

To meet the characteristic requirements of large bandwidth and low delay in 5G application scenarios, mobile or multi-access (lately renamed by ETSI) edge computing (MEC) will be deeply integrated with 5G network architecture during the deployment trend that the 5G user plane UPF is deployed and sink locally to realize local split-flow streaming. Take the V2X RSU product as an example; China Mobile Research Institute and partners released their 5G NR base-station–type RSU product and white paper in 2020.

For the same reason, satellite communication integrated 5G needs an edge to co-locate on or near the ground satellite gateway station, just like 5GS wants an edge server to co-locate on the UPF, or even both the server and the 5G gNB in one unit of RSU on the edge deployment (as in the above example).

IoT also can benefit from the satellite integration in the 5G/B5G ecosystem in the coming years in many ways, beyond the coverage extension and the increase of the available bandwidth that satellites, UASs/UAVs and other HAPS (such as hovering/suspending balloons) can offer together. These new objects are emerging along with the new era ICTs, including the edge computing and B5G technologies (mainly means the continuous working after R17, by 3GPP and ITU); perhaps in the future, satellites may be an essential part of the communication and network layer of IoT. The edge computing, as an enabling ICT of IoT services layer, will be discussed in detail, together with the cloud, in the next chapter.

In the ongoing R17 of 3GPP and beyond, two new features are proposed to expand the reach of mobile connectivity beyond current boundaries. One is the enhancements for NTNs, including both satellites and HAPS (see the next section for further details); another is the connectivity and control of unmanned aerial vehicles (UAVs) including identification, tracking, and authentication. An example will be introduced after the next section.

5.9.1.3 *Introduction of satellite communication*

5G will have to support a higher number of users/devices requiring Internet connectivity with different performance requirements and a higher number of applications and use cases. The IoT is one of these recently emerging use cases, which will involve an even higher number of connected devices aimed at collecting and sending data with different purposes and over different application scenarios, such as smart city, smart factory, and smart agriculture.

In some cases, the terrestrial infrastructure is not enough to guarantee the typical 5G KPIs due to its design and intrinsic limitations. Take the coverage as an example: the terrestrial infrastructure will never be able to cover certain areas, such as oceans and rural and remote areas where there is no chance of or economic advantage in building a terrestrial network like the one in big cities. Resilience in case of temporary or permanent infrastructure unavailability is another key point.

In the last 50 years, communications satellites have been widely employed to extend communications (telephone and Internet) throughout the world, and the satellite network is shown in Fig. 5.56. Currently, there are tens of satellite communication constellations with this purpose, and

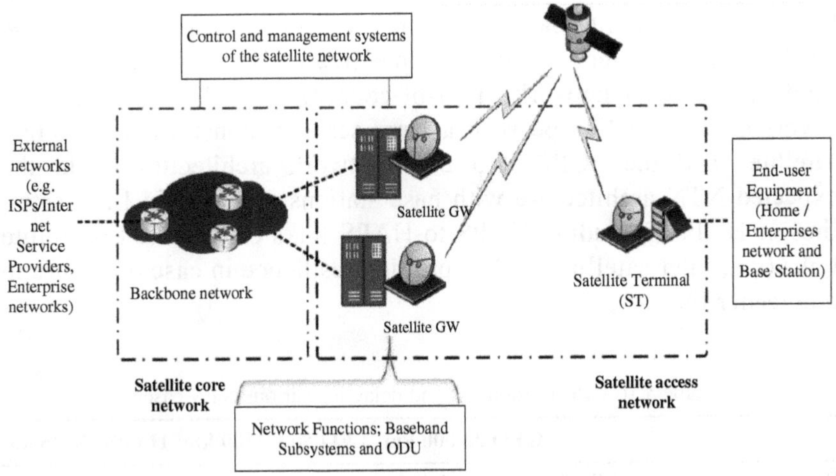

Figure 5.56 Satellite network: satellite access network, satellite core network (sat. core), and satellite gateway.

some others are planned to be deployed to offer global Internet connectivity through low Earth orbit (LEO) satellites. Some preliminary studies already focused on the exploitation of satellite networks for the IoT, envisioning the data exchange between IoT devices and end users through satellite communications. Satellites can act as intermediate nodes directly connecting to the IoT devices or through other intermediate collecting nodes (such as UAVs) in order to offer dynamically deployable real-time connectivity.

Within this section, the following part considers the impact of and need for the IoT environment, the role of UAVs and satellites, and the joint integration of these technologies in the future 5G.

5G technologies over a convergent satellite–terrestrial architecture are evaluated by the 3GPP and the European standardization in 93. From their view, Non-terrestrial networks (NTNs, including primarily LEO satellite) and HAPS are the keys to supplementing the coverage of terrestrial networks and extending service provision to remote areas of the Earth, for example, to support global IoT. Besides the expected deployment modes of LEO and HAPS, such as balloons and UAVs, geostationary Earth orbit (GEO) satellites have the advantage that full global coverage can be achieved with only three satellites, but their RTT is long and they are expensive to deploy. The typical beam footprints and delay budgets for GEO and LEO satellites and HAPS are shown in Table 5.16.

The following two examples include: over-the-air experiments utilizing a GEO satellite backhaul from SATis5 (an organization, whose aim is to build a large-scale real-time live end-to-end 5G integrated satellite-terrestrial network proof-of-concept testbed, and its testbed covers a study in Europe with a large-scale demonstration including satellites and the 3GPP R15 core network architecture.) and the expected NTN architecture with base stations mounted in LEO satellites or HAPS (including HAPS-to-HAPS links or satellite-to-satellite links (i.e., inter satellite link) to provide resilience in case of failure in one feeder link.

Table 5.16 Beam footprint and delay for various NTN cases.

	GEO 36,000 km	**LEO 500–1500 km**	**HAPS 18–25 km**
Beam footprint diameter (km)	200–1000	100–500	5–200
Round trip delay (ms)	270	25	3

5.9.2 *Satellite-5G integration on the edge*

In the discussion of backhaul technologies for 5G, satellites were rarely considered as an effective solution in previous generations. The reasons are ranging from commercial doubts to technological biases. Technical constraints, such as throughput deficits, delay requests, or unsupported network functions, are invoked in the following testbed of Satellite-Terrestrial Integration in the 5G (SATis5).

The main goal of this testbed is to evaluate how satellite communication (SATCOM/Satcom) networks can be best integrated within the 5G environment.

In this section, SATis5 testbed and the over-the-air tests for 5G (GEO) satellite integration are simply introduced, after some prior research including scenarios of 5G integrated satellite–terrestrial networks for enhanced mobile broadband, their QoS optimization of eMBB services, and using satellite access in 5G. Furthermore, SATis5 has selected satellite use cases for eMBB and mMTC to be further investigated and tested through over-the-air demonstrations based on the SATis5 testbed, which also discusses edge delivery and offload for multimedia content and MEC virtual network function (VNF) software (addresses multicast, caching of content to the edge, and update of network software).

5.9.2.1 *Satellite integration into 3GPP network and SATis5 testbed*

Evaluated with over-the-air tests using satellites in the GEO, a 5G edge node concept is presented in Völk *et al.* (2019), which covers a testbed demonstration study in Europe with a large-scale testbed including satellites and the latest standardization for the network architecture which owns an edge tier has been introduced above. In the testbed system for "Satellite-Terrestrial Integration in the 5G (SATis5)" context (including an edge node, which will be in a systematic introduction of edge computing in the next chapter), the Fraunhofer FOKUS Open5GCore toolkit has been deployed as the implementation of the 3GPP 5G core network (providing a 3GPP R15 prototype). As shown in Fig. 5.57, the user equipment (3GPP UE) connects to the edge node, which connects to the central core network node through the satellite backhaul. The backhaul is seen as a transport layer for the messages between the edge node and the central core network

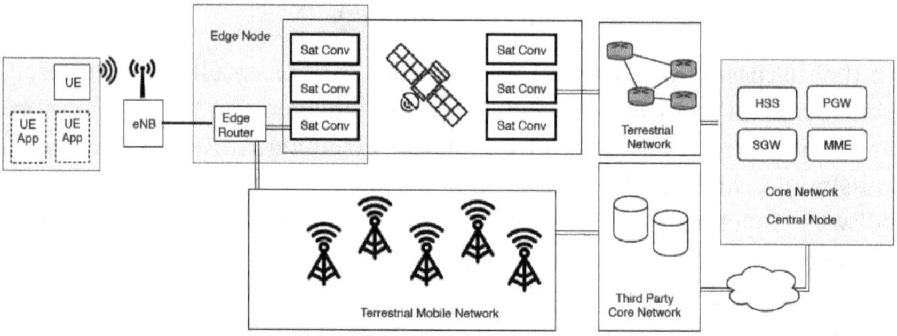

Figure 5.57 In the architecture of the SATis5 testbed, where the Fraunhofer FOKUS Open5GCore toolkit has been deployed as the implementation of the 3GPP 5G core network (R15) for the core network functionality and its integration with 5G NR, an edge node and a central core network node using a satellite backhaul connection among other backhaul opportunities.

site, i.e., as a transparent relay node (RN) between them while at the same time assuring a guaranteed communication quality.

In the SATis5 testbed of Fig. 5.57, an additional network function has been added to the edge node and forwards the specific traffic according to a set of routing policies over the satellite backhaul or an available local MNO network. 4G eNB is used for the RAN part instead of 5G gNB implementations for base stations because the latter was not yet commercially available at the time of their over-the-air experiments (see Völk *et al.* (2019)).

Fig. 5.58 shows the SATis5 testbed that includes more edge node functionalities to deploy further core network elements at the edge of the network. The SATis5 testbed will consist of two star-shaped backhaul networks, with one satellite hub in Munich and the other in Betzdorf. The core network is located in Berlin and connected to the hub locations by a best-effort Internet connection. At each location of the local RANs, there is an edge node, satellite modems with outdoor equipment and at least one mobile base station to provide service to the UEs.

Functions of the existing satellite network are offloaded, allowing SatCore to manage the network as a standard terrestrial 3GPP network. The existing satellite network is modified to comply with standard RAN, (e.g., the SatRAN), as a node to the SatCore. In addition, the remote satellite terminal is modified as a standard UE to the network, which allows it to connect to a SatCore in order to access network services. Thus, the

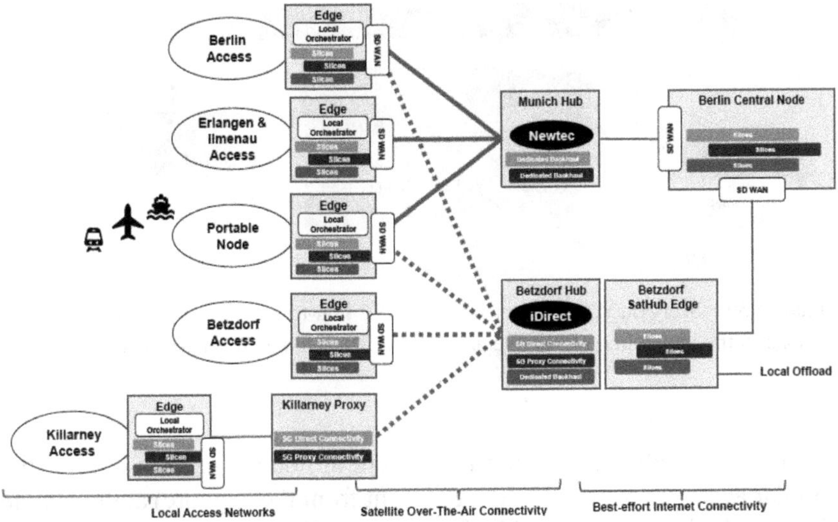

Figure 5.58 Final terminal deployment for the testbed, where the satellite ground segment corresponds to the iDirect velocity intelligent gateway (IGW) system residing at the teleport site introduces a standard 3GPP core network (SatCore) to the satellite hub platform.

existing satellite network (SatRAN and Ni interfaces to SatCore) has been modified to comply with the standard 3GPP core network. Then, SatRAN presents itself as a standard 3GPP cellular RAN, whereas the remote satellite terminal presents itself as a standard 3GPP cellular UE to the network. This enables support for 3GPP services and further for IoT service (e.g., asset tracking), such as authentication, billing, and charging. This also enables the management of the satellite network by the MNO, as if the MNO manages a standard 3GPP 5G cellular access network. Roaming between satellite and terrestrial mobile networks is enabled in such architectures.

The SatCore may be operated by the MNO or the satellite network operator (SNO), and there may even be separate 3GPP core networks for the MNO and SNO networks. The existing non-3GPP-based physical layer (e.g., DVB-S2x/RCS2 based) is used over the satellite, which allows faster satellite integration into 5G. However, the current investigation of 3GPP for 5G NR air interface over satellite, allows the SatRAN function to be fully 3GPP compliant.

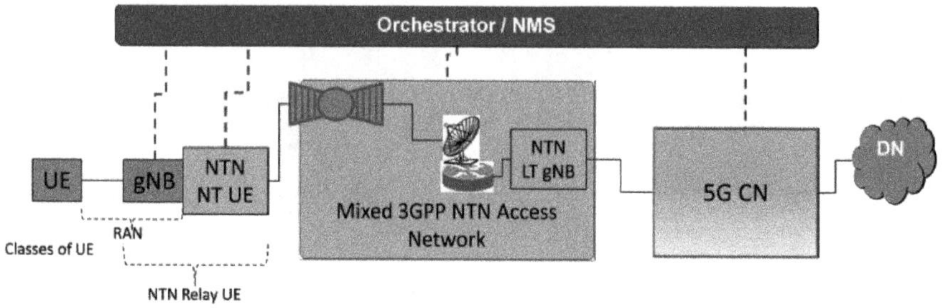

Figure 5.59 Scenario A3: indirect mixed 3GPP non-terrestrial access with bent-pipe payload in the integration of satellite and/or HAPS systems into 5G systems.

The core network residing in the central node is used to operate the cellular access network (the AN, different from the SatCore) at the remote site, and the integration of AN within the satellite hub platform site is used to operate the satellite backhaul network. The satellite network functions are virtualized by transferring their execution environment from a dedicated server to a virtual machine (VM) using the OpenStack pike virtualized infrastructure manager (VIM). Satellite virtual network functions (VNF) include the SatRAN software element, satellite 3GPP SatCore, satellite network management system, and auxiliary deployment using the OpenStack VIM. In terms of management and orchestration, the satellite hub platform system is integrated with the open-source platform. As shown in Fig. 5.59, which is a reference from ETSI SES-DTR/SES-00405-TR 103 611,[21] the integration scenario of satellite networks in the 5G system architecture is called "Scenario A3-Indirect Mixed 3GPP NTN" integration scenario, and 5G UEs are served by an access point (served by a trusted mixed 3GPP NTNs access network). The NTN enabled UE management endorses a multiplexer node role.

New technologies such as virtualization and cloud infrastructure including NFV, SDN/SDR (software-defined radios) at the edge of the cell are considered to meet the 5G requirements and push use cases on the edge.With the virtualization paradigm, a key technology could enable innovations for the satellite ground equipment as well as applications of

[21]ETSI. SESSCN(18)000020)/ETSI SCN TC-SES—DTR/SES-00405 Satellite Earth Stations and Systems (SES); seamless integration of satellite and/or HAPS (High Altitude Platform Station) systems into 5G system, 2019.

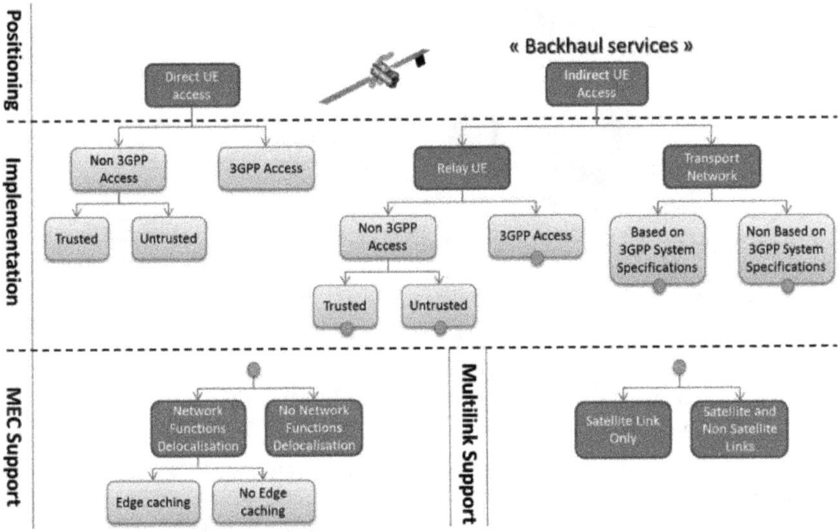

Figure 5.60 Implementation options considered in SaT5G.

Note: Three different types of access between the RN and the 5G core network are: 3GPP access; trusted non-3GPP access; untrusted non-3GPP access, and backhaul options based on the transport network can either be based on 3GPP system specifications (inherently 5G ready), or not; the latter requires an adaptation layer to become 5G ready.

new 5G protocols and algorithms. When considering the non-3GPP access, there is an indirect connection through a 5G satellite access network (bent-pipe satellite case) but with a mixed 3GPP NTN access network instead of a 5G satellite access network (i.e., instead of a 3GPP defined NTN 5G access). Based on the above analysis, as shown in Fig. 5.60, an overview of the different implementation options, including the introduction of MEC is described.

In the over-the-air demonstration, SATCOM networks can be integrated into a standard 3GPP network to provide seamless end-to-end connectivity by satellite. The 3GPP architecture integration results in the satellite network operating as a 3GPP network with the satellite terminal acting as a UE device. The SATCOM network presents itself as a RAN node to the 3GPP core network.

The demonstration illustrates the use of SDN and NFV technologies and their integration with the SATCOM in the context of 5G. Besides satellite integration into standard 3GPP network architecture, the other

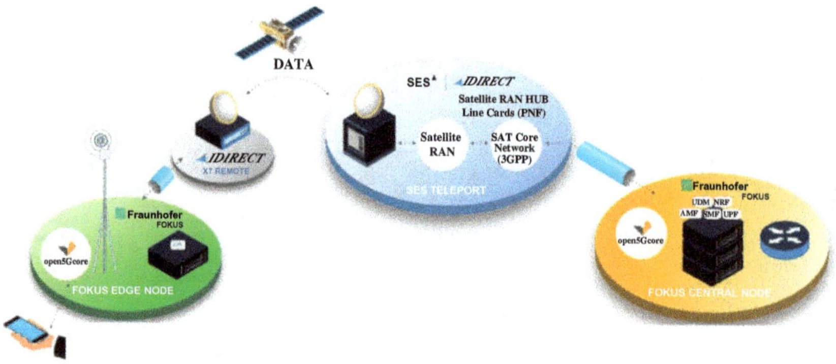

Figure 5.61 Seamless satellite integration into standard 3GPP network telecommunications architecture (setup 1).

Note: LTE network was deployed at the Fraunhofer FOKUS's premises in Berlin, Germany. Through a VPN terrestrial link, the stationary edge node was connected to the remote satellite terminal located in Killarney, Ireland. The remote satellite terminal corresponds to the iDirect's X7 EC satellite router with edge computing capabilities as indoor unit (IDU) and a 1.2 m Ku-band antenna system as outdoor unit (ODU).

two objectives of the demonstration were SDN/NFV and edge node integration into SATCOM, and the network slicing of eMBB use cases over satellite.

As shown in Fig. 5.61, the setup is built upon the following testbed elements by the respective SATis5 project partners. The Open5GCore (from Fraunhofer-FOKUS)corresponds to a 3GPP R15-compliant implementation of the 5G core network. The central entity of the testbed and the applications server are virtualized structures including the rest of the core network. Through a deployed 4G RAN (including eNB), the UE was connected to edge node (hosting the individual decentralized 5G core network functions). iDirect provided the pre-5G-enabled satellite hub platform and remote satellite terminals which incorporate SDN and NFV capabilities and enable the satellite integration into a 3GPP core network architecture, through the satellite hub platform (by providing a SATCOM-3GPP network architecture).

As shown in Fig. 5.61, the remote satellite terminal was connected to the satellite hub station deployed in Betzdorf, Luxembourg through the GEO satellite ASTRA 2F (28.2_E).

In particular, the Ku-band channel bandwidths for downlink and uplink reserved for this experiment were 26 MHz and 6 MHz, respectively. This led to a maximum backhaul UDP throughput of around 60 Mbps and round-trip time (RTT) of around 550 ms.

Through a VPN terrestrial link, the satellite hub platform (shown in Fig. 5.61, as the integrating architecture of SATCOM with a standard 3GPP network.) residing at the SES teleport (in Betzdorf) was connected to the 5G central node of the testbed (residing in Berlin). The 5G core network was deployed with a functional split between the edge node and the 5G core network to assure connectivity to the 5G network through the different backhauls.

In the integration testbed, data from five sensors on a screen represent active devices, such as a phone, a wearable, a car, and a fixed IoT sensor aggregator. All of them were connected and exchanged information as it was routed through the combined space-and-ground network to the core network in Berlin.

Additionally, the NFV-MANO (industry-standard ETSI NFV-management and orchestration) framework describes a standardized set of elements and interfaces that comprise an SDN-NFV system.

In order to introduce the NFV-MANO framework into the SATis5 testbed, virtualized satellite network functions and satellite SDN capabilities are also described from the view of ETSI implementation; for details see Evans *et al.* (2021).

5.9.2.2 *Mobile edge node demo: Connectivity on the move*

The "Connectivity on the Move" scenario could be envisioned as a use case for communications on the move in a disaster relief situation (e.g., earthquake), where the terrestrial backhaul infrastructure has been damaged or is still too expensive (or far/sparse) to deploy, or for the temporary deployments of public events (as the 3GPP defined emergency/critical communications). It is also expected for massive mobile things access in the long run, after the broadband LEO satellite mobile communication system (e.g., the constellation to be discussed in the final part of this section) can provide services to multi-terminal users in the air–space–ground integrated information network

The mobile edge node demonstration shows 5G connectivity "on the move" as illustrated in Fig. 5.62, and it has to manage an unstable backhaul where communication may be blocked for variable durations of time due to shadowing. Some **key characteristics are as follows**:

- **A mobile** cell setting up with an edge integration.
  A mobile and standalone cell is set up in a SATCOM-equipped vehicle for LoS connection to an available satellite, with a mobile edge node integration in the vehicle.

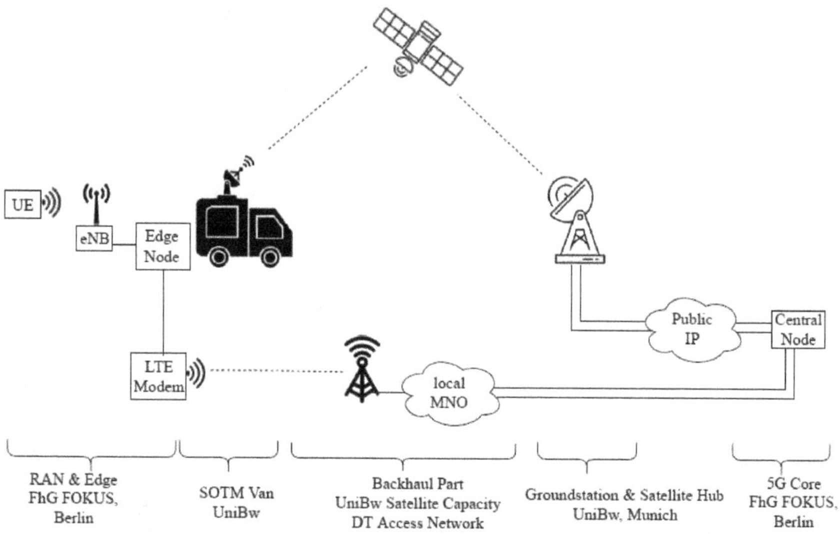

Figure 5.62 5G connectivity on the move demo: SATis5 testbed demo architecture (different with Setup 1), where the iDirect satellite hub and modems offer integration into the overall; the demo is Setup 2 that legacy point-to-point modems are used without a specific API to control satellite resources.

- **The** terrestrial backhaul is an option.
  In the case of a connection to an MNO network, the data traffic can be backhauled on top of this terrestrial network, as shown in Fig. 5.62.
- **Setting of Setup 2** (shown in Fig. 5.62):

(**a**) SATCOM vehicle. An Accelleran E1011 eNB was deployed in the satcom on the move (SOTM) vehicle terminal (from the Munich Center for Space Communications, a major research facility located at the Bundeswehr University Munich (UniBw) in Neubiberg, Germany).

(**b**) Mobile base station deployment showcase and UE. During the testbed demonstration, the LTE band 43 (3.6–3.8 GHz) was assigned from the German regulatory agency.

(**c**) 4.6 m earth station antenna. The transmitting and receiving Earth station was a 4.6 m offset Gregorian antenna. Specifically, during the over-the-air tests, the satellite backhaul was implemented through GEO satellite capacity provided through UniBw in the Ku-band. A small satellite bandwidth of 200 kHz was allocated to the forward link carrier and 200 kHz bandwidth was allocated to the return link carrier.

For the uplink of the forward link, a center frequency of 14.34 GHz was assigned by the operator. This frequency has been converted to an 11.54 GHz downlink frequency.

(**d**) SOTM antenna. In case of an LoS connection to the satellite, the SOTM terminal on top of the vehicle was utilized. This SOTM antenna features multiple onboard tracking sensors, enabling accurate tracking, short initial acquisition, and instantaneous re-acquisition.

(**e**) **Edge node**. The edge node was running on a Lenovo ThinkPad X240. In addition, two Huawei E3372 Mobile Broadband LTE modems were connected with the edge node via USB to backhaul data traffic if the satellite backhaul was unavailable.

(**f**) **SATCOM modem.** The SATCOM modem in Munich was configured to provide access to the central node in Berlin with public IP over the Internet.

- **Hybrid** backhauls. The edge node was connected through an openVPN connection to the central node in Berlin, which includes the main core network functions. In the case when both backhauls are available, the edge node could split the user plane and control plane separately to send the data to the central node over different physical paths.

The connection to 5G network architecture in Setup 2 includes the following: (a) SATCOM vehicle; (b) Mobile base station deployment showcase; (c) 4.6 m Earth station antenna; (d) SOTM antenna.

As shown in Fig. 5.62, a testbed demonstration architecture with edge node capabilities has been developed, as the hardware setup of the SATis5 testbed. The SOTM vehicle (i.e., SATCOM van) was parked in Berlin, Germany (52.53°N, 13.32°E), with mobile base station deployment in it and SOTM antenna on it. Line-of-sight (LoS) to the satellite was given. Shadowing of the SATCOM link occurred occasionally through passing high-build vehicles, such as trucks and buses.

In the case of shadowing, the reconnecting of UE took a few seconds (hold mode of the antenna) or less than one minute (search mode of the antenna), depending on the length of the previous shadowing period. The specific processes for service deactivation, handover, and tracking updates worked as expected.

ICMP messages, which were encapsulated in IP packets within the GPRS tunneling protocol (GTP), were used for validation testing between the UE and the central node. It can be stated that the performance and load management for this specific demonstration were limited by capacity.

This demonstration shows that a RAN can be directly deployed with a satellite backhaul to connect to a 3GPP Release 15 core network. The satellite backhaul can handle large RTT compared to terrestrial radio backhauls (the average RTT over half an hour was 584 ms). Moreover, the demonstration shows that an edge node can handle two different backhauls at the same time. In the case of a blocking of the SOTM link, a backup solution for the UE traffic is provided by offloading the traffic over local MNO networks via two LTE modems. This demonstration shows that even a small satellite bandwidth is sufficient to provide a satellite backhaul for mMTC sensor applications.

At last, a complete E2E 5G network infrastructure is introduced to demonstrate the virtualized and orchestrated backhaul connection of three 5G use cases that embed applications as MEC at the edge of the 5G network and are defined in the SaT5G project and to demonstrate the hybrid multi play using both satellite and terrestrial connections.

Although the average RTT is relatively longer than that of LEO/HAPS, the demonstration means the integration is suitable for non-time-sensitive IoT applications and backup backhauling. possible satellite backhaul applications are eHealth, rapid emergency response (in case of fire or disaster). Continuous efforts besides the SATis5 project are demonstrated as follows, including 5G use cases enhanced with satellite:

- Improved reliability through alternative connectivity independent from terrestrial.
- Providing backhaul for ultra-low latency services deployed at the network edge.
- Mobile and nomadic network deployment use cases.
- Enhanced and mesh IoT and multimedia use cases.
- Global use cases and end-to-end secure.
- Provide convergence with data processing and earth observation.
- MEC supported by 5G.

The use case of M2M through the HAPS relay sees the following parts.

5.9.3 *Satellite–5G integration by the HAPS*

From the optimized 5G architecture views that drives the 5G evolution towards IoE, the reach of mobile connectivity is expanding beyond current boundaries. One expansion point of mobility and altitude is studied continuously by 3GPP, and the object of NTNs includes both satellites and HAPS.

Furthermore, new communication protocols stacks for managing and controlling the user assignment and IoT data, with regard to cells and technology will have to be deployed in the mobile core network for better efficiency in accessing the network resource.

When base stations are mounted in HAPS or satellites, an expected type of NTN architecture is illustrated in Fig. 5.63. The architecture comprises a service link (i.e., access link) and a feeder link (i.e., backhaul link). The feeder link terminates in the ground gateway which is connected to the 5GC. We take this type as Case 0, in which a 5G-gNB or 5G-RAN is located on the air.

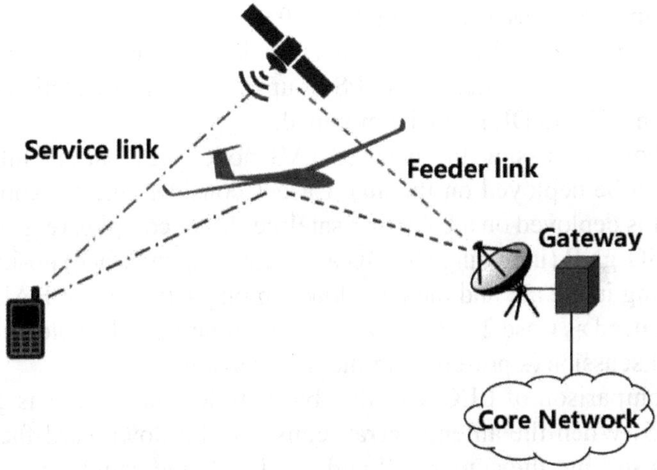

Figure 5.63. Example of NTN architecture (as Case 0), where satellites or HAPS either act as 5G-gNB/5G-RAN on the air (as Case 1, see Fig. 5.64) or satellites act as only relay nodes in a hybrid relay of satellites and HAPS, with the terrestrial 5G-gNB (as Case 2).

The difference between the example of Case 0 by LEO/HAPS service/feeder link (backhaul) and the above SATis5 testbed lies in that the SATis5 offers the iDirect (GEO) satellite hub and modems as an integration into the overall 5G network architecture (with Setup 1 of the testbed in Fig. 5.61); i.e., the (inter) satellite (or HAPS) relay nodes are transparent to the user as an optional backhauling way.

As various concepts such as SDN in the satellite convergence (Sat Conv.) layer are already taken into account in the design of these modems and the satellite hub, which are utilized in a star network topology or satellites constellation topology (or inter-links over the HAPS). An MNO can manage these modems and the satellite hub in its network by itself.

Various business models will be developed for the integration of satellite into a 5G network. The provision of a certain bandwidth by conventional legacy equipment with a guaranteed failure probability as in Setup 2 of SATis5 is a relatively low-cost integration use case, which is also investigated as another branch of Case 0 for mobile support.

Generally, 5G-NR NTNs may exploit the fact that the 5G RAN defines an interface between the centralized unit (CU, in IAB node from 3GPP R16 and beyond) of the base station and the lower layer functions in distributed units (DUs). The lighter and less-complex DU may be mounted on the satellite or HAPS, while the CU may be in the ground station; in the cases (including Case 0 and Case 1), the feeder link/backhaul link carries the CU–DU interface. For example, in Fig. 5.64, DU with antenna arrays under the HAPS or upside-down base station (or IAB node with CU and DU) may be mounted.

Without discussing the detailed IAB node (e.g., parent/child node, which can be deployed on the air), Case 1 considers the situation that a 5G-gNB is deployed on a UAV or a satellite. More complex (e.g., Case 2), such as 5G-gNB (including CU/DU and cascading interface) upside-down suspending in the air, and the inter-links among satellites (or HAPS), will be introduced as Case 2 with the analysis combining IoT deployment, and further discussion is presented in the next section.

A comparison of LEO satellite, base station and HAPS is given in Fig. 5.65. When the antenna array consists of a downward-facing 2×2 panels serving the center cell and six 4×2 side panels each serving an outer cell, as shown in Fig. 5.64, a side panel covers an outer cell in the azimuth domain $\pm\varphi°$ from its boresight, where φ is typically up to 30°.

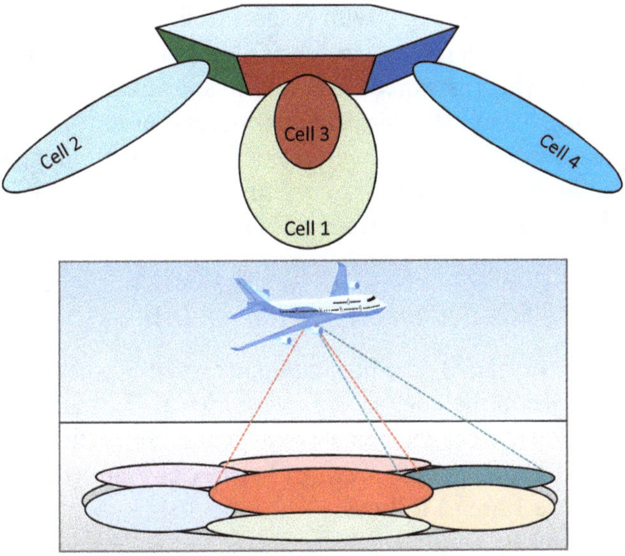

Figure 5.64 HAPS coverage with seven sectors. Case 1: 5G-gNB on the satellite or HAPS (UAV).

Note: Considering the example of a service link configuration with antenna arrays under the HAPS forming sector beams to cover seven cells, the service area is of 100 km radius.

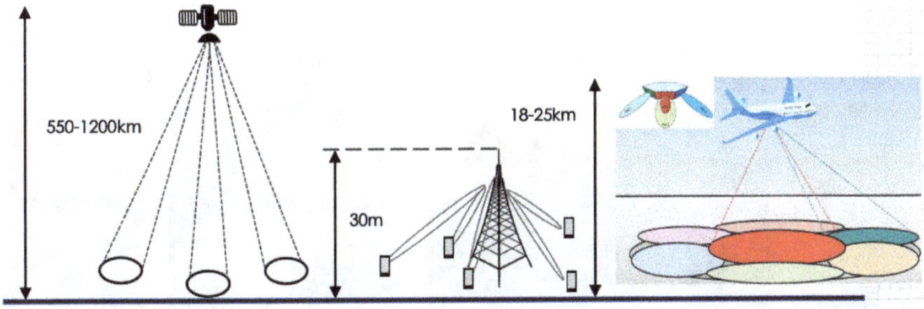

Figure 5.65 Altitudes of LEO satellite, base station, and HAPS.

In Ghosh *et al.* (2019), the HAPS forms sector beams to cover seven cells in a service area of 100 km radius, with a side panel covering an outer cell in the azimuth domain $\pm\varphi^\circ$ from its boresight, where φ is typically up to 30°. The achievable throughput for an outer cell, therefore, depends on the azimuth angle with respect to the side panel's boresight. The relative study of NTN design for 5G NR is ongoing in the R16 and R17 timeframe, which is expected to lead to specifications in R17.

Considering the 5G standardization progress for the NTN reported in R16, the possible network architecture configurations from the user plane UPF viewpoint are discussed. They are divided into two cases as follows (non-terrestrial 5G-gNB and terrestrial 5G-gNB):

5.9.3.1 *Case 1 5G-gNB on the satellite or UAV*

In case 1, UAVs or LEO satellites equipped to be 5G-gNBs (or just the DU of IAB nodes in the later specification after R17 of 3GPP) allow the deployment of 5G cells on demand and offer connectivity to devices equipped as 5G-UE. From the views of IoT device employment, two subdivisions of Case 1 are as follows:

(1) 5G-gNB on the satellite: Figures 5.66 and 5.67 concern the option that the IoT/UE devices are 5G-UE and the access to the 5G network takes place in the terrestrial segment. When UAVs are relay nodes (RNs), including HAPS-to-HAPS or UAV links, for the 5G communication, the RNs only implement frequency conversion and radio frequency amplification to allow data transmission to the satellite.

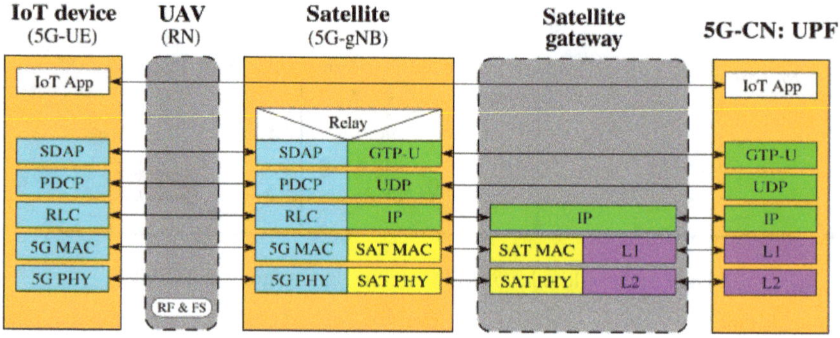

Figure 5.66 5G-UE in the IoT device and 5G-gNB on the satellite.

Note: Satellites act as 5G-gNBs which are equipped with a regenerative payload, and UAV is 5G RN (e.g., integrated access & backhaul, IAB nodes in 5G NR) between 5G UE and 5G RAN if they are transparent payload satellites. The same considerations can be applied for the satellite gateways, which can act as 5G-gNBs or be linked to 5G-gNBs through terrestrial links.

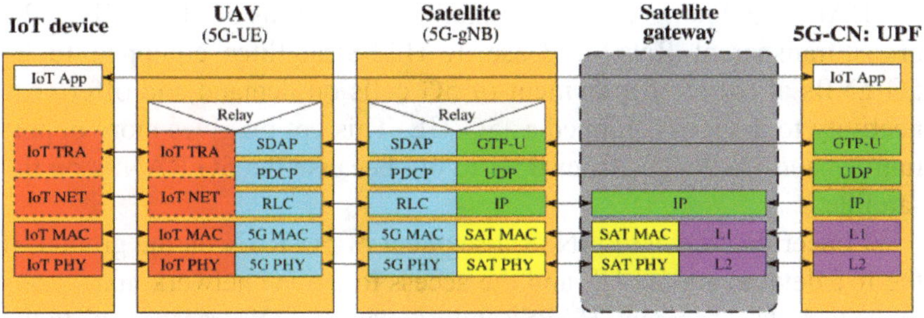

Figure 5.67 5G-UE on the UAV and 5G-gNB on the satellite.

Note: The 5G-gNB functionality is moved on board the satellite, increasing its complexity and leading to additional challenges for the 3GPP. Having a satellite-based flying 5G-gNB is an interesting scientific and technical challenge involving implementation issues to be tackled in both software and hardware. For the same reasons, it is not of immediate application.

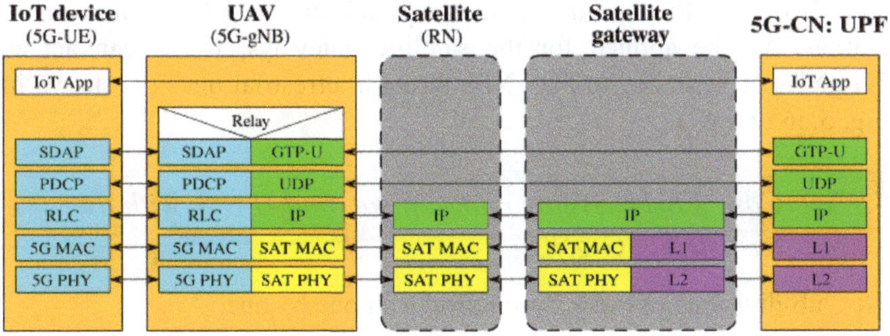

Figure 5.68 5G-UE in the IoT device and 5G-gNB on the UAV.

(2) 5G-gNB on the UAV: The satellites or satellite-to-satellite links (or linked in a sat-constellation) act as RNs or gateway, as illustrated in Fig. 5.68.

As shown in Fig. 5.67, UAVs communicate with the IoT devices through a wireless non-3GPP interface, e.g., one of the Wi-Fi/Zigbee/6LoWPAN or standardized LPWA solution. The case of 5G-gNB on the UAV is shown in Fig. 5.68. It introduces additional hardware/software complexity onboard the UAVs. Even if moving 5G-UE within IoT devices is a scientifically stimulating solution, as the choice to have 5G-gNB onboard a satellite or a UAV was already discussed, from the practical viewpoint; these actions cannot be immediately implemented.

HAPS (including UAVs) or satellites can act as 5G UE, 5G-gNBs, or as transparent RNs. In Case 1, HAPS/satellites equipped to be 5G-gNBs allow the deployment of 5G cells on demand and offer connectivity to devices equipped as 5G-UE. This option gives more opportunities and challenges from B5G to 6G because the 5G RAN is on the satellite.

Concerning the 5G RAN or a segment of 5G RAN on the ground, if the IoT devices are 5G-UE and the access to the 5G network takes place in the terrestrial segment, HAPS/satellites can be "RNs transparent" to the 5G communication and only implement frequency conversion and radio frequency amplification to allow data transmission to the satellite (so-called "bent-pipes"). Then, the following "Case 2", where the terrestrial segment includes 5G CN and 5G gNBs, is to be discussed.

Considering the case 1 of options, when satellites act as 5G-gNBs, they are equipped with a regenerative payload or as RNs between 5G UE and 5G RAN if they are transparent payload satellites. The same considerations can be applied for the satellite gateways, which can act as 5G-gNBs or be linked to 5G-gNBs through terrestrial links (as shown in Fig. 5.66 or 5.67).

5.9.3.2 *Case 2 hybrid relay nodes of sat. and HAPS, with the terrestrial 5G-gNB*

The sub-divisions of Case 2 are introduced one by one.

(1) Satellite as gateway or RN between 5G-UE and terrestrial 5G-gNB.

From the UPF or 5G-RAN viewpoint, Figs. 5.68 and 5.69 show the possible network architecture configurations (for the 5G UE in the UAV/HAPS as an IoT devices/sensors aggregator platform), taking into account the 5G standardization progress for the NTN reported in. In detail, the choice of considering IoT devices as non-3GPP/non-5G devices are depicted in Fig. 5.68. They are equipped with interfaces based on an IoT communication protocol stack (see Chapter 5). In case 2, acting as 5G-UE, the UAV takes charge of the conversion between IoT and the 5G protocol stacks. The difference between these architectures is in the role of the satellite, i.e., in the location of the 5G-gNB. In Fig. 5.68, the satellite is a simple RN, whose only aim is to perform radio frequency processing and frequency switching (including RF and FS) required to transmit from the UAV to the satellite link and vice versa. 5G-gNB is located on the ground close to the 5G-CN and the satellite link 5G-UE and 5G-gNB.

As an extended scenario from Fig. 5.69, the satellite RN node can be located between two HAPS/UAV nodes or on either side of the HAPS/UAV RN node. The satellite RN node and the other HAPS/UAV node joint together into a "co-extender" of RN node in order to cover more area for IoT accessing.

As shown in Fig. 5.69, the satellite plays the role of radio frequency processing and frequency switching (RF and FS) that required to transmit from the UAV to the satellite link and vice versa. 5G-gNB is located on the ground close to the 5G-CN and the satellite link 5G-UE and 5G-gNB.

(2) The satellite is the backhaul between 5G-gNB and 5G-CN. 5G-gNB on the ground close to the UAV, terrestrial 5G-CN may co-locate with the satellite gateway.

As shown in Fig. 5.70, the satellite is still a simple RN, but 5G-gNB is located closer to 5G-UE. 5G-gNB is still located on the ground, and the satellite acts as a backhaul between 5G-gNB and 5G-CN. The main difference between architectures in Figs. 5.68 and 5.69 is that in the latter case, 5G-gNB is located close to the edge of the network, easing the employment of technologies, such as MEC, and allowing a better interaction between 5G-UE and 5G-gNB due to the lower communication delay between them.

Just from the 5G integration architecture, Fig. 5.70 conforms to Case 0 at the point of providing a backhaul option. Their difference is the former supplies an LEO satellite backhauling, the latter supplies a GEO satellite backhauling. Both of them can make full use of the MEC, as mentioned above.

As shown in Fig. 5.70, the satellite is still a simple RN, but 5G-gNB is located closer to 5G-UE. 5G-gNB is still located on the ground, and the satellite acts as a backhaul between 5G-gNB and 5G-CN. The main difference between architectures in Figs. 5.69 and 5.70 is that in the latter case, 5G-gNB is located close to the edge of the network, easing the employment of technologies, such as MEC, and allowing a better interaction between 5G-UE and 5G-gNB due to the lower communication delay between them.

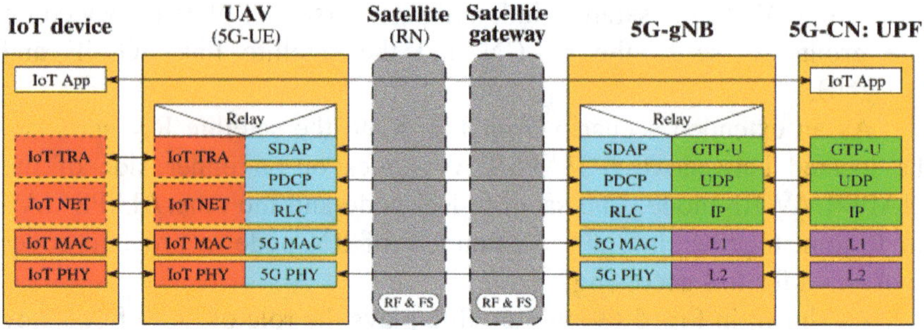

Figure 5.69 5G-UE on the UAV, satellite as RN, and terrestrial 5G-gNB/5G-CN.

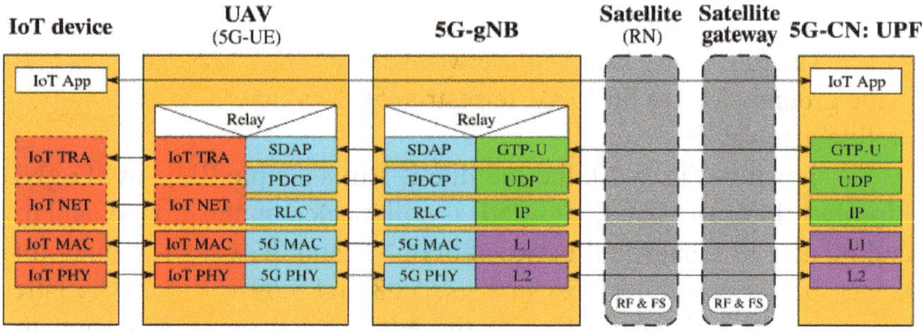

Figure 5.70 5G-UE on the UAV, 5G-gNB on the ground close to the UAV, and the satellite as the backhaul between 5G-gNB and 5G-CN.

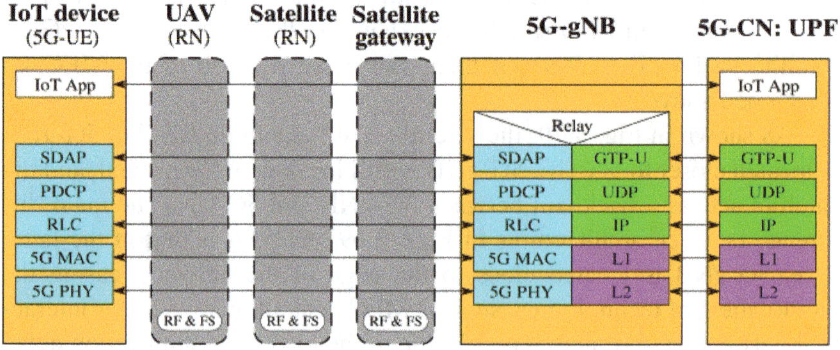

Figure 5.71 5G-UE in the IoT device, UAV and satellite as RNs, and terrestrial 5G-gNB.

(3) UAV and satellite as RNs, and terrestrial 5G-gNB may co-locate with satellite gateway.

Moving 5G-UE in the IoT devices allows both UAVs and satellites to act as simple RNs, as in Fig. 5.71, and when hosting 5G-gNBs on the satellite, it changes into Case 1.

Finally, where the UPF is located, there may be an edge node/server co-locate. For example, when the UPF is near the ground satellite gateway, an edge node can be co-located with the UPF for the IoT devices/services access either through the satellite or 5G/4G wireless air interface.

When the edge node co-locates with a gNB or eNB (Fig. 5.57), sat. conv. in the edge node means the function of the satellite is a RN of the communication between the terrestrial and the edge. Additionally, the network function that is added to the edge node forwards the specific traffic according to a set of routing policies over the satellite backhaul or an available local MNO network. An edge tier or MEC can also locate near the sat. gateway and 5G RAN (or 5G-CN) for their better interworking.

From the views of UAV/HAPS when IoT aggregators or IoT devices are non-3GPP, three kinds of roles are displayed as shown in Table 5.17.

When considering satellites interlinks (satlinks) or inter-HAPS (CU/DU as parent–child links) act as integrated networks of RNs for service link/feeder link, and some works beginning in R18 of 3GPP, satellite constellations are worth further research towards the next generation — 6G.

5.9.4 *Satellite constellations towards 6G*

During the last years, satellite service providers (e.g., Argos, Iridium, ORBCOMM, Inmarsat's Broadband Global Area Network, etc.) have integrated the IoT services into their commercial satellite IoT initiatives (e.g., HIBER, DIAMOND, KEPLER) and have started using nanosatellites for satellite IoT communication. ORBCOMM operates a satellite network dedicated to IoT providing two-way data communications in remote areas of the world via a network of LEO satellites and ground stations. The OG2 satellites provide network redundancy, minimal line of site issues for complete global coverage while VHF frequency furthers signal propagation. The miniaturization of satellite technology for LEO allows using these satellites to serve as a backhaul for narrow-band IoT communication, just like the GEO satellite backhaul in SATis5 testbed in Section 5.9.2.

Table 5.17 Pros and cons of the identified integrated solutions (from the views of UAV/HAPS when IoT aggregators or IoT devices are non-3GPP/None-5G).

UAV/HAPS	Satellite	Sat.Gateway	Advantage	Disadvantage
UAVs may be linked to a 5G cell generated by a satellite in visibility (5G-gNB on-board satellite) or get access to the 5G core network (CN) through a satellite acting as RN.	RN (bent-pipe)	RN (or 5G-gNB)	Simpler IoT devices and simpler bent-pipe 5G-agnostic satellites as the ones already available and deployed; 5G-gNBs' complexity in the terrestrial segment's nodes, which do not have strict resource constraints.	IoT devices not able to get direct access to the 5G network; more complex UAVs with high energy consumption due to protocol conversion.
In case 2, UAVs/HAPS equipped to be 5G-gNBs allow the deployment of 5G cells on demand and offer connectivity to (other) devices equipped as 5G-UE. (either on the ground or in the air)	RN (bent-pipe)	RN	Simpler IoT devices and simpler bent-pipe 5G-agnostic satellites as the ones already available and deployed; 5G-gNBs' complexity in the terrestrial segment's nodes, which do not have strict resource constraints; better management of the 5G cell resources thanks to the 5G-gNB's location closer to the edge of the network and the lower communication delay between 5G-UE and 5G-gNB.	IoT devices not able to get direct access to the 5G network; more complex UAVs with high energy consumption due to protocol conversion
As 5G-UE	5G-gNB (non-bent-pipe)	RN	Simpler IoT devices; regenerative satellites able to deploy 5G cells, increasing the reliability and availability of the terrestrial 5G access network.	IoT devices not able to get direct access to the 5G network; more complex UAVs with high energy consumption due to protocol conversion; more complex regenerative satellites with higher energy consumption, still to be designed, built, and launched.

Note: Summarized from Marchese *et al*. (2019).

When considering these small satellites/nanosatellites networks systems can cover oceans, rural areas, polar regions, and their integration with IoT networks provide new ways of monitoring the climate change, pollution, and global/regional disasters; but how these satellites networking or forming satellites constellations is a problem.

From aspects of the satellite constellations with or without inter-satellite link (ISL), the popular constellations can be divided into three categories, and each of them has the potential integration in the evolution towards the terrestrial–satellite integration into 6G.

The first is satellite constellations without interlink, such as OneWeb, with hundreds of satellites and global ground stations, as shown in Fig. 5.72.

The second is LEO constellations with a full inter-satellite link, such as the constellation of LeoSat (enterprise), which has nearly a 100 (up to 108) satellites and interconnecting ISL technology, as shown in Fig. 5.73.

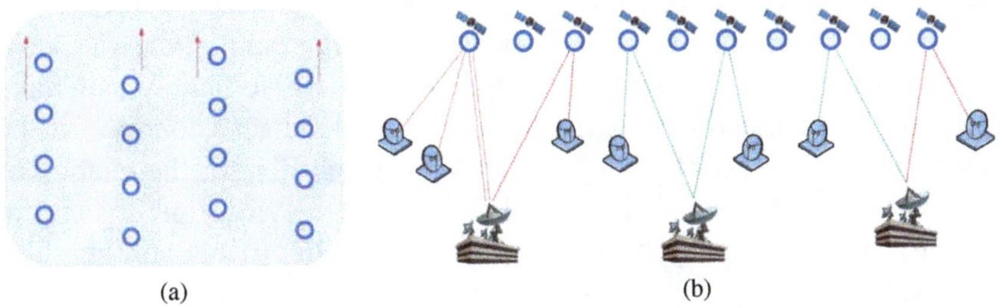

Figure 5.72 Constellation without inter-satellite link can only network based on ground nodes, so it is hard to arrange ground stations on a large scale all over the world, and there is link interruption in the north and south poles: (a) LEO constellations without inter satellite link and (b) network based on ground nodes.

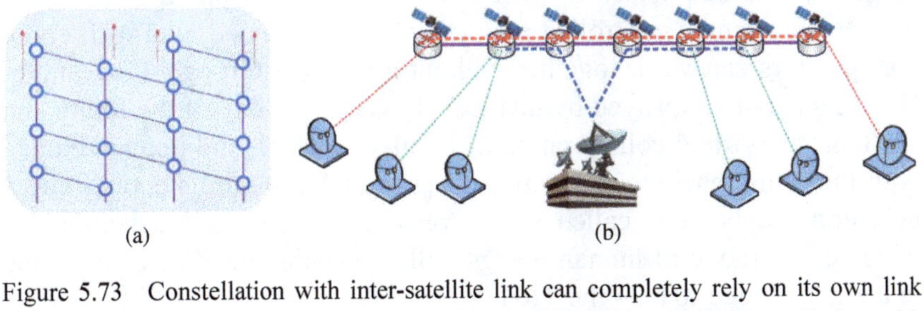

Figure 5.73 Constellation with inter-satellite link can completely rely on its own link network: (a) LEO constellations with full inter-satellite link and (b) constellation with inter-satellite link.

The third is inter-satellite links existing in hybrid, multi-layer satellite constellations (but not full ISLs), with onboard Starlink processing. i.e., the third one belongs to the hybrid of the former two types.

The information exchange between satellites by inter-satellite link cannot be through the gateway station (Fig. 5.72); while for satellites without an inter-satellite link, if they want to exchange information with each other, they must be transferred through the gateway station (Fig. 5.73). Therefore, the constellation with inter-satellite links is more convenient to integrate an IoT use case, but it is more difficult to develop due to the complex ISL technology, including the networking protocol of on-board processing, gateway design, and routing data for data exchange. But for the satellite industry connecting these gateways (satellite ground/on-board gateways, NTN gateways, or LPWAN IoT gateways) is leading to a new satellite application segment.

5.10 TIoT and IEEE P1918.1

Under the influence of the post-epidemic, although many industries have been impacted, tactile Internet (TI) and tactile IoT (TIoT) may undertake the mission of the times entrusted by the non-contact economy in the future. In the context of ITU-T Technology Watch Report, the relation of TI and IoT is described as "The IoT connects devices, or objects, to increase their efficiency by exploiting the potential of networking. The next wave of innovation will create the tactile Internet". In the book, TI and TIoT are used as an alternative for each other.

The TIoT is a shift in the collaborative paradigm, adding human-centered perspective and sensing/actuating capabilities transported over the network to communications modalities so that people and machines no longer need to be physically close to the systems they operate or interact with as they can be controlled remotely. As we expected, two workers or manipulators can work together without a contract through TIoT and/or IIoT (e.g., some improved by uRLLC of 5G) in one day of the future and TIoT lift the virtual collaboration of human–machine and human–human with the same machine/production line remotely. We are stepping into a new era; maybe it is called a non-touch or contactless economic era, where every move of human beings will be synchronized or coordinated in a kind of huge IoT — the TIoT.

5.10.1 *IEEE P1918.1*

From the view of communication, TIoT and TI also enable a paradigm shift from conventional content-oriented communication to control-oriented communication, where there is particular relevance for the realization of human-in-the-loop IoT/ICT applications which are highly delayed sensitive and require tight integration of the communication and control technics and mechanisms in a generally accepted framework.

As the prototype of TIoT in the networking view, TI broadly refers to a communication network that is capable of delivering control, touch, and sensing/actuation information in real time. The TI is currently a topic of interest for various standardization bodies. IEEE P1918.1 standards working group defined a framework for the TI, including a description of its application scenarios, terminology, technical assumptions, architecture reference models, and functional capabilities in 2016. In addition, the group gave the definition of the TI as "a network, or a network of networks, for remotely accessing, perceiving, manipulating, or controlling real and virtual objects or processes in perceived real time". Some of the key use cases considered by the working group include teleoperation, immersive virtual reality, inter-personal haptic communication, live haptic broadcasting, automotive, and drone control. The ongoing work on haptic codecs is broadly focused on various aspects of haptic information exchange.

The TI is envisioned to enable unprecedented applications that will have a marked impact on almost any segment of the society by adding a new dimension to human–machine interaction (HMI or human–system interaction, HSI) of real-time interactive systems (in ultra-low latency). Supported by TI/TIoT, a smart cyber-physical system-based interaction environment is given, where haptic interaction with visual feedback relies on the move and within a certain spatial communication range.

The main objective of this section is to present the reference architecture for the TI based on the latest developments within the IEEE P1918.1 standard. The section provides an in-depth research architectural model of various aspects, including the key entities, interfaces, functional capabilities, and protocol stack, also with an IoT layered view. In the reference architecture of the IEEE P1918.1 for the TI, two tactile edges and a network domain are included (as illustrated in Fig. 5.74), described as follows:

The tactile edges refer to the master and slave domains. The master domain consists of a human controller or a machine controller. The slave

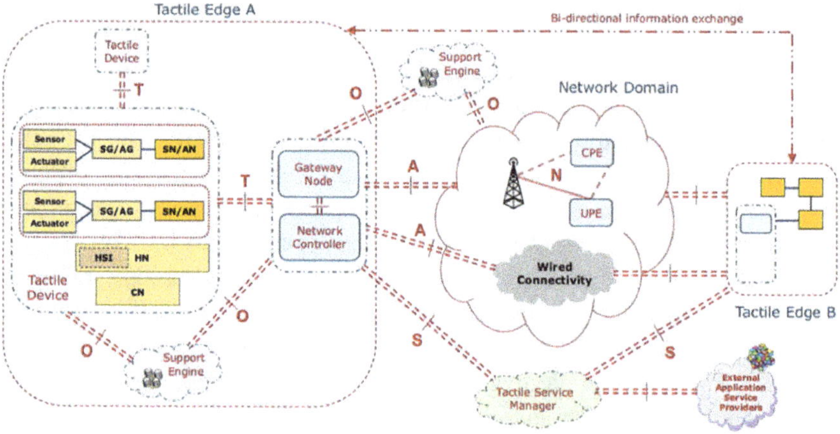

Figure 5.74 Key architectural entities in an organized IEEE P1918.1 TI reference architecture wherein the gateway node and the network controller are part of the tactile edge. The key physical interfaces are also shown.

Note: "A", access interface, provides connectivity between a tactile edge and the network domain. "T", tactile interface, provides connectivity between entities of the tactile edge. "O", open interface, provides connectivity between any architectural entity and the support engine. "S", service interface, provides connectivity between the tactile service manager and the gateway node and the network controller. "N" (network-side) interface, refers to any interface providing internal connectivity between network domain entities. The N interface is the main reference point for user plane or/and control-plane information exchange between various network domain entities.

domain consists of entities, which are remotely controlled by the master domain.

The network domain provides the medium for bi-directional information exchange between the tactile edges. Such bi-directional information exchange may result in a closed-loop control system. The network domain can either provide local area connectivity or wide area connectivity through the Internet or IoT communications and networking infrastructure, according to its needs. The two tactile edges can also exchange information via peer-to-peer (P2P) connectivity, when the tactile edges may also refer to two peer domains.

As shown in Fig. 5.74, the reference architecture consists of various entities that are described as follows:

- **Tactile Device:** The tactile device is the core element of any tactile edge. The nature of the tactile device depends on the underlying TI application. In one embodiment, it consists of a system of sensor nodes (SNs) and actuator nodes (ANs), which are entities with sensing, actuation and limited processing capabilities, respectively, along with necessary connectivity modules for networking capabilities. In a more basic form, third-party sensors and actuators can be connected to SNs and ANs through a sensor gateway (SG) and an actuator gateway (AG), respectively. In another embodiment, the tactile device consists of a human–system interface (HSI or HMI) that converts human input to haptic input. If equipped with networking capabilities, such a device is referred to as the HSI node (HN). In yet another embodiment, the tactile device consists of a controller which runs control algorithms for controlling a system of SNs and ANs. If equipped with networking capabilities, such a device is referred to as the controller node (CN).

- **Gateway Node:** The gateway node is an entity with enhanced networking capabilities that provides interworking functionality between a tactile edge and the network domain. The gateway node can be co-located with the network controller and may exist in the tactile edge of the network domain (see Fig. 5.74).
- **Network Controller:** The network controller is an entity that handles the operation of the tactile edge through intelligent network-side and device-side functions. It further comprises the network management controller (NMC) and device management controller (DMC). The network controller can be co-located with the gateway node, in which case, the resulting entity is termed as the gateway network controller. It may exist in the tactile edge of the network domain.
- **Support Engine:** An entity that provides computing and/or storage resources for improving the performance/experience of the tactile edge. The support engine can be part of the tactile edges or the network domain or both. In one embodiment, the support engine runs predictive intelligence algorithms for enabling the perception of real-time connectivity under the imperfections of wireless environments. In another embodiment, the support engine provides computation offloading capabilities by handling processing operations that are resource-intensive for the tactile devices. Additionally, another embodiment of the engine provides caching capability or has a co-located edge device for caching.
- **Tactile Service Manager:** The tactile service manager is a network domain entity that is primarily responsible for providing the interface to external service and application providers. In one embodiment, it may

also be responsible for session-level functionalities, e.g., authentication and access rights, session establishment, and charging and billing.

- **User-Plane Entity (UPE):** An entity that handles the user-plane functions for the tactile edge inside the network domain, e.g., context activation, data forwarding to external networks, and quality-of-service (QoS) support.
- **Control-Plane Entity (CPE):** An entity that handles the control-plane functions for the tactile edge inside the network domain, e.g., authentication, session establishment, and mobility management.

The functional description of the reference architecture is provided as follows. Note that two variants of the reference architecture can be distinguished depending on the placement of the gateway network controller. In the scenario of Fig. 5.74, this entity is part of the tactile edge. The tactile edges A and B represent the master and slave domains, respectively, or two peer domains. The network domain provides the medium for bi-directional information exchange of control and feedback signals between the tactile devices in the two tactile edges. The network domain may represent wireless connectivity (cellular, Wi-Fi, etc.), wired connectivity (fieldbus system, industrial Ethernet, etc.), or hybrid wired/wireless connectivity.

The support engine can be deployed centrally or distributedly and provides predictive intelligence, computation offloading, and/or storage/caching functionalities, through different manifestations of the edge-computing paradigm such as fog computing, mobile edge computing, and multi-access edge computing (will be introduced in the next chapter).

For predictive intelligence, the support engine runs a model of the TI application which could be obtained in an online or offline manner. The support engine may provide full or partial computation offloading capabilities. The offloading decision is made by either the tactile device or the gateway network controller. As a broader view of ML in the service layer of IoT or TIoT, ML as a service is from the similar thinking of predictive or statistics intelligence in either online or offline manner.

5.10.1.1 *Layered protocol stacks and interfaces (of O/S)*

To provide a generic stack for different interfaces, the working group has adopted the standard TCP/IP protocol stack model, in which different interfaces are specific to the underlying connectivity technology and their different connecting layers also conform to the four-layer architecture of an IoT.

Take the scenario of Fig. 5.74 as an example; Fig. 5.75 depicts the protocol stack for connectivity between the tactile edge and the network domain in Fig. 5.74, i.e., by the gateway network controller. Note that in this case, the gateway network controller has a dual protocol stack, as shown in Fig. 5.75. The stack for the A interface provides connectivity to the network domain whereas the stack for the T interface provides connectivity to the tactile device.

The application layer (Layer 5, the top layer) in the tactile device generates the desired control, haptic, sensing, or actuation information that needs to be transmitted to a tactile device in the other tactile edge. Depending on the nature of the T interface, the tactile device may connect to the gateway network controller at Layer 2 or Layer 3.

The application layer can directly reside over Layer 2 and the gateway network controller connects with any network domain entity at Layer 3 over the A interface. From a control plane perspective, there is Layer 3 connectivity at both T and A interfaces. The control-plane uses the same Layer 1 and Layer 2 as in the user-plane. However, the control-plane protocol (CPP) at Layer 3, which handles typical control-plane functionalities, could be different for each interface.

5.10.1.2 *Access node side*

When the tactile device directly connects to the network domain over the A interface (i.e., the gateway node and the network controller are

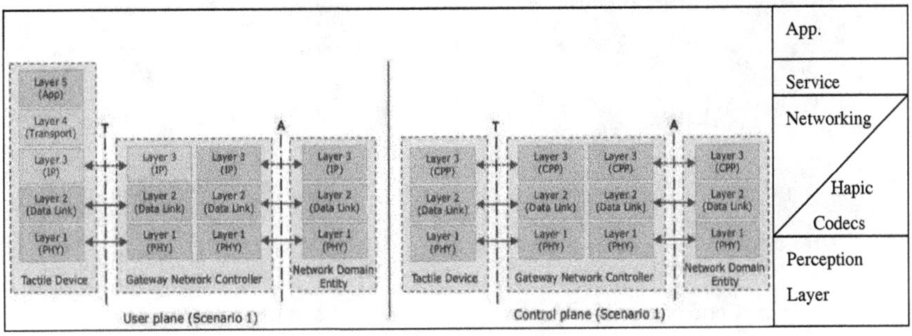

Figure 5.75 Protocol stack for connectivity between the tactile edge and the network domain.

transferred as parts of the network domain), the tactile device connects to the gateway network controller at Layer 3 (as shown in Fig. 5.74).

Figure 5.76 depicts the protocol stack for the O (connecting the support engine and gateway) interface and the S (service) interface. For both interfaces, the respective entities hold a full protocol stack for both the user plane and control plane, according to their specific physical implementation. The protocol stack for various network-side interfaces is specific to the underlying connectivity technology. Hence, it has been deemed as beyond the scope of the working group.

According to the IoT views, the user-side nodes can be classified into two cases:

(i) **Case H: "heavy" node**. The heavy IoT node implements data processing locally before it transfers the tactile information to the "pipelines" of communication or networking. Hence, just the refined data is transferred/received to/from the pipelines. The heavy IoT node shares some of the functions of the support engine by, e.g., sampling the local model and data to sematic model parameters (e.g., as a tuple of vectors or matrices), or other data cleaning/(process) refining methods. One of them, especially for TIoT is haptic codecs, which will be discussed in the following part.

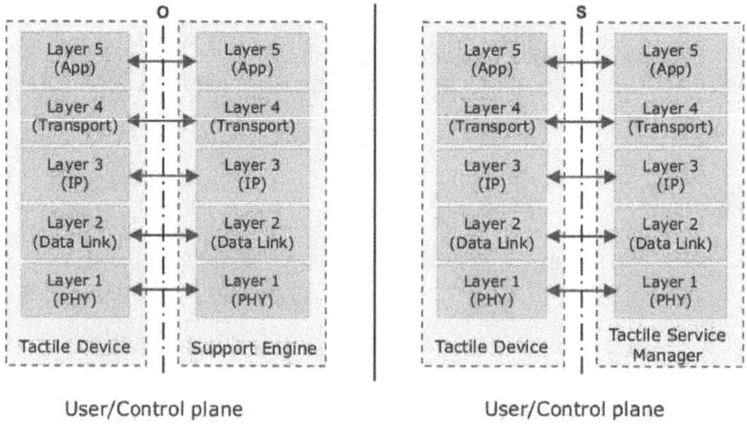

Figure 5.76 Protocol stack for the connecting of the support engine and gateway interface, and the service interface.

(ii) **Case L: "light" node**. On the contrary, the light IoT node (sometimes a sensor/actuator node as tactile device of IoT, with limited processing capabilities) with necessary connectivity modules for networking capabilities, implement just the data acquisition and transmission.

The distributed support engine but around light nodes is needed for the analysis and comprehensions of the local model and data, including the haptic codecs in a model of the tactile application which could be obtained in either online or offline manner.

For predictive intelligence and other functions, the support engine runs on the edge/cloud/fog, a so-called ML-as-a-service aforementioned can be realized to provide computation offloading and/or storage/caching functionalities through deep learning as a data or codecs analysis tool or reinforcement learning as a decision-action model.

5.10.1.3 *Functional capabilities*

To support the envisioned TI applications, the interfaces must fulfill certain performance requirements or capabilities. With reference to the majority of TI applications, such capabilities can be characterized as availability, latency, reliability, and scalability.

The working group has specified two different grades of capabilities for interfaces: an ultra grade and a normal grade. The functional capabilities of the A and T interfaces are summarized in Table 5.18. It can be easily inferred that the desired functional capabilities create a set of stringent requirements that need to be fulfilled irrespective of the underlying connectivity technology. Some of the most important enablers for realizing such functional capabilities are stated as follows:

A. Key Enablers for High Availability: Redundancy is the key to achieving high availability. The IEC 62439-3 standard has specified seamless redundancy protocols for fault tolerance in industrial Ethernet networks.

Such protocols can also be applied for achieving high availability in wireless communications.

B. Key Enablers for High Reliability: Diversity is the key to achieving high reliability. However, diversity in the time domain is not suitable as it

Table 5.18 Functional capabilities.

Interface	Ultra-grade capabilities	Normal-grade capabilities
A and T Interfaces	Availability: ultra-high; >99.99999% Reliability: ultra-high; >99.999% Latency: ultra-low; 10% of end-to-end latency (e.g., 1 ms) Scalability: medium; 1–50 tactile devices	Availability: very-high; >99.999% Reliability: very-high; >99.99% Latency: very-low; 50% of end-to-end latency (e.g., 10 ms) Scalability: high; 50–100 tactile devices

incurs additional latency. Some of the key enablers for high reliability without incurring additional latency include multi-connectivity, efficient channel coding techniques, cooperative transmissions, and packet duplication with multi-path diversity.

C. Key Enablers for Low Latency: Achieving low latency becomes particularly challenging, especially considering its trade-off with providing high reliability. Some of the key enablers for achieving low latency, which could be extended to any wireless technology in the context of the TI, include short packet transmissions, short frame structure, full-duplex communication, lean protocol stack, flexible resource allocation, edge-intelligence, and powerful and efficient hardware designs.

D. Key Enablers for High Scalability: Achieving high scalability becomes particularly important from a network utilization perspective. Some of the key enablers for high scalability include efficient and dynamic multiple access techniques, spectrum aggregation, successive interference cancellation, and interference averaging.

5.10.2 *TIoT and haptic codecs*

In the tactile application environment, enabling remote physical interaction with touch and/or kinesthetic experiences is one of the key technologies that allow motor skills to be available across distances and enables immersive multi-sensory remote exploration of real or virtual **surroundings** where users can see, hear and, in particular, feel remote objects.

From the comparison view, in the sensory and its remote feeling transportation, haptic information needs to be captured, compressed, transmitted, and displayed with minimum latency, according to the information acquisition, processing/communication, and application steps of a typical IoT usage. IEEE P1918.1 Tactile Internet is one of the supporting networks of communication.

Conversely, in TIoT, the compression of haptic information is handled by haptic codecs, which is an important part that enables the bi-directional "pipeline" to the connection from the human side to the remote manipulating side (as shown in Fig. 5.77).

The operator controls the position of the remote robot (teleoperation). Interaction forces are measured during contact and sent back to the operator. Additionally, visual and auditory information is streamed back to the operator.

The provision of high-quality tactile experiences in the context of the TI/TIoT requires three main components: efficient acquisition of tactile object properties, analysis and compression of tactile information, and tactile display technology which ideally can reproduce all relevant tactile dimensions simultaneously. The corresponding tactile "pipeline" (central part of Fig. 5.78) is exacted from the views of object properties, codecs of tactile information and display, according to the tactile information with its comprehensive applications (as shown in Fig. 5.78).

According to Steinbach *et al.* (2018) (the same source as Fig. 5.77), the acquisition of tactile includes the following: (1) human tactile perception of object properties (i.e., object identification); (2) five tactile dimensions (including friction, hardness, warmth, macroscopic and microscopic roughness).

After the tactile perception and acquisition, the display of tactile information includes the following: (1) potential sensing and actuation

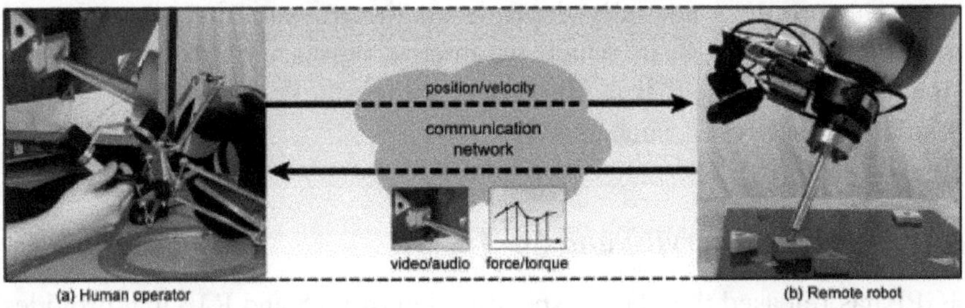

Figure 5.77 Bilateral teleoperation with kinesthetic feedback in a bi-directional "pipeline".

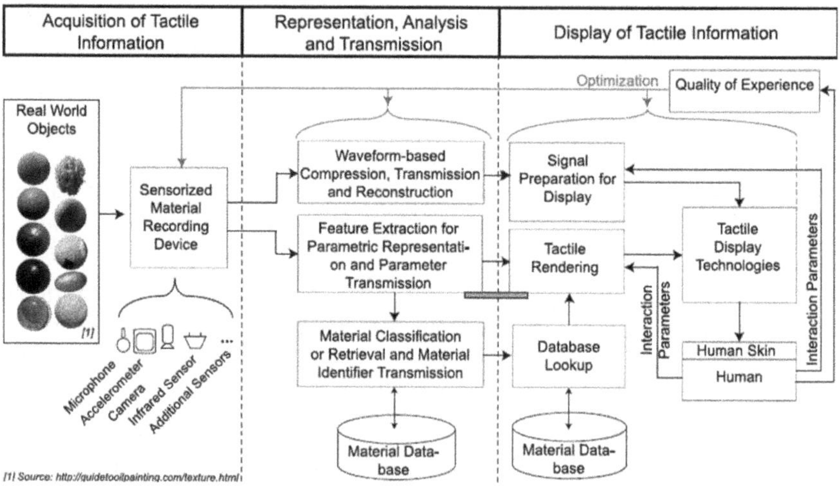

Figure 5.78 Pipeline of acquisition, analysis, transmission, and display for tactile information.

principles for each of the five major tactile dimensions; (2) combinations of tactile dimensions.

Compression of tactile information includes the following: (1) waveform-based representation and compression of tactile signals; (2) feature extraction for parametric representations and classification.

The display part is followed by approaches to collect and display such tactile information as well as how it can be compressed and transmitted. Moreover, in future haptic communication systems that include a large number of different tactile sensors, it is essential to develop tactile codecs that exploit the properties and conceptual limitations of tactile information. The progress not only depends on the transmission scenario and model (see Fig. 5.78, in which parametric representation of the tactile signal is required), either tactile-based or kinesthetic-based, but the communication networks, such as 5G.

5.10.3 *ML as a service and 5G TSN*

3GPP has released the 5G NR specification of R15 and R16 that provides NFV-enabled network with required protocol stack functionalities, the SDN controller with the functionality of programming the core and radio access network, and various enhancements pertaining to ultra-reliable low-latency communication (uRLLC), which is one of the key enablers for the TI. The cellular core network and even cloud-RAN of 5G-driven communication architecture, as shown in Fig. 5.79, opens the possibility to provide an end-to-end flexible architecture based on SDN/NFV slicing in the networking domain and network-aware radio resource management (RRM) & scheduler approaches in the wireless domain.

Hence, the orchestration of network services, such as enhanced mobile broadband (eMBB), URLLC, and mMTC in network slicing environments, as so-called network slicing, is an innovative network architecture technology.

In 5G telecom networks, a single spectrum of the network can be divided logically for different use cases with specific characteristics and network requirements, such as latency, high bandwidth, and security. Furthermore, services in these different slices can be managed separately, enabling privacy and dedicated bandwidth to run critical operations. The technology also offers huge performance boosts for specific use cases, such as tactile slice, smart grid slice, V2V or V2X slice, IIoT, and more, as shown in Fig. 5.79. ETSI OSM and OpenStack have come to some conclusions around network slicing and its readiness. Experts note that end-to-end virtualization, dynamic centralized orchestration, and

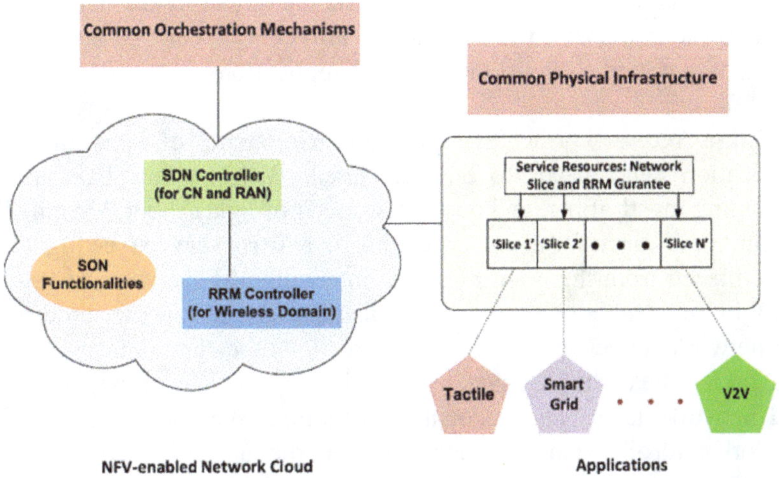

Figure 5.79 Different slices on demand.

quality-of-service manageability are basic requirements for successful net slicing implementation. Such a slicing approach provides more of network on-demand functionality.

Through such a slicing and services supported by 5G coupling, it is possible for the case of multi-player virtual/augmented reality over 5G wireless networks, which is a prominent application of the TI. In this case, the two tactile edges are connected via a 5G wireless network and correspond to an indoor gaming arcade with multiple players and a virtual/augmented reality server.

5.10.3.1 *Network domain and edge computing*

The key functionalities of the 5G core network (CN) relevant to the TI are slicing, edge access, and security.

(i) Slicing: Dynamic application-aware QoS is provided by network slicing (NS) in the NFV/SDN of 5G networks. NFV provides the abstraction as well as separation of network functions from the hardware infrastructure; the network function can be managed as a software module that can be deployed in any standard cloud computing infrastructure. Moreover, SDN provides flexibility by an architectural framework, wherein control and data planes are decoupled and enables direct programmability of network control through software-based controllers. Such an architectural approach enables flexible and dynamic slicing of end-to-end network and service resources, which is particularly attractive to cater to the requirements of tactile as well as other vertical applications.

(ii) Edge Access: For achieving a round-trip latency of 1 ms, the communication delay needs to be considered. Within 1 ms, light travels (assuming mostly fiber, and due to the speed of light) about 200 km. The maximum distance for **a** support engine **or control server** (see Fig. 5.74) to be placed from the point of tactile interaction by the users is 100 km away in the ideal conditions that the distance assumes neither processing nor network congestion delays anywhere along the communication.

Taking the additional signal processing, protocol handling, switching and network delays into account, this requires the support engine and network controller (**control server**) to be in the range of a few kilometers from the tactile point of interaction. Hence, the controller and support engine servers need to be built as close to the base station (access point) as possible.

The concept of putting servers at the edge of the mobile RAN has been coined as the (mobile) edge computing or multi-access edge computing, (MEC) and possibly the best way to enable this proximity is to combine servers into the same box as base stations and access points. As a solution to this kind of **edge box**, a highly adaptive and energy-efficient computing (HAEC) box has been established on how computing design can be built by utilizing optical and wireless chip-to-chip communication to achieve a significant increase in performance compared to today's servers. Hence, the HAEC box can replace a base station and a control/support engine server and in this box, the integration of wireless and optical transceiver functionality is integrated into one 3D-stacked chip, where an individual user can obtain the service of support engine, network controller, even the codecs, and (ML) models of a TIoT on the edge. This kind of edge devices can reduce the latency, as shown in Fig. 5.80.

(iii) Security: In the context of TI, and the data flows and operations conducted on cellular networks, adequate QoS and security for tactile applications must be provided by the core network. Either reducing the number of nodes in the data path or reducing the end-to-end latency can be achieved through the functional decomposition of the mobile core network and moving some of the core functionalities to the access network.

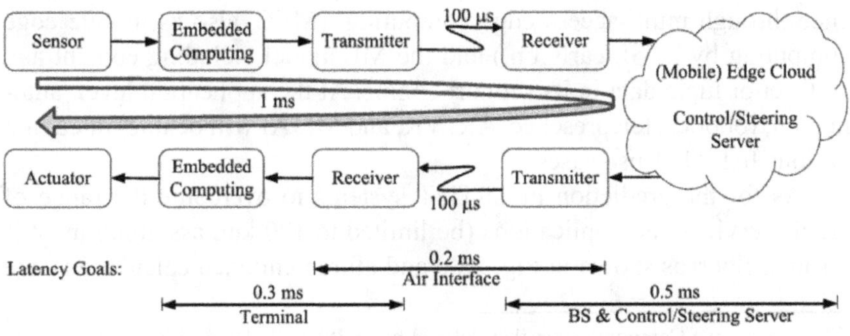

Figure 5.80 Exemplary latency objectives of TI systems

The SDN enabling core network introduces the programmability and the flexibility to tailor the data flow inside the core network with respect to the requirements of tactile applications. This will result in improved service quality and user experience. Current IP security (IPSec protocol functionalities are sufficient for providing the required security in the TI), the placement of IPSec far from the tactile edge significantly increases the end-to-end delays. Therefore, innovative approaches are needed to provide adequate security for tactile applications with minimal delays (e.g., light-weight encryption, and secure consideration for new physical layer, such as Li-Fi). Once more, autonomous components of the TI are considered (e.g., a self-driving vehicle or remote operation), then other security issues will need to be resolved. These are similar to the security of IIoT, which will be discussed in the last chapter. An important issue from the protocol stack perspective is the small packet header to payload ratio. For example, the payload of one packet for a 3-DoF haptic stream is only 6 bytes.

5.10.3.2 *ML as-a-service and an use case in support engine*

At the edges of peer-to-peer connectivity paradigms which are under active investigation within the IEEE 802.15.8-2017standard, or the connectivity over 5G NR specification that provides MEC/TSC[22] interfaces, and the later R17 of 3GPP providing the combination of TSC and TSN (IEEE 802.1), are required to support the TIoT by those content and data enabled by the sensor/actuators and robotic "things", and transmitted over a reliable network (5G-supported MEC and/or TSN or other tactile-supporting networks).

At the same time, intelligence is also enabled close to the user experience through multi-access edge computing, (MEC, also as mobile edge computing by ETSI, early on.) and the ML model including content and skill set or tuple data in its support engine. At the application level, automation, robotics, telepresence, AR, VR, and ML/AI will be integrated into various IoT/TIoT use cases.

As for the prediction in TI/TIoT systems to overcome the range of tactile services and applications (be limited to 100 km, assuming most is through fiber, as shown in Fig. 5.80 and aforementioned calculation), the

[22]Time Sensitive Communication that defined by 3GPP, will play as a bridge of itself to TSN, Time Sensitive Networking (defined by IEEE802.1), in the R16 specification of 3GPP, as the 2nd 5G specification.

TI must support a hybrid composition of the device and human actuation mixing real tactile actuation with intelligence-based predictive actuation. Such predictive actuation should be in close proximity to the tactile edge. Therefore, the edge of the network must be equipped with ML or AI to facilitate predictive caching as well as interpolation/extrapolation of human actions. This necessitates the development of novel ML-as-a-service for edge or cloud architectures.

In TI/TIoT systems, content and skill set data will be transmitted over a more powerful 5G core network or other TSN as well as the next-generation Internet. When the advances in hardware, protocols, and architecture are paramount in diminishing end-to-end delays, the ultimate limit is set by the finite speed of light.

Other more sophisticated techniques need to be invoked to facilitate the required paradigm shift, such as ML-as-a-service in the following use case, which is provided by ML engines or edge AI engines as parts of the functions/services of support engine and can be co-located in the edge box or other edge devices. ML/AI engines are cached and then executed in real-time close to the tactile experience. The respective components in an advanced content-caching example are discussed subsequently.

A. Content caching: With the cloud/edge technology in place, the TI application content needs to be loaded or ported. A typical example would be an ML algorithm, which is tailored to work in the context of a remote dentistry operation or remote vehicle servicing.

These advanced caching techniques and traffic managements approach at the edge of the network improve network performance by de-congestion of the core network and reduction of end-to-end latency (particularly important to the TI). Some work has been conducted on optimum edge caching policies, and one of them is an approach that advocates for proactive caching by using advanced predictive process capabilities as well as improved cloud technologies. With this approach, peak traffic demands are substantially reduced by intelligently serving predictable user demands by caching at base stations and users' devices. The advocated approach pertains to rather long-term windows and file structures, and it forms the foundation for predictive TI caching.

B. Tactile ML engines: The most important contents to be stored are ML/AI engines which predict the haptic/tactile experience, i.e., acceleration of movement on one end and the force feedback on the other. This allows for spatially decoupling of the active and reactive end of the TI because the tactile experience is virtually emulated and allows a much wider geographic separation between the tactile ends (beyond the 1 ms-at-speed-of-light limit).

The algorithmic framework in Simsek *et al.* (2016) is based on simple linear regression algorithms which are able to predict movement and reaction over the next tens of milliseconds, mainly because the skillset-driven actions are fairly repetitive and exhibit strong patterns across the six degrees of freedom. When the predicted action/reaction deviates from the real one by a certain amount, then the coefficients are updated and transmitted to the other end allowing for corrections to be put in place before damage is done, as illustrated in Fig. 5.81.

Algorithms in an instance employed a prediction method for three-dimensional position and force data by means of an advanced first-order autoregressive model. After an initialization and training process, the adaptive coefficients of the model are computed for the predicted values to be produced. The algorithm then decides if the training values need to be updated either from the predicted data or the current real data.

The ML algorithms ported through intelligent edge caching and stored on appropriate cloud/edge technologies aid in enabling the perception of real-time interaction, stabilizing the tactile system, and enhancing the QoE of the TI user consequently.

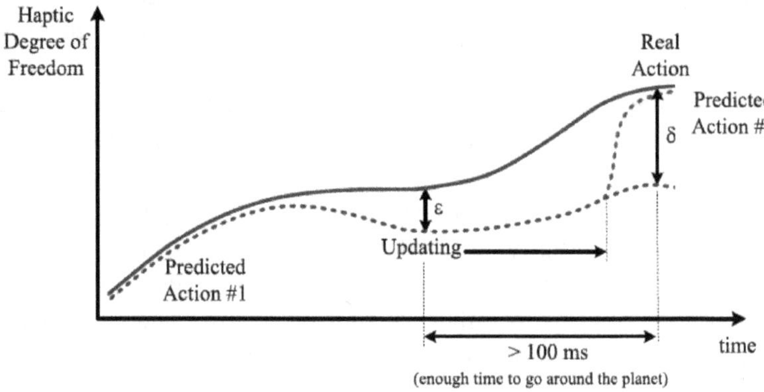

Figure 5.81 Illustration how predictive edge-ML gives the perception of a 1 ms delay while the actual latency due to communications can be much larger.

C. QoE: In a haptic rendering API, kinesthetic and/or tactile rendering mechanisms and graphic modeling, the haptic device includes physical properties of the haptic interface, actuation technology, and performance characteristics (including spatial and temporal). The haptic data describes the data format, acquisition, and encoding of haptic data. The data and models can be trained or refined (or compressed) with the ML-as-a-service for the continuous improvement of QoE, on the edge, even when the wireless condition (such as the channel) is worse.

As for the user, the QoE describes kinesthetic, tactile, and thermal perception attributes, in addition to QoS (quality of service) parameters presented in Fig. 5.82. More QoE-related factors are analyzed in Hamam *et al.* (2014).

Finally, edge computing/MEC in TI/TIoT enables high performance, interoperability, and security in a multi-vendor computing-based system and is focusing on resource allocation at the service level, where support engine including ML as a service, the network controller (maybe co-located with UPF of 5G infrastructure, in an edge box or elsewhere) and logically splitting the software stack (including OS) from the underlying sensory/acting hardware for individual TI/TIoT application transparently.

Further, QoS, and QoE are the performance indicators on either side of the edge for networking service or the experience (e.g., streamed immerse, manipulable, and enjoyable) of TI/TIoT users. One more difference compared to MEC is the need (of support engine on the edge)

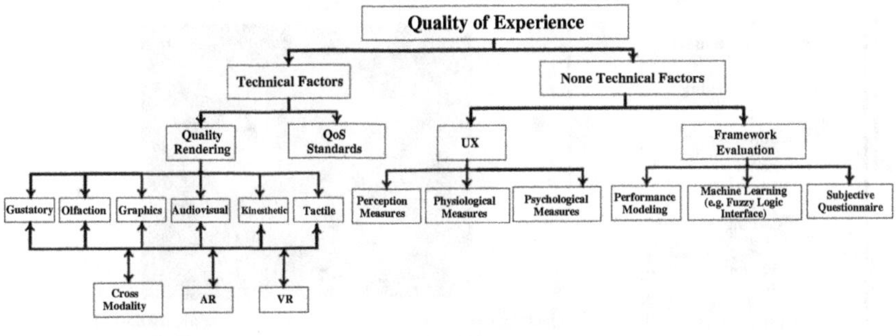

Figure 5.82 QoE evaluation model for TI applications, including media synchronization (QoS parameter with jitter, latency, etc.), fatigue, and user intuitiveness (perception-related), haptic rendering (rendering quality parameter), and degree of immersion (psychological).

to support exotic I/O and accelerator aware provisioning, real-time, embedded targets as well as real-time networks such as TSN, e.g., IEEE 802.1, and deterministic networking (DetNet).

At last, another use case of Internet of robotics things (IoRT) on the edge is given, as shown in Fig. 5.83. In an edge environment, intelligence can be deployed on edge devices in the LAN, as shown in the rectangle (the dotted box) of Fig. 5.83. Data/Information from the sensor of a mobile robot is transmitted from end points to an edge gateway or edge data center, where it is then processed following the six steps, such as feature extraction, representation, ML, knowledge forming, reasoning, and planning. The result is transmitted back to sources for action indication. In edge computing, intelligence and ML algorithms of the edge gateway or appliance are in edge devices, such as programmable automation controllers, object identification, and trajectory finding. Edge computing allows the reduction of points of failure, as each edge device operates independently and determines which information, and also supports the multi-robot collaboration (in perception, decision making, and route optimization).

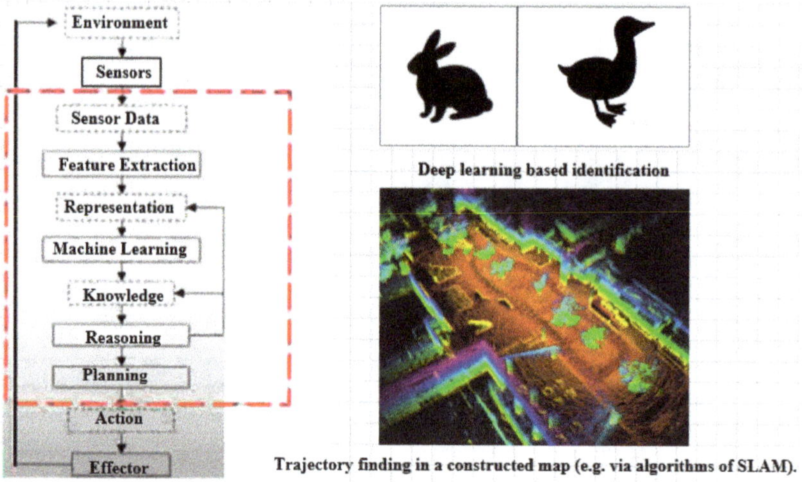

Figure 5.83 Machine learning stack on the edge of IoRT and ML-as-a-service examples.

5.10.3.3 *TIoT in B5G*

Figure 5.84 presents a generalized framework for wireless TI/TIoT in the beyond-5G era including architecture, the main technical requirements, the key application areas, and potential enabling technologies. Subsequently, a comprehensive review of the existing TI works by broadly categorizing them into three main paradigms, namely haptic communications, wireless AR/VR, and autonomous, intelligent and cooperative mobility systems, are discussed in Sharma *et al.* (2020) of the figure,

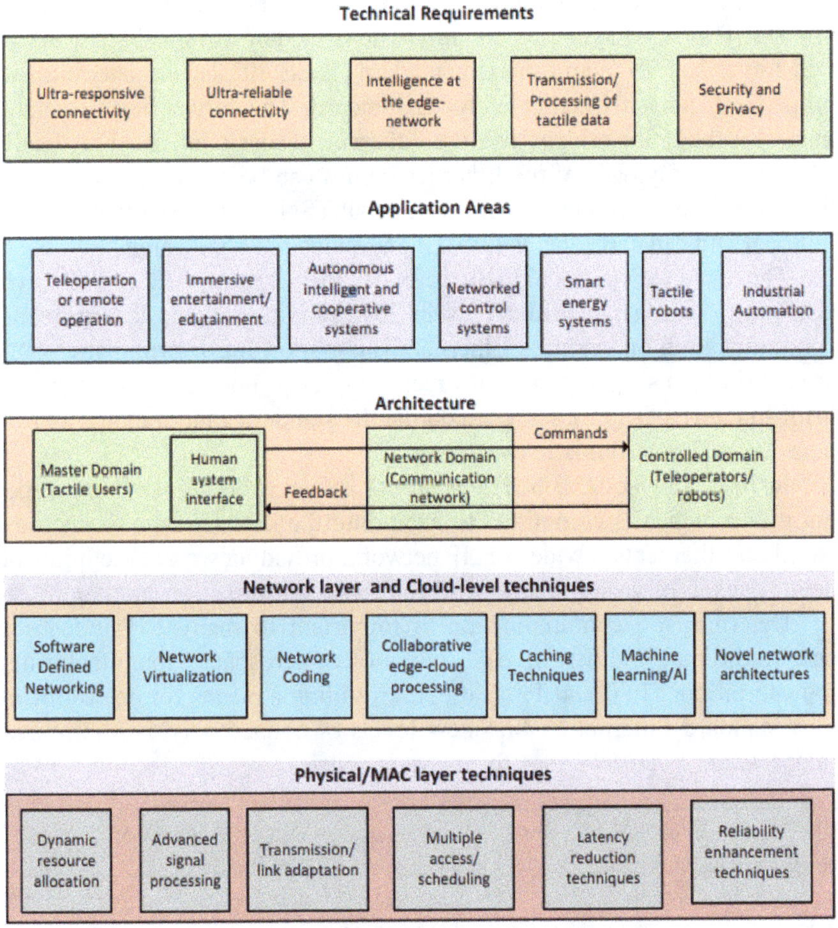

Figure 5.84 A generalized framework for TI in the beyond-5G era.

potential enabling technologies across physical/medium access control (MAC) and network layers are identified and discussed in the followed 5G TSN part.

5.10.3.4 *TSN and 5G*

(1) TSN Introduction: TSN is the IEEE 802.1Q–defined standard technology to provide deterministic messaging on standard Ethernet. TSN technology is centrally managed and delivers guarantees of delivery (e.g., upper latency bounds and low packet loss) and minimized jitter (delay variance) using time scheduling for those real-time applications that require determinism. TSN is a Layer 2 technology. The IEEE 802.1Q standards work at OSI Layer 2. TSN is an Ethernet standard (IEEE 802.3 with deterministic properties), not an Internet protocol standard. The forwarding decisions made by the TSN bridges use the Ethernet header contents, not the IP address. The payloads of the Ethernet frames can be anything and are not limited to Internet protocol. This means that TSN can be used in any environment and can carry the payload of any industrial application.

The goal of the TSN/IEEE 802.1 task group (IEEE 802.1avb task group was renamed the TSN in 2012[23]) is to develop deterministic communication on standard Ethernet. The market for deterministic communication is using non-standard technologies or non-standard Ethernet. Prior to the IEEE 802.1 TSN standards, the standard Ethernet didn't have pure Layer 2 deterministic capability.

In 2015, IETF established the deterministic networking (DetNet) working group, which is committed to extending the deterministic technology based on Ethernet to a wide area IP network, providing worst-case limits of delay, packet loss, and jitter to provide deterministic data transmission.

Deterministic communication is important to many IoT industries and traditional industries, e.g., automotive/aerospace, manufacturing, transportation, TIoT, and TI utilities). Providing a means for determinism over standard Ethernet enables new levels of connectivity and optimization, leading to cost savings for many industries.

---

[23]Research Institute of China Mobile Communication Co., Ltd. White Paper. 2030 technology trends. As discussed in the White Paper, the TSN standard extends AVB technology, with time synchronization, delay guarantee, and other mechanisms to ensure real time, and supports traffic scheduling and shaping, reliability, configuration management, and other related protocols.

The “Deterministic” in TSN consists of five main components as a blow and a standard table is followed.

- ***TSN flow***: The term is used to describe the time-critical communication between end devices. Each flow has strict time requirements that the networking devices honor. Each TSN flow is uniquely identified by the network devices.
- ***End devices***: These are the source and destinations of the TSN flows. The end devices are running an application that requires deterministic communication. These are also referred to as talkers and listeners.
- ***Bridges***: It is also referred to as Ethernet switches. For TSN, these are special bridges capable of transmitting the Ethernet frames of a TSN flow on a schedule and receiving Ethernet frames of a TSN flow according to a schedule.
- ***Central network controller (CNC)***: For TSN, the CNC acts as a proxy for the network (the TSN bridges and their interconnections) and the control applications that require deterministic communication. The CNC defines the schedule on which all TSN frames are transmitted. The CNC application is provided by the vendor of the TSN bridges.
- ***Centralized user configuration (CUC)***: It means an application that communicates with the CNC and the end devices. The CUC represents the control applications and the end devices. The CUC makes requests to the CNC for deterministic communication (TSN flows) with specific requirements for those flows. The CUC is a vendor-specific application. Typically, the vendor of the TSN end devices will supply a CUC for those end devices.

TSN standards can be seen as a toolbox that includes several valuable tools, which can be categorized into four groups: traffic shaping, resource management, time synchronization, and reliability (see Section 5.8.4), TSN tools that are candidates for early TSN deployments in industrial automation, are focused on by Cisco (Farkas *et al.*, 2019)[24] (Table 5.19).

---

[24]Definition of smart factories is given in this article as being developed as part of the fourth industrial revolution. Smart factories require ubiquitous connectivity among and from the devices to the cloud through a fully converged network, supporting various types of traffic in a single network infrastructure, which also includes mobile network segments integrated into the network.

Table 5.19 TSN relative standards.

Standard	Area of definition	Title of standard
IEEE 802.1ASrev, IEEE 1588	Timing and synchronization	Enhancements and performance
IEEE 802.1Qbu and IEEE 802.3br	Forwarding and queuing	Frame preemption
IEEE 802.1Qbv	Forwarding and queuing	Enhancements for scheduled traffic (end devices need time reference for synchronization)
IEEE 802.1Qca	Path control and reservation	Path control and reservation
IEEE 802.1Qcc	Central configuration method enhancements and	Central configuration method enhancements and
IEEE 802.1Qci	Time-based ingress policing	Per-stream filtering and policing
IEEE 802.1CB	Seamless redundancy	Frame replication and elimination for reliability (FRER)

Source: Adapted from 1.ieee802.org/tsn/.

Notes: Not all standards of TSN shown in the table (e.g., generalized precision time protocol (gPTP) in 802.1AS).

TSN guarantees the worst-case latency for critical data by various queuing and shaping techniques and by reserving resources for critical traffic. The scheduled traffic standard (802.1Qbv) provides time-based traffic shaping. Ethernet frame preemption (802.3br and 802.1Qbu), which can suspend the transmission of a non-critical Ethernet frame, is also beneficial to decrease latency and latency variation of critical traffic. Resource management basics are defined by the TSN configuration models (802.1Qcc). Centralized network configuration (CNC) can be applied to the network devices (bridges), whereas, CUC can be applied to user devices (end stations). The fully centralized configuration model follows a SDN approach; in other words, the CNC and CUC provide the control plane instead of distributed protocols. In contrast, distributed control protocols are applied in the fully distributed model, where there is no CNC or CUC.

(2) Deep Learning as a CV Service for Quality Control in Smart Factories through TSN: As introduced in Section 5.8 and above, valuable tools within the TSN toolbox enable deployments in industrial automation. The following use case is a visual quality control using CNN (based on the RetinaNet architecture, a deep learning algorithm) over computer vision to detect the products in the production line (as shown in Fig. 5.85), in a TSN network (as shown in Fig. 5.86), in which the TSN switch supports IEEE 802.1Qbv (time-aware scheduler) and IEEE 1588v2 (precision time protocol, PTP) allowing to slice the available network bandwidth into time slots to guarantee determinism to important traffic. Endpoints (e.g., camera and edge device) only support PTP to synchronize egress traffic with their respective timeslots in the use case.

In the use case, all production modules communicate with each other via standardized interfaces and communication protocols, e.g., the manufacturer-independent standards such as OPC-UA (also TSN supported, see Chapter 8). As shown in Fig. 5.86, an edge device connected via a Hirschmann RSPE 35 TSN switch to the Cisco 6050 IP camera is for the evaluation of the computer vision algorithm mentioned above. The output

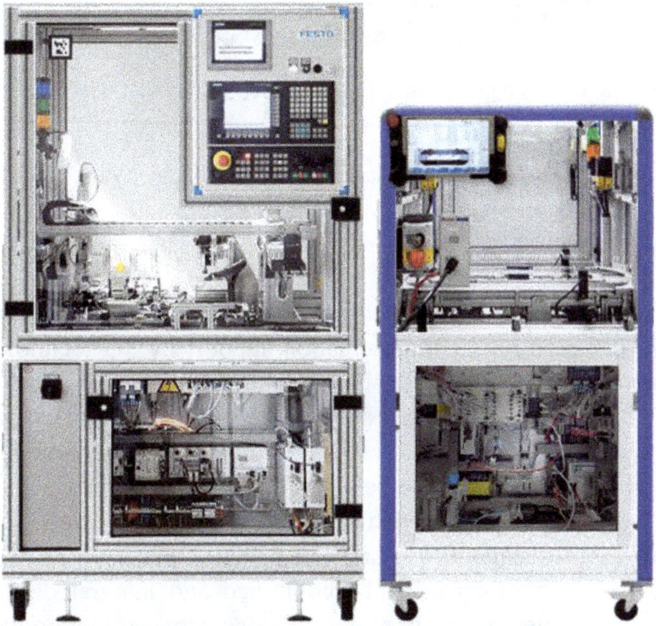

Figure 5.85 *SmartFactory KL* production line modules.

Source: Popper (2020).

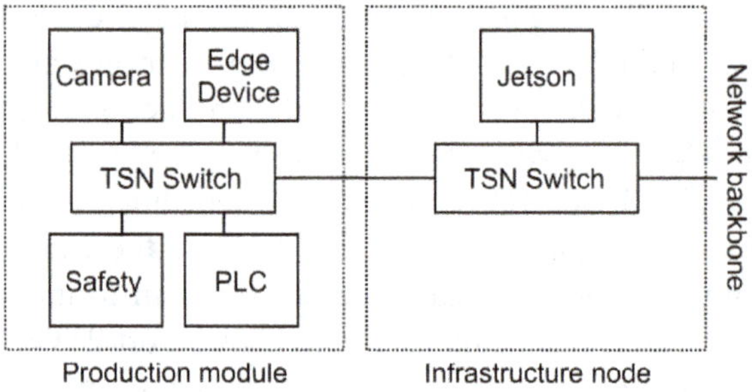

Figure 5.86 Network topology utilizing a shared link.

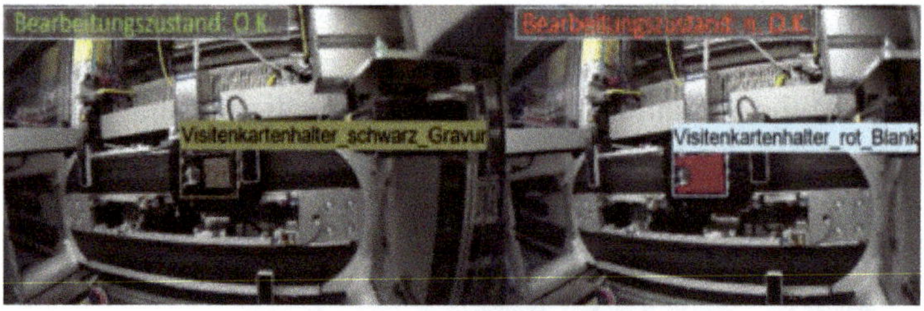

Figure 5.87 Recognized process step of the product: correct (left) and incorrect (right).

of the evaluation represents the label of the recognized current processing state, which indicates a correctly manufactured product or not, as shown in Fig. 5.87.

(3) 5G System (5GS) Integrated with TSN: As for the inherent mobile and multi-machine type communication support by 5G technology, and IPv6, for the tactile or VR/AR-based (immerse) sensory, the ETSI IP6 ISG has completed a work item on IPv6-based TI. The work item identifies the key features of IPv6 for meeting the stringent technical requirements of the TI along with the best practices for different use-cases.

In the R16 of 3GPP, 5G and time-sensitive networking is integrated as the 5G URLLC capabilities providing a good match to TSN features. The two key technologies can be combined and integrated to provide deterministic connectivity end to end, such as between input/output (I/O) devices and their controller potentially residing in an edge cloud for industrial automation. The integration includes support for both the necessary base-bridging features and the TSN add-ons. As illustrated in

Fig. 5.88, the 5G-TSN integration includes TSN components as traffic shaping, resource management, time synchronization, and reliability.

The first step of control plane integration is being carried out for an SDN-based approach. In the fully centralized configuration model of Fig. 5.88, the 5GS appears from the rest of the network as a set of TSN bridges — one virtual bridge per user plane function (UPF), as shown in Fig. 5.89. The 5GS includes TSN translator (TT) functionality for the

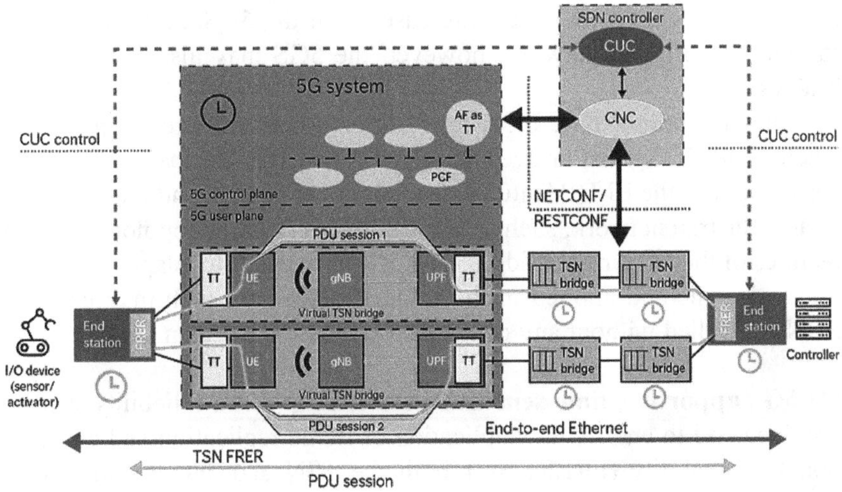

Figure 5.88 5G system (5GS) integrated with TSN providing end-to-end deterministic connectivity (supported in 5G phase-2/3GPP R16.). The green/grey clocks illustrate a case when both bridges and end stations are time synchronized.

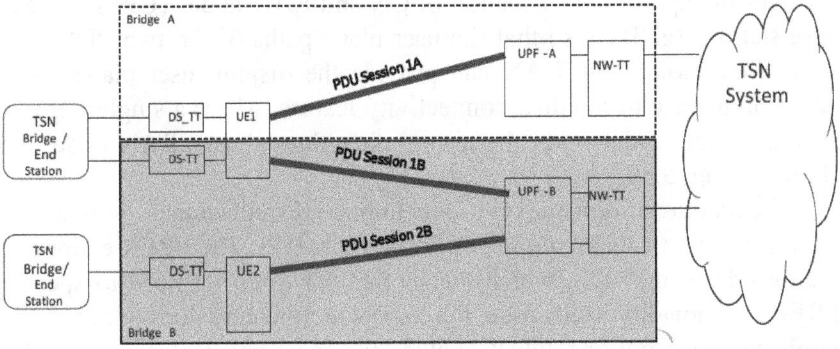

Figure 5.89 Each virtual bridge per UPF.

adaptation of the 5GS to the TSN domain, both for the user plane and the control plane, hiding the 5GS internal procedures from the TSN bridged network.

The 5GS provides TSN bridge ingress/egress port operations through the TT functionality. For instance, the TTs support hold and forward functionality for de-jittering. The figure illustrates functionalities using an example of two user equipment (UE) with two PDU sessions supporting two correlated TSN streams for redundancy. But a deployment may only include one physical UE with two PDU sessions using dual-connectivity in RAN. The figure illustrates the case when the 5GS connects an end station to a bridged network; however, the 5GS may also interconnect bridges.

The support for base bridging features described here is applicable whether the 5G virtual bridges are Class A or Class B capable. The 5GS has to support the LLDP features needed for the control and management of an industrial network, such as for the discovery of the topology and the features of the 5G virtual bridges. The 5GS also needs to adapt to the loop prevention method applied in the bridged network, which may be fully SDN controlled without any distributed protocol other than LLDP.

(4) 5G supporting time-sensitive networking: Ultra-reliability can be provided end to end by the application of frame replication and elimination for reliability (FRER) over both the TSN and 5G domains. This requires disjoint paths between the FRER endpoints over both domains, as illustrated in Fig. 5.89.

A 5G UE can be configured to establish two PDU sessions that are redundant in the user plane over the 5G network. The 3GPP mechanism involves the appropriate selection of CN and RAN nodes (UPFs and 5G base stations (gNBs)), so that the user plane paths of the two PDU sessions are disjoint. The RAN can provide the disjoint user plane paths based on the use of the dual-connectivity feature, where a single UE can send and receive data over the air interface through two RAN nodes, as shown in Fig. 5.89.

The additional redundancy — including UE redundancy — is possible for devices that are equipped with multiple UEs. The FRER endpoints are outside of the 5GS, which means that 5G does not need to specify FRER functionality itself. Also, the logical architecture does not limit the implementation options, which include the same physical device implementing end station and UE.

Requirements of a TSN stream can be fulfilled only when resource management allocates the network resources for each hop along the whole path. In line with TSN configuration (802.1Qcc), this is achieved through interactions between the 5GS and CNC (see Fig. 5.88). The interface between the 5GS and the CNC allows for the CNC to learn the characteristics of the 5G virtual bridge and for the 5GS to establish connections with specific parameters based on the information received from the CNC.

Bounded latency requires a deterministic delay from 5G as well as QoS alignment between the TSN and 5G domains. Note that 5G can provide a direct wireless hop between components that would otherwise be connected via several hops in a traditional industrial wireline network. Ultimately, the most important factor is that 5G can provide deterministic latency, which the CNC can discover together with TSN features supported by the 5GS.

For instance, if a 5G virtual bridge acts like a Class A TSN bridge, then the 5GS emulates time-controlled packet transmission in line with scheduled traffic (802.1Qbv). For the 5G control plane, the TT in the application function (AF) of the 5GS receives the transmission time information of the TSN traffic classes from the CNC. In the 5G user plane, the TT at the UE and the TT at the UPF can regulate the time-based packet transmission accordingly. TT internal details are not specified by 3GPP and are left for the implementation. For example, a play-out (de-jitter) buffer per traffic class is a possible solution. The different TSN traffic classes are mapped to different 5G QoS indicators (5QIs) in the AF and the policy control function (PCF) as part of the QoS alignment between the two domains, and the different 5QIs are treated according to their QoS requirements.

Additionally, 3GPP is planning the non-3GPP TSN integration in its later release (maybe R17), as shown in Fig. 5.90. In most cases, end devices need time reference regardless of whether it is used by TSN bridges for their internal operations.

(5) Time synchronization: Time synchronization in a 5G-TSN combined industrial deployment brings in new aspects, such as generalized precision time protocol (gPTP) and scheduled traffic (802.1Qbv).

When bridges require time reference and they use a TSN feature that is based on time, gPTP is the default time synchronization solution for TSN-based industrial automation, and the 5GS needs to interwork with

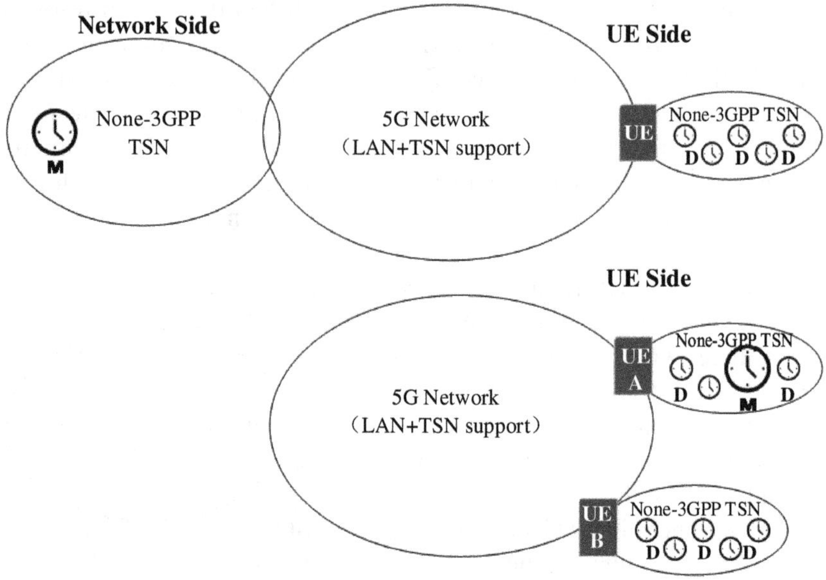

Figure 5.90 Synchronization information integrated with TSN and non-3GPP network.

the gPTP of the connected TSN network. The 5GS may act as a virtual gPTP time-aware system and support the forwarding of gPTP time synchronization information between end stations and bridges through the 5G user plane TTs. These account for the residence time of the 5GS in the time synchronization procedure.

Overall, 5G standardization has addressed the key aspects needed for 5G–TSN integration, and 5G–TSN integration can meet the demanding networking requirements of Industry 4.0 and TIoT, where the features provided for ultra-reliability and low latency for smart factories and smart tactile applications are needed.

A certain level of integration of the two technologies is needed to provide end-to-end Ethernet connectivity to meet the requirements.

Integrated time synchronization by wireless 5G and wired TSN domains provides a common reference time for endpoints. 5G is also integrated with the given TSN tool used in a particular deployment to provide bounded low latency. The disjoint forwarding paths of the 5G and TSN segments are aligned to provide end-to-end ultra-reliability and high availability.

Acknowledgements

For this chapter, the author would like thank the Satis5/SaT5G project for the related published literatures, including the white paper *Satellite is 5G* (November 2020) and its authors. The author would also like to thank the contributions of *IoT and UAV Integration in 5G Hybrid Terrestrial-Satellite Networks* (*Sensors*, 2019) for the use cases and figures in Section 5.9.

As for Sections 5.7 and 5.8, the author would like to thank the funds of China Post-doctoral (No. 4246Z3) and in particular thank Mr. Yuncheng Jiang, who received the B.S. degree in automotive engineering from Southwest Jiaotong University, Chengdu, China, in 2016. He received the first M.S. degree in mechanical engineering from Clemson University, Greenville, USA, in 2017, and the second in automation from Hongkong University of Science and Technology, Hongkong, China, in 2019.

Chapter 6

Services and Platform Layer of IoT

"Creativity takes courage." — Henri Matisse

The demands of the future Internet of Things (IoT) applications and services will require a much larger object space, efficient resource implementation in devices, objects or things interaction across application sectors and business spaces, as well as support for intelligent and trusted mechanisms to provide services. Services and platforms have to support interoperability for any objects to be seamlessly connected. An IoT services and platform layer (i.e., services layer or platform layer) abstracts applications from the things to enable the development of services after they are integrated into the communication and networks layer. The IoT platforms achieve a number of main objectives, such as flexibility (being able to deploy things in different contexts), usability (able to make the user experience easy), and productivity (creating service to improve efficiency, as well as development of new service).

An IoT platform facilitates communication, data flow, device management, and the functionality of applications. The goal is to build IoT applications within an IoT platform framework. The IoT platform allows applications to connect machines, devices, applications, and people to data and control centers. Functionally, IoT platforms cover the vertical value chain of a layered end-to-end IoT system, from sensors/actuators in the perception layer, the connectivity in communication layer, to applications enabling a diversity of services in different sections, such as the Internet of logistics, Internet of vehicles (IoVs), and Internet of industries (i.e., industrial IoT or IIoT), as shown in Fig. 6.1.

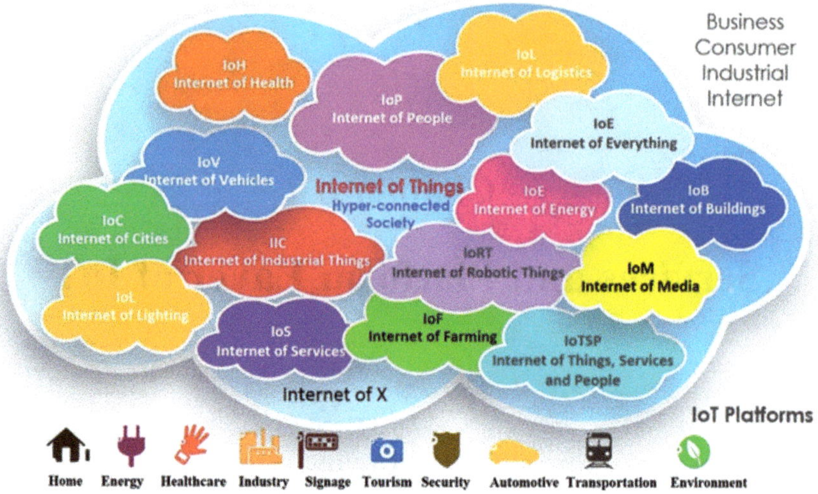

Figure 6.1 Services, platforms, and Internet of X.
Source: Vermesan and Friess (2016).

Horizontally, IoT platforms enable communication between IoT devices, manage the data flow to/from edge/cloud, support application development and provide basic analytics for connected devices, and often have a middleware sub-layer or functional module for heterogeneous devices, communications, services, and data, which increases the flexibility of platforms by the following aspects:

First, new connected objects allow users/developers to optimize functions in a given platform in their daily life. This requires that objects can be seamlessly and securely connected, but they are also identified due to their functionality.

Second, the ingestion of streaming data flow originated on objects/devices and the processing pipelines are usually included in heterogeneous networks and platforms, which require interoperability and even semantic interoperability, in finding services and data to be reused.

Finally, different standardization efforts (e.g., SAREF,[1] W3C, ETSI, 3GPP on MTC, or oneM2M) in a real interoperability environment, to

[1]European Telecommunications Standards Institute (ETSI) TC M2M on middleware. 3rd Generation Partnership Project (3GPP) on Machine Type Communication (MTC). OneM2M, a consortium of the development of standards to improve the ability of M2M

address specific deployment (e.g., safe and easy access for entertainment and comfort and routine activities support), are still on the way.

The platform and service layer of the IoT include many core technologies, including central data processing, storage, query, analysis and management of different functionalities, and OT-oriented examples of IoVs and IIoT (to be discussed in this chapter) based on decision-making, control and implementation from sensing information, cloud/edge computing, and service. In this chapter, the discussion of this layer mainly includes middleware, service-oriented architecture (SOA), and other software organization and implementation methods in line with the structural characteristics of the IoT.

The main objectives of this chapter are to ease the burden of system integrators, release the connection activity/energy of application developers, conform to the usual platform of services deployment, hide device-side technologies, and provide simple abstractions of the sensing and actuation services at the same time.

Another objective is to provide a vertical view across different levels of information aggregation, automation, and at different data scales ranging from real-time robot control in a ROS middleware usage to vertical IoT sections, such as IoVs and IIoT, and platforms, such as edge/cloud. The final point is the introduction of the primitive IoT, and along with IoT grid is followed as the opinions of service framework of generalized IoT service, because the more detailed granularity of services deployment in IoT, the easier it is to enable a re-use/re-arrangement/recombination of data, service, and applications in a wide vision.

Under the premise that IoT platforms and service layer are well-organized by comprehensive and industrial support application technologies, methods, and models, this layer can provide rich specific services according to heterogeneous users' needs, thus forming industrial applications-based vertical sections, which are included on the Internet of X, as shown in Fig. 6.1.

6.1 Middleware

From M2M, IoV to IIoT, the things and their created system intelligence show a large industrial characteristic population of intelligent, networked,

---

solutions. And the Telecommunications Industry Association (TIA) established the TR-50.1 Smart.

embedded, and mobile devices at some level of loosely coupled, even granularity, in some applications/use cases. This increased granularity of intelligence distributed among loosely coupled intelligent physical objects facilitates the need for more adaptability and reconfigurability of systems, allowing them to meet business demands unforeseen at the time of design and providing real business benefits. Among these systems, an adaptable IoT architecture needs a continuous but stable evolution for relative static software architecture.

Software architecture for a system is the structure or structures of the systems consisting of elements and their externally visible properties, and the relationships among them. The service in popular software architecture and its granularity should keep up with the demands for changes, so the new style of software architecture is in its revolutionary way. For instance, with the increasing dominance of the web paradigm, SOA has undergone evolution for the upgraded IoT solutions, in particular for middleware, open APIs, and micro-services.

As for middleware, which is later referred to as a mechanism to combine cyber-infrastructure with a SOA or other software mechanisms (diversity in the following sub-sections), it provides access to heterogeneous sensor resources in a deployment-independent manner. This is based on the idea of isolating resources that can be used/re-used by several applications.

A platform-independent middleware for developing sensor applications is required, such as an Open Sensor Web Architecture (OSWA). The Open Geospatial Consortium (OGC) builds OSWA upon a uniform set of operations and standard data representations as defined in the Sensor Web Enablement Method (SWE). Platform-independent middlewares still work well in robotics (e.g., ROS), vehicles (e.g., AUTOSAR), and industry-related OPC-UA. AUTOSAR platform for vehicle EEA (E/E architecture) design and development is a typical middleware with the SOA view. It will be introduced as a use case in this section. IoT applications can also become technology and programming language independently by taking advantage of middleware (or middleware platform). This helps boost the IoT application development market as application development for a flexible, scalable, and open environment. IoT is not different from building applications for/of/by the web, but a key component for web developers to establish their application market is open APIs.

Open APIs provide a simple mechanism for developers to access the functionality of the platform in question (e.g., Android APIs for mobile devices). Due to the increasing use and power of the Internet, some of these platforms have become open platforms and do not depend on certain programming languages or lock-in between platform developers and platform owners.

From the views of the web of service (WS, or web of things), open APIs relate to a common need to create a market among many companies, as the case in the IoT market. Open APIs permit the creation of a fluid industrial platform, allowing machine learning (ML) algorithms/machine intelligence (e.g., end-end visual execution) and other third-party methods (e.g., SCADA, ERP, or PM/PPM tools) as compact parts of industrial activity/planning of our daily lives. Typically, APIs for the exposition of historical IoT data and events are connected to IoT platforms or middlewares by interfaces.

Before the middleware is discussed, SOA is introduced in the following section, and after the introduction of SOA, IoT middleware and OPC-UA are introduced, and the platform as an IoT (middleware) service will be upgraded as collaborative IoT cloud (C-IoT, presented by Fawzi Behmann and KwokWu, refers to cloud computing in Section 6.3), which will be discussed as a collaborative cloud example after PIoT and IoT grids are presented in the next section.

6.1.1 *SOA*

More and more IoT development and its software architecture have started applying the web paradigm using a SOA and lately the microservices in cloud/edge approach. By extending the web paradigm to IoT devices, they can become a natural component of building any application and facilitate easy integration of IoT devices/services into any enterprise system based on the SOA (e.g., that uses web services or REST (representational state transfer), RESTful interfaces.

As for an evolutional view, SOA could be regarded as a self-refreshing architectural model in the revolution for the Internet of Everything (IoE) era, not only because SOA is supported in communication systems and protocols, middleware of systems, but captures many best practices in previous software architectures. For example, little development of solutions using truly static bindings to talk to other network equipment has taken place. With an SOA approach, such systems can position themselves to stress the importance of highly interoperable and interfaces. Other predecessors of SOA include component-based software engineering and object-oriented analysis and design (OOAD) of remote objects. In some respects (such as software, services in IoT), clouding (or the edge/frog) is deemed as an SOA flourished paradigm, and the container (e.g., docker) applications provide different micro-services to keep up with the fine-grained IoT service. The micro-service is an application-independent building block following the SOA paradigm where a specific end-user application is realized by the composition of diverse services. These services can be programmed in different programming languages and be executed on different platforms and cloud environments.

6.1.1.1 *SOA*

From the view of the World Wide Web Consortium (W3C), the SOA is a set of components which can be invoked and whose interface descriptions can be published and discovered. But CBDI (http://everware-cbdi.com) rejects this definition on two counts: First, the components (or implementations) will not often be a set. Second, the W3C definition of architecture only considers the implemented and deployed components rather than the science, art, or the practice of building the architecture. CBDI recommends SOA is more usefully defined as:

> *The policies, practices, and frameworks that enable application functionality to be provided and consumed as sets of services published at a granularity relevant to the service consumer. Services can be invoked, published and discovered, and are abstracted away from the implementation using a single, standards-based form of interface.*

CBDI defines SOA as a style resulting from the use of particular policies, practices, and frameworks that deliver services conforming to certain norms. Examples include granularity, independence from implementation, and standards compliance. The highlight of these definitions is that any form of service can be exposed with a web services interface. Higher-order qualities such as reusability and independence from the implementation will only be achieved by employing some science in a design and building process that is explicitly directed at incremental objectives beyond the basic interoperability enabled by the use of web services. There are several points worth learning in this definition:

- The components (or implementations) will not often be a set, where a series of service providers needs a clear definition in their context of IoT application and service, including an interface to outside.

- Interface-related principles, such as technology neutrality, standardization, and the negotiation between consumability and protection. Design principles are more about achieving quality services, meeting real business needs, and making services easy to use, inherently adaptable, and easy to manage.
- From software engineering (e.g., developers) and component-based software engineering (CBSE), also along with the enlightening of linguistics, we can learn that a country or a region needs one dialect/language to communicate with each other. But a translator is needed when crossing systems, protocols, and platforms in it.
- Like objects and components, services represent natural/basic building blocks that enable us to organize functions in a familiar way and combine information representation well with behavior. When objects use abstract data types and data abstractions, services can provide a similar level of adaptability through the context.
- If objects or components can be organized as classes or service hierarchy with inheritance compatibility, services can be published and used individually in a limited context, but with collaborations as an integer. This works like the dialects or official languages in a limited region.

On the contrary, hiding internal work to prevent external intrusion should also be considered in the SOA (e.g., language reveals the thoughts to some degree but does not fully reveal the entire thoughts of the individual).

The OASIS (Organization for the Advancement of Structured Information Standards) SOA reference model defines the SOA as "a paradigm for organizing and utilizing distributed capabilities that may be under the control of different ownership domains" and services as "the mechanism by which needs and capabilities are brought together". The central focus of SOA is "the task or business function — getting something done". Together, these ideas describe an environment or an ecosystem, in which business functions (realized in the form of services) address business needs. Service implementations utilize capabilities to produce specific effects that fulfill those business needs. Both those using the services and the capabilities themselves, may be distributed across ownership domains, with different policies and conditions of use in force — this environment is referred to an SOA ecosystem and is modeled in Fig. 6.2.

The role of service in an SOA ecosystem is to enable effective business solutions in this environment. Any technology system created to deliver a service in such an environment is referred to an SOA-based

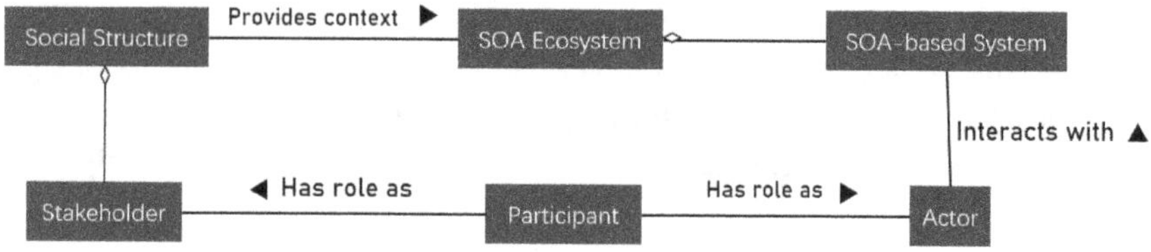

Figure 6.2 SOA ecosystem.
Source: OASIS Devices Profile for Web Services (DPWS).

system (as shown in Fig. 6.2). SOA is thus a paradigm that guides the identification, design, implementation, and utilization of such services. SOA-based systems act as technology-based proxies for activities that would otherwise be carried out within and between social structures.

An SOA-based system is concerned with how actors interact within a system to deliver a specific result — the delivery of a real-world effect. In Fig. 6.2, all potential stakeholders and the roles that they can play include:

How some stakeholders' needs are satisfied by other stakeholders' solutions? How they relate to each other through policies and contracts? How they communicate and establish relationships of trust in the processes leading to the delivery of a specific result? And how to deal with the granular service requirement?

The three key principles that inform the approach to an SOA ecosystem are as follows: an SOA is a paradigm for exchange of value between independently acting participants; participants (and stakeholders in general) have legitimate claims to the ownership of resources that are made available within the SOA ecosystem; the behavior and performance of the participants are subject to rules of engagement which are captured in a series of policies and contracts.

Service composition patterns have two broad, high-level architectural styles: choreography and orchestration. Lower-level enterprise integration patterns that are not bound to a particular architectural style continue to be relevant and eligible in an SOA design.

6.1.1.2 *Service generated scenarios: Primitive IoT and SOA*

The industrial scenario-depended development of IoT is often described as the "nature" of the "fragmented" IoT. But when realized by fine-grained service (e.g., in Section 6.2, where "primitive IoT and IoT grid" will be depicted in detail; but here, just imaging their meanings) — the "soft" architecture of middlewares and services[2] brings us a new way of dealing with or making up the gaps between fragments.

"In a ubiquitous computing environment like IoT, it is impractical to impose standards and make everyone comply". But the ideation of reconstructive/reconfigurable service styles (i.e., primitive IoT), together with middleware, enlightens the author of this book. Since the first book about IoT written in 2013, the author had been concerned about this issue. Therefore, he hopes to propose a set of very basic elements of the IoT, so as to facilitate the splicing (of primitive IoT) based on "service" between the fragmented IoT applications or sectors, and upgrade the service provider with integration (or inheritance from legacy use case), such as from primitive IoT to IoT grid. Furthermore, in an ultra-large-scale network of things and a large number of events that can be generated spontaneously by these things, along with heterogeneous devices/technologies/applications of IoT, the issue also poses new challenges in developing applications platform and makes the existing challenges in ubiquitous computing much more difficult.

Middleware technology plays a role in the scenario-oriented data processing of some industrial applications; however, when it comes to fine-grained services at the "on-premise" level, it has to give up the ability of "one middleware, suitable for almost any class of data", because it is unable to "solve all the problems with one middleware", and we have to reach a compromise of the tradeoff between utility and generality. As for web services, they are not inherently service oriented but merely expose a capability that conforms to web services protocols. Whereas, a sensor/actor/regulator/adjuster (even robotic arm/foot) is a common thing/device in the IoT world, and its service abstraction should follow a series of directions/principles. In this book, we intend to identify the characteristics with a well-formed service style — "Primitive IoT and IoT Grid", and provide guidance for architects and designers on how to deliver

[2]This trend leads to the evolution direction of other technologies in the same era closer to IoT. For example, 5G's service-oriented architecture SBA is the cellular "version" of IoT SOA, together with the different slices of 5G embodies. Another example is the transferring from cloud computing to fog computing or edge computing, which is also to serve fine-grained IoT services on/near the sites. In addition, big data is to process massive and differentiated data generated by fine-grained services.

SOA-based primitive IoT and IoT grid in the applications, which are extended by, but not limited to, the following aspects:

(a) From the user end (e.g., information consumer/regulator/divider), a micro-service architectural style is an approach to developing a single application as a suite of small services, each running in its own process and communicating with lightweight mechanisms, often an HTTP resource API. These services are built around business capabilities and independently deployable by a fully automated deployment machine. Distributed systems have become more fine-grained in the past 10 years, shifting from code-heavy monolithic applications to smaller, self-contained micro-service. Does the shifting also work when the "monolithic" service needs to be disassembled into IoT grids (or primitive IoT)? — especially, when there is a minimum of centralized management of the service, which may be written in different programming languages with different data storage technologies.
(b) From the view of the supplier end (service ability/capability), the question of how to granularize the service in the developing IoT systems and release its potential ability draws along intensive considerations. With lots of examples and practical advice, the following section will take a holistic view of the topics that system/service architects and administrators should consider when building, managing, and evolving IoT grids with a primitive IoT service style. "Adding bricks; into blocks (of a castle)".[3] Before it, middleware provides us with a firm grounding in concepts while diving into current solutions for modeling, integrating, testing, deploying, and monitoring the autonomous services. Then, we will formulate some ideas throughout this section to learn how to prepare primitive IoT/IoT grid in or from middleware and to build a primitive IoT/IoT grid architecture which will influence the following sections in this chapter, such as cloud/edge section and IoV/IIoT section.
(c) In contrast to "Build once, run anywhere", which has described the container (e.g., Docker) in micro-service, "Given your order (in an IoT grid), and get your answer (as the service from the primitive IoT in the IoT grid" explains the main meaning of the style of primitive

[3]As explained by Chinese saying "积跬步, 至千里" or "添砖加瓦" as interpreted by the author.

IoT/IoT grid. Several problems still exist in our consideration, which will help us understand it and middleware, are listed as follows.

- As for the smallest IoT service, which will be defined as primitive IoT, how to implant or plant a new one as the latter adding new function/service in the pre-defined IoT grid, especially when a ML function/layer for diverse industrial IoT use cases are introduced.
- Discover how primitive IoT services allow us to align the system design with the organization's goals (when the primitive IoT services are divisible and reconfigurable).
- Learn options for integrating primitive IoT/IoT grid with the rest of your system (e.g., combining similar parts into an integration or a sector).
- Take an incremental approach when upgrading primitive IoT/IoT grid into an IoT grid/domain model. But how to deploy individual primitive IoT through continuous integration?
- Examine the complexities of testing and monitoring distributed services (e.g., a grid view in Industrial 4.0 and IIoT architecture).
- Manage security with user-to-service and service-to-service models (e.g., in a security grid).
- Understand the challenges of scaling IoT grid architectures (e.g., in the automobile E/EA of V2X or IoV scenarios and collaborative cloud/edge computing).

6.1.2 *Middleware introduction*

6.1.2.1 *What is middleware*

A middleware can offer common services for applications and ease application development by integrating heterogeneous computing and communication devices and supporting interoperability within the diverse applications and services running on these devices. As described by Azure (https://azure.microsoft.com/), middleware is a software that lies between an operating system and the applications running on it. Essentially functioning as a hidden translation layer, middleware enables communication and data management for distributed applications. Because it connects two applications together, data and databases can be easily passed on between the "pipes". Middleware allows users to perform such requests as submitting forms on a web browser or allowing the web server to return dynamic web pages based on a user's profile. As for things, web services (including DPWS, HTTP, or REST/RESTful) and other IoT protocols can work together on the pipes, which play an integrated role as or in an IoT platform. Common middleware examples include the following:

(i) application server middleware (e.g., remote procedure call (RPC)), (ii) object-oriented middleware (OOM), (iii) event-based middleware (EBM), (iv) message-oriented middleware (MoM), such as MQSeries and MessageQ (and others serving the legacy usages); (v) object request broker (ORB) and web middleware (e.g., Orbweb Connect from Hikvision Digital Technology Co., Ltd.,@ http://www.orbweb.com); (vi) middleware of transaction-processing monitors (e.g., the management of process/business/communication in a ticketing system); and (vii) database-oriented middleware (DBM).

Each middleware typically provides messaging services so that different applications can communicate using messaging frameworks like web services, simple object access protocol (SOAP),[4] representational state transfer (REST), and JavaScript object notation (JSON). While all middlewares perform communication functions, the type a company chooses to use will depend on what service is used and what type of information needs to be exchanged. The functions include, but are not limited to, security authentication, transaction management, message queues, applications servers, web servers, database servers, and directories.

Middleware can also be used for distributed processing with actions occurring in real time rather than sending data back and forth, especially in IoT. As for OOM, its contemporary distributed component object model (DCOM) and common object request broker architecture (CORBA), since they no longer work well on the Internet, they were replaced by SOAP. ORB (such as RT-ORB/FC–ORB), whose prototype is original from real-time

---

[4]A messaging protocol specification for exchanging structured information in the implementation of web services in computer network. Its purpose is to provide extensibility, neutrality, verbosity and independence. It uses XML Information Set for its message format, and relies on application layer protocols, most often Hypertext Transfer Protocol (HTTP), although some legacy systems communicate over Simple Mail Transfer Protocol (SMTP), for message negotiation and transmission.

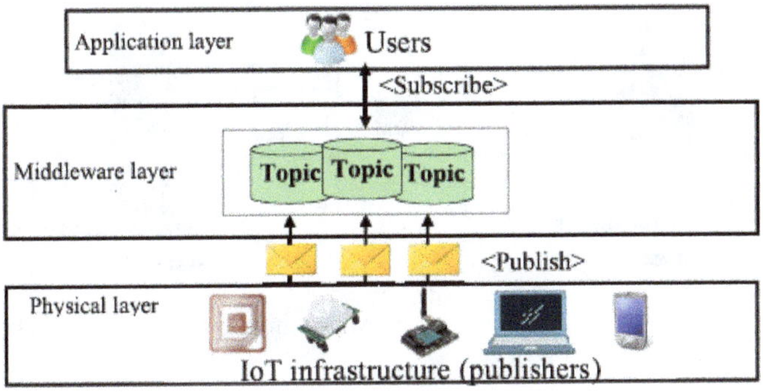

Figure 6.3 General pub-sub model for an event-based middleware (EBM).

ORB middleware, integrates a feedback control or real-time scheduling (FCS) service to improve the communication in some location user cases.

In event-based middlewares (EBMs), components, applications, and all the other participants interact through events. Each event has a type as well as a set of typed parameters whose specific values describe the specific change to the producer's state.

An event system (or event service) may consist of a potentially large number of application components that produce consume events. Events are propagated from the sending application components (producers) to the receiving application components (consumers) through the topic in Fig. 6.3, where the **publish/subscribe (pub-sub)** pattern of EBM contains a set of subscribers as consumers and a set of publishers as producers. Subscribers are provided with access to publishers' data streams through a common database and they are registered for particular events. The notifications about the events are subsequently and asynchronously sent to the subscribers.

This design approach, which is not shown in Fig. 6.4, addresses non-functional requirements, such as scalability, availability, reliability, real-time performance, and security.

MoM is a type of EBM. In the MoM model of Fig. 6.4, the communication relies on messages, including extra metadata compared to events. The following radio frequency identification (RFID) middleware will be introduced as an instance of MoM, and MoM also supports WSN and M2M communications. For example, WebSphereMQ/IBM MQ brokers offer support for M2M communications between services, service providers and service subscribers, conversion between different transport protocols, and homogenization of message streams between subscribers and providers.

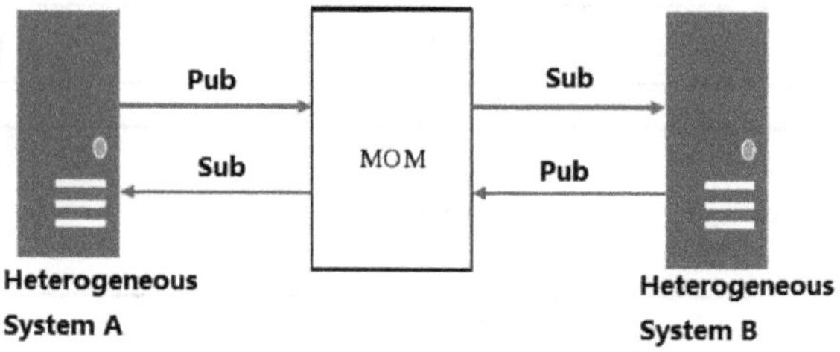

Figure 6.4 The data exchange model in MoM middleware between heterogeneous systems.

Finally, in DBM, a sensor network is viewed as a virtual relational database system. An application can query the database using an SQL-like query language, which enables the formulation of complex queries.[5] Research in this area has been focused on developing a distributed database approach to interoperating systems, such as handling events and in cope with the mobility of the querying (sink) node, and examples can be seen as SINA or COUGAR in Razzaque *et al.* (2016).

6.1.2.2 *RFID middleware as an example of MoM middleware*

RFID middleware is a typical MoM middleware which belongs to a kind of EBM. In a general MoM, messages carry sender or receiver addresses and are delivered by a particular subset of participants, whereas events are broadcast to all participants in a heterogeneous environment (as shown in Fig. 6.4). For instance, message-oriented interaction is used between a RFID reader and the RFID tag with a product ID.

Typically, RFID middleware is an intermediate program to realize data transmission, filtering, and data format conversion between RFID hardware equipment and application system. Various data information read by RFID reader are extracted, decrypted, filtered, format converted, and entered into the enterprise management information system through middleware and reflected on the program interface through the application system for operators to browse, select, modify, and query. Middleware also reduces the difficulty of application development, so

[5]See above, "Middleware solutions in WSN: The IoT oriented approach in the ICSI project".

that developers do not need to face the underlying architecture directly but use procedure call through middleware.

In RFID middleware, information is transferred from one program/module to another or more modules/programs in the form of messages. Information can be sent asynchronously, so the sender does not have to wait for a response.

Based on the development of the enterprise application middleware and combined with its own application characteristics, RFID middleware further expands and deepens the application of middleware in enterprises. As an EBM, its main characteristics are as follows:

- Independence: Between an RFID reader and back-end application, RFID middleware is independent of a certain RFID system and application system and can connect with multiple RFID readers and multiple back-end applications to reduce the complexity of architecture and maintenance.
- Data flow: It is the most important part of RFID middleware. Its main task is to transform the entity object format into a virtual object in an information environment, so data processing is the most important function of RFID. RFID middleware has the characteristics of data collection, filtering, integration, and transmission, so as to transmit the correct object information to the enterprise back-end application system.
- Processing flow: The message-oriented function is to provide sequential message flow and it has the ability of data flow design and management. Data transmission link, data routing, and data distribution need to be maintained in the function. At the same time, the security of data is managed in data transmission, including data consistency, to ensure that the data received by the receiver is consistent with that of the sender.

RFID middleware is between reader and enterprise application over networks, which is equivalent to the neural system of the network. The savant system (see Section 4.1.3) adopts the distributed structure to organize and manage the data flow in a hierarchical manner. It has the functions of data collection, filtering, integration, and transmission. Therefore, it can transmit useful information to the enterprise back-end application system or other savant systems. Savant systems are distributed in all levels of supply chain nodes, such as production workshops, warehouses, distribution centers, retail stores, and even on vehicles. The savant system at each level collects, stores, and processes information and communicates with other savant systems. For example, a savant system running in the store may inform the distribution center that other products are needed, while that in the distribution center informs that a batch of goods has been shipped at a specific time. Sometimes, the collected electronic product data (EPC, see Section 4.1.3) data may be incomplete or wrong due to the reader–writer exception or mutual interference between tags.

Therefore, the savant needs to smooth the EPC data stream read by the reader. Smoothing can clear incomplete and wrong data and minimize the possibility of missing reading. The reader can identify all tags in the read range but does not process the data. The data read by RFID devices is not necessarily used by a single application program. It may be used by multiple applications (including the application systems within the enterprise and even the application systems of business partners). Each application system may also need different sets of data. Therefore, the savant needs to process the data accordingly. This section mainly discusses three key functions of a savant: data filtering, data aggregation, and information transmission.

(1) Data Filtering: When reading a tag, a large amount of data which is not useful for managing inventory or other applications may be generated. For example, a customer moving a product from one shelf to another or a pallet load of articles that passes several readers while being moved in a warehouse is an event that does not produce meaningful data to an inventory control system.

Event/data filtering is required to reduce this data inflow to a meaningful depiction of moving goods passing a threshold. Savant, mainly offered as middleware, performs the filtering from noisy and redundant raw data to significant processed data.

Savant receives data (in EPC format) from the reader, which has a lot of redundant information and wrongly-read information. Therefore, it is necessary to filter the data to eliminate redundant data, so as to transmit "useful" information to the application or a superior savant. Redundant data emerges because in a short period time, the same reader will report the same data repeatedly. For example, in warehouse management, the fixed goods are repeatedly reported and the same items are repeatedly detected in the process of purchase and shipment.

Multiple adjacent readers report the same data. There is a certain rate of missing detection in the reader related to the placement of the antenna, the distance between the object and the reader, and the texture of the article. Usually, in order to ensure the reading rate, multiple readers may be placed adjacent to the same place. In this way, when multiple readers report the detected items, there may be duplication.

In addition to the above problems, in many cases, users may also want to get information about specific goods, new goods, missing goods, or just goods information read by readers and writers in some places. When using data, they want to minimize redundancy and get accurate data close to the requirements as far as possible. This is solved by savant.

The solution to redundant information is to set up various filters for processing. There are many kinds of filters available. The following are four typical filters: product filter, time filter, EPC code filter, and smoothing filter. The product filter only sends product information related to a certain product or manufacturer, that is to say, the filter only sends EPC data of a certain range or mode. Time filters can filter events based on time records. For example, a time filter may only send events within the last 10 minutes. EPC code filter can only send EPC codes that meet certain rules. The smoothing filter is responsible for dealing with errors, including missed and incorrect readings.

According to the actual needs, filters can be pieced together one by one like a toy to get the desired events. For example, a smoothing filter can be combined with a product filter to separate events of interest from an anti-theft application.

(2) Data Aggregation and Event Management: The original RFID data stream received from the reader is single and sporadic information. In order to provide meaningful information to the application or other RFID middleware, it is necessary to aggregate the RFID data. Complex event processing (CEP)[6] technology is used to process a large number of simple/

---

[6]CEP extracts information from distributed event-based (or message-based) systems and is now applied in industrial monitoring, control domains, and the domain of business process management, besides the RFID applications. As a technology to derive higher-level information out of low-level events, CEP relies on a set of tools and techniques for analyzing and handling events with low latency. The feature set for CEP spans from event extraction, sampling, filtering correlation, and aggregation to event enrichment, content-based routing, event compositions, etc.

complex events and sort out valuable events. It can help people analyze simple events and infer complex events, and convert simple/complex events into valuable events, in order to obtain operational information. Here, data aggregation is used to simplify the original RFID data stream into more meaningful complex events, such as the first appearance of a tag in the reader's reading range and its subsequent disappearance. By analyzing a certain amount of simple data, we can judge the tag entry and exit events. Aggregation can be used to solve the problem of temporary error reading, so as to achieve data smoothing.

(3) Information Transmission: After filtering and aggregation, the RFID data needs to be transferred to those entities interested in it, such as enterprise applications, EPC information service systems, or other RFID middleware. Here, a message service mechanism is used to transfer RFID information.

The function of RFID message-oriented middleware is not only to transmit information but also to interpret data, security, data broadcast, error recovery, locating network resources, finding out the path to meet the cost, the priority of messages and requirements, and extended debugging tools. For example, Java message service (JMS) in the J2EE platform is used to realize the message passing structure between RFID middleware and enterprise application or other savants (see Chapter 4 and Section 4.6.2). When the publish/subscribe mode of JMS is adopted, RFID middleware publishes messages to a topic, then enterprise applications and one or more savants can subscribe to this topic message. The message is in the special language of the IoT — physical markup language (PML). In this way, even if the database software for storing RFID tag information or adding back-end application program or replacing it with other software, or increasing the type of RFID reader, the application side can process the data without modification and thus eliminate the maintenance complexity of many connections (i.e., m:n of many different connections).

Other forms of applications of active-RFID data could include sensing of the roadside environment by implanted beacons, weather reports, and noise level monitoring, with the same ideation of middleware design following the three key issues.

6.1.3 *IoT middleware*

As we have already seen, IoT deployments present high heterogeneity at all layers (device, networking/communication, middleware, application service and platform, data/semantics), which restricts interoperability among their elements and them. Though many projects have dealt with the development of IoT architectures in diversified application domains, and a number of operating systems have been developed (such as mbed[7], FreeRTOS, ROS, AUTOSAR, and TinyOS) to support the development of IoT middleware solutions and continuous efforts of semantic interoperability, middleware standardization (e.g., SAREF, W3C, or ETSI, EPC, GS1[8]) has to be devoted to semantic translation or alignment in order to provide easy support for ontology matching among IoT platforms for the addressed interoperability and integration issues.

Despite several efforts to find common ontologies to be reused and different standardization efforts in a real interoperability environment, new ontologies have to be defined to address specific deployment of heterogeneous IoT devices, e.g., IoT middleware discussed here and IoT grids discussed in the next section.

After all, IoT middleware focuses on the design modalities for different abstraction levels that hide underlying complexities and heterogeneities to facilitate interoperability because typical IoT solutions can involve a large number of different devices and sensors and a large set of different actors providing services and information that need to be (re-)composed and accessed with different levels of aggregation.

6.1.3.1 *Introduction to IoT middleware and its requirements*

An IoT middleware provides a software layer between application, the operating system, and the network communications layers, which facilitates and coordinates some aspects of cooperative processing locally or remotely.

From the computing perspective, a middleware provides a layer between application software and system software. In the IoT, it is likely to have considerable heterogeneity in both the communication technologies and the system-level technologies, so a middleware should support both perspectives as needed. Based on previously described characteristics of the IoT infrastructure and the application that depend upon it, a set of requirements for a middleware to support the IoT is outlined in Table 6.1. These requirements are grouped into the following two sets: (1) services such as a middleware should be provided for an instance (the first

[7]Available at: http://mbed.org/technology/os/.

[8]Available at: http://www.gs1.org/pia; or see Section 4.1.

Table 6.1 Requirements for IoT middleware.

Data acquisition middleware	Application supporting middleware	Middleware as a platform
Data management; Event management; Resource discovery; Code management; Interoperability and reliability.	Interoperable; Reliability; Context-aware; Adaptive (intelligence/dynamic); Distributed; Programming abstraction;	Scalability (large network); Security; Availability; Reliability; Real-time (large number of events); Privacy
Examples: RFID, WSN/WSAN	Examples: EPC middleware; Service-oriented middleware (SOM); LBS middleware.	Examples: SCOREDES; OPC-UA

two columns of Table 6.1); (2) system architecture should support when a middleware works in a given platform (the last column).

Generally, the IoT middleware abstracts the complexities of the system or hardware, allowing the application developer to concentrate all his efforts on the task to be solved, without the distraction of concerns at the system or hardware level. Further, the basic division of a functional layout view is based on whether the service layer of middleware is in the perception layer or partly included in the application layer in IoT architecture, also due to the complexities abstracted layers sit on or where the middlewares play their roles, so that the three main sets of IoT middleware are grouped into data acquisition middleware (DAM), application supporting (or application-oriented) middleware (ASM), and platform middleware.

- DAM (mostly as services of data, event, code, and other resources in the perception layer of IoT) focuses on the data/services from the heterogeneity of hardware level. Such a middleware should provide data acquisition and its corresponding sets of services from or for devices/things in RFID, WSN/WSAN, M2M, and supervisory control and data acquisition (SCADA in Section 2.1 and Chapter 5) may be written in different programming languages and use different data storage technologies.
- ASM supports the IoT application across the heterogeneity of system/network level, and the system architecture of the middleware should support different IoT applications and the heterogeneity of network protocols, such as SCOREDES (will be introduced later). Its system architecture should support interoperability, distribution, and some

degree of context-awareness/autonomy (mostly crossing the communication/network layer and the perception of IoT), even with the assistance of a semantic model.
- Platform middleware, includes an extensible platform for a certain industry or application, across the heterogeneity of the IoT platform layer, or supporting the research project of a specialized application (robotic, smart vehicle/automated driving).

Besides the three main types, others will be introduced as engineering-/programming-oriented codes/solutions supporting types, such as VMs (virtual machines) and application-specific middle-wares.

Today, the increasingly complex IoT solutions need more communication applications and middlewares to facilitate the seamless integration of devices, networks, and applications. In this context, the IoT development platform with multi-function (i.e., connection management, device management, application support, etc.) has emerged. With the purpose of rapid development, by reducing cost and providing standardized components in the platform, IoT middleware can share IoT solutions in many vertical industries, such as VM (for coding-facilitated or developing-facilitated), ROS (for robotics development), AUTOSAR (for vehicles), ThingWorx, and EPC (for RFIDs).

The IoT middleware solutions introduced in this section do not cover all the diversity and characteristics of middleware in the IoT architectures, and they are different from resource discovery and management, data, or events management (e.g., potential spontaneous resource (service) (re-) composition, and time-sensitive characteristic). Take EPC as an example, GS1, EPCglobal, and other organizations define the EPC middleware system for different hardware and OS of RFID in order to generate value by providing a standard way of capturing data from objects between the partners,[9] but EPC leaves the interfaces of what/how data could be shared among different business entities in a federated manner/platform, i.e., share relevant logistics data in a secure way (see Section 4.1.3). These will be analyzed in the ASM as a use case.

[9]As mentioned in Section 4.1, EPCIS services store EPC data as well as exchange this data along the EPC global network. The middleware, which is a capturing application between ALE and EPCIS, regulate how the former sends data to the latter. Each company has its own set of components, so the idea is to generate value by providing a standard way of capturing data from objects among the partners involved in a particular application field (including, e.g., suppliers, enterprises, resellers, clients, buildings, and users).

6.1.3.2 *DAM*

Data acquisition middleware (DAM, whose model should be considered as in Fig. 6.5, in its preparing stage) introduced here mainly includes EBM and ABM. Then a use case, together with the analysis of the characteristics of DAM, is followed.

(1) EBM: Besides message-oriented middleware (MoM, including RFID middleware introduced above), Hermes, and EMMA are introduced as main examples of EBM.

Hermes is created for large-scale distributed applications. *Hermes* events can be either type-based or attribute-based.[10] It uses a scalable routing algorithm and fault-tolerance mechanisms.

Apart from scalability, it addresses interoperability and reliability requirements. Hermes has two components, namely event clients and event brokers. Hermes following the typical pub-sub model (as Fig. 6.3), which has the following sub-layers (or functional components): middleware sub-layer, event-based sub-layer, type-based and attribute-based pub/sub sub-layer, overlay routing network sub-layer, and network

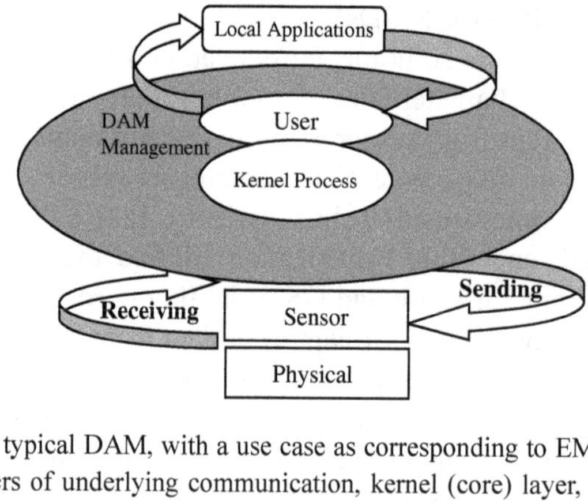

Figure 6.5 The typical DAM, with a use case as corresponding to EMMA (see the next Figure) four-layers of underlying communication, kernel (core) layer, management, and API-interface.

Notes: In the simple model of DAM, local view includes the following: (1) app./user interfaces upwards for either data/state reporting or commands receiving, (2) core/kernel module and common service, which will be described in the usage of indoor monitoring later, and (3) devices interface downwards.

[10] Attributions will be introduced in the example of Robotic middleware in great detail.

sub-layer. The EBM layer provides an API for programmers to use to implement applications. The middleware sub-layer consists of several modules that implement functionalities such as fault-tolerance, reliable event delivery, event-type discovery, security, and transactions. The mobility is limited in terms of dynamic network topology. Hermes does not support composite events or persistent storage of events. Moreover, its support for adaptation is limited to the network level.

EMMA is an adaptation of Java message service (JMS, see Section 5.6.2) for mobile ad hoc environments (see Chapter 4 and the following WSN use case). It is designed for multi-party video communication systems, such as video chatting, where multiple video streams are distributed simultaneously on overlay networks. EMMA is available, reliable, and autonomous through fault-tolerant and resilience (quick recovery) mechanism. Moreover, it offers multiple styles of messaging in order to implement different levels of reliability, and it treats persistent and non-persistent messages differently. Besides, it provides very good performance in terms of delivery ratio and latency. However, the tradeoff between application-level routing and resource usage is not taken into consideration. Relying on its design approach, EMMA is not energy efficient. In an EMMA system, all components are abstracted by CoAP resource interfaces, including node services, resources binding, and distributed processing. The WS-based middleware facilitates its integration with other local IoT services or cloud/edge servers. Although QoS in EMMA (shown in Fig. 6.6) has been discussed, the reliability it supports is limited.

When WSN is constrained and cannot allow a supervisor to monitor and control each distributed system (DS) directly, delegation policies can be deployed to allow a master (leader) supervisor to drive some slave (follower) supervisors (will be shown in the use case part as sink/management nodes). However, the fault-tolerance problem becomes a major concern in which a sub-network will be separate in case of one sink/management failure.

Additionally, GREEN middleware is developed to support pervasive applications for heterogeneous networks and heterogeneous devices (including operating in MANETs and WANs types). RUNES is a component-based middleware for a large-scale and widely distributed heterogeneous network of embedded systems. It introduces a standardized architecture capable of self-organization and dynamic adaptation to a changing environment. GREEN and RUNES support some new components at runtime, such as pluggable pub-sub interaction types (e.g.,

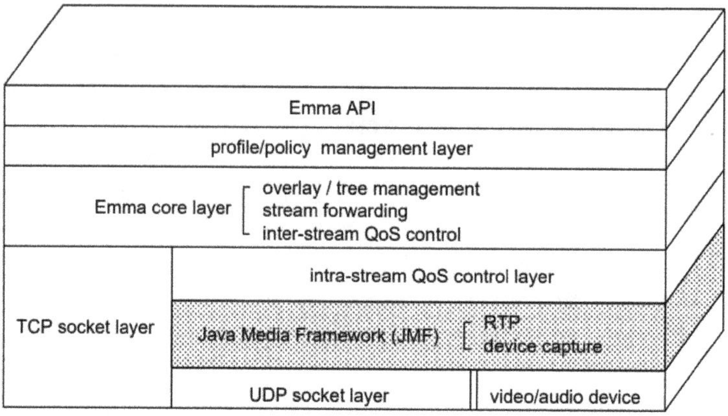

Figure 6.6 EMMA with QoS control.

Table 6.2 Summary of the EBM: From WSN functional requirements.

	Functional requirements				
	Resource discovery	**Resource management**	**Data management**	**Event management**	**Code management**
Event-based approach					
Hermes	CD-DD	RM	DPF	LS	NI
EMMA	CD-DeD, CD-SD	RM	DS	SS	CA
GREEN	DD-ND	RM	DS, DPF	LS	CA
RUNES	CD-DeD, CD-SD	RM, RCA	DPA	SS	CA

Notes: CD-centralized discovery, DD-distributed discovery, DeD-device discovery, ND-network discovery, SD-service discovery. RM-resource management, RCA-resource composition adaptive, DPF-data preprocessing filtering, DS-data storage, DPA-data preprocessing aggregation, LS/SS-large scale/small scale, NI-no information, CA-code allocation, RCL-resource conflict.

topic-based, content-based, context, and composite events). From a functional-requirements view, they are compared to the two detailed earlier in Table 6.2.

At last, TinyDDS middleware enables interoperability between WSNs and access networks. It provides programming language and protocol interoperability based on the standard data distribution service (DDS) specification. The TinyDSS framework allows WSN applications to have control over application-level and middleware-level non-functional properties. Simulation and empirical evaluation results showed that TinyDDS is lightweight with a small memory footprint. It does not address key IoT requirements, such as adaptation, nor offer a topology control mechanism. TinyDDS does not address the heterogeneous infrastructure of an IoT, and it has been designed only for WSNs or mobile devices.

(2) ABM: Agent-based middleware applications are divided into modular programs to facilitate injection and distribution through the network using mobile agents. While migrating from one node to another, agents maintain their execution state, facilitating the design of decentralized systems capable of tolerating partial failures. Typically, ABM heritage the advantages for using mobile agents in common distributed systems based on previous research in the area of distributed operating systems/ middlewares.

Other requirements in the context of ABM include resource management (network load reduction and network latency reduction), code management (asynchronous and autonomous execution and protocol encapsulation), availability and reliability (robustness and fault-tolerance), adaptiveness, and heterogeneity.

Moreover, agent-based approaches consider resource-constrained devices, such as smart messages and Agilla.

Smart messages propose an autonomous network architecture for large-scale embedded systems, which are known to be resource-constrained, heterogeneous, and volatile. Smart messages overcome these limitations by migrating agents to nodes of interest, using application-controlled routing, instead of end-to-end communication between nodes. The main contribution of this middleware is the high flexibility in the presence of dynamic network configurations. However, *smart messages* do not support multiple applications.

Agilla is a mobile agent middleware designed to support self-adaptive applications in wireless sensor networks. Agilla provides a programming model in which applications consist of evolving communities of agents that share a wireless sensor network. Coordination between the agents and access to physical resources are supported by **a tuple space abstraction.** Agents can dynamically enter and exit a network and can autonomously clone and migrate themselves in response to environmental changes. Agilla's ability to support self-adaptive applications in wireless sensor networks has been demonstrated in applications, including fire detection and tracking, monitoring cargo containers, and robot navigation. Agilla, the first mobile agent system to operate in resource-constrained wireless sensor platforms, was implemented on top of TinyOS.

The agent-based middleware solutions presented (i.e., smart messages, Agilla, and Impala) have been designed only for WSNs or mobile devices without the consideration of heterogeneity of an IoT infrastructure and have been tested on a specific hardware/software platform (e.g., TinyOS, Mica2, MicaZ, Hewlett-Packard/Compaq iPAQ Pocket PC running Linux, and Sun SPOTs). These middleware solutions do not address issues such as hard real-time guarantees. Security and privacy are generally not considered. These projects are popular with early adopters, but now they ask for heterogeneity in solutions designed for an IoT environment.

Although agent-based systems can reduce the complexity of designing such systems by defining some higher-level policies rather than direct administration, support self-capabilities (e.g., self-adaptiveness), and support agent-based programming; however, the autonomous characteristics of agents can lead to unpredictability in the system at runtime, especially when the information/states of sensors, network, and environment (where the SNs are situated) are incomplete. Consequently, the patterns and the effects of their interactions are uncertain.

(3) A Use Case of Indoor Environment Monitoring: Functionally, IoT middleware is both a management platform of data/service and a communication "tunnel". It not only supports the upper service for data acquisition but also connects with the operating system to keep the system running normally. The middleware should also be compatible with various standard protocols and interfaces as a supporting platform. For example, in the EPC application based on RFID, it should support the information interaction and management, and shield the complexity of the front-end equipment at the same time. This is why a middleware can be called IoT middleware only when it is used in distributed IoT systems (or just WSN or SCADA). Also, it should be distinguished from system software, application software, and sits in the middle between them.

As previously discussed, the DAM middleware is mainly used in information collection from the end of the IoT, and to utilize/organize the data in the perception layers, where there will be different interface standards between the collection device and the transmission node, along with their heterogeneous tunnels. Other characteristics of data acquisition middlewares are illustrated in Fig. 6.7. The WSN designed for indoor environment monitoring system (a simple indoor SCADA system) is taken as a DAM example and the heterogeneity of hardware-level divers from a thermal sensor, temperature, or humidity sensor.

In the DAM example of Fig. 6.8, the core sub-layer of middleware or kernel functions are unfolded as protocols for API or WAN connections, algorithms for CEP (see Section 6.1.2) or routine data process, and services (including management and security). Other functional analyses are given as follows, which are based on not only this example but other WSN or RFID usages of a typical DAM.

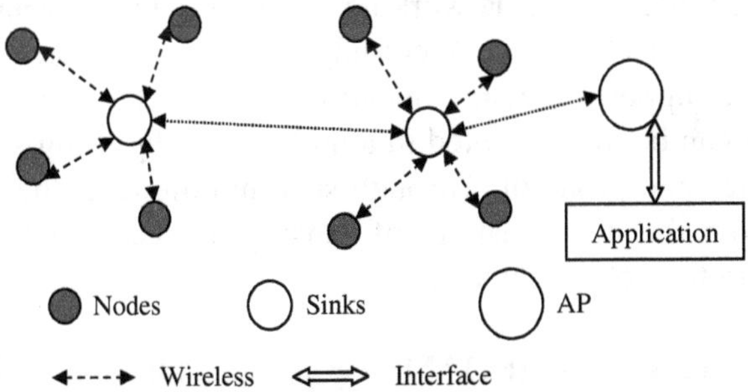

Figure 6.7 WSN *Nodes in ad hoc* environments.

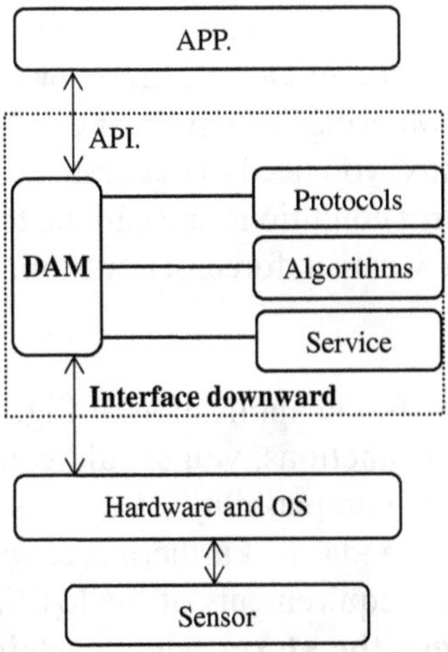

Figure 6.8 Function and software design of indoor environment monitoring system based on wireless sensor network.

- **Acquisition Function:** The information collection middleware in the perception layer is different from the ASM in the application layer, i.e., the communication service when the data transmission nodes such as sensors or RFID are connected with the acquisition middleware, which is mainly used in information collection at the end of the IoT. There are different interface standards between acquisition devices and transmission nodes, such as the access of sensors, OS of devices and communication protocols, as well as the complexity of front-end hardware (especially the complexity of RFID reader).

- **Transmission Function:** In the perception layer, the information collected is transmitted to the network node through the information collection middleware technology. According to different operating software and hardware supporting communication stacks (refer to Section 5.6) or platforms, it can be implemented in a middleware by using standard program interface and protocol. Through such middleware, the information collected from the heterogeneity of sensing devices can be accurately transmitted to the network nodes.

- **Collaborative Function:** DAM also has the function of information collection in a collaborative and distributed way. In the process of information collection, if the information needs to be retrieved from different tables in time or cause-and-effect sequence (set by the logical order of the whole system), the required control information is stored in different database tables (even distributed in cloud/edge). For example, if you want to control the switch of a watering system or air conditioning under a certain temperature and humidity, you need to integrate the collaborative technology to achieve the control conditions and call the temperature information (from cloud service of weather forecast) or humidity/temperature information locally.

- **Extended Functions:** In the application of Fig. 6.8, if you need to add new device/hardware or functions, you should consider the scalability in middleware, such as the compatibility of a class of RFID devices that meet the corresponding standards. Furthermore, with the improvement of the middleware function requirements of the IoT, it is necessary to **judge the function and trigger the alarm when certain conditions are met. The data collection middleware will also have logic functions such as reasoning, forecasting, and prompting (e.g., a message to mobile**

apps.) that are based on the data/information analysis. At the same time, it can keep the synchronous updating and logical consistency of data in the network.

6.1.3.3 *ASM and use cases*

In contrast to the DAM, which ordinarily completes several functions introduced above in the perception/communication layer; ASM sitting between processing/communication hardware and IoT applications provides a rich set of functions needed by many IoT applications. It supports the secure end-to-end data/control exchange between applications of IoT in the service layer (both are discussed in this chapter: the platform and service layer and a similar definition in oneM2M service layer if it is standardized by the architecture of TR-0057).

Different from general middleware, the ASM middleware can be independent of architectures (such as platform/operating system/network, not just the shielding of software/hardware). It supports data flow control, transmission, processing, and management/re-organization (**distributed in the information/semantic level**). Based on these, it provides an open interface to the upper-level application, and also plays a connecting role, which can shield the difference of heterogeneous access downward. For example, in the middleware application of M2M or SCADA, it is more like a middleware platform. Similarly, OPC-UA is introduced separately as the middleware of the standard platform in the next section. Here, SOM, tuple-space and location-based service (LBS) middleware with their use cases are introduced one by one.

(a) Service-Oriented Middleware (SOM): Although almost all the middlewares in IoT usage are SOA-based, the characteristics of service-oriented approaches in SOM show more technology neutrality, loose coupling, service reusability, service composability, and service discoverability. However, IoT's ultra-large-scale network (e.g., EPC, **SCADA** network in use), resource-constrained devices, and mobility characteristics (e.g., **M2M**) make service discovery and composition challenging. A SOM has the potential to alleviate these challenges through the provision of appropriate functionalities for deploying, publishing/discovering, and accessing services at runtime. It also provides support for adaptive service compositions when services are unavailable.

SensorsMW and *KASOM* are SOM for the support of WSN/WSAN applications. *SensorsMW* is an adaptable and flexible SOM for QoS configuration and management of WSNs. It abstracts WSNs as a collection of services for seamless integration into an enterprise information system. This allows easy and efficient configuration of WSNs for information gathering using WS (e.g., HTTP, REST/RESTful). Resources in a WSN are managed to comply with certain QoS requirements, according to SLAs. Importantly, it offers an abstract way to access these resources for high-level applications. Knowledge-aware and service-oriented middleware (KASOM) integrates pervasive embedded networks into the service cloud. KASOM's characteristics provide to developer several tools which facilitate the design and deployed of services in a pervasive network.

More middlewares adopt the SOA design in their support data flow control, transmission, processing, and management. At the same time, more characteristics in a specific application or a certain industry, such as middlewares of tuple space for mobile/distribution and the generalized platform for industry (such as SOCRADES) with plentiful APIs, are emerging. Furthermore, OPC-UA as an integration platform of industrial automation will be discussed in the following part. And either SOCRADES or OPC-UA middleware services can be provided by cloud computing platform as a service (PaaS) model.

(b) Use Case: EPC Middleware System as a Typical SOM: At present, the EPC system is one of the most mature SOM architectures supporting RFID applications. Taking the EPC system as an example, the following usage focuses on the middleware as applied in the EPC system.

Of more specific relevance for IoT are services related to sensor originating data and actuation services and services related to different tags, such as RFID. RFID tags should have the potential to function as low-cost remote sensors that broadcast telemetry back to an information station, which is called the center of EPCIS (as a directory that holds information of available resources and associated service capabilities that can function as a rendezvous mechanism) or backend of a local department. So, EPCglobal (see Section 4.2) middleware for distributing application and the heterogeneous systems/networks is presented as a typical example of ASM and also a SOM platform of RFID usages.

With EPCIS (or a directory in WSN/WSAN), nodes can publish themselves with service descriptions and how to be reached. Applications then

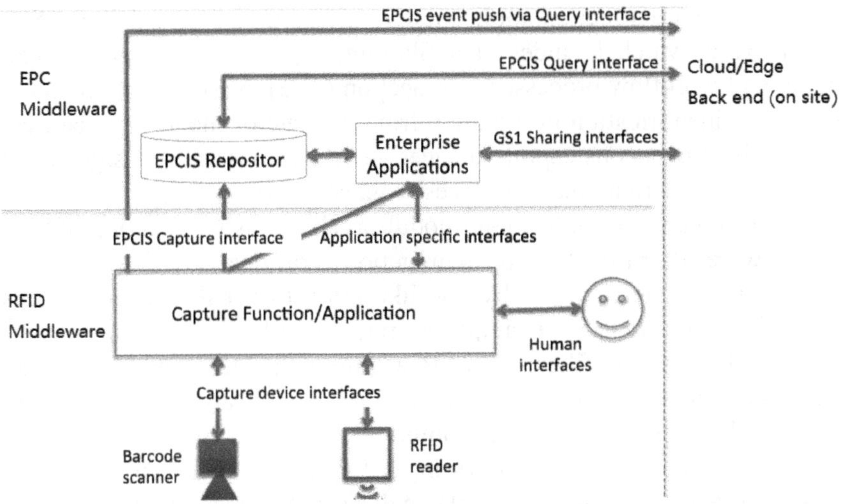

Figure 6.9 EPC (belongs to SoM) and RFID middleware (belongs to MoM) in a simple functional view.

perform look-ups to find which device can provide the sensor reading of interest.

Besides EPCIS, object naming service (ONS, like the domain name service) also helps to resolve an RFID tag ID code to a URL, where information about the tagged object can be found (see Section 4.2), by finding the EPCIS server address corresponding to the ID code, and PML is physical markup language (a special language based on XML for EPC product information[11] exchange).

In detail, as shown in Fig. 6.9, the EPCIS capture interface is an interface from EPCIS to the middlewares specific for RFID, such as savant middleware (see Sections 4.1.3 and 6.1.2) which has been explained in Chapter 4 and the RFID middleware ahead, as a typical MoM.

[11]Regulated by EPCglobal/GS1, as introduced in Section 4.1, it is the acknowledged distributed network-integrated framework at present. RFID technology application is used as the foundation in the global supply chain. The network mainly focuses on logistic fields; it is to increase the visual ability and controllability of the supply chain. RFID electronic tag and reader transfers the electronic product coding data, then the relevant information is shared among the authoritative clients via the Internet.

The capture function/application is a functional module of RFID middleware, which includes data filtering, aggregation, event management, and workflow processes (see Section 6.1.2) to coordinate the readout of the identification information from the heterogeneous data carriers and the heterogeneous capture devices and the provision of designed and desired services to human interfaces (e.g., screens).

In the enterprise applications module as an extensible function of EPC middleware, after filtering, and aggregation of original data flow, services can be pieced together one by one like a toy to get the desired events according to practice. For example, a smoothing filter service can be combined with a product filter service to acquire valuable events, such as an anti-theft application or an inventory alarm application, when certain products become less than a set number.

Besides complex event processing (CEP, refer to Section 6.1.2 and the following Section 6.1.4), more data analysis methods including Big Data, artificial intelligence (AI), can be used on premise or in the cloud/edge, with interfaces of EPC/EPCIS middleware, such as "buy and go" of AMAZON, an example of the judgment of products being taken away or put down in the perception layer of Chapter 4.

(c) Tuple-Space Middlewares for Distribution: Tuple-space middlewares focus on the applications that suit mobile devices in a distributing IoT infrastructure (its heterogeneity is the mixture of wired/fixed and *ad hoc*/mobile), where they need to transiently share data within gateway connectivity constraints, e.g., applications in distributed real-time embedded/operating systems. In tuple-space middlewares, each infrastructure holds a local tuple space structure. A tuple space is a data repository that can be accessed concurrently. All the tuple spaces form a federated tuple space (shown in Fig. 6.10) on a gateway. Applications communicate by writing tuples in a federated tuple space and by reading them through specifying the pattern of the data they are interested in.

Most of these approaches are customizable middleware, which is distinct from distributed operating systems, and designed for classes of systems. So, its abstractions are closer to the application and can be tailored to particular application requirements.

LIME, taken as a tuple-space middleware example, is tailored for a specific environment, ranging from mobile *ad hoc* networks to sensor networks. LIME is a middleware for MANETs developed to address mobile devices' energy limitations. LIME borrows and adapts the

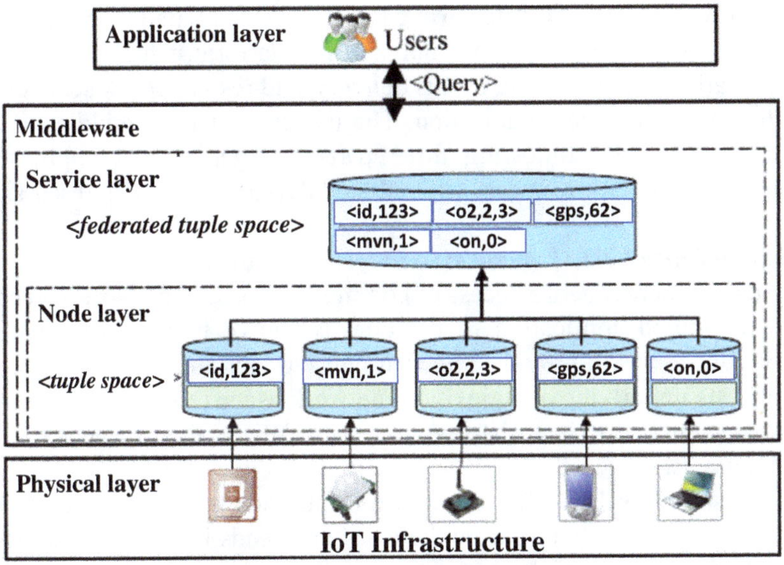

Figure 6.10 General model for a tuple-space middleware.

coordination model from Linda model, and breaks up the centralized tuple space on the gateway into multiple tuple spaces, each permanently attached to a mobile component. Linda tuple spaces are also extended with a notion of location and with the ability to react to a given state.

Access to the tuple space is carried out using an extended set of tuple-space operations, including several constructs designed to facilitate flexible and real-time responses to changes. LIME supports programming abstractions for a changing context dynamically. However, its context awareness is limited (e.g., it is not aware of the system configuration) because it offers limited support for resource management, event management, and scalability and does not provide any mechanism for security or privacy. Another limitation is that an application can access only the federated tuple space of the sensors in proximity. TinyLIME builds on LIME by adding specialized components for sensor networks.

Other similar examples including TeenyLIME and TS-Mid designed only for WSNs, which were originally proposed to address the problem of frequent disconnections, and to improve asynchronous communication.

The following LBS middleware will be introduced as a tuple-space use case, together with a prototype analysis of the ASM.

(d) Use Case: LBS Middleware: Mobile devices related to tuple-space middlewares may be developed into an LBS platform, which needs location awareness in real time, events delivery, and resource/task scheduling with synchronous communication. The use case of LBS middleware is introduced as the following three parts: (i) generalized application supported middleware models; (ii) LBS middleware design; (iii) discussion.

(i) *Generalized ASM models*: ASM is used to hide the distribution details of heterogeneous access of communication and network layer for the distributed application. The model is shown in Fig. 6.11, whose basic function is to provide a unified interface for an application, while hiding the underlying complexity of network usage (e.g., access control, management, and data sharing in a calculation, data structure, and transmission).

As shown in Fig. 6.11, the network interface transfers/receives network layer information to/from the ASM and sends instructions from the upper layer. The core business of the middleware includes service definition, management, and implementation interface protocol and works as a bridge from heterogeneous networks to APIs.

On the one hand, ASM realizes a series of service definitions according to user requirements and realize self-management service functions; on the other hand, it provides the control, execution, and maintenance of user applications and their core business interface, including data storage,

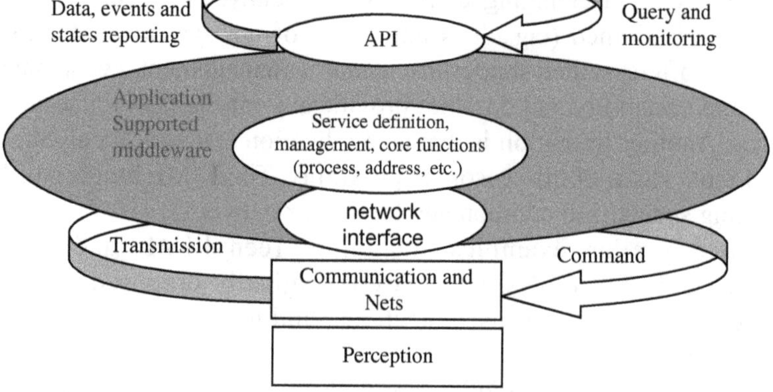

Figure. 6.11 Prototype of ASM.

delivery, sharing (e.g., tuple space) interface and service management, including LBS capabilities and various geographic information system (GIS) services, which are increasingly important for many mobile IoT applications.

(ii) *LBS middleware design*: The user interface is realized as an API sub-layer between the LBS middleware and the app, as shown in the uppermost layer of Fig. 6.11, where the gateway interoperability communications are based on mediators, bridge, or brokers.

It provides a transparent application interface for users, some common-call interfaces between user application and middleware to transfer information.

Nowadays, LBS (location service, LCS in 5G) is a location-awareness service (including, but not limited to, GNSS) based on geographic location information (e.g., GIS, map, and coordination information, details see Section 4.5). LBS middleware **obtains the location information of mobile terminal users through the mobile network of MNO operators, satellite GNSS positioning service or independent third party, or other** location awareness in Fig. 6.12; **sometimes comprehensively using GIS, for location-related information applications prevalent in**

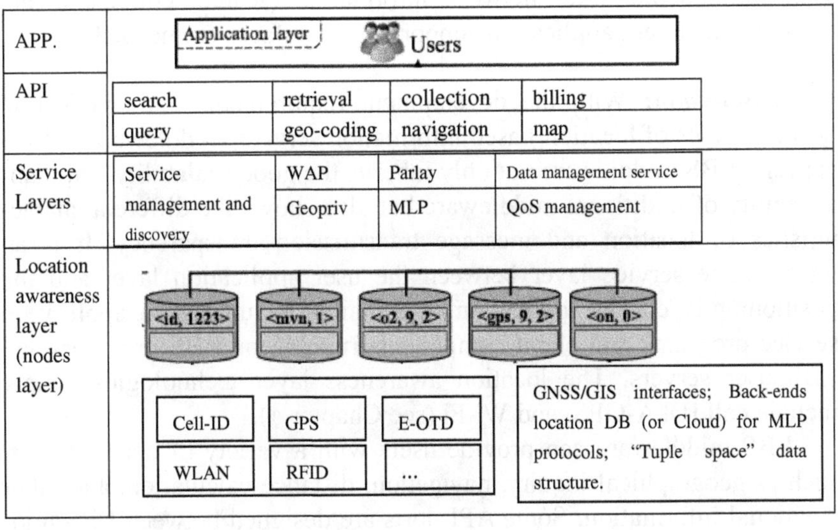

Figure 6.12 LBS middleware in a use case of location service-based location monitoring system of vehicles.

practice systems. In Fig. 6.12, application support middleware has the following functions.

- *Connection function*: The technology and application of LBS involved in middleware span the perception layer and network layer of the IoT in diverse tuple-space relative functionalities. An LBS middleware ecosystem contains equipment, location, communication network, service and content provider (ISP or MNO). Middleware technology in LBS system development can not only reduce the complexity, heterogeneity, and coupling of the underlying positioning technology but also improve the scalability of the LBS system and minimize the influence on heterogeneous communication and interfaces.

- *Management function*: It provides common services, including QoS control, addressing, management, identification, routing, security, service control/triggering, and business billing, together with other network management functions, as well as resource storage and data management. Resource storage and data management include data mining, storage, query, analysis, and semantic understanding for behavior and decision.

- *API function*: According to the different needs in different industries, users and operators for network information (search, collection, and retrieval), different application support and interfaces are needed.

(iii) *Discussion*: With the development requirements and application characteristics of location-based information service, middleware of LBS appears, LBS middleware not only inherits the good scalability and manageability of traditional middleware but also shows the different characteristics of location and message transmission transparency. It is an intermediate service layer between the user application layer and the positioning layer. The application layer mainly includes some application service programs and client components running on LBS providers and LBS user servers. The location awareness layer technologies mainly include cell ID, A-GPS, and Wi-Fi (see Chapter 4).

LBS middleware can provide users with a variety of core services, such as geographical inquiry, navigation, distance calculation, and other positional information. Some API ports are designed between LBS middleware and application program layers; more important geographical information can be provided to upper-level clients via these ports. The services provided by the middleware to the upper-level clients are created based on the basic service of the lower positioning level. The positioning layer acquires the user-end position via multiple methods and then undertakes the storage and processing through GIS; finally, the specific results are offered to different clients.

The intercommunication between the LBS middleware and positioning layer is transmitted via different mobile terminal protocols, which are based on common protocol interface specifications between LBS providers and telecommunication operators.

LBS middleware can provide users with some core services including geographic query, navigation, and distance calculation. It designs some common interfaces (APIs) between the application layer and itself, through which the most important geographic location information services are provided to the upstream users. The service provided by middleware to the upper users is based on the basic services of the positioning layer below. The location layer first obtains the location information of the user terminal by means of a variety of positioning methods mentioned above, then stores and processes the information through GIS, and finally provides the specific results to different users.

The communication between LBS middleware and service layer is transmitted through different protocols generated according to the protocol interface specification of the LBS provider and MNOs (e.g., tuple space conforms to GNSS/GIS message format).

Along with the development demands of position information service and features of the application, the middleware for positioning service shows up, and the LBS middleware takes up the merits of expandability of traditional middleware and easy manageability as well as shows the different features of transparency in positioning and message transmission. LBS middleware is the middle service layer between the client application program layer and positioning layer. Application software mainly contains the composites in between the application service programs and the client terminal. The positioning layer mainly contains Cell-ID, A-GPS, Wi-Fi, etc. (refer to Chapter 4) and the positioning technology detailed in the perception layer.

Figure 6.12 shows the structure of LBS middleware in a vehicle location service system. LBS middleware system is the implementation of data exchange subsystem in vehicle location monitoring system.

The design of the middleware is a high-performance communication middleware for message transmission. It is mainly used to receive data from GPS or BeiDou of positioning terminals and transmit the data processing results to the background monitoring users. At the same time, it interacts with the monitoring users and transmits the user's control instructions to the specific user terminal through the platform.

In the service layer, WAP means a web service for mobile engine, and Parlay interfaces cover the functions of various telecommunication networks (MNOs), such as SMS/MMS, location, billing, availability management, and policy management. Geopriv is included in IETF representations of location in Internet protocols, which analyzes the authorization, integrity, and privacy requirements that must be met when these representations of location are created, and transferred as federated tuple-space data. Mobile location protocol (MLP) is chosen as a mobile device tracking application serving as an interface between the location server (LS) and location client services. Other services are common in the service layer, and some of them will be introduced in the next application support middleware example — SOM as a platform.

The designed LBS middleware described in Fig. 6.12 is mainly based on the message-oriented communication, which combines the high concurrency and long-term performance of terminal TCP connection with the security, timeliness, and volatility of data information. At the same time, it strives to provide a communication framework that can be expanded and make rational use of network bandwidth, making the APIs open and be liberated from the complex underlying network communication, so as to provide stable and efficient information communication services for the whole vehicle monitor system. Some characteristics and connotations are as follows:

- *Self-management*: The positioning layer realizes a subsystem for data exchange based on on-board location monitoring system, above which the service function for self-management is built, and it provides the functionalities of control, execution, and maintenance. LBS middleware can provide for clients the geographical query, navigation and distance calculation, and some other core position information services. The design of the middleware makes the locating system layer for location awareness independent. It is a high-performance middleware to transfer tuple-space information with the receiving of data of GPS and BeiDou locating terminal and to transmit the data processing results to the background monitor user; meanwhile, the interactive action with the monitoring client is done, and the control command is sent to the specific user client via this platform.

The LBS middleware provides self-managed services on the one hand and, more importantly, provides control, execution, and maintenance of the user's application and its core business on the other. These interfaces are used to provide the most important geolocation information services to the upper-layer users. The services provided by the middleware are as follows: First, it obtains the location information of the user terminal with the help of various location methods, then stores and processes the information through GIS, and finally provides the specific results to different users. The intercommunication between the LBS middleware and the positioning layer is transmitted via different mobile terminal protocols, which are based on the protocol interface specifications common to LBS providers and telecom operators.

- *Expandability*: The LBS system constructs the design based on objects and model framework ideation and componentizes the public functional modules for the re-use of modules. Therefore, the focus can be shifted to more extensive issues, avoiding some OS-level details. In addition, due to the multiplicity of GPS/BeiDou terminal products, different protocols of manufacturers have to consider how to be compatible with other navigation systems (e.g., GPS/BeiDou/GLONASS or cellular navigating system); the system development needs to be able to convert the different terminal protocol data into an internal protocol customized for this system.

- *High-performance and reliability*: Based on the client demands and its own features of the whole monitoring system, the system needs at least to support 5000 terminals spontaneous connection online to guarantee the timely response to the new terminal connection requests. It also needs to guarantee the connection response time through efficient spontaneous control methods as well as efficient and reliable transmission of terminal data to the background monitor center (e.g., cloud center). When a great number of terminals are connected, the number of concurrent connections and data cache transfers of the system also increases; therefore, the system middleware must have high processing efficiency to meet the functional normal operation of the application layer. The whole monitoring system data exchange platform is working on the backend network communication server provided by the mobile service operator. As a consequence, the entire system needs to meet the reliability of telecommunication level operation and needs to have certain error tolerance and recovery capability.

• *Scalability and heterogeneous environment support*: For the entire monitoring system, system adjustments may be caused by changes in vehicle terminals, terminal protocols, specific operating environments, and other factors. Therefore, the middleware needs to provide a well-maintained interface in its design and implementation to adapt to changes in the external application environment and to ensure the overall quality of service of the system while minimizing changes in the system architecture. The entire system may be deployed on different platforms and environments depending on the application customer, which requires the system to be cross-platform.

At last, as to the heterogeneous environment compatibility, the whole monitoring system will be aligned due to the change in the onboard terminal, protocol, and specific operational environment. Therefore, a good maintenance interface for the middleware shall be provided during its design and execution period. The holistic system service quality can be ensured at any change of minimized system structure. The entire deployment platform and environment may vary based on different applications, which require a cross-platform performance of the system.

6.1.3.4 *Platforms of middleware*

Common platforms of middleware in the book are explained as comprehensive service management platforms or interconnecting platforms at the middleware level. The former example is the SOCRADES (http://www.socrades.eu) middleware, which abstracts physical things as services using devices profile for WS (such as DPWS[12]) that enhances the real-time performance and shows most of the characteristics of ASM. For example, SOCRADES simplifies the management of underlying devices or things for enterprise applications (e.g., industrial automation).

As shown by the black rectangular part in Fig. 6.13, SOCRADES realized SOA-based integration, and its architecture consists of a layer for service management (e.g., event storage, service monitor) and a layer for

[12]DPWS selects the most appropriate ones, such as WS-Discovery and WS-Eventing above SOAP, for implementation in constrained embedded devices. Several projects such as SOCRADES (http://www.socrades.eu) and SIRENA (http://www.sirena-itea.org) have demonstrated its capabilities, such as interoperability, plug and play, and integration capability. Information model defined in the WSDL file is based on the XML Schema specification for DPWS enabled devices.

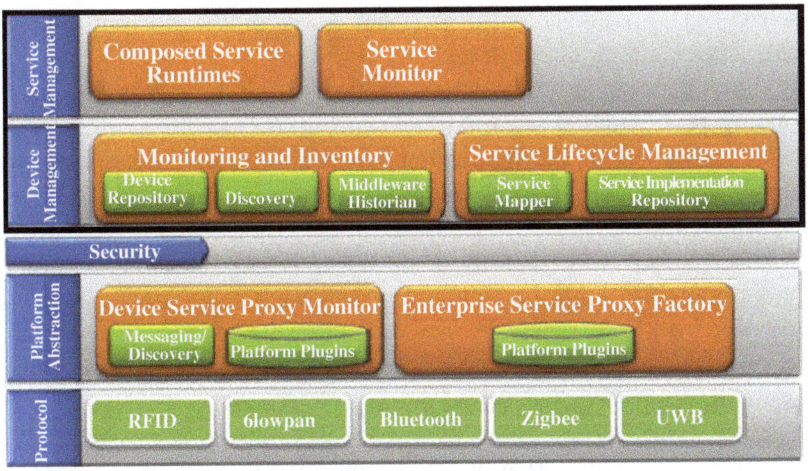

Figure 6.13 Integration architecture of SCORADES.

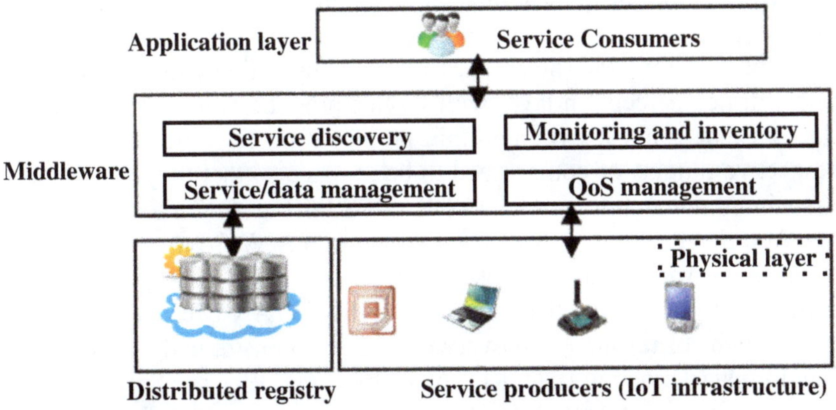

Figure 6.14 General design model for an SOM.

device services management (e.g., device manager and monitor, service discovery, service lifecycle management). Different components in the two layers are unfolded from the middleware layer of Fig. 6.14, to fulfill different requirements as an SOA platform. For instance, the device services management layer's service discovery component, a key contribution of SOCRADES middleware, discovers the services provided by real-world devices or things, while its device manager handles resource management (e.g., device access). It also offers device and service discovery. The management of services' layer provides event management, service monitor, and storage.

The uppermost layer, which is omitted in Fig. 6.13, but as a corresponding part of the application layer in Fig. 6.14, with its interface to service consumers, is the application interface layer — this layer enables the interaction with traditional enterprise systems (such as ERP, MES) and other applications.

The SOCRADES security includes role-based access control of devices communication to middleware and back-end services, and vice versa, and works as a security solution, but it is limited to only authentication. Moreover, direct access to devices or their offered services through this middleware raises the risk of privacy violations.

Platform abstraction in Fig. 6.13 enables the abstraction of all devices, independent of whether they natively support WS or not, to be wrapped and represented as services on the higher systems. In addition to service-enabling the communication with devices, this layer also provides a unified view of remotely installing or updating the software that runs on devices.

Protocols function (heterogeneous communication with devices layer under it, i.e., perception layer with service producers) includes the actual devices that connect over multiple protocols to the infrastructure. The respective plugins of course need to be in place so that they can be integrated into the architecture of SCORADES (as Fig. 6.13 shows).

Additionally, in Fig. 6.13, in contrast to those WS-based M2M communication which is mostly based on IP, CoAP REST-based protocol is a candidate to be the application layer for 6LoWPAN because it includes mechanisms of resource discovery through the constrained environments link format (defined in IETF RFC 6690, by CoRE WG, see Section 5.6.3), which is easily integrated with WEB design system (details in Section 6.1.4). Moreover, it implements a pub-sub mode as a subject/observer design pattern, as above mentioned.

The latter example of interconnecting platforms at the middleware level is the MW2MW (middleware to middleware) of INTER-IoT,[13] which is a sub-project of Horizonal2020. The business data processed by the application of the IoT may span multiple industries/platforms, and different platform integration/applications need to be considered. Therefore,

[13] INTER-IoT designed by "Interoperability of Heterogeneous IoT Platforms" (INTER-IoT) is a part of the European Union's "Horizon 2020".

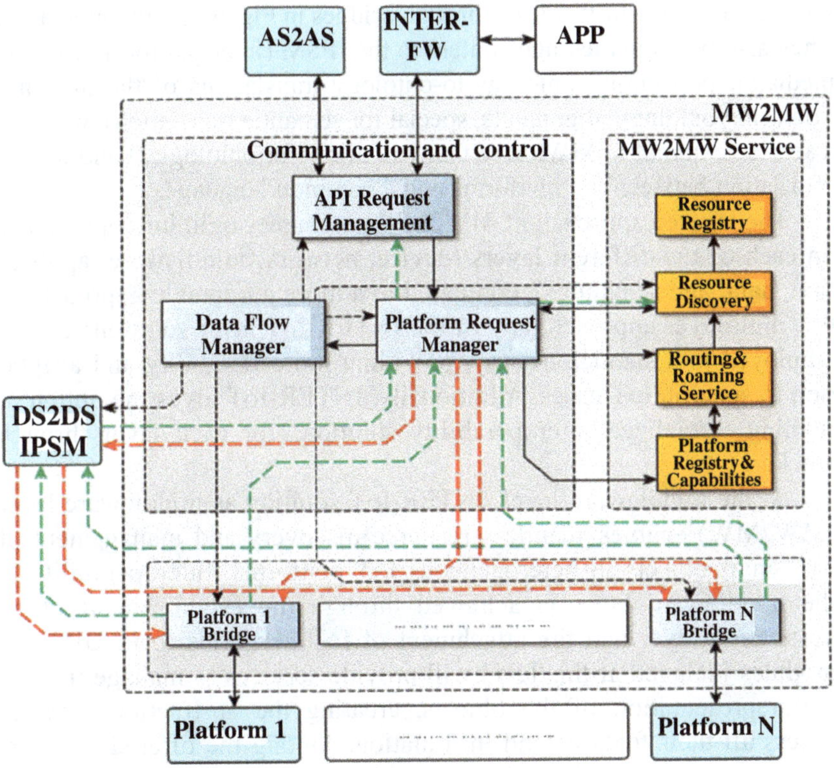

Figure 6.15 MW2MW structure in INTER-IoT.

Notes: Whether WS or not, information from platform bridge up to DS2DS (data & semantics-to-data & semantics)/IPSM, then to request manager, as GREEN flow; on the contrary, the information back to the platform bridge as RED flow.

the introduction of middleware as platforms can make the personalized and compatible/interoperable applications of various platforms be realized, in the multi-platform middleware: MW2MW.

As shown in Fig. 6.15, INTER-IoT MW2MW represents a solution for interconnecting platforms at the middleware level and to enable interoperability among them. With regard to bridges structure (Fig. 6.15), south from the communication and control block, the bridges manage the communication with the underlying platforms by translating requests and answers from and into messages for the queue. Different bridges might need to use HTTP, REST (RESTful or other web services), sockets, or other technologies (IP-based or not) to "speak" to the platforms, but these will be translated northwards (through bridges in Fig. 6.15) into messages. They also pass the message content to the IPSM (inter-platform semantic mediator, performing ontology-to-ontology translations of the information using ontology alignments, special for semantic translation), which is a service external to MW2MW that will allow for ontological and format translation between the platforms and a common language.

The layered approach of MW2MW guarantees tight interoperability on each of the different layers (device, network, middleware, application, data, and semantics), compared to a more acceptable approach. In this multilayer approach, any of the INTER-IoT layer solutions can be employed in a standalone way, providing more flexibility and adaptation to specific IoT cases. Additionally, INTER-IoT gives the option of running virtualized interoperability solutions for each layer through Docker.

At the middleware level, INTER-IoT solution as middleware layer (MW2MW) enables seamless resource discovery and management of IoT smart objects in heterogeneous IoT platforms. Interoperability at the middleware layer is achieved through the establishment of an abstraction layer and the attachment of IoT platforms to it. Different modules included at this level will provide services to manage the virtual representation of the objects, creating the abstraction layer to access all their features and information. Among the offered services, there are component-based interoperability solutions in the middleware based on communication using mediators, bridges, and brokers. Brokers are accessible through a general API. Interoperability at this layer will allow global exploitation of smart objects in large-scale multi-platform IoT systems.

DS2DS/IPSM provides a semantic platform-to-platform translator in the middleware that enables the interconnection and interoperation of any platform at the middleware level, despite the standards and formats employed, and a partially virtualized gateway. Moreover, INTER-IoT has a huge concern on security, layer-solutions, and secure APIs, which can be further integrated into forms of API/integration as a service, i.e., security as a service (in an IoT grid or on the edge, details in Chapter 8). The interoperability framework gives elements, such as natural human interfaces in IoT systems, the existence of ambient intelligent environments (AmI) or the integration of IoT with AI and other integrators on top of it.

Basically, platforms of middleware provide a type of gateways[14] (including ALG gateway and DS2DS/IPSM in Fig. 6.15) or (service-) mediators, whose prototype, named local discovery unit (LDU), enables the dynamic discovery of devices on premise in their coupling with the IoT platform (if necessary, on the cloud/edge collaboration). The resource discovery in Fig. 6.15 is also a compromise to this LDU prototype.

Additionally, every interoperability mechanism can be accessed through an API (which is omitted in the top layer of Fig. 6.13 but shown in the top part as application & services-to-application & services (AS2AS) in Fig. 6.15, with a link to API request manager). The API provided with an integration toolbox facilitates the development of new applications that integrate existing heterogeneous IoT services. The interoperability of API can communicate and interoperate through the interfaces. Then, platforms of the middle with cross-layering allow achieving a deeper and more complete integration and guaranteeing a quick and easy implementation. An additional example of OPC-UA will be discussed as another platform in the next section.

6.1.3.5 *Other middlewares*

Other middlewares discussed here are those that cannot be deduced into the former three (DAM or ASM) directly (e.g., combination of the three), or coding/engineering-facilitated for IoT engineering development (e.g., facilitating potentially spontaneous resource). So, they are introduced as simple as follows:

- **Application-specific middlewares:** *KASOM* has been introduced as SoM middleware for seamless integration into an enterprise information system as well as SensorsMW. But *KASOM* is also specific for knowledge awareness in WSN/WSAN sensors. Its architecture consists of not only

---

[14]As introduced in Chapter 5, some examples of gateways/ALGs (app. layer gateways) include the ZigBee gateway device, which translates from ZigBee to simple object access protocol (SOAP) and IP or gateways that translate from constrained application protocol (CoAP) to hypertext transfer protocol/representational state transfer (HTTP/REST). For some local area network (LAN) technologies, such as Wi-Fi and Z-Wave, the gateway is used for inclusion and exclusion of devices.

security and runtime manager as framework and communication services but also knowledge management services (e.g., service composition rules and context resources). The SOA-based middleware services offer embedded networks for pervasive environments through registration, discovery, composition, and orchestration of services. Most of these services are established on complex reasoning mechanisms and protocols based on the WSAN's contextual model (e.g., semantic description of low- and high-level resources of the WSANs). And their real-life implementations in hospital and health management show the potential in terms of response time, efficiency, and reliability.)

Specific for visual sensor networks, ELLA (middleware of visual sensor networks) is a computer video-specific middleware with publish/subscribe mechanism. The control channel of ELLA can be realized with a decoupling of components. First, CV is publishing images (to be displayed in UI) and tracking results (containing the location in the image and the confidence of the tracked object) in case it is responsible for tracking. Both UI and handover are subscribed to this tracking information. UI uses it to show the bounding box of the tracked object as an overlay to the camera image stream. Handover is informed of the current tracking status with this information and can react to, e.g., a lost object.

As shown in Fig. 6.16, each camera runs a handover and a tracking module. The operator PC runs a user interface. Red solid lines indicate

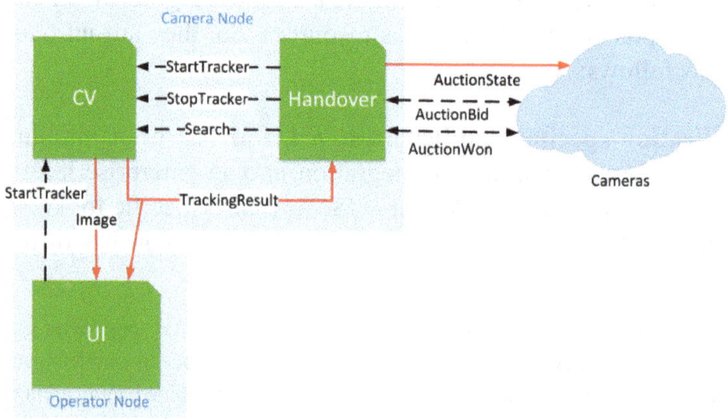

Figure 6.16 The components in our application. Each camera runs a handover and a tracking module. The operator PC runs a user interface. Red solid lines indicate published events, and black dashed lines indicate control messages.

published events, and black dashed lines indicate control messages. So, with the same way of thinking, LBS middleware (introduced in tuple-space middleware) can also be classified as location service-specified middleware.

• **Specific for VM-based middlewares:** In the specific for VM-based middleware architectures, middleware design provides programming support for a safe execution environment for user applications by virtualizing the infrastructure, in order to facilitate potentially spontaneous resource (service) (re)composition, and to satisfy application needs.

The applications are divided into small separate modules, which are injected and distributed throughout the network. Each node in the network holds a VM (module). This approach addresses architectural requirements, such as high-level programming abstractions and self-management, while supporting transparency in distributed heterogeneous IoT infrastructures. VMs middleware not only includes those middleware-level VMs (which are placed between the OS and applications) but system-level VMs (which substitute or replace the entire OS), in order to free up resources that would otherwise be consumed by the OS.

Middleware level VMs add capabilities (e.g., concurrency) to the underlying OSs. Like Maté and DVM middlewares, they are VM-based for resource-constrained sensor nodes (e.g., WSN nodes with TinyOS). When Maté has been extended into a framework for building ASVM (application-specific virtual machine), other capabilities are improved, e.g., ASVMs solve the problems imposed by traditional VM solutions by limiting the generality of the VMs to subsets relevant to application domains. Additionally, MW2MW (mentioned above) SOCRADES and AUTOSAR (AUTomobile Open System ARchitecture) also employ VMs in their design, which facilitates their development.

Other x-facilitated middlewares include ROS (robotics OS) for robotics programming and OPC-UA for industrial automation as a standard for integration. Because supplementation and extension of IoT middlewares driven by the market are growing so fast (e.g., from abstract model to use cases, functionality to data/data format exchanges, and industrial to platform), outlines in the open research field of IoT middleware are summarized above as recommending future research directions.

6.1.4 *OPC-UA as an industrial automation middleware*

OPC unified architecture (OPC-UA,[15] IEC 62541) is more of a standardized IoT middleware platform than just a middleware for IoT. As a middleware platform in process industries for the interoperability between systems and devices coming from numerous vendors as OPC (OLE for process control), OPC-UA is widely accepted as enabling standard for devices from different vendors to understand and communicate with each other.

The OPC Foundation started OPC-UA standardization and improve it for industrial automation, including not only a set of web service (WS) protocols that are compatible with DPWS (devices profile for web services)[16] but also providing a data model enlarging the semantic capabilities of the solution. CoAP and other lightweight protocols are easily translated into HTTP for seamless integration with the web, while meeting specialized requirements such as event-based communication (e.g., EBM), multicast support, very low overhead, and simplicity for constrained environments.

Besides the support for CoAP, XML-based and other protocols (see the later part of this section), OPC-UA as an open middleware standard is independent of the manufacturer or system supplier of the application, of the programming language in which the respective software is programmed and of the operating system on which the application is running. For example, with OPC-UA as an interface (of pipes from industrial word), the machine data can not only be transported but semantically described in a machine-readable way. OPC-UA provides access to a wide variety of data in both vertical and horizontal directions. The spectrum ranges from OPC-UA components directly integrated on the devices and controllers or machines and systems to so-called gateways, aggregating servers and mediators. So, OPC-UA can be used in the daily work to

---

[15]In many references, OPC-UA is OLE for Process Control Unified Architecture, or Open Platform Communications Unified Architecture.

[16]A set of infrastructure services for network discovery of devices and services (WS-discovery), metadata exchange, event publication, and subscription or resource management (WS-eventing). These services allow the implementation of standard profiles, such as basic profile (1.1 and 2.0) and devices profile for web services (DPWS), or of resource management frameworks, such as WS-management or *ad hoc* solutions based on the REST paradigm.

enable interoperability solutions among the most diverse use cases in the industry domains in which IoT interoperability is required.

6.1.4.1 *Introduction of web-based service and CoAP*

As introduced in Chapter 5, constrained application protocol (CoAP) is REST-centric (supports GET, POST, PUT, DELETE), and it can be used to compress HTTP interfaces, as Fig. 6.17 shows. CoAP offers additional functionalities such as built-in discovery, events, multicast support, and asynchronous message exchanges. From the security point of view, several approaches are supported ranging from no-security up to certificate-based using DTLS (datagram transport layer security). CoAP and other simple data representations (such as JSON and SenML) might be sufficient for low-cost sensors and actuators. Some SOA-based middleware technologies, discussed or will be discussed, include: device Profile for web services (DPWS), EXI/XMPP (see Section 5.6.2), CoAP, REST, OPC-UA, distributed service bus, complex event processing (CEP, see Section 6.1.2), DDS, and semantic models. They provide plenty of services and protocols in IoT applications and make up the gaps between Internet and communication technologies (CTs) and operation technologies (OTs) in industrial automation by a shell as a middleware (a bridge between two protocols, see Fig. 6.18), platforms as a middleware (e.g., SCORADES, MW2MW, and OPC-UA) or (service-) mediators as a middleware (to be introduced).

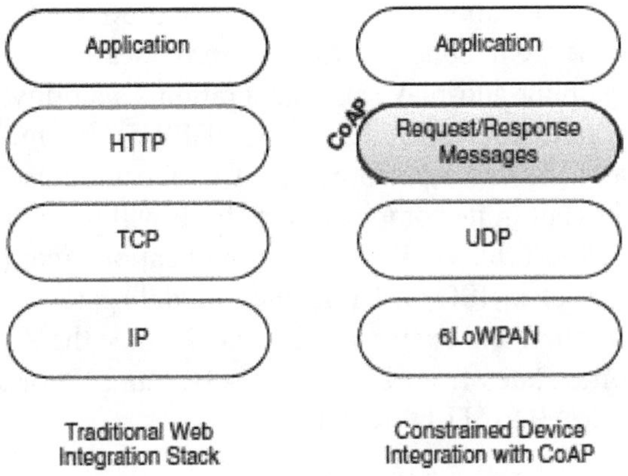

Figure 6.17 CoAP lightweight integration versus heavy HTTP integration.

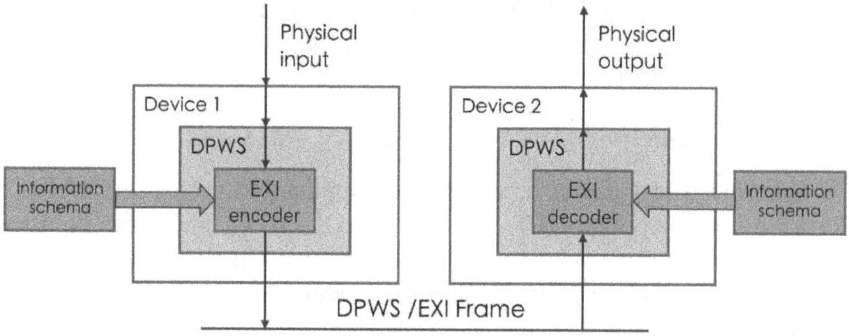

Figure 6.18 A shell as a middleware for DPWS/EXI integration.

(1) Shell as a middleware: A little different with OPC (OLE for Process Control), the technology associated with the DPWS, coming from the information and communication technology (ICT) world, is one of the most applicable sets of traditional web integration stacks. When web services protocols are combined with the efficient XML interchange (EXI, see www.w3.org/XML/EXI) at the device level, DPWS provides capabilities that can be used to cover some real-time requirements.

For example, in order to provide real-time performance in the millisecond range for SOCRADES (see Section 6.1.3), SIRENA (http://www.sirena-itea.org) and EXI projects, a shell of frame working as a middleware for the coupled DPWS with EXI, are demonstrated in Fig. 6.18.

As introduced above, DPWS selects the most appropriate web service protocols, such as the above SOAP (see Section 6.1.2), for implementation in constrained embedded devices. It provides capabilities such as interoperability, plug-and-play, and integration capability. However, if CoAP can be combined with EXI in the "DPWS/EXI middleware" (as Fig. 6.18) in an achievable performance, CoAP can be used for wireless sensor networks (but in its combination of EXI, will be at the cost of real-time supported, see Table 6.1). Similarly, application layer (seventh layer of Ethernet/Internet in ISO/OSI reference model) gateways (ALGs) are also common as shell and examples of ALGs include the ZigBee gateway device, which translates from ZigBee to SOAP and IP, or gateways that translate from CoAP to HTTP/REST.[17]

[17]For some local area network (LAN) technologies, such as Wi-Fi and Z-Wave, the gateway is used for inclusion and exclusion of devices/ service.

(2) Platforms as a middleware: The service bus, the mediator, semantic technologies, and the complex event processing (CEP) are technologies providing the large-scale and migration capabilities, combining and processing information coming through DPWS, OPC-UA, or legacy protocols, in order to manage large-scale platform systems.

The previous discussion points out the potential of some of these technologies with a shell (or bridge) as a middleware view, by which can be used for wireless sensor networks for (near) real-time support, including the lightweight integration for resource-constraint devices with web technologies, e.g., a temperature sensor, a wireless sensor node, etc. Moreover, the devices may also be mobile and rely on a battery for their operation. These distributed devices would probably be used for monitoring and management, while their integration may enhance the quality of information reaching SCADA/DCS systems in a mobile or in a heterogeneous platform. In the progress of heterogeneous but compliant to different protocols (e.g., IPv4/IPv6, 6LoWPAN, Zigbee, Bluetooth, and RFID, etc.) standardization, platforms as middleware are needed and introduced formerly as SCOREDES, MW2MW in Section 6.1.3. As an industrial middleware of standardization, OPC-UA is introduced in the following part.

(3) Mediator as a middleware: Mediator as a middleware is from the aspect of IPSM performing translations of the information using ontology alignments for semantic translation (as stated above in MW2MW) and service mediator organizing/reorganizing services in application layer (or through APIs) of IoT, which constructs the diversity usages/implementations for IoT interoperability. A mediator will be introduced following the section on OPC-UA.

6.1.4.2 *OPC-UA*

As an IoT middleware platform, OPC-UA provides a device (or thing as a machine/equipment) with several kinds of data and services including access rights and all (COM) OPC classic specifications, which are mapped to OPC-UA with platform independence, from an embedded micro-controller to cloud-based infrastructure. Beyond a middle platform, the OPC-UA provides a multi-layered architecture framework (in Fig. 6.19) for innovative technologies and methodologies, such as new transport protocols, security algorithms, encoding standards, or application services, that can be incorporated into OPC-UA while maintaining backward compatibility for existing products.

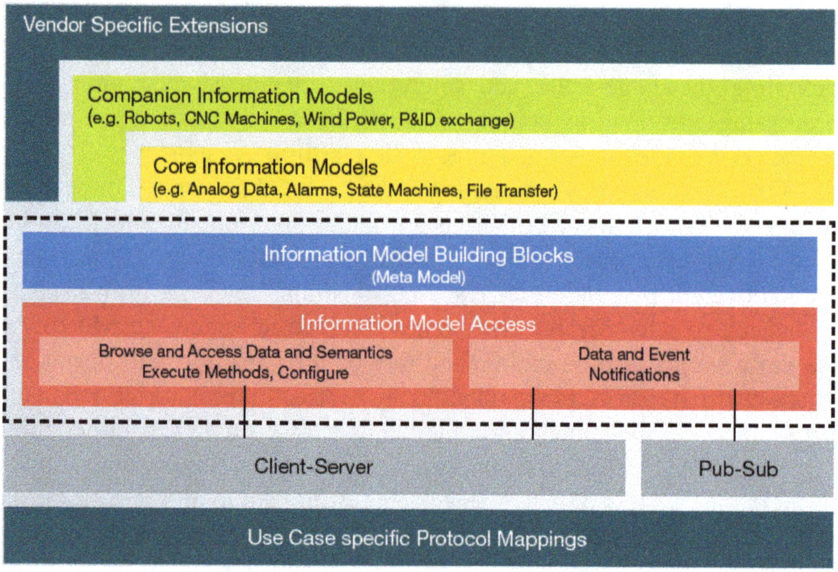

Figure 6.19 A multi-layered architecture framework of OPC-UA.

In the information modeling and access layer of Fig. 6.19, the OPC-UA information modeling framework turns data into information (as a layered pyramid of data–information–knowledge–wisdom pyramid in Chapter 2), with the multi-level structures that can be modeled and extended. As the fundamental element of OPC-UA, the information modeling and access layer define the rules and base building blocks necessary to expose an information model with OPC-UA, which defines several core models that can be applied in many industries and facilitates other organizations building their models upon them, exposing their more specific information with OPC-UA. The necessary access mechanisms defined by OPC-UA in these information models are as follows:

- Look-up mechanism (browsing) to locate instances and their semantic.
- Read and write operations for current data and historical data.
- Method execution.
- Notification for data and events.

The actual transport layer can be extended by additional protocols because of the ability to add new features without affecting existing applications. The independence from the physical transport medium and

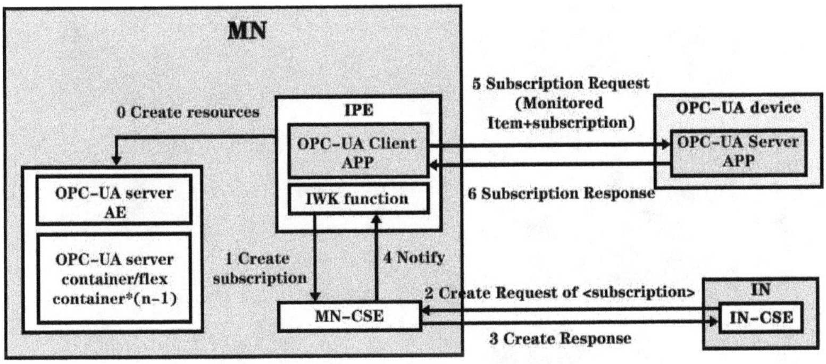

Figure 6.20 Interworking procedure for subscription in OPC-UA.

the transport protocol is an advantage of OPC-UA compared to other pure IoT data protocols (or above DAM). In this layer, the device or machine builder provides the data and services in a secure way. Given the wide array of available hardware platforms and operating systems, platform independence is shown by OPC-UA functions on any of the following:

Hardware platforms: traditional PC hardware, cloud-based servers, PLCs, micro-controllers (ARM, etc.).

Operating systems: Microsoft Windows, Apple OSX, Android, or any distribution of Linux, etc.

OPC-UA provides the necessary infrastructure for interoperability across the enterprise, including machine to machine, machine to enterprise, and everything in between them. Figure 6.20 is an example of its seven steps for subscription in the pub-sub models, where communications among MN-CSE (middle node-cloud service engine), IN-CSE (infrastructure node-CSE), and IWK (InterWorking) function are defined by oneM2M/ITU-T in its standardized service layering for IoT.

6.1.4.3 *OPC-UA and DPWS*

As introduced earlier in platforms of middleware, SOCRADES was dedicated to manufacturing applications with a focus on integration and communication characteristics to be supported by production management and control components distributed across several layers. Among these layers, *SOCRADES* middleware abstracts physical things as services

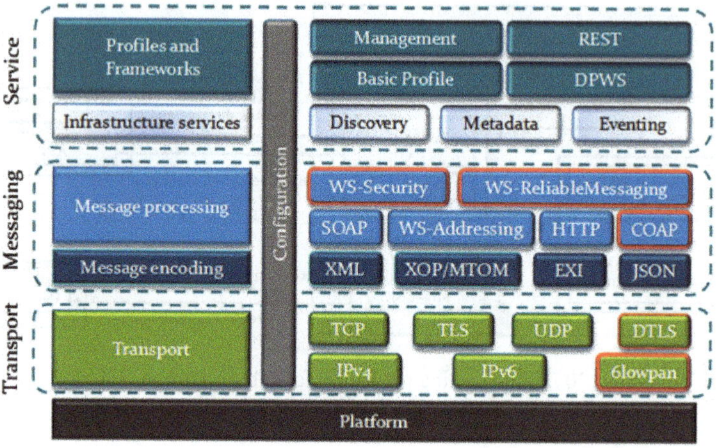

Figure 6.21 DPWS-compliant ESF (redesigned and extended to DPWSCore stack).

using DPWS. As Fig. 6.21 shows, DPWSCore stack integrated embedded service framework (ESF) is another DPWS-compliant platform.

Based on the web service technologies (e.g., WS, REST/RESTful architectures) and the embedded devices utilizing service-oriented, ESF is redesigned (as in Fig. 6.21) and extended to the new version of the DPWSCore stack (http://forge.SOA4d.org) in industrial domain enablement, whose goals, as follows, are the same as middleware:

- To hide complexity from developers, through code generation and high-level APIs.
- To support a large range of (basic/complex) web applications and distinctive mechanisms, such as network discovery and event publishing.
- To support a wide range of platforms, from mono-threaded (or OS-less), deeply embedded devices (e.g., wireless sensors) to complex multi-threaded applications running on large devices, workstations/enterprise servers.

The main features of the ESF (in Fig. 6.21) include:

- Support of standard IPv4/IPv6-based transport protocols: TCP, UDP, TLS, and support for additional protocols, such as 6LoWPAN and DTLS.

- Support of standard message encodings: Besides XML used in several standard messaging protocols, ESF also supports XOP/MTOM, which is used to transport binary data in SOAP messages, EXI, a standard binary format for XML adapted to low-bandwidth networks, and JSON, a popular format used in particular in browser-based applications.
- Support of several messaging protocols, including HTTP, SOAP (directly over TCP or UDP or combined with HTTP), and SOAP extensions such as WS-Addressing.
- Integration with standard profiles, such as basic profile (1.1 and 2.0) and DPWS. For example, services for network discovery of devices and services, including metadata exchange, event publication, and subscription or resource management, allowing the implementation of resource management frameworks such as WS-management.
- A configuration mechanism to select the appropriate components from the above list for their applications.

As shown in Fig. 6.21, based on the abstract definition of a service interface through a WSDL document, the code generator produces a service skeleton ready to be plugged into the ESF service container. The role of the developer is to provide the implementation of the service operations and to configure the ESF runtime with the required protocols. The ESF makes it easy to publish the same services simultaneously by using different protocols in order to extend the reach of available services to a wide range of clients. The ESF also provides a resource manager that allows developers to register resource implementations and provides remote access to those resources through REST/WS protocols. As for the client side, code generation is used to produce service stubs, which can be used by the application to invoke remote service operations or resource access. The configurability of the ESF protocols allows clients to access a wide range of devices.

As shown in Fig. 6.22, if a common stack is compliant with both standards of OPC-UA and DPWS, another inter-middleware platform (differs with MW2MW) arises and the two middlewares can benefit from each other. A component implementing the convergence between OPC-UA and DPWS for embedded devices has been prototyped as described in Fig. 6.22, and more details are discussed in Jammes *et al.* (2014).

Coming from the industrial world, OPC-UA is also a set of web service protocols compatible with DPWS, providing a data model enlarging the semantic capabilities of the solution. CoAP can be used for wireless

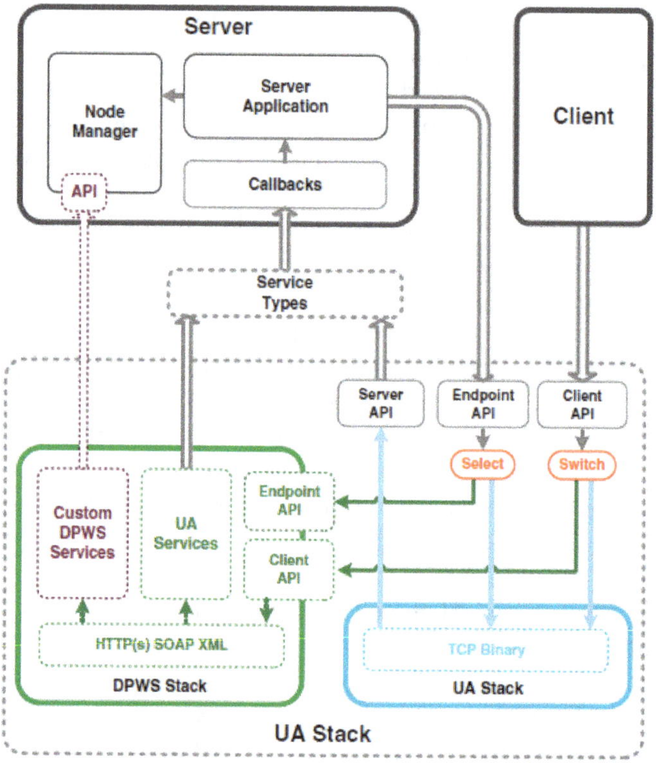

Figure 6.22 Fusion of OPC-UA and DPWS architecture.

sensor networks. It can also be combined with EXI as above-mentioned CoAP followed DPWS. Service bus and CEP are still works in progress with their current impact. Some comparisons among them, either as protocols, or as middlewares, are shown in Table 6.3, and some of them are still on their way toward adaption/improvement for new industrial middlewares.

6.1.4.4 *Services mediator as a middleware compliant to OPC-UA*

The SOA-based concept for inhomogeneous interfaces, middlewares (e.g., SOM), and projects, such as SOCRADES, MW2MW, OPC-UA, and

Table 6.3 Performance and challenges.

Technologies	Real-time	Management of large scale	Event-driven	Semantics
DPWS		X	X	
OPC-UA		X		X
CoAP		X	X	
EXI	X		X	
Service bus		X		
CEP			X	

IMC-AESOP,[18] can be used within automation and integration into production control, automation, and management applications. It can also be effective in the service's mediator as a simplified middleware.

Mediator, originally defined as a bridge between the server and the devices, controls a set of lower-level non-service-enabled devices in IoT scenarios, like the IoT gateway (which allows gradually replacing limited-resource devices or legacy devices by natively WS-enabled devices without impacting the applications using these devices, as an interface for the device to be known/addressed individually by higher-level services or applications.). When a mediator is exposed for more than a gateway, but as a service-enabled device (such as aggregating various data sources, including databases, and log files), it turns into a service mediator.

The service mediator components are now used to not only aggregate various services but possibly also compute/process the data they acquire before exposing it as a service. Service mediators aggregate, manage, and eventually represent services based on some semantics (e.g., using ontologies).

[18] IMC-AESOP (www.imc-aesop.eu) will be introduced in collaborative cloud of section cloud computing. The IMC-AESOP project has proposed a cloud-based information-driven interaction among the different systems. The functionalities of each system or even device can be offered as one or more services of varying complexity, which may be hosted in the cloud and composed by other (potentially cross-layer) services. For more details, see Colombo *et al.* (2014).

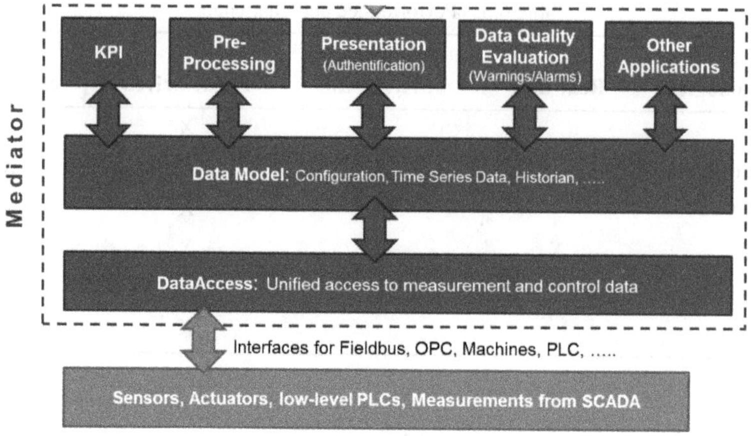

Figure 6.23 Example of generalized middleware platform as a service mediator.
Source: Colombo *et al.* (2014). *Industrial Cloud-based Cyber-Physical Systems: The IMC-AESOP Approach*, Springer.

In Fig. 6.23, as a corresponding part of the dotted rectangular part of Fig. 6.19 (framework of OPC-UA), the service mediator could be used to aggregate various non-WS-enabled devices. This is why the sub-layers in it are explained as data access and data model, which can be extended to an information model. Accordingly, higher-level applications (e.g., from HMI interface, DCS, CMMS/collaborative manufacturing model system, and other higher-level information systems, such as MES/ERP, to the interfaces of OPC-UA, SCORADES, and Fieldbus), could communicate to service mediators offering WS instead of communicating to devices with proprietary interfaces. Benefits are that we do not need the (proprietary) driver integration as a necessity. Furthermore, now the processing of data can be done at the service mediator level, and more complex behavior can be created which was not possible before from the standalone devices.

Several innovative elements are provided in this section of the platform to enhance functionality and have positive differentiators from other interoperability approaches. Finally, in order to promote the business process, including a foresight of industrial middleware, with the support by cloud in a collaborative IoT infrastructure view, IMC-AESOP service cloud was developed as the follow-up industry-driven cloud collaborative approaches in around 2010, after SOCRADES. IMC-AESOP will be introduced as a collaborative cloud case after the following section.

6.1.5 *Robot middleware*

Service robots may accompany us in our daily life/work, and industrial robots will decorate the front of Industry 4.0. In Section 4.6 of the third chapter, we discuss how to perceive the environment information from the perspective of the machine/robot/vehicle (as high-level-things) and then realize the location and map construction in an unknown environment by SLAM technology. Then, they carry out the tasks of path planning, autonomous exploration, and navigation.

For the robot, it needs a set of control systems, along with its ease of development environment. In addition to dealing with SLAM, it also needs to consider the internal motion control, data sharing, external equipment interaction, information fusion, and other services as well as the judgment and response of external access to information, the input and output of functional hardware, robot behavior decision-making and task processing, etc.

More complicated are networked group control tasks such as "robot dance array" (see Section 4.2.4), which involve the cooperation between robots. The robot system is a typical distributed multi-task heterogeneous system. Its openness, compatibility, and portability determine the realization of common basic functions and characteristic functions. For developers, how to face the above problems and integrate multiple elements into a whole system? It needs middleware to support it.

6.1.5.1 *Overview of robot middleware*

The coming of robot era (or Internet of Robotic Things) needs the support of generalization and platform of robot control software in real-time, expansibility, fault tolerance, reusability, and effective utilization of resources. The famous ones among this software are:

RT-middleware and ORiN (Open Robot interface for the Network) in Japan, player/stage system in the United States, and KOMoR (Korea Object-oriented Middleware of Robot) in Korea; Miro, a multi-layer programming and control platform for mobile robots in Germany; "robot standardized modular middleware (Chinese 863 project)" and Tsinghua University's Open Robot Control Middleware in China. The main performance indexes are shown in Table 6.4.

Next, several typical robot middlewares are introduced.

Table 6.4 Main performance indexes and technical standards of robot middleware.

Middleware name	Characteristics	Standard or Tech.
RT-middleware	The component structure of the robot and its functional modules are realized in the software layer (as shown in Fig. 6.24). The robot software development is simplified by the composition of selected modules. The reusable software component, class libraries and standards are available.	CORBA[a]
OrIN	It provides an interface for accessing and controlling robot system from a personal computer and supports a multi-protocol.	HTTP/XML, SOAP[b]
Player/Stage System	Providing a development platform to support different robot hardware and common services for different robots.	Client/Server architecture
KOMoR	It provides interfaces for different operating systems and networks. Other characteristics include scalability, quality of service assurance, resource management, fault-tolerance, and multi-path routing capabilities.	HTTP, SOAP
MIRO	Using distributed object technology to promote the process of mobile robot software development and the interaction between robot and enterprise information system (MIRO is developed by the University of California).	CORBA
Open Robot Control Middleware	Hardware abstraction. Management of various types of peripheral devices, including expansion, replacement, maintenance, scheduling, and channel mapping functions. It provides a unified access channel for upper logic control.	XML, SOAP
ROS1	OS supported: Linux Communication: TCPROS/UDPROS	TCP ROS, UDP ROS
ROS2	OS supported: Linux, Windows/Mac/RTOS, even bare-metal (means MCU); Communication: DDS	DDS, Intra-process API

[a]CORBA (Common Object Request Broker Architecture), regulated by OMG for object oriented software architecture.

[b]SOAP (Simple Object Access Protocol) is an XML-based, RESTful and light weigh data exchange protocol, design for structural/non-structural information exchange on the WEB.

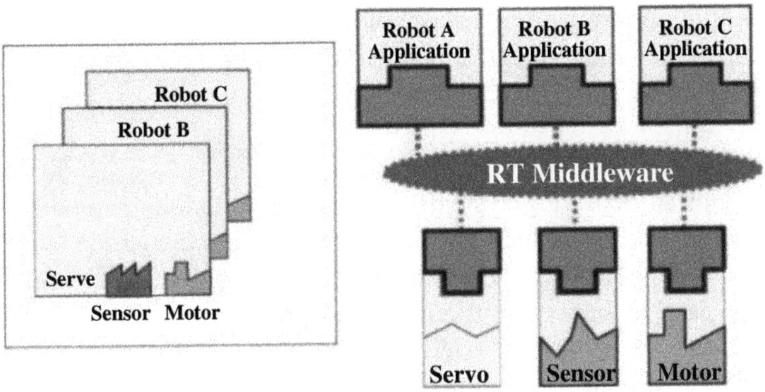

Figure 6.24 Conventional robots vs. modularized robots, where RT-components are integrated through the RT-middleware using a standard interface.

6.1.5.2 *RT-middleware*

RT-middleware is modularized software supporting robot program development for next-generation robots, whose purpose is to improve the efficiency of robot design and making robot systems being constructed more flexible, As a software platform specification originating from Japan, RT-middleware is developed by the National Institute of Advanced Industrial Science and Technology (AIST, the official research institute of Japan). In order to popularize service robots, the institute, as an open strategy, proposed the standard interface specification OMG (object management group) of RTC (RT-component) of a robot and published the standard specification of OMG in 2008, which effectively avoided the problem of incompatibility between machines/companies. At the same time, according to the specification, it has developed and disclosed the intermediate software for RTC application, namely RT-middleware, by which an RT functional element-specific set of interfaces and their distributed object middleware-based component model were defined.

RT-middleware provides control of robot parts (e.g., sensors, processing elements, actuators, and drivers) in the form of components. The component model defines the RT-component used to exchange data with other components. RT-component integrates different functions respectively, which facilitates the flexible expansion of the developed robotic system. Take a robot with arms and recognition ability as an example. The main functions of RT-middleware include: sensor input and output API interface, motor control program, voice and image recognition software, task execution management, and software package management.

6.1.5.3 *ROS* (*robotic operating system*) *middleware*

ROS is not an operating system but provides functions similar to those provided by an operating system, including hardware abstract description, underlying driver management, execution of common functions, message-passing between programs, and program distribution management. It also provides some tool programs and libraries for acquiring, establishing, writing, and running multi computer-integrated programs. ROS is widely used in Europe and the United States. In 2010, Willow Garage Inc. released open-source ROS, which is called ROS1.0, in contrast to ROS2.0.

As an open-source framework for robotics research, the primary design goal of ROS is to improve the code reuse rate in the field of robot development. As a distributed processing framework, ROS allows the executable program to be designed separately and loosely coupled at run time. These processes can be encapsulated in packages and stacks to facilitate sharing and distribution and improve the reusability and modularity of the code.

ROS supports synchronous RPC (remote procedure call) communication based on service, asynchronous data flow communication based on topic, and data storage on parameter server. However, it does not support the real-time and dynamic reconfiguration of a distributed network, until ROS2.0 (codenamed Ardent Apalone) is published in 2017.

The operating architecture of ROS1.0 is a kind of processing architecture that uses ROS communication module to realize the loose coupling of P2P (point-to-point) network connection between modules. It performs several types of communication, including synchronous RPC communication based on service, asynchronous data flow communication based on topic, and data storage on parameter server by using a point-to-point design. ROS consists of a series of processes, which exist in different hosts and are linked by an end-to-end topology during the running process. Although those software frameworks based on the central server can also realize the advantages of the multi-process and multi-host, in these frameworks, the central server (e.g., master node in ROS1.0) will become the bottleneck of the whole network. Once it fails, the whole system will face problems.

6.1.5.4 *ROS2.0 with DDS supported real-time control*

ROS2.0 increases the support of multi-robot system and improves the network performance in multi-robot communication (e.g., in swarm AGVs/UAVs), eliminates the gap between prototype and product by the ease transition from research to application of robots, and it supports micro-controller (MCU, such as ARM-M4/M7, as well as existing X86- and ARM-based architecture). And its corresponding OS expands from Linux to Windows, Mac and RTOS, even “bare-metal”. ROS2 differs from ROS1 in several aspects, as shown in Fig. 6.25.

ROS2 also adds real-time control support to improve the timeliness of control and the overall performance of the robot. As shown in Fig. 6.25, one of the most important concepts in ROS is the “node” (in the application layer of ROS architecture) based on publish/subscribe model (see pub-sub model in Section 6.1.2), which allows developers to develop low coupling functional modules in parallel and facilitate their reuse. The communication of ROS1 is based on TCPROS/UDPROS while that of ROS2 is based on DDS. DDS is a standard solution for data publish/subscription in a distributed real-time system, which will be explained later. The implementation of the abstract DDS layer is provided in ROS2, so users do not need to pay attention to the suppliers of the underlying DDS.

In the architecture of ROS1, Nodelet and TCPROS/UDPROS are parallel in providing a more optimized data transmission mode for multiple nodes in the same process. The data transmission mode is also

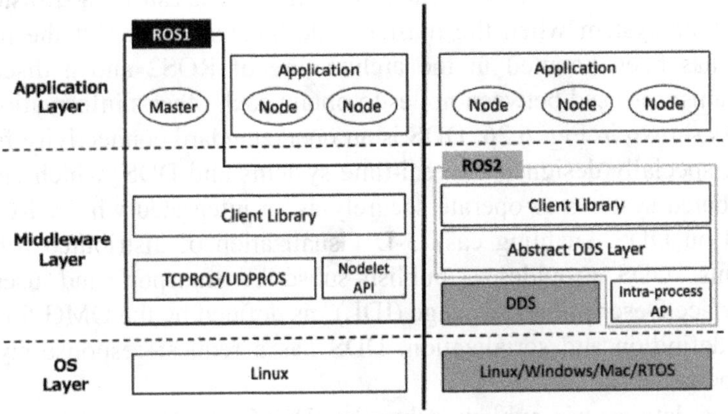

Figure 6.25 ROS1 and ROS2 architecture.

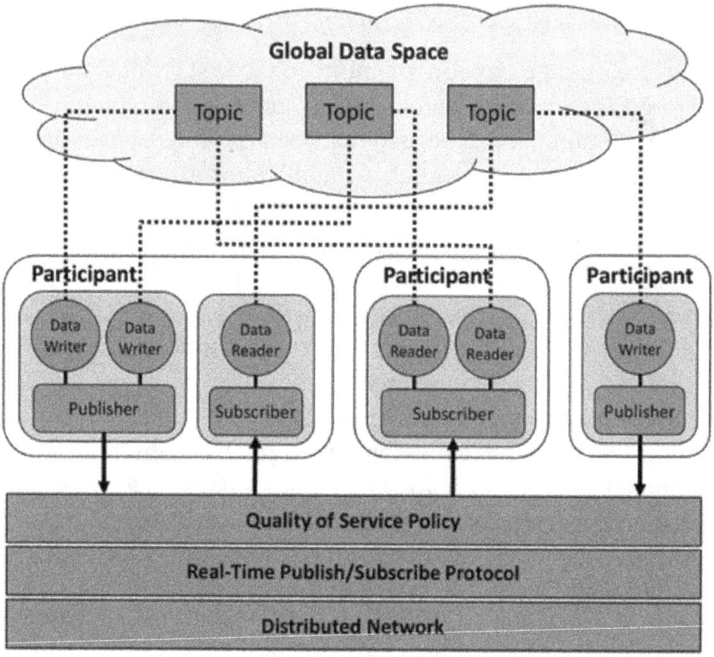

Figure 6.26 ROS2 communication model based on DDS.

reserved in ROS2, but it is called "intra-process", which is independent of DDS.

In the application layer of Fig. 6.25, ROS1 relies on the master node (as the leader node, in the former context), and it can be a disaster for the whole system when the master node breaks down. But the master node has been haunted in the architecture of ROS2 and a discovery mechanism is used between nodes to obtain each other's information.

As shown in Fig. 6.26, DDS is an open-standard connectivity framework, specially designed for real-time systems and DDS, which enables distributed systems to operate securely as an integrated whole. ROS2 is based on DDS, enabling easy 3-D visualization of distributed robotics systems. DDS provides a publish–subscribe transport and uses the "Interface Description Language (IDL)" as defined by the OMG for message definition and serialization. DDS has a request–response style of transport.

The data-centric publish–subscribe (DCPS) model in DDS creates a concept of "global data space", which can be accessed by all independent applications in DDS. Here, every publisher or subscriber is a participant. As shown in Fig. 6.26, each participant can read and write global data space with a defined data type.

The default discovery system provided by DDS, which is required to use DDS's publish–subscribe transport, is a distributed discovery mechanism. This allows any two DDS programs to communicate without the need for a tool like the ROS leader (master). This makes the system more fault tolerant and flexible. It is not required to use the dynamic discovery mechanism however, since multiple DDS vendors provide options for static discovery.

In the ROS2 communication model based on DDS, attributions are defined as follows:

(1) Domain participant: A participant is a container corresponding to a user using DDS. Any DDS user must access the global data space through the participant.
(2) Publisher: The executor of data publishing, which supports the publishing of multiple data types, and can be associated with multiple data writers to publish messages on one or more topics.
(3) Subscriber: The executor of a data subscription supports multiple data types of subscriptions and can be associated with multiple data readers to subscribe to messages of one or more topics.
(4) Data writer: A data writer updates data to the publisher. Each data writer corresponds to a specific topic, and it is similar to a message published in ROS1.
(5) Data reader: Each data reader corresponds to a specific topic, similar to a message subscriber in ROS1.
(6) Topic: This is consistent with the concept of the topic in ROS1 which contains a name and a data structure.
(7) Quality of service (QoS): QoS in ROS2 controls the communication mechanism between all aspects and the underlying layer, mainly from the aspects of time-limit, reliability, persistence, and historical records to meet the data requirements of users for different scenarios.

DDS implementations range from free/open-source to commercial support with enhanced capabilities for performance, security, and safety. Standard bodies in automotive (AUTOSAR), Mil/Aero (FACE), and cross-industry (IIC) have adopted DDS for connectivity in autonomous applications. In short, the robot middleware improves the open ability of "robot development and application". It is the inevitable result of intelligent equipment/device of IoT evolution, along with the continuous assistance of robot middleware which makes the robot technology more accessible through common standards and interfaces.

At present, one development trend of robots is to have a higher level of "intelligence", and the other is to have the ability to access the cloud. The stronger the ability of the robot, the more we should consider the security issues in the application of robots at the beginning of design, such as the event that robots hurt people, and for example, whether people with ulterior motives will "steal" the privacy from robot's mouth. These will be discussed in Chapter 8.

6.1.6 *Security of middleware*

6.1.6.1 *Enlightenment from tuple-space middleware*

One of the most important considerations in choosing a technology is security. As for IoT middleware, security needs to be considered in all the functional and non-functional blocks including the user-level application. Context awareness in middleware may disclose personal information (e.g., the location of an object or a person), or private enterprise, etc. Like security, every block of middleware, which uses personal information, needs to preserve the owner's privacy.

Taking tuple-space middleware analysis as an example, user ID and its associated location message (e.g., GPS message block with IDs in Fig. 6.27) can reveal your history of the places you go. But in time-sensitive usages, as shown in Fig. 6.27(a), problems arise such as security features for tuple-space middleware (as the first dimension in Fig. 6.27(b)), vulnerabilities of real-time properties, and assets (as the second dimension in Fig. 6.27(b)), and fault tolerance (e.g., in the M2M communications).

Just for the views of tuple data privacy-protection, tuple messages as a vector of integers can be batching/encoding as plaintext and then the plaintext can be encrypted as ciphertext by the process shown in Fig. 6.28, from one end of a securing tuple-space middleware (such as the tuple data generating on sites/OS side). At the other end of the securing tuple-space middleware, the tuple messages are decrypted by reversing the process shown in Fig. 6.28.

Furthermore, a privacy-preserving ML algorithm is built by Lou *et al.* on the operations including the usage of homomorphic encryption (HE) in

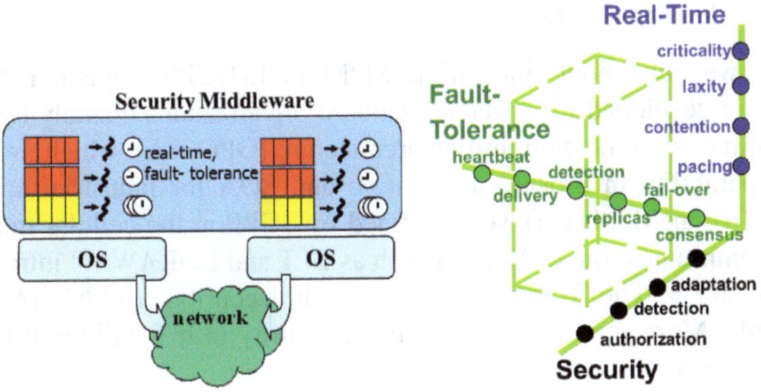

(a) (b)

Figure 6.27 Security features for tuple-space middleware, distributed real-time embedded systems (e.g., SCADA), and for securing mobile ad hoc systems and open platforms (e.g., OPC-UA). (a) A secure middleware in distributed real-time embedded systems or SCADA (e.g., securing mobile ad hoc systems in M2M) and (b) security features for tuple-space middleware (e.g., security in a real-time setting).

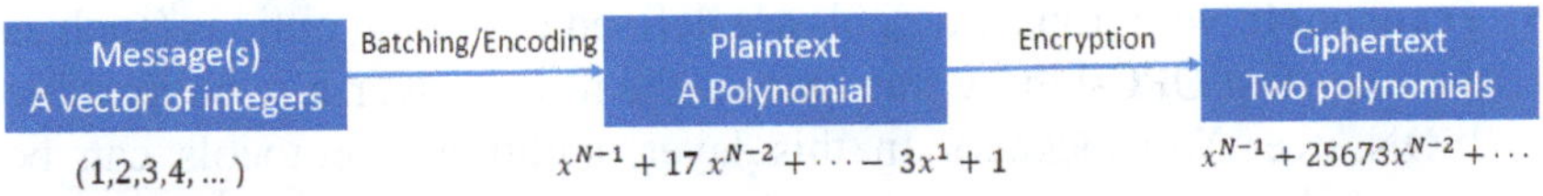

Figure 6.28 Tuple messages as a vector of integers are batching and encrypting into ciphertext.

these privacy-preserving HE operations. They promote these operations to the easy facility (algorithms deployment) to the cloud/edge computing by machine learning-as-a-service. At the same time, securing middleware (special for tuple space and ML on the edge can be generalized in the securing) as a service is drawing more attention in the research of security in IoT.

Accordingly, security as a service on the edge (of IoT grid) is presented by the author in his recent book and will be introduced in the last chapter of this book, by the security discussion of cloud/edge where the homomorphic encryption and multi-party computation (MPC) are introduced in detail.

However, almost all the examples of tuple-space middleware introduced above do not have an in-built security mechanism. But the question leads the author to unpack the security dimension to an open vision — such as security in OPC-UA.

6.1.6.2 *Security in OPC-UA*

When we talk about (industrial) M2M in IoT/CPS, several architectures are developed by different standard organizations, namely (i) open platform communication unified architecture (OPC-UA), which provides interoperability in process automation and SOA for industrial applications, (ii) oneM2M, (iii) MTC defined by 3GPP in the cellular machine type communication, (iv) others such as BLT and LORAWAN introduced in Chapter 5. The following part takes the security in OPC-UA as an example. More generalized opinions of security in IoT will be discussed in Chapter 8.

OPC-UA does not only offer the common ICT mechanisms for authentication, signing/auditing, and encrypted access/encryption but considers the security from an "external" point of view, such as the data accessing and service to or from machines/devices in the cloud or edge. OPC-UA is firewall-friendly while addressing security concerns by providing a suite of controls, as follows:

- **Transport:** Numerous protocols are defined providing options (such as the ultra-fast OPC-binary transport or the more universally compatible JSON over Websockets). In this layer, additional protocols can be extended easily.

  For example, compared with other pure IoT data protocols, OPC-UA is independent of physical transmission medium and transport protocol. As for equipment or machine manufacturers, providing data and services in a secure way needs their consideration.
- **Session encryption:** Messages are transmitted securely at various encryption levels.
- **Message signing:** With message signing, the recipient can verify the origin and integrity of received messages.
- **Sequenced packets:** Exposure to message replay attacks is eliminated with sequencing.
- **Authentication:** Each UA client and server is identified through X509 certificates providing control over which applications and systems are permitted to connect with each other.
- **User control:** Applications can require users to authenticate (login credentials, certificate, web token, etc.) and can further restrict and enhance their capabilities with access rights and address-space "views".
- **Auditing:** Activities by user and/or system are logged providing an access audit trail.

From the views of Microsoft for the vertical application of IoT platform, the importance of OPC-UA in the context of Industry 4.0 and integrated OPC-UA into the Azure Cloud is recognized as the following three points: (1) New OPC-UA servers that support pub-sub functionality can already upload telemetry data directly to the Azure Cloud via JSON/AMQP. (2) A gateway is available for the OPC-UA server with client–server (TCP) channel — in this case, the UA data is converted to UA and forwarded via AMQP. (3) The "Control & Command" return channel can also be configured.

From the views of future smart factories and their intelligence connection by IoT middleware, how to define the adaptive production/flexible manufacturing and their interoperability by means of security M2M standards (which conform to SOCRADES/OPC-UA or TSN/TSC in 5G era) with specific or universal middleware? How to establish a standardized interface independent of the manufacturer in production lines? Some work has been done, such as RAMI4.0, which will be introduced in Section 6.6 on IIoT, but more security questions need further thinking and will be discussed in the last chapter.

6.1.6.3 *Further research*

Although the cyber-physical systems (CPSs)/cyber-physical production systems (CPPSs) are key enablers for industrial and economic growth in the IoE era, security is critical to the operation of IoT and CPS (e.g., systems conformed to OPC-UA). Also, smart factories require autonomic methodologies for security management and self-healing.

In CPSs, malicious attackers can easily modify system measurement data and control input commands to degrade the system performance or even cause irreparable harm. For example, hackers grounded ten LOT Polish Airlines flights at Warsaw's Chopin airport in 2015 by attacking ground computer systems, affecting about 1,400 passengers. What's more, in 2016, the Ukrainian power grid was attacked, where 30 power substations were taken down for six hours, affecting around 80,000 people.

On production sites of CPSS, when the control signal is sent to the actuator through communication networks (by which, a group of sensors deployed by different positions send their messages to a monitoring center to ensure real-time anomaly detection online), it may encounter attacks. An intrusion detection system (IDS) for cyber-attacks is a traditional security method in CPS/CPPS. In addition, false data injection (FDI) attacks in CPSs are discussed with the distributed fusion strategy, which can potentially provide higher accuracy and reliability, as introduced in the above references.

Deterministic dendritic cell algorithm (dDCA), as a bionics technique using the danger theory model of the human immune system (HIS) is introduced by Pinto *et al.* (2020). As opined in the article, when the securing IoT concept is still immature, there increases security-related risks in industrial systems, but CPPSs/CPSs have reached a level of complexity, where the human intervention for operation and control is becoming increasingly difficult, an IDS for OPC-UA based systems is important.

The dDCA approach had evaluated the effectiveness of their research, and a testing data set was generated by implementing and injecting various attacks on an OPC-UA-based CPPS testbed under the dDCA-based danger theory, as shown in Fig. 6.29.

When traditional IDSs are modified and applied to CPS/CPPS intrusion detection, these techniques are limited in the detection of cyberattacks with high accuracy since they usually lack sufficient capabilities to investigate network traffic based on unique proprietary protocols, such as OPC-UA. A CPPS testbed (which conforms to OPC-UA) based on dDCA (including the injection of security threats in the CPPS) is set for measurement (the ability for binary classification), by plotting the true positive rate (TPR) against the false positive rate (FPR) at various

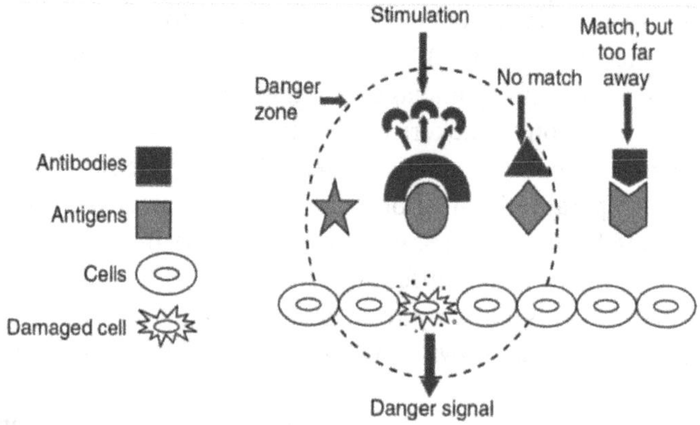

Figure 6.29 Danger theory diagram and the UA attack detection technique based on the dDCA, where the DCA is an abstraction of the danger theory, based on the known functionalities of the biologic dendritic cells of the innate immune system.

Note: The function of dendritic cells, first identified by Steinman & Cohn.

threshold settings when implementing and injecting various attacks on the OPC-UA-based CPPS testbed. The results of their work show that these attacks can be detected by using the dDCA.

As shown in Fig. 6.29, enlightened by the cells collaboration in an organized way to defend danger, we are led to think about how to deploy these mechanics among the grids along with the edge. Maybe it will be called security mechanics of edge grids? Or, is the deployment explained as the collaborative protection to protect from the outer danger? And how to design the mechanics (among grids, after they are organized side by side and joined into a single unit) by using the danger theory model of the HIS, which may be abstracted into an algorithm and which exists under a field of AI called artificial immune systems (AIS)?

When AIS plays the security function of a specific middleware, the protection of the middleware should be considered at the design stage (e.g., the IoT grid preparation of secure/safety service). And the life-cycle support, such as activities/services (testing, maintenance, resilience, updating) also needs to be designed and deployed in the middleware ahead.

Where to detect security vulnerabilities and risk assessments have been discussed under anomaly/outlier detection or abnormal awareness in Chapter 4. But technical and organizational measures have to be in place (refer to Chapter 8). The method of implementing different barriers for security is called defense in depth (including technical and organizational measures). It is a great challenge to protect a critical safety system with completely interconnected systems for the reason that the safety cannot be guaranteed under all circumstances (as there is no 100% safe system).[19] Furthermore, as for an open insight, the security middleware is an interesting point or layer to push and glue all the security issues from all directions (e.g., the upper app. layer and the underlying networks or hardware/software), and at the same time, to solve them probably.

6.2 Primitive IoT and IoT Grids

"Is fragmentation a threat to the success of the Internet of Things?"

---

[19] Sino-German White Paper on Functional Safety for Industrie 4.0 and Intelligent Manufacturing, 2020.

Fragmentation of the IoT becomes a barrier to its role of connecting our daily lives. Conceptually, the IoT has always been "promising" from technology development to product application. Wu Hequan, an academician of the Chinese Academy of Engineering, said that one of the important reasons why the IoT is below expectation is due to "fragmentation", which hinders the effective connection, and even becomes a barrier between the IoT and daily life. In an interview (from May 2016), he said that "fragmentation" may be deemed as the "nature state" of the IoT. "There are many kinds of sensors, including physical, chemical, and biological sensors, and even the same physical sensor shows diversity. It is impossible to have a universal sensor suited to all fields".

6.2.1 *Introduction of primitive IoT and IoT grid*

The increased granularity of distributed IoT modality among loosely/tightly coupled things/physical objects facilitates the need for more adaptability and configurability with a similar view from cells to organisms (a biological view). The former cell is a metaphor for PIoT[20] as a cell, which consists of things, relationships, and services (which are defined as the triple elements of a PIoT); the latter organism is a metaphor for IoT grid, which consists of PIoT. The view not only allows the different granularity of IoT to meet different business demands at different levels but also gives flexibility at the time of design and evaluation of real business benefits.

In a similar way from monolith to micro-service, IoT grid (as shown in Fig. 6.30(a)) can be divided into primitive IoT (as the little water kettles shown in Fig. 6.30(b)). But the service supplying ability in a primitive IoT is tightly associated with physical things (as a metaphor of the "physical gear" — granular services in each kettle). The followed part will discuss the five levels from the very simple things to the high-level IoT grid attributes.

[20] In 2012, the author of this book proposed IoT grids/primitive IoT for the first time in Baidu.com (https://baike.baidu.com/item/%E7%89%A9%E8%81%94%E7%BD%91%E7%BD%91%E6%A0%BC/3695451?fr=aladdin) and in the author's another book-"Internet of things technology and its military applications". Compared with IoT grid, the author prefers primitive IoT to represent the set of IoT elements with minimum granularity.

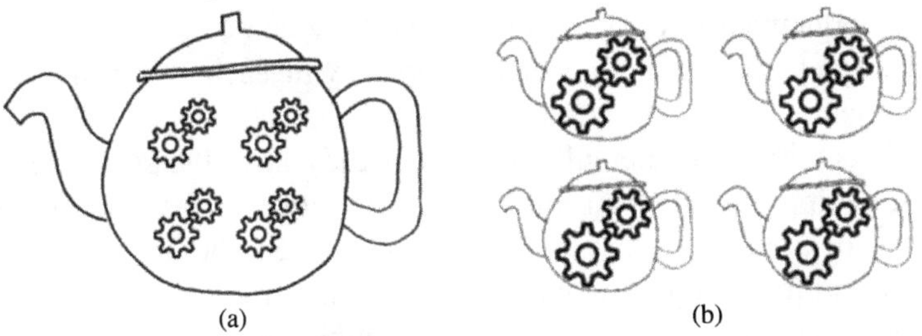

Figure 6.30 IoT grid and primitive IoT. (a) IoT grid (as a big organism) and (b) primitive IoT (as the minimized units of an IoT system, just like cells).

6.2.1.1 *Things in primitive IoT (PIoT)*

(1) Level 1: Fundamental Properties of Things in a PIoT: Some basic properties for things in PIoT are described, but not limited, as follows:

Things with their unique IDs can be physical or virtual ones; things should be environmentally safe/secure, so as to respect the data/information privacy of them or others or people that interact with them, protect their confidential information, and ensure their security.

They can communicate with each other and participate in the information exchange between the real physical world and the digital virtual world. Physically, they can be sensors/actuators/devices or other representations (e.g., gears, even a stone marked with an ID, such as two-dimensional/QR code); virtually, they can bear relations to other physical/virtual things as clients/servers or transmitter/receiver (such as a role of publishing/subscribe, even app. or process piece of a program).[21]

(2) Level 2: Primitive IoT (PIoT) Properties: One "thing" in a PIoT uses the form of service as its interface with other "things" while spreading/registering its characteristics as a server (sometimes also as a client); the "thing" will be in the circumstances of sharing, competition, or collection/collaboration with other "things" for resources, services, and corresponding subject contents (i.e., exchange information through communication). The things can be represented as (or attached with as a

[21]Properties of Things here can also be understood as "assets", which are defined as a fundamental layer of RAMI4.0 (an IoT architecture of Industrial 4.0 that will be introduced later).

sub-functional part) sensors/actuators or service of them as integrity in a PIoT, or organized into IoT grids, so that they can execute certain function, complete certain action, and interact with each other in the same environment.

Things with fundamental attributes already have the speaking potential and equipped with electronic devices/circuit (RFIC as communication component; even SoC, as system on chips) inside (whether used for communication/processing/networking), such as lighting, heating, water supply, and gauge sensor systems, etc. Equipped with potential relations ability (such as communication/networking), they usually can provide services as perception/action and interaction with circumstances[22] under more or less privacy protection. In short, things in a primitive IoT with their services and relations construct a triple element sets as ***PIoT (things, relations, and services)***. A thing can provide multiple *services* with different *relations* through the utilizing of services component (see the following part and Fig. 6.31).

(3) Level 3: Social Alike Attributes: When things in a PIoT can communicate, compute, and share information with others, especially when they can work together and schedule resources across PIoT in order to realize higher-level functions (in a well-organized multi-PIoT system), they create IoT grid, where they can initiate communication, interact independently, and complete missions collaboratively.

Things with "socialized" attribute not only own the first two properties but also have the potential of "intelligence" or already have "intelligence"; IoT grids can actively communicate with the first two kinds of things and manage PIoT/things inside themselves (sometimes by a smart gateway). For example, the networked IoT grid includes palmtop computer/PDA, mobile phone/wearable devices, various environmental sensor systems (humidity, temperature, pressure, contamination, and the WSN containing them), even actuators systems with "hands", as in demanding for manipulation/operation.

In short, normally, they own cyber privacy (data protection against hacking/interruption and sensitivity for cyber threat) and the ability of service, interaction, and management.

The former two properties are more suitable for "things" in primitive IoT, and the third one can be used as the dividing point that separates IoT grid attributes from PIoT:

[22] As so-called integration layer in RAMI4.0.

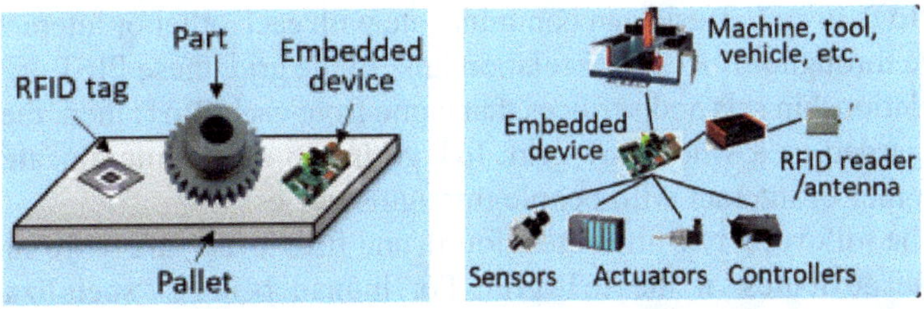

Figure 6.31 The embedded device is an IoT grid that composes of primitive IoT 1 as gear part, PIoT 2 as RFID tag, PIoT 3 as pallet, PIoT 4 as sensor, etc. For details, see Table 6.5.

Table 6.5 IoT grid configuration.

PIoT (thing, relation, service)	Service view from embedded device grid	Meaning
Gear part (gear, on-pallet relation, service as action)	As service component PIoT 1 in the grid	Gear part belongs to the embedded device grid, which sends some action to it. (maybe through another PIoT-controller component)
RFID tag (tag, ID inside for identification, service as information providing)	As service component PIoT 2	Unique code of smart part, with information matrix of the machine list, tool list, and operator list of manufacturing operations
Pallet (itself, physical integration for other component, physical holder)	As service component PIoT 3	Physical part as PIoT of this grid
Sensor (itself, a part of the device, data collection)	As service component PIoT 4	Functional part as PIoT of this grid, with sensing service ability.
Actuator (itself, a part of the device, action)	As service component PIoT 5	Functional part as PIoT of this grid, with actuator service ability.
Controller (itself, regulating each on-board part, controller service)	As service component PIoT 5	Functional part as PIoT of this grid, with controller service.

PIoTs in an IoT grid can communicate with each other or interact with people through services over relation link. In the grid, these PIoT organize the relationship sets and services that come from each PIoT; then, they can be regarded as a whole IoT grid. IoT grids can also communicate with each other or interact with people through services.

The following two attributes (fourth and fifth levels) are more suitable for the attributes of the IoT grid. For human beings, **"socialization"** means extensively that "things" can protect the privacy of the owner/user or from the environment. The provision of standardized "language" across PIoTs and a bunch of service sets in an IoT grid help things break through the limitation of spatial dimension.

(4) Level 4: IoT grid attributions: Things/IoT grid can do many things by themselves and complete tasks automatically. They can understand, adapt to/self-adjust to their environments, and even improve themselves by learning.

From an AI/ML view, these agents (see Chapter 2) of grids may analyze and extract existing patterns from the environment or learn from data, information, and experience of others.

In the long run, they may use their reasoning ability to make decisions, refine knowledge from enriching information selectively, and actively spread/interact with information. In short, they can manage themselves to some degree, obtain resource for the member of PIoT inside them, and act as virtualized agents in the service organization, privacy protection, and compatibility providence, e.g., the distributed advanced metering infrastructure (AMI), SCADA, and WSNs, which are under fully developed conditions. Maybe one day, they can be understood as swarm intelligence.

(5) Level 5: High-Level IoT grid attributes: Similar to the abilities of self-replication, self-motive and full self-management, things of this level can create, manage, and destroy other things. They have advanced intelligence and security protection, which can be understood as strong AI attributes.

6.2.1.2 *Characteristics of IoT grid composed by PIoT*

As for PIoT-upgraded IoT grid, some characteristics, such as intelligence, openness, distribution, and services discovery mechanics (SDM) are analyzed below.

- **Intelligence:** Services in the IoT grid can be found and provided through the relationship sets. Similarly, the upgrading, evolution, and replacement of objects in the grid can also update the relationship sets and services synchronously, which is described as the introspection and intercession capability of the IoT grid, in a self-reflection mechanism. The intelligence of the IoT grid is also reflected in its autonomous ability, which is shown in the following aspects: (1) it can be identified, be searched for and found, and can then provide an interactive interface; (2) it can be self-configured or reconfigured under different conditions; (3) it can adjust itself to achieve optimal performance; (4) it can recover itself; (5) it can protect itself (the security capability of the grid can be understood as the protection of assets); (6) it can understand the internal and external environments of the grid and take corresponding actions (e.g., self-adaptation); (7) the grid runs in an environment as open as possible; (8) it can hide its own complexity from the external environment. In short, a grid is dynamic, autonomous, adaptive, self-learning, autonomous, reflective, reconfigurable, scalable, and evolvable. The grid will evolve from the third level to a higher level (level 4 and level 5).
- **Openness (Different Granularity of Leveled Things from Different PIoT/Grid):** Considering the open architecture of the IoT to maximize the interoperability between different systems and resources, it also brings the corresponding complexity to the application of IoT grid. In a relatively flexible grid environment, defining the elements in an IoT grid as a prototype, abstracting data model, interface, protocol, and binding these into various open technologies (XML, Web services, etc.) to simplify the architecture of the IoT is a good way to reduce the complexity and simplify the whole into parts. It is also necessary to fully consider the universality, independence, and accessibility of IoT grid, so as to expand or evolve to the future IoT architecture (maybe a higher-ranked AI of the IoT modality). The introduction of a physical/virtualized **Grid center** in an IoT grid is also based on this consideration.
- **Distributability and Service Discovery Mechanism:** With the emergence of access methods, such as LPWAN and M2M, the awareness and access in the grid is not only limited to the centralized access for registered services but can be realized by service discovery based on distribution.

Two kinds of services discovery mechanics are taken as examples, one is LBS discovery (e.g., LBS discovery of the IoVs) and the other is relationship-based service discovery, which can be understood by the following instance:

Each IoT grid has only one center, but services are distributed. Take a home grid as an example. When a TV with a remote-control function is bought home by its owner as a member of the family, the TV will register itself with the home grid center and join the home grid. In the registration, it is clear that the main purpose of TV as the "thing" in the home grid is to explain the services that the TV can provide. Then, watching TV or switching off through the remote/local control is the service which belongs to home grid. In addition to the local control, mobile phones, pad, and computers can be selected as the control interface of the home grid. This is because the "objects" in these grids have declared their own functions/services and other attributes to the home grid center when they registered in the "home grid".[23]

Furthermore, when the grid center plays the smart gateway role, by the combination of a service mediator, or an agent running on the gateway as a grid managing PIoT, the relationship-based service discovery can be built. For instance, as a functional prototype, local discovery unit (LDU) enables the dynamic discovery of devices on premise and their coupling with the system integration architecture (SIA) of the system (a use case can be found in Jorge *et al.* (2016).), which has been used in several scenarios as proof of concept for the integration among different devices, both locally and with enterprise systems. When the discovery and interaction are realized in a P2P (peer-to-peer) IoT grid (an example in the second tier of Fig. 6.32), a local LDU service through service mediator/agent on the edge of the grid is implemented in a grid center.

Figure 6.32 gives the user case of IoT grid and a four-tier structure in a special sector. As for event-based interaction between a RFID and reader (product ID via the RFID tag), server1 plays as ID1, and server2 plays as ID2, and so on. Under this circulation, the services component in the second tier from the bottom of Fig. 6.32 plays as distributed readers. And as

---

[23]Take WS (Web Service)-Discovery with WS-Eventing above SOAP as an example, which is just a representation of Grid-based Discovery/register. P2P, LDU, SIA (System Integration Architecture defined by SOCRADES) and naming service scenarios may adapt to the middleware service and as interface to API.

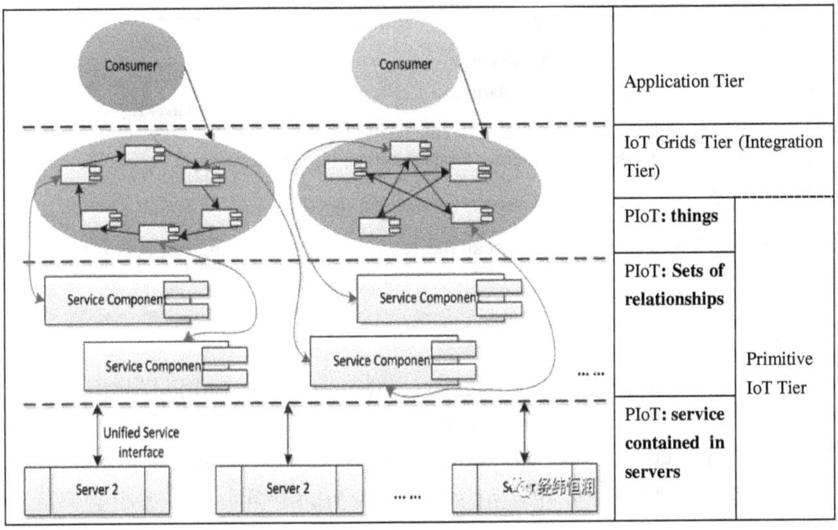

Figure 6.32 Service-oriented primitive IoT and IoT grids (the dotted lines represent the interface between the two adjacent tiers, e.g., the lowest dotted line means the interface between the sets of relationships and server sets).

for the integration between sensor/actuator nodes and anchor/management nodes in WSN/WSAN, the described details also work in the same way.

As for the integration between a programmable logic controller (PLC), a robotic gripper, and SunSPOT wireless sensor nodes are monitored by the SAP manufacturing integration and intelligence software, which is also responsible for the execution of the business logic.

Another server example in Fig. 6.32 can be illustrated as an "order and buy" button (introduced in Chapter 4), an IP-plugged lamp, and a web/can-bus application monitoring the actual node status of a running vehicle or safety analytics.

The localized IoT grid and primitive IoT can meet the remote application requirements through virtualization technology and digital twin (it will be introduced later in this chapter). For example, in the process industry planning of the discrete manufacturing industry, the virtual IoT grid in the system can achieve the consistency of management (the real-time condition of objects) by synchronizing the resource allocation and scheduling with the IoT grid entities.

Things in primitive IoT prototype are shown in Fig. 6.32 as server 1, 2, and 3, which are the simplest modules in granularity as the virtual/physical

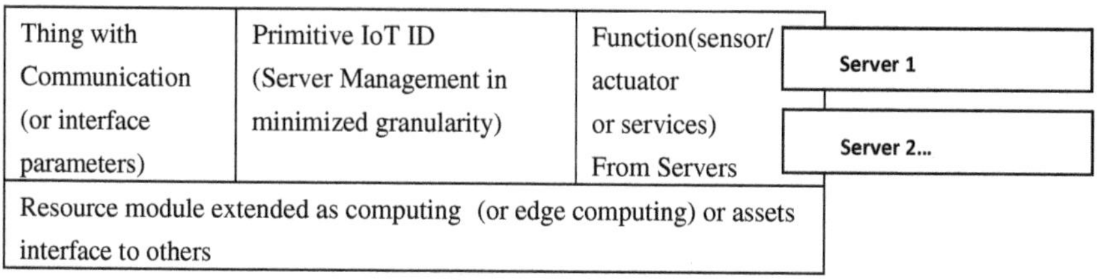

Figure 6.33 Service components bear the relationship from things in primitive IoT to servers.

entities of IoT. In a local IoT user case, they are "assembled" into service grids in the IoT grids tier. From this perspective, a higher-level IoT grid that is composed of IoT grids may be named as IoT zones/domains.[24]

A single primitive IoT as service components is decomposed in Fig. 6.33.

The consumer is in either the application layer (in the four-layer reference architecture) or the platform layer (e.g., for service orchestration). Although these are prototypes and not used productively, the proof of concept paves the way for further consideration towards using such approaches in real-world environments once the exact operational requirements are satisfied. Subsequent follow-up projects, such as the following two use cases, have continued this line of thought and expanded more towards the PIoT/IoT grid utilizing techniques.

The SOA inspired PIoT/IoT grid is the original intention to generalize EPC (see Chapter 4) alike structure (multi-layered, and with middleware, distributed usage, or other characteristics), in order to promote the structuralized PIoT/IoT. From this perspective, we should make every grid structured detailed enough and realize the integration in different granularity through the well-organized relation/communication/network and across grids/sectors/industries.

On the basis of respecting the "property/assets" of IoT grids, we should think about the involved phased development form of the IoT, for example, how to achieve the simultaneous development of IoT industries

[24]Sometimes we need to set up multiple domain controllers or child domain. Controllers in a big network to alleviate the burden of the domain controller, to get high adaptability and the ability of fault tolerance, and there will be an example about vehicle multi-domain in the following parts.

as well as the integration of large-scale systems in a certain specialized industry, and then to the refinement of various sector or grid/domains across industries.

The improved research projects, such as SOCRADES (www.socrades.eu), IMC-AESOP (www.imc-aesop.eu), and Arrowhead, have shed new light on the way that SOAs can be used within automation and integration into production control, automation, and management applications, as mentioned in Section 6.1.

For the consideration of circle-upgrading development, this kind of development is in line with a famous traditional Chinese saying that "longtime separation must be combined in the end, and long-term integration must be divided".

Furthermore, the development of IoT industry standards is being formulated dedicatedly according to the application needs of the industry. If the industry standards are formulated too early and too detailed, the full development of IoT applications in the industry will be bound. Maybe, this is one of the reasons for the question — "Why fragmentation" at the beginning of this section.

If the idea of IoT grid is generalized, only the "rule set" and "interface set" are given to indicate the evolution of individual grid and the communication/relation of grids, and then the "right" of free development for "things" may be gained.

Similarly, if the standard is over-complicated, and beyond the comparison of "interface set" to human language (as a metaphor of the rules in the standard, i.e., a unique language along with its grammar is too dedicated, and wants to cover everything),[25] it is impossible to generalize the use of a common standard or language for all human beings and also impossible to imagine that all countries in the world use the same law.

6.2.1.3 *An evolutionary view of PIoT, IoT grid and beyond*

Considering the complexity/emergency[26] and heterogeneity of modern IoT, a hierarchical analysis is needed from the different levels of things, as PIoT, IoT grid, and IoT zone in an evolutionary view. The

[25] It also works if given a metaphor of human language to the law of a country.

[26] With the author' respect for John. H. Holland, and his book "Emergence: From Chaos to Order" in 1998.

heterogeneous characteristics and diversity of things in the IoT world are described in Table 6.6, which strives to give consolidation of distributed, heterogeneous, and frequently changing information into relatively stable repository items.

From an evolutionary vision, different stages are described in Fig. 6.34.

In the device-centric stage, hardware is getting cheaper, smaller, and networked, and software (e.g., OS, middleware of IoT) is getting smarter, by which diverse high-precision data can flow to enterprises. In the system-centric stage, the software is built by composing collaborative and networked service, distributed cross-layer service mash-ups. Nowadays, we are on the way from the system-centric stage to the higher intelligent IoT Infrastructures stage, where ICT is empowering traditional business relationships and new emerging IoT domain arises.

6.2.2 *Use case: IoT grids in vehicles*

As introduced in Section 6.1, SOA is a software component model that allows services to communicate across different functional units (such as IoT grids and the following case of IoT zones), as well as interfaces of platforms to form applications. In SOA, a service is a self-contained unit of software designed to complete a specific task. The well-defined interfaces among services are in a neutral way and should be independent of the hardware platform, operating system, and programming language that implement the service.

Oriented from SOA, IoT grids aim at services and use EPC information structure for reference, towards the autonomy of themselves, then strive to join each other by splicing up (with a set of interfaces of primitive IoT), and their software architecture conforms to an SOA paradigm.

As the above analysis shows, IoT grids with primitive IoT are not a specific technology or standard; they are a series of directions (or regulations) depicting the service of IoT cells and PIoT policy in constructing or deconstructing an IoT system. From grids into primitive IoT is a top-down method; from primitive IoT to grids, and then to systems[27] (e.g., zones, will be introduced as a use case) is a bottom-up method.

[27]Another example is the systems of systems depending on the grades/levels of granularity.

Table 6.6 The hierarchy in five levels.

Things integration level	Levels included as characteristics	Intelligence	Agent vision	Evolution Stage	Remarks
Things	1	Without	Without	Just things	Fundamental as a cell with ID at least.
Primitive IoT	1,2	Without	Without agent	Primitive	(Thing, relationship, service) as three elements.
IoT grid	1,2,3,	Collaborative intelligence (e.g., at edge computing)	Agent (or a manager of PIoT services)	Device-centric IoT	Grid center as a coordinator/router device/mediator/manager, for management, communication, etc. Additive intelligence at edge will be an option
IoT zone	1,2,3,4,	Networked intelligence at edge computing or fog/cloud	Multi-agent	System-centric IoT	System autonomy
To be upgraded (e.g., by AI/ML, or integrated in the CPS/industry sector)	1,2,3,4,5	In the evolution to higher-level toward distributed intelligence (e.g., swarm intelligence)	Multi-agent Collaboration	Intelligent IoT infrastructures	Important for today, tomorrow, and future; here, taking *Emergence* (a book of John Henry Holland) as an example of swarm-intelligence; another is certain ability, such as crossing IoT industries in a high-level autonomy and collaboration

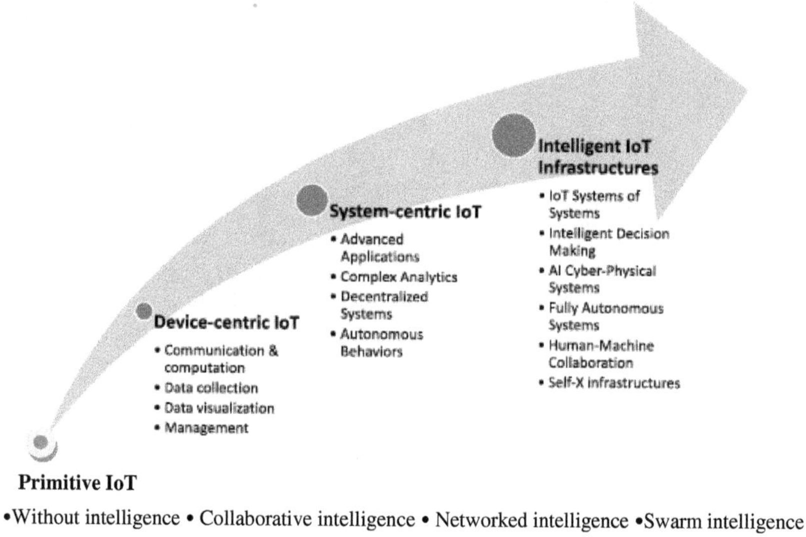

Figure 6.34 Different stages from PIoT, IoT grid/device-centric, IoT zone/system-centric to intelligent IoT infrastructures.

Source: Tsiatsis *et al.* (2018). *Internet of Things Technologies and Applications for a New Age of Intelligence* (2nd edn). Academic Press.

In the three elements group (things, relationship, service) of PIoT, some characteristics shared with SOA are analyzed below.

- **Service:** The core of SOA is to realize the complete separation of service and technology, so as to achieve the reusability of service. The IoT grid also abstracts services as "things" attributes or service capabilities, and things/relationship/service-oriented grids separate services from their hardware platform.
- **Structure:** The main components of SOA involve the following three aspects: service provider corresponds to "things" in IoT grid; service registry (or registry center) corresponds to the IoT grid center/governor/manager; service requester corresponds to ubiquitous resource/service provider internally and externally. Services scheduling across grids can bring more lasting vitality to the business process of enterprises or individuals by SOA industrial services.
- **Intelligence:** The IoT grid can provide services for (remote) users through distributed SOA, and it can make the IoT grid communicate with the same language (protocols) through the Internet/Intranet. This language can be upgraded or evolved, and perhaps has a certain

intelligence, such as self-governance and self-protection. In the future, their integration of device-oriented grids and SOA will show the emergency from a bottom-up view, and may bear or is inherent with an agent of each grid/primitive IoT. So, the following example as IoT grids in vehicles is to describe a flexible/compatible platform towards the next generation of automobile design and production and allow IoT grids combination, upgrade, and extension under the direction, e.g., from IoT grid to IoT zone/domain and the vice versa for granularizing service.

- **Loosely coupled inter-relationship of primitive IoT:** The inter-relationship of primitive IoT in a given IoT grid is loosely coupled. For example, (a) services should be loosely coupled and independent as much as possible; (b) services should be highly cohesive, complete, reusable, and flexible, then a standardized communication service (such as SOC, service-oriented communication) is included; (c) SOA-regulated primitive IoT as cells/units in a given IoT grid, and the well-organized IoT grids form IoT zones, where granular service can reorganize and share resources locally or remotely; (d) service division for the purpose of service reuse and flexible reorganization, namely SORS and service-oriented reuse-shared design; (e) another invisible focus is the software implementation for hosting and adapting SOC and SORS in the service-oriented software (SOS) architecture.

6.2.2.1 *Functions/Hardware-oriented grids and a bottom-up view*

As shown in Fig. 6.35, each sensor/actuator/controller is a primitive IoT unit and dedicated to a set of special services. As for braking sensors or radars, the decision they make is based on the collected data from other sensors, and then they send an instruction to the actuator or other units in the onboard network system (e.g., CAN-BUS). Built-in IoT grid consisting of a group of primitive IoT units not can only provide services onboard/built-in but also can transmit the acquired information to repair shops, automobile factories and big data companies for further analysis.

If one plans to add an additive/extra function into a vehicle, he/she wants the hardware plug & play but it doesn't work without a prior design of primitive IoT/IoT grids according to forecasting modularization in a vehicle. No extra wired/wireless connection, computing, and memory, can meet the requirement without a design in advance.

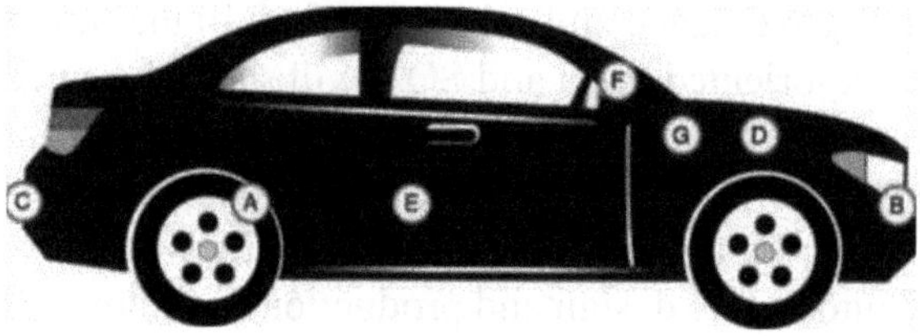

A. Braking sensor
B. Radar
C. Trunk sensor and camera
D. Engine sensor
E. Door sensor
F. ACC control
G. Master controller

Figure 6.35 Multiple PIoT units/small devices connected form an IoT grid and then, with the same bottom-up view, IoT grids unified into an intelligence zone/domain.

Notes: Some of the relatively complex devices contain two or more embedded devices or system on chips as IoT grids or PIoT units, like using some small building blocks to build a large device, which communicates with other similar onboard devices (over SOC). They together "evolve" into an intelligent IoT zone by the grids integrated way.

But the bottom-up view in preliminary IoT grids can alleviate the question or dilemma, as follows:

By sorting and inventory from the endpoints of the vehicle hardware to the center hardware, the same or similar services can be summarized as the function of a specific IoT grid. For example, the sunshine and rainfall sensor can provide information on light intensity and rainfall. In this way, a service of sunshine and rainfall can be abstracted out. As long as the IoT grid hardware is present, the service will be ready (e.g., OTA). After that, we can continue to explore the grid upside, mine the corresponding functions of hardware, and extract or upgrade service from the data provided and the functions designed. Then new services join the existing onboard IoT grids well.

The bottom-up method is a popular service-defined way in the traditional automobile manufacturing industry but not enough nowadays, especially when more intelligence or regular updating are expected for vehicles. This method can only be solved by the anticipated increase in hardware. Some inspiration from Tesla's vehicles E/E architecture may help us to attempt to unlock the dilemma that anticipated software features and service upgrades through the prepared embedded hardware for the vehicle' grids and zones. This requires a decentralized department of hardware and distributed IoT grid design, especially when the software in/between IoT grids of the vehicle E/E architecture needs upgrading frequently. For example, the OTA-ready mode needs the top-down view to analyze the existing and expected services together.

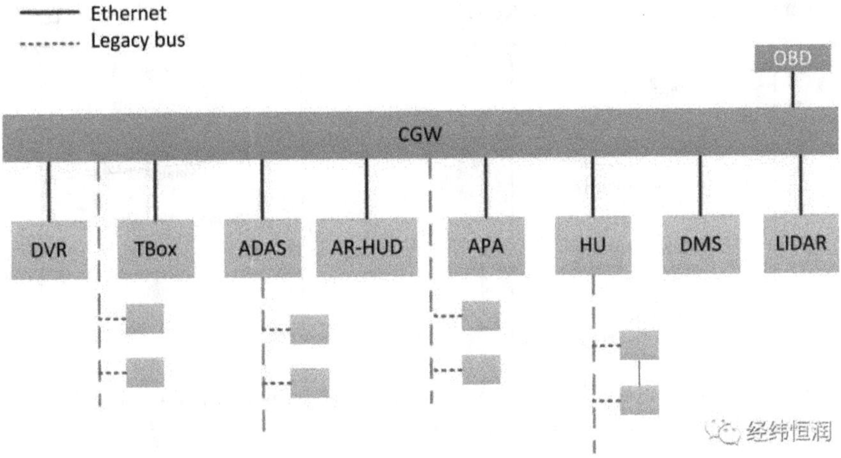

Figure 6.36 E/E architecture of vehicle: From primitive IoT to grid, then to system and systems of systems.

6.2.2.2 *Service-Oriented grids and their top-down views*

With the rapid development of built-in Ethernet, the design idea of SOC in vehicles is facing a shift. A new generation of Ethernet technology has been independently developed in the Chinese automobile industry, such as Singulato. Inc., and some of them have been in mass production and on the market. From the perspective of IoT grids, which focuses on the field of automotive electronics in this section, SOS architecture and the implementation of SOC are introduced with the top-down view. As shown in Fig. 6.36, IoT grids are embodied as driving video recorder (DVR), telematics box (T-box), advanced driving assisting system (ADAS), head up (HU), and so on. Each of them contains a set of primitive IoT and one can play the role of client/server to another. Some of the messages among them are shown in Fig. 6.37. So far as ADAS grid is concerned, it contains a braking sensor, HD-maps, and other primitive IoT (e.g., LBS from GNSS or tracking from TBox).

Service-oriented middleware over IP (SOME/IP) is a series of communication protocols defined by AUTOSAR.[28] Here, SOME/IP is

[28]AUTOSAR — Automotive open system architecture is a development partnership of automobile manufacturers (OEMs), suppliers, and tool vendors and developers for standardized software architecture in automotive control units (ECUs).

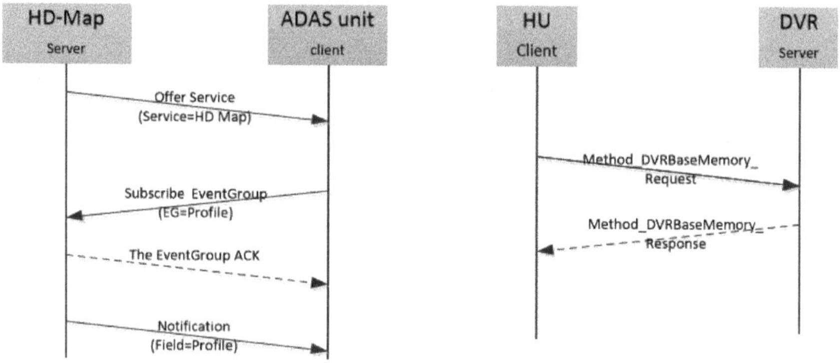

Figure 6.37 Communication from ADAS grid to the primitive IoT of HD-Map, and communication between the two PIoT-DVR and HU.

taken as an example to explain communications in a grid or between grids. DDS and other IoT protocol (e.g., MQTT, AMQP[29]) with persistent publish/subscribe (PPS) service can also undertake the communications realized by SOME/IP, with well-defined QoS and low-latency high-reliable operation guaranteed (e.g., in AOS of Huawei).

SOME/IP absorbs the RPC mechanism and successfully inherits the model of the server–client. SOME/IP service discovery enables clients to flexibly and reliably find the server and subscribe to the service content they are interested in. Clients can use the model of request–response or fire & forget to access the services by the server, and servers can use notification to push the service content that clients have subscribed to. Because Ethernet adopts switch networking mode, the interaction of Ethernet nodes in the topology can be forwarded in layer 2 (OSI/IOS

[29]As introduced in Chapter 5, a common aspect of MQTT, AMQP, and DDS is the adoption of the pub-sub communication model. Compared to DDS, MQTT does not support real-time operation; DDS is focused on supporting timely data distribution among devices (e.g., M2M, robotic things in Section 6.1.5). MQTT and AMPQ rely on TCP/IP sockets, while DDS specifies a reliable real-time pub-sub wire protocol DDS interoperability wire protocol specification (DDS-RTPS) aimed at a UDP/IP stack or other data encapsulations (TCP/IP or direct shared memory inside a node). CoAP can also run over 6LoWPAN. MQTT also enables the bypassing of TCP/IP by using a modified standard called MQTT-SN. This standard supports the direct transport of MQTT-SN messages over 6LoWPAN or ZigBee. Details see Section 7.1.

reference model), and nodes in the network can dynamically establish the relationship between service provision and consumption, independent of other additional mechanisms and components.

As shown in Fig. 6.36, HD-map is a primitive IoT that belongs to the ADAS unit (grid) and publishes the map service, for the ADAS subscription (the real-time pub-sub mode in Section 6.1.5). ADAS unit subscribes to the event group, and HD-Map Server (PIoT) sends the "ACK" back. Then, the server starts to transmit the information (such as lane line data) to the ADAS control unit. Another example is the request and response mechanism between HU and DVR. When HU wants to obtain DVR memory information, the HU client sends a request to the DVR. After receiving the request, the DVR (PIoT) replies to the response according to its current status.

HD map, HU, and DVR are all PIoT, and the shifting of communication roles is based on situations. For example, the HD map changes to a client when it needs to be updated. When DVR needs to publish the video for online analysis or remote diagnosis, DVR becomes a client. ADAS grid contains more PIoT than HD map, braking sensor. Other PIoT of the ADAS grid include the speed control from the PIoT of ACC, balance control, and so on.

The description of the PIoT service interface is shown in Table 6.7. A unified description of the service interface is an important component of cross grid or PIoT communication. In the system design phase, the service interface description should be uniformly designed based on the data types provided in a PIoT, which is given as the example of DVR PIoT in the following table, and it differs from the service role of request–response.

Table 6.7 Example of services decomposed in PIoT communication.

Description	IVI want to get DVR memory size.
Service ID/Method ID	0 × 0101/0 × 0001
Message Type	Response
Payload	Unit16 BaseMemory (unit:GB)
Description	IVI want to get DVR memory size.
Service ID/Method ID	0 × 0101/0 × 0001
Message Type	Request
Payload	void

Besides the group (things description, relation as service ID, and request–response service), further definitions of addressing information and payload are given in Table 6.7, by SOME/IP.

6.2.2.3 *From domain to multi-domain*

The current vehicle E/E architecture (EEA) is mostly in the distributed stage (as shown in Fig. 6.38). All nodes with Ethernet communication capability in the vehicle are hung on the gateway discretely and connected to a single zone with the concept of the central domain controller, central processor, or high-performance computing (HPC) node. There is no problem to realize SOC by way of the centralized zone, but it is difficult to realize SOA because the functions of each node are too scattered.

It is hard to re-arrange abundant resources for the service re-use and consumption of new functions after initial planning. Therefore, it is also difficult to realize the function reconfiguration without appropriate system prerequisites. This is one of the reasons why the next generation of

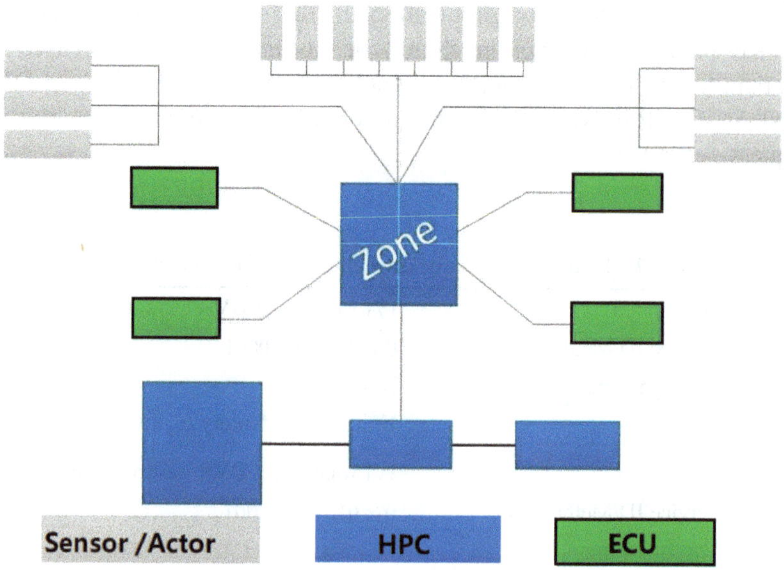

Figure 6.38 From grids to zone, as a cluster of grids/systems integration views.

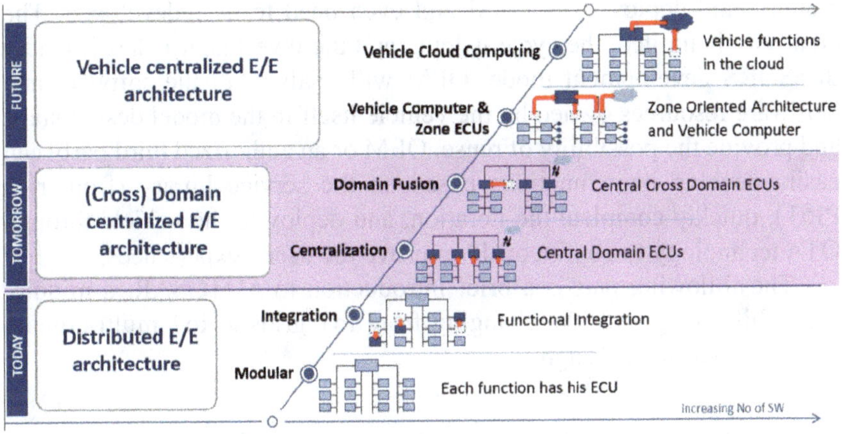

Figure 6.39 Evolution of E/E architecture.

Notes: The top part depicts the distributed Multi-zones E/E architecture of next generation vehicle, and each zone is connected to the zone GW (gateway).

Source: V. Bandur, G. Selim, V. Pantelic and M. Lawford. Making the case for centralized automotive E/E architectures. *IEEE Transactions on Vehicular Technology* 70(2): 1230–1245, Feb. 2021, doi: 10.1109/TVT.2021.3054934.

electronic and electrical architecture (E/E or EEA, e.g., multi-zones, as shown in Fig. 6.39) is on the way, that is, a new architecture is needed to cater to the new development needs. Based on the principle of clustering multi-zones (i.e., logic moving up and service moving down), more implementation logic can be placed in the de-centralized zone nodes with distributed hardware as sensor/actuator and ECUs.

Compared with Fig. 6.38, service-oriented reuse-shared design (SORS) is the extended SOA for the next generation of EEA, as illustrated in the multi-zone EEA in Fig. 6.39, which depicts the aforementioned upgrading view: (1) from PIoT to IoT grids, and integrated by vehicle gateways; (2) from IoT grids to multi-domain, but in a single zone; (3) from multi-domain to multi-zone, with the integrated by zone gateways (as the second part of the top future level shown in Fig. 6.39).

As shown in Fig. 6.39, each zone will be connected to the backbone through different classes, and the top class 3 is zone gateways. The backbone includes HPC or vehicle computer as a whole.

The design of SORS followed the direction of PIoT to IoT grids in service reuse and shared design and has a great influence on the new functions. In the traditional development mode, new functions can only be planned and deployed by OEM and even need to be redeveloped. The creativity is limited, the cycle is long, and the investment is large. Under the SORS development mode, OEM will analyze all the software and hardware resources owned by the vehicle itself in the model design stage and provide the possibility of reuse. OEM or an authorized third party can easily develop new functions based on the service library (from rich PIoT), quickly complete the iteration, and deploy to the vehicle through OTA technology to continuously improve the users' experiences.

The following part is a brief introduction to AUTOSAR, a middleware shift along with the changing from IoT grids to IoT multi-domain in-vehicle software design.

6.2.2.4 *AUTOSAR software architecture in grid view*

A significant amount of computing power is required to activate an autonomous vehicle. Recent advances in GPU technology, such as NVIDIA's DRIVE PX and Xavier series AI platform, designed specifically to enable AI/deep learning from built-in cameras, combined with continued improvements to EEA and the electronic control units (ECUs, of which there are almost hundreds per vehicle) and improved communications, such as automotive Ethernet mentioned above and AUTOSAR (see Fig. 6.40). Huawei's built-in designed platform series is also partly based on the same requirement of computing power and networking inside a vehicle, which includes MDC300, MDC600, and MDC700 series.

The communications platform as a middleware as AUTOSAR was improved by SOS architecture, and the AUTOSAR Adaptive Platform (AP) emerging these years after the classic AUTOSAR shown in Fig. 6.40.

The AUTOSAR architecture uses a layered architecture that includes application software (ASW), run-time environment (RTE), and basic software (BSW). To decouple hardware from application software and RTE, it is sub-divided into several layers. The BSW is further subdivided into an inter-service layer, ECU abstraction layer, and MCAL, as shown in Fig. 6.40.

The grid example of AUTOSAR ARA (in Fig. 6.41) embodies the idea of service-based architecture: the running environment (ARA) is divided into PIoT with different services — each primitive IoT as a virtual service unit to support the whole ARA (the platform service integration as

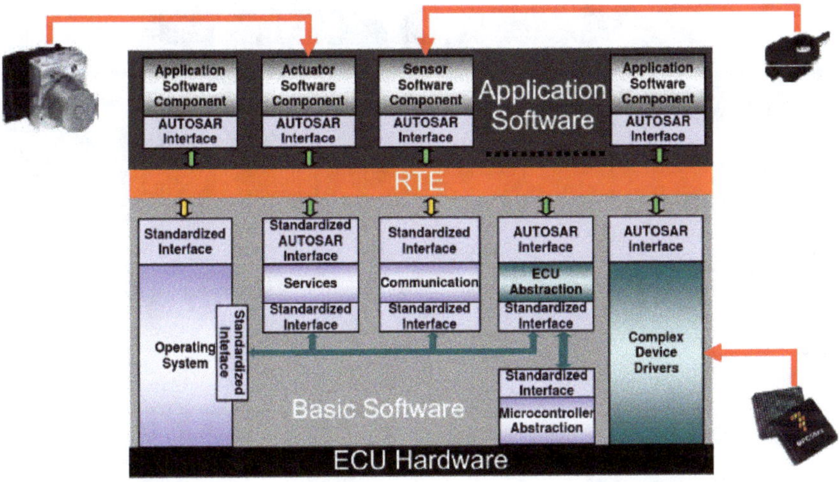

Figure 6.40 Classic AUTOSAR as a middleware of the ECU hardware and application software.

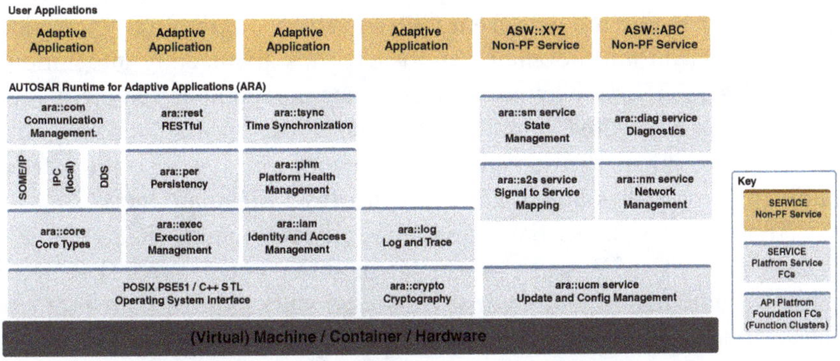

Figure 6.41 AUTOSAR adaptive platform in a grid view.

AP foundation), above which user application (the top grids as user application of Fig. 6.41) can be developed.

The SORS revolution is coming along with the increasing use of intelligent sensors and actuators in automation proportionally, which increases the need for suitable interfaces to either interact with or provide the means or participate alongside a common interface. Without appropriate system

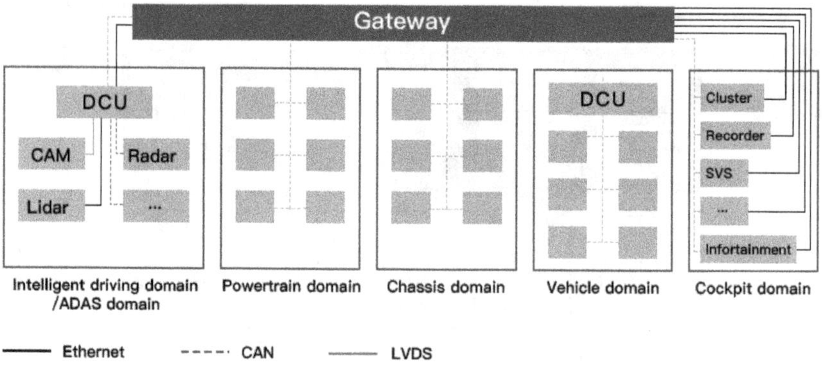

Figure 6.42 Built-in network system of Ethernet and CAN in multi-domains view of iS6 of Singulato Inc. (www.singulato.com).

prerequisites (e.g., service/PIoT design and its integration into a grid/domain) and such interfaces, it is not possible to achieve the integration of sensors or actuators in an Ethernet-based network.

The way from embedded computing to adaptive computing platform more or less is like the way from CPS in vehicles to the IoT connecting intelligence with multi-domain (multi-IoT grids architecture integrations in vehicles), so the new terms connecting and autonomous vehicle (CAV) or intelligent connected vehicle (ICV) were made during the past years, especially in China. The transitional built-in network system is introduced in Fig. 6.42 (a multi-domain EEA example from Singulato Inc.).

Another example is from an research and development (R&D) project of the University of Wismar, in which a modified open-source BACnet™ (building automation and control networks) stack is used as a protocol stack for device-to-device communication between sensors and actuators. As hardware, Mbed OS-compatible ARM cortex-M-based micro-controllers are used. The target is device-to-device communication for virtually any sensors or actuators. Therefore, the primary tasks of devices utilizing a modified embedded BACnet stack are the extension or provision of Ethernet communication abilities via BACnet/IP. The flexibility of BACnet to project virtually any source of information as a group of standardized objects and services allows integrating a wide range of individual devices into Ethernet networks via a common interface. Combining an established Ethernet network for multi-device communication and protocol with an RTOS provides all necessary means for a built-in interface for the integration of "PIoT" as each onboard device/service into Ethernet-based IP networks via BACnet/IP.

The Ethernet-based multi-device/domain methods facilitate the development of ADAS (L1/L2/L3 included), whose markets occupation rate as predicted by Strategy Analytics. In China, the penetration of ADAS in passenger cars will rise from about 26% in 2020 to 70% in a long run. The EEA of domains/zones will lead to functional changes inside and 5G IoVs (e.g., NR V2X, will be introduced later) will unlock the potential of multi-zone evolution from the outside (e.g., OBU/T-box).

It is clear that the fusion of sensors, actuators, computation, and communication technologies with the evolution of the EEA upgrade revolution can enable any method of transport to become autonomous. That means autonomous vehicles (AVs) are from their inside intelligence technology strategy. But the systems they comprise together with intelligence outside and the connected infrastructures are representatives of not only the intention from on-board CPS Systems to IoVs but also the assistance of network outside, where thousands of autonomous vehicles are continuously interacting with one another, with the outside driving environment, and potentially innumerable cloud/edge-based application servers. Then, how to manage these new systems is a significant challenge. IoV/V2X, edge computing, and 4G/5G-based network is facing a turning point these years, which will be introduced shortly in the coming sections in this chapter.

Finally, different levels of AV as L0–L5, defined by SAE J3016, are listed in Table 6.8 for further discussion.

6.2.3 *A grid view in industry sectors and RAMI 4.0*

The emergence of the IoT with its billions of envisioned devices poses a challenge to the design, management, production, and maintenance of these, which is expected to extend to the vertical value chains as different IoT industries (or sectors) and to the horizontal value chains as layered platform (for interaction), ranging from perception/assets, network/communication, software/data platform, to digital service/application.

The previous section gives an automotive application platform in the IoT grid and PIoT view, especially in EEA design and functional development, and the upgraded software SORS is also discussed and followed by a middleware example of AUTOSAR for software development. It is just one aspect of the IoT industry sectors.

IoT industries are broader than industrial IoT contents. But industrial IoT is more complex from the view of prototype, production, department, maintaining, and upgrade/replacement. Three group elements (things, relationship, server/service) of PIoT, which play as the cell of two-dimension IoT industries value chain or 3-D industrial IoT product view (e.g., the following RAMI4.0), show some kind of permeability.

In Section 6.4 and the relevant IIoT section of this chapter, we will cover more in-depth the IoT reference architecture model for edge computing (RAMEC)[30] of Germany and Industrial Internet Consortium(IIC) reference models and architectures. One reason for this part is that the fragments of most IoT applications are required to be united in certain organizing views, i.e., primitive IoT presented in this section is a minimized service set for reuse, which constructs/composes the IoT grid Layer/tier and further as components of IoT zone. Another reason is that the organized view from IoT grid to IoT zone in the IoT-A and IIC references architectures is reused similarly, in the bottom-up view from primitive IoT to IoT grid. So, concepts from primitive IoT to IoT grid and IoT zone-described can be better understood in a unified view (architecture views, viewpoints, stakeholders, concerns, etc.)

6.2.3.1 *The value chain of two dimensional domain of grids*

The IoT grid is not a standard but a service-oriented regulation exploration or the conceptual model which either links an entity in the physical world to the service it can afford or helps to decompose the application of an IoT sector with a grid vision. The latter includes not only RAMI4.0, but RAMEC (by Fraunhofer FOKUS) in sections of cloud and edge computing and other conceptual model of industry architectures in the section of IIoT & manufacturing.

As shown in Fig. 6.43, if we regard the horizontal X axis of grid coordinates as the services of different industry sectors and regard the vertical Y axis as the layered different platforms, the industry sectors are clustered as example sectors of M2x, B2x, and G2x (machine to everything,

[30]European Edge Computing Consortium (EECC, @https://ecconsortium. eu/) gave the first iteration of the reference architecture model for edge computing (RAMEC) to accelerate the adoption of software-based, interoperable, programmable, secure, and easy to use industrial ICT infrastructures. Meanwhile, the edge computing paradigm was described as an approach to execute certain services closer to devices and thereby supplements centralized cloud computing solutions. Details are provided in Section 6.4.

Table 6.8 Automation level of AV.

Level	L0-No Automation	L1-Driver Assisting	L2-Partial Automation	L3-Conditional Automation	L4-High Automation	L5-Full Automation
SAE		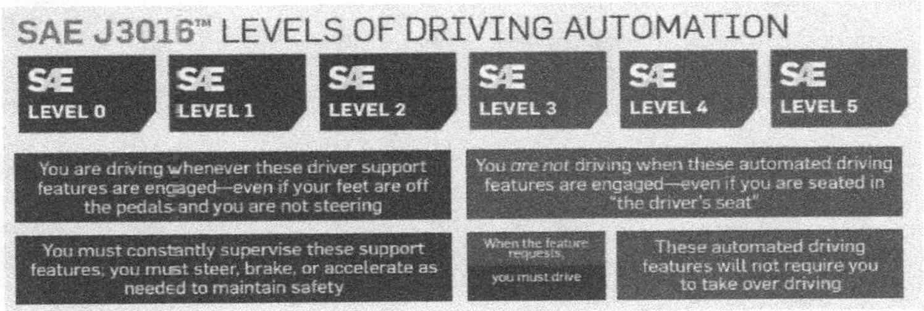				
ADAS Features	FCW (Front Collision Warning); LDW (Lane Departure Warning); TSR (Traffic Sign Recognition); FCTA (Front Crossing Traffic Alert); RCTA (Rear Crossing Traffic Alert); BSD (Blind Spot Detection); LCA (Lane Change Assist); DOW (Doors Opening Warning); RCW (Rear Collision Warning)	ACC (Adaptive Cruise Control); FSRA (Full Speed Range, or ACC Stop & Go); AEB (Automatic Emergency Brake); AEB-C (Automatic Emergency Brake — Cycling AEB); AEB-P (Automatic Emergency Brake — Pedestrian AEB); AEB-V (Automatic Emergency Brake — Vehicle AEB); LKA (Lane Keeping Assist); LKA-LC (LKA — Lane Centering LKA); LKA-LDP (LKA — Lane Departure Prevention LKA); ELK (Emergent Lane Keeping); ISA (Intelligent Speed Adaptation); IHBC (Intelligent High Beam Control)	TJA (Traffic Jam Assist); HWA (Highway Assist); APA(Auto Parking Assist); RPA (Remote Parking Assist)	TJP (Traffic Jam Pilot); HWP (Highway Pilot)	Autonomous Vehicles (AV)	Full Autonomous Vehicles (AV)

Source: SAE.

business to everything, and governments/games to everything, which have been extended to wearable device/service). Along the X axis (as shown in the vertical direction of Fig. 6.43), hyper-connectivity and multi-data value chains in vertical industry sectors, such as business sector, publish sector, and machine sector, are unfolded and extended into the application of agriculture, commerce, smart utilities, intelligent transportation, logistics, etc.

Along the Y axis (architecture axis), the horizontal layered value chain includes the perception and device/product layer, infrastructure, and network layer, data/software platform, and digital service layer.

Each block of the value chain, as shown in Fig. 6.43, is described as IoT domain, which can be decomposed into IoT grids, and can be further decomposed into PIoT if necessary, for their better fitting into the right position of the whole value chain. It is one of the important viewpoints of this section.

The hidden Z axis vertical to the X–Y plane includes sensor as a service, systems of CPS as a service, product/production-as-a-service (a view of RAMI4.0), and so on. From the perspective of product, when IoT grid is applied in the decomposed scenarios with product-as-a-service, the minimum granularity service of a product belongs to its corresponding PIoT. It will be further discussed in the following part.

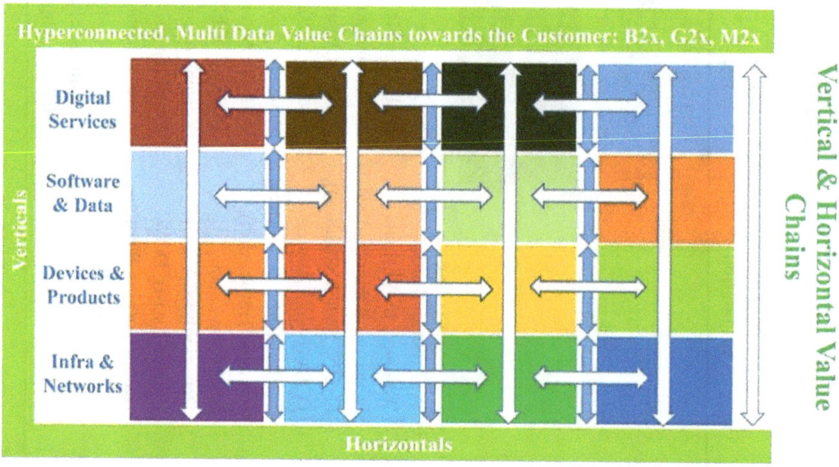

Figure 6.43 Gridded value chains of vertical and horizontal, where the hidden Z axis is to-everything services (e.g., business/games/machine/production-as-a-service).

Notes: The hidden Z axis will be unfolded as product view or product-as-a-service, in the next figure.

6.2.3.2 *A Grid analysis of RAMI4.0 and IMSAs*

Before the introduction of RAMI4.0, assets as the bottom architectural layer are explained here. The objects/devices/things and places represented as physical entities are the same as assets mentioned here, which are explained as "an item or property that is regarded as having a value", according to the Oxford dictionary. A physical entity can potentially contain other physical entities; e.g., a building is made up of several floors, and each floor has several rooms. Similarly, IoT zone/domain is made up of several IoT grids and each of them has several PIoT (e.g., parking grid includes: the car, the destination parking location as a certain goal, how to park the car as the relations of the former two PIoT, and the services linked to problem solving). Therefore, the term asset is more related to the business aspects of IoT than objects/devices/things because in the parking grid, either the car or the parking location has a virtual representation in the software of an IoT system, but each of them and the associated service are digital assets in this business application.

On some occasions, a human user can choose to interact with the physical environment by means of a service or application, or an IoT grid, and the IoT grid is also a user when it needs service from other IoT grids, following the same opinion of IoT grids model as mentioned above. In an IoT sector, similar grids come into a bigger domain, and then the domain fits into a value block in two-dimensional value chains or into the three-dimensional value model below.

As shown in Fig. 6.44, as a service-oriented technical architecture, the RAMI4.0 (Reference Architectural Model Industrie 4.0) was presented in Germany, combining all elements and ICT components in a layer and life cycle model. In RAMI 4.0, the bottom of the six architectural layers (as the layered Y dimension) is deemed as a physical/virtual entity of asset that brings us value on certain occasions, which is also included in the perceptual layer in this book.

In the hierarchy X axis, a smart factory can be abstracted as a pyramid model in which the enterprise stays on the top and is refined down to the control device level.

The Z axis represents the life cycle of each producing-related stage, e.g., the type stage and the instance stage. Along with the hierarchy level dimension (X axis in Fig. 6.44), the product life cycle is taken as an instance in Fig. 6.45.[31]

[31] "RAMI4.0 — a reference framework for digitalization", where Product Life Cycle Value Stream is introduced as the Standardization "IEC62890".

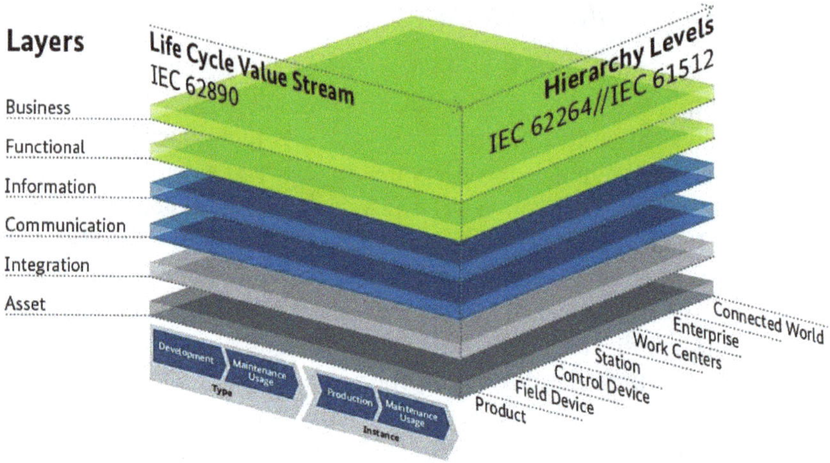

Figure 6.44 RAMI4.0 maps the whole lifecycle and working scope of an industrial product or service along three axes. The X axis shows the attribution from the product, field device to enterprise, and the connection to the world, as a top-level above the enterprise, in the X axis of hierarchy level.

Source: Anna Salari.

As shown in the RAMI 4.0 model, the layered architecture Y axis represents different views of the product or service, such as the business view, functional view, communication view, and the asset view. The production life cycle axis covers the full life cycle of a product/service while taking all participants such as suppliers and integrators into account.

RAMI 4.0 provides a standard framework for tracking details of a product or a service and breaks down complex processes into easy-to-grasp packages. For example, a safety function (including data privacy and IT security) in the hierarchy axis can be mapped to relevant devices. In the architecture axis, the function is described in detail in the functional layer. In order to achieve the required safety goal, different production phases may be involved, e.g., the material quality needs to be defined in the design phase while being guaranteed in the purchase/delivery phase.

In the complex yet necessary 3-D model of RAMI4.0, along with the production lifecycle axis (Z axis) as decomposed in Fig. 6.45, primitive IoT are designed as service prototype and "assembled" into the IoT grid

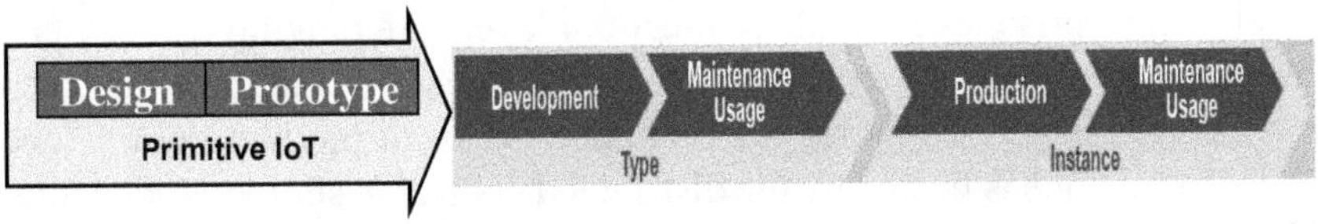

Figure 6.45 The preparing stage as an IoT grid before "type" stage, when "**Product/service-as-a-primitive IoT**" is designed.

usage before the "type" stage, and after their integration/unifying into IoT grids, a "type" is prepared to upgrade to an "instance".

The preparing stage plays the role of fundamentals of each layer (e.g., assets/integrations in perception layers) of IoT and each stage of the product lifecycle in RAMI4.0. From the information view, the virtual "assets" also offer value (e.g., not only the patent or idea but also the program or app./service), and it also needs preparation for the design as PIoT service capability and its logical "location" (i.e., where the requirement of service happens) at a certain IoT grid before its construction plan.

The compromising target (of IoT grids) may not be the described product or service directly but only one feature of it (e.g., intelligence/security/availability/integrity or just an involved control device or control command in the hierarchy axis). For a security example, a comprehensive attack can be achieved within the whole scope of the RAMI model. It may start from a lower level to compromise a higher-level target (e.g., a factory station). In the architecture axis, it comes with its own business purposes, compromises important functions, as well as goes through a specific communication topology. At last, the attack can be deployed at the beginning of the lifecycle and will be only triggered at a given point, as part of an advanced persistent threat (APT).[32]

So, the security service of PIoT in each IoT grid may be deployed one by one along with the hierarchy axis/the architecture layer (e.g., communication layer). Accordingly, the security analysis should not be limited to a single security IoT grid of a certain level or layer of phase (or stage of life cycle) of the RAMI model.

RAMI 4.0 aims at common standards requirements for digitized industrial production with hierarchy axis aspects (from device/equipment

[32] Sino-German White Paper on Functional Safety for Industrie 4.0 and Intelligent Manufacturing, 2020.

level to enterprise level), and architectural layers are ranging from assets/resource integration, inter-connecting/communication, and information to the business layer. The integration/connection from product/field device to control device is hosted by the distributed control in station/work center (or a higher-level IT/IoT systems, such as SCADA or enterprise information system), then the sharing value spreads from distributed work centers to an enterprise level and to the connected world, where they are regulated by IEC62264/IEC61512, including networks and protocols; common rules for cyber-security and data protection, the shared common language (including signs, alphabet, vocabulary, syntax, grammar, semantics, pragmatics, and even culture), and so on.

6.2.3.3 *IoT grids in the leveled IoT view*

In certain cases, the term "thing" interchanges with the word "physical". So, the term physical entity is used instead of the term physical asset/thing in contrast to virtual entity, and sometimes, in (industrial) IoT, physical entity is represented as a sensor/device, and virtual entity is represented as the service it offers. For example, in the following scenario, the assets represent (physical) sensor, field devices, controller, and so on.

The RAMI 4.0 model maps the whole lifecycle and working scope of an industrial product or service along three axes. In the hierarchy level axis of Fig. 6.46, a smart factory can be abstracted as a pyramid model in which the enterprise/company (either local or distributed but its connection to each other or the world in RAMI 4.0 view) stays on the top and is refined down to the distribution or machine controller level, field device level, and so on, as shown in the field device level of Fig. 6.46, where the product/service-as-a PIoT level and IoT grid-as-a-service level overlap on it.

From the Y dimension of RAMI4.0 or the leveled Fig. 6.46, "connecting as a service" is an easy understanding expression, which focuses on the distributed control and information integration through the network.

Below the connection as a service level axis, existing asset/device management considers the operations applicable to various physical assets. When referring to the monitoring of the operations and the control (distributed control or machine level's local control) of their behaviors, in their majority, such operations have been up to now strongly coupled with

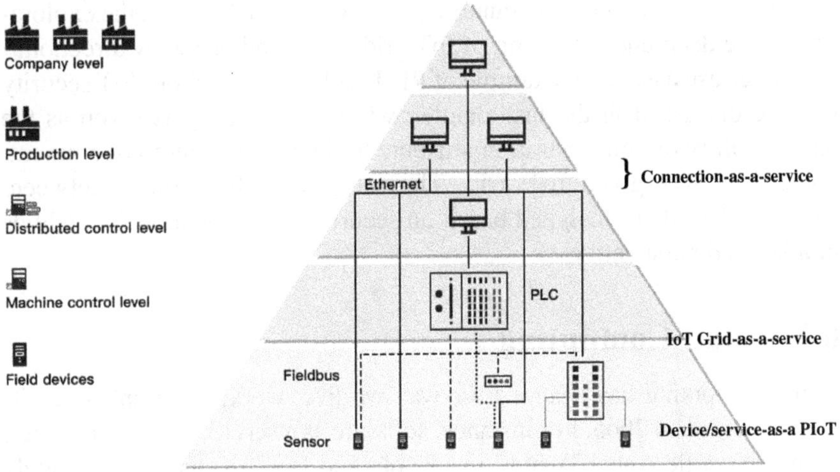

Figure 6.46 Pyramid model with IoT grids.

Notes: Below the distributed control level, the machine grid is described as "**IoT Grid-as-a-service**", which is composed of many "**device/service-as-a PIoT**".

what the devices and underlying systems are capable of, bound with (mostly) proprietary protocols.

In order to give a flex view when facing fragmentation, a flexible combination of IoT grid-as-a-service is presented here, just try to cover the possible spectrum of functionalities which can be de-composed as device/service-as-a-PIoT and improve the current static but strongly coupled proprietary protocols.

However, in the last couple of years, a significant movement has been witnessed towards open protocols, mostly over IP (e.g., HTTP, MQTT, Wi-Fi, and Ethernet), that are slowly finding their way into widespread industrial settings. And open protocols give the grids remote joint/splicing/fusion capability and provides the possibility for the implementation of digital twin technology (e.g., local IoT grid and the remote one are in online synchronization).

But the flexibility and easy splicing up capability below the "connecting as a service" level are still within our expectation, especially in the machine controller level.

If "fragmentation" is the bottleneck of development in the early stage of the IoT era, then how to format the fragments of IoT in a gridded view is something we are now encountering, and what benefits us in the exploration of the deep understanding of IoT grids may lead us a new direction.

Other use case as an example of PIoT and IoT grids about IoT security is to be discussed in the last chapter, where the security is given as the responsibility or administration attribute to the management/government/ownership of a given IoT grid. The relationship/function of/between/among IoT grids is analyzed based on security scenarios/models/methods in a layered perspective.

6.3 Cloud Computing

Cloud computing has changed the way we live, work, and think since its inception around 2005. For instance, software as a service (SaaS) instances, such as Google Apps, Twitter, Facebook, and WeChat, have been widely used in our daily lives. Moreover, scalable infrastructures, as well as processing engines developed to support cloud service, are also significantly influencing the mode of business processing and the scope of IoT, for instance, Google File System, MapReduce, Apache Hadoop, Apache Spark, and so on. As the extended concept of cloud computing, fog computing/edge computing[33] are also resources (serving paradigm) that meet our demand according to the request and allocation of scenarios where the fresh data-process and fresh outcome as feedback are necessary.

Since IoT was first introduced for supply chain management, the concept of "making a computer sense information without the aid of human intervention" had been widely adapted to other fields such as healthcare, home, environment, and transports since about 1999. Now with IoT, we will arrive in the post-cloud era, where there will be a large quality of data generated by things that are immersed in our daily life, and a lot of applications will also be deployed at the edge to consume these data for industry, society, and individuals.

More and more IoT-created data will be stored, processed, analyzed, and acted upon close to, or at the edge of, the network. Some IoT applications might require a very short response time, some might involve private data, and some might produce a large quantity of data which could be a heavy load for networks. Cloud computing is not efficient enough to support these applications. With the push from cloud services and pull from IoT, the edge of the network is changing from a data consumer to both a

[33]Edge computing will be discussed in the next section in detail.

data producer and a data consumer. Here, in order to contribute to the concept of edge computing, the analysis of why we need edge computing and the definition is given, then a vision of edge computing is discussed in the next section.

Several case studies like smart home and building as well as collaborative cloud or edge are introduced in this section and the next to further explain edge computing in a detailed manner. The remaining parts of this section are organized as follows. Section 6.3.1 discusses the need for cloud computing as well as gives its definition. In Section 6.3.2, we show some case studies about cloud computing, and in Section 6.3.3, a collaborative cloud platform as IMC-AESOP is introduced.

6.3.1 *Cloud paradigm*

Cloud computing is one of the greatest aspects of the evolution of ICT for IoT as it allows virtualized and independent execution environments for multiple applications to reside in isolation on the same hardware platform, in large data centers and distributed infrastructures. Covers the main features of the technology. The National Institute of Standard and Technologies (NIST) gives the definition that cloud computing is a model for enabling convenient, on-demand network access to a shared pool of configurable computing resources (e.g., networks, servers, storage, applications, and services) that can be rapidly provisioned and released with minimal management effort or service provider interaction.

Figure 6.47 summarizes the main aspects of cloud, characteristics, the layered architecture, and the standard service models. With different *as a Service* models, the architecture of cloud can be split into several layers: data center (hardware), infrastructure, platform, and application. Each of them can be seen as a service for the layer above and as a consumer for the layer below. Cloud services can be grouped into the following three main categories: **software as a service** (SaaS), **platform as a service** (PaaS), and **infrastructure as a service** (IaaS). SaaS refers to the provisioning of applications running on cloud environments. Applications are typically accessible through a thin client or a web browser. PaaS refers to platform-layer resources (e.g., operating system support, software development frameworks, etc.). IaaS refers to providing processing, storage, and network resources, allowing the consumer to control the operating system, storage, and applications.

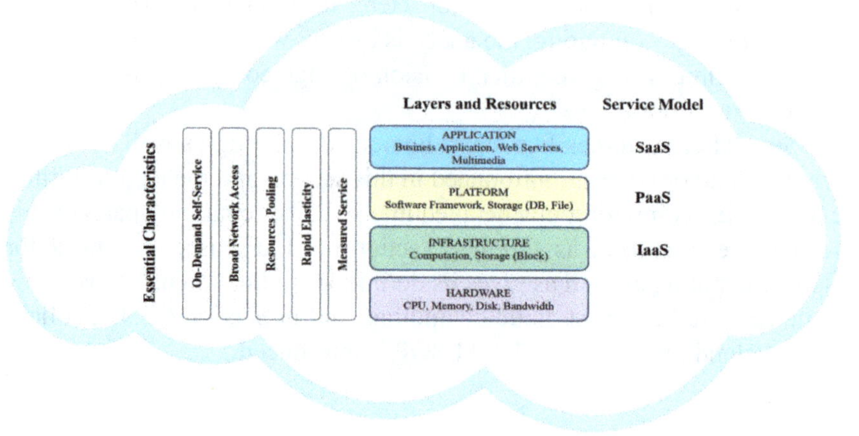

Figure 6.47 Cloud paradigm.

Between the IaaS and PaaS, there may be **container as a service** (CaaS, in Fig. 6.48), where a service resides in an abstract hosting environment known as a container and provides a specific programming metaphor. A service/application container can store and retrieve services as their implement in CaaS, and the service/application running in a container only has access to a subset of the underlying available resources, devices, data, etc. that are needed to run the containerized application.

As shown in Fig. 6.48, **function as a service** (FaaS) is a recent development that is based on the concept of running code in the cloud without the need for provisioning or managing servers. The term "Serverless Computing" is also used for this concept, more or less, as a marketing term.

FaaS is practically targeted to decrease the work of provisioning and server management for the developers, where there is no continuous process on a server that waits for an API, but instead, a specific event triggers the execution of a particular piece of code that implements the desired function. FaaS offers shorter start-up times and the increased ability for an application to scale up or down. For example, in building the backend of an e-commerce case, one can build a service that will have an application with all the necessary functionality from payment processing to shipment tracking. One also can approach the same problem by designing several micro-sized services, such as an authentication/authorization service, a payment service, and an inventory service. By dividing modules in a

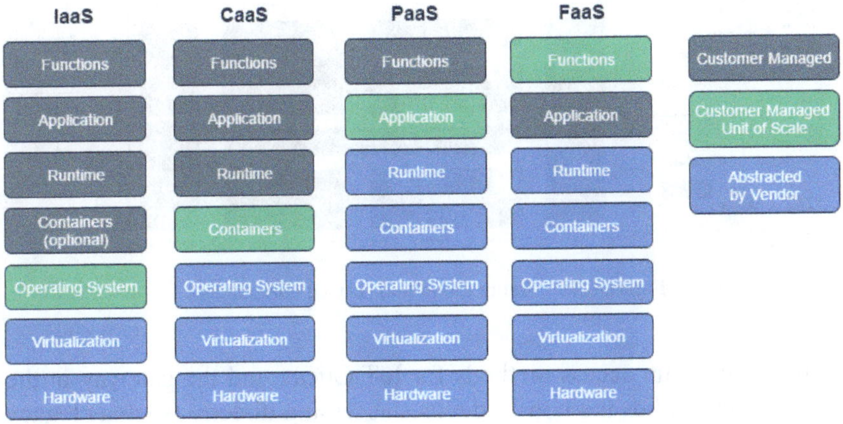

Figure 6.48 Different cloud computing service models.

huge service into separate services, one has the system architecture with independently scalable components running as separate services.

IoT can benefit from the capabilities and resources of the cloud to compensate for its technological constraints (e.g., storage, processing, communication, etc.). Cloud can offer an effective solution for IoT service management and composition as well as for implementing applications and services that exploit the things or the data generated by the things. Cloud can benefit from IoT by extending its usage to deal with physical things in a more distributed and dynamic way and for delivering new services in a well-formed manner.

Cloud computing, along with edge/fog computing, provides an opportunity to unify the real, digital, and virtual worlds. IoT enables the building of very large infrastructures that facilitate the information-driven real-time integration of the physical world, sensing/actuating, processing, analytics, with the digital, cyber, and virtual worlds on a global scale.

In the following part, two examples are described from different aspects, one is Azure cloud, another is Google cloud. Then, collaborative cloud and edge computing are introduced.

6.3.2 *Azure and Google clouds as examples*

As Chapter 5 introduced, in the Azure cloud example, a typical backbone of cloud computing department is shown in Fig. 6.49, where its left part

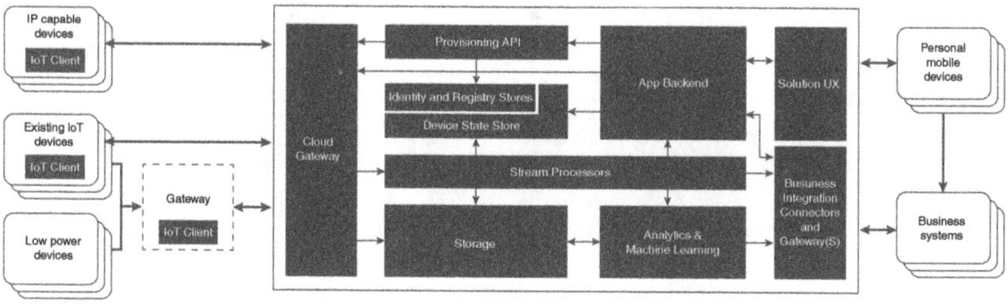

Figure 6.49 Azure cloud and service components.

shows three main access methods for IoT Client, and the gateway in the dashed area applies the non-IP devices accessing directly (such as legacy or some low-power devices and parts of existing IoT client) for an alternative (e.g., devices organized by *ad hoc* or other IoT protocols).

The arrowed line represents the data flow and the IoT clients in the rectangle represent different types of IoT components in IoT device libraries. Take three types as examples here:

Type I. As for IP-capable devices, they send/receive data by AMQPS/MQTT/HTTPS to/from IoT hub of cloud directly.

Type II. Even IP-capable devices or other existing IoT devices, send/receive data by MQTT/HTTPS to/from an IoT protocol gateway, then to/from IoT hub by AMQPS/HTTPS. The IoT protocol gateway plays as an intermediate between the custom and the cloud supplier but as a part of the cloud.

Type III. As for non-IP devices, such as low-power devices, they send/receive data to/from IoT devices with IP-capable or an IoT field gateway locally, where the IoT devices with IP-capable play as an intermediate between non-IP devices and the cloud by AMQPS/HTTPS, or the local IoT field gateway play as an intermediate between non-IP devices and the IoT protocol gateway mentioned in Type II.

IoT solution backend of Azure cloud is unfolded into three main parts. First, event-based device-to-cloud ingestion is an important component of stream processors for real-time analytics, e.g., cloud-scale telemetry ingestion from sensors, websites, apps, and any streams of data. Second, a reliable cloud-to-device message is another important component because non-continuous or unstable network connections (for example,

GSM or satellite) may cause errors when devices interact with cloud-based services because of intermittent service. The final points are the per-device authentication and secure connectivity, as shown in Fig. 6.50. Other components in the Azure example, include the app backbone supporting UX solution for personal mobile device applications and streaming data analytics (included ML) for business integration and business level application.

As shown in Fig. 6.51, another example of deployment is the cloud IoT edge that extends Google cloud's data processing and ML to edge devices (e.g., robotic arms, wind turbines, oil rigs, edge router, etc.), so they can act on the data from their sensors in real time and predict outcomes locally.

Google's cloud IoT edge can run on Android Things or Linux-based operating systems, and it is expected that more edge OS will appear.

As shown in Fig. 6.51, the edge OS is composed of two runtime components, edge IoT core and edge ML, and takes advantage of Google's purpose-built hardware accelerator ASIC chip, edge TPU, which is a purpose-built small-footprint ASIC chip designed to run TensorFlow Lite **machine learning (ML)** models on edge devices.

Besides Google's hardware accelerator, more and more semiconductor companies are providing dedicated micro-controllers and microprocessors with hardware dedicated to accelerating ML (DL, in particular, see Section 4.6) processing coupled with tools for easy mapping of algorithms in those architectures.

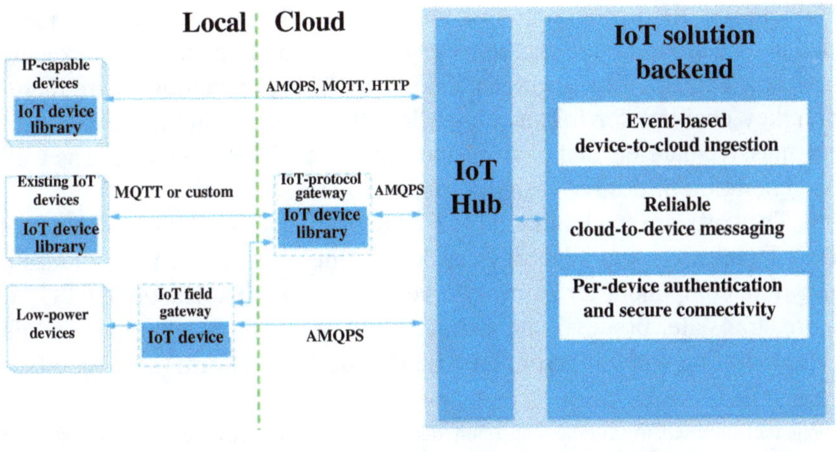

Figure 6.50 Device connection domain and data processing domain in Azure IoT.

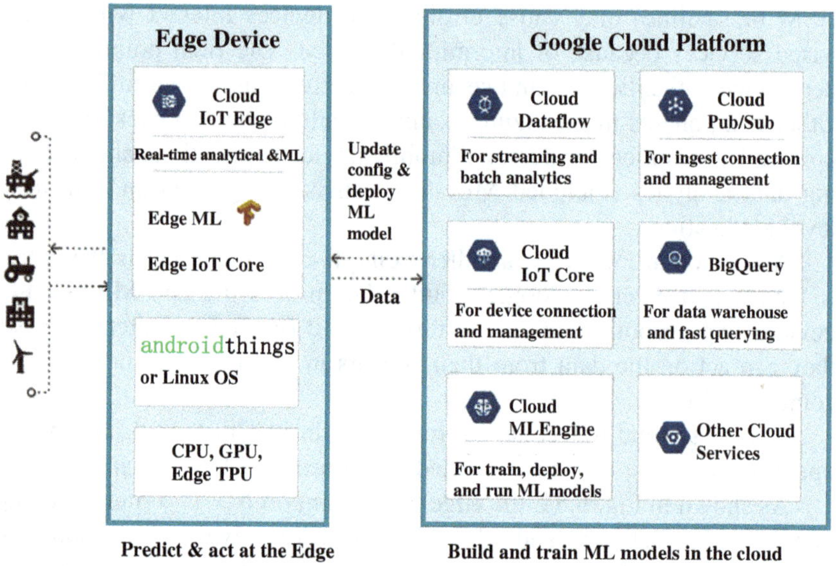

Figure 6.51 Edge with cloud in Google.
Source: Google.

Either the edge of the data center or cloud, it is concerned with ML in the perspective of processing large amounts of data for gathering insights. The use of analytics, ML, and AI in IoT solutions is rapidly gaining momentum.

Dedicated hardware accelerators built on graphics processing units (GPUs) and field-programmable gate arrays (FPGAs) are being embedded in data centers/edge centers/edge devices[34] to more efficiently execute different ML and AI algorithms. Combined, these technologies are therefore key enablers for IoT, as they allow the collation and aggregation of the massive datasets that devices and sensors are likely to produce as well as generation of desired insights and automating operations.

The software stack of cloud IoT edge extends Google's cloud services to IoT gateways and edge devices, where the cloud IoT edge includes a run-time component for gateway-level devices (with at least one CPU) to store, translate, process, and extract intelligence from edge data, while interoperating with the rest of Google's cloud IoT platform (see Fig. 6.51).

[34]The real-time sensing components (cameras and lidars) and hardware accelerator serving for auto-driving are co-located with the roadside RSU, which is an instance of edge devices deployment in smart road/high way.

6.3.3 *Collaborative cloud in industrial IoT sector*

In the post-cloud era, the performance of IoT cannot be evaluated by using a simple mechanism since it depends on components and performance of involving technologies. Moreover, huge amounts of data, network traffic, and heavy reliance on the cloud are the other factors that influence the performance of IoT. Especially in collaborative manufacturing systems (CMS or CM model systems) or collaborative automation of industrial, cloud facilitates resource-sharing, and enables the convergence of IoT and cloud for the users to access the services irrespective of the location by an Internet connection. The convergence of IoT and cloud follows a cloud-based IoT approach or IoT-centric cloud approach, which promotes the collaborative automation (or CMS/CMMS) from the collaboration on sites (such as SCORADES mentioned in Section 6.1.3) to a new stage — collaborative cloud, as IMC-AESOP introduced below.

- **From distributed service bus to service cloud:** The first seeds of the so-called collaborative cloud for distributed service are planted by the DSB approach, which aims at decoupling service consumers from service producers in the industrial process control system. Large-scale distributed systems can benefit from service bus-type middleware architecture (which belongs to SoM of ASMs) as the bus acts as a broker between the numerous service consumers/providers, avoiding a potentially huge number of point-to-point connections.

As shown in Fig. 6.52, the service bus as a middleware is based on a distributed architecture to share information among all middleware instances, i.e., devices and systems of different protocols and handled by an instance of the service bus are exposed through a normalized data model, where this information is shared with the other instances.

The middleware of the service bus (in Fig. 6.52) allows adding protocol connectors and application modules to manage various devices and services, but such management operations are applied through a common abstract layer locally. Allowing a management operation to be routed to the adequate service bus instance handling the targeted device or service on sites becomes inadequate. In order to push the distributed architecture of the service bus from the common abstract interface layer to the remote collaboration which enables the management of large-scale systems in the cloud, the collaborative cloud for distributed point-to-point connections is required.

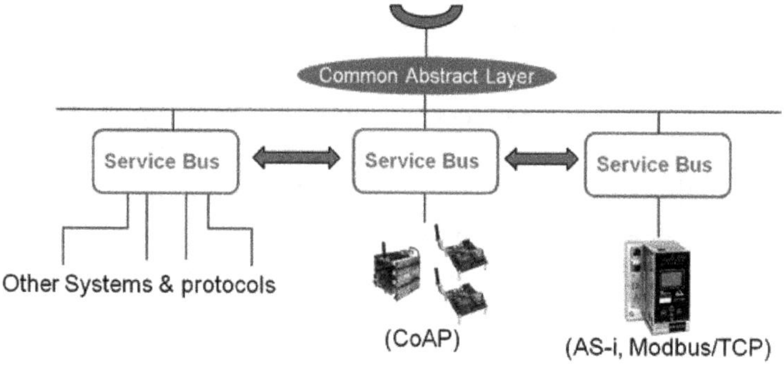

Figure 6.52 Service bus middleware model.

The idea that point-to-point connections should be open (i.e., service bus should immigrate from local to the cloud) has been used in several scenarios as proof of concept for the integration among different devices, both locally and with enterprise systems collaboration in the cloud.

The following examples are not only due to the improvement of collaborative demands but also the post-cloud era utilizing technologies (e.g., Paas/IaaS in SOCRADES, IMC-AESOP in the following part). Examples include the following:

- Integration and collaboration between a PLC, a robotic gripper, and SunSPOT wireless sensor nodes, while these are monitored by the SAP Manufacturing Integration and Intelligence (SAP MII) software, which is also responsible for the execution of the business logic.
- EBM user case as the interaction between a RFID reader (product ID via the RFID tag), a robotic arm (used to demo transportation), a wireless sensor which monitors the usage of an emergency button, an IP-plugged emergency lamp, and a web application monitoring the actual production status and producing analytics.
- Production planning, execution, and monitoring by SAP MII of a test rig controlled by power line communication (PLC, another expansion for PLC is Programmable Logic Controller) and communication over OPC (see Section 6.1.4).
- Passive energy monitoring as the usage of sensors and gateways.

These industrial scenarios are prototypes for collaborative cloud and the proof of improvement paves the way for considerations towards using such approaches in real-world environments once the exact operational requirements are satisfied. Then, subsequent follow-up projects, such as IMC-AESOP, FAR-EDGE (http://www.faredge.eu), Productive4.0 (https://productive40.eu/), Arrowhead, have continued this line of thought and expanded more towards the cloud utilization. Among them, IMC-AESOP will be introduced in the following.

- **Integration PaaS in collaborative SCADA/DCS system:** With the continuous progress promoted by European R&D projects after SOCRADES and advanced cloud technologies and concepts in the industrial automation in around 2010, IMC-AESOP is proposed as an SOA-based approach, which covers different application areas, such as SCADA/DCS.

Functionally, as the collaboration architecture of DSB, some of the services identified in the IMC-AESOP architecture are listed as follows:

- Gateway functionality through a variety of connectors;
- Registry as a central repository for IMC-AESOP services;
- Code/configuration/model repository;
- Event broker for loose-coupling between event producers and consumers;
- Security services and DNS service;
- Historian/logger;
- Time service for time synchronization between IMC-AESOP services;
- Native interface (web services) to higher-level information systems (MES/ERP/CMS).

Cloud-based SCADA/DCS platforms are offered by cloud providers to support developers to build IoT solutions on their clouds. From the platform as a service (PaaS) aspect, the IMC-AESOP platform is described as in Fig. 6.53, where the upper part interfaces to business process/enterprise system and the lower part is shown as DSB abstract interfaces for the layout of the open services in the cloud of things, which are distributed in the real world as device collaboration or cooperation among things/objects.

As mapping from the industrial process environment to a "service cloud", (i.e., devices/services and applications distributed across the different layers of the enterprise expose their characteristics and functionalities), IMC-AESOP service cloud was developed as the follow-up

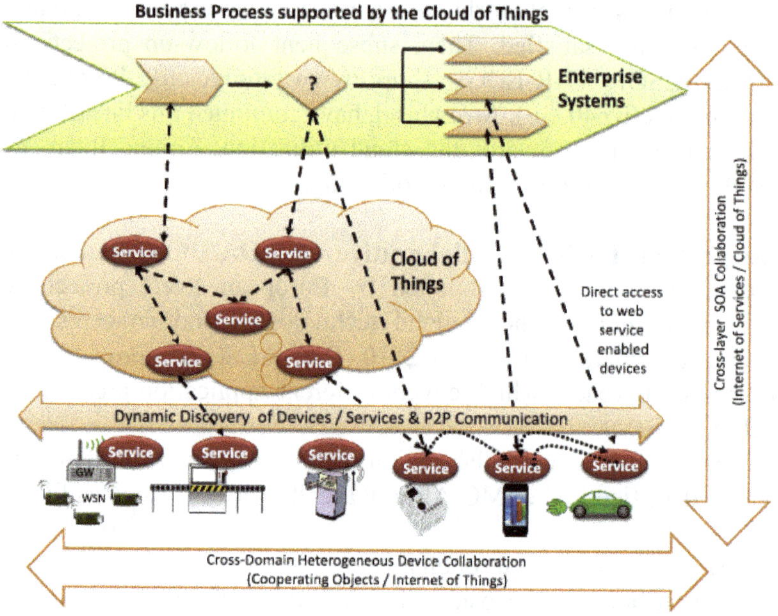

Figure 6.53 A collaborative cloud platform in IMC-AESOP.

industry-driven cloud collaborative approaches (as shown in Fig. 6.53), dealing with visionary approaches bundled around the cloud. Additionally, these devices and systems in Fig. 6.53 are able to access and use those "services" located in the cloud (e.g., supported by a collaborative and distributed middleware/cloud-based OS), then they have the potential to change significant parts of modern factories pertaining to devices, systems, and processes.

- **IMC-AESOP approach: A User Case in CPS:** IMC-AESOP gives a cloud-based collaborative vision with technologies and methods that even take a more key role as they empower the backbone of the approaches under development, such as SOA/SOM, distributed large-scale process monitoring and control system (distributed SCADA/DCS[35] or CPS),

[35]**Supervision Control and Data Acquisition (SCADA)**/distributed control system (DCS) as real industrial use cases of **the IMC-AESOP** that may empower collaborative industrial systems. And it has paved the way from web-service enabled systems to cloud-based industrial cyber-physical systems. As a European research and development project,

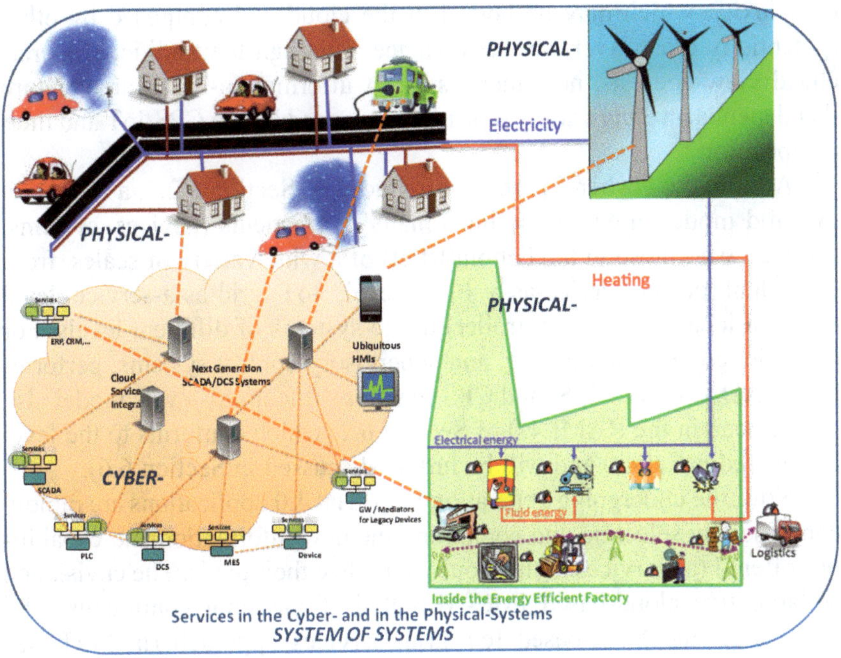

Figure 6.54 IMC-AESOP infrastructure view: A distributed dynamically collaborative cloud for CPS in the energy domain.

industrial automation, and industrial Internet/industrial IoT, where technologies have to be selected and used in an industrial context about integration, real-timeliness, distribution, event-based interaction, service-enablement, etc., are approached from different angles.

From aspects of the collaborative manufacturing cloud, IMC-AESOP is realizable due to the distributed, autonomous/intelligent, proactive, reusable systems, which expose their functionalities, capabilities, and structural characteristics as services located in a "service cloud", (service in the "cyber-" part in Fig. 6.54), which support the applications (such as the "physical-" part related heating, electricity generator, energy, and logistic business for mobile apps together with their monitoring and managements).

In the IaaS, as Fig. 6.54 shows, the functionalities of each system or even device can be offered as one or more services of the varying

---

the IMC-AESOP (http://imc-aesop.org/) is also a part of the Collaborative Project initiative of the European Union's 7th Framework Program.

complexity, which may be hosted in the cloud and composed by other (potentially cross-layer) services. Hence, although the traditional hierarchical view coexists, now there is a flat information-based architecture that depends on a big variety of services exposed by the CPS/IoT and their composition.

Around the "cyber-" part, as introduced in Section 6.2.3, a five-level pyramid model in enterprise links many components (devices, systems, services, e.g., those in the bottom level) of a wide variety of scales, from individual device/service-as-a PIoT level, IoT grid-as-a-service level (under a local machine controller) to the systems of different levels. For example, control, monitoring, and supervisory control systems, performing SCADA, DCS, MES, and CPS functions (the multi-levels model also can be seen in the RAMI 4.0 of Section 6.2, which conforms to the level axis of Industrial 4.0 and will be further discussed in Section 6.6).

Now, the undergoing generation industrial 4.0 applications are rapidly composed by selecting and combining the new information and capabilities offered (as services in the cloud) to realize their goals. The envisioned collaborative cloud-based IMC-AESOP is flourishing continuously by cloud/edge and SOA-based IoT grids/services approach (in PIoT, see Section 6.2), and the IMC-AESOP project vision is carried out by the first set of industry pilot applications. But there are four major challenges that may need to be addressed:

1. Low latency SOA. Determine the real-time limits of bringing SOA inside the high-performance control loops of process monitoring and control (e.g., Is it possible to provide service-oriented solutions targeting the milliseconds level performance range, in a TSN/IEEE802.1 environment and the later-discussed TSC of 5G/6G?)
2. Super-large-scale distributed process control and monitoring system. Is it feasible to dynamically design, deploy, manage, and maintain an open plant/enterprise-wide system, with thousands of devices and systems operating? If so, then which part of the infrastructure should be pushed to the edge? In either way of real-time or large-scale, new challenges are foreseen, i.e., dynamic resource management, orchestration techniques, and dynamically offloading from clients/hosts to the cloud, while overcoming existing individual challenges of cloud and IoT.
3. IoT grid-level collaboration. Every technological design has to focus on making data and components/services easy to use and profitable to every single user in an open and democratic way. This is the reason

why we stick to discuss the problems inherited from PIoT/IoT grid in the former section.

Low-leveled and small-granularity collaboration among IoT grids is a vital requirement of IoT environment, especially when the applications of IoT is decomposed into grids, then into PIoT if the real-time service is necessary (e.g., scheduling and control in the product line). Further discussion arises when the local grid needs real-time linking with its twin grid in the cloud, and they may be named grid twins.

4. Interface to multi-access edge computing and cloud-edge collaboration. Although IMC-AESOP service cloud gives an approach for a distributed dynamically collaborative system (e.g., SCADA/DCS). From aspects of distributed dynamically IoT system, how to design and benefit from a unifying interface to IMC-AESOP or OPC-UA and other SOA-based industrial automation systems, in the mobile edge computing/multi-access edge computing (MEC) and cloud collaboration environment, need more research.

At last, the following section with a case discussion will partly explain how edge computing fits in the cloud/edge collaboration when dealing with the increasing demand for distributed resources (computing, memory and power) in various sizes of service.

6.4 Edge Computing

Compared with the cloud computing model, edge computing/edging can respond to users' needs more quickly, reliably, and save more energy. Starting from saving some deficiency of cloud computing model, the concept and difference between fog computing and edge computing are introduced, then the following part elaborates **two** reference architectures of edge computing, and finally summarizes the challenges faced by it.

6.4.1 *Edge computing and fog computing*

Imagine a day in the future, when each person, wherever he/she is, is linked by an edge software called "IoT edger talk" in his hat/glove/glass/shoe/ring/watch and on-wrist devices or even inside one's hand, just as a smart and virtual assistant (In China, the box-like DUER is a popular AI assistant now) through the pervasive cloud and edge. But the hardware (device or component) cannot be so heavy to feel it anytime; then, where to distribute the weight or computing ability in diverse sites? Smart distribution and its inborn flexibility are on their way to us.

By now, smart gateways oblige the data aggregation, filtering, protocol translation, information processing (re-organized and considering semantic model), and security in home/industrial IoT sectors while the integration of more functions into smart devices/grids and gateways closer to the edge reduces latency. Together with the edge computing (EC) paradigm, they play the promising roles in intelligent IoT by moving intelligence to the edge, local devices can generate value and optimize the processing of information and communication. This allows for protocol consolidation by controlling the various ways devices that can communicate with each other. More edge computing paradigms are emerging, such as transparent computing, fog computing. and mobile edge computing (MEC, by ETSI in 2014, and it has another explanation as multi-access edge computing by ETSI in 2016[36]). MEC emerged in the context of 5G architectures and enables an open RAN as well as being able to host third-party applications and content at the edge of the network.

Almost the same time as EC emerged, fog computing (fogging) appears when things of IoT/IoE need clouding to be closer to them, instead of facing each other across the remote distance of wire/wireless range far away, by providing "closer" resources (such as computing) — just like a traditional Chinese saying goes, "distant water cannot quench present thirst".

Fog computing, as well as edge computing, means that resources of computing, storing, applications, and services are nearby devices that are on the edge of the network rather than almost all in the centralized cloud. Fog or edge computing is an extended concept of cloud computing, which means that data can be stored and processed in the smart gateways or local edge devices. This is because data is increasingly produced at the edge of the networks; therefore, it would be more efficient to process the data at the edge of the network also.

As predicted by the Cisco Internet Business Solutions Group, by 2023, the number of cellular IoT connections is forecast to reach 3.5 billion worldwide. The digitization of assets, equipment, vehicles, and processes in a factory means that the number of connected devices will increase

[36]ETSI Industry Specification Group (ISG) described MEC as Multi-access Edge Computing in the first released specifications (including a "Framework and Reference Architecture") in 2016.

exponentially. Nowadays, the estimated number of connected devices needed in a typical smart factory is 0.5 per square meter.[37] These require a change in IoT digital infrastructures.

6.4.1.1 *From cloud back to the edge of IoT*

"As for the general trend of the world, a long-term division tends to combination, and a long-term combination tends to division".[38] From the developmental history of computer and networks, the computing paradigm has been back and forth between the centralized and distributed computing modes:

Since the 1960s, the computing paradigm shifts in the context of distributed computing from mainframes to client-server models and back to centralized cloud approaches. Then, the distribution of intelligence back to the topological edge of the network followed. As for cloud around IoT, the same steps are shown in Fig. 6.55.

From centralized IoT networks and cloud to the distributed cloud, as shown in Fig. 6.55, the trends of cloud development will include not only the decreasing dependency and load on the network caused by the natural evolution and the enhancement of data privacy and protection but also the collaboration of both cloud with an edge and edge with an edge. The collaboration is shown in the right parts of Fig. 6.55, as a forecast from 2025 and beyond. Nowadays, the edge computing paradigm accelerates the trends, with its contemporary new technologies and enabling application domains. such as 5G, AI, IIoT, or digital twins.

As the edge computing market is estimated to generate a value of up to EUR 19 billion by 2023, the technological approaches and their benefits in the area of edge computing cause more and more interest in order to build an industrial edge-based ecosystem by making infrastructures interoperable, programmable, secure, and easy to use.

Edge computing processes the data of some IoTs devices, such as home appliances and automobiles, through some edge devices with weaker computing power than the cloud but more distributed. Some IoT applications might require a very short response time, some might involve

---

[37] The author cited that average number based on data from different manufacturing sites. In dense areas, the connection density could be up to one connected device per square meter.

[38] From Chinese classical fiction — *The Romance of Three Kingdoms*. Here gives another translation as "The world's great matter gets united after longtime division, and divides after longtime union."

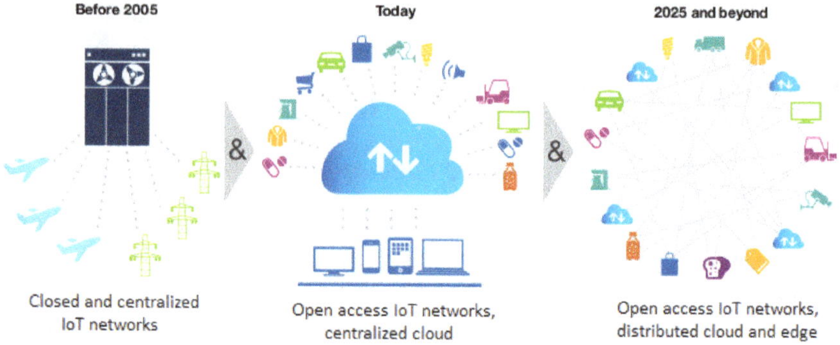

Figure 6.55 IoTs and cloud development.
Source: IBM and Samsung bet on Bitcoin Tech.

private data, and some might produce a large quantity of data which could be a heavy load for networks. Cloud computing is not always efficient enough to support these applications for data processing when the data is produced at the edge of the network. And processing in the local ground intelligent device does not need to be completely sent to the cloud for processing.

In the next part, some reasons are listed to figure out why edge computing is more efficient than cloud computing for some resources and services, followed by a comparing table which gives some understandings of edge computing with its requirement and architecture.

In the scenario of IoT, any natural or virtual object can be assigned an independent address and have the ability to transmit data on the network. These things can create a large amount of data. Edge computing is an effective way to deal with the increasing number of IoT devices and to satisfy the accompanying data processing needs.

In the edge computing environment, a large number of data processing will take place in a router (intelligent gateway or similar local edge devices), without the need for remote transmission. Fog computing extends cloud computing mode to the network edge. Although fog computing and cloud computing use the same resources (network, computing, and storage) and share many of the same mechanisms and properties (virtualization, multi-tenancy of different levels), this extension is meaningful because some fundamental differences lead to the development of fog/edge computing: addressing the applications and services that do not conform to cloud computing mode with/without the local routing mechanics.

For example, when an application requires very low latency, cloud computing releases the user from many implementation details that include the exact location information of computing or storage. This kind of free releasing is optional. When a significant delay is unacceptable (such as in games or video conferences), free release becomes a disadvantage: the service object cannot be quickly and accurately addressed. In addition, some applications and services include the following:

- Geographically distributed applications (sensor networks for pipeline monitoring and environmental monitoring).
- Mobile applications in a fast speed (railway scheduling).
- Large distributed control system (smart grid, intelligent traffic light system).
- LBSs and traffic control on the IoVs.

6.4.1.2 *Edge and cloud/fog computing*

There are also applications in the IoT that affect the user experience because they are sensitive to time delay, location, and context. Cisco's Ginny Nichols gave the term fog computing. The metaphor comes from the fact that fog is a kind of cloud close to the ground, just as fog computing is centralized at the edge of the network. According to Cisco, fog computing extends the edge of cloud computing in terms of geographic distribution and hierarchical structure. From the perspective of the IoT, the purpose of fog computing extension is to serve the computing needs of "things" better. In terms of the demand for cloud computing in the IoT at this stage, fog computing may be the appropriate option. In the IoT platform, the physical functions and resources required by users are integrated and abstracted into resource pools independent of physical location and resources in the cloud, which of course, can expand the ability and nature of computing and enrich the application forms and integration modes of various clouds in the IoT. When IoT applications need timely processing and response, they need "cloud" as a resource provider to be closer to "things". This kind of "cloud" is named "fog". Compared with "cloud", which is composed of server clusters and located in the center, "fog" locates from the edge of the cloud to the edge of end devices, and it is more widely distributed geographically and has a larger range of mobility.

Fog is hence by definition the tier between cloud data centers and smarter end devices, thus at the level of the WAN infrastructure and the

Internet itself, those typically composed of micro-data center, gateway, and edge nodes. From a cellular network view, the edge nodes include routers, switches, and small/macro base stations, which are shown in Fig. 6.56.

Along with fog computing, edge computing is already at the forefront of the demand, where it meets the needs of more computing resources caused by more intelligence. As shown in Fig. 6.56, if data analysis of an edge device or node is processed locally, without sending it to the cloud, we can minimize latency. In this case, all event aggregation must be based on the distributed system deployment of the network (considering the location of IoT devices such as sensors and fog nodes).

In practice, the architecture of fog computing is in some of the known IoTs platforms (MS Azure IoT suite, IBM Watson IoT platform, and ThingWorx IoT platform), and we can see such a structure: a high-performance platform connected to data flow processing through a gateway. Established in 2015, Open Fog Consortium (OFC) is a prominent consortium working on defining an open and interoperable fog computing

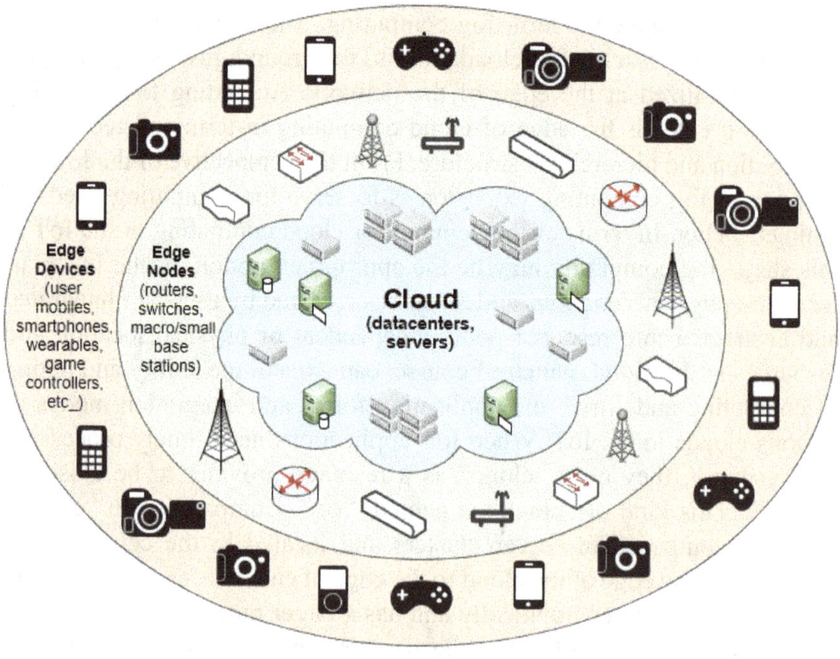

Figure 6.56 From cloud to edge nodes and to edge device in a cellular view.

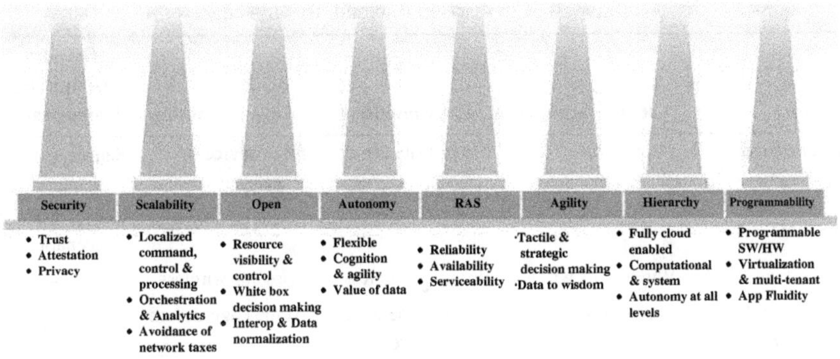

Figure 6.57 Eight pillars in Open Fog RA include security, scalability, open, and so on.

architecture. It gives eight pillars, as shown in Fig. 6.57, in its "Open Fog Reference Architecture for Fog computing" (Open Fog RA). OFC was combined as a part of IIC, Industrial Internet Consortium, in December of 2018.

In Table 6.9, a detailed comparison of cloud, fog, and edge, considering features, benefits, and motivations for why distributed processing is of particular relevance for IoT, is summarized.

6.4.1.3 *What is edge computing*

However, more and more networks of IoT are facing limitations of network bandwidth and the disadvantage of geo-distribution, which are the bottleneck of cloud computing. In the meantime, the transformation from cloud to edge is also promising. According to the forecast released by IDC (an international data company), by 2022, more than 40% of cloud deployment structures will accommodate edge computing. IDC also predicts that by 2025, more than 50% of the data in IoT need to be analyzed, processed, and stored at the edge of the network. Edge computing could have as big an impact on our society as cloud computing.

Edge computing refers to the enabling technologies allowing computation to be performed at the edge of the network, on downstream data on behalf of cloud services and upstream data on behalf of IoT services.

The rationale of edge computing is that computing should happen in the proximity of data sources. For example, a smartphone is the edge between body things and cloud, so the "edge" for the body things belongs

Table 6.9 Comparison of cloud, fog and edge.

Feature	**Cloud computing**	**Fog computing**	**Edge computing**	**On-sites computing demonstration**
Distribution	Data center	Micro Data center	Edge device or gateway	Sensor and actuator (i.e., OT) scenarios
Access	Wireless or wireless	Wired or wireless	Wired or wireless	
Access to the service	Through server	Through the edge/ fog server	At the edge device	
Distribution	Data center of a country and regional/global	Local/Metro	Premise/site/edge device	
Latency	High	Low	Minor	
Benefit. (and number of users)	Scale, cost, efficiency, and power saving. (millions)	Resilience, efficiency, cost reduction, data ingestion, federation. (billions)	Autonomy, safety, performance, cost reduction (number to be defined and restricted by latency and collaboration)	
Location of resources (i.e., processing and storage)	Center	Distributed/Edge	Edge	
IoT work load	Large scale analytics, knowledge, and cognition training	Aggregation, data ingestion	Pre-processing, control loops, programmability	
Control	Centralized	Distributed	On Site/premise	
Mobility	Not supported	Not supported	Supported	
Virtual infrastructure location	Enterprise server, ICT or mobile operator	Enterprise server, or user defined	Without	

to the phone; likewise, a gateway in a smart-home is the edge between home things and cloud, so the "edge" for the home things belongs to the gateway, and a micro data center and a cloudlet is the edge between a mobile device and cloud. Edge computing is interchangeable with fog computing, but the former focuses more on the things itself, while the latter focuses more on the infrastructure side.

From the view of GE (General Electric Company), "edge" refers to the computing infrastructure that exists close to the sources of data, e.g., industrial machines (e.g., wind turbine, magnetic resonance (MR) scanner, undersea blowout preventers), industrial controllers such as SCADA systems, and time-series databases aggregating data from a variety of equipment and sensors. These edge computing devices typically reside away from the centralized computing available in the cloud. As shown in Fig. 6.58, besides industrial machines, there are sensors and controllers in the perception lays of IoT.

In terms of technical architecture, the mutual collaboration between cloud computing and edge computing should be reflected in the superposition of a layer of distributed computing ability on the IoT platform close to "things", just like the human peripheral nerve and central nervous system. In this way, the IoT can acquire and discharge the "resources", i.e., the demand of cloud in time and the edge on time. The cloud computing in the data center and the never (or seldom) delayed sensitive applications

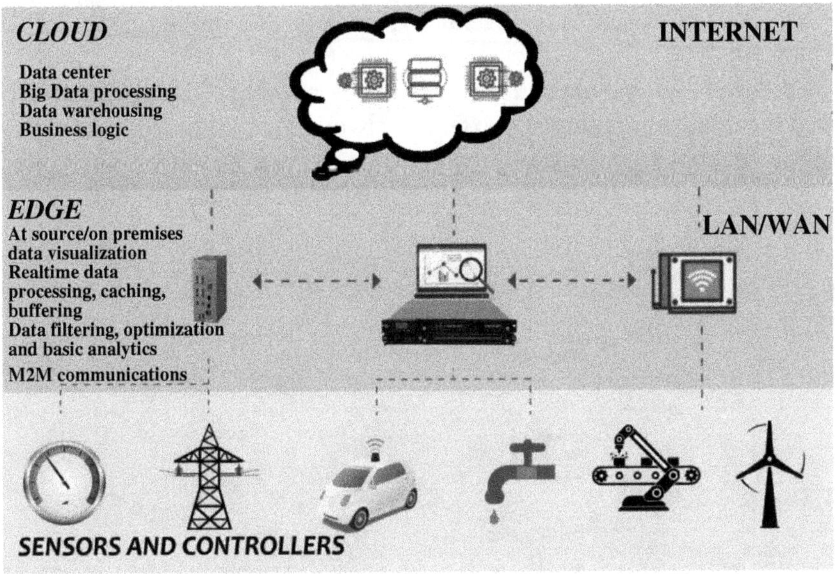

Figure 6.58 "Edge" is defined as any computing and network resources along the path between data sources, such as sensors or controllers, and cloud data centers.

"catching up" of edge computing are also important in the network deployment of IoT applications, in addition to location sensing and low latency, mobility support, and geographical location distribution are also needed. Then, mobile edge computing (MEC) arose.

6.4.2 *Requirement analysis and architecture of edge computing*

From IIRA (see Section 5.9.1) views, as is also stated in the description of the function in the IIRA, "edge analytics" is a better term to describe the function of edge. Edge analytics range in sophistication from simple (e.g., the average value of temperature sensor data in a building) to complex, such as insights involving the application of a model of the diffusion of thermal energy across the rooms in a building floor based on the thermal properties of the physical objects on the floor. It is typically used for the following three purposes: (a) as one function implementing local real-time control, e.g., as low latency in Fig. 6.59; (b) for reducing the amount of data transported to external systems because of financial or efficiency reasons, e.g., as dealing with sensors of high bandwidth; (c) the edge/local security and privacy protection in analytics. In the complexity of IoT protocols, the purposes over several IoT sectors are further discussed in Fig. 6.59.

Edge computing expands the network computing paradigm characterized by cloud computing and extends network computing from the center of the network to the edge of the network, so as to be more widely used in fitting not only geographical distribution application but mobile

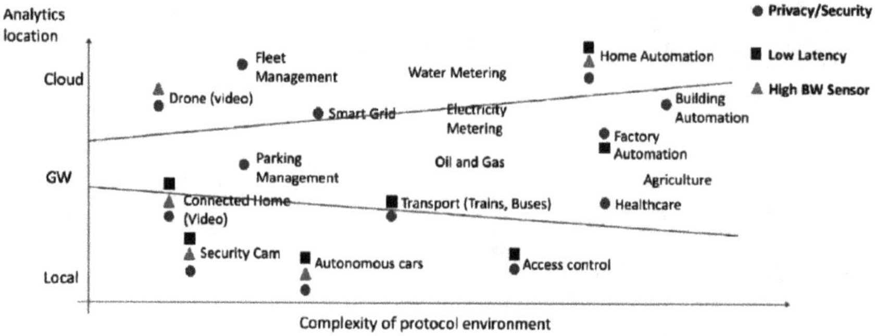

Figure 6.59 The conditions need analytics and local/edge storage the most.

applications and their service types, e.g., the transport and autonomous cars in Fig. 6.59; this is why sometimes it is called mobile edge computing — mobile EC (MEC) can be seen as a cloud service running on the edge of mobile network to perform specific tasks in mobile or cellular networks. For details, see the next section.

6.4.2.1 *Advantages of EC and its requirement for IoT*

Edge computing can provide services of computing, storage, and other resources close to users and edge devices in the IoT sectors, as shown in Fig. 6.60, such as surveillance of SCADA, monitoring utility, vehicle and transportation, and IIoT.

Unlike the cloud, edge computing is an integral part of distribution network infrastructure. The demand for edge computing in the IoT is reflected in the following aspects.

(1) Sensor/actuator data processing needs to be buffered and refined (e.g., data decreased or fitting) by "edge computing" before entering the cloud.

With edge computing, edge devices can process the data from sensors/actuators and filter out the content that needs to be transferred to the data storage unit and database locally for analysis. The distributed architecture of edge computing includes edge nodes and edge intelligent devices (e.g., gateways or edge devices shown in Fig. 6.58). Data

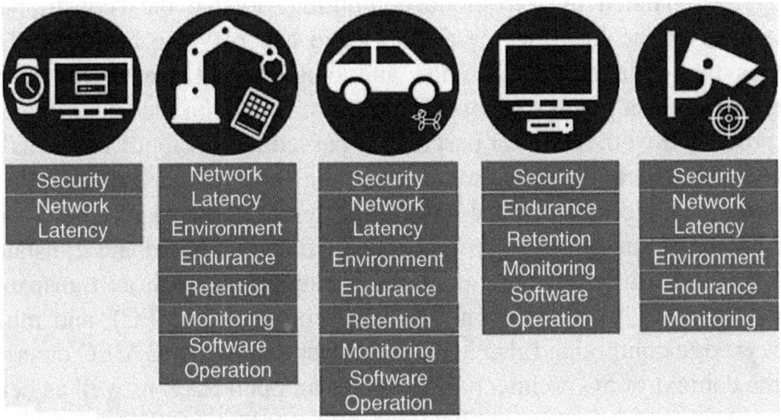

Figure 6.60 Demand from the edge.

collection, computing, and intelligent processing are performed in edge intelligent devices. Then, intelligent processing is embodied in edge nodes that support data sharing, collaborative decision-making (such as intelligence vehicle and multi-agents), data filtering, and give priority to data. Additional functions include service delivery, computing offload, IoT management, data storage and caching. The "smart data" selected at the edge will be decided whether to be transferred to the central "cloud computing" for further processing or not. Edge computing must meet the challenges of response time, latency, endurance, reliability, and security (as shown in Fig. 6.60). Especially, when the rate of data generated by edge devices is much faster than the processing capacity of the cloud (or the communication pipeline), it needs "edge buffering".

(2) The filtered and aggregated data can be divided into what "edge" can do and what "cloud" should do.

Not all data from the terminal device/equipment needs to be processed by cloud computing. Following intelligent processing, such as quality filtering and aggregation analysis of intelligent edge device, the edge data is analyzed with idle computing resources supplied by the near-the-edge node (gateway or other nearest edge node, and another base station nearby is another option in cellular edge or MEC) for processing, which can reduce the amount of data sent to the cloud.

If more functions are integrated to the edge of smart devices and gateways, it will play a better role in reducing latency.

In short, the edge can determine whether the data is processed in "edge" or handed over to cloud computing, so that the "constrained" resources of the local device and its edge can play the best role. This means the collaboration of edge and cloud **to deal with the rapid increasing data generated by IoT devices**. If data on the "edge" cannot be processed well, then it or part of it is passed to the cloud. The collaboration and differentiation between "edge/fog" and "cloud" will need to be summarized and deduced according to different scene requirements, and even some communication protocols need to be integrated and translated. So, there are different edge computing paradigms, such as transparent computing, fog computing, mobile edge computing (MEC), and multi-access edge computing (also MEC). The last paradigm, as MEC emerged in the context of 5G architectures, enables an open RAN as well as being able to host third-party applications and content at the edge of the network.

(3) Edge computing is closer to the need of "things" for data process in their physical location.

When an "edge" service is a part of a wireless network, whether Wi-Fi or cellular, local service can determine the location of each connected device in one "edge grid". This generates a smart home use case and can be extended to LBSs. After all, the edge computing close to the "thing" needs to know where the serving "thing" can cover. For us, it looks safer to see the devices that process our "needs nearby" than far away to the cloud.

In edge computing, the hierarchical processing of data avoids the massive data stacking at the edge. In the low-delay networks or time-sensitive networks (TSN, especially in IIoT scenario), it can achieve rapid data refinement; this mode of information acquisition, hierarchical processing in time, and transmission of synchronization can achieve large-scale data throughput near the "things". This is supporting the development of touch, smell, and taste, towards the future IoT, such as IIoT, TIoT, and IoRT. We had reviewed the "pyramid" process from data and information to knowledge and wisdom in Chapter 2.

6.4.2.2 *Hierarchical IoT with edge computing*

As mentioned above, edge computing is a decentralized computing infrastructure in which data, processing, storage, and applications are distributed in the most logical, efficient place between the data source and the cloud. From the four-stage IoT solution architecture, the generalized edge IT is shown as a platform of services layer in IoT. As shown in Fig. 6.61, where the perception layer of IoT is simple as sensors/actuators in stage 1, there is an "OT" interface between it and things. Then, the network's layers are simple as internet gateways in stage 2.

The four-stage model is represented in Fig. 6.61 with many alternative implementations of hardware and software at each stage, but all of them are subject to the same set of design constraints. In this model, stage 4 represents the data centers and the cloud, stage 3 is organized into small, dispersed data centers representing the essence of edge computing, stage 2 represents the gateway-base processing devices, and stage 1 is represented by the edge physical devices.

The landscape of future computing is evolving, including new computing paradigms such as distributed AI in the IoT. For example, future decentralized and distributed architectures and computing paradigms for IoT/IIoT inspired by neuromorphic computing with hybrid implementations

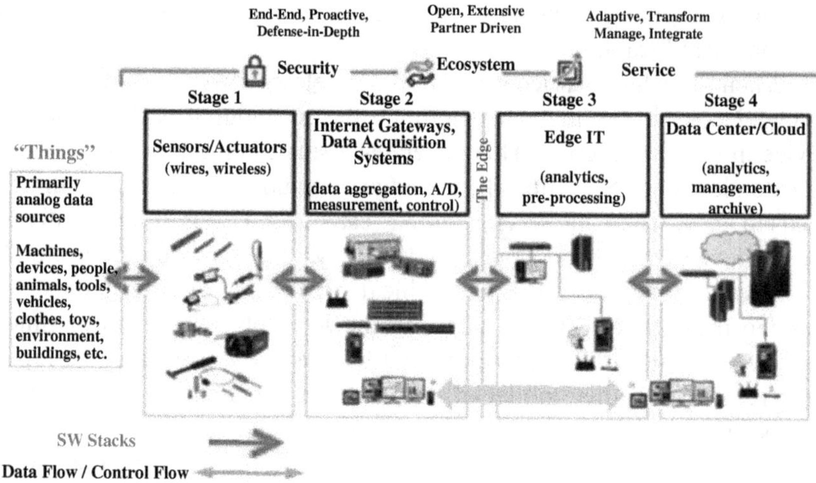

Figure 6.61 Four stages in IoT solution architecture.

based on architectures for neural DL that could provide computing and the structural optimizing in such systems leading the edge–cloud collaboration paradigm.

- Across stage 1 and stage 2, networks, especially the scene of the cellular paradigm, are under transformation to become virtualized through NFV and SDN that separates network control from the infrastructure. This virtualization can be seen in Fig. 6.61 and enables the transformed network to become a release for application workloads in stages 2 and 3, such as distributed IoT applications.

Virtualization technologies applied to data centers and network infrastructure are considered as part of ETSI multi-access edge computing (MEC), and ETSI explained MEC formerly as mobile edge computing in 2015. Either mobile edge computing or multi-access edge computing is deemed as a key part of 5G by ETSI, and MEC is expressed in the following part as either of them, if without specification of the meaning of MEC. ETSI has released a set of specifications on MEC that are publicly available, and some of them will be discussed in the next part.

- From stage 2 to stage 3, here manufacturing industry of cellular mode is taken as an IIoT (industrial IoT) example. The connectivity requirements of the manufacturing industry are matched by the capabilities of cellular networks. To enable smart manufacturing, different network deployment options are depending on the case-by-case needs and the digitization ambitions of the factory. For example, in 4G networks, virtualization and dedicated core networks (DECOR) can be used to map local private networks and virtual networks running within a mobile operator's public network. In 5G network, non-public network (NPN) with dedicated radio base stations and evolved packet core in-a-box (edge box as a gateway is another option[39] for traditional IT operator) can be deployed on the premises to ensure that traffic stays local to the site.

In this case, on-premises cellular network deployment with local data breakout ensures that critical production data do not leave the premises, using QoS mechanisms to fulfill use case requirements and optimize reliability and latency. Critical applications can be executed locally, independent of the macro network, using cellular network deployment with edge computing.

- From the view of stage 3, edge IT enables high-performance, interoperability, and security in a multi-vendor computing-based ecosystem, where edge computing is focusing on resource allocation at the service level, while transparent computing concentrates on logically splitting the software stack (including OS and middlewares) from the underlying hardware platform to provide cross-platform and streamed services for a variety of devices.

As shown in Fig. 6.22, whether data flow or control flow, compared to MEC, one more difference is the need to support exotic I/O and accelerator aware provisioning, real-time, embedded targets, as well as real-time networks,[40] such as TSN, e.g., IEEE 802.1. The real-time networks supported communication pipeline in 5G and MEC is called time-sensitive communications (TSC). In the long run, any edge node will

[39]Taking Azure cloud as an example for better understanding, Azure Stack Edge, previously Azure Data Box Edge, brings the compute power, storage, and intelligence of Azure right to where you need it — whether that's your corporate data center, your branch office, or your remote field asset. A hybrid of cloud and Edge for IoT solutions according to your own business logic is created more conveniently. Even in the offline state, the edge also can realize the artificial intelligence and advanced analysis that partly release the necessary of connecting simplify the procedure and reduce the IoT solution cost.

[40]In the 5G specification, Time Sensitive Communication (TSC) gives another option. A similar solution as edge computing technology is represented by CMU's Cloudlet, which enables new classes of mobile applications that are both compute-intensive and latency-sensitive in an open ecosystem based on cloudlets. The Cloudlets have lately been transformed to Open Edge Computing. More details can be found at http://openedgecomputing.org/.

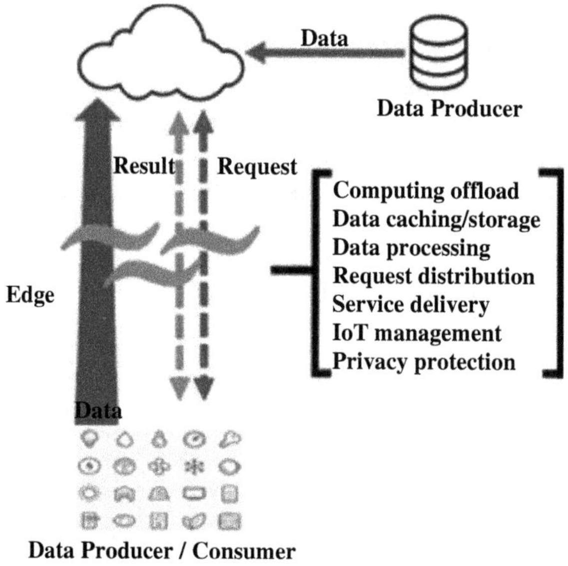

Figure 6.62 A typical edge paradigm.

offer computational and storage resources to other users in close proximity using a standardized mechanism, whomever it is defined and provided by.

- From the view of stage 4, although edge computing is characterized by openness, operators open the networks to third parties to deploy applications and services, while their differences enable edge computing technologies to support broader IoT applications with various requirements; but the joint services integrated with edge computing and cloud edge collaboration is a more effective service architecture. Edge computing extends cloud computing and services to the edge of the (devices) network, bringing the advantages and power of the cloud closer to where information is created and acted upon. Cloud computing pushes intelligence to edge computing. Their collaboration can make full use of the different advantages of cloud computing and edge computing and flexibly deploy and respond to the business requirements with different characteristics.

For better understanding, the data characteristic of edge computing itself as producer and consumer is illustrated in Fig. 6.62. As for those jobs in the network, the edge itself needs to be well designed to meet the requirement efficiently in services such as reliability, security, and privacy protection. At the edge, the things can not only request service and content from the cloud but also perform the computing tasks from the cloud. At the same time, edge computing is pushing intelligence and computing power closer to the source of the data and promoting the user experience of devices. In order to fully realize the value of the massive amounts of data being generated by devices, machines, edge nodes, and other things, edge computing and cloud computing should work together.

As a typical edge paradigm presented in *Edge Computing: Vision and Challenges* by Shi W *et al.*, the things not only are data consumers but also play as data producers. It is illustrated as the two-way computing streams in edge computing. **Edge can perform computing offloading, data storage, caching and processing, as well as distribute request and delivery service from cloud to user.**

6.4.2.3 *The reference architectures of edge computing as RAM of EC*

At the 3rd Edge Computing Forum organized by Fraunhofer FOKUS in 2019, more aspects were discussed, such as the identification of reference architectures, open standards, available implementations, reference technology stacks, and evaluation within use cases. Furthermore, best practices and experiences gained from recent testbeds were presented. More than 100 decision-makers, key experts, innovators, and early adopters from companies, such as IBM, Siemens, Huawei, Vodafone, etc., attended the forum.

In order to build an industrial edge-based ecosystem by making infrastructures interoperable, programmable, secure, and easy to use, additional topics such as the identification of reference architectures, open standards, available implementations, reference technology stacks, and evaluation within use cases, are organized by giving a RAMEC, as Fig. 6.63 shows.

As shown in Fig. 6.63, RAMEC combines all elements and IT components in a layer/level and cross-layer model. Most of the areas covered in the RAMEC include aspects of 3-D views as the following.

From the Z-axis view, which is conformed to the typical four-layer IoT architecture. They are:

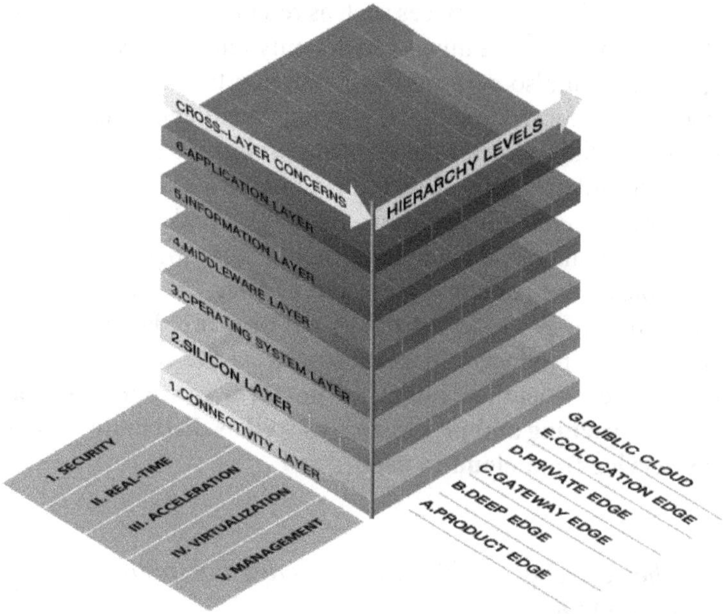

Figure 6.63 RAM of EC by Fraunhofer FOKUS, One of the best industrial associations in European, with 3D visions.

- Connectivity (Physical connection of networks, e.g., TSN/5G)
- Silicon (e.g., x86/ARM)
- Operating Systems
- Middleware (e.g., OPC-UA)
- Information (e.g., Distributed digital twins)
- Applications (e.g., Distributed AI/PLCs)

From connectivity, silicon to operating systems, they consist in the network and communication layer of IoT in the North Bound. Their unified working is as an interface to South Bound, where lie the sensor and actuator layer of IoT.

From the X-axis view of cross-layer concerns, there are:

- Security and safety (e.g., TPM)
- Real-Time (e.g., RTOS)
- Acceleration (e.g., Edge TPU)
- Virtualization (e.g., Unikernels)
- Management (e.g., Kubernetes)

From the Y-axis view of cross-layer concerns, there are:

- Product edge
- Deep edge
- Gateway edge
- Network edge
- Private edge
- Collocation edge
- Public edge

While there are many outcomes that edge computing can enable for industrial organizations, and these outcomes included most of the critical aspects for industrial organizations, e.g., a summary from the IIoT aspects is given from GE as follows: (a) low/intermittent connectivity (such as a remote location); (b) bandwidth and associated high-cost of transferring data to the cloud; (c) low latency, such as closed-loop interaction between machine insights and actuation (i.e., taking action on the machine and controlling AGV); (d) immediacy of analysis (e.g., a technician working in the field to check machine performance); (e) access to temporal data for real-time analytics; (f) compliance, regulation, or cyber-security constraints.

The business implications of edge computing are compelling, and at least six directions need to be discussed as follows:

(1) **Predictive maintenance and flexible manufacture:** EC in digital twin may reduce costs and security assurance in testing and maintenance of production. As for flexible manufacturing, product-to-service is an extension of EC function, as the small-quantity and multi-batch modes are beginning to replace high-volume manufacturing.
(2) **Energy efficiency management in IIoT:** EC can reduce energy consumption and maintenance costs, especially in smart manufacturing and customization of production modes.
(3) **Flexible device replacement:** Flexible adjustments to production plan with higher reliability and rapid deployment of new processes and models.
(4) **Safety surveillance:** For example, in chemical industry, EC is used to build intelligent petroleum refineries with different types of machine sensors, where the process is carefully analyzed to improve

productivity and workplace safety. As an extension of this point, remote safety monitoring in oil and gas production also works.

(5) **Industrial automation:** Edge computing infrastructure adopted in factories helps them automate their workspace so as to reduce costs, improve security, and ROI ultimately.

(6) **Reliability and sustainability of production:** As for various energy production industries, EC can be used to reduce their energy losses and make their energy equipment reliable and efficient. As for various semiconductors manufacturing companies, EC is used not only to reduce the failure rate of microchips but also the mechanical level of fault detection in predictive maintenance of manufacturing in IIoT scenarios.

In a word, IoT, edge computing, cloud computing and 5G/B5G are brothers and sisters in the future IoE era. They add human intelligence alike techniques to themselves and strive AI to make the world smart, tightly woven and super-efficient. 5G and MEC are discussed in the next part. Reference architecture with security in the IIoT scenario will be discussed in the last part of this section.

6.4.3 *MEC and 5G*

As mentioned above, mobile edge computing (MEC) can be seen as a kind of network architecture that enables cloud/edge computing capabilities and an ICT service environment at the edge of the cellular network. By running applications and performing related processing tasks closer to the cellular users (human, IoT device or program), network congestion is reduced and applications perform better. As the GE news once described a demonstration of a private LTE network for Industrial IoT,[41] "Industrial companies often have local connectivity needs and operate in remote locations or temporary sites, such as mines, power plants, offshore oil platforms, factories, warehouses, or ports — connectivity for these environments can be challenging. A standalone LTE network to serve devices and users within a localized area can help improve performance and reliability for these industrial settings".

Nowadays, more opportunities for the merge of MEC and cellular have been arising as evolution to a higher-level of automation will increasingly lead to a higher share of 5G-connected devices. Both high

[41] From website of GE company.

bandwidth and consistently low latency are necessary to support large data volumes and real-time critical data as well as to ensure consistent and secure communication (a private MEC-5G zone as a use case will be illustrated in the following part).

As we are stepping into the 5G era, the multi-access edge computing (MEC) standard is developed in the ETSI Industry Specification Group/ ISG multi-access edge computing (ETSI ISG MEC) from mobile edge computing. The ETSI ISG MEC is the leading voice in standardization and industry organization concerning MEC.

As designed to open up opportunities for industrial companies looking to optimize their assets and operation, the MEC not only releases connectivity from the edge to the cloud but also the connecting assets to MEC platform and using the innovations emerging from 5G wireless technology. The MEC will help IIoT unlock efficiency, increase manageability, and drive sustainability.

It is also expected that more network intelligence will reside closer to the source when regarding IoT applications. This will push for the rise of cloud/fog and MEC-distributed architectures, along with 5G-enabled ICTs. The technical definition of integration architecture of 5G and MEC is given by ETSI and is shown in Fig. 6.64.

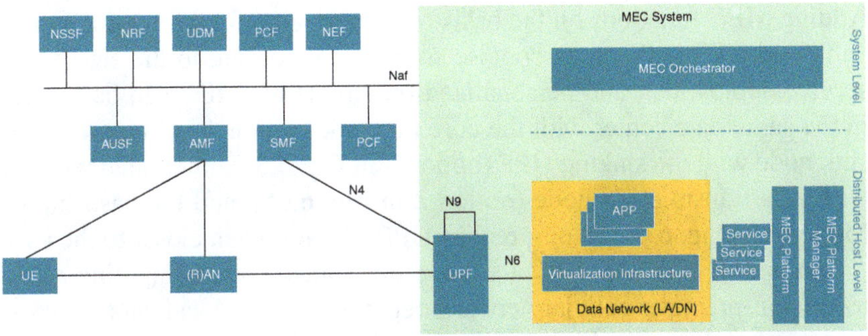

Figure 6.64 Integration architecture of 5G and MEC defined by ETSI.

Notes: N3: Interface between the RAN (gNB) and the (initial) UPF. N4: Interface between the Session Management Function (SMF) and the UPF. N6: Interface between the Data Network (DN) and the UPF. N9: Interface between two UPF's (i.e. the Intermediate I-UPF and the UPF Session Anchor); AMF (access and mobility function), SMF (session management function), PCF (policy control function), UPF (user plane function), etc. are control plane elements defined by 3GPP. UE means user equipment.

Source: 3GPP and ETSI.

The critical component of the 5G core network: user plane function (UPF), which is the link between the 5G core network and MEC can provide data diversion (east–west shunting of data) and traffic statistics. As shown in the left side of Fig. 6.64, 5G network, includes core network (as access and mobility management function (AMF), seen in Section 5.8.4), PCF and other control plane elements, as well as UPF), radio access network (RAN) and terminal (UE). On the right is MEC, which includes the MEC platform, management choreography domain, and multiple services provided by apps.

The joint point between the 5G network and MEC is UPF, which focuses on the user plane interface function of the core network, and the MEC data must be forwarded by UPF before it can flow to the external network (cellular networks). In other words, the MEC platform in distributed host-level responsible for edge computing needs to be connected to the UPF of the 5G core network.

The design of the 5G core network is very flexible. In order to reduce the detour of data transmission, the deployment position of UPF is generally lower than that of the control plane network component, which is called UPF sinking (e.g., to province/city/on premise).

The UPF is a critical new component for supporting the new generation of service-based architectures.

For MNO operators, the location of deploying MEC is very flexible. Adding MEC functions on the basis of edge UPF to form edge-integrated enhanced UPF is the most concise solution. According to the size of the service deployment and personalized requirements, MEC can be located in the same data center with the core network (option 4 in Fig. 6.65), the sink node with the sinking UPF (option 3 in Fig. 6.65), integrated with the UPF in a transmission node (option 2 in Fig. 6.65), and the base station (option 1 in Fig. 6.65) as on-premise UPF which is even closer to the user.

In option 1 of Fig. 6.65, the open distributed edge computing architecture on-premises cellular network deployment with local data breakout ensures that the critical production data do not leave the premises, using QoS mechanisms to fulfill use case requirements and optimize reliability and latency. Critical applications can be executed locally, independent of the macro network, using cellular network deployment with edge computing.

As for internet service providers (ISPs), although they are also actively promoting edge computing, they can only support MEC by docking with UPF of operators because they have no cellular network in hand.

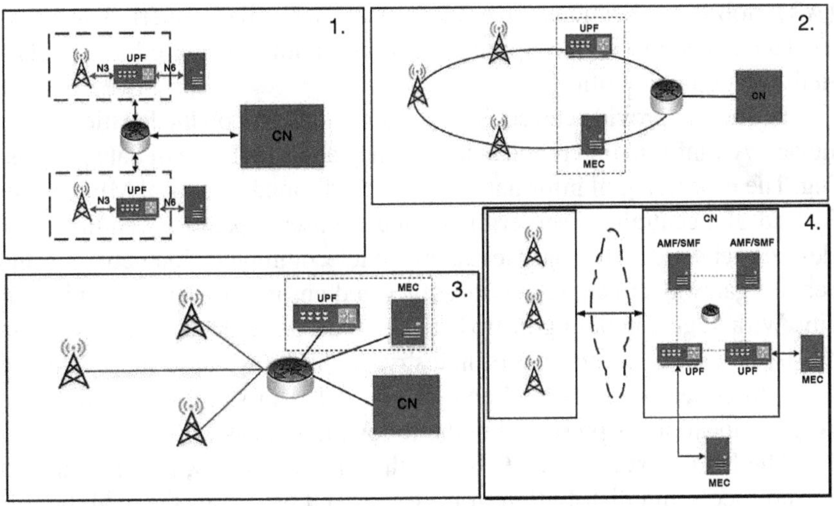

Figure 6.65 The four options of UPF in 5G and MEC: (1) MEC, UPF, and base station are integrated together. (2) MEC and sinking UPF are integrated in a transmission node. (3) MEC and UPF are located in the same sink node. (4) MEC and core network are deployed in the same data center.

As shown in the user case of the next part, the edge computing platforms of ISPs need to connect with the UPF of various operators and then connect to the base stations of different operators through UPF, so as to deliver services to each user.

IoT assets and devices are connected by mobile infrastructure, and cloud services are provided to IoT platforms to deliver real-time and context-based services. MEC uses the power of local computing and different types of devices to provide intelligent services. Data storage, data computing, and data control can be separated and distributed among the connected edge devices (servers, micro servers, gateways, IoT nodes, etc.). Besides advantages, such as improved scalability, local processing, contextual computing, and analytics, making it well suited to IoT application requirements, MEC is offering low latency, proximity, high bandwidth, and real-time insight into radio network information and location awareness, enabling the development of many new types of IoT applications and services for industrial sectors.[42] In the 5G era, augmented reality

[42]The Next Generation Internet of Things — Hyperconnectivity: How Cloud IoT Edge works?

(AR) mobile applications have inherent collaborative properties in terms of data collection in the uplink, while computing at the edge and data delivery in the downlink.

In order to provide correct information depending on the location of the device, AR information requires low latency and a high rate of data processing. The processing of information can be performed on a local MEC server instead of a centralized server to provide the user experience required. IoT devices generate additional messaging on telecommunication networks and require gateways to aggregate messages and ensure low latency and security. With edge computing in IIoT, latency can be reduced by 10–20 ms in 5G-based critical controlling of industry. Architectures used for leveraging MEC to collect, classify, and analyze the IoT data streams with different types or locations is presented in the following use case.

The MEC server, or MEC box with a smart gateway, manages different protocols and distribution of messages and processes the analytics.

The MEC environment supports the creation of new value chains and a new type of ecosystem, which provides new opportunities for not only mobile operators, application, content providers, and ISPs but also for the MEC platforms in the 5G era, along with the collaboration and cooperation the edge computing can provide.

6.4.4 *User cases of edge deployment of Azure*

"The intelligent cloud and the intelligent edge" describes the view of Microsoft to enable new edge computing scenarios for partners and developers with Azure Edge Zones, which is pushing the intelligence from the edge to the local mini datacenter, and to cloud, from local (private) networks to cellular networks (e.g., 5G), and to anywhere in IoT/IoE.

As for family and smart building, edge computing is contributing the following:

1. Security cameras, telephones/cell phones, televisions, cars, thermostats, and other home and building sensors, just as a small part of daily use, can create data that can be mined and analyzed at all levels with EC.
2. Digital twin in fault monitoring and predictive maintenance of building infrastructure.
3. Energy management, including energy saving and energy contributing.
4. As for commuting management and optimization in a city, various transportation companies are using edge-powered IoT devices and

computing services to help find suitable parking areas, reduce parking time, and downtime in **transiting**. AI algorithms are working with these edge devices to optimize parking distribution and collect real-time traffic and navigation data among blocks. EC analysis of real-time is used to make informed decisions and **transiting schedule arrangements during the connection of different transportation.**

Details and other use cases will be discussed in the next section.

In the 5G era and beyond, not only the intelligent cloud and the intelligent edge but also the connection between them and their collaboration with 5G and stakeholders are also important. Azure Edge Zones combine the capabilities of Azure, 5G technology partners, and mobile carriers together, and they will allow the following:

- New frontiers for developers working with high-density graphics and real-time operations in industries such as online game streaming and mobile platforms.
- Local data processing for secure workloads, latency-sensitive data analytics, IoT, and media services.
- Real-time IIoT and AI analytics for optimizing, building, and innovating for robotics, mixed reality, and automation tools.

As shown in Fig. 6.66, Azure Edge Zone actually comes in three different offerings. Normal Azure Edge Zone (i.e., Standard Azure Edge Zone, as the left part of Fig. 6.66) are small-footprint extensions of Azure located in population centers distant from Azure regions.

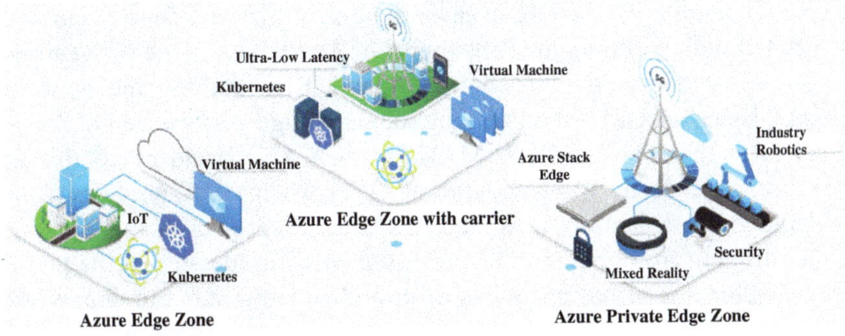

Figure 6.66 Three kinds of Azure Edge Zones: (Normal) Edge Zone, Edge Zone with carriers, and Azure Private Edge Zone.

This kind of Azure Edge Zone deployment along with several footprints is away from core Azure services of a data center (or population center, such as AT&T in the New York city). The closer to the user, the delay reduces more high-performance requirements for business, industry or other entertainment applications, such as streaming of game and online controlling, require this scenario of edge computing deployment as simple as best, and as near as possible to the data center, no need for other platforms. When edge computing needs a connection to the Internet, the issue of network latency needs to be considered as the main problem especially for traffic flow which goes through the network of mobile carriers.

As shown in the center part of Fig. 6.66, Azure Edge Zone with carrier (5G) is located in mobile operators' data centers in population centers. For example, one use case scenario sees developers building optimized and scalable applications using Azure and directly connecting to 5G networks by building upon previously announced integration with AT&T to enable next-generation solutions on the edge, leveraging consistent Azure APIs and tooling in the public cloud.

In order to find a solution to the network latency, under this edge condition, different Azure Zone services are introduced into the Edge Zone over the WAN/MAN/SD-WAN. Those under development/testing applications and services with Microsoft Azure Portal tool may directly be deployed in operators hosting edge,[43] to meet the requirements of different businesses and applications. Under ideal conditions, for the application of low-latency requirements, and only one hop can be sent to close to the edge side of the user, the latency can be reduced within or below 10–20 ms, such as in AR, game streaming applications, etc. So, 5G plays an important role in uRLLC and eMBB, which means the realization of ultra-reliable low latency and enhanced mobile bandwidth, even in extremely massive density circumstance but really needing the deployment of Azure Edge Zone with carrier.

When it comes to the solution from MS to address the network latency issues faced by the previous standard edge zone, different Azure services to the edge via WAN/MAN/SD — WAN should be combined. MS Azure is experimenting with this at AT&T when MS Azure Edge Zone is deployed in Atlanta, Dallas, and Los Angeles. However, this scene is quite different from the core 5G net-based MEC introduced in the previous Chapter 5. The basic stations of providers are utilized to deploy the

[43]That is an edge server near the base station and it is hosted by operators of mobile networks.

server, the traffic in application/service can undertake convenient management in the overall network service and edge, which is limited to some services, permitted by the operator and can be utilized in Azure practices, unlike the application based on cloud-native core and 5G MEC.

Azure Private Edge Zones are located on premises, as shown in the right part of Fig. 6.66. This kind of private edge zone gives an important way to promote the development of 5G edge ecology, where it gives a bridge to industrial robotics, mixed reality, tube pipeline of TSC, as above-mentioned option 1.5G is coming with several core arguments: ultra-high bandwidth, extreme density, and ultra-low latency. What does that mean? The mobile network carrying things will be dozens of times, even hundreds of times, than the scale of things now. And some of them really need MEC to reduce latency, such as things of IIoT and IoV.

6.4.5 *Use cases for smart driving and smart building*

As most data is too noisy, its transferring to the cloud will be latency sensitive or expensive. Edge computing technologies for IoT require developers to address issues such as unstable and intermittent data transmission via wireless and mobile links, efficient distribution, and management of data storage and computing. Edge computing interfacing with the cloud computing to provide scalable services and finally mechanisms to secure IoT applications. The edge computing model requires a distributed architecture and needs to support various interactions and communication approaches to be used broader in consumer/business/industrial domains. To do this, it needs to provide peer-to-peer networking, edge–device collaboration (self-organizing, self-aware, self-healing, etc.), distributed queries across data stored in edge devices as well as in the cloud and temporary storage locations, distributed data management, (e.g., for defining where, what, when, and how long, in relation to data storage) and information governance (e.g., information quality, discovery, usability, privacy, security, etc.). In this context, the research challenges in this area are discussed in the following sections.

6.4.5.1 *Transportation scenarios of ultra-reliability and low latency*

According to Peter Levine, the General Partner of Andreessen Horowitz (a venture capital corporation), the cloud will shortly take a back seat in the edge computing. In this way, we will soon see the most processing occurs at the edge device level. Levine has an interesting metaphor for edge computing:

"Think about a self-driving car, it's effectively a data center on wheels, and a drone is a data center with wings and a robot is a data center with arms and legs and a ship is a floating data center…". He adds, "these devices are processing vast amounts of information and that information needs to be processed in real time". What he means is that even the split-second latency required to pass information between these systems and the cloud simply is too long. Drones can reach any remote place that humans cannot access to. And the edge computing enables them transmitting the data in real time and respond to it. For example, if drones detect any emergent matters, they can immediately send valuable messages to the person nearby.

Autonomous vehicles from some technology giants, e.g., Google and Uber, are developing the edge device to carry out real-time processing and transmission of key data between vehicles. It is promising that autonomous cars can save tens of thousands of lives and avoid car casualties worth billions of US dollars.

For example, the principle of driving an autonomous is simple: the camera and sensors in the car capture the video and information needed, the server analyzes the road conditions from sensors (including the video from this car or not) in real time, and then, all the surrounding information is returned to the data center of the car for real-time control. But if the time of either processing or transferring delay is beyond the estimation we can bear, by the time the command/message received by the steering control returns to the steering controller, an emergency situation may have occurred, and not to mention that if the perception information is from an RSU.

One way is to strengthen the capacity of the vehicular network and the front-end processing capacity, together with the capacity of the vehicular data center (e.g., the Huawei MDC). The enhanced MEC along with the arrival of 5G provides another way, for the improved connecting capabilities, e.g., the reduced latency and the URLLC slicing (see Chapter 5) for mobile vehicles.

Edge computing can provide a rich set of IoV services to meet the requirements of safety, information entertainment, real-time traffic sharing, etc. because it can be distributed along with the road, along the traffic lights, and along with the cellular network. The edge distribution, in terms of safety, helps the detection of pedestrians, riders, and other vehicles by the so-called edge grids with RSUs that are placed along the road side. In terms of traffic condition, the intelligent control of traffic lights should be handed over to several blocks covered by the nearby network. In terms of a driver, "I need to know the best path timely rather than being blocked in the cloud navigation". The real-time traffic information about the congestion of the adjacent blocks need more edge distribution (just several times larger coverage than the sight distance in a city environment) rather than the information being transmitted to the cloud for processing and then being transmitted back.

For intelligent control of traffic lights, low delay and heterogeneous edge devices are closer to the neighborhood that drivers care about than clouds. Edge computing supports mobility and real-time interaction based on position sensing (such as the interaction between the cycle of traffic lights and real-time road condition perception), which expands abilities of local computing, interaction, and collaborative decision-making. In the edge, the aggregated "intelligent data" that will affect the global when it is sent to the cloud computing data center for further global data analysis, so as to achieve location-based context awareness widely. In this way, after quality filtering and aggregation analysis, it can more intelligently suggest the distance, speed, path, and real-time control of traffic lights of the driving vehicle. This idea can meet the needs of location-related edge computing for the automated driving as well. In short, navigation applications can move the navigating or searching services to the edge for a local area, in which case only a few map blocks are involved. And traffic content filtering/aggregating could be done at the edge nodes to reduce the data volume to be transferred.

6.4.5.2 *Smart home and building with edge computing design*

In order to raise the intelligence degree of smart building and reduce the uncertainty of the controlling or management process, some products and OS have been developed and are available on the IoT market benefiting the home environment, such as smart light, smart TV, and robot vacuum. However, adding a Wi-Fi module to the current electrical device and connecting it to the cloud is not enough for a smart home. In a smart home environment, besides the connected device, cheap wireless sensors and controllers should be deployed to room, pipe, and even floor and wall. These things need a "smart management" on the edge; for one reason, the

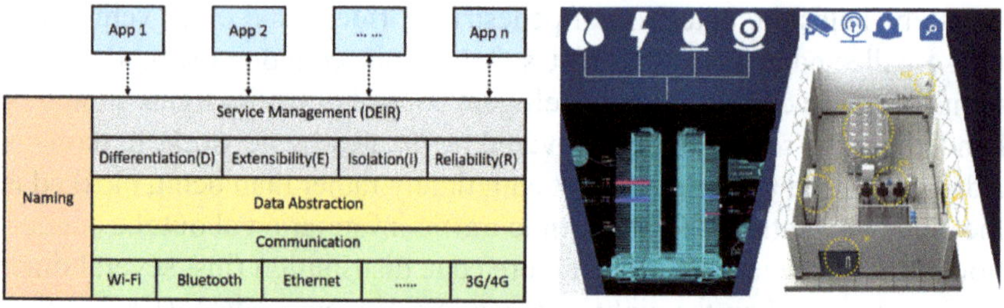

Figure 6.67 Structure of edgeOS and the smart home/building environment.

data and control actions owned by stakeholders is rarely shared with each other due to privacy concerns and the formidable cost of data transportation. Another is the heterogeneity of both the products and the APPs.

Edge, as a physical small data center that connects the cloud and end-user with data processing capability, can also be part of the logical concept. Collaborative edge connects the edges of multiple stakeholders that are geographically distributed despite their physical location and network structure is proposed. Those connected things and edges provide the opportunity for stakeholders to share and cooperate data. Two of the promising applications in the smart building and smart home are the smart service and smart management connected everything in it, as shown in Fig. 6.67.

As shown in Fig. 6.67, the demand of geographically distributed data processing applications, i.e., secure monitoring, fire precaution, requires data sharing and collaboration among enterprises in multiple domains. To face this challenge, the collaborative edge is presented for geographically distributed data by creating virtual shared data views.

Similar to the concept of edge zone, the virtual shared data in a smart building is exposed to end users via a predefined service interface.

Take the structure of a variant of edgeOS as an example. Through the interfaces in the service management (in Fig. 6.67), applications leverage the specific services for end users. These public or specific services are provided by participants of collaborative edge. Considering the amount of data, the data transportation pressure and privacy protection, this data should be mostly processed and consumed in the home or building.

With an edge gateway running a specialized edge operating system (edgeOS), the things can be connected and managed easily in the home, the data can be processed locally to release the burdens for Internet bandwidth, and the service can also be deployed on the edgeOS for better management and delivery.

EdgeOS needs to collect data from mobile devices and all kinds of things through multiple communication methods such as Wi-Fi, ZigBee, or a cellular network. Data from different sources need to be fused and massaged in the data abstraction layer.

On top of the data abstraction layer is the service management layer. Requirements including differentiation, extensibility, isolation, and reliability will be supported in this layer.

Moreover, the computation only occurs in the participant's data facility so that the data privacy and integrity can be ensured. The chance of edge computing in an industrial edge that connects various field devices, converts and adapts industrial protocols, also emerges these days; see the next part.

6.4.6 *Further discussion*

After the eight pillars of EC was presented in "Open Fog Reference Architecture for Fog Computing" by IIC, IIC introduced the reference architectures of MEC in its white paper "Introduction to Edge Computing in IIoT" in 2018. In the white paper, edge computing in the IIoT sector is introduced by means of a three-tier architecture and five cross-tier functional perspectives in a unified view.

As shown in Figure 6.68, the three-tier architecture refers to the edge, platform, and enterprise tiers described in RA, and the cross-tier functional perspectives refer to the separate functions that certain functions have to be performed across each tier, including data management, connectivity communication, policy orchestration, industrial analytics, and security.

In Figure 6.68, the inclusion of security as part of the cross-tier functional perspective shows that security was given full attention in the design of the IIoT edge computing architecture as an essential part of the basic architecture, spanning the entire architecture from the edge, platform, and enterprise layers, indicating that each layer should be considered separately, with additional security considerations overall. In the white paper, a separate chapter discusses the security for IIoT edge computing, arguing that the addition of more information components and communication connections in industry introduces new attack vectors that require innovative approaches to security monitoring and protection.

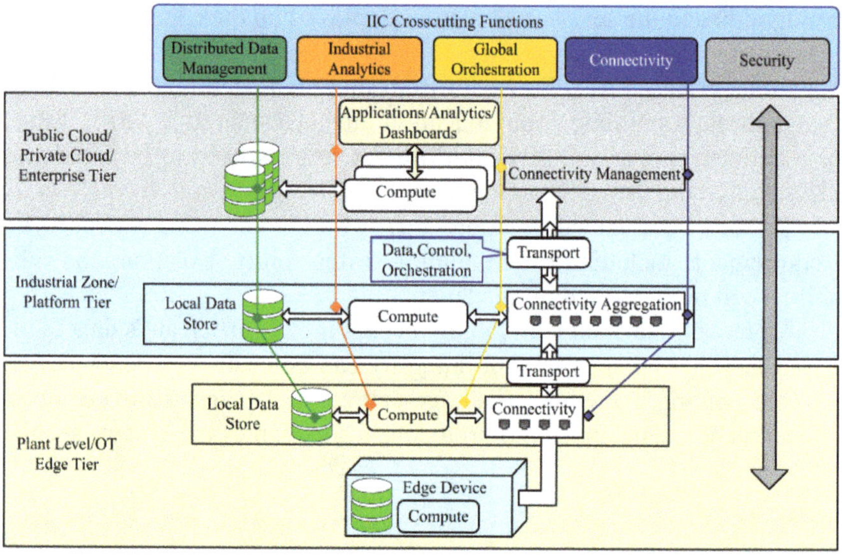

Figure 6.68 Reference architecture of edge computing, with security in IIoT scenario.

Functional safety, security monitoring of computer and network nodes, timely patching, and updating, etc. will be introduced in the last chapter.

On the OT edge, the concept of an edge controller gains more popularity.

The edge controller means an industrial edge device that connects various field devices, converts and adapts industrial protocols in a unified access to the edge computing network, and encapsulates device capabilities in the form of services to achieve physical and logical communication connections over an industrial platform. The edge controller hardware architecture is designed with a distributed heterogeneous computing platform, which generally uses a heterogeneous computing architecture to support fully distributed control, the collaborative operation and seamless integration of multiple controllers, and is currently the mainstream implementation scheme for various real-time inbound hardware platforms. The system can run real-time and non-real-time tasks or operating systems on the same hardware platform, and meet the requirements of system diversity and portability, and improve the security, reliability, flexibility, and resource utilization efficiency of the overall platform system: the application of space–time isolated multi-task and multi-thread scheduling

Table 6.10 Some basic security considerations in an IoT security framework.

<table>
<tr><th>Security from OT Tier to Platform Tier</th><th colspan="2">Security from Platform Tier to Cloud/Enterprise Tier</th></tr>
<tr><td>• Network accessibility.
• Network fingerprinting.
• Communication protocol security.
• Monitoring, alert and response capabilities.
• Firewall.</td><td colspan="2">• Network accessibility.
• Network fingerprinting.
• Communication protocol security.
• Network ports exposure.
• Monitoring, alert and response capabilities.</td></tr>
<tr><td colspan="3">Overall Security</td></tr>
<tr><td>Authorization</td><td>Integrity</td><td>3rd party libraries and components</td></tr>
<tr><td>• Access control.</td><td>• Integrity check.</td><td>• Vulnerabilities.</td></tr>
<tr><td>Privacy</td><td>Communication</td><td>Accounts</td></tr>
<tr><td>• Privacy assessment.
• Data protection.</td><td>• Encryption.
• Relay protection.</td><td rowspan="3">• Default passwords.
• Password complexity.
• Login Lockout.
• Hardcoded or backdoor accounts.
• Cleartext passwords.</td></tr>
<tr><td colspan="2">Control center application</td></tr>
<tr><td colspan="2">• Web application.
• Mobile application.</td></tr>
</table>

mechanism combined with the transformation of optimal scheduling algorithms to achieve the task scheduling mechanism.

Finally, the edge security consideration from three kinds of perspectives is discussed in Table 6.10. Along with the rapid development of edge computing, the efforts of encapsulating secure service in the end to end of logical communication connections between devices and the collaboration platform among multiple stakeholders (builders/users/platform and service providers) are more and more important.

6.5 IoV(V2X) and Autonomous Driving Vehicles

More and more LBS-based service providers are emerging around us. Baidu/Google map has opened LBS Platform and integrated APIs, aiming to explore the potential of IoV applications with many ISPs and "third partners". As discussed in Sections 4.5 and 4.12, IoVs cannot be separated by LBSs, which is original from cellular networks and now cultivated and thriving in the 5G and IoE era. From 2001, "Positioning Star", "parent–child communication", "automobile GPS navigation service", and other LBS services were provided by China Mobile Inc. in China. Some map operators (e.g., Baidu in China) open their LBS platform in order to find more stakeholders to join the application of IoVs and other location-associated markets. Such operators of mobile networks, those following the evolutional standard of 4G/5G and beyond, give rise to a wealth of new possibilities of connection, bring new functionalities to the individuals, and/or make transport easier and safer in IoVs. In this section, the concept of IoV connected with the concept of IoT represents future trends for smart transportation and mobility applications in the IoE era. IoV is creating new mobile ecosystems based on security and convenience to mobile/contactless services, driving assistant information/autonomous driving, and transportation applications in order to ensure security, mobility, and convenience to harmony-centric transportation and services, among all elements equally related in the evolving smart transportation of IoE. At the same, smart sensors in the road, traffic control infrastructures, pedestrians, wherever they are on/off the vehicles or on/off the road, need to be considered as a part of IoV because they collect information about road and traffic status, weather conditions, and so on in the representation and exhibition of traffic scenario in IoT. Moreover, IoV in 5G, i.e., a branch of V2X which hold or support the network of connecting cars and people, and other instructions will be introduced in this section.

6.5.1 *LBS and IoV*

IoVs service originated from the application of LBS in the field of transportation. Now, LBS has played a wide and important role in many fields, such as smart city, traffic facilitation, path optimization, vehicle navigation, mobile communication, and infotainment, and has formed an important direction of IoT development in the field of transportation — IoVs.

LBS system is a comprehensive information platform that integrates location, data communication service in real time, geographic information storage and processing, and so on. As mentioned in Sections 5.4 and 6.1.3, location service has two meanings: determining the geographic location of (mobile or not) equipment or users, and then providing various information services related to location.

In 1994, American scholar Schilit proposed the concept of context-aware computing and pointed out three goals of location service: where are you (spatial information), who are you with (social information), and what resources are nearby (information query).

In 1996, Federal Communications Commission (FCC) required all mobile network operators in the United States to provide a location information service for E911 emergency calls. At that time, the location accuracy provided by the task of E911 could not fully meet the needs. After that, mobile network operators have invested huge efforts to improve location technology in their cellular networks, in order to get a return on the investment of the E911 business. Then, operators launched a series of LBS businesses, such as scenic spots, restaurants, or gas stations finding.

Around 2000, with the application of 3G technology, 3G network has enriched the service content that commercial application provided by LBS is no longer limited to a cell phone. At that time, traditional automobile manufacturers began to upgrade the vehicle information system, and the functions of positioning, navigation, anti-theft, and security of vehicle electronic equipment are more abundant with LBS. Institutions and platforms such as Mobility2000 and intelligent vehicle highway system (IVHS) have developed rapidly in the United States.

A contemporary concept, Telematics, richer than Prometheus — a monitoring system & time-series database,[44] emerged in Europe. Vehicle information and communication system (VICS), advanced safety vehicle (ASV), and other vehicle platforms and products have emerged in Japan. The application of IoT technology, such as RFID and Bluetooth/Wi-Fi beacon (see Section 5.5), partially solves the problem of positioning when satellite positioning is not available or in indoor environment.

Afterwards, in Japan, ETC, which is enriched by RFID and IEEE 802.11p (see Chapter 4 and Section 5.3), becomes an evolving technical way in Japanese V2X development.

In May 2002, AT&T and GO2 launched the world's first mobile LBS application under the authorization of FCC in the United States, which is used for automatic location identification (ALI). Users of GO2 can locate

[44]PROMETHEUS (Program for a European Traffic with Highest Efficiency and Unprecedented Safety, @ https://prometheus.io/) is a plan proposed by Mercedes Benz in 1985 and then expanded into a vehicle platform in Europe. Its development fields include: vehicle AI processor, real-time pattern recognition, various sensors and processing devices, digital communication technology, system comprehensive application method, and evaluation model development.

themselves by using ALI provided by AT&T and search the list of geographic locations near themselves to meet their needs of certain services.

In 2010, Foursquare Company gave a dazzling success model for its LBS social network service in the United States. The company of Foursquare provided comprehensive platform services integrating location services, social networks, and game elements.

At present, more and more mobile location services are combined with other mobile Internet applications (e.g., WeChat and YouTube), with the characteristics of interaction and sharing.

For example, in Fig. 6.69, LBS and mobile LoCation Service (LCS in 5G) are supplying the location of cell phones in a cellular network, where using location information as a real label can improve the interaction efficiency and confidence. LBS's characteristic capabilities and various GIS services, wherever indoor/outdoor, are also important for many IoT (e.g., IoV) applications.

Not only vehicles but also more specific positioning relevance for IoT need location services, especially sensor originating data, actuation services, and services that relate to different tags like RFID, two-dimensional

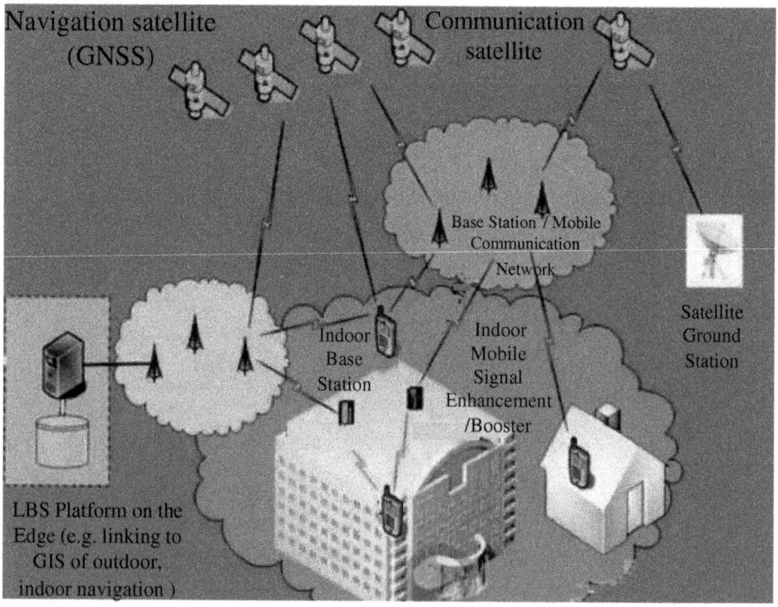

Figure 6.69 The integration positioning of indoor/outdoor and open space, and the LBS/LCS application scenario towards 6G.

code (e.g., indoor AGV location), or signal footprint of Bluetooth beacon location (see Sections 5.6 and 4.5), where services should be provided locally and in detail in the presentation of their position.

From the aspect of WSN or WSAN (see Section 4.2), information of available resources and associated service capabilities can be functionalized as a rendezvous mechanism, where nodes in WSNs can publish themselves in such a directory with service descriptions and how to be reached. Then, applications (e.g., of LBS) perform look-ups to find out which device can provide the sensor reading of interest.[45]

From the cellular aspect, such as 4G/5G by 3GPP, a series of specifications are released in LBS and V2X, such as requirements for support of assisted global navigation satellite system (A-GNSS),[46] functional stage 2 description of location services (LCS),[47] 5G system (5GS) location services (LCS), stage 2,[48] functional stage 2 specification of user equipment (UE) positioning in NG-RAN.[49] Among these and follow-up work of 3GPP, device-to-device communication, side link in LTE-V2X and 5G NR V2X, proximity service (ProSe in R17) are paving a cellular way including location enhancement indoor/outdoor and V2X in different stages (including M2M related aspects of Section 5.7).

The benefits of IoV, according to Frost & Sullivan analysis[50], are listed as follows:

- A World Health Organization report states that nearly 1.25 million fatalities are caused every year because of road accidents, mostly due

[45] This will be taken as an e.g., in the primitive IoT grid of section. END of this chapter. A directory of LBS based sensors that holds a directory with service descriptions in a location of primitive IoT grid for inter-service of each other will be described latter.

[46] 3GPP TS 38.171 V15.1.0 (March 2019) in Release 15.

[47] 3GPP TS 23.271 V15.1.0 (September 2018) in Release 15.

[48] 3GPP TS 23.273 V16.0.0 (June 2019) in Release 16.

[49] 3GPP TS 38.305 V15.0.0 (June 2018) in Release 15. In NG Radio Access Network (NG-RAN), UE Positioning may be considered as a network-provided enabling technology consisting of standardized service capabilities that enable the provision of location applications. The application(s) may be service provider specific. The description of the numerous and varied possible location applications which are enabled by this technology is outside the scope of the present document. However, clarifying examples of how the functionality being described may be used to provide specific location services may be included. This stage 2 specification covers the NG-RAN positioning methods, state descriptions, and message flows to support UE Positioning.

[50] TechVision Group of Frost & Sullivan. V2X Vehicle to Everything for Connected Cars.

to an error during driving. The primary aim for the adoption of IoV is to avoid collisions and reduce fatalities.
- Several work hours are wasted globally as a result of traffic jams. IoV technologies are capable of optimizing the road space with their intelligent systems and reduce road congestion.
- Wastage of fuel and the resulting greenhouse gases play a significant role in global warming. The technologies in IoV enable fuel-efficient vehicles thereby reducing the waste of fuel and the emission of greenhouse gases.
- In addition to safety and reducing road congestion and with the evolution of cellular technologies for connectivity, connected cars will enable various intelligent navigation systems and multimedia services in the short to medium term, resulting in a better travel experience.

Towards 5G and beyond, from WSN and IoV to other IoT LBS applications (e.g., GNSS/GIS), whether indoor/outdoor or in open space (described in Fig. 6.69), present and future needs of IoVs are primarily described below in the coming IoE era.

6.5.2 *Different stages of IoVs*

As one of the symbols of modern society, the invention of automobiles has greatly promoted the scope and efficiency of human mobility. But at the same time, automobiles also bring many problems to human society: traffic congestion, environmental pollution, casualties, and property losses caused by traffic accidents. These problems have become some factors restricting social and economic development. Traffic safety, traffic jams, and environmental pollution are three major problems in the field of transportation. With the rapid development of the automobile industry, how to solve the contradiction between vehicle and road, traffic and environment has become an urgent problem.

The IoVs can not only realize the real-time access and management of vehicles through the LBS-based vehicle location service but also are promising to realize the interconnection and information sharing between vehicles, vehicles and people, and vehicles and roads, along with the traffic efficiency improvement in a macroscopic and harmonious way. After the information of a vehicle, road, and environment is collected, and it is processed with aggregation and **filtration** through calculations, then the outcome becomes available as information for sharing and publishing to multiple parties on the information network platform (described as an IoV service and platform as mentioned above). Vehicles can be effectively guided and supervised according to different functional requirements as well as intelligent interaction and mobile Internet application services. Then, conditions of traffic and environment are improved continuously. This is the original purpose of IoVs, and it has undergone almost 30 years of development.

- **Early stage of IoV (from the 1990s to 2000s):** If LBS is a hint foreshadowing later developments into IoV service, the concept of telematics[51] also embodies the early stage of the understanding of IoV as applications in connecting vehicles via the Internet.

From that stage, the collection of IoV related concepts is improved by the interconnection between vehicles directly, and then between the vehicle and the cloud. Two important communication technologies for vehicles connection arise. One is DSRC for VANETs (see Section 5.4), and the other is the cellular mobile connection for automobile access and supported by mobile network operators (MNOs). Almost at the end of the early stage (almost from the 1990s to 2000s, as defined as early stage here in the book) of IoV, in Japan, the Vehicle Information Communication System (VICS) was presented along with the Japanese Intelligence Transportation system (ITS) of overall frameworks in 1996. In the same year, VICS began its service.

- **Middle stage of IoV (from the 2000s to 2010s):** This stage of IoV is called the middle stage (almost from the 2000s to 2010s) in this book, and the connection-based vehicle applications can only be described as "connected vehicles" with "vehicle information networks". In Japan, ETC service began in 2001 and the plan of Smartway was proposed in 2004. Then, through the on-board unit (OBU), vehicles could transmit the collected information to the VICS center, and the comprehensive, processed information was transmitted back to the navigation system by VICS function wirelessly

[51]The word "telematics" was derived from telecommunication and informatics during the 1990s in Europe. When it was coined, it referred to the information technology and its network interconnection system for entertainment and services, such as vehicle location and navigation and voice interaction. Then, through the computing, communication, satellite navigation, and cellular technology, it was embodied as an "on-board unit", which was built into the broad category of automobiles, aviation, ships, trains, etc.

(e.g., DSRC in ETC usage compliance with IEEE 802.11p, see Section 5.1), so that the driver could understand the vehicle operation report and traffic conditions[52] in real time. According to statistics, for the same destination, vehicles using the VICS system could reduce vehicle travel time by about 22% and increase average speed by about 5%, than those without VICS system. The increased VICS units shipped in Japan were shown in Fig. 6.70, and the mechanisms of VICS information are depicted in Fig. 6.71.

At this middle stage, smart transportation or ITS thrived by using IoT and its contemporary communication technologies, such as DSRC or VANET, and mobile cellular networks. IoVs were deemed as "the applications of IoT in automobile and transportation" at this stage. From a technical view, the frame of IoV was gradually formed as the realization of the interconnection among vehicles, vehicles and roads, vehicles and pedestrians, vehicles and networks, and other V2X-connected things (e.g., infrastructures and people), so as to achieve the purpose of intelligent transportation through the effective coordination of people, vehicles, and roads. In the following part, several technologies about the connected vehicles will be introduced that developed from the middle stage to the latter stage or nowadays.

In the middle stage of IoV, each vehicle/person/traffic light can be used as a source of information and connected to the network through wireless communication; after the collection and processing of information, the refined information is shared to realize the interconnection between

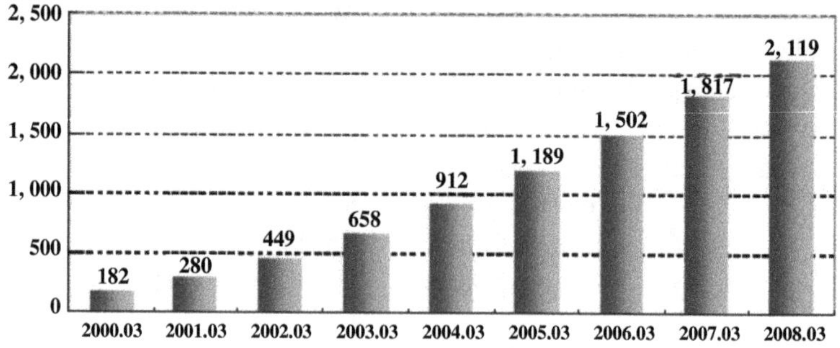

Figure 6.70 VICS progress by increasing units shipped in the middle stage of IoV.
Notes: Unit: 10,000 vehicles.

[52]Traffic conditions, such as main cross section blocked or not, road in building or re-building, and traffic control lights condition, were refreshed every 5s, and they were displayed on the on-board navigation system on digital maps.

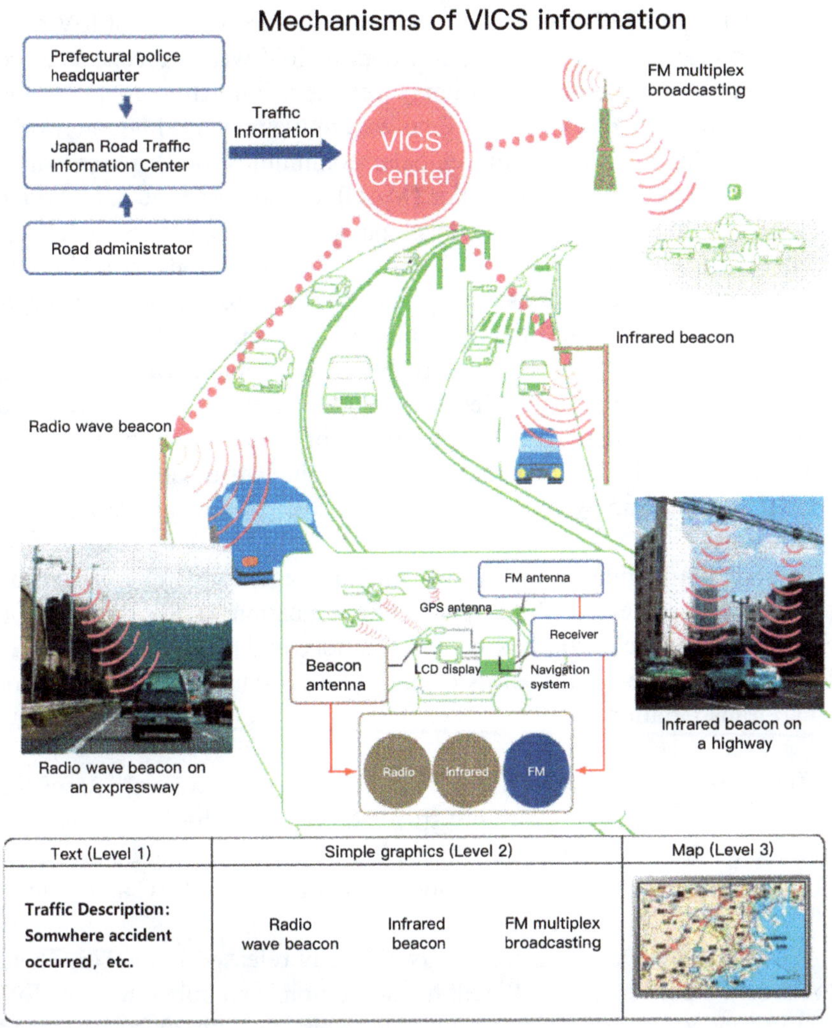

Figure 6.71 Mechanisms of VICS information.

Source: Ministry of Land, Infrastructure, Transport and Tourism of Japan.

vehicle to vehicle (V2V), vehicle and road (V2R), vehicle and urban traffic infrastructure (V2I), vehicle and network (V2N), and realize safety, environmental protection, and comfortable driving experience. The key is that the IoVs should be able to reduce traffic congestion and accidents.

From around the 2000s, the serial standards of the United States (US) on IoV were constructed by IEEE and SAE, which included IEEE 802.11p,

IEEE 1609, SAE J2735, J2945, and so on. In the US, vehicles of IoV were called connected vehicles (CV), corridors of IoV were called connected corridors (CC or Internet of corridors). Vehicle-to-infrastructure (V2I) and vehicle-to-vehicle (V2V) at that time were in vehicular ad hoc networks (VANETs) for the purpose of vehicular communication. VANET was a class of mobile ad hoc networks (MANETs, see Section 5.4), which played an important role in the development of intelligent transport systems (ITS). A combination of V2V and V2I applications in IoV could significantly reduce collisions while changing lanes as well as while intersecting. According to the data from the US Department of Transportation, the applications of IoV technology based on vehicle wireless access (e.g., DSRC) effectively avoided about 80% of traffic accidents, reduced thousands of casualties, and saved billions of dollars in property losses. For this reason, developed countries all over the world had invested a lot of money and manpower to carry out large-scale research and test of IoVs technology.

From the beginning of the IoV middle stage, IEEE had issued the standard of dedicated short-range communication (DSRC) based on 802.11p for vehicle wireless communication, and China had officially launched the development of its communication standard towards ITS or smart transportation.

• **Developing stage of IoV (from the 2010s to nowadays):** From the 2010s, IoV progressed to a new stage. Along with the ICTs, the IoVs became another symbol of our smart cities. The connecting communication technologies of IoVs evolve along two directions: DSRC and cellular V2X.

In 2010, the DSRC standard was officially released in the US. Then, towards the concept of intelligent transportation, four subsystems of IoV were proposed as a whole: central subsystem, vehicle subsystem, road subsystem, and pedestrian (passenger) subsystem, as shown in Fig. 6.72.

Subject to the cost estimation of the central subsystem, the early development of the subsystem was not so smooth, in contrast to its corresponding (intelligent transportation) system of the European Union. The vehicle subsystem includes the communication among emergency vehicles, commercial vehicles, convenient vehicles, maintenance and infrastructure maintaining or construction vehicles; the cooperation between the designed vehicle subsystem and pedestrian subsystem was realized by WAN (wide area networks) mobile communication; the cooperation

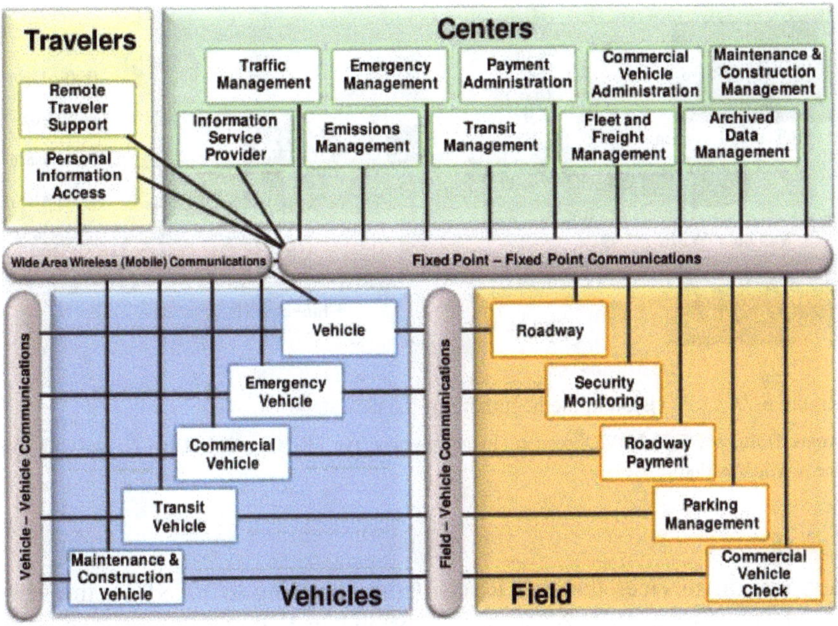

Figure 6.72 Four subsystems of proposed IoV in the new stage of US: Centers (central subsystem), vehicle subsystem, field (road subsystem), and travelers (pedestrian) subsystem.

between vehicle subsystem and road subsystem was realized by RSU (road side unit) to achieve safety monitoring, roadside payment, parking management, commercial vehicle inspection, etc.

At the beginning of the new stage, contributions of the US in IoV are: V2V in-vehicle subsystem, as Fig. 6.72 shows, and the networking scheme in V2R (or V2V2R) technology with road subsystem; that is, VANETs (vehicle ad hoc networks).

VANET had been the focus of the government and automobile manufacturers in the US for a long time. And it was a multi-hop mobile wireless communication network (DSRC, where its application layer introduced WAVE message set, see Section 5.4), and composed of vehicles with the OBU and RSUs. The user communicated with the vehicle via OBU (for vehicle to vehicle) and RSU (for a vehicle to infrastructure). The vehicle transmitted the perceived information to RSUs through VANET wireless communication mode (DSRC), and RSUs sent it to the corresponding server through wired/wireless WAN. Then, vehicles obtained various

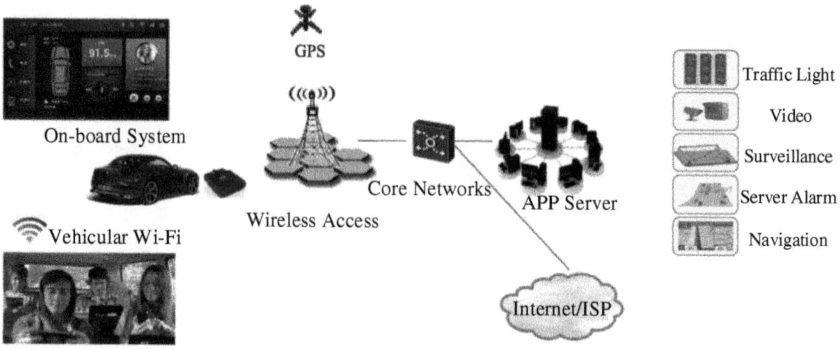

Figure 6.73 IoV vision in the beginning of the new stage.

Notes: DSRC and Cellular V2X scenario in the new stage (i.e., 3G/4G era), and they pushed CVs into the new IoV period.

application services through RSUs. Corresponding to VANETs, the academic term of an IoV or V2X networking in that stage was connected vehicles (CV as mentioned above), which was extended to the connected and intelligent vehicle (CAV) later and nowadays.

The leading work of the IoVs in the US has affected the middle development of the IoVs in Europe, Japan, and other countries and regions. However, their underlying standards of the IoVs all refer to the DSRC standard more or less. Along with the popularization of 3G/4G technology in the middle development, the pervasive scenario of IoV applications from the perspective of the intelligent transportation system is shown in Fig. 6.73.

During the middle stage, plenty of tests have been done by NHTSA (National Highway Traffic Safety Administration) and RITA (Research and Innovative Technology Administration) of the US for V2X experiments from about 2006 to 2009. The impact of connected vehicles, considering a wider and open vision, such as ITS, traffic, and environment improvement, was reported[53] as follows:

[53]*Source*: US Department of Transportation (US DOT), and Frost & Sullivan Report about the Three Big Impact of Connected Cars (https://ww2.frost.com/wp-content/uploads/2018/12/FS_Global_Connected_Car_Brochure_Final.pdf).

- Accident reduction — During harsh weather conditions, or poor visibility, proper implementation of connected traffic management systems can reduce accidents by 25%.
- Travel-time reduction — Intelligent traffic system applications can reduce travel time by 23% for emergency vehicles (hospital ambulances, fire engines) and by 27% for other vehicles.
- CO_2 Emission reduction — Optimized use of lane management systems and traffic management systems can reduce carbon dioxide (CO_2) emissions by 11% and can account for fuel saving up to 22%.

6.5.3 *C-V2X and DSRC*

C-V2X and dedicated short-range communication (DSRC) are communication and network technologies for vehicle wireless communication to everything (i.e., vehicle to everything, V2X) in IoV, where they are striving for more elements connected in the evolving transportation system for improvement in the long run.

As mentioned above, V2X technology is a new generation of ICT that connects the vehicle to everything, where V represents the vehicle, X represents any object of interaction with the vehicle, and the current X mainly contains the vehicle, people, traffic side infrastructure, and network. The information mode of the V2X interaction includes: interaction between car to vehicle (vehicle to vehicle, V2V), between vehicle to road (vehicle to infrastructure, V2I), between vehicle and person (vehicle to pedestrian, V2P), and vehicle to network (vehicle to network, V2N). Then, C-V2X means the V2X technology based on cellular networking.

6.5.3.1 *DSRC-based V2X*

In different countries and regions, the standards and technical routes of the IoVs are different.

In the US, IEEE 802.11p-based DSRC technology was developed specifically for V2V applications that require critical latency of ~100 ms, very high-reliability, and security authentication with privacy safeguards. The DSRC standard has been subjected to extensive testing by automakers and select large-scale trials in the 2010s. Stakeholders have completed work on the use of DSRC to protect vulnerable road users.

Dedicated spectrum for transportation safety applications in the 5.850–5.925 GHz band (at that time) has been allocated by FCC to ensure operation without interference that DSRC-based V2V systems plan to leverage.

In Japan, the underlying layer of the DSRC is still the same as that in Europe and the US and is based on IEEE 802.11p. But a different standard (Association of Radio Industries and Businesses ARIB STD-109) is used, and Japan's DSRC uses a different band (760 MHz) in its substantially different physical layer. However, more attention is paid to the construction of ETC[54] facilities and the RSU units, and their steady deployment is still upgraded along with the VICS system mentioned above. The application frequency band of ETC in Japan is 5.8 GHz, which is a little different from that of the US. However, Europe pays more attention to V2I and its application towards ITS.

In 2016, the European Commission adopted a strategy that aims at promoting an integrated European market to support common priorities, and the strategy would leverage both cellular communications and European Telecommunications Standards Institute — Intelligent Transport Systems — G5 (ETSI ITS-G5), a standard based on IEEE 802.11p and similar to DSRC. Spectrum resources for V2X communication in Europe have been allocated in the 5.9 GHz band, similar to the US. The typical DSRC-based V2X scenario is shown in Fig. 6.74, where V2V and V2R are via DSRC.

6.5.3.2 *C-V2X of R14 in 3GPP*

From the new stage, with the development of V2X and 4G/5G cellular technologies, the results of greater data throughput, lower latency, higher security, and more massive connectivity have greatly contributed to the development of intelligent driving and intelligent transportation. Through the "vehicle–road–cloud" collaboration, on the one hand, intelligent and

[54]ETC (electronic toll collection) system is an automated payment system for expressways, bridges, and tunnels. Toll gates communicate with an in-car radio transmitter to deduct the fare from an ETC card which is linked to a special credit card. For more details see Chapter 1.

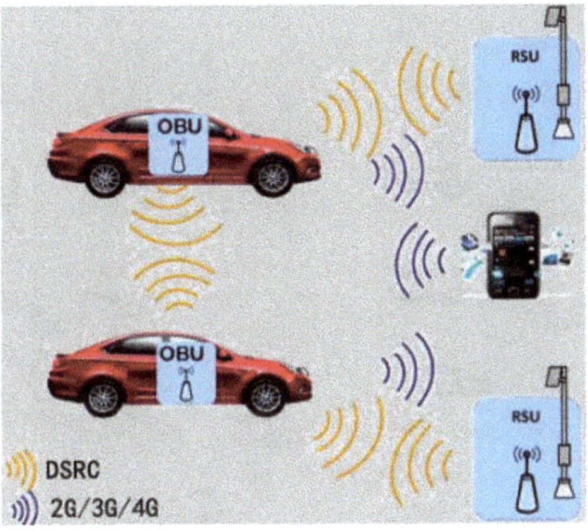

Figure 6.74 VANET (DSRC-based) and cellular scenarios.

connected vehicles[55] provide a safer and more intelligent road in the interactions of travel. On the other hand, the empowered intelligent road conditions integrated perception, dynamic collaborative traffic control, and other functions promote the development of intelligent traffic as the infrastructure of V2X.

In R14 of 4G stage by 3GPP, extensive research had been done in C-V2X (i.e., LTE-V2X in 4G stage), such as "LTE support for V2X services", "architecture enhancements for LTE support of V2X services", "security aspect of LTE supports of V2X services", "radio access networks (RAN) aspects of LTE-based V2X Services", and so on. They defined vehicle-to-everything (V2X) features encompassing all aspects of the 3GPP work needed to support vehicle-based communications: enhancements of the air interface, protocols, and impacts on the LTE core network. There are two modes of operation for V2X communication,[56] as shown in Fig. 6.75.

The working scenarios that C-V2X can support include both those with cellular network coverage and those without cellular network deployment. In terms of specific communication technology, C-V2X can

---

[55] Intelligent connected vehicles (ICV) is a popular name for vehicles obtained service in V2X networking, especially in cellular networking. In China, the "C" in C-V2X also represents collaboration besides cellular.

[56] 3GPP TR 21.914 V2.0.0 (March 2018). 3GPP TR 21.914 V2.0.0 Technical Report.

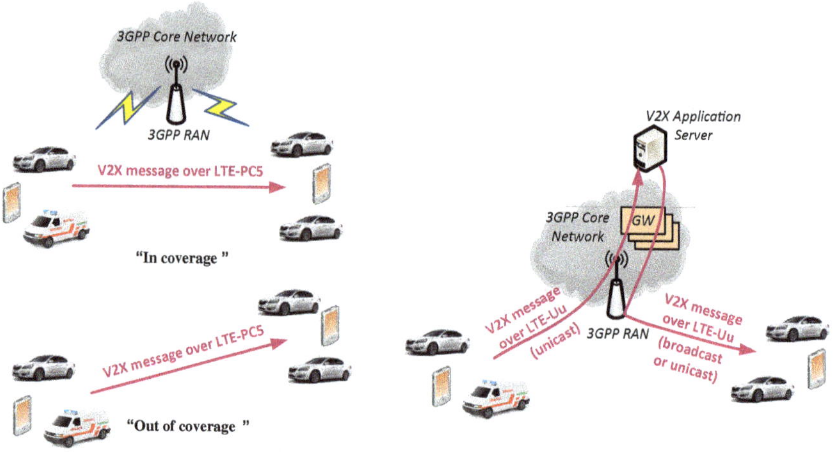

(a) **V2X communication over LTE-PC5** (b) **V2X communication over LTE-Uu**

Figure 6.75 V2X communication over PC5 interface and LTE-Uu interface.

provide two kinds of communication interfaces, namely the Uu interface (cellular communication interface) and PC5 interface.

These two communication interfaces may be used by a UE independently for transmission and reception. V2X communication over PC5 is supported using a side link (direct connection communication interface) when the UE is inside LTE network coverage, i.e., "served by E-UTRAN" and when the UE is out of network coverage, i.e., "not served by E-UTRAN". Under this condition, an OBU with a 3GPP UE inside is the onboard terminal installed in the vehicle, while RSU is installed on the roadside. The information exchange between the vehicle and the road is realized through the communication with LTE-Uu or LTE-PC5 between OBU and RSU.

For V2X communication over LTE-Uu, which is supported only when the UE is inside network coverage, a UE may receive V2X messages via downlink unicast or broadcast while transmitting V2X messages via uplink.

Through the V2X Server in the cloud/edge, the collaboration of vehicle, road, and cloud can provide more enabled applications. For example, intelligent and connected vehicles with their networking service have become a widely recognized IoV development trend in China. China planned to utilize unified cellular standards for V2V and V2I communication in 2018. Then, an important step had given the country's large population and growing global economic importance toward C-V2X in recent years.

6.5.3.3 *Comparison of DSRC and C-V2X from a technical view*

The current C-V2X landscape includes LTE-V2X by R14, 5G NR-V2X by R15, and R16 of 3GPP. These differences around the world illustrate that there are strategic planning and deployment choices to be made. The C-V2X 3GPP standard was completed in March 2017, and 5G C-V2X (in R16) was completed in 2020 with products underway. Table 6.11 compares DSRC, release 14 C-V2X, and 5G C-V2X at a high-level.

As mentioned in Table 6.11, the DSRC support for V2I is limited because in VANET, the connection between vehicles to infrastructure by RSU is one hop and it cannot guarantee that the connection from the nearest vehicle to RSU is within the range of the communication coverage.

Since 2019, China began to launch regulatory and testing efforts in R14 C-V2X. Then, products or modules of R14 V2X began to change the "limited" regulatory/testing efforts. For backward compatibility design of 3GPP, a 5G V2X-enabled vehicle or RSU will be supported both by LTE-V2X services (e.g., the basic safety for which LTE-based V2X was designed) and some expected advanced services, e.g., for automated/autonomous driving.)

With a focus on enabling vehicular safety for longer-range and enhanced-reliability use cases, C-V2X has several advantages over DSRC, including the following:

- Enhanced safety for longer range and enhanced reliability in cellular networking, especially 5G.
- More consistent performance under traffic congestion and better coexistence with other technologies.
- Evolution path towards 5G (R16/R17) for emerging applications with URLLC, eMBB, and mMTC (including mobile/cellular IoT networking capability) around vehicles.
- The extended sensor ability and its upgraded capability in compatibility.

In order to enhance safety and efficiency, C-V2X in R14 and DSRC already support low latency and reliable exchange of messages among

Table 6.11 High-level comparison of attributes for DSRC, LTE V2X, and 5G V2X.

Key Elements	DSRC/ IEEE8021.11p	R14 C-V2X	5G C-V2X(R15-R16, expected)	Remarks
Out-of-network operation	✓	✓	✓	R14 cellular communication technology provides long-range connectivity of up to two kilometers.
Support for V2V	✓	✓	✓	DSRC provides medium range connectivity of 300 to 1000 meters.
Support for safety-critical uses	✓	✓	✓	DSRC is highly suitable for V2V applications and moderately suitable for V2I applications.
Support for V2P	✓	✓	✓	
Support for V2I	limited	✓	✓	C-V2X more suitable for V2I applications and moderately supports V2V applications until D2D (PC5) arise.
Support for multimedia services	×	✓	✓	
Network coverage support	limited	✓	✓	
Regulatory/testing efforts	✓	limited	×	
Very high throughput	×	×	✓	
Very high-reliability	×	×	✓	
Wideband ranging and positioning	×	×	✓	
Very low latency	×	×	✓	
Proposed applications:	Collision detection, electronic toll collection, traveler information services.			

vehicles and the infrastructure. However, 5G V2X along with emerging applications in IoV are expected to be increasingly autonomous with many advanced safety and non-safety functionalities. Continuous advancements in V2X technologies are needed to meet emerging requirements. Some of them will be introduced in the next part.

Here is an example of sensor sharing, which is envisioned to be a promising feature for vehicles to significantly enhance vehicles' visibility beyond their immediate line-of-sight (LoS) vicinity. Sensor sharing requires the exchange of a large amount of data (e.g., a series of objects or camera feeds) among vehicles and even infrastructure, and in many cases, very low latency and high reliability are necessary to ensure timeliness and accuracy of the received data. Given the expected high vehicle density in many congested urban areas, and evolved V2X technology that can support very high capacity and data rates, as well as low latency, is needed to enable sensor sharing.

The following two testing scenarios are from Qualcomm, Inc., and they show consistent performance is enabling vehicle communication use cases. One is for the comparison in **longer C-V2X range than DSRC; the other is for** the comparison in limited visibility of the opposite traffic scenario where a vehicle follows a large truck has.

As shown in Fig. 6.76, C-V2X can achieve LoS and non-LoS (NLoS) V2V ranges of 443 m and 107 m, respectively, compared to 240 m and

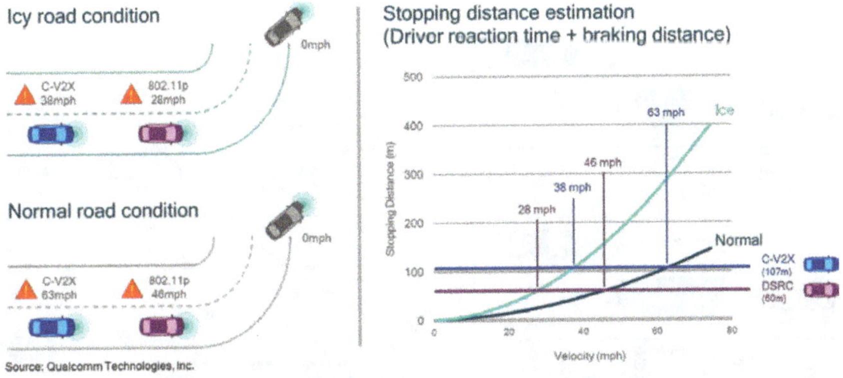

Figure 6.76 A disabled vehicle behind a blind curve is transmitting alerts to approaching vehicles under both icy and normal road conditions. If DSRC is used, an approaching vehicle must maintain a speed below 28 mph and 46 mph for icy and normal road conditions, respectively, to stop in time to avoid an accident after receiving an alert.

60 m, respectively, for DSRC. And the test is based on link-level simulation analysis and the stopping distance estimation consistent with CAMP deceleration model.

Figure 6.76 illustrates a scenario of a disabled vehicle after blind curve use case. With C-V2X, the incoming vehicle receives the alert earlier at a longer distance away. Therefore, it can stop before reaching the disabled vehicle even if it is traveling at a higher speed, for example, 38 mph and 63 mph for icy and normal road conditions, respectively.

The longer range can be translated into earlier alerts and better visibility of unexpected and potentially dangerous situations; furthermore, it allows vehicles to travel at higher speeds while still being able to stop in time to avoid hazardous conditions.

Figure 6.77 illustrates a do-not-pass use case scenario where a vehicle following a large truck has limited visibility of the opposite traffic. At the same time, a second vehicle is approaching the first vehicle from the adjacent lane. The higher the vehicle speeds, the faster the two vehicles approach each other and the more dangerous is the situation if the first vehicle is selected to pass the truck.

Similar to the first example, the longer C-V2X range allows the first vehicle to receive the alerts earlier, thus allowing it to safely pass the truck even if it is traveling at a higher speed compared to the case when DSRC is used.

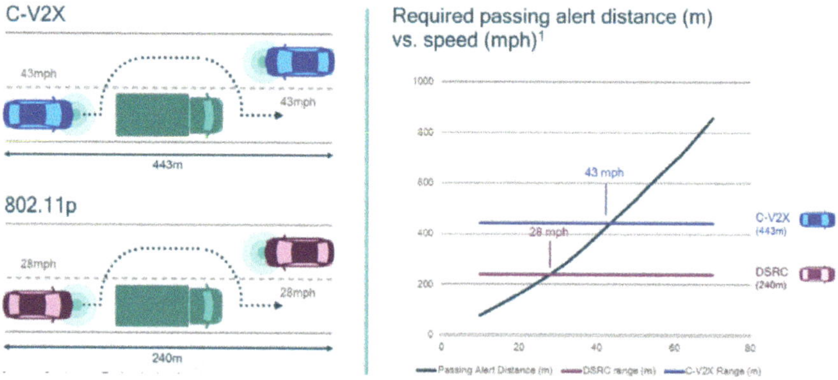

Figure 6.77 In the do-not-pass warning use case, with V2V communication, the second vehicle ahead can send warning alerts, which are used by the first vehicle (followed) to decide whether it should pass the truck in between them.

Note: Required passing alert distance vs. speed calculations based on AASHTO "green book".

As for the consistent C-V2X performance even in congested conditions, safety messages are generally transmitted more or less periodically for a given duration. C-V2X is designed to leverage these quasi-periodic traffic arrival patterns to deterministically pre-allocate resources for subsequent traffic arrivals. This semi-persistent scheduling mechanism ensures that resources are available when traffic arrives. There is no need to go through resource contention procedures for subsequent traffic, thus allowing C-V2X to maintain low latency even as vehicle density increases.

6.5.3.4 *Comparison between different countries and regions*

In the application of 760 MHz broadcasting frequency band, Japan mainly considers V2I and V2V at crossroads; the former includes the cooperation between RSUs and vehicle OBUs, while the latter includes the cooperation between vehicles: the exchange of location, speed, etc. For example, in 2014, Japan carried out a 760 MHz communication performance verification, evaluated the service performance of V2V and V2I cooperative communication in a controllable environment, and their applicability for emergency vehicles (e.g., ambulances) based on data exchange and analysis.

In recent years (2015–2016), V2V and V2I cooperative communications which were able to serve the autonomous driving system were developed in Japan. From the perspective of intelligent and connecting vehicles (ICV), on the one hand, it carried out the road test for ordinary drivers under real conditions; on the other hand, it deployed the application of a safe driving assistant system in trams, road construction vehicles, and public transport systems. From the perspective of cooperative V2I construction, Japan still develops its infrastructure along with ETC facilities (as mentioned in Table 6.12). After 2017, the cooperative V2X of IoV gradually upgraded to the safe driving support system for different levels of automation service (six levels from L0–L5 as SAE J3016 described). These works lay the groundwork for cellular-ADAS (advanced driving assistance system) based on the C-V2X network. Subsequently, the concept of C-ADAS gradually appeared, that is, an advanced driving assistance system based on the cellular network. From then on, the "C" in C-V2X implies another meaning besides cellular — cooperative. Table 6.12 describes the different technology roadmap and framework among the US, Japan, and Europe.

In Europe, the idea of cooperating in V2X or ITS arose early in 2008 when the European Union issued its action plan of cooperative ITS.

Table 6.12 Differences among U.S., Japan and European on their IoV respective development.

Country	Policy in priority	Frequency	Standard framework	Technology roadmap	Methodology	Marks
The United States	1. Safety/ Collision-avoidance; 2. Mobility/accessibility; 3. Context awareness in IoV	5.9 GHz	Low layer: IEEE 802.11p; Medium layer: WSMP; High layer: BSM	Emphasis on V2V, with DSRC	ISO/IEC and IEEE 42010:2011-based structure and software engineering related standard. Development: encouraging vehicle manufacturers to adopt complementary sensing and communication (V2V, V2I) technology with built-in sensors for the ADAS high-level automated driving system.	The US hopes to lay the V2X infrastructure foundation for autonomous driving, and by 2040, roadside infrastructure will be deployed.
Japan	1. Safety/ Driving-assistant; 2. Mobility/accessibility in IoV	5.8 GHz/760 MHz	Low layer: ARIB STD-T75; Medium layer: EC-006; High layer: T75/RC005	Based on the steady progress of ETC facilities practically.	ETC upgrades in roadside units; V2P cooperates between pedestrian and vehicle terminal; millimeter-wave radar is deployed in RSU to collect pedestrian and bicycle data at intersections and other key sections, and data is shared based on V2I.	In cooperative intelligent transportation, dynamic traffic operation environment recognition based on cooperative communication data exchange (such as automated driving infrastructure in SIP-adus[a]) is realized.

EU	1. Safety/prediction and warning; 2. Context awareness in IoV 3. Mobility/accessibility in environment	5.9 GHz	Low layer: ITS G5[b] (assess layer)/LTE-Medium layer: GeoNetworking/ BTP High layer: CAM/DENM/ LDM	Focus on the development of V2I, and its synergy in ITS. Consider a variety of wireless communication.	GeoNetworking makes use of geographical position information for packet transport and supports the communication among individual ITS stations as well as the distribution of packets in geographical areas.	Emergency and aid vehicle warning, fault or anchored vehicle warning, obstacles and weather warning have been realized.

Notes: [a]SIP-adus is a Japanese research program on connected and automated driving led by the Japanese government that began in 2014. Beginning from 2016, the project prioritized five themes (dynamic map, human-machine interfaces (HMI), cyber-security, pedestrian collision reduction, and next-generation transport). Large-scale field operational tests started in October 2017 around the Tokyo area in order to integrate and evaluate achievements. Its contents reflect the latest progress in the theory, technology, and application of automated driving and related fields.

[b]ITS-G5 is defined by ETSI, and its radio air interface is based on IEEE 802.11p (DSRC in the US), which is an approved amendment of the Wi-Fi standard (IEEE 802.11p) to add wireless access in vehicular environments (WAVE). ITS G5 works independently of cellular networks, it supports V2V and V2I low-latency short-range communication in the 5.9 GHz frequency band and uses orthogonal frequency-division multiplexing (OFDM) and a carrier sense multiple access (CSMA)-based protocol in the MAC layer. ITS-G5 facilitates high reliability under high vehicle speed mobility conditions. Enhancements towards more advanced services such as autonomous driving are addressed and on-going.

Then, in October 2009, under the joint efforts of CEN, CENELEC, and ETSI, the European Union began to mandate C-ITS standard. In February 2014, the first edition of the C-ITS standard was completed. Later, as mentioned in Table 6.12, the preferred V2I strategy outlined by the European Commission serves as the foundation for implementing the necessary legal framework that enables the commercial deployment of cooperative intelligent transportation systems.

In Europe, the cooperative intelligent transportation system (C-ITS) is used to refer to the infrastructure based on V2X and the cooperative technologies of IoV, which are considered to be the most important characteristics of C-ITS different from traditional ITS. Cooperative ITS is a group of technologies and applications that allow effective data exchange through wireless technologies of IoV among elements and actors of the transport system, very often between vehicles (vehicle-to-vehicle or V2V) or between vehicles and infrastructure (vehicle-to-infrastructure or V2I) (but also with) vulnerable road users such as pedestrians, cyclists, or motorcyclists.

Finally, in terms of IoV infrastructure for (connected) automated driving, Europe has developed the *ERTRAC — Connected Automated Driving Roadmap 2019* and proposes infrastructure support levels for automated driving (ISAD) based on digital infrastructure support for connected and collaborative automated driving, as shown in Table 6.13.

6.5.4 *IoV in 5G Era*

With the rapid development of cellular technology, the connotation of the IoVs is constantly enriched and extended. At present, the communication technology of the IoVs is generally replaced by V2X, where "X" stands for everything, that is, everything that can be connected to the IoVs. Therefore, C-V2X is V2X technologies based on cellular communication defined by 3GPP (3rd generation partnership project). They include V2X communication technology and systems based on LTE and 5G, which can be seen to be a powerful supplement to DSRC-based technology.

6.5.4.1 *5G fitting V2X by network slicing*

5G use cases have diverse requirements, including high data rates for eMBB, low power consumption and high scalability for mobile IoT

Table 6.13 Network-linked collaborative autonomous driving classification supported by digital infrastructure in Europe

Items	Classification	Name	Description	Digital maps and static road marking information	VMS, warning, accident, atmospheric information	Information on traffic conditions	Guidance speed, vehicle spacing, lane choice
Digital Infrastructure	A	Cooperative driving	Based on the acquisition of real-time information on vehicle movements, the infrastructure is able to guide individual vehicles or formations of vehicles in order to optimize the overall traffic flow.	✓	✓	✓	✓
	B	Collaborative Perception	The infrastructure is capable of acquiring information on traffic conditions and transmitting it in real time to self-driving vehicles.	✓	✓	✓	
	C	Digitization of dynamic information	All static and dynamic infrastructure information is made available to the autonomous vehicle in digital form.	✓	✓		

(*Continued*)

Table 6.13 (*Continued*)

Items	Classification	Name	Description	Digital maps and static road marking information	VMS, warning, accident, atmospheric information	Information on traffic conditions	Guidance speed, vehicle spacing, lane choice
Traditional Infrastructure	D	Static information digitization/ map support	Digital map data and static road sign are available. The map data can be supplemented by physical reference points (landmarks). Traffic lights, temporary road construction, and variable message signs (VMS) still need to be identified by the automated vehicle.	✓			
	E	Conventional infrastructure/ not supporting autonomous driving	Traditional infrastructure cannot provide digital information and requires autonomous vehicles themselves to recognize road geometry and traffic signs.				

Note: ISAD (Infrastructure Support levels for Automated Driving) is from "ERTRAC — Connected Automated Driving Roadmap 2019".

(mIoT, the same as cellular IoT in Section 5.7), and ultra-low latency and high-reliability communications (URLLC) for mission-critical services. Meanwhile, the ever-increasing mobile data traffic volume means that 5G must support more spectrum bands and types, from sub-6 GHz to mm wave, as well as licensed, shared, and unlicensed allocations.

At the same time, a number of cities and infrastructure providers offer solutions with ITS combined cellular platforms for vehicles services, including but not limited to LBSs, e.g., IoVs are embracing more things around the mobile IoT besides the vehicles and V2X infrastructure through edge computing or MEC, in an open vision. With more details included in IoV, more dangers can be predicted and avoided ahead. Here, the technical scenario of 5G NR-V2X is taken as an example as 5G's end-to-end capabilities of network slicing. Then, IoV in its integrated way to a smart vision of ITS is analyzed. At last, the expected benefits of 5G-based V2X will be introduced.

As the development of 5G technology expands the scope of use cases with one technology fit all, it is anticipated that broader adoption of 5G cellular will occur for C-V2X, especially for V2I and V2N. A number of trials are ongoing around 5G, and V2X is one of the preferred use cases. This being said, the ITU and countries need to allocate 5G spectrum, operators need to deploy 5G, and OBU manufacturers need to evolve their existing products to support 5G new radio (NR) when available, if the desire is to fully leverage 5G's end-to-end capabilities. As introduced in Section 5.8.3, network slicing is an enabling technology that seemed to fit all use cases in autonomous driving or safety/emergency services, e.g., an ultra-reliable low-latency (URLLC) network slice would be required in the network of V2N for V2I or V2V use cases. At the same time, some assistant or personal mobility services would require either a best-effort slice or an eMBB slice in the case of streaming infotainment video (as the early-stage requirement of IoV, together with telematics built-in).

For example, a given vehicle could access different slices, with passengers watching an HD and real-time map, while a see-through application detects a road hazard ahead and triggers an emergency message for the cars around to slow down or stop to prevent an accident.

According to this multi-slice requirement of 5G, slices could come from one "device" or multiple devices. In the case of one device, as illustrated in Fig. 6.78, 3GPP defined that a given device can support up to eight different slices with a common access and mobility function

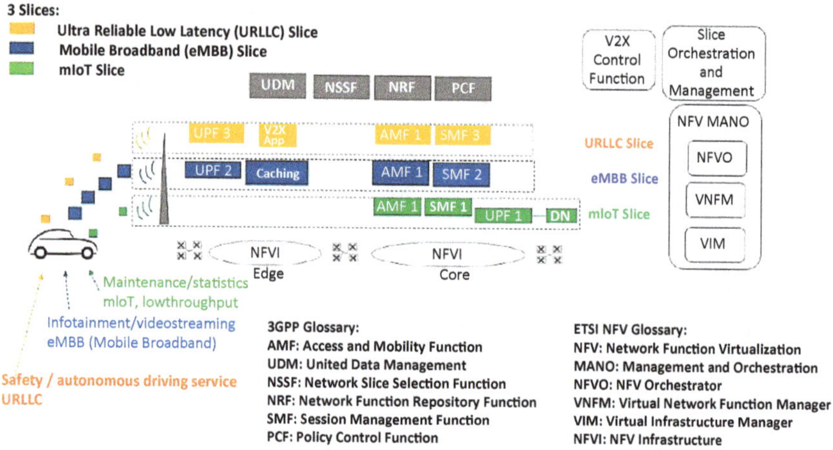

Figure 6.78 Technical scenario of 5G NR-V2X network slicing example.

(AMF) for all the slices and a session management function (SMF)[57] per slice. In Fig. 6.78's example, there are three network slices attached to the same device and sharing the same AMF instance. Slice no. 1 is mIoT and sends data to the core and the data network. Slice no. 2 offers caching at the edge, while slice no. 3 offers access to an edge V2X application.

6.5.4.2 *A unified technology vision of IoV in 5G era*

In 2019, the FCC chairman proposed to reallocate 5.9 GHz wireless spectrum resources, hoping to allow C-V2X and unlicensed Wi-Fi devices to share the band. Subsequently, the FCC redistributes most of the spectrum in the 5.9 GHz band and uses 20 MHz of 5.905–5.925 GHz for C-V2X wireless communication technology.

As for the communication technologies are concerned, new rules are adopted by the European Commission in its C-ITS roads, as foreseeing the use of complementary technologies, by offering different advantages: low latency for safety-critical services and high coverage using existing cellular networks. While the current decision includes detailed

[57] 3GPP TS 23.285.

specifications for mature intelligent transport systems-G5 (ITS-G5) technology for safety-related services, additional technologies may be integrated.[58]

At present, the IoVs related organizations in Europe, the US, and Japan are promising, and maybe work together to form a compatible IoV operation platform. The basic IoV communication organization from a technical vision can be seen in Fig. 6.79.

6.5.4.3 *ITS vision of smart Columbus and Chinese CAV roadmap*

More and more mIoT supported applications and platforms are emerging in ITS, ranging from connected vehicles to smart logistic, from connected residents to connected visitors.

In the 2020s, when the US examined the IoVs from the perspective of intelligent transportation and smart city, Smart Columbus has a vision that starts with the reinvention of mobility, which adopts electric vehicle (EV) to sustainable transportation and others as access to convenience jobs, smart logistics, residents' connection, and visitors' connection. All the five perspectives are unified in the vision of smart Columbus, leading to a bright future, as shown in Fig. 6.80.

Intelligent-connected vehicles, Chinese smart expressways with digital infrastructures and further extended sensors supported RSU/OBU are on their way to the "new four modernizations" of the automobile industry now. The following table gives the Chinese ICV and smart mobility roadmap. Autonomous driving will be introduced in the next part of this section with extended sensors.

With the help of all-round connection and efficient information interaction among people, vehicles, roads, and cloud platforms, at present, C-V2X is developing from information service application to traffic safety and efficiency application and will gradually evolve to collaborative service application supporting automatic driving as the smart mobility stage of the Chinese upgrading stages listed in Table 6.14. On the "new four modernizations" of Chinese automobile industry, C-V2X

[58] The European Commission has today adopted new rules stepping up the deployment of cooperative intelligent transport systems (C-ITS) on Europe's roads.

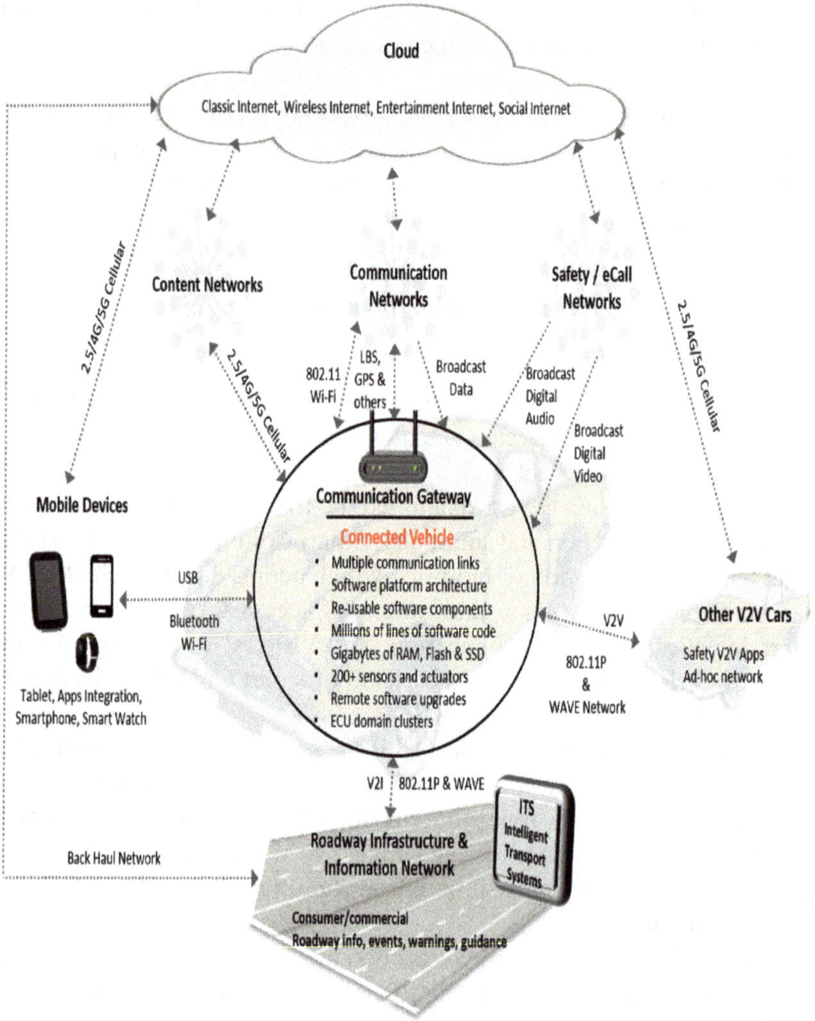

Figure 6.79 Technical scenario of IoV (gateways can be set at edge or MEC. Smart phone/watch with apps integration is an interface for pedestrian or other moving elements in/out of IoV scope, through cellular, Wi-Fi, and Bluetooth or other LPWAN of IoT).

typical integration and application are unfolded into the following four ICV-related aspects:

- **Improve Driving Safety:** Improving driving safety is the most important significance of C-V2X. Through the multi-source perception

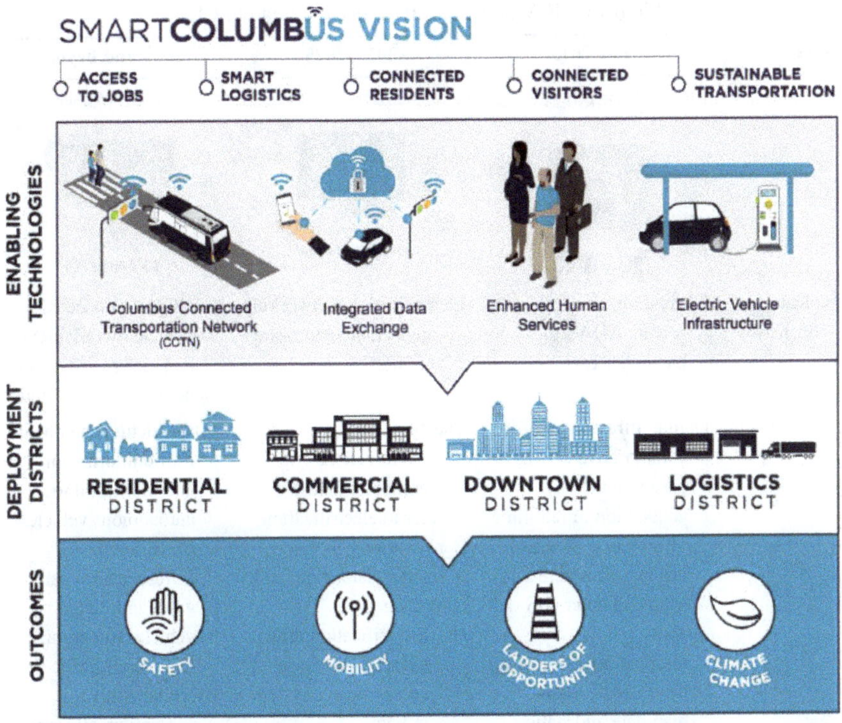

Figure 6.80 ITS vision of smart Columbus of the US.

fusion of C-V2X vehicle device/equipment as OBU and intelligent roadside RSU, the real-time situation of the road environment is perceived, analyzed, and given for decided assistance. In the case of possible danger or collision, the intelligent network vehicle gives an early warning, providing more reliable, safe, and real-time environmental information acquisition for vehicle travel.

Typical C-V2X traffic safety applications include the warning of traffic ahead from intersections, accidents ahead, blind areas monitoring, road emergencies, etc.

- **Improve Traffic Efficiency and Driving Safety:** Improving traffic efficiency is an important role of C-V2X. C-V2X can enhance the traffic perception ability, realize the network connection, and the congestion reminder, build the intelligent traffic system, optimize the route guidance by dynamically allocating the road network resources,

Table 6.14 ICV and smart mobility roadmap in China.

Stage	**1996–2015**	**2015–2025**	**2025 and beyond**
	Telematics  2G/3G/4G	Intelligent Connected Vehicle  Cellular-V2X (LTE-V)	Smart Mobility 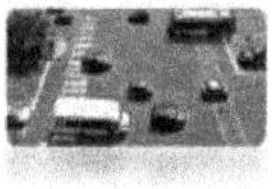 5G (NR-V2X)
Typical Scenarios	Navigation, emergency rescue, ADAS for passenger cars.	Electrification, networking, intellectualization, and sharing.	Intelligent-connected vehicle by OBU/RSU and many digital and network infrastructures.
Key Enablers	Digital infrastructure for collaborative driving — based on the acquisition of real-time information of vehicle driving, such as Baidu Map and other GIS apps. Traditional infrastructure can provide digital map data and static road sign information. Map data can be supplemented by physical reference points (landmarks). Construction of traffic lights is still needed.	The “new four modernizations” of automobile industry refer to electrification, networking, intellectualization, and sharing. (1) Electrification refers to the field of new energy power system in EVs; (2) Intelligence refers to unmanned driving or driving assistance system; (3) Networking refers to the layout of the IoVs; (4) Sharing refers to car sharing as Uber/DiDi for mobile travel.	Infrastructure can obtain traffic information and transmit it to autonomous vehicles in real time. Infrastructures can guide individual vehicles to optimize the overall traffic flow. By collaborative perception, all static and dynamic infrastructure information is provided to autonomous vehicles in digital form.

provide the priority of way for the urban mass public transport vehicles and special vehicles, improve the urban traffic operation efficiency, and further improve the traffic management efficiency, especially the ability of regional collaborative control.

Typical C-V2X traffic efficiency applications include front congestion alert, traffic light signal broadcast, and speed guidance, the priority of special vehicle intersections, etc.

- **Provide travel information services:** Providing travel service is an important part of the C-V2X application and a means to comprehensively improve government supervision, enterprise operation, and people's travel level. Typical applications of C-V2X information service include severe weather warnings, electronic signs in the vehicle, etc.

- **Support for automatic driving:** Vehicle road coordination is an important means of supporting automatic landing. Through local information collection, analysis, and decision-making, it provides collision warning, driving assistance, and information reminder services for intelligent network vehicles, providing auxiliary decision-making capabilities for automatic driving, improving the safety of automatic driving, reducing the cost of vehicles adapting to various special road conditions, and accelerating the landing of autopilot vehicles.

  Typical application scenarios of automatic driving include vehicle formation driving, remote control driving, autonomous parking, etc. The basic and enhanced business scenarios of IoVs are introduced in the following as use-cases analysis. They are mainly divided into three categories: security, efficiency, and information service.

6.5.4.4 *5G-V2X use-cases*

5G Automotive Association (5GAA) is an organization created to connect the telecom industry and vehicle manufacturers and to work closely together to develop end-to-end solutions for future mobility and transportation services.

In the evolution from LTE-V2X to 5G NR V2X and beyond, end-to-end solutions for intelligent transportation, mobility systems, and IoVs include the automotive industry, vehicle platform, hardware and software solutions (HW/SW). From the views of IoVs, the work of 5GAA ranges from connectivity and networking systems of communications, devices, and technologies that are designed and adapted to future needs for advanced sensing, to communication and computing technologies that should be integrated into vehicles to improve these statistics and save lives.

Beyond saving peoples' lives, these technologies will also enable fully autonomous driving, which will profoundly transform transportation into the intelligence interconnection of IoVs. The sample use cases of 5G V2X are listed in Table 6.15.

Among these cases, the extended sensors, platooning, and remote driving are introduced, and they are all based on the 3GPP and 5GAA views.

Table 6.15 Sample use-cases enabled by C-V2X.

5G V2X assistance scenarios	Function	Remarks
Left turn assistance	Alerts are given to the driver as they attempt an unprotected left turn across traffic, to help them avoid crashes with traffic from the opposite direction.	Alerts ahead.
Intersection movement assistance	Informs driver when it is not safe to enter an intersection — e.g., when something is blocking the driver's view of opposing or crossing traffic.	For example, a god's view and the see-through case
Emergency electronic brake lights	The driver is alerted to hard braking in the traffic stream ahead. This provides the driver with additional time to look for and assess situations developing ahead.	Driver alerted ahead
Queue warning	Intended to engage well in advance of any potential crash situation, providing messages and information to the driver in order to minimize the crash or take mitigating actions later. The infrastructure will broadcast queue warnings to vehicles in order to minimize or prevent rear-end or other secondary collisions.	Platooning
Speed harmonization	Determines speed recommendations based on traffic conditions and weather information. It detects the developing roadway or congestion conditions that might necessitate speed adjustments for upstream traffic and broadcasts such recommendations to vehicles long before they reach the affected area.	Collaboration
Real-time situational awareness	Provides mechanisms for vehicles to receive real-time information about city/roadway projects, lane closures, traffic, and other conditions that may necessitate adjustments to driving patterns.	Dynamic adjustments

Software updates	Provides mechanisms for vehicles to receive the latest software updates and security credentials required to ensure their safe operation.	For example, OTA
Remote vehicle health monitoring	Provides mechanisms to diagnose vehicle issues remotely. As driving becomes more autonomous, this becomes the key mechanism for remote supervision of vehicle functions and its health.	Online diagnose
Real-time high definition maps	Provides situational awareness for autonomous vehicles at critical road segments in cases of changing road conditions (e.g., new traffic cone detected by another vehicle some time ago).	HD maps generators and consumers
High-definition sensor sharing	Provides mechanisms for vehicles to share HD sensor data (Lidar, cameras, etc.) to enable better driving coordination for platoon and intersection management.	The following mentioned extended sensor (connected sensor sharing in IoVs)
See through	Provides abilities for vehicles such as trucks, minivans, cars in platoons to share camera images of road conditions ahead of them to vehicles behind them.	See the followed part
Vulnerable road user discovery	Provides the ability to identify potential safety conditions due to the presence of vulnerable road users, such as pedestrians or cyclists.	A typical IoV services, either from RSUs or sensors sharing in cellular and VANETs *ad hoc* meshing

6.5.4.5 *5G C-V2X as a new sensor for longer detection in uRLLC usages*

Release 16 C-V2X incorporates 5G NR design features to enable new use cases for automated driving with more stringent requirements. 5G NR-based C-V2X will deliver higher throughput, lower latency, and better reliability and will be enhanced to support both unicast and multicast in addition to broadcast communication. It will also enable wideband ranging and positioning to deliver more precise (e.g., sub-meter) location accuracy.[59]

With these enhanced capabilities, 5G C-V2X will become a new type of sensor with ultra-long range and high accuracy by leveraging vehicles as moving sensor platforms. For example, in a typical "see-through" use case scenario, a vehicle following a large truck with limited forward visibility can receive high-quality and real-time video feeds from cameras installed on the trunk or other nearby vehicles to gain visibility. Figure 6.81 gives the V2N based see-through perception scenario.

As an example, vehicles send messages that provide non-line-of-sight (NLoS) awareness to other vehicles. This is particularly important intersections/on-ramps or where environmental conditions (e.g., rain, fog, snow) impair the range of the onboard sensors. As shown in Fig. 6.81, the red car warns about the cyclist behind it, which the yellow car cannot see.

From a V2X service view, a piece of useful information affects the associations between traffic participants and related services, e.g., a person moving closer to a camera (vehicle) is associated with the device and services offered by the camera of this vehicle for other vehicles or pedestrians. In such cases, the temporal availability of the associations between an IoT grid and services needs to be captured, as additional attribution in the real-time IoT grid. It is important to observe that several of these pieces of information as PIoT that serve an IoT grid can contribute

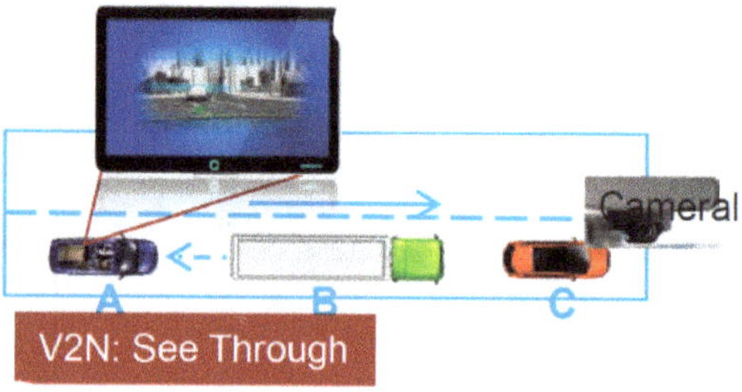

Figure 6.81 V2N-based see-through perception scenario in the intersection NLoS view.

[59] 3GPP Technical specification TS 22.186.

themselves to information sharing, by high-reliability networks such as 5G, or an edge-cloud collaboration service platform (see the last use case of this section).

In another example, a cloud-based sensor analytic platform can be established to deliver visibility and accuracy unrivaled by traditional stand-alone sensors that operate only under line-of-sight conditions. Using 5G C-V2X, this cloud sensor platform can collect a large volume of raw and/or processed sensor data from vehicles in a region. Then, the data is analyzed in real time (e.g., using AI) to identify important objects and events and pinpoint their locations. The results are then streamed to vehicles in real time together with other relevant data, such as an HD map.

Apart from the enhanced visibility and accuracy, this new C-V2X sensor also provides access to high-quality sensor data to vehicles with less-capable onboard sensors, e.g., the side link (SL) in Fig. 6.82, for information exchange directly and thus further improves road safety.[60]

From 5GAA views, extended sensors refer to the ability of vehicles to obtain information about objects around them, which is beyond the view of their own onboard sensors. Other nearby vehicles can detect these objects process them, then broadcast them out to aid other vehicles around

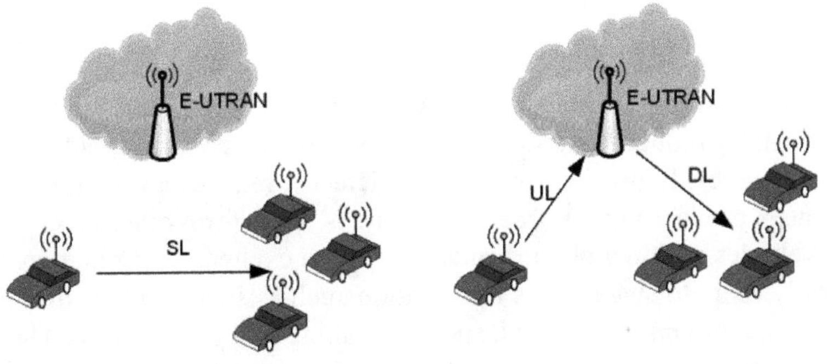

Figure 6.82 SL for information exchange directly in V2V (D2D-PC5 mode) and uplink/downlink for UE to cellular V2X, by uu-interface (eNB base station).

[60] 3GPP TS 22.071: "Location Services (LCS); Service description, Stage 1". 3GPP TS 23.032: "Universal Geographical Area Description (GAD)". 3GPP TS 36.331: "Evolved Universal Terrestrial Radio Access (E-UTRA); Radio Resource Control (RRC); Protocol specification". 3GPP TS 36.214: "Evolved Universal Terrestrial Radio Access (E-UTRA); Physical layer — Measurements". 3GPP TS 36.302: "Evolved Universal Terrestrial Radio Access (E-UTRA); Services provided by the physical layer".

in building up a more complete picture of the traffic environment. Current work on this aspect is taking place in ETSI ITS and 5GAA. And the traditional ADAS is changed into another new words-collaborative ADAS, by the connected sharing sensors.

Extended sensors enable the sharing of raw and processed sensor data (for example, cameras, radar, LIDAR) among vehicles, RSUs, pedestrians, and V2X application servers. The sensor data that a vehicle can share ranges from a photo of a perceived object to its real-time video stream. The availability of sensor data from multiple disparate sources enhances situation awareness of the vehicles and pedestrians and thus improves road safety. Extended sensors also enable new features and capabilities, such as cooperative driving and precise positioning, which are necessary for autonomous driving.

The potential communication requirements between two V2X nodes to support extended sensors include:

- High bandwidth to support burst transmission of large quantities of data.
- Less than 10 ms latency.
- High message reliability of 95%.
- High connection density to support congested areas (e.g., there are 15,000 vehicles per mile at a congested highway intersection).

6.5.4.6 *Platooning and remote driving*

Platooning allows vehicles to form a tightly coordinated "train" with significantly reduced inter-vehicle distance, thus increasing road capacity and efficiency. It also improves fuel efficiency, reduces accident rate, and enhances productivity by freeing up drivers to perform other tasks.

Vehicles within a platoon must be able to exchange information periodically (e.g., to share status information such as speed and heading) and to send event announcements, such as braking and acceleration. The following are several aspects of platooning that must be supported through reliable V2V communications:

- **Joining and leaving a platoon:** to allow a vehicle to signal its intention to join or to leave a platoon at any time while the platoon is active and to support additional signaling to complete the join/leave operations.
- **Announcement and warning:** to indicate the formation and existence of the platoon so that nearby vehicles can select to join the platoon or to avoid disruptions to the platoon.

- **Steady-state operation group communication:** to support the exchange of platoon management messages also to indicate braking, acceleration, which road to take, the change of platoon leader, etc.
- **Specific requirements for the operation vehicles:** to meet the platooning requirements for the operation vehicles in the limited scene or just within the operation area. For example, distance control between two operation vehicles and real-time scheduling among them.

Given the small target inter-vehicle distance while the vehicles are traveling at relatively high speed, V2V communication must be able to support reliable, high duty cycles and secure message exchange to ensure effective and safe platooning operation. The following are some key V2V communication requirements to support platooning:[61]

- 25ms end-to-end communication latency among a group of vehicles (10 ms for the highest degree of automation);
- 90% message reliability, and 99.99% for the highest degree of automation;
- relative longitudinal position accuracy of less than 0.5 m;
- 10 to 30 messages per second of broadcasting rate;
- dynamic communication range control to improve resource efficiency given the varying platoon size and to limit message distribution for privacy reasons.

Remote driving enables the remote control of a vehicle by a human operator or by a cloud-based application, via V2N communication.[62] Several scenarios can leverage remote driving including the following:

- **Provide a backup solution for autonomous vehicles.** An example is during the initial autonomous vehicle deployment when a vehicle is in an unfamiliar environment and has difficulty navigating, and a remote operator can take control.
- **Provide remote driver services** to youth, elderly, and others who are not licensed or able to drive.
- **Enable fleet owners to remotely control their vehicles.** Examples include moving trucks from one location to another, delivering rental cars to customers, and providing remotely-driven taxi services.

---

[61] 3GPP TS 22.186.
[62] 3GPP TS 38.331: "NR Radio Resource Control (RRC) protocol specification".

- **Enable cloud-driven public transportation and private shuttles,** all of which are particularly suitable for services with predefined stops and routes.

Remote driving can be used in a way to lower the cost of fully autonomous driving for certain use cases because of the lower technical requirements (e.g., a smaller number of built-in sensors and fewer computation requirements for sophisticated algorithms). The following are some potential V2X requirements for supporting remote driving:

- Data rate up to 1 Mbps downlink and 25 Mbps at uplink (assuming two H.265/HEVC HD stream up to 10 Mb/s each);
- Ultra-high reliability at 99.999% or higher (URLLC);
- End-to-end latency of 5 ms between the V2X application server and the vehicle;
- Vehicular speed of up to 250 km/h.

Remote control/driving will be required when an obstacle blocks a level 4 or 5 autonomous vehicles, rendering it unable to decide on a pathway or approach to safely bypass it. Examples of obstacles include blocked lanes due to a proximate accident, unexpected or never-experienced situations where the vehicle is unable to decide on a safe action.

When the vehicle encounters such situation, it will stop or find a position with minimum risk and then request the assistance of a remote-control operator to take control and drive it around the obstacle. For the remote controller to understand the obstacle and determine the pathway the vehicle takes, the controller will utilize the streaming sensor information (e.g., video, LIDAR, radar) that has been made available to users.

Besides the above mentioned, if the operation vehicles work in a strictly limited working area, such as the sightseeing bus in scenic area or mining trucks, the remote control is also important for the embarrassed navigation before an emergency, especially when the vehicle itself does not know how to proceed or handle the encountering situations.

Although the services with predefined stops and routes are arranged ahead, an enabling edge-driven non-public transportation controller is needed as a backup for security. The so-called "edge controllers" are particularly suitable for operational vehicles and the control scenarios of IIoT and TIoT. Additionally, the secure and high available communication is often needed by an end-to-end vertical way (e.g., TSN), either onboard or not, in a built-in model and a relative open IoV platform. See the following parts.

6.5.4.7 *Autonomous vehicle use-case*

• **Built-in IoT model:** As for a driver, high-level ADAS or autonomous driving vehicles interacting with the physical world is the key for the IoT/IoV service platform in vehicles, which we call as built-in OS that needs to be captured in the domain model (Fig. 6.83). The first and most fundamental interaction is between a human and an agent (of the application) with the physical world object or place. Therefore, a user and a physical entity are two concepts that belong to the domain model. A user can be a human user or an agent (e.g., a driving agent in automated driving or an agent in the responsibility of telling us a predicted danger), and the interaction can be physical (e.g., parking the car in the parking lot or automated valet parking (AVP) of L4 of SAE, see Section 6.2.2). The physical

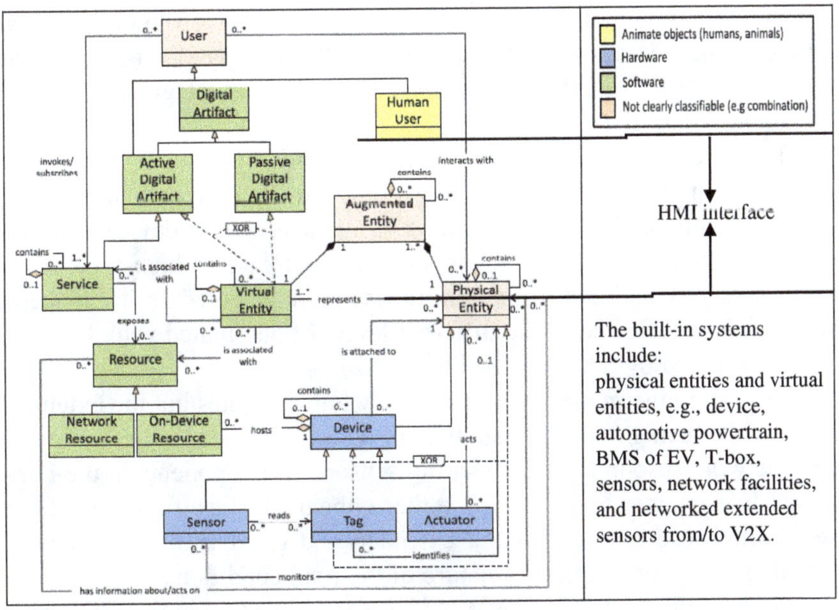

Figure 6.83 SOA-based built-in IoT domain model.

Source: IoT-A.

interaction is the result of the intention of the human or a driving agent to achieve a certain goal (e.g., braking or turn left/right). On other occasions, a user can also choose to interact with the physical environment by means of a service or application, e.g., from environmental sensors to the control of ACC of ADAS.

This application is also a user in the domain model. A physical entity, as the model shows, can potentially contain either an IoT grid/domain hardware which has physical attachments to device/actuator or other entities, or both of HW and SW (integration as an IoT grid, see Section 6.2), where the latter has a virtual representation as virtual entity, linking to service from other IoT grids locally or the network resource of IoVs (e.g., the traffic light service). For example, the onboard physical entity is made up of several IoT grids as the ADAS grid, automotive powertrain grid, BMS grid, T-box grid, etc., and each composed grid may have several service/resource links from HD map/DVR PIoT.

From an open IoT vision, objects, places, roads, and things can be represented as elements of an IoT grid or PIoT, as Section 6.2 mentioned earlier in the chapter. In this section, a physical entity is the example of IoT grid in E/E view of IoT domain model.

According to the IoT domain model of IoT-A, the concept of a digital artifact is an artifact of the digital world and can be passive (e.g., a database entry) or active (e.g., application software) or an integration of them (e.g., a middleware as AUTOSAR).

The model captures human-to-grid, application (active digital artifact or human intention)-to-grid, and grid-to-grid/PIoT service interaction when a digital artifact, and thus a user, interacts with a device that is a physical entity. The model captures this special case of high-level auto-grid being physical and virtual entities as an augmented entity concept, which can be reflected in the different levels of automated vehicles from L0–L5, defined by SAE (see Section 6.2.2).

Sensors in the model include not only onboard ones but the extended sensors above mentioned. As shown in Fig. 6.83, the sensor can be hosted by a network resource (as the sharing sensors or components in the horizontal IoV manner in Fig. 6.84), either onboard for itself and the above see-through use case or not but extended and fixed with the RSUs for building up a more complete picture of the road conditions.

Overall, the domain model provides a technical tool in the E/E design of vehicles in the IoVs. When these vehicles in an open area or a more complete IoV environment, the current work of the description is

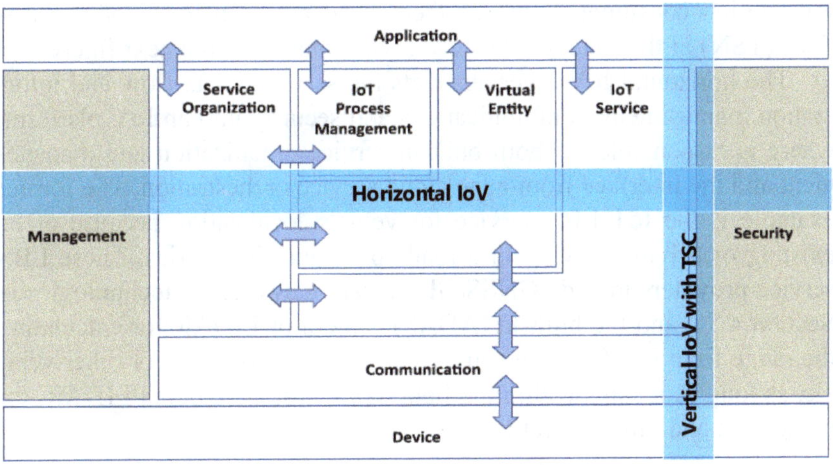

Figure 6.84 IoV structure and horizontal IoV focus on the platform.

concluded into the four layers IoV architecture, conforming to the IoT architecture proposed in this book, as shown in Fig. 6.84.

A device layer located at the perception layer of IoT is not only a physical entity that could have a sensor, actuator, or tag instantiation, grid, MEMS with self–controller, even wheeled robot or other CPS system, as its physical representation; but the road, the obstacle, the traffic conditions, other vehicles or extended sensors, etc. in an open environment. Therefore, an instantiation of a device depends on the realization of it, and any information from dimensions of physical packaging to the physical placement of sensors, actuators, tags, processors, on-board or not from a traffic controller or traffic light signal from IoVs even by wired/ wireless communication interface between grids and service bearers (e.g., RSU), etc.

An on-board device example also contains an automotive power train as an IoT grid, or power system (BMS grid), sensors and actuators as PIoT as service on device could be captured in the device description.

From an IoT grid view, PIoT-as-a-service description should contain three elements as an identifier or name for a thing/device, service, and the relation of the service deployment, either expressed in global (or relative) coordinates or local on-board system (e.g., a device control command from the upper APPs for remote driving). The top application layer includes a user/driver, a controller, an agent for self-driving, or an information consumer. Some of them need time-sensitive communications (TSN) in the functional safety environment; see the next figure.

The horizontal IoV layer abstracts the services, data flow and information management, communications and security into an IoV platform, where is responsible for both built-in service organization and management and the interface from edge/cloud service orchestration. The former example is the IoT LBS service for vehicle localization because of its existing or driving/moving in a road space and time series. These LBS service providers include GNSS/GIS, location awareness technologies in Section 4.55, and the built-in (ADAS) camera or LIDAR for calculating the range from itself to a person moving close, an obstacle or other vehicle, as long as it stays within the field of view of the camera/LIDAR, for navigation and other operations.

• **A vertical IoV view and functional safety:** Vertical IoV focuses on the end-to-end information sharing in real time, and controlling-based collaborations of human–agent, and the collaborations of/with edge/cloud (e.g., human–remote agent, and human–human).

First, a human driver or built-in security guard should control the vehicle well through real-time operations or the controlling-based collaborations of human–agent, if the driving assistance agent is from an ADAS grid (the augmented entity in Fig. 6.85). Second, the end-to-end vertical extension refers to the edge end or edge device, e.g., an RSU in the intersections for non-line-of-sight (NLoS) awareness to other vehicles (the above-mentioned extended sensor example). Another example of the second point is remote driving with an end-to-end TSN support for a command from the edge/cloud end. And the final lies in the cloud service that opens both vertically and horizontally to an IoV cloud, for real-time environmental conditions (e.g., rain, fog, snow, and traffic congestion prediction before intersection/junction at on-ramps).

In Fig. 6.84, we call the “vertical” IoV not only because it penetrates through the device/perception layer, the communication layer, service platform layer, and application layer vertically; but it is vertical to the traditional five major systems of motor vehicles as: (1) engine systems, (2) body and chassis system, (3) electrical/electronic system, (4) **powertrain system**, and (5) emission control systems.

The cross-part of vertical IoV and security is considered from functional safety design that penetrates through either an ADAS (HW/SW) grid development or different levels of autonomous vehicles (L0–L5)

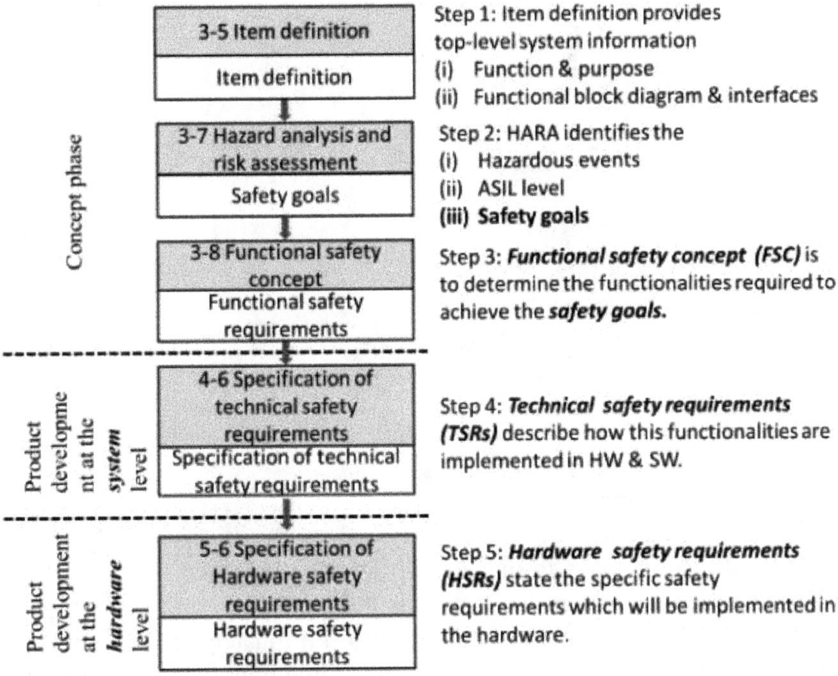

Figure 6.85 Functional safety design.
Source: ISO-26262.

defined by SAE, especially for the MCU or E/E development (e.g., by tier1/tier2 of the automotive industry). Following ISO-26262, this cross part is unfolded as the five steps shown in Fig. 6.85.

Details of the Fig. 6.85 are beyond the scope of this book, but the uncovered security parts will be introduced in the next part.

• **ICV Use Case in Closed Sites: The end-to-end vertical capability is unfolded into** the overall architecture of IoV including the whole structure of "end to the cloud", which improves traffic safety and efficiency through the cooperation of vehicles by V2X, as shown in Fig. 6.86.

In closed sites, such as a park or a mining area, an intelligent and connected vehicle (ICV) is taken as a bus or a mining truck for sightseeing in the park or mining trip in a given operation and closed site. From the view of **horizontal IoV**, the corresponding functional platform in Fig. 6.86 includes the collaboration between vehicles, edge (MEC), and cloud, as shown in Fig. 6.86.

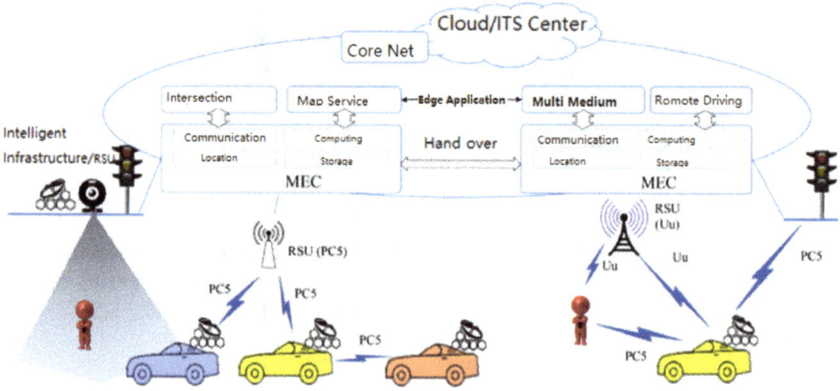

Figure 6.86 A use case of ICVs scenarios based on edge-cloud collaboration in China.

Note: When the upgraded V2X with edge computing, from telematics, the collaboration between pedestrian and vehicle emerges.

Without some ways to manage all the data on which they run effectively, self-driving cars or ICVs will not be able to go too far before they encounter delay and bandwidth challenges. Fortunately, edge computing will allow them to process this data locally while transmitting information about road conditions and location to nearby vehicles, as shown in Fig. 6.86. Edge data centers (e.g., RSU includes intelligent V2X infrastructure in Fig. 6.86) can process more important data locally while passing additional vehicle data back to the management central network (or manufacturer's cloud for online diagnosis). As a result, the versatility architecture of edge–cloud collaboration networks will make it possible for these vehicles to function outside the reach of traditional cloud computing, which is essential for transportation and the operation in closed sites.

In the operation sites, marked cloth, hat or wireless on-wrist (or in caps V2X module) with pedestrian works as mIoT apps with their interface to the cloud or edge of monitor center (MC), and when these on-site IoT devices (onboard OBU and fixed RSU included) receiving real-time instruction from MC, safety tips or alarm is given if necessary. Furthermore, tips help vehicles negotiate with each other or allowing the MC do the decision in front of a crossroad or busy segments.

Apps at the edge include platooning, remote driving, and cooperative communication.

Until now, the concept of IoV may be furthered as the collective networking of communication infrastructure and applications in

automobile and transportation, where things in or off a vehicle are connected to achieve the smart deployment of/for transportation-related resource and the improvement of efficiency and safety (such as ITS and VICS).

6.5.5 *The security of IoV*

> "There are no dependent machine values; machine values are human values." — Shannon Vallor

As a multi-disciplinary technology, the IoV has rich research content, which not only requires the background knowledge of information technology but also requires researchers to have a full understanding of automotive, communication, and traffic, especially traffic characteristics with V2X. On the basis of building a vehicle–roadside collaboration technology framework based on intelligent data processing and vehicle communication, at present, increasing connectivity is causing widespread disruption across the automotive industry. Frost & Sullivan's analysis indicates that connected vehicles will comprise nearly 86% of the global automotive market by 2025, thereby giving rise to many vulnerable threat points for hackers. Cyber-attacks and data-breach incidents will pose severe risks to the automotive industry as they directly impact driver safety, data privacy, and service continuity. Hence, proper guidelines and regulatory mandates will be critical to ensure the safety and security of automotive customers in the near to long term.

Approved on September 28, 2018, Senate Bill No. 327 (state of California in US) goes into effect on January 1, 2020. The bill requires "a manufacturer of a connected device, as those terms are defined, to equip the device with a reasonable security feature or features that are appropriate to the nature and function of the device, appropriate to the information it may collect, contain, or transmit, and designed to protect the device and any information contained therein from unauthorized access, destruction, use, modification, or disclosure".

National Highway Traffic Safety Administration (NHTSA) also prepared cyber-security guidelines and a database of best practices to make automotive computer systems more secure. The security of onboard systems is just one aspect of IoV security.

Toward safety and security of IoVs, more security-related aspects are listed as follows:

- End-to-end security framework approach and privacy, trust, and safety in order to secure the grid from hackers and acts of cyber-sabotage. Security needs to be built into every device (/IoT grid, as a service) starting at the base of the software stack or communication protection.
- Providing a secure solution for connecting and protecting ICT systems (e.g., by building secure Internet gateways/secure grid edge and infrastructure) enable control systems to collect local data from the systems while blocking attacks.
- Edge intelligence with smart devices (or services) delivers manageability, security, and connectivity, while driving down the cost of development and deployment in smart transportation.
- Privacy by the design of the LBS systems that will ensure that the data generated by using the monitoring systems will not leak customers' sensitive information. This requires the same security principles that apply to the LBS/LCS from MNO and ISP enterprise, also applied at the consumer level, and conform to some degree of QoS/SLA regulated by industrial/commercial standards for privacy protection (e.g., the GDPR of European Union in 2018).

The following part will discuss a vehicle cracking example, then some V2X security consideration follows.

In a car hacking experiment conducted in the US at the end of July 2015, network engineers Miller and Valasek remotely controlled a Jeep Cherokee car on St. Louis highway. They used laptops to intrude into the electronic system of the jeep through its Internet entertainment system, then remotely controlled the speed of the jeep, operated the air conditioner, wiper, radio, and other equipment. This is just one scenario where security is threatened.

In case of the city transportation, the driving security threats may threaten the safety of drivers and passers-by. Although IoV can bring us convenience, if it infringes our privacy, we may fear to use it.

6.5.5.1 *Wi-Fi or can attacks to vehicles*

As mentioned in Section 6.4.7, Wi-Fi-enabled devices could easily be connected by others if not protected properly. Some automobiles with cellular-based Internet connections actually share these connections with passengers by acting as a Wi-Fi hot spot. Wi-Fi security assessment methodologies have been around for years and access point hacking has been frequently documented in recent times.

In the on-test Jeep sample from IOActive (https://ioactive.com/), the 2014 Jeep Cherokee has the option for in-car Wi-Fi, which is a hot spot that is only accessible after paying for the service on the web (or for the vehicle info-control system, in the sample, is Uconnect 8.4AN/RA4 radio manufactured by Harman Kardon).[63] One observation testers made was that the Wi-Fi system could be accessed by individuals without advanced knowledge of automotive systems.

The default Wi-Fi encryption method is WPA2 with a randomly generated password containing at least eight alphanumeric characters. Due to the current strength of WPA2 and the huge number of possible passwords, this is a secure setup, but how does an attacker gain access to this network?

One way is that the user has chosen WEP or no encryption at all, both of which are available options. But the attacker would have very little problem in gaining access to the wireless access point by either cracking the WEP password or just joining the access point.

Another attack scenario exists if the attacker has already compromised a device connecting to the Wi-Fi hot spot in the car, such as a laptop computer or mobile phone. If the owner is paying for this service, chances are that they are regularly connecting to the wireless network via a phone or other devices. In this case, if the attacker gain access to one of these devices, they will already be connected to the car's wireless network. This scenario has too many prerequisites to be possible.

In their test, even under the default WPA2 setting, it is still possible for the attacker to access the network by disassembling the "WifiSvc" binary from the OMAP chip (which can be acquired by dumping the binary from a live QNX instance). Then, one can identify the algorithm used to construct the random password. The algorithm is given by testers.

The Uconnect info-control system contains a micro-controller as HW (OMAP chip in their test) and software that allows it to communicate with other electronic modules in the vehicle over the controller area network — interior high-speed (CAN-IHS) data bus. In vehicles equipped

[63]The vehicle info-control system as the Uconnect system, manages the source for infotainment, Wi-Fi connectivity, navigation, apps, and cellular communications.

with Uconnect access, the system also uses electronic message communication with other electronic modules in the vehicle over the CAN-C data bus. The Uconnect system in the 2014 Jeep Cherokee runs the QNX operating system (OS) on a 32-bit ARM processor.

6.5.5.2 *Cracking on the Uconnected system*

One important service that runs on the QNX[64] system, or embedded IoT program, is the PPS service (see Section 6.1). These files in respective directories are essentially places to write data so that other processes can use them as input. Think of them as UNIX pipes with some data-handling capabilities to aid in the parsing of data structures. These PPS files just provide insight into how processes communicate without any direct communication access to the CAN bus. It is even possible to use these files along with the PPS subsystem to send arbitrary CAN messages; they exploit two ways to jailbreak the Uconnect device in their test for saving time. One may work with any version through changing the inserted USB stick:

First, insert the USB stick with a valid ISO (ISO package used for updates and reinstallation of the OS) on it into the USB port on the Uconnect system; after verification of the USB stick (e.g., for an updating process) and restarting the head unit, a new USB stick is inserted when the power is off. Second, it is not clear what check it runs on the new USB stick, but it aborts the update and just reboots into normal (non-update) mode, and the new one can contain modified files. Finally, hex edits the original ISO to change the root password. The update runs from the ISO, including the code used to verify the validity of the ISO. Therefore, attackers can stop that code from running the integrity check if desired.

Another one is bypassing the ISO verification process with a bug of specific version 14_05_03 (OS versions), which could be considered a legitimate jailbreak.

CAN attacks steps, as concluded in their tests, are listed as follows:

- **Identify the target:** An IP address of the vehicle is needed. You could just pick one at random or write a worm to hack them all. If you know the VIN or GPS, you could scan the IP ranges where vehicles are

---

[64] QNX is a kind of embedded real-time UNIX operating system, which complies with POSIX (Portable Operating System Interface).

known to reside until you find one with corresponding VIN or GPS. Due to the slow speed of devices on the Sprint network (MNO in the test), to make this practical, you would probably need many devices, possibly up to a few hundred, to parallelize the scan.

- **Exploit the OMAP chip of the head unit:** Once you have an IP address of a vulnerable vehicle, you can run code using the execute method of the appropriate D-Bus service, as discussed earlier. The easiest thing to do is to upload an SSH public key, configuration file, and then start the SSH service. At this point, you can SSH to the vehicle and run commands from the remote terminal.
- **Control the uConnect system:** If all you want to do is control the radio, HVAC, get the GPS, or other non-CAN-related attacks, LUA scripts are given in their test. Most of the functionality can be done by using D-Bus without actually executing code, just by using the provided D-Bus services. If you want to control other aspects of the car, you can have a modified v850 firmware ready to go and follow the instructions above mentioned to flash the v850 with the modified firmware. This requires an automated reboot of the system, which may alert the driver that something is going on.
- **Perform cyber-physical actions:** Utilize the modified firmware, send appropriate CAN messages to make physical things happen to the vehicle by sending messages from the OMAP chip to the modified firmware on the V850 chip using serial peripheral interface (SPI).

As the research of IOActive, a cellular original CAN attack based on the intrusion of cellular modular (e.g., GM's OnStar in their test, used to retrieve traffic or weather information) may lead to the holy grail of automotive attacks since the range is quite broad (i.e., as long as the car can have cellular communications). Even if an on-board telematics unit does not reside directly on the CAN bus, it does have the ability to remotely transfer data/voice, via the microphone, to another location. Researchers previously remotely exploited a telematics unit of an automobile without user interaction. On the testing Jeep, all of these features are controlled by the radio, which resides on both the CAN-IHS bus and the CAN-C bus.

D-Bus system can be accessed anonymously and is typically used for inter-process communication. The D-Bus service is exposed on port 6667 running on the Uconnect system, by which executing code in an unauthenticated manner during their test. The testers think that exposing such a comprehensive service like D-Bus over the network poses several security risks from abusing functionality to code injection, and even memory corruption, caused by the command of vulnerabilities injection.

6.5.5.3 *Security in V2X*

5G security is still being developed by 3GPP for the device to network communications. Release 15 and 16 (R15/R16) was completed and the phase started by now. C-V2X security is unlikely to be updated with Release 15. However, the enhancements developed for network access and associated security aspects will apply to the network-enabled mode of communication. As for the direct mode of operation, the security design for the C-V2X of R14 included LTE-V2X is expected to remain unchanged, namely specifying the reuse of the application-level security already defined by IEEE for DSRC systems.

Notably, LTE Release 14 does not support vehicle identity privacy when it sends V2X traffic via the network. Architectural changes would be required to support user/vehicle anonymity from the operator. In China, the following three aspects of security for V2X of R14 are ongoing:

- Define device-to-network authentication methods and transport;
- Specify provisioning and storage of 3GPP credentials for devices;
- Specify network functions and protocols necessary for secure device operation within the operation network.

According to "Cellular V2X Communications towards 5G", it is possible to deploy public key infrastructure (PKI) security, where devices use a digital certificate to authenticate to the network (likewise the network). It can be speculated that this should favor V2X systems where devices are vehicles provisioned with digital certificates and wishing to access the network for V2X applications. So far, 5G security design is being developed to achieve the following goals:

- **Enhanced subscriber/device privacy:** This is a major change from 4G LTE in that the new subscriber permanent identifier (SUPI) is never allowed to be transmitted over the air in the clear. Instead, the sensitive part of the SUPI travels over the radio link protected against spoofing and tracking, which was not the case with the 4G international mobile subscriber identity (IMSI).

- **Enhanced security support at the network level, along with the capability for flexible authentication and authorization schemes:** A new network function is specified: the security anchor function (SEAF) which maintains the security anchor deep in a network (in a physically secure location). SEAF also provides flexibility in deploying other functions (for example, AMF and SMF). In R15, the SEAF is collocated with the AMF (for device-to-core network).
- **Support various types of devices that have different security capabilities and requirements:** Secondary authentication enables support for non-3GPP access links and sessions authorized by third-party servers, such as for IoT, V2X, and industrial automation. This functionality is related to the access control for network slices. For example, IoT devices may require different credential provisioning and authentication methods. The details for this type of industrial scenario are still being worked on.
- **Support user data and signaling encryption and integrity protection:** These features are essential for a secure system, which is why 5G supports them. A new feature is data path integrity protection, which may be especially important for certain new services (e.g., IoT). There is also the potential for the user plane security to be terminated in the network instead of the base station.
- **Separate device credential management and access authentication from data session setup and management:** This split results in a separate security context between the device and the AMF which is used for mobility management (therefore, only to grant the device access to the network). A different security context is established for session management, between the device and an SMF, used to authorize access of the device to specific services (e.g., slices or specific data networks such as corporate networks, industrial systems). This new type of access control employs a separate authentication and authorization procedure flexibly (therefore, based on the extensible authentication protocol (EAP)).
- **Support secure slicing:** There could be several services instantiated as a network slice, each with different security requirements. Access to a slice is granted based on the primary authentication and subscription information, but this authorization is carried out by the respective SMF. In this way, the access security is contained within that network slice and does not rely on the AMF, which may serve multiple slices that may have different security requirements. Moreover, an attack mounted

on one slice does not result in an increased risk for the attack on a different slice of the same network.

Overall, what 5G security is achieving is the increase of user privacy, resistance to cyber-attacks on the network, and better device hardware security. This goal will be achieved with stronger authentication/authorization schemes between device and network — both radio access network and core network functions — secure credential provisioning and storage on the device, and new network functions that support device-to-network communications security, with the integrity- and confidentiality-protected signaling and data traffic.

The V2X system and the device link to the radio access network can leverage the 5G system security for vehicle device authorization, authentication, and access to the network.

6.6 IIoT and Smart Manufacturing

Nowadays, we are rapidly moving beyond bespoke detailed solutions tailored for specific problems, and we have built upon reusable and more infrastructures with general purpose and tools, referring to them as IoT, IIoT/Industry 4.0, etc. In IIoT, the enormous innovation potential of IoT technologies lies not only in the production of physical devices but also in all activities performed by manufacturing industries, both in the pre-production (ideation, design, and prototyping) and the post-production (sales, training, maintenance, and recycling) phases.

It is also known that IIoT acquires and analyzes data from connected devices, CPS, locations, and people (e.g., operator), along with its contemporary new terms, such as 5G, edge computing, and other ICT technologies with their applications. It is drawn upon its combination with monitoring devices and actuators from operational technology (OT). IIoT helps regulate and monitor industrial systems, and flexibly integrates and reorganizes production resources, thus enhancing OT capability in the smart value chains that facilitate the decision-making of distributed production.

6.6.1 *Introduction*

Towards the IoE era, the traditional, fragmented processes of design, production, and customer fulfillment will be replaced by the management of the end-to-end design-to-customer fulfillment, where products are designed based on customer requirements (granularity decided by customer-focused manufacturing) and their production cycles are shorter. Differently, they do not finish with product delivery; the product service extends to service maintenance and continuous product design. Autonomous sensors in a machine and manufacturing services will facilitate the operational performance model for predictive maintenance. Furthermore, three main reasons for IIoT value chain analysis are as follows:

(a) The requirement of the autonomy production is far beyond the close loop of production–consumption–usage–upgrading/elimination–reproduction, dual-direction information transition; therefore, the internal self-balance mechanism in manufacturing is necessary for a close loop of IoT enabling dynamic configuration and monitoring of the operational capabilities of the company. So, IIoT starts to concentrate on networks in/with plants, quality control, and efficiency improvement. Specifically, after the interfaces and data sets are given, the distributed agent for manufacturing, besides when to work and how to distribute the workforce (e.g., flexible manufacturing) with the automation, should be combined with machine intelligence (e.g., ML).
(b) Enhanced OT capability integrated into the smart value chains enabling the decision-making of distributed production. The promise of the IIoT includes significant wealth in the coming years: a management consulting firm, McKinsey & Co., estimates that the IIoT will create USD 7.5 trillion by 2025. The Industrial IoT combines minds and machines–people and machine data together, accelerating the transformation of digital industrial.
(c) Flexible integration of production resources (workforce, information, sensors, and networking) makes the autonomy of IoT across the grid (resources) easier. Figures 6.87(a) and 6.87(b) show modular machine design with HM collaboration and machine adjustment with Sick's appropriate technology in man-made wood procession, respectively. And Fig. 6.87(c) shows the continuous condition monitoring that can be applied in servo design and online remote diagnose.

In short, the IIoT connects business and processes by breaking the boundary of the grid borders of heterogeneity, resource reallocation and service from companies, and plant the OT (real-time supported or not)

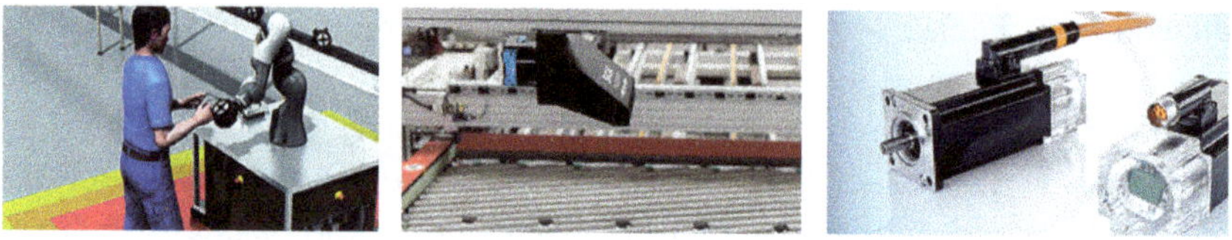

(a) (b) (c)

Figure 6.87 Flexible integration of production resources. (a) HM collaboration in smart design and safe motion control; (b) machine adjustment with Sick's appropriate technology in man-made wood procession; (c) continuous condition monitoring can be carried out in the servo for actuator.

Source: https://www.sick.com/.

into different factories, embracing ICT in a super-integrated supervised scenario and pushing the service, security, openness, and intelligence into smart manufacturing of a new stage.

6.6.2 *Industrial IoT and I4.0*

Compared to IoT, Industry 4.0 (I4.0), smart manufacturing, and IIoT are relatively new terms, and their descriptions and usage vary significantly. Thus, it is important to clarify their definition for better understanding.

IIoT is defined as IoT applied in the industrial environment, by ENISA (European Union Agency for Network and Information Security) in the Baseline IoT Security Recommendations. Industry 4.0 is a much broader concept that encompasses IIoT and smart manufacturing/factory in the fourth industrial revolution era.

The goal of IoT is to realize the complete integration of human society, the information world, and the physical world and is on its long evolution towards IoE. Industry 4.0 synchronizes with this goal and tries to build a controllable, credible, scalable, safe, and efficient physical device interaction in the industrial scene, thus fundamentally changing people's traditional understanding of the industry, as shown in Fig. 6.88.

In the upgrading steps, as the traditional industrial barriers disappear, a variety of new activities and cooperation forms will be produced in the practice of innovation economics.

6.6.2.1 *Industry 4.0*

Nowadays, the role of the IIoT is becoming more prominent in enabling access to devices and machines, which are in manufacturing systems,

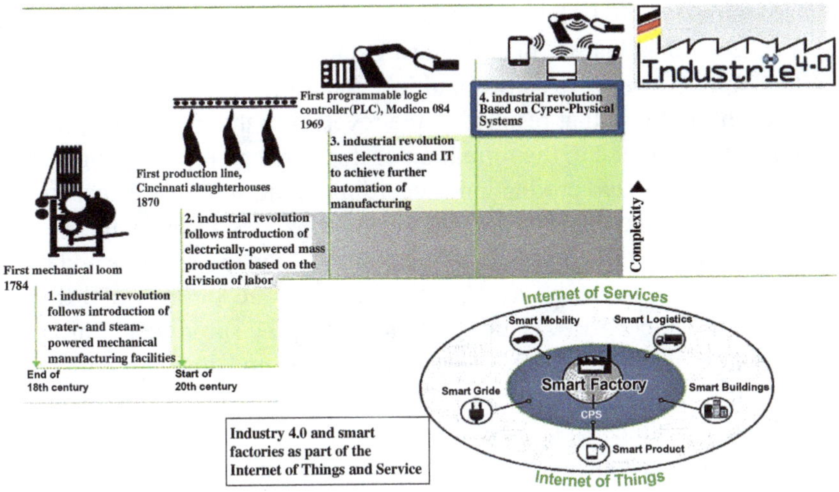

Figure 6.88 Steps from first industrial revolution to the fourth industrial revolution.

hidden in well-designed pattern, principle, and methodology of Industry 4.0. Industry 4.0 is just a pronoun for the new fourth industrial revolution, including interoperability, autonomy, information transparency, technical assistance, and distributed decisions, which make traditional manufacturing smart (see the right corner of Fig. 6.88).

The concept of I4.0 transforms the basic mode from centralized control to decentralized enhanced control to establish a highly intelligent and digital industrial production and organization mode. Such transformation is emphasized by ENISA on its Industry 4.0 definition — "a paradigm shift towards digitalized, integrated, and smart value chains enabling distributed decision-making in production by incorporating new cyber-physical technologies such as IoT".

In the process of creating new value chains, during which ICT are applied, the division of labor and resources in the industrial chain will be reorganized optimally and efficiently. The value chain of Industry 4.0 has three supporting points: First, product leads production and ICT technology services the production. Second, it makes the machines/devices more intelligent, being able to talk to each other in their collaboration and even communicate with products and production (before and afterward, e.g., designing, prototype, planning, and maintaining). Finally, it makes the products reflect the social value of environmental protection, safety, reliability, and sustainable development.

In terms of IIoT, Industry 4.0 is an innovative "set of rules and connection" of industrial manufacturing and resource distribution in the vertical application of IoT grids and IoT zones (see Fig. 6.89).

Recent progress that resulted in the reversal of the traditional production process logic led to the formation of this concept, representing a shift towards decentralized production. According to the shift and its accompanying ICT enabler, Industry 4.0 is divided into zones and conduits with a layered architecture in Fig. 6.89. Zones can be divided into grids and even subdivided into sub-grids (e.g., primitive IoT) according to different manufacturing scenarios. Under the same rules, the sub-division of vertical IIoT in Industry 4.0 integrates with each other and develops collaboratively with its communication relationships (in Fig. 6.89). The value of intelligent manufacturing itself is multi-objective, not only to do a good job in one product or a single production line but also to minimize the waste in the production process more widely.

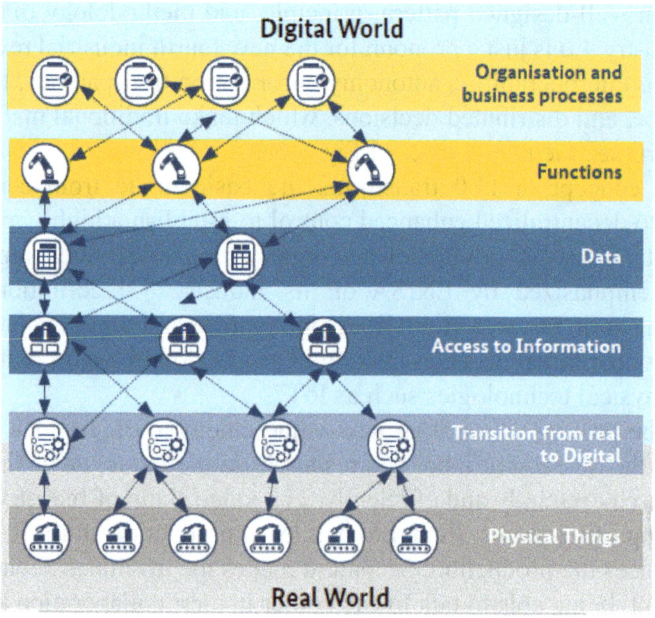

Figure 6.89 IoT zones and conduits in I4.0, where the communication/connection can be organized either in one-to-one or m-to-n relations as required by the related business functionalities.

More specifically, the IIoT should **first** aim for the cost–performance ratio of the whole life cycle of the product; the design and manufacturing process, including post-maintenance and reproduction, can be matched with the user demand and the ideal price (forecasting, evaluation and other statistics of data science). **Second**, it should make the whole system smart enough to make automatic adjustment according to the change of the product condition (e.g., demand/requirement) in the manufacturing process and realize the real-time "autonomy (or self-introspection)" of the system status based on the dynamic planning. **Last**, it should realize zero failure, zero hidden danger, zero accident, and zero pollution in the whole manufacturing process, which is the highest level of smart manufacturing in future IIoT (possibly can be realized in Industry 5.0 or beyond).

The infrastructure design and the layout of zones and conduits in such solutions need to be developed in line with the results of the security risk assessment, which has to consider the possible impact on the safety risk reduction required by the I4.0 and intelligence manufacturing (IM) workspace.

In the long run, we are just on the way to intelligent IIoT through both the shift of intelligent/digital in production and organization and the shift of decentralized production. Therefore, the value chain of IIoT lies at the corresponding three points, as follows: (1) Through industrial automation/Industry 4.0/Industrial Internet and IIoT, the horizontal integration of resources between (within) enterprises/factories can be realized. (2) Integration and intelligent application of end-to-end engineering digitization throughout the whole value chain. (3) Within the enterprise (factory), vertical integrated and networked manufacturing system (beyond the horizontal combination/re-organization) can be flexibly realized.

As mentioned in Section 6.2.1, at the beginning stage of intelligence (device-centric IoT), a product/device is not merely processed by machines — it communicates with other devices in producing context with relevant information and instructions. When a production-related device in manufacturing (e.g., production lines) is no longer isolated, and devices of device-centric IoT become integral parts of the overall network by communication and distribute computing (e.g., edge or cloud computing, especially in discrete manufacturing), the collaborative-intelligence stage upgrades into the system-centric IoT stage, which introduces complex analytic and flexible decentralized systems in the networked intelligence environment.

The character of system-centric IoT is that its functions are not bound to hardware but distributed throughout the network. In these new systems, now internal communication can be observed across an organization's hierarchical levels, which will be introduced in the next section.

System-centric IoT connects production to information and communication technologies. It merges end-user data with machine data and enables machines to communicate with each other. As a result, it has become possible for components and machines to manage production autonomously in a flexible, efficient, and resource-saving manner.

From the viewpoints of intelligence, new characteristics include not only the IoT systems of systems but also the AI ability both on different CPSs and flexible organization of external interactions. Intelligence IoT infrastructure benefits include, among others, higher product quality, greater flexibility, shorter product launch time, new services and business models. It is important to note that the data flows depicted in the decision-making or autonomous systems of Intelligence IoT, which refer to physical productions and data (e.g., the exchange of digital twins). Data flows are at least bidirectional, e.g., customers may provide feedback to the production/manufacturing process.

6.6.2.2 *Vertical IIoT grids*

At the recent international symposium, a rapid survey on the application and value creation industry of the IoT shows that the application of the IoTs in the industrial field will benefit the most. The survey selected six different perspectives with "Internet of Things, value and industry" as (1) IIoT applications now vs. five years, (2) tech./development impacting IIoT applications, (3) obstacles or challenges, (4/5) value from IoT systems: ACTIVE/PASSIVE, and (6) your vision. The analysis is shown in Fig. 6.90.

The top three benefits of IIoT applications are logistics for industry and supply chains, discrete manufacturing, and industrial services. The rest are batch processes, energy (oil and gas), and power electric industry (smart grid).

However, service improvement and production discretization in intelligent manufacturing are still urgent problems. The application of IoT in industry 4.0 is not only reflected in the customized solutions but also in different IoT vertical industrial services, where the IoT grid seems to be

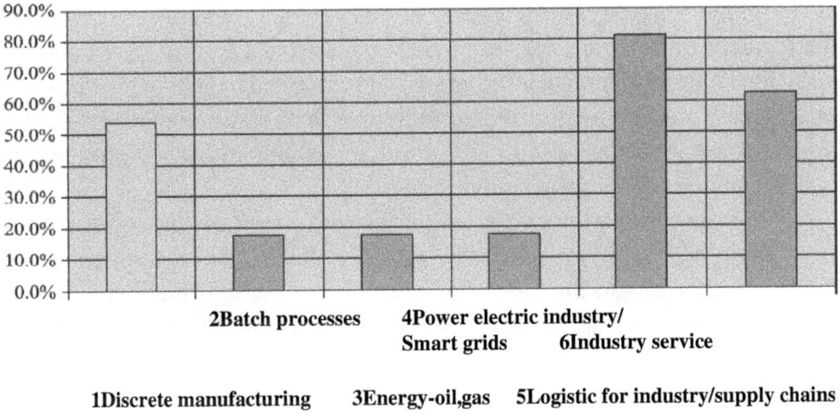

Figure 6.90 Sub-division of industry of IIoT.

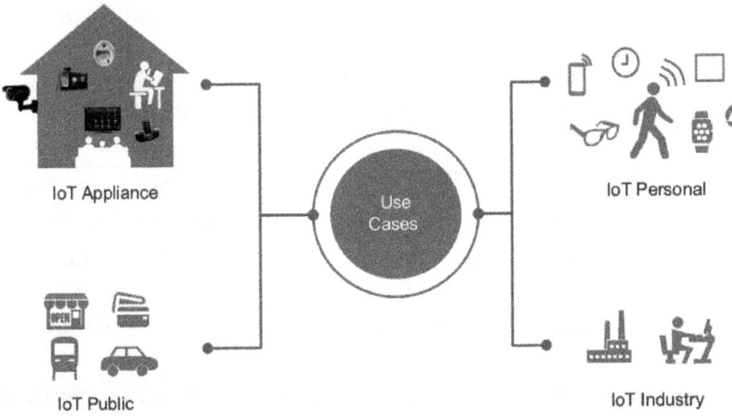

Figure 6.91 Four parts (IoT sectors/domains/grids) as use case grids/examples of IoT vertical industrial services.

more suitable for integration, deployment, configuration, and usage (see Fig. 6.91).

As shown in Fig. 6.91, from the perspective of industry, IoT industrial is no more than a vertical grid of industrial IoT. The core reason is that it needs not only the installation and configuration of equipment but also the development direction of independent intelligence. In short, according to the concept of IoT grid, the "big grid" of industry 4.0 is divided horizontally into the IoT, cloud computing, big data management, intelligent equipment, etc. Vertically, it is subdivided into industrial logistics and supply chain, industrial production service, discrete industrial production, batch production, and other fields.

From the application on the right corner of Fig. 6.91, the IoT industry, as to the IIoT, is only an industry grid for the industrial application of the IoT. According to the industrial use cases of the IoT, there can also be a personal grid (wearable grid), smart home grid, smart transportation grid, etc.

In succession, the concept of "Internet of Things+" (industry) grid such as agriculture 4.0, business x.0, smart tourism x.0 will appear, showing that the grid of various industries will sooner or later move to the independent intelligent road of vertical functional autonomy and horizontal information union.

In the process of rapid industrial transformation and technological layout update by using the IoTs technology, the IoT grid can lead to its intelligent way from inside. It is hoped that the IoT grid can provide good thinking for the independent intelligent road of IoT, and more practical work of IoT grid needs further research.

The development of IIoT/IoT urgently calls for standards. From the "horizontal perspective", each standard in the perception layer, network layer, platform layer, and application layer does not open enough to provide cross-sector integration ability. In the vertical view, the application specifications of each industry are still in the state of "separation" and lack of function (service) format.

However, the application of IoT is gradually moving from vertical and single solutions to cross-industry, cross-application, and cross-standard collaborative application or multi-objective application. Therefore, there is an urgent need for a long-term standardization based on standards but higher than standards. In response to the background of the digital economy, the internal standardization reconstruction of the "system of the IoT" is consistent with the self-renewal business model, product service portfolio, and customer multi-objective (such as security) requirements. The product concept of product-as-a-service can be embedded into the standardized "grid" and can develop in the direction of horizontal cross platform and vertical cross industry.

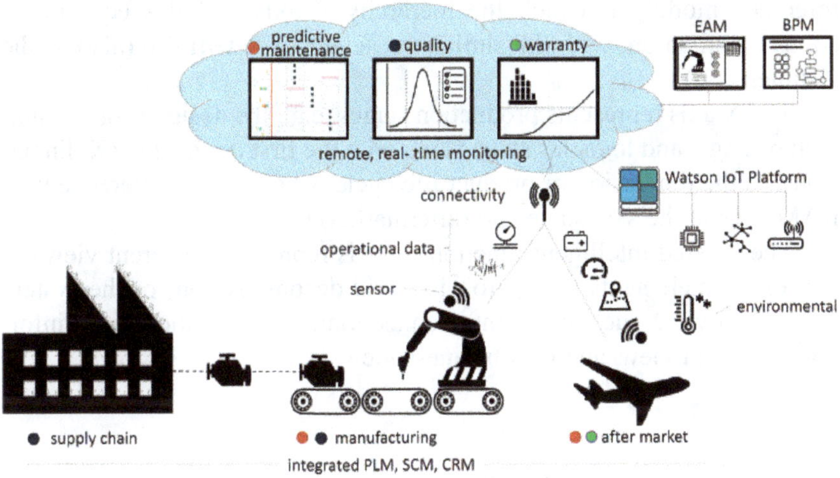

Figure 6.92 The hierarchy level integration among the collaboration between supply chain grid, manufacturing grid, and aftermarket grid in the aviation IoT sector.

6.6.3 *The value chain of IIoT grids in IMSA*

The IIoT grid is not a standard but a service-oriented regulation exploration or the conceptual model (inherited from Section 6.2) that either links an entity in the physical world to the service that can give in order to be discussed in detail in an IIoT sector or helps to decompose IIoT with a gridded vision. The latter includes not only RAMI4.0 (see Section 6.2) but (RAMEC) mentioned in Section 6.4 and other conceptual model of industry architectures in IIoT (e.g., IMSA of China). Figure 6.92 gives a multi-grid collaboration scenario of the supply chain, manufacturing, and aftermarket.

In the above occasions, a grid user can choose to interact with the physical environment by means of a service (e.g., PIoT) or applications (e.g., a set of PIoTs inside a grid), and the collaboration between two grids needs a platform for service inter-working. As shown in Fig. 6.92, the Watson IoT platform is an example in the opinion of the IoT grids model introduced in Section 6.2. Figure 6.92 just describes the hierarchy level of IMSA in Fig. 6.93.

As shown in Fig. 6.93, the Chinese Reference Architecture Model IMSA (Intelligent Manufacturing System Architecture) is a 3D reference model, in which the hierarchy Z axis includes equipment, control, and so on, with the similar six levels of RAMI 4.0 (also as the Z dimension).

The X axis represents production stages, e.g., the design stage, manufacture stage, and logistics stage along with the first dimension (X dimension), as the dimension of product life cycle, where some difference with RAMI lies in the sale stage and (aftermarket) service.

The layered intelligent functions Y axis represents different views of the resource elements (e.g., PIoT/IoT grid decomposition) or the system integration view, such as the interconnection/communication view, information fusion view, and new business view.

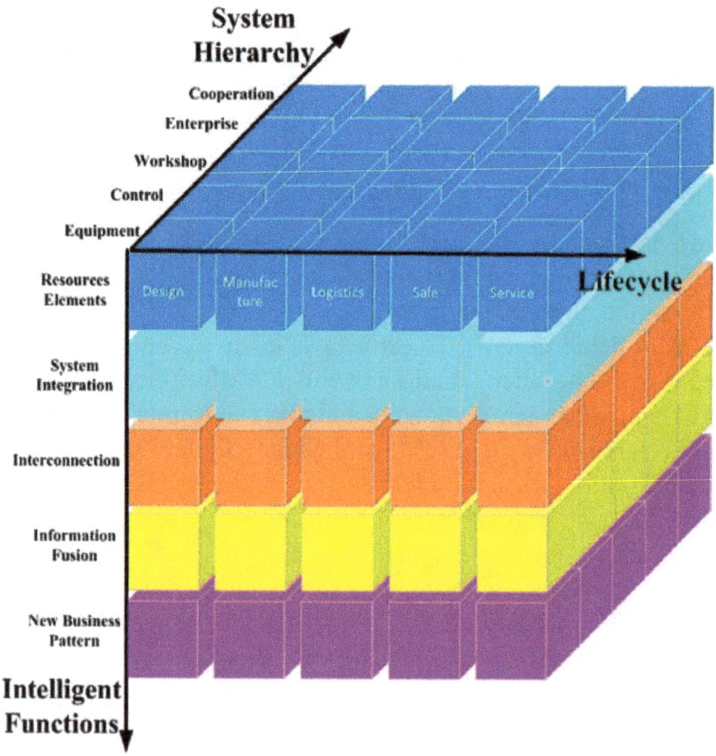

Figure 6.93 Intelligent manufacturing system architecture of China.

Source: Sino-German White Paper on Functional Safety for Industry 4.0 and Intelligent Manufacturing.

The intelligent function axis of IMSA (in Fig. 6.93), in contrast to the layering axis of RAMI4.0, considers not only technological assets (resource element) in the view of layered architecture but integration/interconnection/fusion of information as platforms, where the intelligent function penetrates into the building blocks of networks, CPSs, IoT grids, cloud/edge/Big Data, safety/security, and applications marketplaces are also considered.

Taking security as an example, in dealing with an unexpected attack, those IoT grids mean the search space of checking point is significantly increased. However, for the given attack, the RAMI or IMSA model with IoT grids insight provides a break-down view to analyze, discover, and prevent or mitigate the attack with the knowledge (e.g., patterns recognition) of the composed grids inside. The following use case is taken from a safety working IIoT view, which also covers some intelligent functions, such as edge-cloud collaboration and risk management.

6.6.4 *Healthy workforce: TRW use case as a safety grid*

With the emergence of an ageing workforce in Europe, active and healthy protection is one of the major societal concerns in the smart home/city and smart industry sectors. In fact, human and organizational factors are still involved in almost 90% of all workplace accidents and incidents.

The ageing workforce may exhibit more limited physical and cognitive responses. According to the World Health Organization, the European workforce will be older than ever before, making up for 30% of the working-age population.

The European Commission estimates that muscular-skeletal disorders (MSD) accounts for 50% of all absences from work lasting three days or longer and for 60% of permanent work incapacity. Furthermore, up to 80% of the adult population will be affected by an MSD at some time in their lives. In the last few years, it has become apparent that this situation will even worsen. For this reason, it is necessary to improve the quality and comfort of the workforce.

In order to find out new solutions and take benefit from the IoT technologies, TRW (pronounced as Tier One, in Germany) trial developed an IoT-based worker-centric safety management system, whose aim was to reduce accidents and incidents in the production workplace.

The TRW as a use case of IIoT application is focused on the monitoring and assessment of the ergonomic risk that can affect the blue-collar workers on the production lines in order to perform more effective prevention strategies than the traditional prevention strategies.

Current procedures and systems are not customized to the limitations or characteristics of the workers, so the results are not trustworthy when customizing specific plans and current human-based surveillance are not effective enough. So, the TRW trial specially provides the following functionalities: (1) real-time data collection through Kinect sensors; (2) continuous data processing for ergonomic risks detection; (3) events management; (4) web services and applications for corrective actions performance (e.g., web services for sending messages or warnings related to the risks detected.

The platform of TRW trial (see Fig. 6.94) is based on the smart factory platform (GEs: general ends and SEs: special ends), and new components and services developed for the trial TRW platform, which takes advantage of functionalities related to data gathering, complex event processing (CEP, see Section 6.1.2), context information management, and event information delivery, among components related to IoT service, e.g., monitor, sensors data repository, risk/action repository, etc., in Fig. 6.94.

System monitors and collects real-time data of the skeleton and movements of the workers in the production line through Kinect sensors (see Section 4.4). Risk/action repository service collects and processes the data in order to detect "unsafe" events based on the defined rules (e.g., angles of the body or frequency of movements higher than the threshold values). In case of event detection, different services or actions previously set up are delivered, e.g., messages or warnings are sent to the blue-collar workers and prevention technicians.

Preliminary intermediate KPIs already demonstrate a reduction of 13% in the number of accidents and incidents in the factory as well as a performance improvement of 80% in the number of risks detected and alarms activated.

The third service interface (e.g., ISP or MNO) in the cloud can be seen as a map service widget and security policy assessment in Fig. 6.94. TRW trial introduces and accepts IoT technologies in the local manufacturing on the edge as well as the cloud (e.g., workflow management, alert

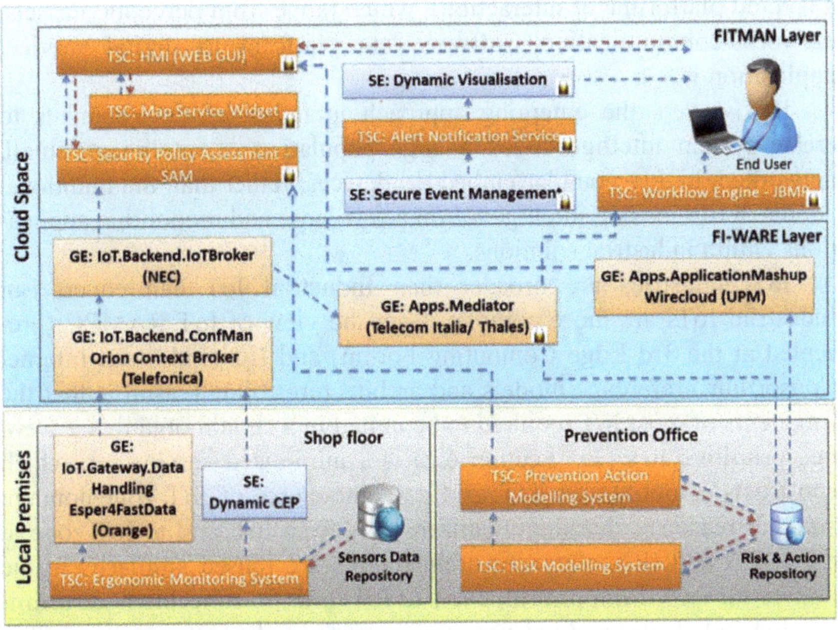

Figure 6.94 Future Internet platform for safer and healthier workplace.

Note: FITMAN SEs, FI-WARE GEs, and trial specific components (TSCs) developed to provide problem-able specific functionality not otherwise available through GEs and SEs.

notification service, secure event management, etc.), in order to get the workplace of the near future of the ageing era, providing the necessary balance between security and privacy concerns. The implementation of IoT technologies of industry supports the innovative human-in-the-loop model, is getting a participative approach for the workers' empowerment solution, and improving the value chain of IIoT.

6.6.5 *Further discussion*

The emergence of the IoT and its billions of envisioned devices poses a clear challenge to the design, management, production, and maintenance, and is expected to extend to the vertical value chains as different IoT industries (or business) and the horizontal value chains as a layered platform (for interaction), which range from perception/assets, networks/communication, software/data platform to digital service/application.

IIoT covers the emerging approach in industrial environments to create system intelligence by a large population of intelligent, small, networked, highly granular embedded devices, rather than the traditional approach of focusing intelligence on a few large and monolithic applications within industrial solutions.

IoT industries are broader than Industrial IoT can cover. But Industrial IoTs are more complex from the view of IoT RAMEC (presented at the 3rd Edge Computing Forum) and IIC (Industrial Internet Consortium) reference models and architectures. One reason is that the fragments of most IoT required to be united in a certain organizing view, i.e., primitive IoT (see Section 6.2) is a minimized service set, which constructs/composes the IoT grid as components of IoT zone/domain. Another reason is that the organized view from IoT grid to IoT zone in the IoT-A and IIC references architectures are reused similarly, in the bottom-up view from primitive IoT to IoT grid. So concepts from primitive IoT to IoT grid and IoT zone are described to be better understood in a unified view (architecture views, viewpoints, stakeholders, concerns, etc.). Along with the upgrading level, connection as a service in IIoT may be supported by 5G slice, such as edge computing for IoT grid, from devices/equipment/things onsite, to workshop/enterprise edge, and the cloud cooperation.

The healthy IoT case from TRW and FITMAN projects of Germany, as an example, describes some intelligent care including a risk/action repository service, which collects and processes the data in order to detect "unsafe" events. From the insight of AI (such as ML), forecasting is a key issue in the prominent IoT use case of predictive maintenance, as well as the predictive for human diagnoses, which is used to determine the health of a piece of machine/equipment/asset or human and to understand when any maintenance or exercise/health examination might be needed. Forecasting involves predicting new outcomes based on previously known results. Depending on the IoT use case, different forecasting time frames can be applied. For example, trajectory forecasting of moving objects can be real time, whereas machine degradation is more long term.

Forecasting can be data driven or model driven depending on the problem requirements. Model training and usage are necessary for IIoT applications and the former can be based on training sets or via reinforcement learning. In a word, more research across different disciplines is working towards the IIoT era and the IoE era.

Chapter 7

Application Layer of IoT

"The Unity of Knowledge and Action".
— Wang Yangming

Between the technologies and Internet of things (IoT) markets — how the industrial structures will be formed around these solutions, despite very similar technology implementations? This is covered in more detail in this chapter, which focuses on vertical applications and industrial examples.

Vertical application refers to the vertical procedures and associations within a given industrial sector, where it is concentrated individually on a special industry, such as health, food, resident, and so on. But it does not mean that each industrial application is constrained in its domain without any connection to others, e.g., the use case of the food from farmer reaching the table/restaurant of resident linking food, resident with healthy keeping, and they may share the platform of IoT.

Although each industrial application has its own structure that is purposed towards the achievement of the goals of a particular industry, as mentioned earlier, the purpose of IoT grid is to break the vertical applications and to improve the interconnection across platforms, industrial services, and data barriers. This is one of the key differences between the M2M and IoT markets — the former cares more for vertical communication solutions.

The Application Layer lies in increasing complexity because of not only the heterogeneity of devices themselves but also the constellations they take part in. In Fig. 7.1, the use of functionalities of vertical industrial applications show the crossing/relating aspects in modern IoE applications.

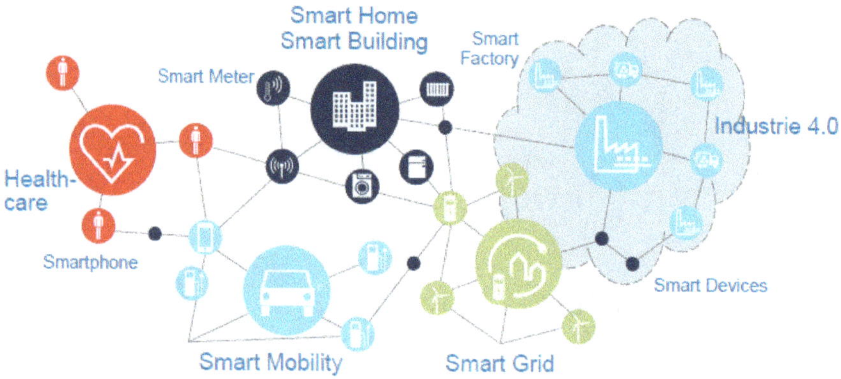

Figure 7.1 Verticals in IoT application layer.
Source: Bosch© Rexroth AG.

The desired applications are not monolithic from their providers, but on the contrary, they are dependent on multiple layers, levels, and grids that are developed from other stakeholders. Hence, managing different devices requires significant overhead in order to be able to effectively integrate, monitor, and control/reconfigure them, in the comprehensive and heterogeneous architecture of applications.

IoT service and platform layer provides significant support for comprehensive applications, where the data interflow and cooperation and sharing could be achieved by the service from devices/sensors integration platform (e.g., a middleware).

As illustrated in Fig. 7.1, the outlook of the IoT application layer contains healthcare, smart home/building, smart mobility, smart energy/traffic, smart residence/food, and so on. Some of the verticals will be discussed here.

In Section 5.6, six protocols of CoAP, XMPP, MQTT, AMQP, DDS, and JMS have been introduced in the context of communication and networking technologies. Others will be introduced in the following.

7.1 Protocols of Applications

As requirements for many IoT applications accelerate the development of protocols that address the resource-constraint environments, and the demand of fulfilling the blank in Fig. 7.1 in diverse IoT sectors, application protocols of IoT are summarized in this section. In fact, a lot of protocols have been introduced in the **Communication and Network Layer** and the **Services and Platform Layer** of Chapters 5 and 6. The following is only a brief supplement of them.

- **IEEE 1888:** IEEE 1888 is an application protocol for environmental monitoring, smart energy, and facility management applications by supporting reading and writing of time-series data using the extensible markup language (XML) and simple object access protocol (SOAP). The data is identified using universal resource identifiers (URIs).
- **Session Initiation Protocol:** Session Initiation Protocol (SIP) is a text-based protocol that can use different underlying transports, such as TCP, UDP, or SCTP. It is standardized by IETF as RFC 3261. The protocol handles session establishment for voice, video, and instant messaging applications on IP networks, such as Internet multimedia conferences, Internet telephone calls, and multimedia distribution. It also manages presence (e.g., XMPP). The invitation messages are used to create session descriptions that enable edge devices to agree on a set of compatible media types. The protocol elements called proxy servers are used for the route requests of the user's current location and the authentication services by implementing call-routing policies. A registration function is defined by the protocol to enable users to update their current locations for use by proxy servers. SIP supports end-to-end and hop-by-hop authentication, as well as end-to-end encryption using S/MIME (secure multipurpose internet mail extensions).

Together with CoAP, XMPP, MQTT/AMQP, DDS introduced in Sections 5.6 and 6.1, IEEE 1888 and SIP are compared in Table 7.1.

In addition, more data/information models or platform/specific domain relative applications protocols are introduced as follows:

- **MQTT-Sensor Network:** The MQTT-Sensor Network (MQTT-SN) is an open, lightweight publish/subscription protocol designed for constrained devices, i.e., wireless sensor network (WSN). The protocol is based on MQTT and adapted to the specific requirements of the wireless communication environment (e.g., short message length, low bandwidth, high link failures, etc.) and devices (e.g., low-cost, long-battery life, limited processing, and storage resources, etc.).

Table 7.1 Overview of IoT application protocols.

IoT Protocol	Functions	Transport	Format	Applications	SDO
AMQP	Message orientation, queuing, and pub/sub Data transfer with delivery guarantees (at least once, at most once, exactly once)	TCP	Binary	Financial services	OASIS
CoAP	REST resource manipulation via CRUD Resource tagging with attributes Resource discovery through RD	UDP	Binary	Low-power and lossy networks	IETF
DDS (RTPS)	Pub/sub messaging with well-defined data types Data discovery Elaborate QoS	UDP	Binary	Real-time distributed systems (military, industrial, etc.)	OMG
IEEE 1888	Read/write data into URI Handling time-series data	SOAP/HTTP	XML	Energy and facility management	IEEE
MQTT	Lightweight pub/sub messaging Message queuing for future subscribers	TCP	Binary	Enterprise telemetry	OASIS
SIP	Manage presence Session establishment Data transfer (voice, video, text)	TCP, UDP, SCTP	XML	IP telephony	IETF
XMPP	Manage presence Session establishment Data transfer (text or binary)	TCP HTTP	XML	Instant messaging	IETF XSF

Several changes have been introduced in MQTT-SN compared with MQTT, e.g., the topic names are replaced by topic IDs, which reduces the overheads of transmission. Topics do not need registration as they are preregistered, and messages are split to send only the necessary information. The clients connect to the broker through a gateway device, which resides in the WSN and connects to the broker and reduces power consumption. When in an offline procedure for clients who are in a sleep state, the messages can be buffered and later read by clients when they wake up.

Three components of MQTT-SN architecture are used, namely clients, gateways (GW), and forwarders. MQTT-SN clients connect themselves to an MQTT server by an MQTT-SN GW using the MQTT-SN protocol; the MQTT-SN GW may or may not be integrated with an MQTT server. When utilizing a stand-alone GW, the MQTT protocol is used between the MQTT server and the MQTT-SN GW, having the function to translate the messages between MQTT and MQTT-SN. MQTT-SN clients can access a GW through a forwarder in case the GW is not directly attached to their network. The forwarder encapsulates the MQTT-SN frames that are received on the wireless side and forwards them unchanged to the GW and releases the frames that are received from the gateway and sends them unchanged to the clients.

- **Secure Message Queue Telemetry Transport:** Secure Message Queue Telemetry Transport (SMQTT) is an extension of MQTT with an encryption-based lightweight messaging protocol. Four main stages of SMQTT are setup, encryption, publish, and decryption. Compared to an MQTT session, SMQTT session has the following four levels: setup, encryption, publish, and decryption. The protocol uses a similar MQTT broker-based architecture with the difference that both the subscriber and publisher need to register with the broker using a secret master key. The data is encrypted before being published by the publisher and then is decrypted at the subscriber end and diversity encryption algorithms can be used.

Table 7.2 gives the description of IoT data/information models from different organizations.

In classic OPC, only pure data was provided, such as raw sensor values with only limited semantic information, and the tag name and engineering unit. OPC UA offers a more powerful capability for semantic modeling of data. It uses type hierarchies and inheritance in model information. The OPC UA node model allows for information to be connected in various ways by allowing for hierarchical and non-hierarchical reference types. This facilitates exposing the same information in many ways and depends on the use case.

Table 7.2 Some of the IoT data/information models.

Date/Information model Type or Service Platform	**Organization**	**Description**
DPWS data model	Devices Profile for Web Services (DPWS) (see Section 6.2)	Information model defined in the WSDL file is based on the XML Schema specification for DPWS enabled devices.
OPC UA data model	OPC Foundation (see Section 6.2)	Information model based on object-oriented techniques to represent data for Object Linking and Embedding for Process Control (OPC) and OPC UA.
Lightweight M2M (LwM2M) Platform	OMA (see Section 5.7)	Device management protocol of LwM2M, is designed to meet the requirements of applications by transferring service/application data. The protocol uses a simple object-based resource model with resource operations of creation/retrieval/update/deletion/configuration of an attribute. The protocol provides data format support for TLV, JSON, Plain Text, Opaque, and transport layer support for UDP/IP and SMS. M2M functionalities, such as LwM2M server, access control, device, connectivity, firmware update, location, connectivity statistics and uses DTLS for security are included.
RESTful HTTP (REST) data model	W3C/IETF	Representational state transfer (REST) uses the HTTP methods such as GET, POST, PUT, and DELETE to provide a resource-oriented messaging system where the interactions can be performed simply by using the synchronous request/response HTTP commands for receiving, modifying, and sending data. Based on TCP/IP, REST uses the request/response architecture at the client side, having a larger header compared to other IoT Protocols (e.g., higher bandwidth requirements) and applying SSL/TLS for security.
oBix data model (http://www.obix.org/)	Open Building information eXchange	A restful approach is based on an object-oriented data model to represent data for the mechanical and electrical systems in smart buildings. It includes classes and even method signatures and objects composed of other objects. It offers a standard library providing the basic object types and classes with special purpose such as a watch, history, batch operations, etc.

7.2 Digital Twin

Digital twin (DT) technology sounds very advanced, but maybe it originated from the simple demand of human desire. One day, a kid asks his/her parents, “Dad and mum, why did you bear another baby again?” “En, you should have an alternate as a substitute account for one favorite game when playing a game in a bad situation”. Obviously, that is a joke. However, perhaps there is another you only existing in the information world — your DT — only if the DT technology could be used on humans.

7.2.1 *Introduction*

DT is a young concept that was born in this century, but it plays an important role in industrial IoT. It is a digital network and intelligent reflection relationship between the real world and the virtual world, by which the lifecycle active trace of things could be recorded in both the physical world and the digital world simultaneously, so the operation characteristics of things or the equipment could be recorded or observed in the network world. In the view of deep consideration, DT constructs a parallel virtual space in the information world that opens a time–space door to the dimension of information.

As Chapter 1 mentioned, the author of this book argues that human beings cannot grasp the wisdom of nature completely but only understand it based on technology/science and cognition for now. As a member of nature, humans evolved over generations gradually. There is a time axis associated with “network code” of gene, which is perpendicular to the existing space. Our network, only existing in the present time–space network, cannot transfer wisdom from the time axis, but nature inherited all the wisdom along with the time axis in form of genes. As a particular technology, the gene could not be deciphered entirely so far.[1] However, there may be an entrance of a time–space analysis model for transferring wisdom by a data twin in the long run.

In Section 6.2, how to abstract an embedded device into an IoT grid is discussed (shown in Fig. 6.31). In the discussion, a device gird is modeled as the abstracted composition of Primitive IoT (PIoT), and each PIoT embodies one thing (RFID tag, Pallet, Raspberry Pi, or others in Fig. 7.2(a))

[1] Is the human understanding of time and space acquired or inherited? The exploration is still on the way.

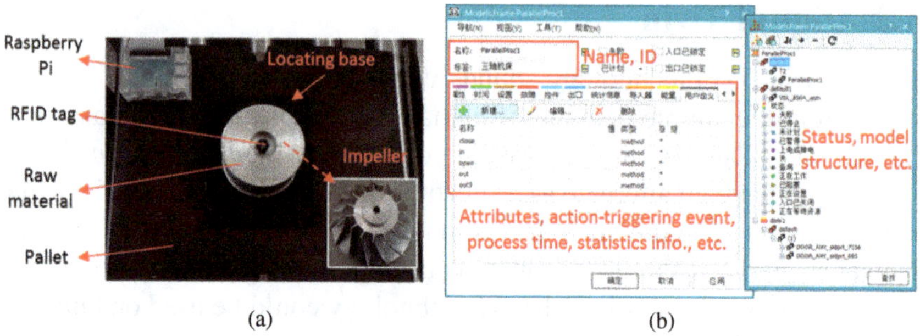

Figure 7.2 DT-CPPS for the real-time manufacturing data being synchronized to the DT model. (a) Physical shop floor (PSF) configuration and (b) cybershop floor (CSF) configuration.

in a triple-element sets as PIoT (things, relations, services) virtually. Different PIoT in the grid can provide multiple services with their relations through the utilization of services components (such as attributes, even-triggering events, and statistical information in Fig. 7.2(b)). The example is further extended to a DT-based Cyber-Physical Production System (DT-CPPS), which builds a physical shop floor (PSF) and corresponding cybershop floor (CSF) and discusses their interconnection and interoperability in Fig. 7.2.

In DT-CPPS, the responsive production scheduling strategies for real-time disturbance responses are discussed, and the application contains different responsive scheduling strategies which are built in two modules, i.e., disturbance recognition and responsive scheduling, and the former acts as the input of the latter. For a smart manufacturing shop floor, real-time monitoring, simulation, and prediction of manufacturing operations are vital to improving production efficiency and flexibility.

7.2.2 *Characteristics of DT*

The concept of DT was proposed by Grieves at his production life-cycle management (PLM) course at the University of Michigan, in 2011. Then DT was drawn into the maintenance of aircraft and was defined as simulation processes that concentrated multiple physicals, multiple scales, and multiple probabilities on constructing a complete virtual model based on the physical model of aircraft, which reflected the aircraft's life cycle by utilizing the historical data and real-time updated data (e.g., by sensors).

In an old project of NASA, two identical space aircraft needed to be made, which were called twins for each other, and the one on Earth was designed for reflecting the situations and states of the other. On the one hand, the twin was used to train staff on flight preparation; on the other hand, the twin could be used to simulate another operation state during flight, for aircraft being reflected and predicted precisely, and for assisting astronauts to make the right decision in an emergency.

Later, aiming at maintaining the spacecraft and keeping it in good working condition, the US Department of Defense proposed the following:

First, a digital aircraft model was constructed and synchronized with real aircraft state by real-time sensing completely. At the end of every flight, the situation and load could be analyzed according to the flight data in data space rather than reconditioning by a maintainer. However, the representation of data twin is the same shape, rather than the difference, in essence. Like the shadow of real things, data twin was the virtual model of the data world.

From the view of IoT analytics, "A DT is a digital abstraction or representation of a physical system's attributes and/or behavior on three distinct dimensions". In addition, in its report, a three-dimensional (3-D) cube analysis is used to frame the various DT offerings in the market, which includes the following: (1) Hierarchical levels; (2) Lifecycle phases; (3) Most common uses and input data types, and results in over 250 DT classifications, as shown in Fig. 7.3.

From the x axis which represented the six lifetime phases from design to decommission, it is similar to that of RAMI 4.0 (in Section 6.2.3, before the two phases, "type" and "instance", the author inserts "Service Design and Prototype" as a grid preparation phase) in the production life cycle. In Fig. 7.3, the other two axes represent the six hierarchy levels from information to multi-system and the seven most common uses, respectively.

Nowadays, from the aspect of IoT applications, the main models or use cases of DT includes manufacturing and equipment process model, simulation analysis model, product definition and development model, and measurement and test model (after production). The simulation analysis model enables users to see the possible situation of the actual physical product/asset in operation state by its DT. Take the "Digital Thread" project as an example, intent, feedback, and specify mechanisms for capturing and communicating requirements in a well-defined 3-D product models

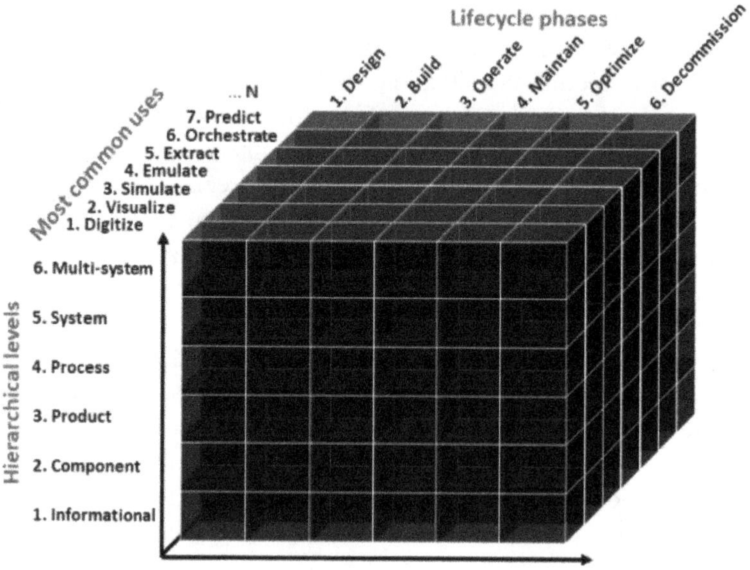

Figure 7.3 The DT cube.

Notes: Each combination of these 3-D results in different DT classification-252 different combinations possible in total. For simplicity, the model does not consider the different input data types.

Source: DT insights Report 2020 Cube Analysis.

have four-folded meaning as follows: (i) identify the common information elements that are needed to integrate the product life cycle; (ii) promote and promulgate standards for representing this information; (iii) define and demonstrate a framework and technologies that support access of trusted information, in context, wherever it is needed during the lifecycle; (iv) define and demonstrate mechanisms for providing a feedback cycle from inspection stage back to design.

All the data models could be communicated on a dual way, the state and parameter of real physical product will feedback to data model by an information system which concentrated on the intelligent manufacturing system. The feedback mechanism which demonstrates the utility of such a data environment from inspection to design use case will be further analyzed. The corresponding results will provide the technical underpinning for new standards and tooling that enable manufacturing systems to become smart.

From the view of IBM, the end-to-end DTs let owners/operators reduce equipment downtime while increasing production, and a service

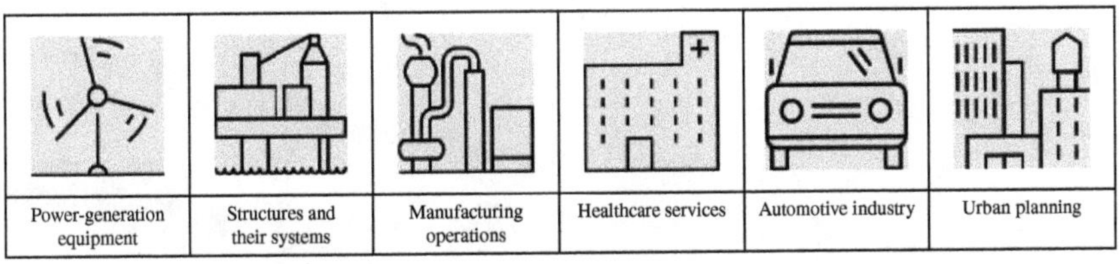

Figure 7.4 Applications of DT.

lifecycle management (SLM) solution is discovered and created in DT (as mirror and monitor of PLM). Some industry analysts speculate that the DT market could rise sharply until at least 2026, climbing to an estimated USD 48.2 billion, at a CAGR of 58% from 2020 to 2026. DTs are already used in the following applications, as shown in Fig. 7.4.

Moreover, some companies (IBM and Siemens included) tried to bring machine learning (ML) or AI technology to DT to assist in constructing intelligent data models and utilize the number of sensors to obtain real-time data and state information. As shown in Fig. 7.4, with a high-level overlapping application sector of IoT, the DT, as a virtual representation of the IoT physical object or system across its lifecycle PLM and SLM, using real-time data to enable understanding, learning, and reasoning, is one element connecting the IoT and AI.

Combining with ML/AI algorithm, data analytics and context information could be used in understanding and learning modeling. Model-based control and time-series prediction could be used in predicting optimization, and abnormal state under process automation of normal operation could be predicted for pre-diagnosis, as shown in Fig. 7.5.

The evolution of DT shows a similar mode to that of the IoT upgrading that was described in Section 6.2 (in Fig. 6.34). For example, after the data and service of PIoT are integrated into a device/grid-centric IoT, the IoT grid shows some collaborative intelligence in its process or information context in an IoT system/zone, for its further integration into the IoT zone/system. At this evolution stage, promoted by IoT communication and network layer, the networked intelligence emerges both in an IoT system and its DT. From the system-centric IoT upgrading to intelligent IoT infrastructure, especially in industrial sectors (IIoT), the predict-optimizing and automation (in different levels, the six-levels of driving automation is an example described in Section 6.2.2) are along with the advanced DTs, which should be included in an IIoT platform layer for information running through design, manufacturing, and product support

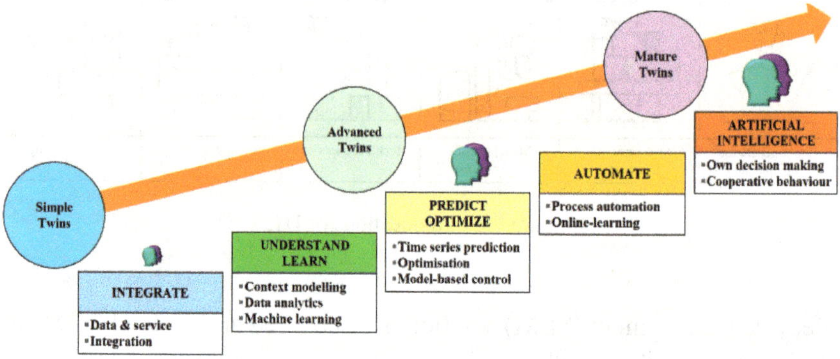

Figure 7.5 DTs evolution.
Source: IBM.

processes, enabling the integration of smart devices and systems/multi-systems.

Some technologists believe that DT technology based on ML or AI makes it possible to perform appropriate detection or predictive maintenance without being close or unable to approach the device. As this technology becomes more mature, it may eventually reach the entire industrial sector on a large scale. It will be used by companies to plan equipment service and production line operations, predict when equipment will break down, improve operational efficiency, help with new product development, etc. In the future, this technology is expected to be completely integrated with industrial production, driving Industry 4.0 into a new phase of intelligence across the board.

7.2.3 *IIoT and DT*

The DT concept model was proposed by Prof. Michael Grieves in his book *Virtually Perfect: Driving Innovative and Lean Products through Product Lifecycle Management*. As illustrated in Fig. 7.6, it contained the following three parts: (a) physical products in real space; (b) virtual products in virtual space; (c) the connection of data and information that ties the virtual and real products together.

On the virtual side, the amount of available information and numerous behavioral sensing are added in visualizing the product for the test and performance capabilities. As an efficient integration with IoT in

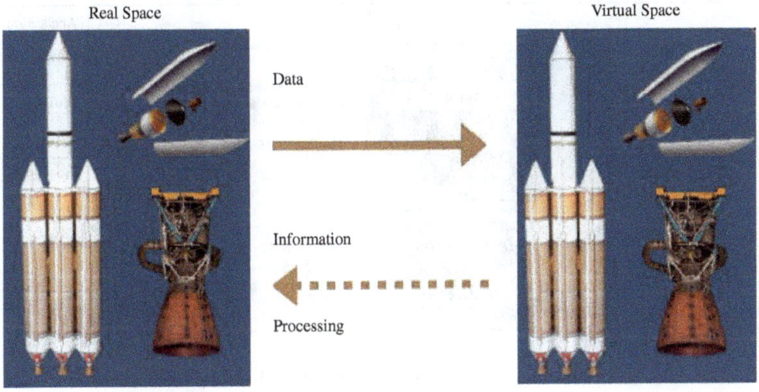

Figure 7.6 Model of mirror information analysis.

Source: Digital Twin White Paper: Manufacturing Excellence through Virtual Factory Replication.

linking physical space to virtual space, the characteristics of DT are as follows:

- DT concentrates on the integration of various data of the physical object, and it is also a reflection of the physical object.
- DT existed in the life cycle of the physical object, and it evolved simultaneously with the accumulated relative knowledge.
- DT could not only describe the physical object but also be optimized with a model.

Nowadays the concept of data twin is applied and certified in many fields. For example, in Siemens, DT is used to predict behavior, optimize performance, and validate the most complex products. It helps the manufacturer to construct the Industry 4.0 system model of integration manufacture process at information space and complete the whole digital process from design to production. For improving user's experience on the complex scenario, a 3-D Experience platform (Dassault Systèmes) with data twin technology was constructed by Dassault Aviation Company, which improved the product design model by utilizing reflection of users continuously and optimized the product in the physical world.

As discussed in RAMI4.0 (in Section 6.2) and **ISMA (in Section 6.6.3)** aforementioned, the 3-D architecture of Industry 4.0/IIoT is similar to that of the DT cube above. In the layers axis of the 3-D model RAMI4.0, six major aspects are shown vertically, i.e., device,

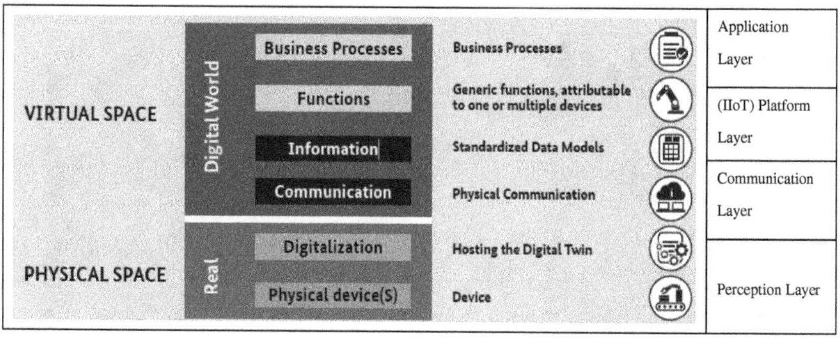

Figure 7.7 RAMI4.0 in architectural dimension.

digitalization/integration, communication, information, functional, and business. They represent the physical device properties decomposed according to their functionalities, and together with the corresponding aspects of four IoT layers are shown in Fig. 7.7.

In a design typical for layered architectures from the six aspects, data/service or an event may be exchanged among them, but only among two adjacent ones, and of course within each layer. In the physical space, a device or a physical grid in the above DT-CPPS use case (with its inner components links as PIoT), based on its functional context, is abstracted as the digitalization which hosts its DT.

As shown in Fig. 7.8, following a common semantic model with "Communication" to any other endpoint, or the device is already linked with an IoT communication platform, the given device is connected to an administration shell that is handling functions required to establish the functions of the "DT". The administration shell may be a part of every device or hosted by a dedicated piece of equipment handling the DTs of one or multiple devices.

In Fig. 7.8, the administration shell is understood easily because it is named as "Grid center" in Section 6.2. This administration shell covers all functions required to integrate devices into an I4.0 and IM (an I4.0/IMSA instance in Section 6.6.3) application. Such a shell may cover either a single physical device (e.g., a sensor), a functional group of devices (e.g., a PLC grid including its field devices), or a complete production unit (e.g., a machine or a processing unit).

From the deployment viewpoint, the device and its administration shell can be decoupled into the perception layer and the communication layer of IoT, respectively. But the administration shell links the DT of the

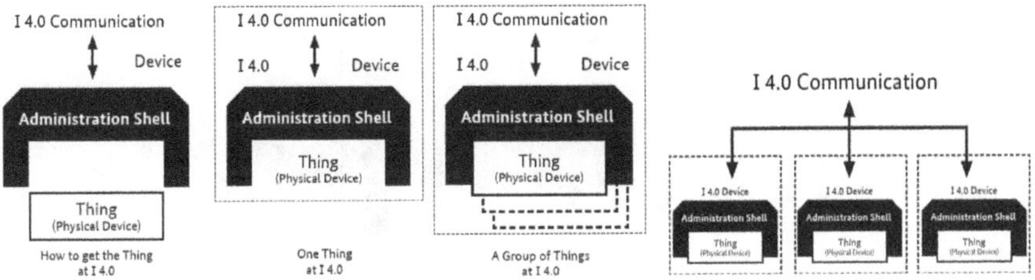

Figure 7.8 Integrating things in I4.0, where an "administration shell" is used to turn any things/devices to an I4.0 component.

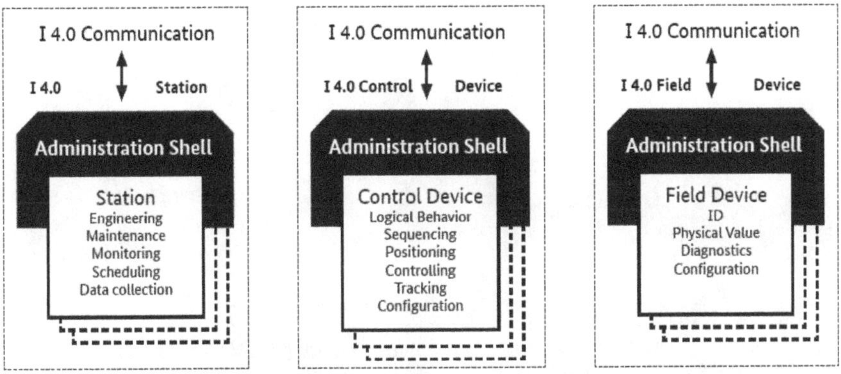

Figure 7.9 Three kinds of communications related I4.0 elements.

device from its digitalization to its functionalities, which may be hosted in a higher-level IT system (e.g., an IoT/IIoT platform).

Based on the possible ways for integrating things in I4.0 and IM (definition of each in Sino-German White Paper on Functional Safety for Industry 4.0 and Intelligent Manufacturing, 2020), there are in principle three kinds of I4.0 elements of relevance to the subject matter discussed in Fig. 7.8, in which an I4.0 and IM component in the context of this section is either a (control/field) device or a station. Each device/station is equipped with an administration shell. Such an administration shell can either be used to handle an individual component (as shown in Fig. 7.9); alternatively, multiple components can be hosted in the same shell, as shown in Fig. 7.10.

The "administration shell" covers both the virtual representation and the technical functionality of the different kinds of devices, as shown in Figs. 7.9 and 7.10. In the latter, the device in it can be described as a device grid (e.g., ADAS grid in-vehicle), with a non-loose on-board integration to a computing station (e.g., HPC of in-vehicle Domain/Zone

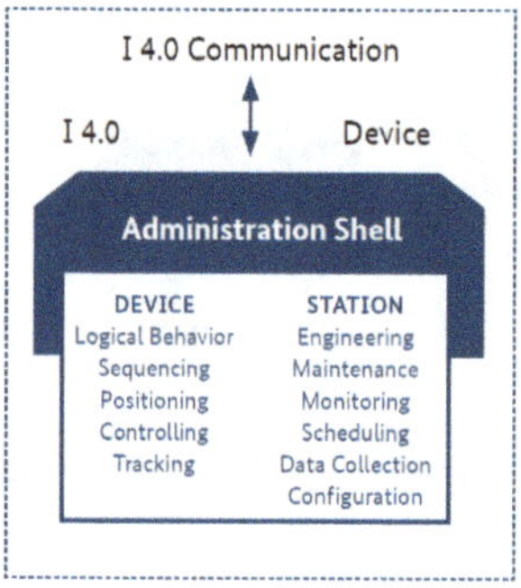

Figure 7.10 I4.0 Device.

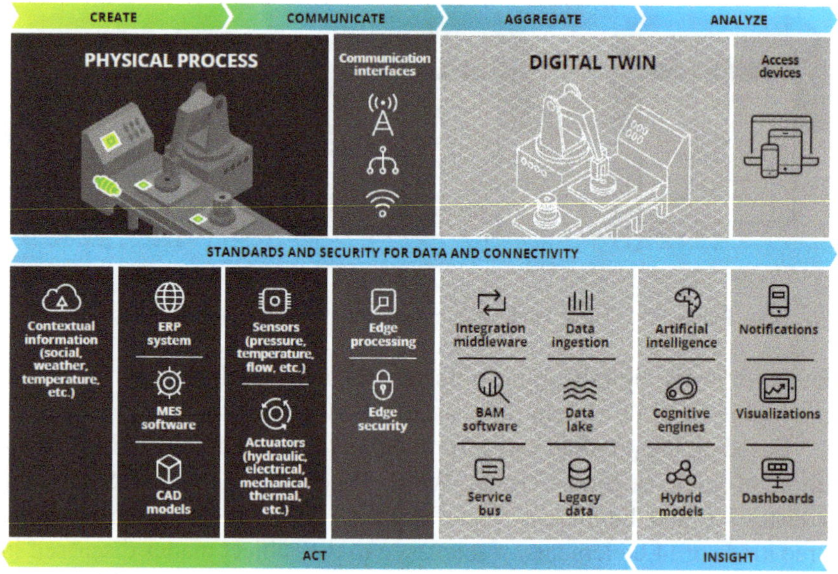

Figure 7.11 DT representation.

Source: Deloitte University Press.

are detailed in Section 6.2.2). However, it is also feasible to define a safety/security-related administration shell, which will be further discussed in the next chapter.

Finally, by layered integration from devices to communication and platform, in that way from IoT grid to IoT domain/Zone (details in Section 6.2), higher-level systems or IIoT platforms are able to access all

I4.0 components in a well-defined manner, which streamlines the creation, communication, aggregation, and analysis in the DT representation of an IIoT aspect, as shown in Fig. 7.11.

Once connected, the value chain of DT is beyond the product lifecycle management (PLM) and service lifecycle management (SLM), and the DTs for IoT will possess at a minimum the following attributes:

- Correctness — give a correct replication of the IoT ecosystem and its devices.
- Completeness — updated *vis-à-vis* the functionality in the real-world system.
- Soundness — exhibit only the functionality available in the real-world system.
- Abstractness — free from details specific to particular implementations.
- Expandability — adapt easily to emerging technologies and applications.
- Scalability — must be able to operate at any scale.
- Parameterized — accessible for analysis, design, and implementation.
- Reproducible — be able to replicate the same result for the same input as the real system.

The IoT DTs can expand the interface between man and machine through their virtual representation and advanced technologies on levels, such as AI and speech, which enable people and devices/machines to take actions based on operational data at the edge, which ranges from data/device edge, administration/grid edge to edge computing processing and edge security/safety.

The following use case is a real-time temperature sensing indoor system for the DT as an interface between a management machine and the temperature agent.

7.2.4 *Use cases*

Through the virtual representation of a person in a given room or region, a real-time temperature sensing IoT system for individuals is built in the post-epidemic era. If the use case is advanced by more sensors and actuators, such as the ones for heating, ventilation, and air conditioning (HVAC) control, it can be used in building automation systems (BAS), smart buildings, or smart energy (e.g., energy-saving use case in the next section).

- **Device and Communication:** The hardware of this part consists of low-cost infrared (IR) sensor beams, a temperature sensor, a lighting sensor, and a wireless communication system, which are all packaged into a shell (or an IoT grid) as nodes in different rooms environment. The internal components of a node are shown in Fig. 7.12. This is not shown in the figure, but as a part of the built WSN, it is the "Kill A Watt energy usage monitor" for collecting plug-load information for any electronic devices or appliances plugged into the apparatus.
- **Platform and DT:** A countably finite set of regions/rooms R, where R = {R1;R2; ... ;Rm}, and here m = 4. In each room, one sensing agent (or more) is ready to record the temperature when a person is an occurrence with his occupancy time (as shown in Fig. 7.13). In the use case, the temperature records of a person in time series are his DT in the

Figure 7.12 The sensors inside a node (with connections removed for clarity). The components are (from left-hand side moving clockwise): an xBee communications module, a TEMT6000 light sensor, two Sharp 2Y0A02 distance sensors, an Arduino micro controller, and a TMP102 temperature sensor.

virtual space: As shown in Fig. 7.14, the agent (functional abstracted from the in-room sensing node) in the room (i.e., R3) is hosting the DT of individuals.

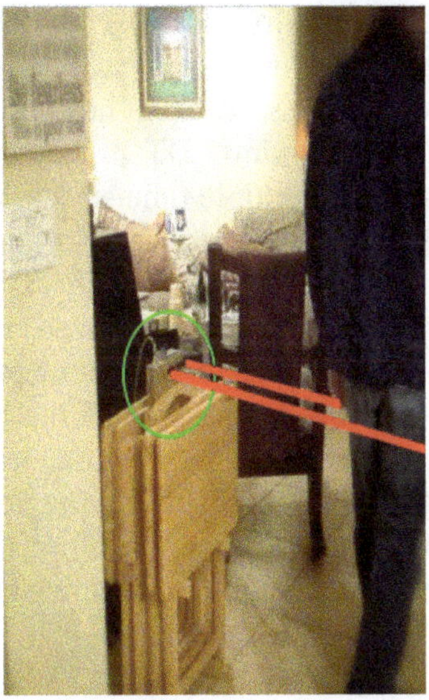

Figure 7.13 When staff/resident crossing in front of a node, the red lines represent the IR beams emitted by the sensors. Then his temperature is recorded.

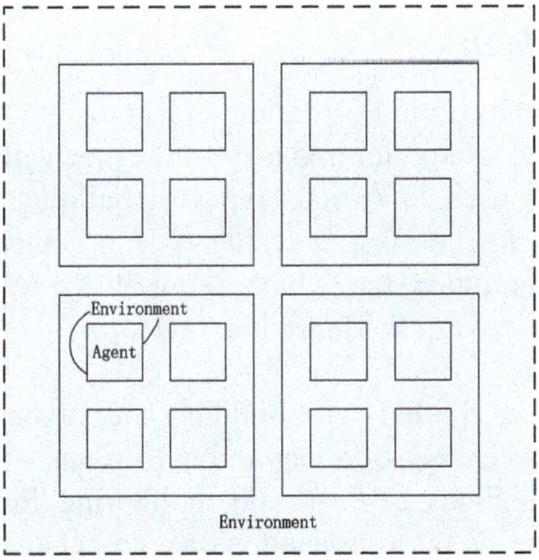

Figure 7.14 In the four-room example, each agent in a given room is hosting a certain range of inside room environment.

- **Application:** When the sensing agent detects a resident/office staff in one room by IR, his temperature is recorded as {ID, room, temperature, time} as the DT data sets of the human.

The above is a simple DT-IoT use case modeled by one-dimension temperature data abstraction from the physical space (i.e., room, person, and their relation is described as the agent hosting DT service) to virtual space. From an OT or IIoT view, DT processes multiple physicals/scales, multiple data spaces, multiple time–space, which pertain to products/production and their different phases. In an interview with Mr. Cao Dewang, the founder of Fuyao Glass Industry Group, he said, "in the production process, every optimal (or optimized) link or stage should be combined into the assembly line to form an optimal assembly line". From the author's view, how to "assemble" the best production links/stages into a production line should be a near-scope goal of DT. There is no doubt that AI or ML will help to achieve the goal in the involvement of training a deep learning (DL)/deep reinforcement learning (DRL)/semantics or service model using plenty of time-series data outputs from sensors.

7.3 Applications in Smart Building and Smart Energy

7.3.1 *Smart building*

Smart building means a kind of building or home automation where IoT devices can be used to monitor and control the mechanical, electrical, and electronic systems used in various types of buildings (e.g., public and private, industrial, institutions, or residential) in home/office automation and building automation systems. In this context, the following three main areas are being covered in the literature:

- The integration of the IoT with building energy management systems in order to create energy-efficient and IoT-driven "smart buildings".
- The possible methods of real-time monitoring for reducing energy consumption and monitoring energy-wasting behaviors.
- The integration of smart devices in the built environment and how they might know how to be used in future applications.

Technically and socially, energy consumption and monitoring in public spaces and work environments are two of the most important problems to solve. On the one hand, the building sector plays a crucial role as far as energy consumption is concerned, thus efforts and resources are incurred in making them more efficient. On the other hand, the technological solutions of energy-wasting control that enable efficient energy use not to spread out among old buildings, the lack of resources for the implementation of new technology that would adapt to their infrastructure, and the disparity of requirements among all the users' comfort/preferences level because of the difficulty to deploy automatic energy management systems in buildings.

However, the misuse of energy or potential wasteful behavior in public buildings generally is due to careless usage of these resources (not turning off lights, leaving monitors or PC working all night, needlessly using lifts, etc.), and users have no direct awareness of the generated energy bill. The following example is based on the combination of WSNs and real-time locating systems (RTLS) to collect information that enables monitoring, replicating, or interacting with the environment where the context-aware information is taking place. WSN and RTLS provide dynamic, efficient, and flexible infrastructures that collect contextual data regardless of the chosen location.

The RTLS permits determining what behavioral habits users follow and gives guidelines on how to improve these habits in their works. A virtual organization of agents supports the social machine (a kNN algorithm in the social machine classifies the users into different groups based on their previous energy performance). This gives intelligence to the worker/player and enables the learning process, updates contextual information, monitors users' actions, provides information to workers or players, and facilitates the deployment, configuration, and communication of the WSN and RTLS deployed.

The framework of the context-aware framework for collaborative learning applications (CAFCLA) is shown in Fig. 7.15, which contains the IoT perception layer as tablet, smartphone, location beacons, and temperature, luminosity, on/off, and consumption sensors; the communication layer as Wi-Fi, ZigBee, 4G/3G/GPRS; the service layer as context-awareness WSNs, RTLS, management social computing, virtual organization of agents; and the application layer as API and Web interfaces.

In the communication layer, the ZigBee protocol (IEEE 802.15.4) is established through which information will be transmitted between

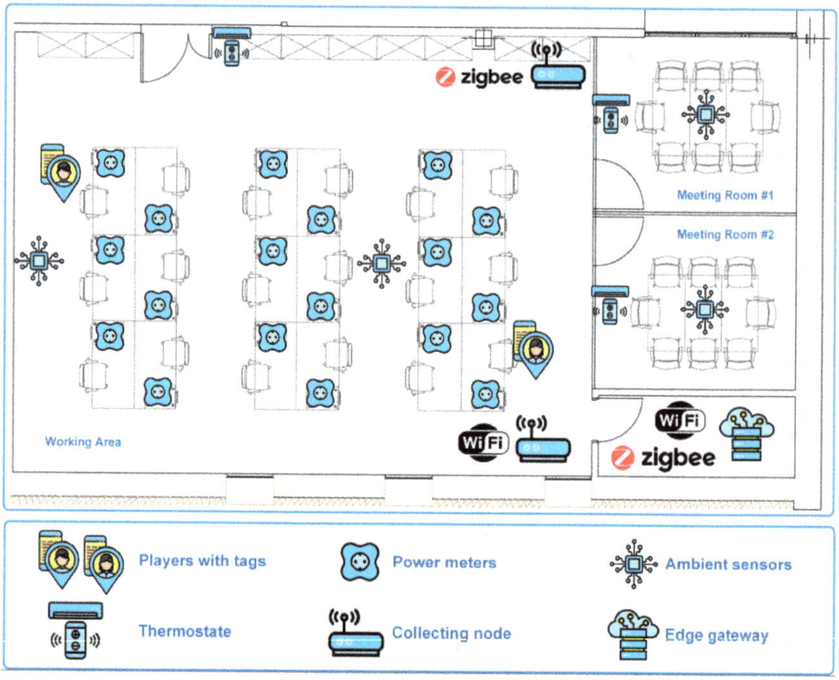

Figure 7.15 IoT devices and edge layer in the evaluation scenario for energy efficiency in public buildings (as CAFCLA framework).

sensors and beacons. Wi-Fi transmits the information to the server and the devices of the participants. Above this layer, the following four functions are realized, including applications:

- The real-time contextual status of the environment (temperature and luminosity sensors), the instant and historical energy consumption of each job site (electricity consumption sensors in the working area of Fig. 7.15), and the status of lighting and HVAC[2] systems (on/off sensors), for not only the environmental and consumption parameters that draw the context providing real-time information to users but also the analysis of the data and their use by other parts of the system.

[2]HVAC (heating, ventilation, and air-conditioning) is extended as application and development of automatic control in HVAC system.

- To provide the location, CAFCLA integrates n-Core Polaris, which allows determining the position of users with up to one-meter accuracy based on the ZigBee protocol. In order to locate, n-Core requires a set of beacons to be deployed, as mentioned in Section 4.5.4 (indoor location beacon). Beacons collect the signal sent by tags that are worn by the players. This signal, together with its associated data, is sent to the server that implements the location engine, which calculates the position of each player. Players wear an n-Core Sirius Quantum tag responsible for sending the signal, and it is also equipped with an accelerometer that determines whether the user is moving. The beacons send these data to the server in the same way that sensor data are sent through Wi-Fi data collectors.
- The contextual information layer integrates the location engine and all the logic needed to perform effective data collection through the IoT devices forming the Physical layer. Furthermore, in this scenario, this layer exploits the features of the n-Core platform as the n-Core Polaris RTLS system to provide the system with sensing and locating capabilities.
- The management layer includes a social machine as well as all the logic and intelligence that allows for the management of the serious game.

Finally, the application layer develops the interaction interface for both configurations (e.g., the configuration of players/workers who are rewarded or penalized depending on their behavior in energy savings within a work environment) and development. In the example, several tools are established, such as the collaboration between players (e.g., deciding on meeting times) and the necessary contextual information at any time that allows players to make decisions that could be taken in order to be rewarded (e.g., turning off the monitor when the work is finished).

Another example of HAVC use case in sensor fault diagnosis with distributed intelligent algorithms on the edge is shown in Fig. 7.16. The figure shows a reliable and energy-saving EC use case in smart building (automation).

The distributed intelligent fault diagnosis algorithm for detecting and isolating multiple sensor faults in large-scale HVAC systems is developed by a team of researchers led by Professor Marios Polycarpou, Director of the KIOS Research and Innovation Center of Excellence, Cyprus. Through modeling the HVAC system as a network of interconnected subsystems, the design of a set of distributed sensor fault diagnosis agents (as

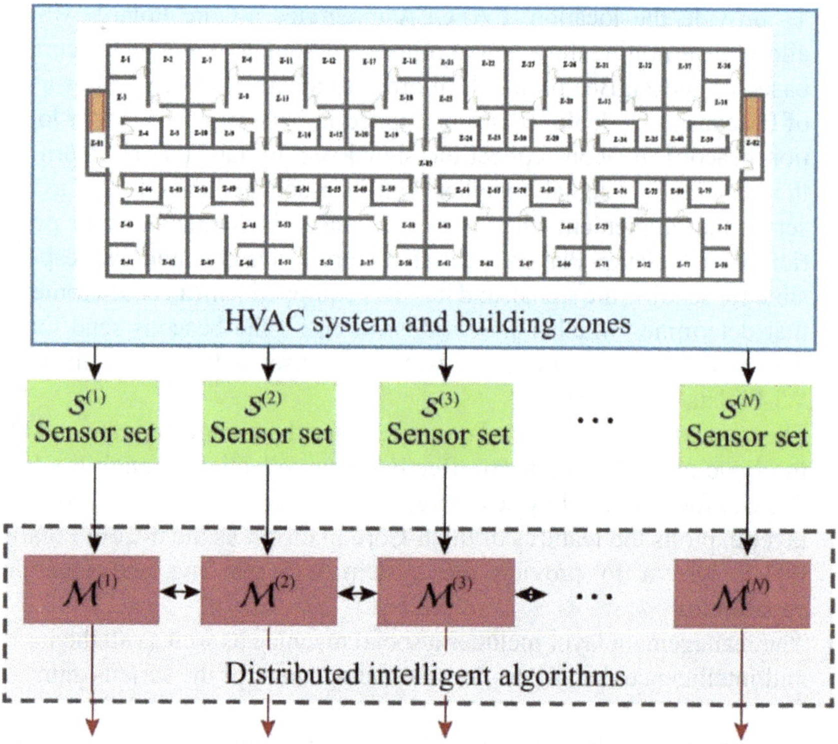

Figure 7.16 A distributed intelligent fault diagnosis algorithm for detecting and isolating multiple sensor faults in large-scale HVAC systems.

$M^{(1)...(N)}$, in the figure) in a sequence of computer-implementable instructions is capable of isolating multiple sensor faults by applying a combinatorial decision and diagnostic reasoning on the edge, as indicated by the dotted rectangle in Fig. 7.16.

Simulations are used to illustrate the effectiveness of the proposed method in the presence of multiple sensor faults applied to an 83-zone HVAC system and to evaluate the sensitivity of the method with respect to the sensor noise variance.

According to Professor Polycarpou, "The operation of heating, ventilation, and air-conditioning (HVAC) systems in our homes, workspaces, and public indoor spaces are based on the use of feedback measurements from sensing devices to make adjustments for maintaining the desired temperature. The presence of faulty measurements disorients the system and may create uncomfortable indoor conditions and/or significantly waste energy".

This study presents an algorithmic approach that can be applied either on existing building management systems or plug-in IoT as a system of physical computing devices that are interconnected via a network for collecting and sharing data — to notify the users and operators of the building about the presence of faulty measurements as well as the location of any faulty sensors. Combined with the utilization of thermal models of the variation of temperature in HVAC equipment and building zones, the diagnostic algorithms implemented in a multi-agent framework as a self-organized system consists of several intelligent agents. These agents interact with each other to solve complex problems that would be difficult for them to solve singularly, which enables the development of advanced methods for detecting and isolating sensor faults. In this framework, a wireless smart sensor can communicate with its neighboring sensors to enhance the fault diagnostic process in terms of reliability, robustness, sensitivity, and scalability.

The goal of the research team is to develop lifelong diagnostic systems for smart buildings, which are able to continuously monitor their operation over the lifetime of the buildings, to detect, diagnose and self-heal any faulty behavior, and to learn from their prior experiences, as well as from the experiences of diagnostic systems from other smart buildings.

From Deloitte's smart cities research, smart building has been expanded from the initial definition to a Smart City 2.0 version, which encompasses not only connected infrastructure but also the goal of higher quality of life for citizens. Smart City 2.0 uses three dimensions — data, digital, and (user) design — to enhance citizens' experience and city-wide decision making.

In the perception layer of IoT, smart buildings seek to encompass a logical, physically proximate grouping of smart things (as physical assets shown in the left part of Fig. 7.17). The digital assets that create a fabric throughout the connected IoT platform, including digital automation and cloud storage, which are combined in optimized building and operational automation with intelligent space management to enhance the user experience, increase productivity, reduce costs, and mitigate physical and cybersecurity risks.

The IoT platform in Fig. 7.17 bears not only communication but also data collection and analysis (e.g., ML). As their most basic function, smart

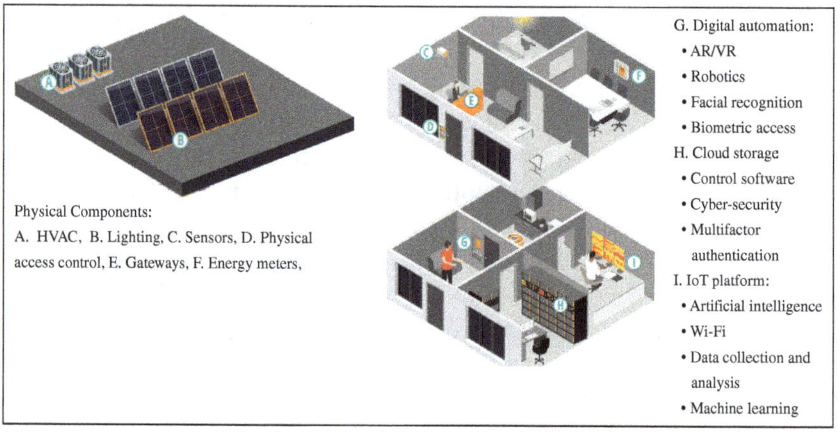

Figure 7.17 The smart building framework consists of the physical assets within the building, the digital assets that create a fabric throughout the connected space, and the use cases that are enabled by the marriage of physical and digital assets.

Notes: Other extended use cases include Virtual assistant, Room reservation, Usage-based maintenance, Location awareness, and Smart parking.
Source: Deloitte analysis.

buildings are digitally connected structures that span industries, including office buildings, factories, shopping malls, hospitals, academic campuses, stadiums, airports, military bases, and residential buildings. In Deloitte's view, the common thread running through these use cases (from A to I in Fig. 7.17) is human — these are all spaces in which humans can converge and interact with each other, utilize the advanced technology to perform their necessary functions, and benefit from a digitally enhanced experience.

As shown in Fig. 7.17, smart buildings (2.0 by Deloitte) are digitally connected structures that combine optimized building and operational automation with intelligent space management to enhance the user experience, increase productivity, reduce costs, and mitigate physical and cyber-security risks.

Finally, as mentioned in Sections 5.7.4 and 6.1.4, the OneM2M platform is a federated interworking model, where several heterogeneous IoT platforms are interconnected. An IoT platform includes various modules: big data management and storage, real-time and batch analytics, security and privacy, semantics, etc. As shown in Fig. 7.18, interoperability between the central IoT platform and the pilot site IoT platforms (e.g., industry, home, and health platforms) is addressed in this platform.

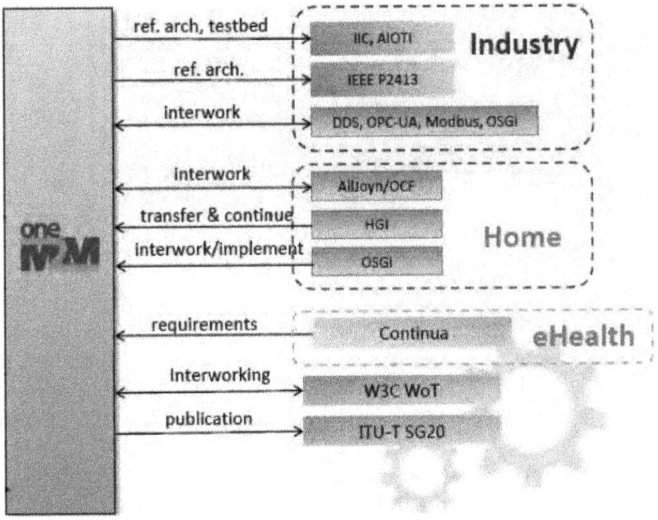

Figure 7.18 OneM2M interworking overview.
Source: OneM2M.

7.3.2 *Smart energy*

Smart energy is one of the scenarios in which IoT is applied to achieve efficient energy use, and it plays an important role in distributed energy systems as they turn from energy consumers to the so-called "energy prosumers" in their development of buildings, industries, countries, and universities. In order to obtain energy efficiency from applications capable of controlling, measuring, and managing energy consumption in buildings, grids, and households, countless researches have provided new hardware solutions (sensors, controllers, or smart meters) and integrated IoT platforms. Despite the efforts done to make users understand the importance of reducing energy consumption in public spaces, work environments, or at home, this problem continues, and it is necessary to find a solution to it. The following example is an OneM2M platform-based home/building energy use case.

As shown in Fig. 7.19, numbers of energy-consuming devices (e.g., switches, power outlets, bulbs, televisions, etc.) already integrate IoT connectivity, which can allow them to communicate with utilities to balance power generation and energy usage and optimize energy consumption as a whole. The OneM2M platform provides a functional architecture as device (app control)-middleware (horizontal)-communication networks

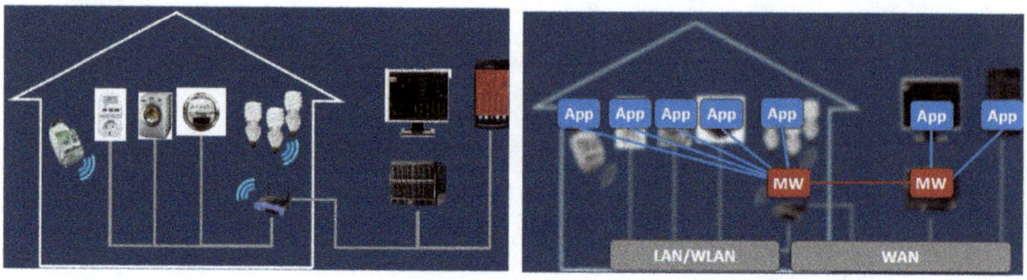

Figure 7.19 A home/building energy management use case based on the functional architecture of OneM2M.

Notes: OneM2M provides both a single private network/proximal network (e.g., smart home) and connecting "things" in reach: Monitor, control, automate, no hierarchy, with service enablers as discovery, advertisement, introspection, on-boarding. Its interworking protocol examples include the consumer-side OCF, IoTivity, dotot, KNX, and the Industrial-side OPC-UA, DDS, Profinet, Sercos.

in Fig. 7.19. Through these platforms, devices allow for remote control by users or central management via LAN/WAN or WAN/cloud-based communication (the bottom part of Fig. 7.19) and enable functions like scheduling (e.g., remotely powering on or off heating systems, controlling ovens, changing lighting conditions, etc.).

Smart energy-enabled automation of building operations, notably with climate-energy control and fault diagnosis in HVAC systems as the two use cases in smart buildings, which have had benefits of more than a decade of technology evolution, such as IoT, cloud/edge analytics, and mobile devices.

The IoT benefits related to optimizing the control of building operations and secure building access are well documented and reveal some of the most directly attributable outcomes from smart buildings. Optimizing and improving the operations of the facility can lead to a variety of recouped costs and start from major savings on bills related to heating, cooling, lighting, and maintenance. For example, on average, 50% can be saved by moving to a connected lighting system. This can be achieved by creating a digital control tower for building operations, which provides real-time insight and leverages ML and artificial intelligence to calibrate services across a building.

- **Smart Grid:** In order to stabilize and facilitate buildings, industries, and countries (or participate) in energy trading as well as for structural condition monitoring and proactive maintenance, smart grid is presented. For example, monitoring energy consumption and other parameters allows for a 40% reduction in energy consumption. As for buildings, smart grids offer semantically annotated properties of the technical equipment within specific energy flexibilities (i.e., for shifting electrical and thermal loads). Based on the above mentioned, the following use case employs the technologies developed in a sustainable smart town (SST) to dynamically discover the flexibilities of smart energy and analyze its potential as well as their demand for applications that are necessary to manage and offer energy to the smart grid or the energy market. Other aspects, such as achieving better efficiency and resource management, reducing carbon emissions and costs, improving demand response (DR) systems and **MG/DER/DG,** or **improving knowledge and system automation by data correlation (such as temperature, humidity, luminosity, or other sensors, weather information, user, segment and building profiles, etc.)** may be included in two kinds of use cases, namely industrial/commercial environments and energy IoT environments.

As shown in Fig. 7.20, the SST of Fujisawa in Japan provides an IoT-based energy platform (in the center of the figure), in which information can be used by energy retailers, grid operators, and renewable energy to deploy fitting applications to buildings, factories, and individuals. The SST uses semantic enrichment of grid data and data analytics to enhance

Figure 7.20 Smart Grid in Japanese SST.

smart grid applications and reduce the need for manual engineering, maintenance, and setup of energy systems.

As for the use of renewable energy resources (RER) and an increasing number of energy production and self-consumption solutions for homes and businesses, the town's first green technology logo is a 400-meter-long solar panel, and wind power generation is followed.

The primary consideration of the SST project is the regional characteristics based on the concept of living comfort, energy-saving and recycling, and smart community lifestyle, including the imagination of future life mode planning of the energy, security, mobility, health, and so on. The SST also encourages electric vehicles (EVs) and free bicycles for individuals to commute.

- **Industrial Use Case of Micro-Grid (MG):** As mentioned above, smart energy environments can benefit from IoT approaches by sensors and intelligent devices that have transformed the energy industry by allowing access to a deeper understanding of how energy is spent and what factors influence its consumption. Stimulated by the IoT technology, RER and distributed energy resources (DER) call for a large number of proposals and approaches nowadays. They are based on the definition of micro-grid (MG) by IEEE standard 2030.7–2017, as "a group of interconnected loads and DER with clearly defined electrical boundaries that act as a single controllable entity concerning the grid and can connect and disconnect from the grid to enable it to operate in both grid-connected or island modes". The following use case is based on the grid-connected DER, also from an IoT view. DER decreases the cost of electricity transmission infrastructure by using RER between grids and supply consumers (prosumer). Further, grid-connected DER mode, together with micro-grid management system (MGMS) at the different control level, manages the connection of MG to a utility grid defeats the risk of unavailability owing to natural resource features and offers other benefits related to participation in the electricity market as a prosumer.

Figure 7.21 illustrates a conceptional MG structure, which is adapted to the role of generation, transmission, distribution, operator, and consumer of smart grid. As can be seen in Fig. 7.21, the maintainer acts as a service provider and the aggregator in the market domain. The performance of each entity is clarified as follows:

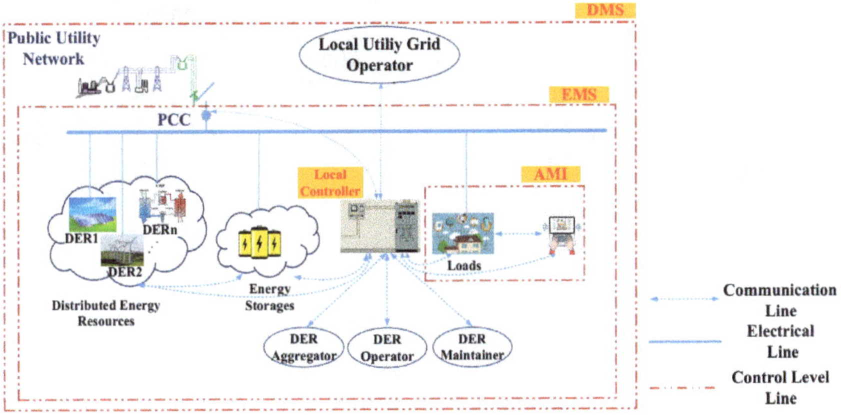

Figure 7.21 MG structure in a distribution management system (DMS).

MG Aggregator: This participant is in charge of gathering information about energy marketing participants for MG.

MG Operator: This party monitors MG and controls its performance through local and remote services.

MG Maintainer: This agent is responsible for the accurate performance of MG by providing maintenance services in case of failure according to the received reports.

MG Controller: Aggregator, maintainer, and operator interact through this part with each other and DER, facilitating the energy management system (EMS) control level.

Local Utility: Local utility is the MG utility neighbor who connects to MG through the point of common coupling (PCC) and interacts with MG to coordinate the provision of ancillary services (AS) in grid-connected mode.

As well as embedding MG in the smart grid domain, Fig. 7.22 conveys a hierarchical control strategy of smart MG by introducing three supervisory levels, namely advanced metering interface (AMI), EMS, and distribution management system (DMS).

AMI: The first or the lowest control level is related to load control. This control level is considered in the scope of MG and in this book. As introduced in Section 6.2, this level is PIoT level, in which energy

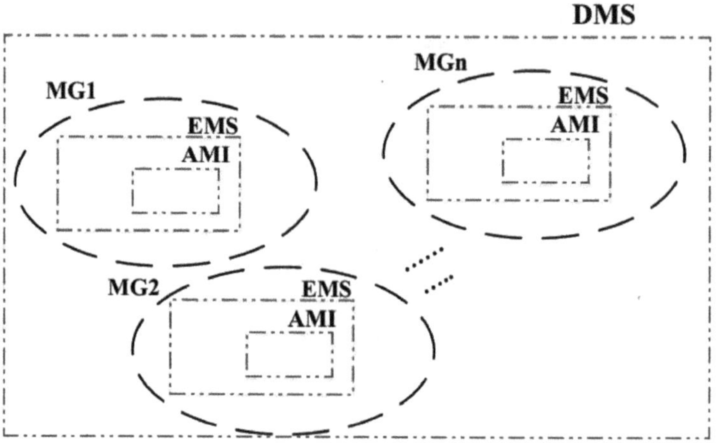

Figure 7.22 DMS supervisory level domain as an IoT domain.

consumption monitoring of smart appliances is a primitive IoT service, and the service is provided directly through a smart meter. The PIoT service as control level is also responsible for sending this information to the higher level, which is EMS (IoT grid level).[3] AMI makes it possible to cooperate with PIoT from the service/device of the same AMI or others in the same EMS, in responsive loads (RL), load shedding, peak shaving, and other DR services.

EMS: The second control level of MG is EMS, which is responsible for controlling demand and supply in MG based on information receives from DER, energy storage (ES), and loads. EMS has a key role in MGMS and provides a schedule for each MG element operation through the optimization algorithm in both grid-connected and islanded modes of MG. EMS decides MG contribution in ancillary services (AS) provision for the utility grid in a way that determines the contribution portion of each source. Commonly, MGMS (hardware as local controller in Fig. 7.21) works as an IoT grid center (see Section 6.2) and manages different PIoT roles, including $DER_{1...n}$, ES, the above-mentioned MG

[3] In this context, the author of the reference shares the consensus of the author of this book in PIoT-IoT grid-IoT domain/sector/zone (three levels as aforementioned), but the word "grid", which can easily lead to confusion, is referred as IoT grid in previous chapters of this book. In this section, smart grid is a terminology in energy domain.

aggregator, **operator, maintainer, controller, and** local utility as AS provider.

DMS: The third control level is responsible for the control, monitoring, and reliability of the distribution (IoT grid) network as the domain/zone level. This supervisory control level reveals when MG will be able to work in grid-connected and supply loads from the main SG (e.g., a higher energy coverage smart grid in a city or country) or provide AS for utility and, in case of any failure in one MG, it will disconnect from the main SG. There could be several MGs in DMS territory, with the same idea that there are several IoT grids in an IoT domain/zone, as shown in Fig. 7.22. The hierarchical control level of MG can be implemented through a centralized or decentralized approach. In the centralized approach, each element receives set points from a central controller (IoT domain/zone center) and follows a global objective. In decentralized approach, decision-making in each level of control (IoT grid center, as a local controller or an edge controller) is distributed as a multi-agent system (MAS). In distributed fashion, each element has been considered to be an agent which independently decides to participate in SG or MGMS (to some automation degree). This offers advantages such as plug-and-play patterns without the need for dedicated communication infrastructure, fast response to system failure, power grid consisting of independent entities, and the network between each MG(EMS) or IoT grid, may be ad hoc meshing (see Section 5.3) or be included in 5G NPN or slicing as discussed in Section 5.8.4.

This use case helps us understand the PIoT/IoT grid in Section 6.2, which deepens the IoT grid organizing approaches from the decentralized approach and the centralized approach. Moreover, due to the advantages of edge characteristics when deploying MAS, trends toward the implementation of SG in the form of multi-MG have been augmented recently. Each IoT grid or MG can either join a higher lever IoT domain or DMS, or self-coordinated with the collaboration by other IoT grid, in a multi-MG or MAS environment. The proposed edge (local) control level of individual MG without a centralized approach can be considered as an IoT grid center in EMS locally (as the local controller in Fig. 7.21).

- **Edge Computing Use Case:** As mentioned above, an energy management system can be located on the edge of a local IoT grid or MG; the same way can be achieved in a CAFCLA-based energy efficiency system (the edge use case is also based on the above-discussed CAFCLA).

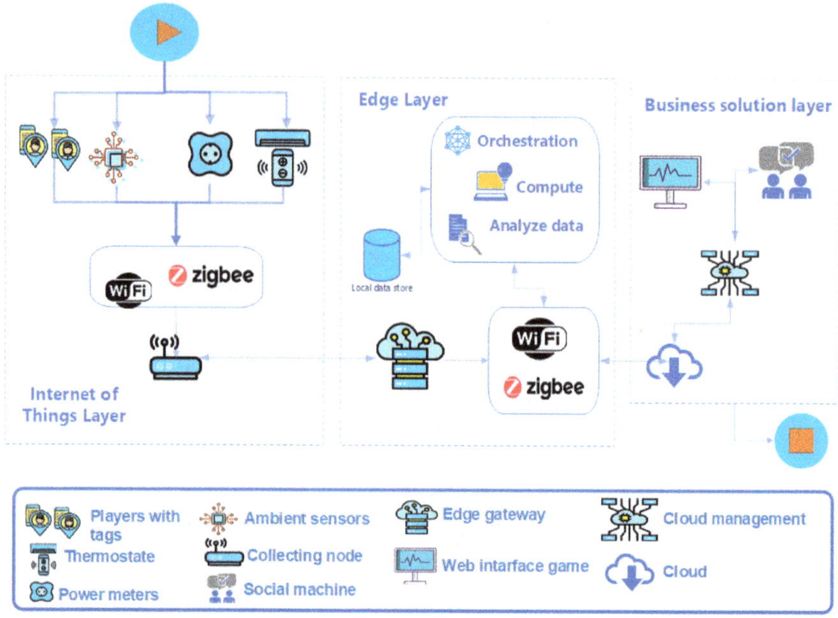

Figure 7.23 Data-flow chart of the edge experiment in the energy efficiency system.

The edge computing structure in the experiment is shown in Fig. 7.23. In the edge layer, the orchestration, monitoring, and updating of the technological resources needed for the management of the organization's activities (e.g., working/gaming and energy-consumption monitoring). The edge layer filters and pre-processes the data generated in the IoT layer (as the IoT service and platform do, see Section 6.4) in real-time, sending to the cloud center used by business intelligence applications. On the edge side, the edge devices in charge of pre-processing are low-cost solutions, such as microcomputers based on educational architectures (such as Raspberry Pi or open architectures such as Orange Pi based on Raspberry Pi with the ability to work with Linux, with RAM between 256 MB and 1 GB and SD cards).

If greater computing capacity or online data availability is required, this edge layer supports edge gateways (or routers) that function performs as an intersection between the devices of the IoT layer and the cloud; the edge gateways should offer different interfaces for communication standards, such as Ethernet, WiFi/WLAN, Bluetooth, Zigbee, CAN Bus,

SCADA, cellular access (e.g., 3G/4G/5G) or for an IoT platform as OneM2M, OPC UA.

The application (business solution) layer of the energy efficiency system was deployed in Google Cloud using the App Engine as PaaS (platform as a service) to provide the backend of the system, including the RTLS system and the Google Cloud SQL to provide the relational database (DB).

Base on the discussion of MAS and the edge layer in SG or the energy efficiency/management system, the following flexible EC (FLEC) architecture is introduced in short, with the objects of the review of Section 6.4, and the crossing layer MAS FLEC method, which may be used in the granular collaboration (e.g., agent, PIoT level) between the perception (device) layer, edge layer, and platform layer.

As Section 6.4 mentioned, edge computing can respond to the service demand quickly and efficiently on the data-generation side because of the shortening of the transmission link, and the local processing of data can also improve the degree of users' privacy protection. **Furthermore, edge computing reduces the dependence of services on the cloud and can also provide basic business services in the offline state.** A FLEC architecture is presented in Fig. 7.24, in which the role of the service management layer is enhanced by giving its function to manage the device, edge,

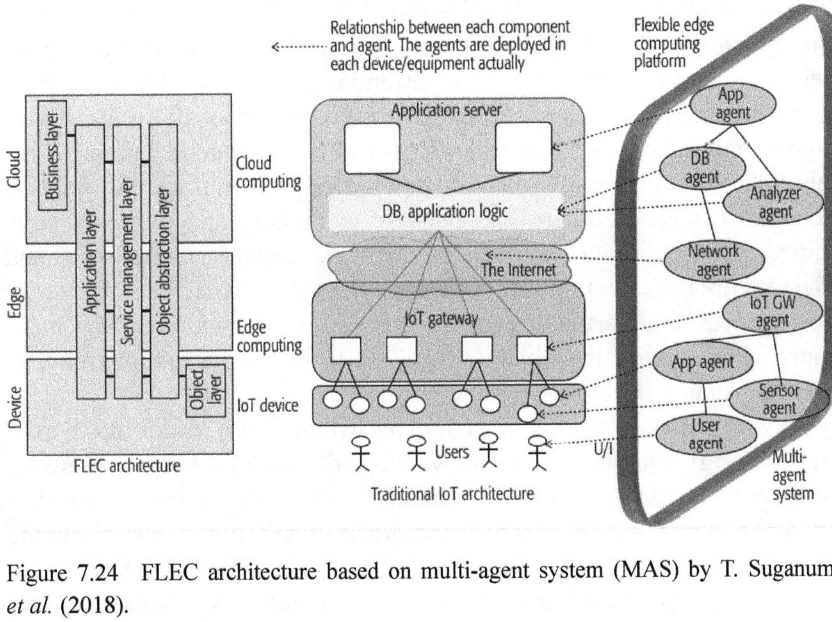

Figure 7.24 FLEC architecture based on multi-agent system (MAS) by T. Suganuma *et al.* (2018).

and cloud interactively. The object abstraction function in the perception layer is also extended so that it can manage all components of EC from sensors and devices to an edge device (e.g., the above-mentioned gateway/router or computer locally deployed) to make it the foundation for the enhancement of the service management or the platform layer.

In the FLEC platform (the right part of Fig. 7.24), different agents play different roles. The agent from the perception or device layer can be deemed as PIoT, which can be combined with other PIoT in the same layer and organized into an IoT (edge) grid. In the IoT grid level, an IoT GW agent may play the role of IoT grid center, which manages the PIoT and its service and provides the grid level service to the network agent (in the platform level), or to the app/user agent, as shown in Fig. 7.24.

The penetrating FLEC platform crossing perception layer, platform layer, and application is composed of MAS, and each agent is provided by a special service with reflecting the actual situation. The FLEC architecture has advantages including the improvement of overall system performance, flexibility, and scalability enhancement, quick response to changes in IoT components, improvement of user's QoE (for more details see Refs. Suganuma *et al.* (2018) and Tightiz *et al.* (2020)).

7.3.3 *Energy internet and Internet of energy*

Energy internet is a new development form of the energy system. It realizes the integration of energy flow, information flow, and business flow. More and more business model and service model innovations are stimulated in energy internet. Energy internet can be understood as that which comprehensively uses advanced power electronic technology, information technology, and intelligent management technology to connect a large number of new power network, oil network, natural gas network, and other energy nodes composed of DER devices, distributed energy storage (ES) devices, and various types of loads and prosumers (e.g., MG mentioned above), with the objectives of energy and information two-way flow in a shared business network.

It was 2014 when economist Jeremy Rifkin first introduced the concept of energy internet in his book, which had aroused widespread interest in the third industrial revolution. He said, in the coming era, we need to create an energy internet so that hundreds of millions of people could produce green renewable energy in their homes, offices, and factories. The extra energy should be shared with others, just as we shared information on the Internet.

The information flow in energy internet includes state monitoring data, energy (resource) user management data, energy supply network data, etc. Some key concepts in energy internet include prosumer, MG, virtual power plant (VPP), smart grid, and smart energy, and some of them have already been introduced. A VPP is based on some new technologies as an energy big data analytics, cloud/edge, and IoT, and it is described as a cloud-based distributed power plant that aggregates the capacities of heterogeneous DER to enhance power generation as well as trade or sell power on the electricity market.

From the perspective of cloud, Hadoop and virtualization technology (e.g., NFV), distributed redundant storage and data management, and energy big data analytics are included. In the stage of energy internet, the management and sharing of resources with edge computing will achieve closer to the user's prosumer and sharing of energy, as discussed above, when considering data or energy generation, especially from the view of "edge autonomy". From the perspective of the collaboration between energy "edge autonomy" and "cloud autonomy", the advanced stage of energy internet development will go from energy use and share over the Internet to green autonomy of energy over IoT. All energy-related resources will be integrated with the concept of the IoT to achieve broad connectivity, autonomy, sharing, and collaboration. This new stage may use another new term, i.e., the Internet of energy. It is a technological term that refers to the upgrading and automating of electricity infrastructures for energy producers and manufacturers. The term is derived from the increasingly prominent market for IoT technology, which has helped develop the distributed energy systems that make up the Internet of Energy. The characteristics are as follows:

- Internet of Energy allows energy production to move forward more efficiently and cleanly with the least amount of waste. Benefits of using it include increased efficiencies, significant cost savings, and a reduction in the wastage of energy.
- Ultra-high voltage (UHV) transmission is a system that allows energy to be transmitted rapidly over long distances. UHV solves the problem of energy production being located too far from load centers. China first implemented UHV in 2009, but its development is constantly expanding to meet demand.
- While the UHV extended the coverage, the "edge autonomy" will push the edge intelligence to the self-organized MGs.

Take China and energy usage as an example. Although China is one of the world's largest producers of renewable energy, it still experiences shortages and energy crises because it cannot deliver energy at a level that can sustain its population. This results in power outages and gaps. The infrastructure for a massive number of EVs with sufficient charging stations is one of the solutions, together with the constructing storage sites — particularly in cities that use the most energy — in order to store excess energy efficiently and close to where it will be needed. Economic benefits provided for companies that supply renewable energy, such as solar and wind, since more energy will be retained and sold, in addition to providing relatively low storage costs.

From the technological views, the benefits of the Internet of Energy are as follows:

- Integrate traditional and emerging energy generation to achieve cleaner, safer, and more economical energy delivery.
- Operators will realize transparent and visible monitoring and analysis in energy circulation and also realize two-way communication over prosumer smart meters and consumption pattern analysis.
- Intelligent devices that collect and analyze massive data will be able to enable emergency plan operation according to emergencies.
- The intelligent IoT devices will achieve distributed energy management based on real-time data and situational awareness rather than based on historical data mode.
- When a component needs attention or repair, the predictive ability of maintenance will remind the operator in time, so as to reduce unnecessary uninterrupted inspection.
- The adaptive analysis will enable the system to automatically balance energy load, reduce local pressure, and prevent overheating.

A large number of distributed MGs and medium-sized energy and power plants can be combined with the self-organization mode of VPP. With this edge concept, the coverage of MG can be isolated from the central main grid (e.g., the SST use case), and energy supply can be realized from some internal energy sources, such as roof photovoltaic equipment, wind or thermal energy, power plant (or energy storage station on the edge) for "edge autonomy". In addition, if is more or not enough, energy on edge will collaborate with other MGs in energy "cloud autonomy".

As IoT devices and services are already integrated with SG/MG and smart building/office/factory, the release of power is done via remote connectivity, which can allow them to communicate with utilities to balance power generation and energy usage and optimize energy consumption as a whole. These devices allow for remote control by users, or central management by a cloud-based interface, and enable distributed functions like "edge autonomy". The smart grid is upgrading from a utility-side IoT application, in which systems gather and act on energy- and power-related information to improve the efficiency of the production and distribution of electricity, to the use of advanced metering infrastructure (AMI), Internet-connected devices, electric utilities which collect data from end-users as well as manage distribution automation. All these make IoT devices to be like transformers which push the Smart Grid to Energy Internet, and the Internet of Energy.

From the developmental views, the benefits and business values of the Internet of Energy are as follows:

(1) Data to the micro level, resource management to the macro level, and the two tendencies combine at the edge.
Energy data is from user oriented to "things/devices oriented", and resource/energy management is from low-level mode to high-level mode as cloud/edge, which has the ability to coordinate a wider range of energy resources. Figure 7.25 is a basic unit of the Internet of Energy in LAN diagram, which can be implemented in a family, factory, building, etc. The energy mode based on distributed self-sufficiency is divided into three parts: consumption load and state prediction, the "plug-and-play" and other energy devices, and RER generation. In the LAN grid center, intelligent energy management realizes the real-time consumption and RER generation of monitoring and management. The LAN unit connects to the upper grid (MG or DMS in energy WAN) through grid gateway (EMS as mentioned above).

(2) The systematic combination of energy network and consumption network.
Internet of Energy is an intelligent wide area network that combines energy and IoT deeply and organically. At the different levels of country-to-country, district-to-district (in a region), point-to-point (in a family), and even granularity (in MG or IoT grid/PIoT level), we should realize the combination of sharing and unification, sharing and hierarchical

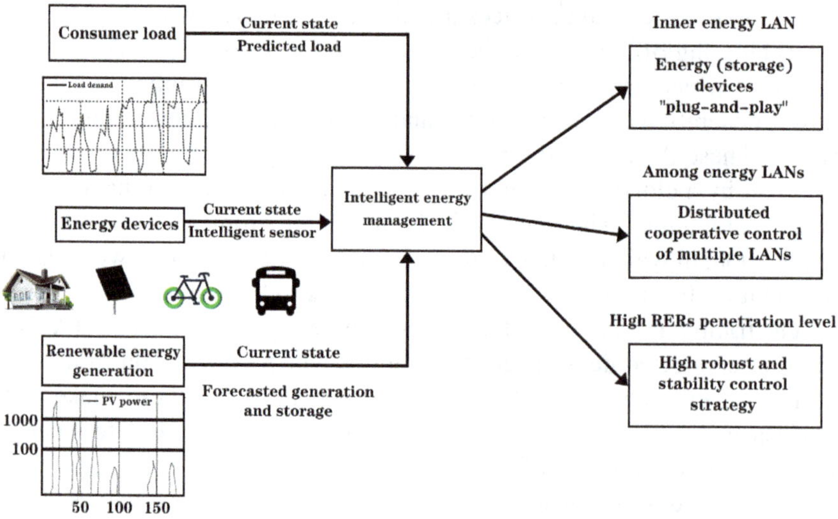

Figure 7.25 Energy LAN on the edge as a smart local grid (SLG).

autonomy (edge/cloud level), green energy cycle, and ecological environment protection.

(3) Integration of Internet of Energy and ecological environment.
Energy consumption is due to human dissatisfaction with the pursuit of comfort from science and technology, resulting in the consumption of materials and energy to meet human needs. But energy is facing depletion, forcing us to weigh energy consumption and scientific and technological development. Energy is something like water and air to humans now. The attitude towards energy should be viewed over a longer historical period. The earth itself is an ecosystem, and the speed of biological evolution and the ability to adapt to the transformed environment is in a balance, and species extinction is a piece of circumstantial evidence.

If we break this balance, we may open a Pandora's box, which will have an impact on the environment, water, and air, and challenge the survival of organisms. Earthquakes, haze, and pollution may result from the breakdown of this balance. Therefore, human beings need to look at energy, technology, environment, and human beings (biology) from a larger perspective. The western exploration of unknown laws is open, while the eastern exploration of unknown laws is convergent. However, uncertainty theory (e.g., Schrodinger's cat) tells us that the laws under certain conditions may get different results when the conditions go further to the micro or step back to the macro.

We must be cautious with the development and utilization of energy. If we can raise our cognition to the impact on the ecological environment through the IoT and promote the dimension of the integration of things, energy (e.g., service), and ourselves (e.g., relation in PIoT), with granular and deeper understanding (e.g., PIoT/IoT grid in Section 6.2) of Internet of Energy, we may find the sustainable way for the utilization of energy.

(4) Renewable energy is the main, and non-renewable energy is the auxiliary and gradually eliminated.
In coming years, as the world works toward harvesting renewable energy sources, the use of non-renewable resources is expected to fall, which will reduce the need for outdated infrastructures that handle resources such as coal and oil.

A large number of various types of distributed renewable energy generation technologies and systems on the Internet of Energy will increase the permeability, connectivity, and proportion of renewable energy in the energy market. It is necessary to predict and study a series of new scientific and technological problems, and the first is to explore whether nuclear energy should be eliminated from the long-term comparison of energy benefits and environmental damage.

The dynamic energy supply with time-sharing, planning, and demanding will be considered with more overall characteristics, which will be used to restrict each other with price (electricity price and energy generation cost), realize the multi-objective overall optimization of green energy consumption, sustainable energy supply, dynamic regulation and energy storage, and ecological environment protection, and realize the current and long-term consistency: energy self-evaluation, self-optimization, self-planning, self-evolution, and self-balance. Related markets are shown in Fig. 7.26.

For example, General Electric (GE) is using the Internet of Energy to augment its operations by using sensors to collect data from its equipment. It then feeds the information into its asset performance management software to be analyzed. This process allows GE to monitor all its equipment in real-time. As a result, it has realized benefits such as a 5% reduction in unplanned downtime, a 75% reduction in false positives for faulty machinery, and a 25% reduction in maintenance costs. All of this contributes to increasing not only the company's overall productivity and

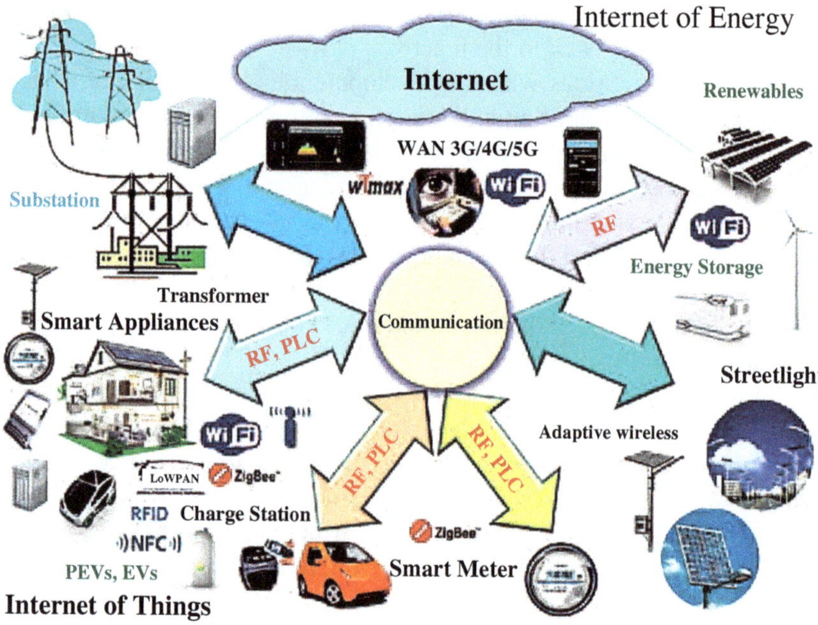

Figure 7.26 Markets of Internet of energy.

profitability, such as edge-aided utilities' decision-making regarding load balancing, forecasting, and other business decisions, but also its customers' profitability by enabling them to use weather data, energy market pricing data, and many other data points to optimize the efficiency of their business operations.

The Internet of Energy will not only change the expected operation mode of the Energy Internet but also consider the response from the user's (DER and RER as energy prosumers) side, and it explores the local and regional changes of load, by predicting and adapting to environmental changes (e.g., temperature drop, earthquakes, and other emergencies). Considering the random characteristics of new energy access, new energy (consumption and storage) mode and new technology innovation, such as edge/cloud in the control, optimization, and scheduling of energy, the Internet of Energy will face greater challenges.

Perhaps we can imagine that before the real energy crisis comes, the Internet of Energy Things will meet the needs of human energy consumption just like the alternation of the sun and the moon, the cycle of the seasons. We will not feel like a system but a gift from nature.

The autonomy of the Internet of Energy can consciously reduce the damage to the ecological environment, to the extent that the ecological environment can repair itself, and provide intelligent planning for the energy consumption of human technological development, avoiding the energy consumption produced by human beings.

Comparative analysis of Smart Grid, Energy Internet, and Energy IoT concepts is shown in Table 7.3.

7.4 Applications in Smart City

In the last two decades, the concept of the "smart city" has gained popularity in scientific discussion, though smart cities do not have an official definition. It is believed that the wide use of smart ICT (information and communication technology) can make the critical infrastructure components and services of a city more intelligent. Smart cities have no definite concept. In terms of ICT, smart cities can be seen as ICT infrastructure of the city with interchangeable concepts, such as a digital city (Cocchia, 2014), an information city (Sproull and Patterson, 2004), and an intelligent city (Komninos, 2013). A town called a smart city is characterized by an intelligent ICT infrastructure that can improve the control efficiency compared to the manual process. This example of an energy view can be found in the SST of Section 7.4.2. Other examples range from air pollution control, fire control, and tracking of vehicles to those that would be more efficient by using an intelligent ICT infrastructure, such as M2M/IoT and edge/cloud computing (e.g., sensing networks, data analytics, and increased processing power).

Issues of smart cities are the development of smart community and nature-friendly urban planning. As mentioned earlier, nature is a finite resource that needs to be managed intelligently and carefully to sustain and support society's needs and to take a long-term view of survival and development.

There are several stakeholders involved in the development of the smart city, such as business, community, and government. Each stakeholder has an important role in developing a smart city system. For the business and technology aspects, see Fig. 7.27.

Although the advancing ICT has made data sensing, collection, and real-time analytics much easier, the demand for an open and well-formed infrastructure is increasing. For smart city residents, there is a foreseeable gap between the constant information enabled by ICT, and their

Table 7.3 A Comparative Analysis in the evolution stages of energy systems.

Evolution stages	Essence	Objectives	Source	Capability	Stages	Technical Views
SM	Smart	Decentralized energy system, centralized energy system	Electricity, hydroelectricity, thermal power	Coverage	From second industrial revolution	Digitalization, automation, and other intelligence; IoT only for condition monitoring of power equipment
Energy Internet	Energy Sharing	Distributed energy system	Wind, light, storage, and other new energy sources (batteries, flywheels, and other energy storage, solar energy, etc.); water, electricity, nuclear, and other types of energy	Coverage, Connectivity	The period from 2014 and beyond, when the world reaches 10 energy-consuming products per capita, may just be the beginning	Big data, interactivity, edge computing, and IoT for monitoring, management, and the innovative representation of energy systems in the third industrial revolution
Energy IoT/ Internet of Energy	Energy autonomy network	Smart and connected energy system. Balancing and cycling of energy supply, energy storage, and energy consumption.	Modular, plug-in, and networked energy (Produce, store, and consume for oneself)	Regional (cross-regional) load balancing and balanced forecasting, phase-out of high-consumption energy, and access to	In the future, the IoT will be fully applied when personal holds hundreds of portable appliances, each household holds thousands of and each business runs	Microscoping, convergence, sustainability, cloud computing, and big data to form energy cloud autonomy. IoT for monitoring, management, forecasting, and overall optimization. Smart, environmentally friendly, recycling, bioenergy

	Integration of energy supply equipment networks and electricity consumption networks. Integration into smart (eco) cities, smart planet	low-consumption new energy sources; energy cloud autonomy	tens of thousands of appliances
Energy Eco Network	**Searching for the tiniest particles of energy, possibly all derived from bioenergy** In addition to operating every individual asset in the VPP, the central control system uses a special algorithm to adjust to balancing reserve commands from transmission system operators and to grid conditions — just as a larger, conventional power plant does. Furthermore, the VPP can react quickly and efficiently when it comes to trading electricity, thus adjusting plant operations according to price signals from the power exchanges. **Decentralized units create collective intelligence** A VPP is a pool of several small- and medium-scale installations, either consuming or producing electricity. Individual small plants can in general not offer services as balancing reserve or offer their flexibility on the power exchanges as their production or consumption profile varies strongly, they have insufficient availability due to unforeseen outages or they simply do not meet the minimum bid size of the markets.		

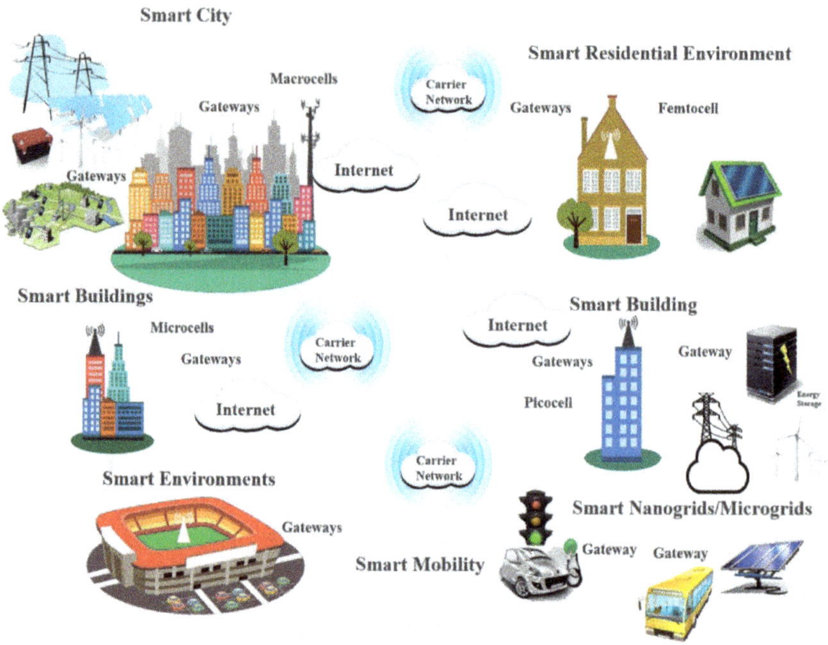

Figure 7.27 Smart City applications and technologies landscape.

Source: Vermesan and Friess (2015). *Building the Hyperconnected Society IoT Research and Innovation Value Chains, Ecosystems and Market*. River Publishers, Vol. 43, pp. 80, 192–195, 203.

limited information-accessing capability, as well as the diversity of platforms.

7.4.1 *Resident grids in comprehensive views*

"People oriented" is the core concept of smart city construction. Its connotation is to focus on the "people" in the urban civilization ecosystem, to meet the needs of the "people" in the city in terms of healthcare, food, living, transportation, and education, and to provide safe, efficient, convenient, and green urban work and life services for urban residents.

Specifically, "healthcare" refers to telemedicine and mobile healthcare, especially health services for the early warning of cardiovascular and cerebrovascular diseases as well as sub-health warning and other intelligent medical services. "Food" refers to food safety services such as food traceability and illegal additive detection. "Living" refers to the safe, comfortable, green, and smart home for residents. "Transportation" refers to intelligent transportation, intelligent logistics, etc. "Education" refers to distance education, public education, etc. In the construction of these application systems around people's livelihood, such as smart healthcare, smart food, smart home, smart community, smart logistics, smart education, and smart transportation, we can try to introduce the "IoT grids" serving people's livelihood, such as people-oriented "healthcare (clothing), food, living, transportation, and education".

1. People's livelihood grid: The concept of livelihood grid originates from Section 6.2. If the vertical "grids" of a smart city are divided into many sectors that can provide residents with "healthcare, food, living, transportation, and education", the data and service of physical entities can be relatively easily obtained in these vertical industries. In these vertical sectors, according to the technology (or platform) that can provide services, they are further divided into horizontal grids. For example, the IoT, cloud computing, big data, geographic information, urban infrastructure network (wired, wireless, satellite, etc.), and other functional grids. They are used in different domains within a city, such as municipal administration, social security, medical and health, along with the x axis of Fig. 7.28.

From the IoT view, sensor, identifier, encryption system, GPS, RFID, server, storage, data analysis, software management system, mobile payment, QR code, NFC, and others — all of these are folded into the horizontal three-level grids, as shown in Fig. 7.28. These technologies, which are independent of each other in their functions, are applied in various sectors to provide specific industry applications and services for each vertical grid. Horizontal grid overlay based on multi-technology application and vertical grid fusion based on cross-industry can form a larger grid across the city, which is represented as the intelligence of a city, as the z axis. Based on the "people's livelihood grid" components in Fig. 7.28, this book defines the following six elements of smart city characteristics along one dimension (the smart management of y axis) of Fig. 7.28: smart governance, smart economy, smart mobility (including IoT app-x), smart environment, smart people, and smart living.

Along the y axis, smart mobility is described as the spread of mobile devices and IoT-based city infrastructures (as one of the smart city pillars), which has sparked a new era of possibilities for the penetrating application sectors (such as MA, SS, etc. mentioned in the note accompanying the figure), with the capabilities of the three surrounding layers (above these, the smart usage of mobility or IoT application is constructed).

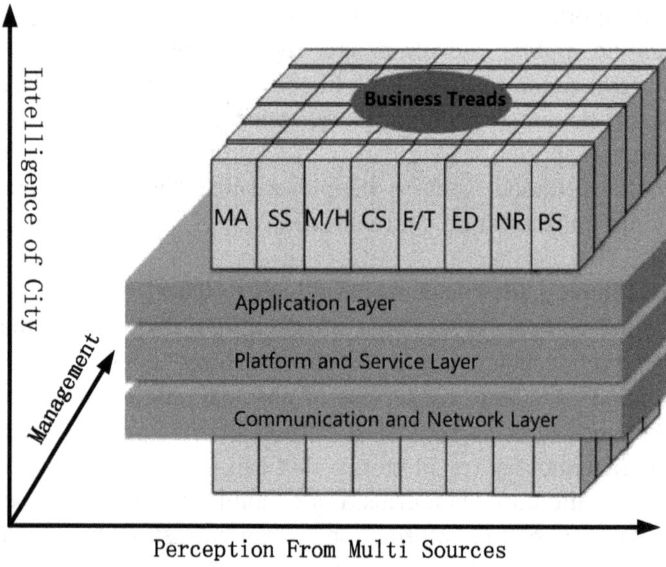

Figure 7.28 An IoT grids vision of the smart city.

Notes: MA-Municipal Administration; SS-social security; M/H-medical and health; CS-community service; E/T-education and technology; ED-economic development; NR-nature resource; PS-public security/safety.

"People's livelihood grid" is the primary stage of the comprehensive application of the IoT and other new-generation ICT technology to serve people's livelihood and smart city construction. The construction and full development of these "people's livelihood grids" can be focused on the livelihood fields such as healthcare, food, living, transportation, energy conservation and emission reduction, food safety, drug safety, social security, education, product quality, and other vertical industrial applications. Then, the fine level of urban management will be improved and a comprehensive infrastructure will be formed.

On the level of multi-source perception, it is possible to see that the device/equipment is becoming more intelligent in every grid of the IoT, which is also convenient for data collection and analysis. The "smart" industry in a smart city is no longer the vertical extension but develops in the same format as the widespread Internet.

Similarly, the construction and full development of "the people's livelihood grid" is not only the development mode of the IoT at present but also the way for the smart city to go through in its infancy. After the formation of the top-level design planning and standardized system of the smart city, the grid format division and development of smart cities can avoid the restriction of too strict norms on the free development of new industries but also the waste due to extensive patterns and the lack of overall planning. Next, “Smart” is explained in several directions.

2. Municipal administration: Under the promotion of the government, the IoT will be widely used in various fields of smart cities and improve the efficiency of government affairs. The application of electronic identity identification (EID) service in the field of the IoT solves the problem concerning the management of the residents’ identity in smart cities. For example, an ICT company in China proposes a five-in-one application plan for smart cities, which can integrate the most common people’s livelihood activities, such as household registration, election activities, driver license verification, water, and electrical and medical services. All verification information is kept in a unified way, and all institutions do not need to collect citizen data repeatedly. The comprehensive management plan makes the life of the citizens more optimized and the city more intelligent.

The registration information of the household registration can prove the identity of a citizen, check his/her nationality, age, blood type, and so on; the election certificate is a proof that the citizens have the right to vote in an election activity; in the context of the IoT, driver license validation becomes very simple — after the verification terminal is connected to the IoT, it can query online and verify offline. Water and electricity are the most important aspects of life for the citizens. At present, the water and electrical supply are divided into different systems in many cities, and it is inconvenient to read and pay for the meter. When they are integrated in to the same IoT management (system or platform), water, electricity, and gas services will be smart, greatly facilitating the lives of citizen and improving management efficiency.

Hospitals and families can be connected by medical intelligent sensors at both terminals of the hospital and the family. A telemedicine center can be established to conduct remote consultation, remote monitoring, and remote diagnosis.

The five-in-one application scheme of the smart city centering on EID service also considers the secure communication between the center and users, which promotes the intelligent management of urban residents through the secure links of identity information collection, network transmission, unified management, and business processing.

3. Electronic bills: As a mobile communication network terminal, the mobile phone has a great advantage in the application of the IoT. In recent years, in the application of the electronic bill of compound RFID/NFC SIM card, the communication between mobile phone and terminal equipment, such as vending machine, access control, and so on, has been realized. So, there are mobile phone card swipe, mobile phone sign-in, mobile payment, and other applications so far. In the financial field, not only the mobile online bank is realized through the network but also the function of the POS terminal can be realized when the mobile phone is combined with the additional hardware module.

4. Urban security: Ian McLoughlin, a professor of the Department of Electronic Engineering and Information Science in University of Science and Technology of China, pointed out that smart cities collect data from cities and their residents through various sensing technologies, and at the same time, they also bring about privacy conflicts and trust crisis. He said that before looking forward to the real smart city, we should first deal with the problem of security. But the existing research on the IoT security is not enough. The security of the IoT restricts its development and application, restricts the industrialization process and scaling up application of the IoT technology, and restricts the presentation of "Smart" in smart cities.

The ubiquitous things that collect data on large-scale in urban applications, e.g., the environmental monitoring devices such as sensors used to obtain data, are liable to easily expose information. Especially in wearable computing, the information obtained directly or indirectly through the monitoring of people's physical environment may be uncovered through people's personal devices and environmental interactions with others. The leakage of individual information, whether in quantity, quality, or sensitivity, will cause great concern for privacy protection. For the construction of a smart city, security is the foundation of the overall architecture.

7.4.2 *Use cases of smart city*

This section **discusses the role of IoT** technology and application as a drive to realize the smart city in terms of three use cases based on the OpenMTC platform. OpenMTC (developed by Fraunhofer FOKUS) is an integration platform, based on the oneM2M standard, for conducting applied research and developing innovative M2M and IoT applications. Its horizontal service approach easily integrates devices from different Industrial IoT verticals, independent of the underlying hardware or network infrastructure. This platform serves as a standard-oriented middleware for M2M/IoT applications and services oriented to facilitate research and development. For example, it is the availability of a standard application programming interface (API) to access data and information, and the OpenMTC SDK aims to provide developers with a convenient but flexible tool to write oneM2M compliant applications. This includes network applications (NAs), gateway applications (GAs), device applications (DAs), as well as interworking proxy entities (IPEs).

As shown in Fig. 7.29, the three use cases are as follows:

- **Mobile tracking system:** After the vehicle position is obtained from the GPS module, and the processed data in the onboard monitoring system module (HW/SW as an ARM microprocessor with MicroC OS/II-operating system and monitoring application) flows to a GSM module, the position and time data of the vehicle is transferred to the server OpenMTC. As shown in Fig. 7.29(a), the data accepted on the server side consists of longitude and latitude position and also timestamp when the data is captured. Data and coordinate of the vehicle taken periodically to show the tracking of vehicles from time to time in the

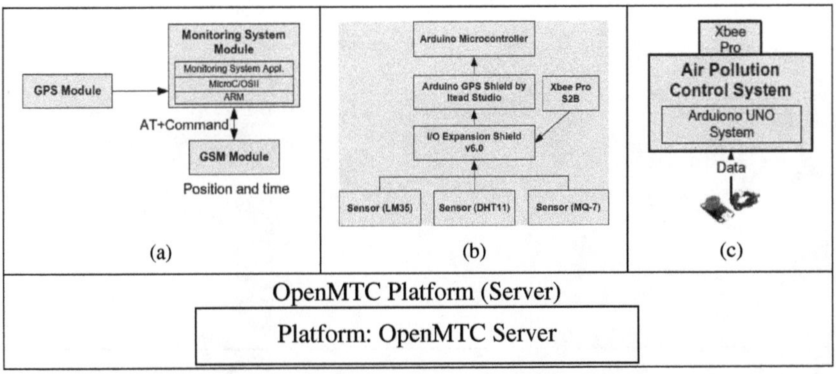

Figure 7.29 OpenMTC-based three use cases (device side structures): (a) mobile tracking system; (b) early warning forest fire system and (c) air pollution control system.

map application (e.g., Google Map), which can be accessed through any device. Figure 7.30(a) shows the application of the system.

- **Early warning system of forest fire:** On the device side, an on-device app is a set of sensor networks and gateways connecting to the gateway service capability layer (GSCL) of OpenMTC. Sensors in the sensor network (HW/SW as microcontrollers, XBee Pro S2B, GPS module, power supply, and I/O expansion shield) are used to acquire the early warning of forest fires in the surroundings. As shown in Fig. 7.29(b), the processed data from the microcontroller flows to the gateway, in which the on-device app (as ZigBee coordinator node) forwards the received data to network service capability layer (NSCL) in OpenMTC platform through GSCL. On the platform side, the collected information is sent to the early warning system of forest fire periodically. Figure 7.30(b) shows the application of the system.
- **Air pollution control system:** On the device side, two sensors (PM and CO) are included in the end node (its HW/SW includes a microcontroller,

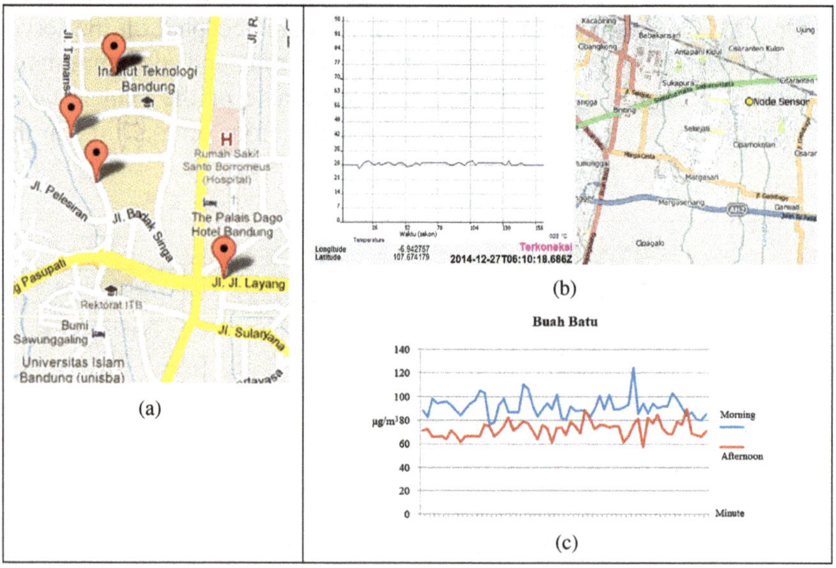

Figure 7.30 The applications (app side) of the three use cases: (a) an app of mobile tracking system in Bandung City, Indonesia; (b) an app of early warning forest fire system in Kamojang forest, Garut, West Java, Indonesia; (c) an app of air pollution control system in Bandung, Indonesia.

XBee, and expansion shield), as shown in Fig. 7.29(c). On the gateway side, data is sent by the M2M device through M2M Gateway (ZigBee coordinator node XBee), to the M2M Server (OpenMTC server), and in the gateway, the data conversion to XML format is completed. Air pollution monitoring data in the server will be processed to be able to do a push notification to the M2M. The application displays it through the website. Figure 7.30(c) shows the application of the system.

7.4.3 *MONICA project*

MONICA project addresses several challenges in eleven pilots of six major European cities[4] by using a large number of IoT wearables and sensors and demonstrates to developers and service providers the ability of the MONICA platform to cooperate with other smart city IoT platforms, open data portals, and generic enablers.

As one of the five large-scale pilot projects funded by the European Commission, the main focus of the MONICA project is on how to leverage multiple existing and novel IoT technologies to address real-world challenges in open-air event scenarios. More specifically, MONICA demonstrates a large-scale ecosystem that uses innovative wearables and IoT devices with closed-loop back-end services integrated into an interoperable, cloud-based platform capable of offering a multitude of simultaneous and targeted applications.[5] Related MONICA use cases are described in detail in Table 7.4.

Along with the smart mobility dimension (one of the pillars in a smart city), the spread of IoT-based healthcare solutions in future generations promise to transform the healthcare industry by enabling breakthrough computing and communication capabilities, where individuals are monitored online by connected wearable sensors, enabling interoperability of personalized health and wellness-related information, patient's vital parameters, as well as data on physical activities, behaviors, and other critical parameters that affect the quality of daily life. With the same vision of IoT technology, the smart city is enriched by IoT applications in smart buildings/energy, smart industry, smart healthcare, and smart farming (agriculture).

In the following section, smart farming is taken up as an example.

[4]These pilot cities include: Tivoli Gardens in Copenhagen, Denmark; Kappa FuturFestival in Turin, Italy; Hamburg, Germany; Lyon, France; Bonn, Germany; and Leeds, England.

[5]IoT_The_Call_of_the_Edge-Everything_Intelligent_Everywhere_.

Table 7.4 Use cases in MONICA.

Scheme	APP	Feature
Crowd monitoring	To predict and handle emerging incidents in large open-air events. These applications are primarily based on data from crowd wristbands and CCTV cameras.	Crowd count: to know the number of people being in a specific area. – Crowd density: estimating crowd size and density shown as a heat map. – Crowd flow: detecting anomalies such as fights, explosions or high-risk queues. – Redirection: redirect visitors to safer areas using large screens or APPs.
Ambient intelligence (AmI) device assistance	Smart glasses, staff wristbands, activity recognition wearables, CCTV cameras, mobile phones, and environmental sensors (e.g., for the detection of strong wind). For example, ambient sensors, robots, and connected devices at home enables elderly people to live in their homes safely and independently. This smart environment can monitor their health status and prevent them from becoming frail as well as keeping them remotely in touch with their doctor.	Incident detection and notifying about type of incident and related location, for instance, through smart glasses and staff wristbands. – Report back to control room, for instance, through smart glasses and staff wristbands. – Detect person falling or fighting, for instance, through CCTV, activity recognition wearables. – Report incident using a mobile phone APP. – Monitor wind speed, for instance, through environmental sensors, to detect high risk for tall amusement rides.

Missing person	Quickly finding a child (who is missing) or a friend is also relevant at some events. For the location of people, staff and crowd wristbands, tracker GPS devices, and mobile phones could be used.	Some features are reported as follows: – High-precision location (staff wristbands). – Approximate location (crowd wristbands, trackers GPS devices, mobile phones).
Healthy monitor	Health/security incidents. By leveraging the IMU of the staff wristband, certain health incidents can be detected. A wrist-worn accelerometer is used for recognition of abnormal activities related to stewards and security staff visitors in crowded environments.	A network of intelligent sensors that are able to collect, process, transfer, and analyze valuable information in different environments, such as connecting in-home monitoring devices to hospital-based systems. An instance of increased efficiency of health centers in Brazil is the health monitoring of cancer patients and sleep apnea diagnosis projects which aim to use IoT devices to monitor the health of patients in order to perform early diagnosis and save lives.
Sound monitoring and control	To give their performers and audiences the best music experience, an acoustic system provides sound zones at the venue.	Information about the sound levels is displayed and used for different purposes, i.e., moving to a quieter zone, checking that regulations are met, studying health aspects, etc. Sub use cases include sound field control system, quiet zones, and monitoring.

7.4.4 *Blockchain on the IoT edge*

As discussed in Section 7.3.2, the computational requirements of smart grids may be moved to the edge of the network. Similarly, the Global Edge Computing Architecture (GECA) with blockchain technologies for their implementation in real-time locating systems, and information exchange between multiple devices connected to the smart grid, or between SG/MG are discussed in a social edge computing project, in which databases (e.g., Oracles) are used for verifying and sending data to the blockchain and work as intermediaries between the blockchain and the devices that generate data sets with values for temperature, humidity, market prices, payments, heart rate, movement, solar radiation, and more. The generated data are regulated by microcontrollers with less computer resources and reduced storage capacity and must be sent to the edge layer, which has computing modules with filtering and pre-processing capabilities. Moreover, in the following use case, rich APIs such as Raspberry Pi can be used in the edge solution.

- **Data-agnostic devices:** The data-agnostic devices in platforms and systems are responsible for the integrity of the data collected by the different sensors which are guaranteed following the blockchain for the IoT paradigm. The guaranteed integrity ensures that no data are modified by any other element of the network or spurious data are injected into it. In this way, neither the origin nor the value of the data can be repudiated by any other observer component of the data. For the confidentiality/integrity/availability of the data, it is possible to implement smart contracts that are automatically executed if the agreed conditions are met and in which the nodes that sign these contracts cannot repudiate their compliance.
- **Authentication:** Effective authorization and distributed transaction are realized through the use of smart contracts in the public domain. In the private sphere, a licensed blockchain is used.
- **Analysis and management:** Cloud provides the capacity for data analysis and visualization through case-based reasoning and other learning techniques. The storage and management service are provided in the cloud.
- **Application:** In the application layer, a knowledge-based social machine is developed to supervise and update the connected technological resources, and APIs make it possible to call cloud services so that they are available through a web browser or some APPs.

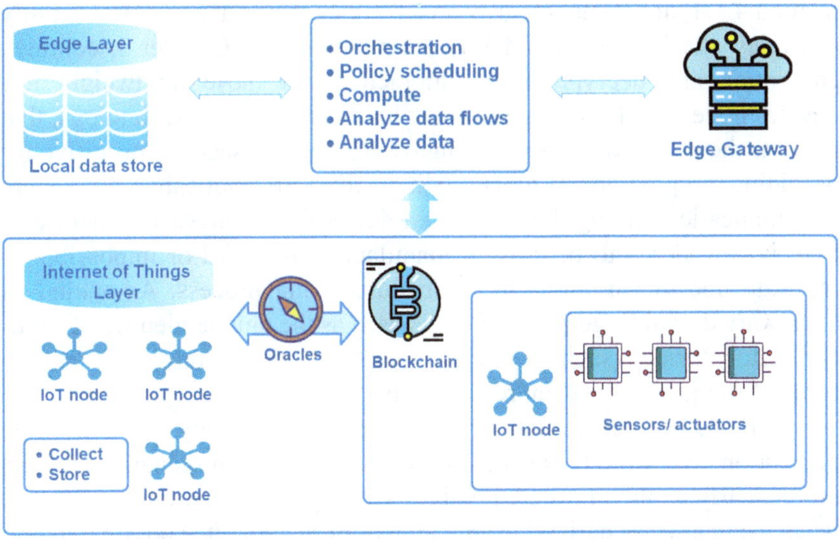

Figure 7.31 Blockchain as a security service in the IoT platform for the confidentiality/integrity/availability of data.

Notes: The Crypto-IoT boards developed by the BISITE Research Group of the University of Salamanca, for the security of data exchange. Each board is formed by a USB module in host mode for connection to micro servers such as Raspberry Pi, Arduino, BeagleBone or neural processing modules, I2C sensors in plug and play modes, an ATSHA204A encryption chip with SHA-256 technology and XBee technology to support heterogeneous communications, such as ZigBee, Wi-Fi, LoRa, RPMA, or Bluetooth.

In short, the GECA and blockchain combination in Fig. 7.31 presents a system that is compatible with IoT models, and the blockchain capabilities, by which security, reliability, and trust links of IoT nodes are considered.

Except for the security technology as PKI-infrastructure depended, in the following parts, the blockchain-based DID and VeChain, and PUF of hardware-level are introduced as infrastructure-independent technologies. Distributed ledger technologies (DLTs)/blockchain still have to demonstrate their value and applicability in IoT systems being supported by PKI (public key infrastructure) as well as physical unclonable function (PUF) technologies.

PUF: Device/asset security exists in the countering of attacks from "data and firmware attack" "transmission attack" (e.g., the front end as SCA in

Section 4.1.4) and "data integrity attack" (e.g., the back end as traceability and relay attack in Section 4.1.4). As mentioned in Chapter 3, complex encryption and decryption are impractical for those lightweight IoT devices/nodes. PUF is a lightweight hardware security technology that protects the data and firmware as hardware-specific security primitive for providing cryptographic functionalities that are applicable for secure communication among the embedded devices. The physical structure of PUF is considered to be easy to manufacture but hard or impossible to replicate due to variations in its manufacturing process. As a kind of "firmware digital fingerprint", PUF is used as the unique identity of semiconductor devices (such as microprocessors), with cryptography advantages of uniqueness and unpredictability.

PUF has become a relatively simple and fast security solution in the perception layer of IoT. Fig. 7.32 shows the application scenarios that can more clearly explain how PUF solves security problems. In Fig. 7.32(a), when using a secret derived from a PUF as protection, it is possible to mix this secret with the parameter. This prevents the encrypted parameter values stored in the one-time programmable (OTP) memory from being hacked. When the secure AI module starts processing, only the PUF value needs to be used to process the mixing process again so that the encrypted parameter can simply be decrypted to its original value. The encryption method used in this case is XOR, as shown in Fig. 7.32(a).

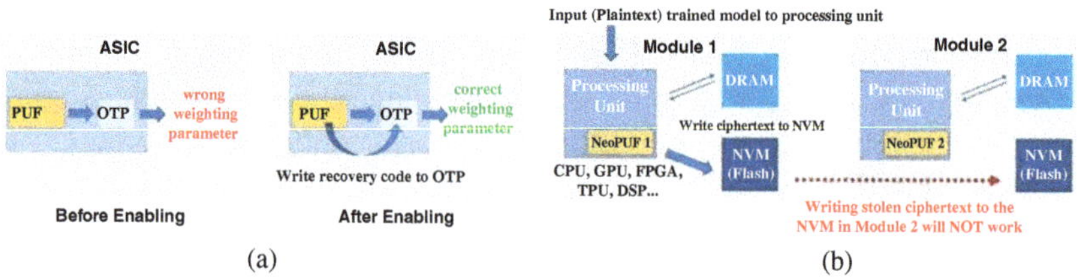

Figure 7.32 The encryption and decryption process of PUF. (a) The encryption method used in this case is XOR, such as: A (secret value derived from PUF) ⊕ B (parameter in OTP) = ciphertext A (secret value derived from PUF) ⊕ B (parameter in OTP) ⊕ A (recovery code) = plaintext and (b) bind data to a specific model by using unique PUF values in each module. If the data in the bound module and the unique PUF value are simply mixed as cipher text, even if this encrypted data is stolen during transmission to an external NVM, it cannot be used in other modules. This is because the data requires a specific PUF value used in conjunction with the module to handle the decryption process.

In order to deal with transmission attacks, such as data leakage during transmission, the process shown in Fig. 7.32(b) is used to prevent data leakage and misuse in other modules.

Combinations of several of these technologies have strong potentials of increasing even further the safety, security, and privacy capabilities of DLTs. However, in most cases, this combination may require support from the hardware devices, especially when providing more processing power is required at the edge.

VeChain*:** VeChain is a blockchain platform designed to enhance supply chain management and business processes. Its goal is to streamline these processes and information flow for complex supply chains through the use of DLTs. For example, the ***VeChain platform contains two distinct tokens: VeChain token (VET) and VeChainThor energy (VTHO). The former is used to transfer value across VeChain's network, and the latter is used as energy or "gas" to power smart contract transactions.[6]

When IoT is in conjunction with blockchain, it can be used to track, process, and exchange transactions among connected devices. However, the development of new privacy-preserving approaches should manage the cost of cryptographic operations to foster the adoption of blockchain technologies.

***Distributed Identifier*:** A distributed identifier (DID) is a new type of identifier without a central issuing and controlling agency that creates and controls the identifier. Instead, DIDs are created and managed by the identity owner, an approach known as self-sovereign identity, as shown in Fig. 7.33. On the issuance side, ZK credential is used as an essential for attestation. On the user side, services of access include attestation, claims, and ZK proofs. On the service provider side, verify claims and access of grant/deny are provided by the verifier.

DID acts as a persistent verifiable identifier through cryptography and can be used to encrypt communication channels for safe and secure

---

[6]Public and private blockchains are the two most common types. They are widely used in various cryptocurrency networks and private enterprises. The third category, the licensed blockchain, has also gained attention. The comparison of the three sees: https://www.investopedia.com/news/public-private-permissioned-blockchains-compared/ and (https://www.investopedia.com/terms/v/vechain.asp.

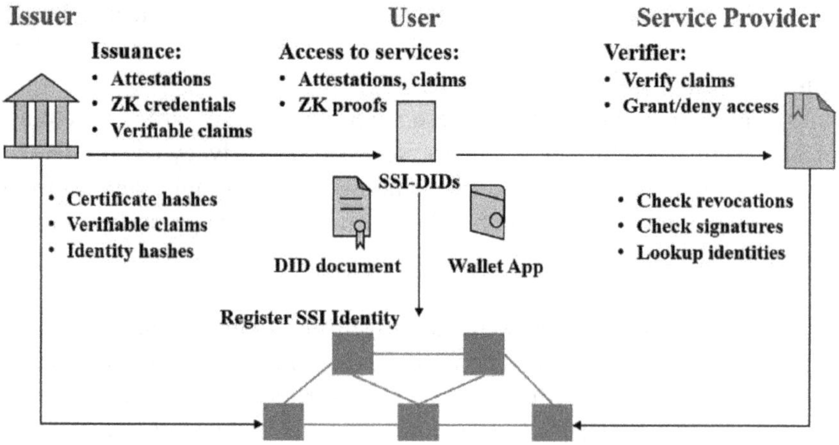

Figure 7.33 Blockchain-based self-sovereign identity management.

messaging. A typical DID contains one or more public keys that can be used to authenticate the DID.

One or more services can be used for interaction via protocols supported by those services. Finally, DID contains metadata, such as digital signatures, timestamps, and other cryptographic proofs. An entity can have a different number of DIDs for many different purposes. In 2016, a generic format of a DID was introduced by the developers of the DID specification for multiple blockchains which followed the same basic pattern.

Further, privacy-enhancing by using decentralized identifiers for the IoT devices is necessary for protecting the privacy of the users and owners of the devices, such as the following:

- Secure infrastructure should consider the control of periodic integrity and authentication verification in the blockchain to effectively prevent malicious nodes from intruding, resist DDoS attacks, and prevent tampering with the device firmware.
- Lightweight and scalable blockchain solutions can be used to solve some traditional security and privacy challenges in IoT environment against the lack of protection of privacy or safety threats.
- In applying DLT to identity management, the evaluation of some proposals (i.e., uPort, Hyperledger Indy, and ShoCard) is analyzed in Vermesan *et al.* (2020) and Lo *et al.* (2019).

7.5 Smart Agriculture

As we know, "good soil produces good rice". Smart agriculture is not only referred to as reducing waste and enhancing productivity in a safe agriculture environment but also throughout the whole process of agricultural production with the help of sensors (light, humidity, temperature, soil moisture, etc.) and automation of irrigation systems.

1. Accurate management: In traditional agriculture, watering, fertilizing, and medication depend on farmers' experience and feelings. Now, in the facility of IoT for agricultural production, we can see another scene:

Should vegetables, melons, and fruits be watered? How to keep an accurate concentration of fertilizer and medicine? How to implement demand–supply of temperature, humidity, light, rainfall, and carbon dioxide concentration? A series of crops that was once "empirically" dealt with in different growth cycles have been "accurately" monitored with real-time, quantitative, and "precise" control by the information technology intelligent monitoring system. Farmers, operators, or agricultural technicians only need to press a button, make a choice, or completely listen to the "instructions", and then they can yield a rich harvest. This is smart agriculture.

In the large-scale production of farmland and orchard, the agricultural environmental parameters that need to be carefully grasped are not only "over ground", but also "underground": organic matter content, temperature and humidity, water content, pH parameter, etc., as well as information on the plant's own growth characteristics (with key requirements for different growth stages).

The real-time collection, transmission, and application of this information are of great significance for the fertilization, irrigation, and other fine agricultural management for the cultivation of crops. Crop growth is highly dependent on the environment. In the communication with an agricultural expert, we learned that a certain kind of tomato will lose one-third of its yielding if a water shortage happens during its growth.

2. Environment monitoring and smart cultivation: The IoT can realize real-time monitoring of temperature, humidity, illumination, and other "over ground" parameters in a crop production environment, soil temperature and humidity and other environmental parameters related to crop itself such as leaf surface humidity and temperature through a variety of wireless sensors, such as light, temperature, and humidity. At the same time, to achieve remote management and control, cameras and other monitoring equipment are arranged to collect real-time video signals. Through CV or mobile phone, agricultural experts or technicians can remotely observe the crops, control the temperature and humidity at any time and can remotely control the designated technological process, such as automatically opening or closing the irrigation system, greenhouse switch roller shutter, etc. Among them, the main functions of the IoT can be summarized as follows.

- ***Data collection***: The temperature, humidity, illumination, soil moisture, and other data in the greenhouse are transmitted to the data processing system through wired or wireless networks. If the parameters reported by the sensor exceed the standard, the system will give a threshold alarm, which can be controlled automatically with intelligent adjustment of relevant equipment.
- ***Video surveillance and automated harvester***: In the seedling stage, users can watch the actual image in the greenhouse through the mobile phone (PAD) or computer anytime and anywhere and monitor the crop growth process remotely; in the stage of irrigation, the video monitoring of water-supply gate and water amount control can be realized, together with technical support remotely.

In the harvesting stage, the automated harvester positioning itself and finding the optimized path by multi-sensors, including video, LiDAR, and GNSS, and the operation site monitoring facilities are carried out. The operation status and location information of various sensors are organized in real time by the automated harvesters to maximize the operational efficiency of agricultural machinery, as shown in Fig. 7.34.

- ***Data storage and analysis***: The system can store historical data to form a knowledge base for processing and queries at any time. The system will display the time distribution and spatial distribution of the collected values to users in an intuitive form and provide daily, monthly. and other historical reports. The smart agricultural application of cloud computing, database and data mining technology can deeply analyze large-scale and long-term agricultural data, and it is easier to discover knowledge through a large number of data.

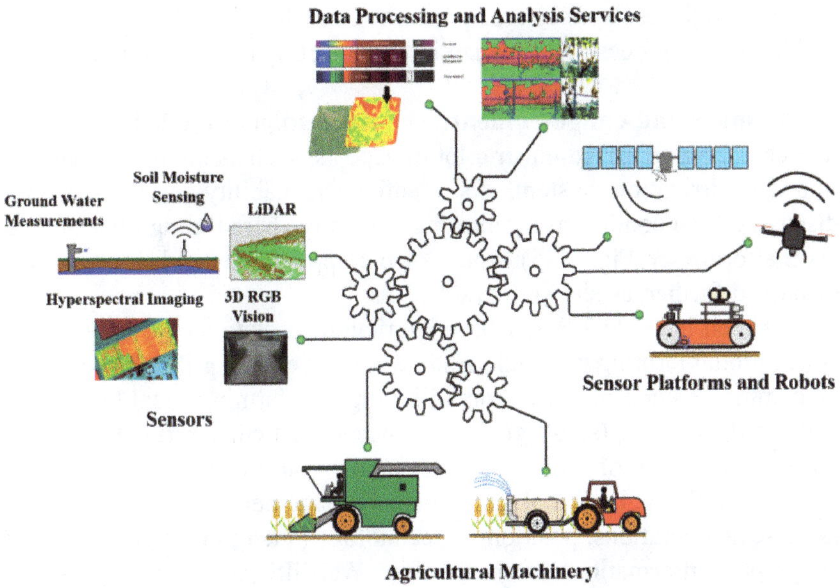

Figure 7.34 The automated harvester in smart agriculture.

- ***Remote control and guidance*:** Users can control all kinds of equipment in the greenhouse remotely at any time and any place through the Internet. When the agricultural technicians are needed to give remote guidance, they give diagnosis opinions through the network, and further track the effect through the network, so as to realize the dual-way flow of information.
- ***M2M use case*:** The adjustments of sensors and actuators can be done through M2M communication, for spraying, sunlight control, and so on. In the long run, the application of M2M can be provided as the basis for the development of smart agriculture.

In addition, in livestock and aquaculture, smart IoT systems can be realized in the management of the healthy breeding process. For example, in breeding, RFID can be used to identify the individual animal and provide personalized feeding, animal physiology care, and health services. With the development of IoT technology and its application in smart agriculture, eventually the agricultural IoT will realize a whole set of traceability system from farmland to dining table (including agricultural products logistics, agricultural products traceability, and management), and the whole process will realize interconnection and integration.

3. Summary and enlightenment: The application of the IoT in agriculture can be summarized under a lot of aspects, such as intelligent cultivation and irrigation system, food safety traceability, and the above discussed field conditions monitoring from anywhere through IoT analytics platform (see Fig. 7.35). Some of the applications and functions are discussed further, as shown in Table 7.5.

As seen in Table 7.5, IoT-based agriculture solutions not only targets conventional farming but could also be new levers to uplift other growing or common trends in agricultural like organic farming, quality control, and family farming (small groups or spaces, particular cattle and/or cultures, preservation of specific or high-quality varieties).

As for the agricultural machinery management and scheduling in large-scale operations, positioning technology (such as GPS, Beidou) and geographic information system (such as WebGIS) can be used to determine the location of the object and display it on the electronic map. A good agricultural machinery management mechanism can improve production efficiency and reduce operating costs. On the one hand, it can record the working track of agricultural machinery and make the administrator view the farming situation in the whole farmland; on the other hand, it can also be used as asset management to prevent the agricultural machinery operators from misuse.

Figure 7.35 IoT analytics platform for smart control, smart monitoring, and smart planning.

Table 7.5 Main functions of the IoT in smart agriculture.

Applications	Main functions	Notes
Precision agriculture	Data acquisition, video monitoring, data storage, data analysis, remote control, alarms, environmental parameters monitoring, etc.	Remote agricultural diagnosis, disaster forecasting, and smart cultivation
Food safety	Safety control throughout the food production cycle	Food safety traceability, food storage, and logistics
Quality control	Access to all information and quality control of agricultural products from production to sale	Organic farming, crop growth monitoring, genetically modified food enquiry, grading according to food quality (nutritional elements)
Information access and agricultural machinery management	Agricultural consultation, agricultural training, dynamic scheduling for agricultural machinery management; UAV seeding and pesticide spraying (as shown in Fig. 7.36)	Information platform based on mobile, real-time, and video monitoring/interaction for the information transmission and processing, e.g., location-based services (LBS)

Figure 7.36 UAV pesticide spraying.

In order to realize the friendly, harmonious, and coordinated coexistence for the sustainable development of human and nature, and in terms of fine management and intelligent cultivation, IoT technology (system) can help us to explore the internal relationship between agriculture and time/season rules, land/soil and people. Also, IoT gives us the right tools to explore how to improve the climate, soil condition, and the environment for both agriculture and us, to explore more suitable conditions for agricultural production (greenhouse, smart cultivation, etc.) and to explore the relationship between local management and large-scale industrialized agricultural production. Furthermore, this section enlightens us on how to explore and achieve the optimal combination of local benefit and overall benefit, current benefit and long-term benefit.

7.6 Application of TIoT

From the discussion of touch (tactile) or movement sense in Chapter 4 and Section 5.10, we know that IoT senses provide sensory information similarly as we do. The sensory information provided by the mechanoreceptors in our muscles, tendons, and joints is collectively referred to as the kinesthetic sense, which seems similar to touch/tactile but the resulting information is very different. The kinesthetic acquisition contributes to human perception of limb position and limb movement (velocity) in space and the perception of applied forces/torques acting on the human body. This information also helps in determining physical properties of touched objects, such as viscosity, stiffness, and inertia, something like an INS linking to our brains for space sense (see Section 4.4.6), especially when considering the position, velocity, angular velocity, force, and torque that all fall into the category of kinesthetic signals.

Kinesthetic haptic interfaces (devices) are used to capture the position/orientation information and provide force/torque feedback to the user. Similar to other IoT senses mentioned in Section 4.4, kinesthetic and other perceptual information can be captured in terms of input to a TI/TIoT system explained in Section 5.9.2, e.g., a human operator. Kinesthetic information codecs in an important aspect for TIoT, but in this section, we only discuss some use cases from the views of input end and the output end in TIoT systems.

7.6.1 *Finger kinesthetic perception schemes and AR*

The augmentation of kinesthetic information into the user's field of view enables the creation of many assistance systems, e.g., maintenance, city guides, driver-assistance systems, medicine, and the work of police and firefighters. Kinesthetic information refers to the position/orientation of

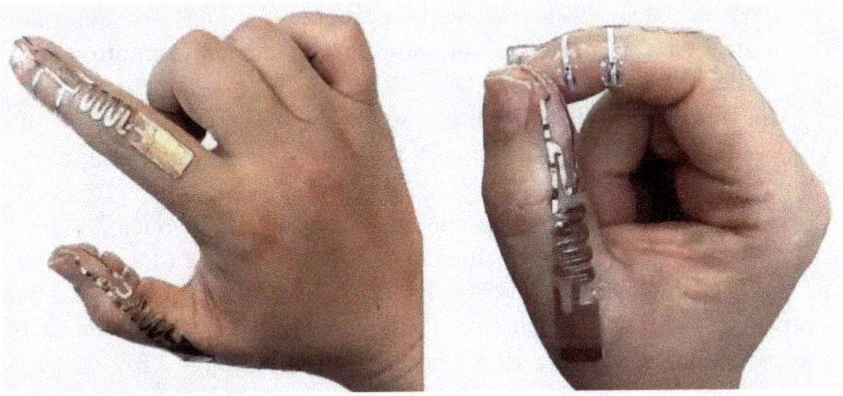

Figure 7.37 Tip-Tap is wireless and battery-free. It could be used in factories, hospitals, gyms, and many other applications.

Source: University of Waterloo.

human body parts and external forces/torques applied to them. Hence, as for finger kinesthetic in some exquisite TIoT scenarios, such as surgery and industrial teleoperation, the acquisition of position/orientation of fingers is important. In Fig. 7.37, a gesture input scheme is introduced as Tip-Tap, which is described as a wearable input technique that can be implemented, without batteries, using RFID tags. It recognizes two-dimensional discrete touch/kinesthetic events by sensing the intersection between two arrays of contact points: one array along the index fingertip and the other along the thumb tip. A formative study identifies locations on the index finger that are reachable by different parts of the thumb tip, and the results determine the pattern of contact points used for the technique. Using a reconfigurable 3 × 3 evaluation device, a second study shows eyes-free accuracy of 86% after a very short period, and adding bumpy or magnetic passive haptic feedback to contacts is not necessary. Finally, two battery-free prototypes use a new RFID tag design to demonstrate how Tip-Tap can be implemented in a glove or tattoo form factor.

In the processing chain of an input haptic, signal conditioning in combination with data compression is required, and this is common for sensor/actuator nodes in TIoT. Intelligent compression methods, which significantly reduce the amount of data to be stored or transmitted, play a central role in the aforementioned communication and system architecture, e.g., in which the minimal algorithmic delay and communication supported by TSN are highly recommended. In addition to compression algorithms and short transfer times, the support engine running ML algorithm for predication can minimize the end-to-end latency and improve QoE (see Section 5.9.3).

This kind of tactile or gesture input can be widely used in VR/AR-based TIoT use cases, especially for those operations without physical touch to the object.

The above Tip-Tap can be concluded as an RFID-device AR, as a part of wearable computing, which encompasses a range of systems and technologies that deliver real-time, hands-on guidance to ensure tasks are completed safely and efficiently. The wearable Tip-Tap gives us assistance when holding the steering wheel is possible through TIoT far away or when surgeons cannot be present but can give a hand (finger operation) remotely.

When TIoT acts as a bridge between physical operation and digital infrastructure, AR brings remote interaction with the physical environment in real-time. Let us take the example of workers and engineers accessing real-time IoT data on the shop floor, where it adds the most value. Augmented reality devices (handheld, finger-held, or head-mounted) are aware of the spatial configuration of the environment of the worker and can therefore sense what the worker is looking at to intuitively display only the data needed for the operation at hand. These applications of AR and TIoT can be extrapolated to manage maintenance in remote locations, in conditions of low visibility and high temperature, and other hazardous conditions.

One of the most important features that make this kind of standardization possible is the inference service or functionality that needs to be integrated into different TIoT systems. This ensures that before all steps are completed, the pre-analysis and the prediction of the next steps in the correct sequence before allowing the user to move on to the next phase of the process. This kind of AR-TIoT eliminates most sources of human error and ensures that the right parts, processes, and sequences are always followed correctly, as discussed in the IEEE P1918.1, no faults and no (less) latency forward are necessary.

7.6.2 *Inference as a ML service*

As for AR-TIoT in healthcare, the proposed "Enhancement of Sensor Data Transmission" by inference infers sensed data before transmitting them to the requestor networks in order to reduce data volume and

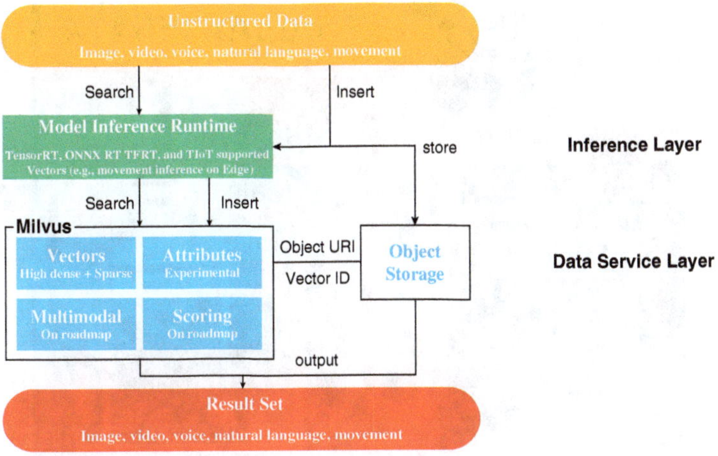

Figure 7.38 Inference as-a-service for unstructured data in Milvus framework.

bandwidth to save battery power consumption. For implementation, various AR/VRs are used to determine optimal inferencing of data processing such as finer or coarser rates followed by beacon data points to be added to increase the accuracy as high efficiency does not necessarily mean it will represent the original data accurately. Figure 7.38 is a framework analysis of open-source vector similarity search engine, Milvus, which is adapted from the online seminar on inference-as-a-service in the Milvus framework.

Milvus is a project assistant by Intel. Along with the edge of support engine in a TIoT infrastructure, an inference layer or inference service includes the most critical devices/service that have direct interactions with an ID service, operation, and AR support in IoT environments, such as TSN, UAVs control, and actuators. Inference service can be used to accelerate processing and analysis of raw input data (unstructured or structured), e.g., learning from a series of input gestures or body movement, the next time finger/body movement can be inferred in ML algorithms. Besides these motion inferences, the trajectory of objects and false/danger pre-alarm can also be inferences.

Given the constraints imposed by an embedded device, the inference model will often be trained on an edge processing device (support engine or an edge box/edge server) than the one running the inference. This section explains the inference as an ML service or inserted inference layer for its selection option of the edge deployment in TIoT use cases.

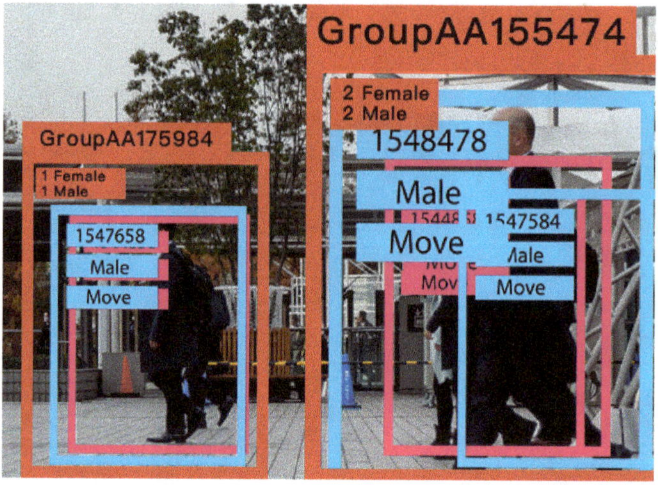

Figure 7.39 Example of object classification using embedded deep learning. *Source*: Texas Instruments.

Take the inference model performing the deep learning inference as an example, as shown in Fig. 7.39. Some vectors and attributes are optimized to the point of using 1-bit weights and can perform simple functions like key phrase detection. The optimizing is high to save communication consumption from end to end, with a tradeoff of limited edge/ inference layer functionality and precision.

The smaller inference model may not be integrated into the support engine of TI/TIoT infrastructure if the application is not so complex. When evaluating the size of the engines or inference model, make sure that either structured or unstructured data are compressed to the right size for the input of TI applications. A limitation on these inference/support engines comes when the application needs additional processing aside from the deep learning inference. More often than not, the engine will need to be used alongside another processor or another edge device in the TI system, functioning as a deep learning co-processor. An integrated system on chip (SoC) is often a good choice in the embedded space.

7.6.3 *TIoT and remote diagnosis*

Tele-diagnosis, tele-surgery, and tele-rehabilitation are just some of the many potential applications of TI. In healthcare, by using advanced tele-diagnostic tools, medical expertise may be released from the bounding to the location of the physician. When TI could be available anywhere, anytime for allowing remote physical examination even by palpation (examination by touch), the physician will be able to command the motion of a tele-robot at the patient's location and receive not only audio-visual information but also critical haptic feedback.

The same technical principle of tele-operation makes tele-surgical interventions possible, relieving the patient of costly travel to the surgeon. Future tele-rehabilitation techniques will benefit from the progression of tele-robotic technologies. Envisaged tele-rehabilitation systems see patients wearing an exoskeleton — a robotic device — commanded by the therapist to steer and correct the motions of the patient. The possibility of embedding rehabilitation into the patient's home and everyday life promises higher therapy success rates as well as improved cost-efficiency.

INTER-Health is the healthy application of IoT, which is based on the INTER-IoT (see Section 6.1.3) platform from the European Union's "Horizon 2020". BodyCloud is its assistant communication platform specifically addressed to the creation and management of body sensor networks (BSNs) and the integration of wearable sensors, medical sensors (at home), and fixed devices (at the medical center, e.g., hospital).

One of the goals of the INTER-Health pilot is demonstrating how to prevent chronic diseases by monitoring subjects' physical characteristics, nutritional behavior, and activity. Using IoT devices on the premises (BMI, waist circumference, weight, blood pressure), the physical characteristics of each subject are measured, and the subject under a management program measures his characteristics with phone and IoT devices. The healthcare professional in charge of monitoring each user will have access to the history of all the measurements through a dedicated web application.

INTER-Health enables the remote measurement of different physiological parameters by means of medical IoT devices such as weight scale, blood pressure monitor, and physical activity rate monitor, as shown in Fig. 7.40. Sensors interact with an IoT platform (BodyCloud) and provide measurements through the connection with a smart gateway employing Bluetooth communication, which receives the measures from the devices and sends them to the BodyCloud platform through 2G/3G/4G/WiFi/ADSL connectivity. The BodyCloud creates a smart gateway on a mobile phone, thus enabling a smartphone to become an IoT gateway for the medical sensors. Doctors have access to a web medical application that allows them to follow up the monitoring of patients remotely.

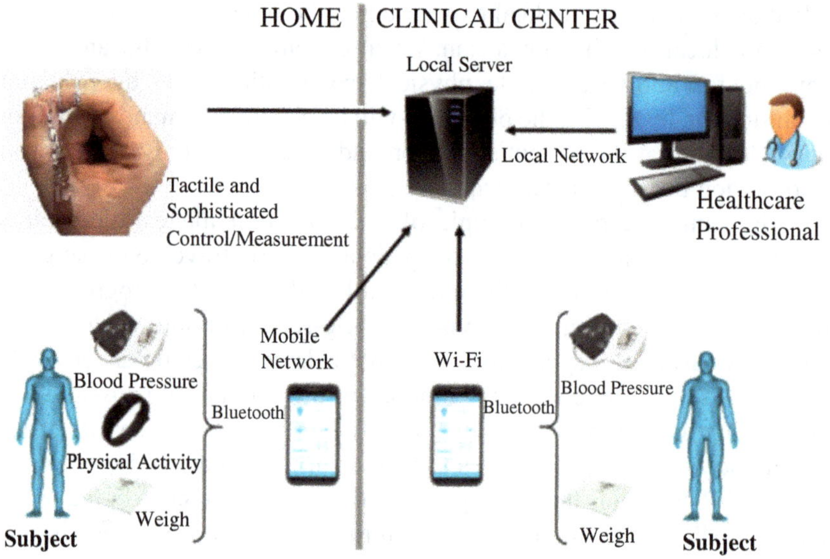

Figure 7.40 Real-time and near real-time demands in TIoT system.
Source: INTER-Health.

When exploiting IoT wearable devices in real-time demands on TIoT, from the view of ITU, high-fidelity interaction is fundamental to the safe deployment of tele-medical technologies: the physician, surgeon, and physiotherapist need a realistic impression of the remote patient's status. High fidelity requires deterministic real-time behavior of the communication channel, which is not achievable with current communications technologies.

Sophisticated control approaches do exist to stabilize the system in the presence of packet loss and 100-millisecond latency, but the fidelity is significantly decreased. To achieve the high fidelity required for telemedical applications, it is necessary to achieve end-to-end latency of 1–10 milliseconds and highly reliable data transmission.

Finally, other promising TIoT use cases are summarized in Table 7.6, which also includes some technical considerations.

At the end of the section, two figures are used to describe the deepening relationship between AR and IoT. When TIoT acts as a bridge between physical assets and digital infrastructure, AR realizes digitization through real-time interaction with the physical environment. As shown in

Table 7.6 Applications and analysis of the Tactile Internet.[a]

Section	TI/TIoT use cases	Technical aspects
Industry automation.	The sensitivity of control circuits of industrial robots when controlling devices moving rapidly requires an end-to-end latency significantly below 1 millisecond per sensor. In typical scenarios of industrial control with closed-loop systems, at intervals of roughly a millisecond, a master station will contact all sensors and actuators and present the acquired data to the control application. Every sensor must be accessed within an end-to-end latency period.	Communication demands for high data rates from the example case of optical sensors employing a high resolution and very high frame rate, such as those needed to monitor the quality of a surface. Security is of utmost importance as potential attacks could occur wirelessly, without the attacker physically present.
Remote-controlled robots.	Construction and maintenance in dangerous areas is an application area providing a good example of the potential of remote-controlled robots. Such robots have great commercial and societal relevance, as demonstrated by projects such as the planned deconstruction of nuclear plants in Germany, repair work in damaged nuclear or chemical plants, off-shore construction tasks, removal of satellite debris in low-earth orbits, or maintenance work on the outside of space stations.	Remote-control or telepresence solution with real-time, synchronous visual-haptic feedback. These solutions require system response times (including network delays) of less than a few milliseconds. Communications infrastructure providing this level of real-time capability, mobility support, and high reliability and availability is not available today. New technologies and networking concepts will be required.
VR	Haptic feedback is a prerequisite for high-fidelity interaction, allowing the user to perceive the objects in the VR not only audio-visually but also via the sense of touch. This allows for sensitive object manipulations as required in tele-surgery, micro-assembly, or related applications demanding high levels of sensitivity and precision. When two users interact with the same object, a direct force coupling is brought into existence by the VR and the users can feel one another's actions.	Typical update rates for the physical simulation and the display of haptic information are in the order of 1000 Hertz, which corresponds to an ideal round-trip communication latency of 1 millisecond. A consistent local view of the VR for all users can thus only be achieved if delays are kept very small.

(*Continued*)

Table 7.6 (*Continued*).

Section	TI/TIoT use cases	Technical aspects
AR	The augmentation of dynamic content or up-to-date information enables the real-time virtual extension of a driver's field of view. Dangerous events caused by drivers' not seeing people or obstacles in fog or rain, or as a result of curved roads or car blind spots, can now be captured by other vehicles able to transmit their view to following vehicles in the form of a projection onto the windshield.	The visual combination of real and computer-generated content require delays of only a few milliseconds in order to avoid irritating the user. This holds not only for data transmission over fast networks but also for low-delay sensors and visualization techniques; and the new algorithms needed to enable the distributed computation of demanding processes, such as 3D-scene capturing of view correction.
CAV and Road Traffic	Through communication — the data exchange among vehicles (V2V communications) and between vehicles and roadside infrastructure (V2I communications) — a vehicle turns from an autonomous system into a component of a more efficient cooperative one. The data exchange provides information on a vehicle's vicinity as well as non-visible surroundings. Vehicles detect a highly dynamic object by radar or video, such as a pedestrian, and disseminate this information to neighboring vehicles. It is expected that fully automated driving will change individual mobility entirely. With small distances between automated vehicles, in particular, in platoons or road trains, potentially safety-critical situations need to be detected earlier than with human drivers.	Vehicle safety requires a very low end-to-end latency of below 10 milliseconds, the time needed for collision-avoidance systems to intervene before a collision occurs. With a bi-directional exchange of data for the negotiation of automatic cooperative-driving maneuvers, a latency of less than 1 millisecond would be needed.

Note: [a]The Tactile Internet ITU-T Technology Watch Report August 2014.

Figure 7.41 AR and IoT assistance in maintains.

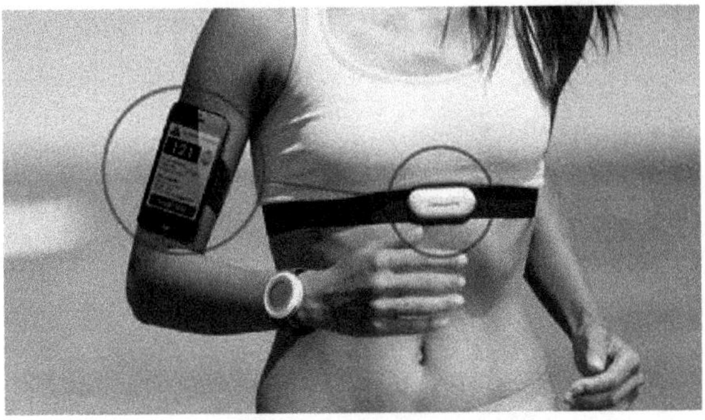

Figure 7.42 Wearable AR devices.

Fig. 7.41, workers and engineers in the workshop access real-time IoT data by an AR class, where the class adds the most value of reference and real-time information. Augmented reality devices (handheld devices or headwear devices) understand the spatial configuration of the worker's environment, so they can perceive what the worker is looking at, so as to intuitively display only the data needed for the operation at hand. These applications of augmented reality and IoT can be used for maintenance remotely or under low visibility, extreme temperature conditions, as well as other hazardous conditions.

As to the wearable AR device, some features have been discussed in this domain: it is unmonopolizing of people's attention, unrestrictive for people's activities and movements, and controllable at any time. It can perceive the environment attentively with multi-modal sensing ability, and the user can interact and communicate with other, obtain observable and auxiliary information needed in the work or movements, as shown in both Figs. 7.41 and 7.42.

Chapter 8

IoT Security

"No security without privacy".

— A remarkable title in *People's Daily*, dated April 26, 2012.

8.1 Introduction

There is a wide range of challenges of Internet of things (IoT) security to be discussed in this single chapter with a new view in order to face this issue correctly, and then we propose some new developments to keep IoT safe and secure for us. In this chapter, key aspects and recommendations are made for further evaluation.

With the development of information technology (IT), security and privacy are already challenges on IT systems; these challenges become much more important on the IoT systems considering that the attack target has significantly been enlarged as well as the amount of data generated and handled.

More and more individuals and things would be linked to IoT, and their behavior could be expanded to many devices/nodes of IoT through "butterfly effect" spreading, therefore the effective scope would be expanded rapidly. The relation of individuals would be more tightened in IoE era, and the insecurity factor of individuals would also spread to a wider scope if left without enough attention. Therefore, the damage level of attack is more than that caused by a single device or an application. The security problem becomes more serious than before when we step into IoE era.

A civil survey has showed that 90% Americans consider that it is very important to control their information being collected or obtained. Users are assuming that the level of data security and privacy protection is lower now than even before. When it comes to the IoT, consumers worry that security and privacy will become the two biggest obstacles to the acceptance of the IoT.

However, these fears are reasonable in some ways. On the one hand, perhaps IT/IoT users worked in a default environment of insecurity without a systematic caution. On the other hand, the fears were proved right by researches that an insecure IoT equipment or even low-end device could lead to invasion of the whole system. Although default security is a goal, many devices have intrinsic security vulnerabilities.

Although security is a broad concept, the impact becomes more important considering that IoT devices have not enough processing capabilities, as in RFID device and other low-end devices introduced in Chapter 4, in contrast to IT systems, and they have a limited autonomy because they work mostly on batteries. They use generally different wireless connectivity solutions and some of them are not compliant with existing security standards. Last but not the least, the implementation of the applications, for instance SCADA for real-time control system (see Section 6.1), requires a high level of security to keep end-to-end data integrity, confidentiality, and service availability. The SCADA users are very concerned by these aspects. Securing IoT systems with high level of personal data protection is mandatory to uphold the user and systems trust. Furthermore, if without enough protections of devices and correct user directions for security or safety, accumulation of risk occurrence and management disturbances may break off the development of IoT.

These aspects should be solved integrally with guidance, cooperation, and mutual understanding among us, so as to accomplish positive economy effectiveness and social effectiveness. If the consensus was achieved by the stakeholders, there will be the following four gains: achieve economic growth in a trusted IoT environment, achieve standardization and regulation in dealing with the security dilemma, increase the flexibility and security resilience of key infrastructures (e.g., cloud/edge for IoT), and help realizing the scaled-up growth of the IoT.

The potential utilization of IoT was developed in smart city and home, as Fig. 8.1 shows; they are the top two fields supplying smart connections and services. The third safe and security aspect, also together with the

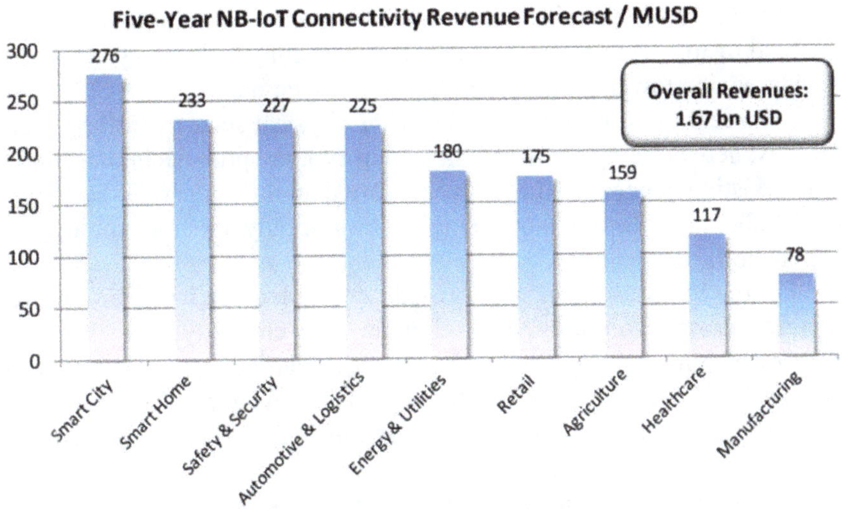

Figure 8.1 The earnings forecast of NB-IoT operation and service in Germany.
Data source: https://www.huawei.com/minisite/4-5g/img/NB-IOT.pdf.

former two, supply the raising job opportunities and new businesses for the promotion power of IoT, from just NB-IoT views of Huawei research.

In terms of safety and security, they have their individual specific concept, but the main topic in this chapter is limited to security and privacy protection. With the development of IoT research and technology application, the interconnecting number of devices around us has increased to several billions over the years. Mobile phones and devices and IoT systems are becoming more and more smart, which make them work autonomously, in medical application, transport, industrial control and security, in constructing a sustainable development field which contains energy utilization and environment monitoring. But each coin has its two sides. Securities relating to IoT are also particularly prevalent among things, connectivity of systems and people living in the IoE era. How to build a trusted and healthy IoT environment in a long run is a serious problem which is worth our persistent attention.

“Every aspect and every data level in every link of IoT is a potential risk”. IoT security arose greater interest recently but without enough caution so far. IoT security contains not only physical security, data security, network security, information security, and encryption but also security consensus, privacy, and data protection rules, security management and safeguarding mechanism, security organization, and implementation. So, the field of IoT security also exceeds to the existing technology and need a wider vision towards the comprehensive utilization.

IoT security is not only the fusion of physical security, information security, network/cyber security, data security, encryption technology, and other existing concepts. But it covers more than the security issues mentioned above and beyond some single views of only about technology or application.

For the IoT, it is not easy to provide a complete security framework. It needs cross-technology, cross-domain, and cross-layer mechanism. Moreover, human's cognition of the new thing "IoT" has not reached the level of consensus that "protecting the IoT means protecting one's privacy and security". The security of the IoT can not only be constrained to protecting the devices and platforms of the IoT from attack and tamper (from the perspective of things) nor can it just satisfy the information security and privacy protection of people (from the perspective of people); Moreover, the security of IoT should not only obtain a certain degree of social recognition but also be restricted by laws and regulations.

Just like protecting a child who just begins to "talk", he may easily tell you all the private details of himself and his family, including the access code; but his "limited capacity" needs the protection of law and guardian. Many "resource-constrained" objects use simple processors and can only consider lightweight encryption. They are easy to be cheated and cracked. Of course, the safety of children is related to our future. The security of the IoT is related to the future of the IoT.

The above discussion inspires the following three clues in this chapter:

(1) Things with single service capability need to be protected before they can evolve to autonomous intelligence;
(2) Technical level, including security technology and security strategy;
(3) Humanistic analysis, including the security analysis of people and things, the security concept of the IoT, the security of things, moral counseling, and legal constraints (the protection of communication between grids in the functional safety or security environment).

In the following sections, first of all, how to understand the "IoT security" from the perspective of humanities is given. Second, the deepening of the concept of IoT security from technical levels and different functional perspectives (e.g., IoT security relative technology and strategy) is considered; finally, the concept of "IoT security grid" is proposed in the last section as an edge security use case.

This chapter focuses on the security of the IoT and its technologies and strategies from the perspectives of perception layer security, network layer security, platform layer, and application layer security. The purpose of this chapter is to discuss the technologies and methods needed to achieve security and privacy protection in a super-connected world. From the perspective of security, in the application layer, the management service layer of the four-layer structure of the IoT is abstracted as the security management of the IoT applications. In fact, the security management of the IoT will run through all levels of the IoT. Moreover, more security algorithms such as homomorphic encryption, security multi computing, and federated learning are also introduced in order to understand IoT security deeply.

8.2 The Baseline of IoT Security

IoT business value lies in the data it gathers — data that's often mission critical and on a tremendous scale. "Will my IoT data be vulnerable?" From the views of Vodafone in the protection of data from theft or tampering as it moves over the network, 76% of businesses say that IoT security should be treated as an end-to-end solution, and 91% say it is important for them to work with an end-to-end solution provider for IoT.

One lies in owning the infrastructure for seamless security. IoT data originates at the very edge of the infrastructure, far beyond the protection of the corporate perimeter, in remote devices like cars or security cameras. It is a long journey to the data center. If a breach happens at any stage in that journey, sensitive data is at risk. Responsibility for securing the data as it moves from the SIM, or embedded SIM, or the device in LAN/PAN through the wireless and core networks around the world attributes to the central management platform and the data centers where it is hosted.

Another lies in supporting multiple layers of data protection. By providing hosting and private cloud environments for applications, data never have to leave the protection of MNOs. Edge or cloud protection to host applications offering a range of secure backhaul connections between data/edge centers and our data is expected in seamless security, without the risks associated with integrating solutions from multiple providers. It also means benefits from greater accountability and agility in a holistic view of the risks facing personal or IoT data.

Some responsibility from a data company/ISP or MNO operator really means something to IoT security baseline. In terms of opinions from the book, the innovative application supported by the IoT can improve the efficiency of social production and our daily lives (if efficiency is emphasized unilaterally, kindness from nature to things and us, and examination of themselves would be ignored). Although driven by clear business opportunities, IoT is favored by more and more stakeholders and market participants; however, IoT security needs to be thought in a broad framework.

IoT security, which derived from human security necessity, is calling for a feeling and requirement from ourselves to IoT related things. Similarly, the baseline of IoT security should originate from the right vision of the security by human beings. In facing the polluted environment and the polluted data, IoT security and human security are mutual in needing for consideration ahead in avoidance of the long-lasting punishment.

8.2.1 *What is IoT security?*

"Do not do what you do not want to do to others".[1] This proverb means that things which you don't want to do would not be done by others. However more and more data should be collected, stored, and applied in IoT domain. So, the data security is a very important topic in IoT.

8.2.1.1 *Empathy alike from human security necessary*

More things in IoT become useful for us to satisfy human need.

As in Fig. 8.2(a), the top needs of a human for self-actualization, releasing potential abilities, reflect the same top expectation of IoT as high-level automation AI systems or machines (an extension of human intelligence).

The layered IoT architecture consists of perception layer, communication (and networks) layer, and application layer, while the bottom layer below perception includes things/devices that are composed of components and circuits, which is called physical/device layer requiring basic needs as energy and protection from destruction. When things in IoT

[1]A famous traditional saying from Confucius-"己所不欲勿施于人". And another explanation for this proverb is "What you do not want done to yourself, do not do to others".

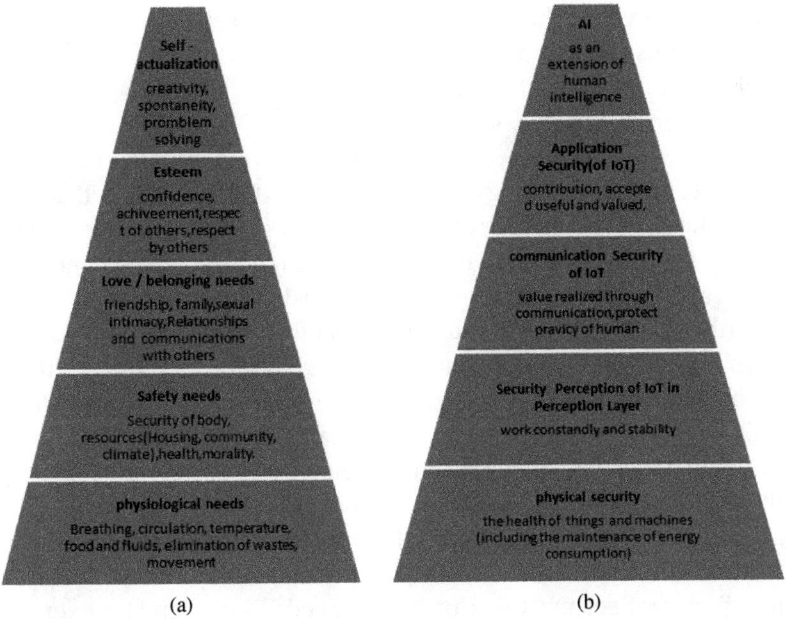

Figure 8.2 Maslow's hierarchy of requirements theory diagram and IoT security analysis. (a) Maslow's hierarchy of needs and (b) Things in IoT as a part of society of security needs.

develop in a structured and organized way, such as working in cooperation within IoT teamworks, they become smarter and tend to form a IoT society or likewise. Then communication security layer in Fig. 8.2(b) shows that things are granted more value with communication of others in IoT as well as privacy protection. As Maslow's hierarchy of needs enlighten us, each layer needs protection especially when they are undeveloped. Most things in IoT are resource constrained (sensors, actuators, and GPS devices) with less memory, lower data processing, and other capabilities (constrained by their size or power) than those of a computer. But they can share our privacy between things or machines, even when uncovered in the Internet. IoT (as a part of society extension) needs security protection for humanity's sake. Analysis of each layer in IoT hierarchy is shown in Fig. 8.2(b).

Almost all information is a certain expression of human will or demand, and IoT security is a kind of self-protection demand and self-identity of human beings. On the one hand, IoT security is related to human security and privacy; on the other hand, when IoT has not evolved to a similar level of human intelligence, but when humans can make things serve us in each corner of our life and work, shall we first try to treat things as partners like children or pets?

As shown in Fig. 8.2, security is also one of the basic requirements. The homogenization analysis of "things" can avoid draining the pond to get all the fish (the analogy of achieving all the benefits but at some unbearable cost). Even for pets, humans will give or consider a certain degree of safety to pets from their own needs (such as feeding and avoiding starvation). This is the inspiration of Maslow's analysis.

Further from Fig. 8.2, human physiological needs correspond to "things" and "health" needs of machines (e.g., physical security); "things" must be at least structural integrity, being undamaged, whereas human security needs correspond to the functional needs of "things" in the IoT which help understand the perception security in the perceptual layer normally and stably. Human social needs correspond to the transmission and communication security needs of "sharing our minds with language", just like some of the functionalities of the network layer in the IoT, and "things" can reflect the value of "being needed" to a greater extent and coverage in network communication. The need for human being to be respected and self-actualized also partly correspond to the value that the IoT can realize in the application layer — which is recognized in "things-systems" information sharing and interaction and in "things-person" communication and service.

On the top, the demand for human self-realization, corresponding to "things" can assist human beings to form new forms of wisdom — artificial intelligence (AI). This is also the highest value of self-realization for either the things or the IoT — at least for now in the viewpoints of mankind, e.g., the Alpha Go can defeat mankind sometimes.

Security is a requirement. IoT security is a concept derived from human security needs; the feeling and identity of a kind of security technology pushing oneself to "thing". Maslow's analysis enlightens us on the homogenization security and human self-identity between the IoT world and our society.

8.2.1.2 *IoT is the reflection on human social relations*

From the traditional Chinese point of view: "the unity of nature and mankind, and the mutual understanding of things and us"; first, the integration of heaven (*Tian* in Chinese) and man: heaven means the material world and its laws or principals, which can be extended to the nature and the society. Things or nature have their own working laws, and the society has also its laws; these laws are consistent and at least should not be contradictory.

Second, there is no contradiction with the various interpretations of "heaven": this sentence at least leads us not to oppose human beings against "material world, nature, ecological environment".

As some blind sense of human self-realization begins to affect physiological needs (through the deterioration of the ecological environment), it is necessary to reflect whether the needs of human self-realization respect the "common interests of people and things" — the overall security of society and environment. Human beings and the material world should respect each other in the same planet.

One's self-actualization has laws and morals to adjust if it affects or suppresses others' self-actualization. But what if the present self-realization of the whole human being deprives the foundation of the future human security needs — environment and the sustainability? Let's stand at the point of view and turn our attention to the right side of Fig. 8.2: IoT security hierarchy analysis.

Third, "knowledge of things": Defective thinking could turn back methodology. Try to consider the rights of existence (security), rights of development, rights of communication, rights of value realization, not only because things have their own data but also the data can reflect the privacy of users; the overexploitation and blind occupation threaten the nature resource or other's data, and affect the development of the whole society.

IoT security is the way of human and environment security from the macro view, and it is also the way of human security for the sustainable development from the views of ourselves.

8.2.1.3 *Necessary security for harmonious coexistence between people and things*

Not all the meanings of things done can be understood in time; nor could we begin to explore until something meaningful is found, which is the dialectical relationship between the stolen sheep and repair (as the traditional Chinese saying — "It's not too late to mend the fold after the sheep had been stolen"). Here, trying from "harmony" to see the Chinese saying (from Yangming Wang, an ancient Chinese philosopher) — "things and us are interlinked, heaven and mankind are combined".

Zengdian's (who is one of students of Confucius in China) study exceeded concrete things and was aimed at the wide philosophy domain. His behaviors and viewpoints are very magnificent. However, he is still a simple man, satisfied with common daily life. Moreover, his mind fused with nature, up to sky, down to river (*The Analects of Confucius*, volume 6). The phenomenon which Zengdian hold and described in the fusion with the nature is some kind of realm of life which everyone should make an effort to practice,[2] **for** more peace, more kindnesses and beauties in life, nor leak of malice, evil idea and evil behavior. It is well known that there would **occur** security threat after the leaked data is used by someone with evil intentions.

Harmony is not only a kind of beauty from human views but also the views of nature. Harmony is the original intention of mutual respect, inter-dependent security, and sustainable development.

The IoT gives humans the opportunity to connect with things. Before the emergence of IoT, Confucius taught us that the harmony between man and nature is a realm; after the emergence of IoT, should we also consider the harmonious coexistence between man and "thing?" This is an open topic, but the "existence" security of objects and machines should at least be considered. For example, how to ensure the safe, stable, and reliable operation of things?

The threat of IoT security incidents is also breaking this harmony at the cost of people suffering from it. For example, IoT devices around the world could be infected by powerful malware "Mirai". In the world of people and things, people gradually pay attention to IoT security. For example, Tim Kleiner, deputy director of the Günther Oettinger office of the European digital economy commissioner, said that it is not enough to focus on just one IoT component, and that we need to look at the whole network, the cloud, and to establish a government framework for certification. However, the security of things would be protected and dignified in order to keep security for your, for us, for IoT ecosystems, and for the sustainable development that is also necessary for harmony.

---

[2]From Zhu Zhirong's Aesthetics and the Realm of Life (speech at Kunshan Research Center on July 5, 2010), the author wants to lead to the discussion that the natural science and the humanities are twinned and the same way, as detailed in that the harmony gains more beauty and kindness for us, and for the nature.

8.2.2 *Insight and extension of IoT security*

IoT security idea is being accepted by people. In order to deepen the understanding of IoT security, this part shifts to the discussion of some insights and extension around IoT security concept.

8.2.2.1 *Extension of IoT security is that "things" is fully respected*

We should not only just think that protecting the privacy of things is that protecting our privacy but should realize that protecting the security of things is that protecting our security. Human beings exist in the objective material world; their respect for "things" is that respecting the environment on which human beings live and develop together in the harmonious coexistence between human beings and the nature. This would extend to the realm of "big IoT security", which leads to the discussion on natural environment protection and social development. "IoT security" is a humanities topic which covers cognition, management, technology, law, and many other aspects.

8.2.2.2 *Connotation: The information security and privacy protection of people involved in things*

The connotation of IoT security can also be understood as narrow IoT security, which mainly includes the following two aspects: information security and privacy protection.

Privacy protection is that protecting the information that individuals or groups do not want to be known by outsiders. Privacy contains a wide range. For individuals, an important kind of privacy is personal identity information, that is, the information can be traced directly or indirectly to a person through connection query. Contrary to this is the Six Degree Separation theory 60. The other is identity-related information that one wants not to be known by outsiders, such as addiction, family, occupation, health, sexual orientation, and other information which individuals wanting to control the known range, which have potential commercial value. For the collective, privacy generally refers to sensitive information representing various behaviors of a group, such as personal information that the group wants to be known within family members.

Information security generally refers to ensuring the confidentiality, integrity, authentication, non-repudiation, and availability of information. IoT information security, in addition to the "thing" security, can be extended to ensure that users control the resources of the IoT system, to ensure the safe, stable, and reliable operation of system. The security of the IoT also includes the effective control of the information related to "people" and "things" of IoT. In a sense, it is a larger realm than IoT information security.

Privacy protection is closely related to information security, but the emphasis is different. The main concerns of information security are the confidentiality, integrity, and availability of data, while the main concern of privacy protection is that seeing whether the system provides the protection of privacy information (such as anonymity that contains hidden behavior, hidden part of privacy, e.g., *k*-anonymity by Samarati and Sweeney in 1997). Generally speaking, privacy protection is a kind of information security problem, which can be regarded as a manifestation of data confidentiality. For example, if data contains privacy information, the breach of data confidentiality will cause the disclosure of privacy information.

Privacy concept, in depth, has more than 100 years of research history, covering all fields of social science (such as philosophy, psychology, and sociology), there is no clear definition that meets both the development needs of the times and the practical testing 61. This literature provides the concept of privacy, privacy protection along with the evolution of IT, which is shown in Table 8.1.

Only in credible and innovative IoT ecosystem, social and commercial benefits could be achieved by prioritizing security and privacy. According to statistics, 95% users can be identified by analyzing four visited locations.[3] Whether or not it serves (belongs to) your "thing",

---

[3]"Data Trigger How to Solve Personal Privacy Security Problem". http://www.boiots.com/news/show-14665.html. Date: January 27, 2016 14:07:52 Source: WEB. A study was published in Nature's Open Access Journal, Scientific Reports. By analyzing mobile phone movement data for 1.5 million people over a 15-month period, the researchers found that only four space-time points (i.e., the approximate time and location of individuals using mobile phones) were sufficient to determine 95% of individuals. Research shows that in order to keep up with technological progress, privacy laws need to keep pace with the times. Four temporal and spatial locations are enough to identify most people for a simple reason — Human mobility is unique. It is similar to human fingerprints. Each

Table 8.1 Privacy evolutions as IT in different periods.

Period	Original feature description	Notes and remarks by the author
Era of privacy baseline: 1945–1960	Limited information technology development, high public trust in government and business sector, and general comfort with the information collection.	Limited information technology development, high public trust on government and business, and collection of information that can be accepted by the public.
First era of privacy evolution: 1961–1979	Rise of information privacy as an explicit social, political, and legal issue. Formulation of the Fair Information Practices (FIP) Framework and establishing government regulatory mechanisms.	As an obvious social, political, and legal issue, rights of information privacy have arisen.FIP framework is formed and government regulatory mechanism is established. The information is standardized and controlled. The Six-Degree Separation theory emerged simultaneously.
Second era of privacy evolution: 1980–1990	Rise of computer and network systems, database capabilities, federal legislation designed to channel the new technologies into FIP, Some nations made data protection laws.	With the advent of the computer age, the functions of network system and database have been embodied, guided new technologies into the FIP framework, which is designed in federal legislation. Some countries have enacted data protection laws.
Third era of privacy evolution: 1991–2003	Rise of the Internet, data mining, and terrorist attacks dramatically changed the landscape of information exchange and caused user privacy concerns and the attention of the researchers.	(Internet age coming) Internet, data mining, and the occurrence of terrorist attacks dramatically changed the pattern of information exchange, aroused the users' privacy issues, and attracted the attention of researchers.

(Continued)

Table 8.1 (*Continued*)

Period	Original feature description	Notes and remarks by the author
Fourth era of privacy evolution: 2004-present	Rise of Web 2.0, cloud computing, IoT, and big data l collected a lot of personal information, privacy concerns rose to new highs.	New generation of IT — including Web 2.0, rise of cloud computing, IoT, and big data, collecting a lot of personal information. Privacy issues have risen to a new height.
(Extension form the above 4th Era) IoT 1.0	At the technical level, a security certification scheme must be able to cope with dynamic systems, dynamic threats and real users working in real organizations. It must complement, rather than conflict with, existing safety certification mechanisms. Anderson (2009)	Certification: "A comprehensive assessment of the management, operational, and technical security controls in an information system, made in support of security accreditation, to determine the extent to which the controls are implemented correctly, operating as intended, and producing the desired outcome with respect to meeting the security requirements for the system" from NIST SP 800-37 (2011).
(Extension form the above 4th Era) IoT 2.0	It is an open question if existing applications might continue running on top of certified, and properly modified of course, products. Assessments should take place to this direction. Re-writing existing application will prove to be a big challenge. ENISA (2014).	Security certification in IoT is used to ensure that a product satisfies the required security requirements, which can be both proprietary requirements (i.e., defined by a company for their specific products) and market requirements (i.e., defined in procurement specifications or market standards). In the latter case, these requirements are also defined to support security interoperability (EU Commission, 2017).

whether it is leaked by the social information you know, whether it is analyzed that location, shopping information, and other data, the IoT has been able to lock individuals with very high accuracy and dig out personal information systems.

The next discussion in this chapter will include privacy protection and information security in an IoT security model, and there are some privacy related technologies and strategies.

8.2.3 *A layer model of IoT security*

When IoT is mentioned, it may be easier to think with personal security and network security of IoT devices that are often contacted in life, such as wear and home, but in fact, IoT will involve many fields, such as trade, energy transport, social undertakings, urban management, and so on in the future, including upgradation applications of Industry 4.0, manufacturing 2025, and the Internet+ industry; these national economy and human livelihood planning and trends will take the IoT as an important basis. If infrastructure and industry networks (for instance, the electronic payments) are attacked, then the property and life might be threatened, and the country's industrial construction might also be affected. Therefore, it is urgent that IoT security should be understood and mastered with a whole frame macroscopically. Further, if it can be divided into levels or regions in a large framework, and the connotation of the issue of IoT security might be very clear. This chapter about the IoT security system framework (shown in Fig. 8.3) is only a starting point of IoT security; we are facing the era of connection of all things, increasingly serious security threats, and its privacy protection problem which cannot match well with the application of security technology.

The network security system framework consists of the following four parts: IoT security in perception layer, in communication and networks layer, in service and platform layer, and in IoT application layer. Some non-functional views are also given in the frameworks, such as the above-mentioned security of cognition, and its management system,

---

person's trajectory is rarely the same as that of others. Researchers even found that just two random space-time points were enough to identify 50% of people. Identification is not enough by moving data alone, but researchers point out that individuals can be identified by combining public information such as personal home addresses, work addresses, and Twitter IDs.

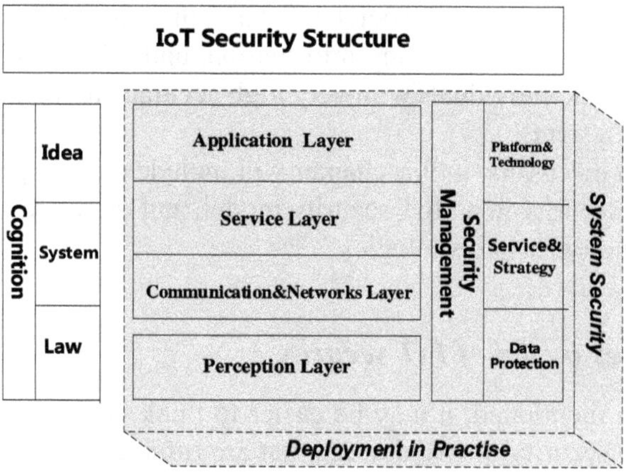

Figure 8.3 IoT security system framework.

Notes: Security Awareness in IoT perception layer, includes physical security. Security management below the networks layer and the IoT platform. The additional two dimensions from the IoT security plane will be further discussed as security functions/services, and the components/deployment in a reference architecture of secure network infrastructure in Section 8.4.

which affects the IoT deployment most. Among them, the underlying technology of the IoT layer security are physical relative security, corresponding to the underlying physical requirements of Maslow's demand model, which has been discussed in Chapter 4. When referring to the physical data protection, the blockchain is given as an example technology in Section 7.4.4, together with the introduction of physical unclonable function (PUF).

IoT security management is mainly about the macro-view of IoT; it also includes the IoT security design, IoT security standards, and so on. These two points are introduced in Section 8.4. Next, every layer security technology and security policy will be discussed according to the four-layer structure of the IoT.

The idea is that the security cognition of the IoT can strengthen the positive energy of "security"; the regulation strengthens the security idea and prevents the violation of the security idea morally; the law further strengthens the idea and the regulation, restricting the "negative energy" with punishment. For example, the IoT security concept at least lets us know that peeping at other people's privacy in the IoT world is as immoral as peeping at others bathing. The relevant legislation can consider evidence and punish peeping behavior.

The management of IoT security is a series of organizational norms for the effective organization and implementation of IoT security technologies and strategies in the IoT system, ensuring the user's security and managers' control over IoT security. After all, users do not need to immerse themselves in technical details.

The next discussion in this chapter will converge to technical issues, corresponding to Fig. 8.3, the middle part of the IoT security system framework, i.e., technical layer of IoT perception security.

8.3 Security in Perception Layer

If skin did not exist, fur would also not exist. So, the security and privacy protection of things and information collected at perception layer are the prerequisites of IoT security in technical and functional views. The quantities and qualities of data which are collected by IoT are more and sensitive, and they are related to security. Therefore, the privacy protection in IoT world is very necessary.

Privacy protection should run through all processes of the product design, should start at the front end of product design, and should satisfy the expectations of the people of the European Union.

For respecting and protecting people's privacy, the concept of privacy design should be used to resist all behaviors of collecting a large number of data for IoT application. Therefore, enhanced privacy control and IoT security technology and strategy should be used for IoT infrastructure.

8.3.1 *Perception security technology*

Privacy protection and IoT information security have been fundamental challenges of IoT security studies for a long time. The simplest IoT security scheme is that encrypting or decrypting of data collected at one point and decrypting or encrypting of data transmitted at another point. However, there have also been a lot of questions over this scheme even if the best encryption technology was employed.

8.3.1.1 *Lightweight encryption*

There is a common principle that one might not bring a key heavier than the lock. The IoT perception devices could not be operated with complex encryption mechanism for the limited resources, processing ability, telecommunication, and storage volume. So, a lightweight encryption, which is easy to carry, with less resource cost and less scale, should be developed.

More securities could be supplied by lightweight encryption. It is well known that AES way is used on limited equipment based on group widely. It is discussed that the application and usability of public encryption mechanism used on limited equipment in the reference. The importance on encryption management scheme is also discussed in detail. And two encryption management schemes are also provided in the reference. One is Hash function based on symmetric encryption like SHA-3 and lightweight function Hash is one of the future development directions (e.g., signature). Another is asymmetric encryption like encryption management scheme based on ECC (Ellipse Curve Cryptography). Although smaller key than standard public key should be used, the fault is its lower executive efficiency.

It is easy to intercept key when swapping key without encryption in IoT perception layer, especially on attack situations. However encryption algorithm not only satisfies for energy efficiency but also develops in optimized security performance continuously. It should be considered that encryption algorithm optimization, password allocation and storage, especially lightweight design for public key and private key mechanism, together with the end-to-end security design.

8.3.1.2 *Signature and authentication*

Upon a super-link IoT world, data flow is of high coupling and open, which denotes the data flow may be illegal tampered at storing, processing and transmitting even if data transmits in security tubes. However these multi source data flows also could be protected by information level protecting mechanism completely. The malicious data without authority would be recognized with asymmetric encryption security signature scheme.

Signature: Signature means non-completeness data will not be adopted. Signature is the technical ways for validating completeness of data. It could also be used for validating identity of data source. There has a simply method for signature validating that MAC should be added between sender and receiver in order to ensure message completeness. There has also some questions should be considered as follows,

(1) The PKI/PKC infrastructure and application special design for things of IoT.
(2) The signature scheme about top secret or private like bank data or account data (e.g., digital currency).
(3) The signature rights about things and holding accountability.

When considering the signature for limited equipment running codes, code signature should be used to protect equipment from executing unsigned code and lower the probability of attack.

Many sorts of code can be signed, including tools, applications, scripts, libraries, plug-ins, and other "code-like" data. In addition, we can create signed installer packages in firmware or hardware level. The efficiency on code signature depends upon security of signature key since it as a authentication mechanism. All executing code upon perception level should be signed in order to avoid malicious code executing which covering on normal code. Like signature, it also needs Hash function or PKI to achieve the completeness of system in order to avoid accessing, tampering and executing unauthorized.

Authentication: Authentication is a validating and authorizing mechanism upon IoT perception level, is also a technical method that validating data operator and ensure secure dialog/session. It is considered from two points as follows.

One is validation authorization management among inner nodes of perception level. Key management mechanism of IoT perception level is the recognition and validation basis among other nodes in IoT perception level, secure dialog could be constructed through authorization under this basis. Identification and authentication methods should be used to authorize perception level normally and mutual authentication between nodes is established by sharing key.

Another is IoT perception level nodes authorization for users. As the entity out of IoT perception level, users often manage or access perception level nodes and collect data. When users want to access IoT perception level, authorization should be obtained from authorization center in IoT perception network first and relative nodes would be accessed only with relative key (e.g., access control systems). It is worth noting that the entity is not only people but also a computer program or the agent.

8.3.1.3 *Watermark*

In IoT world, many heterogeneous networks, various perception equipment collect, store, and process data, and the data are transferred to information partly relying on models, service, and middleware. However, intelligent decision could be made by only combining these data with its context. Similarly, malicious attack could be accomplished only if perception data and its context could also be fused sufficiently.

For example, for avoiding personal information use maliciously, Mr. Zhang gives "Zhang X bank" as his account name when he registers at the X bank website, and he gives "Zhang Y insurance" as his account when he registers at insurance company named Y; similarly, he would know which company leaked his personal information when he answers the phone and the caller may recall him as Zhang X or Y which denotes his account.

In the above example, Mr. Zhang hid part of his name and added sign of cooperation organizations as a simple watermark in order to avoid malicious use of personal information. Moreover, Mr. Zhang could also judge which caller according to the watermark he added. So, the watermark not only protects the user's proprietary rights for privacy but also pursues the malicious use of privacy. The utilization of watermark should consider some questions as follows:

- Compatibility with other secure techniques.
- Completeness of equipment and applications between ports or ends.
- Privacy design should rely on variety of perception data.

There is a privacy design solution, in which every data entity could authorize someone to collect, store, and process the personal data and only for special and relative purpose. Contrary corresponding privacy design should be made according to different scene which needs variety of privacy data, such as relative privacy data should be processed according to special applying scene. It would be discussed in the following chapter on wipe scene sign. Similarly, one could agree with the other one for getting and processing his private data and could also hide his personal data not related with the other one.

Other perception security techniques are secure router technique of perception level and access control technique.

Security technique application based on data security and privacy protection start from perception data port, through many middle processes, such as data arriving at applying port through different middleware after data leaving the perception layer. There may be some leaks of data when passing through such processes. There are also some leak possibilities when applying even if at the security perception layer, such as SCA attacks. Thus, checking leak security strategy should be developed for avoiding unforeseen leaks.

8.3.2 *Perception security strategy*

There is an example for explaining the relationship between security strategy and security technology. People often set more complex passwords with numbers and letters and avoid birthday, certificate, and telephone number, thus it might be secured. However, these passwords might still be intercepted and cracked. Nevertheless, security technique is more secure by combining theory and practice.

8.3.2.1 *Compressed sensing (CS) on data*

Compressed sensing technique 23 used on WSN could be used to compress data which are collected from sensors. Compressed sensing is suitable for compressing data which are the same step with data collection and lightweight lossy encryption. CS with lightweight lossy encryption is the kind of security strategy in the view of application.

In fact, we are all living in a CS world unknowingly. From CD to MP3 and VCD to DVD, language is a compression of motion communication with expression, gesture, and spot. All this are compressed in a phone. The development scene of human beings could be reflected on technique development field; in other words, the reason and target of technique development are social development.

It needs enough memory and process ability when analog signal of sound and video transfer to digital signal. However, with the development of society, these memory and processes become insufficient. How to deal with this situation? The simultaneous compressing and collecting is proposed.

For IoT, when the volume on local data processing can be reduced, in other words, when one and one barrel of water should transfer to the big barrel on backstage and extract useful information, is it necessary having more extracting water to be transferred to backstage if one and one barrel of water can be extracted locally? The extraction denotes CS and encryption. A kind of technique that real-time extracting CS encrypting key could support data encryption of IoT sensing equipment and it utilizes channel measure for extracting keys without any key allocation mechanism. This should defend against detecting attacks, such as an SCA attack, efficiently.

CS contributing to secure strategy should extend to communication technology. The principle like the transfer from time domain to frequency domain in communication principle should be extended to cover more than CS.

8.3.2.2 *Wiping scene mark*

The scene relative marks of who, where, and when are often mentioned in our first writing class. It could protect privacy if one of the following was wiped.

(1) Anonymity: Anonymity denotes hiding who. For ID is the only one sign of IoT, anonymity technique could protect privacy through fuzzing perception information like ID, namely updating or hiding local or global original perception information.

(2) Anonymize location: Anonymity location denotes hiding where. LBS is one of the important IoT applications. User's location privacy protection is an important service of IoT when users apply LBS like GPS. The location protection method is as follows:

- A trustworthy third party should be brought in between user and the LBS provider in order to anonymize user information;
- User should send location message to the trustworthy third party when user needing to visit LBS server;
- *Privacy protection service* makes sure that the sent location message doesn't contain the user accuracy location when none is necessary but instead of a mask block including many other user's LBS information (the k-anonymity as an example will be given in Section 8.7).

(3) Anonymize time: Anonymized time denotes the hiding of when. It is well known that time is very important in web and privacy, such as people should only be at one place at the same time. The methods of anonymized time are as follows:

- Time should be hidden in unnecessary fields or applications automatically, such as time information of image (or video) should be anonymized after a period of monitoring when no unusual action occurs in a public entrance monitor.

- Another option is reducing time precision by cutting and adding random disturbance for the time expression in IoT applications.

(4) Anonymized scene factors and relationship: Scene should be extended to six factors that is when, where, who, why, how, and what. It should be considered as privacy protection method when one or two factor is wiped for breaking the relationship of these scene factors.

(5) Reducing data precision: Partly anonymity, pseudonym, or disturbance could also be accomplished by lower data precision suitably. But these methods could not achieve complete anonymous. The principle of attack is like the mosaic recover program that scene analysis (e.g. the correlation factor) might recover part core data.

8.3.2.3 *Discussion*

One method of privacy protection service denotes making the minimum data to avoid scene correlation attacks. The principle of Occam's Razor–Ockham's Razor means that entities should not be added or multiplied unnecessarily. Some ways of privacy protection service are as follows.

- **Minimum privacy data:** Minimum privacy data could be transferred to the network by designing privacy protection service content. IoT engineers should have the ability to know necessary and unnecessary information with their professional knowledge. The best position of minimizing privacy data located in the perception layer, the source of data generating.
- **Privacy protection agent in middleware design:** Information collecting middleware should also use privacy data in authorized service and provide data protection upon or across the perception layer. A kind of privacy agent technique was proposed in reference. On one side, agent should contact with user, on the other side, it should also have contact with supplier. So, the supplier only gets necessary information, while user could set the priority rights of agent, and set and control privacy agent strategy.
- **Key management strategy:** Key management of perception layer not only contains about generating and allocating but also updating and

propagating mechanism. Integrating key management and distributing key management are two usual methods of key management.

Finally, it should be explained that hardware security of perception layer is not equal to security of perception layer of IoT simply. Perception security technique not only includes security strategy of privacy protection, whatever perception security technique or perception security strategy is not independent on security of network layer and application layer of IoT. In this section, the secure analysis of heterogeneous devices in the perception layer is given for the related security technologies used to enable secure perception. The secure networks as a whole are the issues included in the following section.

8.4 Security in Networks and a Reference Architecture

In the evolving IoT market, security goes beyond securing the information exchanged among the IoT nodes. The entire operation of an IoT ecosystem depends on protection at all levels, from single devices to communications. Moreover, devices must exhibit a high level of resilience against a growing range of attacks, including hardware, software, and physical tampering.

Security is therefore critical to IoT technologies and applications, and end-to-end security is essential to enabling the implementation of trustworthy IoT solutions for all stakeholders in IoT ecosystems and IoT value networks to enable the development, deployment, and maintenance of systems in IoT applications and provide a common framework to enable the growth of IoT value network solutions.

The standard security services that are valid for the Internet framework and technology, such as authentication, confidentiality, integrity, non-repudiation, access control, and availability, should be extended to also apply to IoT technologies but adapted with their particularities and constraints in mind. These will be covered as security technology and mechanics in the following section.

First of all, a 3-D IoT security layered architecture capturing the IoT systems functions and cross-cutting functions is presented in Fig. 8.4. In this figure, the system security hierarchy on Z-axis includes equipment/device, edge, workshop, enterprise. and cooperation as the integration of

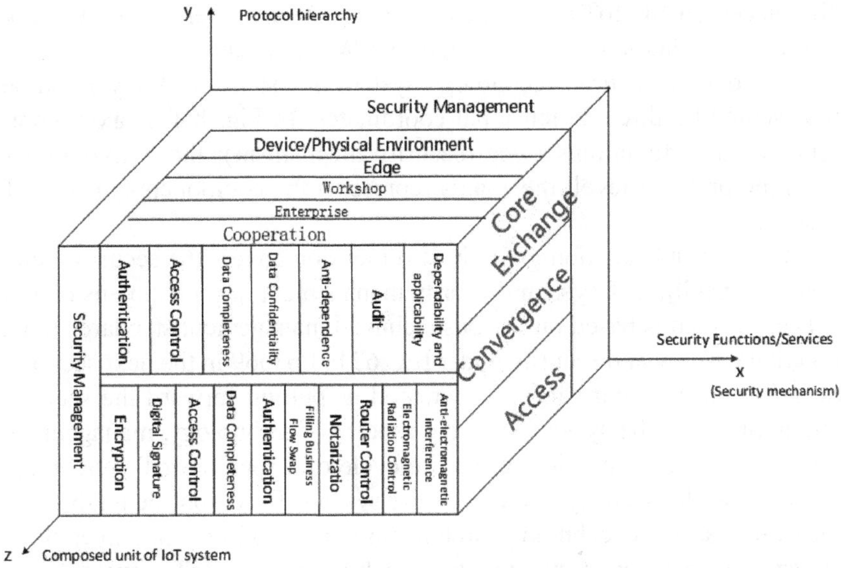

Figure 8.4 Security technological system of information system.

systems on different sites, which is described in I4.0/IMSA as hierarchy levels.

8.4.1 *A reference security architecture of IoT network layer*

It can be seen from the above that the security of the IoT is the integration of a series of security cognition, security technology, and security management to realize the confidentiality, integrity, authentication, non-repudiation, and availability of information, ensuring the control of system resources and ensuring the safe, stable, and reliable operation of the system, for managers, users, and other stakeholders. The network layer of the IoT mainly includes the integration of network security, information security, and infrastructure security. The network layer of the IoT can be divided into access layer, convergence layer, and core exchange layer, as shown in Fig. 8.4. IoT network security technology has been covered with a lot of discussion and model analysis. In Fig. 8.4, we try to build network layer security technology architecture. It should be emphasized that the IoT does not necessarily have to be IP access, for example, in the section of "M2M technology", the MTC service development of 3GPP and the

"ID" access in NB-IoT deployment; they also need a reference framework of security technology system supporting WAN coverage.

The overall security technology system of IoT network layer can be represented by three-dimensional coordinates: In Fig. 8.4, X axis represents security function/service (security mechanism); the Y axis represents the protocol level; the Z-axis represents the components of the IoT system.

The security function given in X dimension covers the security function of a specific IoT system. Security management in each dimension is a concept, which is based on various technical management standards (e.g., functional safety and security under IEC 62443/63069 in the next section). Security management can be understood as putting forward the security requirements of the system from the aspects of technology, management, process, and personnel during the life cycle of a specific IoT system and formulating the security strategy of the system. Based on the analysis of the overall security technology architecture of the IoT network layer, there are specific technical requirements in each layer of the IoT network.

(1) Secure access (sub-) layer: Perceptual information enters the network at the access layer. The security technology of access layer mainly includes sensor network/WSN security, gateway security, the key management, etc. For example, denial of service (DoS) attack and denial of sleep attack on the nodes/devices in perception layer; node identification, authentication, and access control; node hardware level damage (anti-EMI for physical security) and network repair (self-healing); integrity authentication, message verification, watermark technology, and other mechanisms to ensure the confidentiality and security of task or service deployment and execution; (lightweight) cryptographic protocol and key management, and the security level setting by multi-factor authentication (MFA) with password included (compound identification and authentication) technology and mechanics. This layer is the transition sub layer from the perception layer to the network layer, some of which overlap with the security technology of the perception layer and the communication sublayer of IoT.

(2) Convergence (sub-) layer security technology: The convergence layer is located between the access layer and the core exchange layer, which connects the user's traffic of the access layer and performs local routing, filtering, balancing, and other processing. Consistent with the information security technology system in Fig. 8.4, other considerations are as follows:

When the IoT network layer uses the satellite network, security technology for data link, and other private networks to carry the private data flow (e.g., IIoT data or semi-public like 5G slicing); the security technology of heterogeneous network convergence; wireless spectrum management technology in wireless network; network invulnerability technology; secure routing technology; cognitive radio technology, etc.

In fact, this layer shows some edge characteristics, such as the M2M convergence on the MEC of cellular RAN (or base station).

(3) Core exchange (sub-) layer (wide area application or platform oriented) security technology: This layer usually refers to the WAN bearer, which is consistent with the information security technology in X–Y plane of Fig. 8.4. In addition to the existing SSL (a communication encryption protocol between a website and its users) and TLS (transport layer security and authentication protocol) security protocols, we should focus on the following:

Access control of hierarchical perceptual data (database); behavior authentication, record, and evidence collection (e.g., notarization of secure acts); information (cyber/software) security; digital signature (watermark), authentication, cryptographic algorithm, data (information or evidence) tracking technology, etc. These can be extended to a variety of IoT terminals and systems to achieve end-to-end security, especially for an IoT platform or the applications in it. For example, if compared with the ISO/OSI network reference model, the core exchange layer covers the layers from the fourth to seventh, but this layer is always involved in a platform as OneM2M or OPC UA, from the business or functional applications view.

In short, the IoT network security architecture needs to provide a comprehensive security technology guarantee for the whole network security of the IoT system.

Now, it seems that the IoT through the network layer achieves a wide area bearing, many applications need IP access, access to IP network security — network security technology; is included in a general IoT network layer security technology, and it has been under more study. It is only listed here and will not be discussed in detail. Before the access layer of IoT network layer, the part of perception layer security has been discussed in detail in the section of perception layer security of IoT. Network security management system and network security organization system, which are inseparable from network security technology system, will not be discussed here. In the section of IoT application layer security, we will try to discuss the technologies and strategies that IoT as a large and unique information system should consider from a more macro perspective, combined with the application scenarios of IoT.

8.4.2 *Security technology and mechanics*

Different IoT topologies as the system hierarchy in the Z-axis of the reference security architecture requires different security configurations and strategies, and this is especially true at the edges, where devices can be diverse, small, and possibly out of reach for security updates. The edges are therefore vulnerable, providing entry points for malicious attacks, which are difficult to track and therefore easily propagate throughout the whole IoT ecosystem.

As edge devices, from the hierarchy level view, often range from unsophisticated edge devices (e.g., router, field/controller devices of EMS in Section 7.3.2) to local management station, it may be difficult to build security into the design. However, it is here that edge collaboration among IoT grids may come to the rescue. Edge devices may form IoT zone/domain, where they collaborate and share resources and functions in the presence of perceived danger (see Section 4.7). Each edge device, now belonging to an IoT defense zone, will exhibit collective intelligence and be able to evolve and adapt to new requirements and threat situations. The collaboration on the edge helps to identify the threat and define its landscape. For example, blockchain technology has been developed for scale and with interoperability in mind; hence, it is often generalized as DLT. Its security mechanism, based on public ledger and consensus, is applied across the communication stack and the network, whether this is centralized, decentralized, or distributed (see the example in Section 7.4.4.).

Nevertheless, in spite of all security advancements, guarding against single scenarios of fraud, hacking, and other breaches still needs a comprehensive view of both the security plane (*X*–*Y* plane) in Fig. 8.4 and the security management, which are crossed by secure access layer, secure networks layer, and secure core exchange or application layer. Some of them are listed in Table 8.2.

Table 8.2 The security mechanics and management.

Security technology or mechanics	Contents	Remark
Identification	The act of allowing a device or service to be specifically and uniquely identified without ambiguity. This may take the form of RFID tag identifiers, IP addresses, global unique identifiers, functional or capability identifiers, or data source identifiers.	Bio-ID is also discussed in Chapter 4.
Authentication	The act of confirming the truth of an attribute of an entity or a single piece of data by using passwords, PINs, smart cards, digital certificates, or biometrics to sign in. In contrast to identification, authentication is the process of actually confirming the identity of a device or confirming that data arriving or leaving are genuine and have not been tampered with or forged.	MFA
Authorization	The function of specifying access rights to resources and ensuring that any request for data or control of a system is managed within these policies. Authorization mechanisms tend to be centralized, which may be a challenge in IoT systems that tend to be increasingly decentralized, without an authority involved. Whatever the degree of democratized authorization, where more entities can grant permissions, the authorization system must be consistent, persistent, and attack resistant.	Access control (AC) using attribute-based AC see Section 8.6.
Availability	As with mainstream information assurance, the system must provide data and resources in a timely manner for a set percentage of the time (e.g., 99.99% uptime availability).	Resilience in the IoT is also included, which is critical that many devices are available or retain their critical functionality, even if the system has undergone an attack.

(*Continued*)

Table 8.2 (*Continued*)

Security technology or mechanics	Contents	Remark
Confidentiality	A set functionality that limits access or places restrictions on certain types of information, with the goal of preventing unauthorized access.	Confidentiality is usually achieved through encryption and cryptographic mechanisms and is essential within an IoT ecosystem where a large amount of information is exchanged among the nodes.
Integrity	It is defined as providing consistency or a lack of corruption within the IoT system. It requires the final information received to correspond with the original information sent and that data cannot be modified without detection. Malicious modification of the information exchanged may disrupt the correct functioning of an entire IoT ecosystem.	A critical measure in information assurance.
Non-repudiation	An aspect of authentication that enables systems to have a high level of mathematical confidence that data, including identifiers, are genuine. This ensures that either a transmitting or receiving party cannot later deny that the request occurred (cannot later "repudiate") and provides data integrity around the system.	This is of particular importance in terms of tracking illegal activities within an IoT system, as it allows for accountability to be enforced. Whether non-repudiation needs to be enforced under certain circumstances will depend on the particular applications.
Root of trust	An immutable boot process within an IoT system based on unique identifiers, cryptographic keys, and on-chip memory to protect the device from being compromised at the most fundamental level.	The chain of trust extends the root of trust into subsequent applications and use cases. Given that IoT systems rely on a

		large number of devices that collect and process information, it is paramount to ensure their credibility so that they are honest and leverage correct outputs. For examples, see Section 8.6.
Secure update and patching in time	The mechanics enable IoT systems and devices to install new firmware from authorized sources without the firmware being compromised. Software updates are critical processes and are susceptible to a number of threats and attacks. During an update, the device receives the firmware wirelessly and installs it, removing the previous version. However, to reassure that the process is being done properly and securely, the sender of the firmware should be verified as trusted, the firmware should be validated as not compromised, the initial security keys should be protected, etc.	Additionally, depending on the services that the device offers, the downtime during a firmware update may need to be kept at a minimum. If not properly protected, devices may be open to manipulation, typically through the installation of malicious code on a device.
Access control	A flexible and secure control system in which subject requests to perform operations on objects are granted or denied based on assigned attributes or roles of the subject, assigned attributes or roles of the object, environment conditions, and a set of policies specified in terms of those attributes or roles depending on conditions. As ABAC is still in its maturation phase, a new model called ABAC-them was introduced. It focuses on combining simplicity and expressiveness, and its main characteristics are	MAC (mandatory access control); RBAC (role-based access control); ABAC (attribute-based access control). For examples, see Section 8.6.

From services or management views, security is often related with a certain IoT sector, or IoT solution; see the following part.

8.5 IoT Security and Secure Communication

As introduced in Sections 6.6 and 7.2, the fourth industrial revolution (I4.0) has arrived in the industrial IoT (IIoT) sector. As characterized by the increasing digitization and interconnection of production, systems, value chains, and business models, RAMI 4.0 and intelligent manufacturing system architecture (IMSA) are presented and published in respective reference architecture models by Germany and China. The alignment of both models was agreed upon (see the white paper entitled *Alignment Report for Reference Architectural Model for Industrial 4.0*).

Based on the general functional safety standard IEC 61508 and domains-specific standards, e.g., IEC 61511 for the process industry (e.g., in the Industrial Automation Control System/IACS, or SCADA mentioned in Chapters 5/6), IEC 62061 or ISO 13849 for the machinery sector, and ISO 26262/ISO 21448 for the automotive industry; and the functional safety alignment work of both Platform Industrial 4.0 (Germany) and Intelligent Manufacturing Standardization Administration Group (IMSG of China); an I4.0/IM functional safety platform design is introduced in this section. From OT view, the relation between safety and security will be discussed in the following part. The relative RAMI4.0 and IMSA have been introduced respectively in Sections 6.2 and 6.6. For the DT abstraction details, see Section 7.2.

8.5.1 *Functional safety and security*

With more intelligent and digital technology required for IoT, the potential threat and security related attacks draw a wide range of challenges in the increasing number of information technologies, communication devices, and smart devices when being integrated into modern control systems. Although this can increase efficiency and reduce costs for industries, the overall infrastructure will become more susceptible to internal failures and more vulnerable to cyber-attacks.

In such a degree of complexity and interconnection among systems, as the RAMI4.0 or the DT cube-hierarchical levels mentioned above, dangerous events may be triggered in one corner but spread further in the adjacent layers or levels and of course within each layer. In this section, the bottom-top safety extraction and security analysis are given, which is a following part of the above-discussed I4.0/IM, RAMI4.0, and DT.

The anticipating functional safety in general is a kind of an attribute of physical devices (or the way such devices are used, e.g., in an IoT grid). As introduced in Section 7.2.2, for a given device, the connection to an administration shell that is handling functions required to establish the functions of the "digital twin", is explained in an IoT environment (e.g., an administration shell with different kinds of I4.0 elements). The administration shell may be part of every device or may be hosted by a dedicated piece of equipment handling the digital twins of one or multiple devices.

This administration shell covers all functions required to integrate devices into an I4.0 and IM application. Such a shell may cover a single physical device (e.g., a sensor), a functional group of devices (e.g., a PLC including its field devices, as shown in Fig. 8.5(a)), or a complete production unit (e.g., a machine or a process unit). In Fig. 8.5(a), the integrity of the safety function is related to the administration shell, which might provide safe and non-safe communication with its affiliated plus devices.

Each device/station equipped with an administration shell can either be used to handle an individual component or, alternatively, multiple components/devices can be hosted in the same shell, as shown in Fig. 8.5(b).

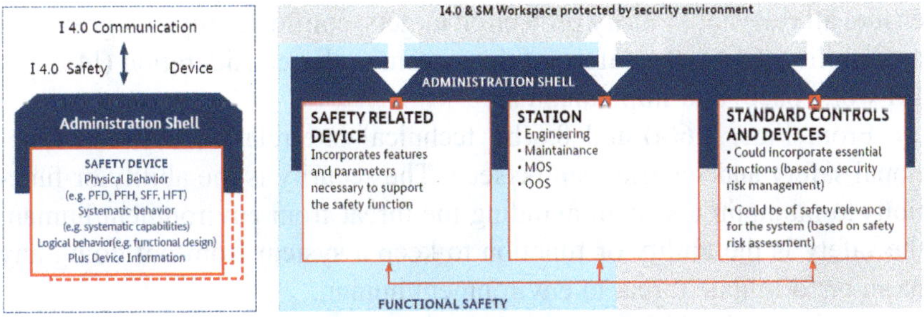

(a) (b)

Figure 8.5 Safe Administration Shell and the security environment. (a) Safe Administration Shell and (b) I4.0 & IM security environment for IM operational environment.

Notes: For probability of failure on demand (PFD), probability of failure per hour (PFH), safe failure fraction (SFF), hardware fault tolerance (HFT), see IEC 61508, which gives functional safety of electrical/electronic/programmable electronic safety-related systems.

Source: IEC 62443/63069.

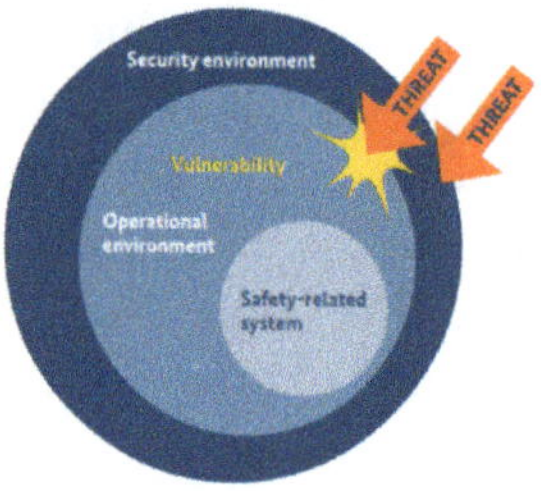

(a)

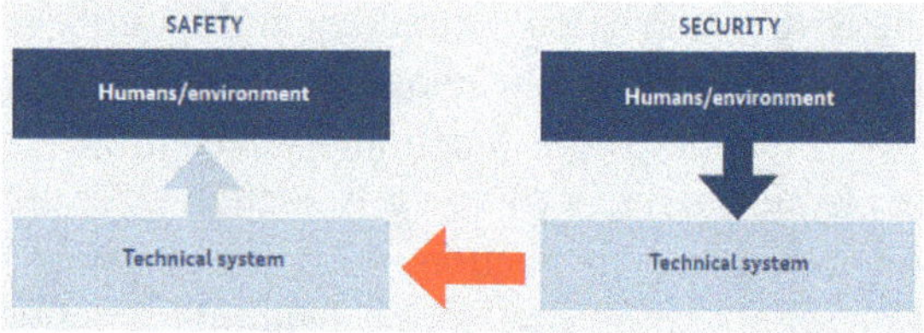

Security Design→Technical Estimation → Technical system under safety requirement→ Safeguard Implementing Management for safety

(b)

Figure 8.6 (a) Security environment and its coverage of the operational environment of the system (from IEC 63069) and (b) interrelation between functional safety and security (from IEC GUIDE 120).

In Fig. 8.6(a), safety-related devices and safety stations can be allocated in the I4.0 and IM workspace, under the protection of security environment, which is introduced in IEC 63069, by providing all security countermeasures necessary to meet the overall safety, a sufficient level of security, and the dedicated risk reduction realized though functional safety. In order to achieve these, sufficient protection for the operational environment of an I4.0 and IM workspace is described in Fig. 8.6(a).

In essence, all the security countermeasures in the security environment are defined based on a security risk assessment for the OT control system in the manufacturing domain. Basically, this is required in order to ensure all relevant security protection targets, confidentially, integrity, and availability (CIA), the safety of the system under consideration (I4.0 and IM workspace) and implemented.

From Figs. 8.6(a) and 8.6(b), technical interrelation between functional safety and security can be seen. The security is the ability or functions to maintain a system avoiding the threat from environment/human; the safety is the ability or function to keep a system from not doing any harm or formulate threat to environment/human.

In Fig. 8.6(b), if the process from threat to hazard is considered as an "event chain", the first half is the responsibility of security policy (before invading the systems), the latter half is the responsibility of safety (capability of system to prevent and control failures from random, to systematic, even to intended). For example, the threat may attack the end-user control (EUC) or EUC control systems instead of safety-related systems to trigger shutdown frequently and result in the field operators wrongly thinking that the problems do not lie with the safety-related systems.

8.5.2 *Communication in safety/security*

As introduced in Section 7.2.3, communications in/between I4.0 device/stations/workspaces and further linking to an IT system (for applications or business functions) or platform by administration shell (or other data models) is discussed. A safety station or a workspace is built up following the same concept applied for a safety device too; however, a station is connected to the area of business processes and interfaces between this part of the I4.0 and IM workspace and the data-handling domain (e.g., transformation in data model/information level, see Section 7.2.3).

Based on the safety communication covered by the measures of the security environment (see IEC TR 63069 in the footnote), safety-related components (including communication) in an I4.0/IM workspace constituting the operational environment are shown in Fig. 8.7.

If the administration shell is safety related, safety-related communication through the I4.0 and IM workspace is possible by allowing the connection of safety-related devices and stations, which is allocated somewhere in the I4.0 and IM workspace.

If such solutions are used, the related communication must be investigated for potential attack surfaces regarding security threats. Following the concept of defense in depth (see the next section) and the consideration of the criticality of essential functions as per IEC 62443, different architectural decisions on the implementation might be made.

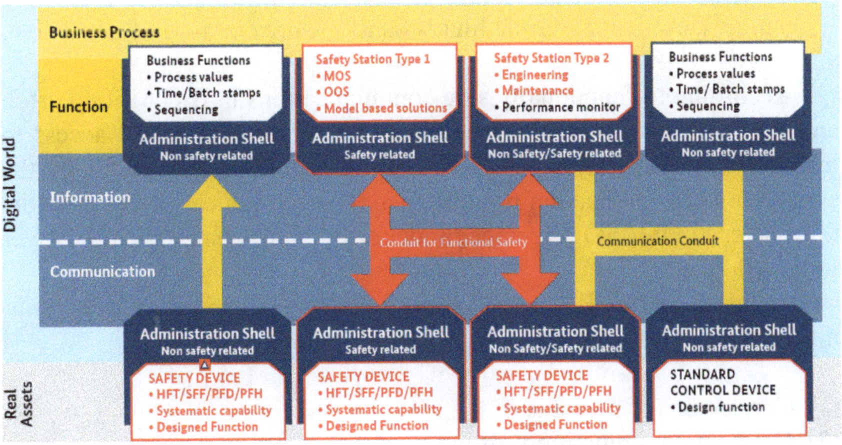

Figure 8.7 Communication in workspace.

In Fig. 8.7, the conduits (either safety related or not) between devices/stations shells (as different functional grids in Section 6.2), between a shell and an IoT zone (see Section 6.2), or between IoT zones are composed of different communication channels, protocols, and technologies (as introduced in the entire Chapter 5) at different levels. Some of them are packaged into a middleware, a platform middleware, or a platform (e.g., OPC-UA) according to the business scenarios (see Section 6.1). A bottom-up view, has been introduced in Section 6.2, and after that, with the discussion of IoT/I4.0 in Section 6.6.2, the layout of IoT zones and conduits in I4.0 is also shown. In the layout, different levels of conduits from device (physical grid), DT transition, to information/data, and to functions facilities the security risk assessment, which has to consider the possible impact on the safety risk reduction required by the I4.0 and IM workspace. For example, the following parts will be exposed as the functional safety below the information/data level, and the secure communication over the information/data level (through a public platform, such as OPC-UA). Either of the two parts is due to the constantly escalating threat of cyber-attack from enormous attacks conducted on industrial facilities worldwide, and the demand for secure and safe transmission protocols on I4.0 and IM applications growing in recent years.

- **Functional safety communication:** In particular to industrial communication and IoT (in the communication layer of IoT), this communication is the link to surrounding devices/systems and, from a security point of view, is therefore a highly sensitive area in need of protection.

According to functionally safe communications in IEC 61508 Part 2, and Fig. 8.7, this level of safety communication is below the access to information (fourth layer in RAMI4.0) and should be guaranteed by the safe/secure communication protocols (in the communication level, as the third layer in OSI/ISO reference model or the third communication layer in RAMI4.0).

At this level, the IEC 61784 series of standards in industrial communication deals with the following communications errors:

(1) Corruption (of messages);
(2) Unintentional repetition (of messages);

(3) Incorrect sequence (of messages, e.g., commands in the wrong sequence);
(4) Loss (of messages);
(5) Unacceptable delay (message data too old);
(6) Insertion (messages from unexpected sources);
(7) Masquerade (messages generated by functionally non-safe elements and treated as functionally safe messages);
(8) Addressing (delivery of messages to wrong recipients).

Countermeasures for the above lists in industrial communication and processes are also included in the IEC 61784 series, as shown in Fig. 8.7, as sequence numbering, time/batch stamping, time expectation, connection authentication, and cyclic redundancy checks (CRC) for data redundancy.

OPC UA safety communication is application independent and does not pose requirements on the structure and length of the application data. The most basic type of safety communication in Fig. 8.7 is bidirectional communication between two safety devices or between safety device and safety business function (Functional Entity), which are named as automation components (ACs) in OPC UA (either as safety provider or safety consumer, or both). In their communication state machines, the session between safety protocol data units (SPDUs) may also be protected by end-to-end latency guarantee.

- **Secure communication over the information/data level:** This communication is the link to public/semi-public networks or open platforms. The former (as the information layer of fourth layer in RAMI4.0) is given in detail in Chapter 5, ranging from LAN/PAN/WAN, satellite IoT to cellular IoT and proprietary LPWANs. The cellular network is a semi-public example because NPN and slicing are included in 5G technologies (see Section 5.8). Each of them has its own secure consideration. For example, Zigbee and its underlying IEEE 802.15.4 related security have been introduced in Section 5.5. Some of the former in security communication are discussed in Table 8.3. The latter will be introduced in the next section, as platform security.

By including confidentiality, integrity, and authentication, secure communication is always relevant when leaving protected networks

Table 8.3 Review of security technologies used in the LAN/PAN device domains to offer security objectives (e.g., authentication, integrity and confidentiality).

Forum(s), references	Security Targets (including the three basic pillars: confidentiality, integrity, and authentication)	Security technology
WiFi alliance	• Security technologies of WiFi • Authentication, encryption, integrity, replay protection	• WPA2 that uses counter mode with cipher block chaining message authentication code protocol (CCMP) based on 128-bit AES-CCM block cipher • Cryptographic hash function • Key management • Replay protection • WPA2 can be used in two modes: • Shared key: relying upon the use of a key shared by all Wi-Fi clients and access point • Enterprise, relying upon the use of an external AAA server
Bluetooth special interest group (SIG)	• Security technologies of Bluetooth • To enable authentication and pairing of Bluetooth devices, to encrypt the transmitted data, and to check integrity of transmitted data packets in Bluetooth network	• Frequency-hopping spread spectrum • Master clock is shared to slaves • Binding of devices is done through selected pairing mechanisms • Different security modes • Link keys to establish authenticated and/or encrypted ACL links

		• SAFER+ block cipher (not for encryption!) • E0 stream cipher • Secure simple pairing (SSP) with elliptic curve Diffie–Hellman (ECDH)
Bluetooth special interest group (SIG)	• Security technologies of Bluetooth low energy (BLE) • Similar problems to solve as in BT	• AES-CCM block cipher • Data can be signed with connection signature resolving key (CSRK), MAC, counter • Privacy feature to change private address on a frequent basis
ZigBee alliance	• Security technologies of ZigBee • Authentication, encryption, integrity checking, countermeasures against replay-attacks	• 16-channel hopping • Key establishment, key transport, frame protection, ad device management implemented mostly at the network (NWK) and application support sub-layer (APS) • AES-CCM to offer confidentiality and authentication, AES-CBC-MAC to offer authentication or AES-CTR to offer confidentiality. 32-, 64-, or 128-bit MAC and 128-bit key • Key sequence counter
ZigBee alliance	Security technologies of ZigBee RF4CE (lower power and simplified version of ZigBee for remote control and Zigbee input devices, see "https://zigbeealliance.org/solution/rf4ce/")	• Three-channel hopping • Simpler pairing mechanism than in ZigBee • AES-CCM with 128-bit key
EPCglobal	• Default security technologies of EPCglobal UHF Class 1 generation 2(v1.2.0) RFID tags • To prevent unauthorized writing and disabling and counterfeiting of RFID tags	• 32-bit KILL and ACCESS passwords • Locking of memory • Unique unprogrammable TID numbers

(protected by the security environment) and passing through public or semi-public networks. This does not only apply, e.g., if the internet or cellular network is used for communication. It must also be assumed that external access is possible when WLAN (WiFi) routes are used, which leads to the edge security issues (see the following section).

Security communication in the area of industrial communication is covered by the IEC 62443 series. Overall, the origins of the various methods vastly vary. However, all cryptographic methods have one thing in common: they have to withstand critical analysis by other recognized cryptologists in order to gain general acceptance. Other confidentiality, integrity, authentication, and credential mechanics are also important in the construction of a trusted chain or environment. The interaction of safety and security plays an important role for the entire automation system, or at least for the safety part of the system, and this applies in particular to industrial communication.

8.5.3 *Secure network technologies*

The emergence of the IoT ecosystem has led to the revision of the conventional network security paradigm. In the communication and networks layer of IoT, in essence, interconnect heterogeneous network segments, where the heterogeneity is expressed in terms of functional capabilities and information capacities. This encompasses, for instance, the interconnection of a WAN/cellular IoT with low-power network segments like WSNs in multi-hop communication schemes or through LPWAN gateways (see Sections 5.6 and 5.7). The security of communications involving several segments of the communication path from source to destination is secured using distinct credentials possibly managed by distinct parties involving rekeying operations at each transmission node.

From the view of end-to-end security, credential and its management model provide some reasonable security, according to the various parties involved in credentials distribution and management needs to trust each other, which will be discussed in the edge security use cases. This requirement is difficult to achieve in the case of M2M communications, and it is generally accepted that end-to-end security involving the use of a single set of credentials from source to destination is a better model.

However, when the communications pass through open networks or platforms, the deployment of end-to-end security is a challenging task as it requires solving the problem of trust distribution, either from a quality

Table 8.4 Secure network access and related security technologies.

Forum(s), references	Security technologies	Security contribution
IETF's IP security protocol (IPsec) concluded working group	IPsec	IPsec WG developed a security protocol in the network layer to provide cryptographic security services to support combinations of authentication, integrity, access control, and confidentiality. IPsec has been implemented, e.g., over 6LoWPAN (see Section 5.5).
IETF network working group	• EAP based authentication • EAP/TLS • EAP/TTLS • EAP/SIM • EAP/AKA • EAP/PEAP	EAP is an authentication protocol commonly used to secure access to wireless networks and point to point connections.
IETF's transport layer security (TLS) working group	• TLS/DTLS • To choose cipher suites for providing (mutual) authentication of end-points, encryption and integrity of transmitted data	Specifying new TLS and DTLS protocols and extensions to them. They run on top of transport layer protocols and provide, e.g., confidentiality and data integrity between two communicating applications. Both have been implemented, e.g., over 6LoWPAN.

of service (QoS) aspect, or from a security aspect, at a wide area interconnection level. At this level, different forums and organizations contribute many security technologies, as shown in Table 8.4. Secure network access and related security technologies.

In the perception layer, the secure communication in the device domain or the above workspace domain has been introduced from the view of IEC 63069 and IEC 62443. In IEC 62784-3, some principles for safety/security communication are given. In the communication and network layer, the corresponding security for IoT capillary communications occurs in diversity communications (typical LAN/PAN proximity networks). As shown in Table 8.3, the owner of this network has the responsibility to secure those communications occurring between the devices or the safety workspace and the gateway. Then, Table 8.4 lists the major network technologies, or security technologies used to secure the network access. These technologies provide, e.g., interoperability for secure communication in WANs but in some cases also secure the interoperable communication between devices in WANs and devices in LANs/PANs, even in a multi protocols platforms.

In some cases, there is a need to secure the connection between the gateway/device and the access point to the Internet (WAN) and keep the interworking of protocols in a secure environment. The platform security will discuss these cases.

8.6 Security of Platform and Application

The IMSA part of Section 6.6 is just a preparation of the securing IoT on the edge. Based on Chapter 6, it is seen that platform and service layer for the IoT architecture need to be defined in order to establish a solid basis for multiple stakeholder system for IoT applications, which can be found in Chapter 7. In addition, platform principles for solving the heterogeneity of technologies are needed to enable communication between objects and applications, which have not initially been designed to communicate together but support the heterogeneity of communications, as discussed in Section 6.1. An objective of the horizontal platforms is for the system architecture and application of autonomic computing principles. Such horizontal architecture is based on open standards to enable connectivity and interoperation with multiple IoT domains and heterogeneous devices and to enable reaching wide acceptance as a basis of multiple stakeholder IoT systems. In such a way, several different IoT domains could become capable of deploying the platforms, enabling interoperability, lowering the development cost, and boosting the arising IoT markets by contributing towards transferring from vertical towards more horizontal M2M markets.

8.6.1 *Platform security*

On a technical level, platform security approach requires standardization to take place on multiple levels: semantics, information modeling, communication protocols, perception layer (including data link layer and physical layer, at least); the latter two have been introduced above in functional safety device/workspace/communication, and the more relative standards in IIoT are IEC 61508, IEC 62443, and IEC 61784-3. From a platform view, semantics, information, and IoT details should be embraced by a common cyber-security convergence of IT and operational technology (OT) allowing a common IoT platform to be shared by IT and OT traffic while guaranteeing different levels of security (e.g., QoS) demanded by diverse IT and OT applications. In this section, some security technologies on a platform level are introduced and some importance aspects and use cases are discussed.

As introduced in Sections 5.7 and 5.8, cellular communication (e.g., 3G/4G/5G) infrastructure by MNOs is playing a more and more important role in IoT communication and networks layer, which is regulated by 3GPP, GSMA, OMA, and other stakeholders. From a generic security case, when using 3GPP communications to protect the radio transmission and networks, the SIM/UICC/eUICC card holding credentials used to secure the access to the wide area network is managed by the MNOs to achieve network access security. For example, when a device with its unique identities from international mobile subscriber identities (IMSIs) uses its SIM for device authentication which enables network level authentication and session key distribution based on the LTE authentication and key agreement protocol. A challenge-response protocol uses symmetric cryptography for LTE-M, NB-IoT, and EC-GSM-IoT supported algorithm negotiation to enhance overall security, as described in Section 5.8.

Some common security aspects are discussed in Table 8.5, and some platforms in the table can be seen as the M2M platform views. Platform layer often involves IoT communications and applications in a given sector, so the following security in platforms is discussed from some common platforms, such as M2M, JSON (middleware or WS aspect), OneM2M, and OPC UA. In the next section, security technologies

Table 8.5 Security in platforms.

Forum(s) or organizations	Security technologies	Security contribution
Open mobile alliance (OMA) LwM2M	• WTLS • To offer data integrity, confidentiality, and authentication of end points • GotAPI provides a total secure framework for applications to access external devices and internal apps through device Web APIs using Web technologies	To secure communication between a LwM2M client and a LwM2M server and protection against message replays Similar to TLS but originally meant to be used devices without TCP/IP Works over UDP or WAP datagram protocol (WDP) Using CBOR-based CBOR object signing and encryption (COSE) in OSCOR (see Section 5.6.3)
3rd generation partnership project's (3GPP) service and system aspects (SA) working group 3	MTC security from 3GPP, 5G relative security will be introduced in the following platforms security	• IMS security • Security of multimedia broadcast and multicast service (MBMS) • Generic bootstrapping architecture (GBA) • Key establishment mechanisms • Ongoing: security for system improvement for machine-type communications • Lawful interception
• IETF's JavaScript object signing and encryption (JOSE) working group • Used, e.g., in/by SAML 2.0, WS-Federation, OpenID OAuth 2.0[a], (see Section 5.6.3), XMPP, ALTO and to provide integrity of exigent (alarms)	• JSON security • To provide authentication, integrity and confidentiality, access control, and resource control	Standardizing integrity protection and encryption security services in order to increase interoperability of security features between protocols that use JSON

ETSI	ETSI M2M security architecture[b]	• Pre-provisioned device/gateway credential types, e.g., SIM/AKA or X.509v3 certificates • Defining M2M bootstrap procedures based on GBA, TLS, or EAP/PANA • Securing M2M service connection by GBA, TLS, or EAP/PANA • Securing mId (interfaces the M2M Gateway or device service capability layer and the M2M network service capability layer) by TLS or DTLS, XML security or relying access network security
OneM2M (Industrial Internet Consortium, IIC)	• Entities using proven authentication/authorization/encryption	Security service and access control in sensor/actor/data sharing, selective communications
OPC-UA(field-level safety communications for entities/applications/workflow), based on IEC 61784-3 series standards (functional safety for fieldbus)	• Cyclic communication, watchdog (local clock of the consumer suffices) • 32-bit CRC-polynomial • "Properness" shown for all data lengths between 1–1500 bytes • Calculated PFH-value suffices for SIL4 • IDs are used to detect authenticity errors such as misdirected telegrams • A monitoring number (MNR) is used to detect timeliness errors	The key aspects of the work for OPC UA safety are: • Uses OPC UA client/server (OPC UA pub/sub with or without TSN later on) • Unidirectional, bidirectional, and multicast communication patterns • Arbitrary network topology: line, tree, star, ring, mesh, and so on • Arbitrary structured user data, length: 1–1500 bytes • Dynamic establishment of safe connections during runtime • No requirements on regular (i.e., non-safe) network participants • No need for synchronized clocks • Unlimited number of network components and terminals • Unlimited data rate

(*Continued*)

Table 8.5 (*Continued*)

Forum(s) or organizations	Security technologies	Security contribution
OPC-UA (security architecture model): Defense in depth of the OPC UA security architecture	• Trusted information (by confidentiality, integrity, and authentication/CIA), including: encrypting messages on the transport layer, integrity and authenticity by signing messages on the transport layer, and availability by restricting the message size and returning no security related codes • Access control (AAA Framework), including: Authentication by username and password or X.509 certificate on the application layer; authorization to read, write values of a node or to browse the information model based on the access rights of the information model, access rights of the user or of the user's role; accountability, by generating audit events for security-related operations.For details, see Section 6.1.6, or the next table	• The OPC UA security model for administrators • X.509 certificate standard • Symmetric/asymmetric encryption • Message signing validates communications integrity • Message encryption keeps communications safe from prying eyes • Application identification provides measure of trustworthiness

Notes: [a]OAuth 2.0 is a framework that controls authorization to a protected resource, such as an application or a set of files, while OpenID Connect and SAML are both industry standards for federated authentication. WS-Federation created by Microsoft is an extension of WS-Trust, providing a federated identity architecture.

[b]See Section 5.7.4, or Ref. ETSI Technical Specification 102 690 Machine to Machine communications (M2M) Functional Architecture. V2.1.1. Available at http://www.etsi.org/deliver/etsi_ts/102600_102699/102690/02.01.01_60/ ts_102690v020101p.pdf.

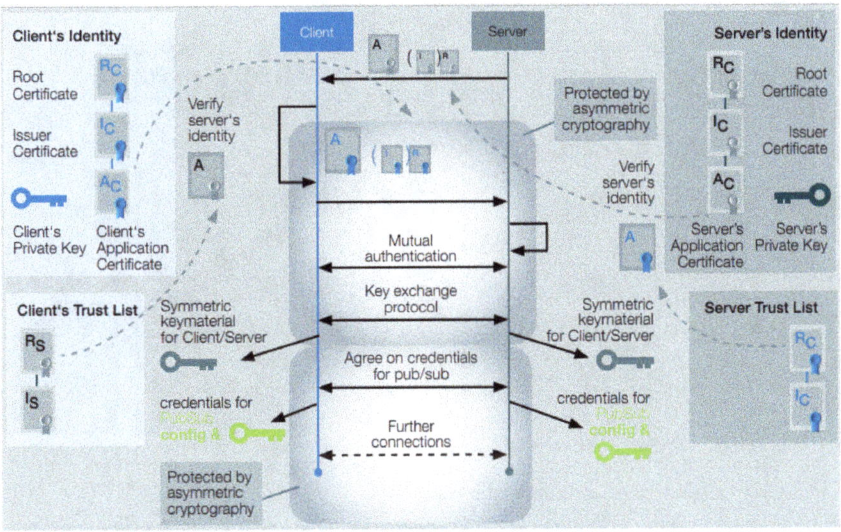

Figure 8.8 Mutual authentication plus obtaining credentials for Pub-Sub.
Source: OPC-UA.

applicable for application layer will be introduced from the views of IoT application layer, including the higher layers in ISO/OSI network reference model (e.g., seventh layer).

Security for the platform of field-level connections is taken as an OPC UA example, as shown in Table 8.5. In the details of OPC UA platform in Fig. 8.8, every field-level connection in the platform is authenticated and optionally encrypted by standard OPC UA security mechanisms specified for the client/server and pub-sub communication. The connection establishment is entered after an OPC UA secure session establishment is completed with the use of asymmetric cryptography with certificates and private keys (see Fig. 8.8). In this phase, the mutual authentication and the symmetric key exchange for the connection establishment are done. Thereafter, the connection manager (CM)[4] maintains the connection by this secure session up to the operational state of the connection.

[4]Connection manager (CM) is a service responsible for establishing connections between FEs (Functional Entity). It uses connection configuration data such as partner communication address, update rate, and QoS settings, to set up communication with one or more communication partners.

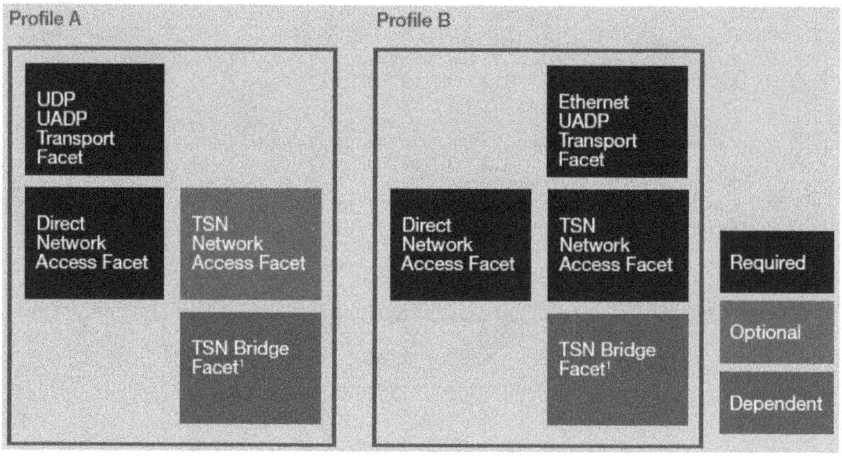

Figure 8.9 Structure of communications profiles.

Notes: If an automation component (AC) supports the TSN bridge facet and is implemented with an embedded Ethernet bridge, then it shall implement the TSN bridge facet.

In the OPC UA platform, standardization of information models for field-level devices in online and offline scenarios supports Ethernet TSN for deterministic communication and IT/OT convergence, and maps of application profiles (e.g., Profile A/B in Fig. 8.9) related to real-time operations on Ethernet networks including TSN, which requires a high-level QoS, such as latency and glitter (see Section 5.9). In Fig. 8.9, when a field level communications device allows for two communication profiles to be used with Pub-Sub communications, at least four communication facets are constructed in layers two, three, and four of OSI/ISO networks reference model. In the network access layer (layer three in OSI/ISO networks reference model), TSN is given as an optional. In more of the communication profiles with their optional facets, each profile can be used on a per-connection basis. Thus, if a controller conforms to multiple profiles, a control system engineer can make the optimum selection for each connection.

Finally, some additional contents covering the last item, security architecture model of OPC UA, is given in Table 8.5.

The security concept "defense in depth" realizes the information assurance by using multiple layers comprised in IoT platforms. As a result, an attacker must break through several barriers before compromising the whole system. In Table 8.6, the security features that OPC UA

Table 8.6 Defense in depth using the OPC UA security architecture.

Restricted data flow	Transport integrity and application authentication	Transport confidentiality and application authentication	Information model access control	Role-based/ user-based access control	Accounting	Availability	Security maintenance and incident handling
Non-permanent connectivity, firewall, network segmentation	Secure channel with security mode = "Sign", application certificates, trust list, revocation list, certified authority	Secure channel with security mode = "Sign and Encrypt", application certificates, trust list, revocation list	Least privilege (read, write, browse) for each node	Least privilege for each role, least privilege for each user, no privilege for deprecated roles and users, username/ password authentication, certificate based authentication, two-way authentication	Generate audit events for security related operations as: (Un) authorized connections, listing devices, rouge devices, access violations, read, write, discover attempts	Delay processing of open secure channel, in case of bad open secure channel requests, alarm incidents	Global discovery server (GDS) that provides pull/push management for: Provisioning certificates updating trust list, updating revocation list, renewal of expired/ compromised certificates

offers within the different layers are shown. Within each layer, several requirements can be fulfilled by using the corresponding OPC UA feature to improve the overall security.

8.6.2 *Security of service and strategy management*

8.6.2.1 *Data protection and encryption*

Data protection technology studies the verifiable authenticity of data, including the authenticity of data during processing. In short, it is to deal with the problem of "has my data been moved by others". When multiple entities participate in collaborative computing with private data, how to protect the security of each entity's private (private or confidential) data is a problem. That is to say, when multi-party cooperation is needed for calculation, each party only knows its own private data, and each party's private data will not be leaked to other parties, and there is no central trustor who can access any party's data. When the calculation is finished, each party can only get the correct final result but cannot get others' private data. This requires data protection in cloud computing. The current data protection system can realize the following: in the process of privacy (or secret related) data storage and processing, even if the calculation itself is executed by one or more untrusted processing units, the validity of the calculation results can be checked by verifiable calculation. Implementation of data protection system in the cloud is being tried. In addition to the protection of privacy data, whether the perception data of the IoT is processed correctly also needs data protection to verify. For example, cloud users can use data protection mechanism to check whether their data (or confidential data) has been correctly processed; on the contrary, if not handled correctly, incorrect (or malicious) handling should be easy to identify.

When data in a computing process performed by a cloud provider, this can be very useful if the process allows the authenticity of the computing operation data to be maintained. Homomorphic signature (homomorphic encryption) is a common technique that allows modification and maintains authenticity (see the next section). All of these privacy protection issues should be considered in a secure cloud service, such as QoS and SLA.

8.6.2.2 *QoS*

QoS refers to network control mechanisms that can provide various priorities to different devices or data flows or guarantee a certain level of performance to a data flow in accordance with requests from the application program. QoS guarantees are important if the network performance is critical, especially for real-time control applications.

The most common approach to delivering QoS in industrial automation networks was by providing differentiated services to different types of traffic. In this approach, some types of traffic are treated better than others by classifying the traffic and using tools such as priority queuing, enabling faster handling, higher average bandwidth, and lower average loss rate for the chosen types. However, this only provides a statistical preference, not a hard and fast guarantee. Different types of industrial Ethernet traffic (such as motion, I/O, and HMI) have different requirements for latency, packet loss, and jitter. The service policy should differentiate services for these types of flows. In open platforms, such as QoS, requirements of an OPC UA application should be configurable with no or only little dependencies to the underlying network technology.

Based on platforms and middleware, the hiding network details from the application makes it easier for the application builder to migrate applications (e.g., OPC UA applications) from one network technology to another or even to interconnect applications over different network technologies.

As to TSN, it provides standardized mechanisms to deliver guaranteed service by reserving specific resources from the network for specific types of traffic. Such network guarantees must be mapped to the network application or middleware (e.g., OPC UA Pub-Sub model).

Take TSN QoS mechanisms of OPC UA field-level communications as an example, the field-level communications define provisions for identifying important OPC UA traffic at the field level with both Layer 3 DSCP (differentiated services code point, defined in IETF RFC 2474, etc.) and Layer 2 CoS (class of service, defined in IEEE 802.1Q) tags for use in non-TSN managed networks.

The IEC/IEEE 60802 TSN profile for industrial automation defines a selection of QoS mechanisms specified by the IEEE 802.1 TSN task group for use in converged industrial automation networks.

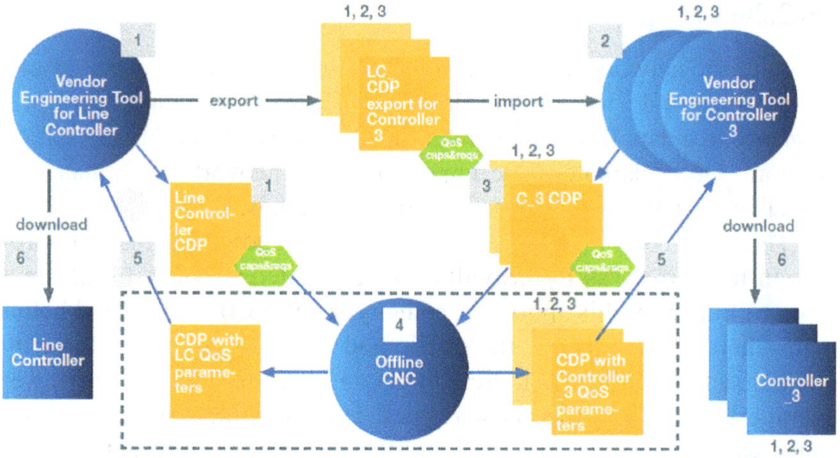

Figure 8.10 Example: A system with a line controller configuring three subordinate controllers.

Notes: C: Controller (e.g., PLC, DCS), caps & reqs: Capabilities & Requirements, LC: Line Controller, CDP: Configuration Descriptor Package.

Converged networks promise to enable OT which includes traditional field buses (e.g., PROFINET or EtherNet/IP), and traffic to operate the plant, e.g., HMI/SCADA/MES communication to PLCs, and IT applications to share the same physical network infrastructure without hampering operation of the other. For many industrial control applications, this implies that certain bandwidth, latency, and deadline requirements must be met, especially in situations where there is contention for network resources.

The configuration descriptor in OPC UA defines the functional entities (FEs), communication data sets, required QoS, and data necessary for connection establishment (such as unicast or multicast addresses for OPC UA Pub-Sub). In addition, for a field or I/O device, the configuration part may also contain parameterization data.

As in the field-level OPC UA, CM is an integrated service responsible for establishing connections between FEs. It uses connection configuration data such as partner communication address, update rate, and QoS settings, e.g., QoS option and their parameters (including TSN), to set up communication with one or more communication partners.

In workflow examples (as in Fig. 8.10), if the system with a line controller and three subordinate controllers without TSN, and configuration descriptor package (CDP) contains an index that helps to navigate through the stored information and a digital signature from the author (in this case the development engineer of the system integrator), the control engineer checks the validity of the signature and uses the CDP index to browse and find the publication information in a Pub-Sub mode, to set up the corresponding subscription and connection objects in the controller.

If the case of the above system with TSN, additionally, the CDP for each controller includes the QoS capabilities and requirements provided by the TSN mechanisms for each controller. The QoS capability is part of the product descriptor of the controller (contained also in the CDP), while the QoS requirements are part of the configuration descriptor.

In Fig. 8.10, QoS capabilities and requirements (caps & reqs) of all controllers (LC, C_1, C_2, and C_3) are imported from the CDPs into the offline central network configuration (CNC) to calculate the information needed for the TSN configuration (e.g., QoS parameters/TSN stream settings data). The output of the calculation is entered into QoS parameters/ TSN stream settings descriptors — one for each controller C_X.

8.6.2.3 *SLA*

Service-level agreements (SLAs) is facilitated with a high degree of control in a common virtualized environment, e.g., cloud computing, for a service-oriented offering. SLA SECURITY service ensures the security and integrity of the data produced, transmitted, and used within such IoT solutions. This is a critical area for the creation of trust within the IoT-enabled digital economy.

Without the assurance of the integrity of data (i.e., that the data has come from the sensor that it says it has, that the device has not been tampered with, and that the data itself has not been tampered within in transit), the decisions made upon such data can be of poor quality and even dangerous.

Some of the stakeholders are illustrated in Fig. 8.11, with viewpoints from upstream users of the data produced in IoT SLA solutions.

- From the data protection aspect, the following three recommendations should be considered:
  (1) **Data security:** At the time of designing IoT companies should ensure that data collection, storage, and processing would be

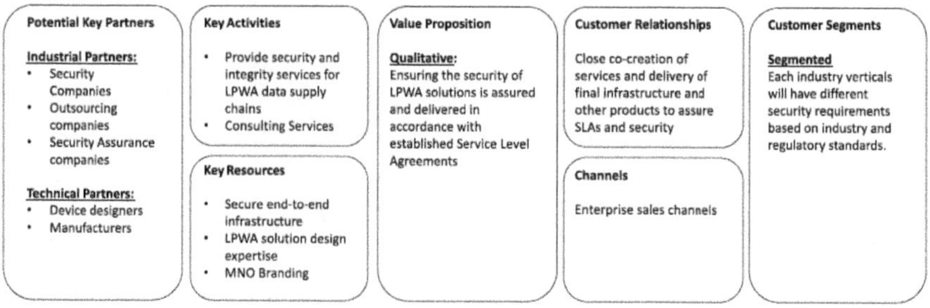

Figure 8.11. SLA security framework.

secure at all times. Companies should adopt a "defense in depth" approach and encrypt data at each stage.

(2) **Data consent:** Users should have a choice as to what data they share with IoT companies and the users must be informed if their data gets exposed.

(3) **Data minimization:** IoT companies should collect only the data they need and retain the collected information only for a limited time.

- From aspects of integrating and processing heterogeneous data collections, efficient methods for correlating, associating, filtering those data are taken into consideration. Further, their structural characteristics (due to the different data models) and also their quality, e.g., trust, freshness, provenance, partial or total consistency, are called for.
- From the cloud end, an "SLA-Guided Data Integration on Cloud Environments" was presented in dealing with integrating big data collections that are both weakly curated and sometimes described through metadata or schematics. The approach proposes three steps starting from query processing to the delivery of result sets. Given a query and a set of QoS preferences (cost, data provenance, service reputation, execution deadline, and so on), in Fig. 8.12, the system processes it in three steps. These steps generate intermediate results that are stored as knowledge to reduce the overhead of further query evaluation processes. Moreover, an integrated SLA is generated to archive negotiated rules obtained during the integration. For an incoming query, the whole process is monitored to determine whether the integration SLA is being honored.

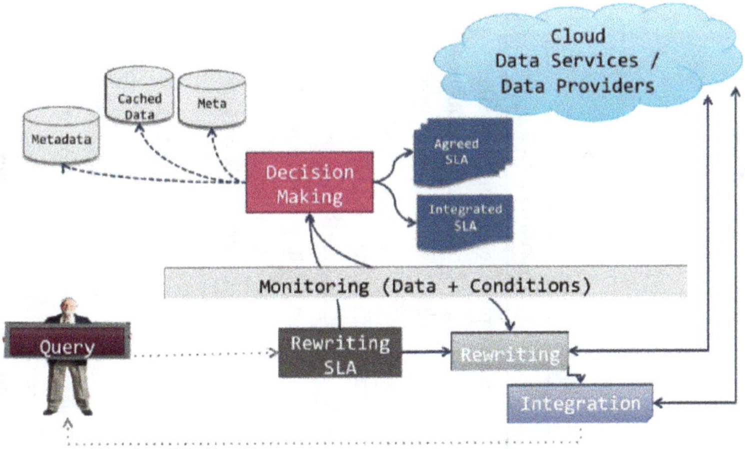

Figure 8.12 SLA-guided data integration architecture, where the system processes it in the following three steps: (i) SLA derivation, performed to filter possible data and services providers using a set of matching algorithms based on graph structures and RDF specifications; (ii) query rewriting for computing possible service compositions giving partial or exhaustive results according to defined SLAs; (iii) results integration into an answer.

8.6.3 *Security for applications layer*

A variety of applicable systems needs to be considered in the application layer of IoT, together with the corresponding security problem, network heterogeneity in terms of interoperability (e.g., WAN vs. LAN), and supported protocols. This interoperability requires defining dynamic configuration mechanisms and adaptive protocols to ensure end-to-end security for applications in public or semi-public networks.

From the devices end, most of them are involved in applications producing or consuming data which need to be secured from the source to the destination, either using hop-by-hop (e.g., different communication segments) or end-to-end security. In application domain security, the application providers or the service providers are typically responsible to manage the associated credentials.

Table 8.7 lists security technologies that have been or can be used at application layer, e.g., as M2M services and those also used in IoT platforms.

Table 8.7 Security technologies applicable for applications layer.

Forum(s) or organizations	Security technologies	Security contribution
W3C's XML security working group	• XML security • To provide authentication, integrity, and confidentiality	XML signature provides integrity, message authentication, and/or signer authentication services for data. XML encryption specifies a process for encrypting data and representing the result in XML. XKMS specifies protocols for distributing and registering public keys
IETF's web security (websec) working group	HTTP strict transport security (HSTS)	HSTS is designed to allow web sites or http servers to tell users' browsers or http clients that they want to communicate only over an encrypted connection
IETF's domain name system security (dnssec) working group	• DNSSEC • To provide secure DNS	Enhancements to the secure DNS protocol
IETF's simple authentication and security layer (SASL) concluded working group	• SASL • To provide authentication.	A framework for authentication and data security in Internet protocols. Application protocol that uses SASL can in theory use any authentication mechanisms supported by SASL

IETF	• HTTPS • Authentication of end-points, protection against man-in-the-middle (MITM) attacks, encryption of communication	Usage of TLS to secure HTTP connections
• IETF's authentication, authorization, and accounting (AAA) concluded working group, RADIUS extensions (radext) working group, diameter maintenance, and extensions (dime) working group • 3GPP	• AAA protocols • To authenticate entity's identification • To authorize the entity • To account aka track a network resource consumption	• Diameter • Radius • 3GPP EPS AAA
• MIT (Kerberos) • OpenID foundation	• Trusted key distribution centers (KDC) • Authentication and key exchange, sometimes also access control	• Kerberos 5 • OpenID • Single Sign-On (SSO)
SMQTT and SMQTT-SN (see Section 7.1)	Key/Cipher text policy-attribute based encryption(KP/CP-ABE) using lightweight elliptic curve cryptography	• Dos detection • Edge device security

In the application layer of IoT, different security technologies could be applied for enabling application security as shown in Table 8.7. There is very strong need for defining guidelines for the use of security technologies as in the IIoT domain. OPC UA gives an application example in the cases of very sensitive to misuse or time sensitive requirements for reliability, e.g., TSN. When both ends of the communication are mobile, there is the need, e.g., for advanced credential management, creation of trust, bridging mobile asset network and WAN security, adaptive secure elements, and horizontal end-to-end security solutions in a given platform. For example, creation of trust is traditionally established in hop-by-hop manner between M2M asset devices and M2M applications (e.g., LwM2M and OneM2M, see Tables 8.2 and 8.5).

This kind of model can be challenging in M2M systems because of M2M information content may be business critical and it may contain high privacy requirements. Therefore, these areas are also open for future research.

8.7 Cloud/Edge Security

Either of the edge[5] or cloud is due to the constantly escalating threat of cyber attacks, from enormous attacks conducted on industrial facilities worldwide, and the demand for secure and safe transmission protocols on IIoT (e.g., above I4.0 and IM) applications is growing in recent years. At the same time, the most obvious risk of connecting-as-a-service (see Section 6.2.3) is that it creates an expanded attack surface with countless points of vulnerability.

Distributed architectures and computing paradigms for IoT/IIoT inspired by neuromorphic computing with hybrid implementations based

[5]On the edge side, HW/SW in edge (upper than an on–board OS) with microservices are described here as an example and also as an extension from Section 6.4. Software architecture for IoT gateways includes a Linux-based OS, a scripting language such as Node.js, and a local Web server for simple local requests including Apache and nginx. Examples associated with microservices are Linux containers (e.g., kubernetics/k8s), open service gateway initiative (OSGi) bundles, scripts and actors in an actor model (e.g., akka@https://akka.io). These penetrating or hop-by-hop services arose more back doors when providing convenience.

on architectures for neural DL that could provide optimizing computing in such systems leading computing paradigm.

Embedding sensors/actuators, storage, computing, and advanced AI capabilities in IoT edge devices and integrate them within mesh or infrastructure architectures in the communication and networks layer, will enable dynamic, intelligent, responsive, peer-to-peer IoT end devices that exchange information with enterprise IoT platforms and conduct peer to-peer exchanges with other IoT devices operating across different industrial sectors. All the above trends need new methods and further design to keep the cloud and the edge secure.

8.7.1 *Secure by design*

"Secure by design" is the inclusion of security design principles, technology, and governance at each and every stage of the IoT journey. When an organization looks at creating, deploying, and leveraging connected technology to drive its business, security must be integrated into every component, tier, and application to preserve the integrity of the IoT solution and minimize the risk of cyber threats.

IoT technology requires a broad set of capabilities to help organizations achieve high levels of cyber-security. IoT platforms have numerous built-in security features, such as user access control, secure network protocols, and data encryption capabilities.

When developing IoT solutions around a standard platform, organizations develop security solutions for IoT devices in a consistent manner. In contrast, when organizations develop IoT platforms from scratch, it can unknowingly increase the potential for cyber-related risks.

- From platforms view, standard tools, methods, and technologies (see Section 8.5) of them can not only promote good design habits but help developers build strong security into their solutions from the outset, to meet different levels SLA and stakeholders. Typically, IoT platforms are commonly designed and tested holistically to validate that there is a high level of security deployed at every level, not only within individual components but for all components working together as a whole. Because platforms are used by more than one company, they benefit from "real-world" testing that helps expose hidden or otherwise unknown vulnerabilities, i.e., platforms have the potential to increase cyber risk because they provide a bigger and potentially more lucrative target for attack. When a vulnerability in a platform is found by hackers, typically they don't just gain access to one system but to many or even all systems that use the platform.

- From a functional view, because hazardous events can also be influenced by security attacks and not only by technical failures related to the system design in the interconnected IoT systems, based on the understanding of the systems and their risk, and the management of their complexity and security (see Section 8.4), the method of implementing different barriers for security is called Defense in Depth (including technical and organizational, as shown in Section 8.6.1) in order to prevent attacks, to detect security vulnerabilities, with risk assessments (example as shown in Fig. 8.13), technical, and organizational measures in place.

The challenge to protect a critical safety system in IIoT with completely interconnected systems is very high and safety cannot be guaranteed under all circumstances (although there is also no 100% safe system), but the desired security coverage is still from device/edge device, fog/cloud to applications as a security pipeline. An example of the two parts of the pipeline is taken as shown Fig. 8.14.

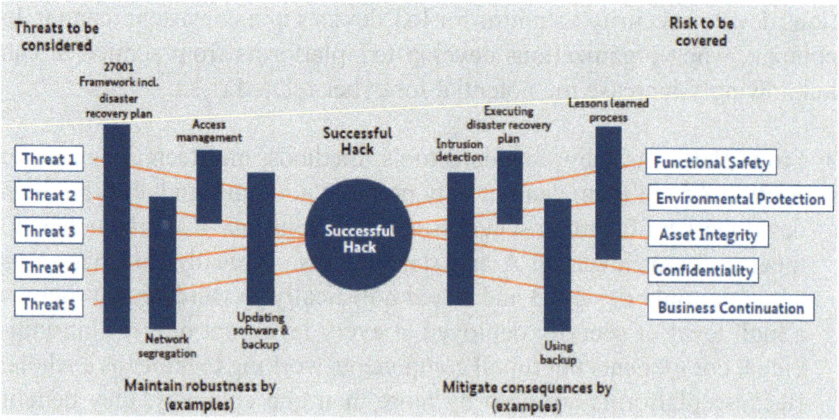

Figure 8.13 A generic security-related risk assessments model and context elements. *Source*: IEC 62443-1-1:2009.

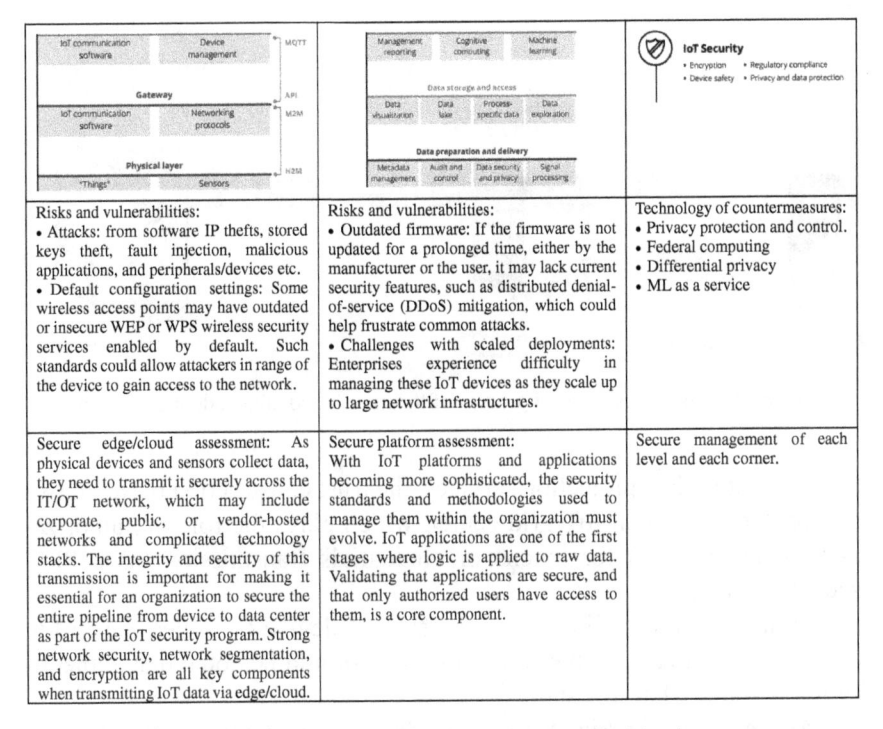

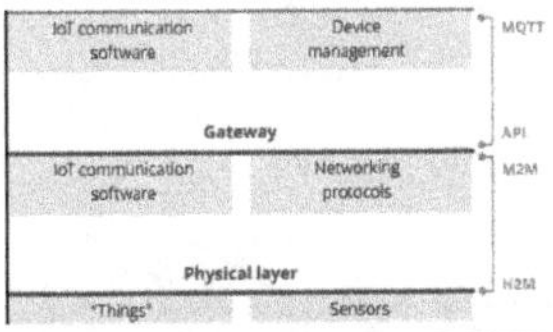	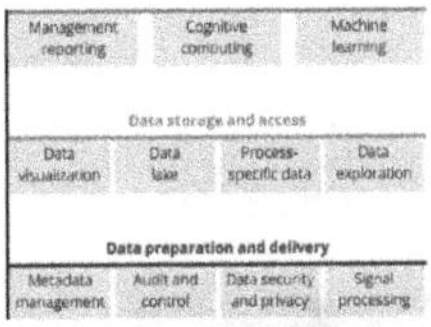	
Risks and vulnerabilities: • Attacks: from software IP thefts, stored keys theft, fault injection, malicious applications, and peripherals/devices etc. • Default configuration settings: Some wireless access points may have outdated or insecure WEP or WPS wireless security services enabled by default. Such standards could allow attackers in range of the device to gain access to the network.	Risks and vulnerabilities: • Outdated firmware: If the firmware is not updated for a prolonged time, either by the manufacturer or the user, it may lack current security features, such as distributed denial-of-service (DDoS) mitigation, which could help frustrate common attacks. • Challenges with scaled deployments: Enterprises experience difficulty in managing these IoT devices as they scale up to large network infrastructures.	Technology of countermeasures: • Privacy protection and control. • Federal computing • Differential privacy • ML as a service
Secure edge/cloud assessment: As physical devices and sensors collect data, they need to transmit it securely across the IT/OT network, which may include corporate, public, or vendor-hosted networks and complicated technology stacks. The integrity and security of this transmission is important for making it essential for an organization to secure the entire pipeline from device to data center as part of the IoT security program. Strong network security, network segmentation, and encryption are all key components when transmitting IoT data via edge/cloud.	Secure platform assessment: With IoT platforms and applications becoming more sophisticated, the security standards and methodologies used to manage them within the organization must evolve. IoT applications are one of the first stages where logic is applied to raw data. Validating that applications are secure, and that only authorized users have access to them, is a core component.	Secure management of each level and each corner.

Figure 8.14 An analysis use case from edge/cloud.

8.7.1.1 *Managing security risks at edge devices*

Although many edge devices include native security capabilities, such as wireless APs or virtual private network (VPN) servers designed to block a malicious user or device connection. Organizations must consider how best to implement these security features and other security methods such as device configuration and management, encryption, cryptography, system visibility, continuous monitoring, and access control to prevent the device from being exploited.

In order to discuss the security service belonging to a IoT edge grid for the responsibility or administration attribution in a given IoT grid, the access control process for a subject device is analyzed as an edge use case. The following use case is a location awareness-based access control system among edge devices indoor, to achieve the trust building process (as the seven steps shown in Fig. 8.15) with indoor positioning technology. The ultimate goal is to show that when the geographical location is closer

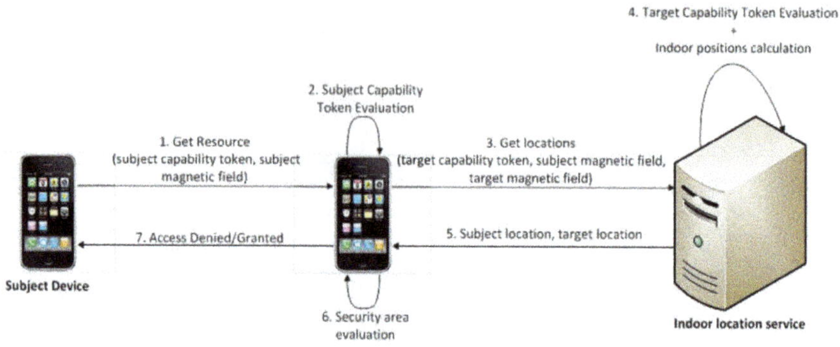

Figure 8.15 The access control process of location-based edge indoor environment.

to the target of data protection services, the trust construction between two device depends on an IoT grid center, which plays the role of authorization manager (AM) for tokens or credentials transmission (as a PIoT secure service).

In the previous offline phase, the subject device contacted the AM to obtain a token to access the smart object. It should be noted that authentication is required at this stage.

As described in Fig. 8.15, once the subject device is successfully authenticated, the authentication manager evaluates the policy and generates (if allowed) a credential representing the permission set associated with the smart object. When a new device joins the IoT grid (AM on the edge) covering area for existing resource access, the self-governor or the intercession ability within the IoT grid embodies as the secure PIoT service, which establishes a trust link among members in the given IoT grid.

- **MFA on access control:** MFA can be implemented both for systems designed to control administrative access to edge devices and for VPN connections. Alternative methods for MFA, such as authenticator applications, software tokens, and phone call verification are more secure to protect devices. The Bio-ID or composite feature identification can also be involved (see Section 4.3).
- **Secure update in time:** Attackers are continuously finding new flaws in existing devices and their embedded software. Once the vulnerability is found, it is essential to patch it as soon as possible to prevent an attacker from using it to gain unauthorized access to the device. For patching edge devices details, see Section 8.3.

- **Ensure encryption between multiple edge devices:** Synchronization/asynchronization between devices may include valuable information, such as cryptographic keys and credentials, but this communication is often unencrypted by default. Use a truly random mechanism for the source of entropy during cryptographic key creation (e.g., RFID secure communication under EPCglobal regulation, see Section 4.1.4).

  The asynchronization security algorithm for multiple communication with RSA (Rivest–Shamir–Adleman) algorithm is taken as an example: A user of RSA creates and then publishes a public key based on two large prime numbers. The prime numbers must be kept secret. Anyone can use the public key to encrypt a message, but only someone with knowledge of the private key can decrypt the message.
- **Lightweight algorithm for real-time encryption/decryption:** For instance, when PRINCE algorithm is used for real-time encryption and decryption for on-chip flash, it is fast because it can decrypt and encrypt without adding extra latency, as compared to AES.
- **Visibility and automated monitoring:** Automated monitoring can provide detailed and holistic system visibility in which software is used to scan the network and analyze logs for anomalous behavior. For example, AI algorithms run over those devices and the data generated help in understanding the behavior of the network, monitor, analyze, and report on network events for anomalies and possibly malicious activity. Another way is carrying analysis within a security camera to analyze certain situations (unknown people, objects, etc.). Data privacy and security concerns associated with edge devices can remain intact with the use of data locally on the device.
- **Access control PUF:** Physical unclonable function (PUF, see Section 7.4.4) secure all networking equipment physically so that the devices remain out of reach of unauthorized personnel. Physical root login should be disabled and networking devices should only be accessible via a secure console. Ensure all default passwords are updated during the installation process. In edge computing, the demands of robust security functions at edge devices are high. By restricting access, the risk of intentional or accidental manipulation of resources and data can be avoided.

8.7.1.2 *Secure cloud infrastructure*

Cloud computing is one of the fastest growing industries in the field of ICT, which plays an increasingly important role in strategic support and innovation leading to national economic and social development. Today, with the acceleration of cloud computing into the landing stage, cloud security is becoming more urgent. Especially in the process of building user confidence, security is the first consideration of cloud computing vendors.

In terms of cloud computing security, there are a series of certifications and standards, such as ISO27001 (information security management system) international certification, trusted cloud certification, information security technology cloud computing service security guide, and so on. Their improvement is further promoting the establishment of trust system in cloud computing market, which is undoubtedly a great benefit to the development of cloud computing. Today, with the rapid popularization of cloud computing in China, "cloud computing security is the focus of the government". Today, when "data are resources and data are assets", cloud security is not only about enterprise security but also about national security. The cloud security technology is discussed in Fig. 8.16.

In Fig. 8.16, cloud service is regarded as an independent layer below the application layer, which is higher than the network (or communication) layer and supports the privacy management of IoT. Cloud computing itself can provide storage, facility management, process control and analysis, advanced analysis, privacy management, and data security services, and the enriched resources supporting services cover the management of data/device, the analysis of data flow, ML techniques, and beyond the reach of the resource constrained "thing". At the present stage of development of the IoT, it is not realistic to solve the problem of "resource constrained" things due to the limitations of cost, bandwidth, access mode, material technology, etc. However, a powerful cloud can implement security services and so on.

As mentioned in the previous discussion on application layer technology, more and more IoT systems use cloud computing to realize IoT data storage and processing, device management, process processing and analysis. Cloud computing is a good partner of IoT, which can support large-scale storage and processing of data collected by many constrained devices in IoT, sharing some functions with edge devices. However, the cloud is a double-edged sword and it brings new threats to security, especially about privacy.

Cloud security not only needs to realize the security protection of the cloud platform itself but also needs to be able to use a series of cloud security technologies, such as encryption to protect the IoT data

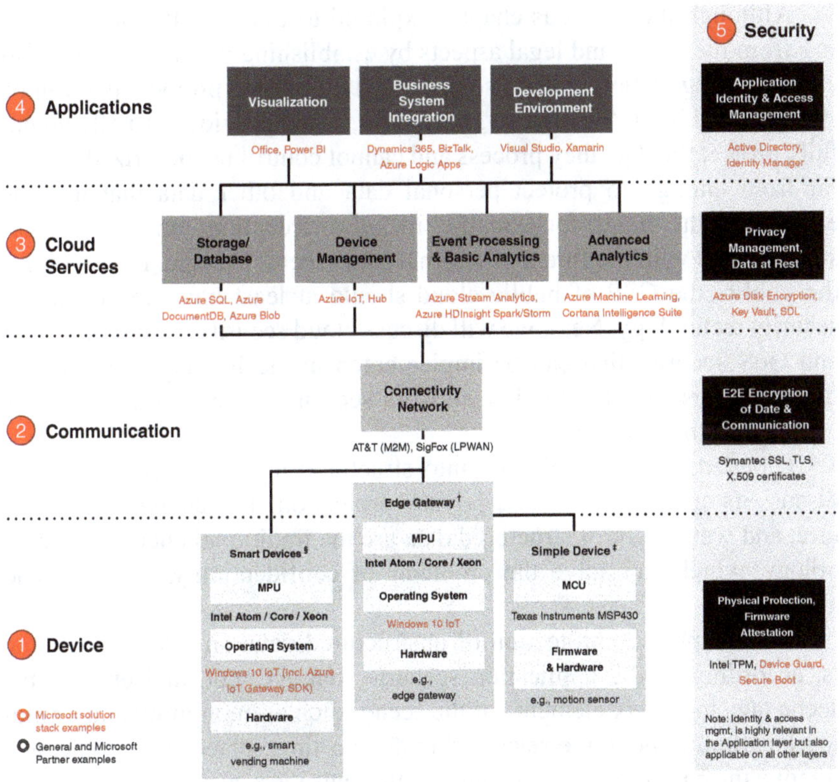

Figure 8.16 Schematic diagram of cloud services and cloud security in the IoT.

Source: Azure.com.

entering the cloud storage. If the application transforms the data into information in the cloud, the cloud service provider (CSP) can also access the data from the physical world. Naturally, as a third-party CSP, it has inherited all privacy issues from the cloud. At present, third-party suppliers have become part of the infrastructure to provide cloud services, such as computing and storage for IoT applications. Third-party suppliers also have to face IoT security technologies and strategies based on cloud architecture environment to solve the security problems in cloud environment. The research objects of IoT cloud security are as follows: Based on the security of cloud platform itself; to ensure the availability, data confidentiality, integrity, and privacy protection of IoT services.

Although the previous chapter explored to establish the order of the IoT from the moral and legal aspects by establishing words, morality, and calling for legislation, it has also discussed the trusted protocol that can be strengthened in SLA. However, nowadays, cloud providers usually do not fully protect the data they process and cannot control unauthorized access, far from enough to protect personal data and other data that may be exposed in the cloud, for example, illegal interception, emergency measures to deal with the threat of internal trade secret leakage. However, for the public, the CSP of public cloud should at least have confidence in security technology. Next, we will discuss cloud security technology. SLA and QoS security that can be implemented in the IoT network security have been discussed in the IoT network security strategy and will not be repeated in this section.

Cloud data can be divided into structured and unstructured data to discuss its confidentiality and privacy protection. The encryption, signature, and watermark of structured data are the traditional encryption technology, which can solve the problems of confidentiality, integrity, and authenticity.

For the privacy protection of unstructured data, an effective method is, according to the application scenario, remove, cut, and encrypt the scene tags in the six elements of the scene, such as anonymity and/or hiding location, remove the relationship among time, place and people, and remove the causal relationship among the cause, process, and result of the event. This is discussed in above Section 8.2 and a genetic difference privacy (DP) details will be discussed in the following section.

8.7.2 *Cloud and edge security policy and technology*

As introduced in Section 8.2, many anonymity heuristics models are used to preserve the privacy of individuals in research databases. Anonymization (the removal of "identifiable" attributes, such as names, addresses, SSN, and IP addresses) is the most commonly used technique. As many organizations mentioned (e.g., GDPR), in personal data processing method and process, controllers should take appropriate technical and organizational measures, such as pseudonymization, to store additional data and personal data separately. Unless additional data is used, personal data cannot point to a specific data subject.

For example, in an IoT system, the component of the identity management FC manages the different identities of the involved services or users by the use of multiple pseudonyms to achieve anonymity. The component maintains a hierarchy of identities and group identities.

However, such heuristics in anonymization or pseudonymization, devoid of any formal guarantees (e.g., SLA) can fail in "linkage attacks", which motivates the need for a robust definition of privacy — one that is immune to attacks using auxiliary knowledge, including knowledge of a data curator.

As shown in Fig. 8.17, a secure edge analysis together with measures is given in the following:

(1) "*k*-anonymity" is a database- or dataset-oriented privacy protection concept model that prevents joining attacks by generalizing and/or suppressing portions of the released micro-data so that no individual can be uniquely distinguished from a group of size *k*. In the *k*-anonymous tables, a data set is *k*-anonymous ($k \geq 1$) if each record in the data set is in distinguishable from at least ($k - 1$) other records within the same data set. The larger the value of *k*, the better the privacy is protected. *k*-anonymity can ensure that individuals cannot be uniquely identified by linking attacks (or linkage attacks).

k-anonymity model in turn led to other models such as confidence bounding, l-diversity, t-closeness, (α,*k*)-anonymity, etc. In particular, all known mechanisms try to minimize information loss and such an attempt provides a loophole for attacks.

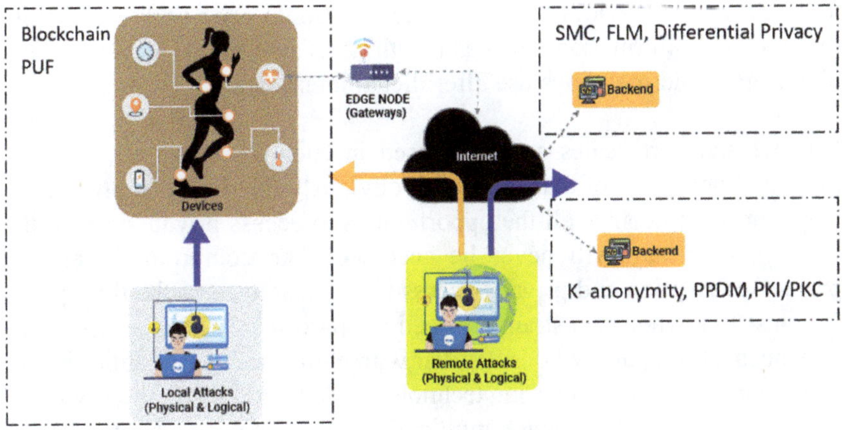

Figure 8.17 The attack scenarios and counter-measure technologies.

(2) Privacy-reserving data mining (PPDM) in dealing with data mining, which is often a key component of information systems, homeland security systems, and monitoring and surveillance systems.

When a wrong impression is given as privacy intrusion, this lack of trust has become an obstacle to the benefit of the technology. For example, the potentially beneficial data mining research project, terrorism information awareness (TIA), was terminated by the US Congress due to its controversial procedures of collecting, sharing, and analyzing the trails left by individuals. Motivated by the privacy concerns on data mining tools, a research area called PPDM emerged in 2000. The initial idea of PPDM was to extend traditional data mining techniques to work with the data modified to mask sensitive information. The key issues were how to modify the data and how to recover the data mining result from the modified data. The solutions were often tightly coupled with the data mining algorithms under consideration. In contrast, privacy-preserving data publishing (PPDP) may not necessarily tie to a specific data mining task, and the data mining task is sometimes unknown at the time of data publishing. Furthermore, some PPDP solutions emphasize preserving the data truthfulness at the record level, but PPDM solutions often do not preserve such property.

(3) Differential privacy (DP): Data collected from many people does not allow the identification of a single individual but still allows meaningful statistical calculations in a DP model. The technology can realize the anonymous authentication service of IoT devices, and the data anonymization of IoT devices helps to protect personal privacy. For example, the sensitive information (such as health data) sent by IoT devices to the cloud can avoid malicious use after illegal interception.

(4) PKI and certificates are often used in encryption and exchange of privacy. Encryption of data privacy is obviously the most comprehensive way, but it also denies all the opportunities to access private data, or the encrypted privacy will never be accessed. The compromise between privacy encryption and privacy access is the guarantee of the third party. It is just like when two strangers need to share secrets for the first time, they need a third party who is familiar with both sides to give authoritative trust guarantee. The supporting technologies include PKI public key infrastructure (certificate), secure multiparty computing, and homomorphic encryption.

(5) Homomorphic encryption. When the data is a computing process performed by a cloud provider, this can be very useful if the process allows the authenticity of the computing operation data to be maintained. Homomorphic signature (homomorphic encryption) is a common technique that allows modification and maintains authenticity.

Homomorphic encryption is an encryption function based on homomorphic principle, which encrypts the data directly without knowing the decryption function. Its formal definition is as follows: let x and y be the elements in the plain text space m, which are the operations on M, and EK () be the encryption function with the key space K on M, then the encryption function EK () represents homomorphic encryption computation:

$$A(EK(x), EK(y)) = EK(xy).$$

Homomorphic encryption protocol can protect the privacy of source data and intermediate results. The disadvantages of the algorithm are poor performance, a large amount of computation, and high communication overhead.

Homomorphic encryption was introduced by Ron Rivest, Leonard Adleman, and Michael L. Dertouzos in 1978. It was defined as a way to delegate processing of your data without giving away access to it by Craig Gentry. General encryption scheme which being mainly aimed at data storage security means that encrypted data would be decrypted by the user who has the password after it was sent, and the encrypted data should not be changed. However, homomorphic encryption is aimed at data process security, which supplies a scheme that could process encrypted data. Users could process the encrypted data not leak and change any original content of data. The expectation result would be obtained after the processed encrypted data was decrypted by the user who has the password.

Consider an example to explain homomorphic encryption. Alice bought some gold, and she wants to make it into a necklace, but is afraid that the gold might be stolen by the worker during this process. So, is there a way by which the gold could be processed by the worker but not be stolen? There is a feasible way where Alice should make a transparent box with a pair of gloves and lock the gold in it; the worker wearing the gloves could process the gold, while not getting any piece of the gold from the locked box. Alice would then fetch the gold necklace and pieces of surplus gold after unlocking the box. The diagrammatic sketch is shown in Fig. 8.18.

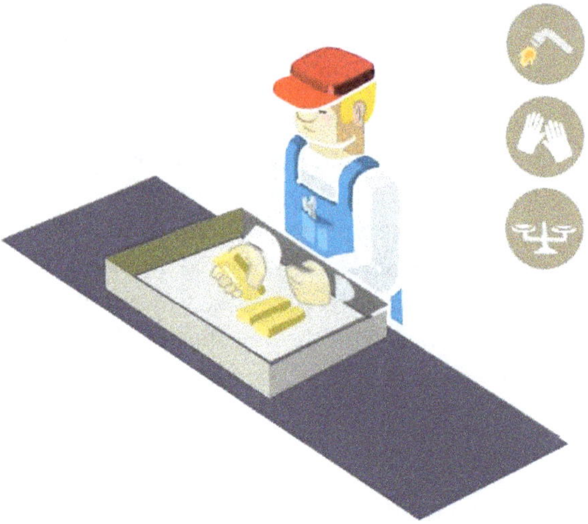

Figure 8.18 The diagrammatic sketch of gold processing in locked box.

In Fig. 8.18, the relationship among box, gloves, gold, lock, processing, and locking could be abstracted as follows:

- Box corresponds to encryption algorithm.
- Lock on the box corresponds to password.
- The action of putting the gold in the box and locking the box corresponds to homomorphic encryption of data.
- Processing corresponds to homomorphic characteristic.
- Unlocking corresponds to decryption.

Homomorphic encryption could be used in realistic scene with cloud in order to obtain security and processing. But the efficiency probably will be lower. A simple homomorphic encryption application example based on cloud computing scene was constructed. Alice will submit a ciphertext which is encrypted data with key and function to cloud; cloud will return encrypted operation result after function is worked on the ciphertext in cloud; Alice obtains the operation result after decryption. Here, the function is the homomorphic encryption function.

There should be at least two kinds of homomorphic encryption functions which are fully homomorphic encryption (FHE) and somewhat homomorphic encryption (SWHE). FHE has the characteristics of

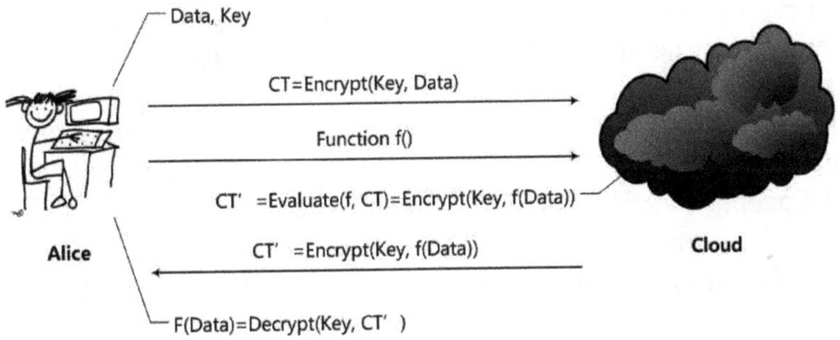

Figure 8.19 Homomorphic encryption at cloud computation scene.

multiplying homomorphism and adding homomorphism, but SWHE only has one characteristic.

An instance of Elgamal encryption scheme to explain multiplying homomorphism is shown in the last part of this section as an appendix.

(6) Secure multiparty computation (SMC) is introduced in the following. SMC prohibits any data sharing other than the final data mining result. Clifton *et al.* present a suite of SMC operations, including secure sum, secure set union, secure size of set intersection, and scalar product, that are useful for many data mining tasks.

(7) Access control approach, such as MAC (mandatory access control), RBAC (role-based access control), and ABAC (attribute-based access control). Even though roles and authorization, various encryption technologies, digital signature, and other complex protocols are constructed, such as MAC classification and management and RBAC (role-based access control) assigned roles and corresponding permissions, all of these help to improve the robustness of the cloud. Various types of secret sharing protocols can help solve different potential threats. However, for a multi-user cloud, it is necessary to set up a trusted distributed access control mechanism, which can extend its privacy access function. For example, in cloud computing, the privacy and security protection of medical IoT need such a cloud security solution to deal with personal highly sensitive medical data and its service data.

As for the hierarchical access control mechanism, both the access control based on resource hierarchy and the access control based on node hierarchy can be applied to data protection in cloud (edge/fog). This chapter only proposes the direction of confidentiality exploration for a large number of unstructured data in distributed architecture.

In summary, the security and privacy of the IoT system is regarded as the key to wider application in the public IoT. At present, it can improve its security and privacy from the technology, make the security of the IoT, and let people benefit from their work and life at ease, and avoid the disclosure of information, privacy or its exposure to the public. This security purpose is consistent with cloud computing (fog computing). This chapter discusses the cloud security of IoT in this section, and some of the hotspots are also concerned with cloud security (security cloud). The access control use case is given in the next section. The following part is an introduction to SMC.

8.7.2.1 *SMC*

With the transfer of Internet from IT to data technology, there are many puzzles that would be always encountered in day-to-day life. For example, the patient diagnostic data would be acquired and analyzed but not leaked in a hospital, the election data should be counted but not issued in the election records by a government, the production level of manufacture should be identified by industrial standard agency but not be known by any competitive parties. SMC could solve these puzzles to some extent, which was originally introduced by Andrew Yao in 1982 as secure computation between two parties in order to solve Millionaires' problem which described a situation in which two aggressive millionaires named Alice and Bob met at a street. Now, how to select the richer one without disclosing their assets? Owing to the advantages of privacy of input, correct computation, and decentralization, SMC is becoming an actively researched field in modern cryptography.

SMC could be described by two different aspects, namely the number of parties and computation scene.

(1) **The Number of parties:** There would be two parties of computation, and multiparty computation is according the number of parties.
Garbled circuit and oblivious transfer are the core of two-party computation (Fig. 8.20). One party could transfer calculation logic to Boolean circuit; every gate of Boolean circuit could be encrypted next, and all the encrypted circuit and relative input tags which could not be cracked should be sent to another party. Finally, the computation results would be

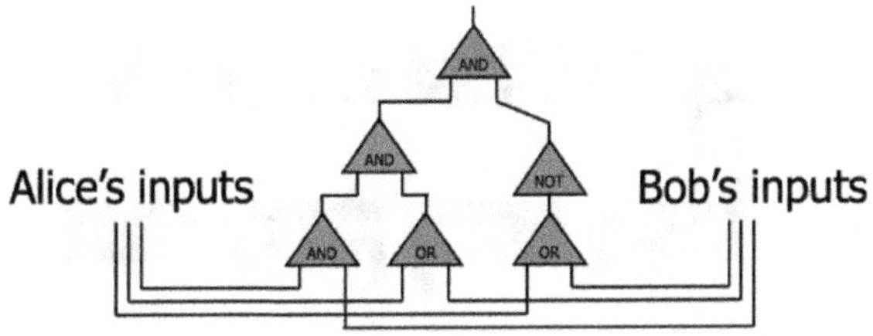

Figure 8.20 Garbled circuit applied to Millionaires' problem.

obtained by selected tags with oblivious transfer technology according to input and the encrypted circuit would then be deciphered.

There are also many schemes introduced for solving the multiparty computation problem after the above-mentioned **Yao's protocol for SMC,** such as BMR Goldreich–Micali–Wigderson (GMW), which is based on garbled circuit, and Boneh, Gentry, and Waters (BGW) which is based on secret sharing, SPDZ protocol, and so on.

(2) **Computation scene:** There are two different scenes that are special scene and general scene according to the computation scene. It points to special computation logic in special scene, such as the size comparison, intersection comparison, and so on. Garbled circuit, oblivious transfer, and homomorphic encryption are always used for general scene which should have the characteristic of completeness and be used at all scenes theoretically.

SMC is very important at secret sharing scene and privacy protection scene; nowadays, it is always applied in joint data analysis, data security inquire, data trustworthy transfer, and so on. It is further used in financial industries, manufactures, medical industries, electronic government administration, and so forth.

A common instance is as follows: iCube, which is the first SMC financial program, is developed based on blockchain technology. Figure 8.21 illustrates the architecture of iCube. A series of protocol which supports combination, computation, and protecting the privacy of participants, was added on the lower layer, so that obtaining data combination sharing computation under the privacy protection on information. Of course iCube support various trans-chain protocols in order to link data assets in future quickly.

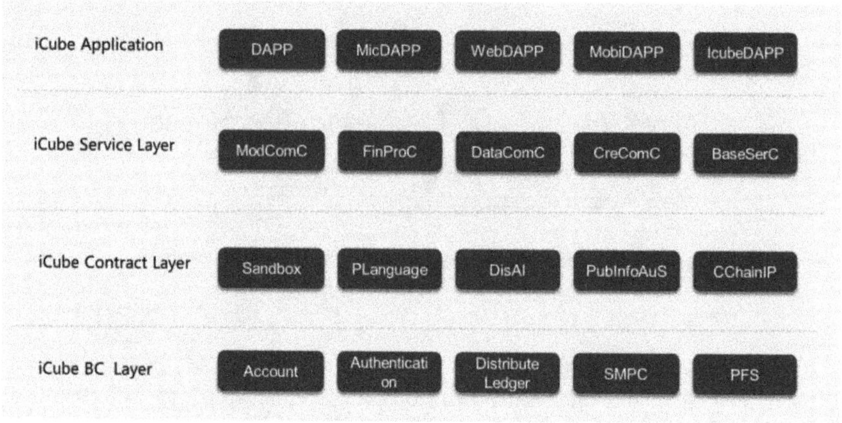

Figure 8.21 The architecture of iCube.

(3) **SMC based on secret sharing:** Secret sharing originated with cryptography; it is used for sharing secret which is always separated to several parts by some algorithm in order to send to receiver securely. It could be combined before use.

There is a formalization principle for secret sharing, i.e.,

$S(s,t,n) \rightarrow \{(s_0), (s_1), \ldots, (s_n)\}$,

where S represents the secret which is needed to be separated, t represents reset threshold, and n represents separation numbers.

It should have a function F, for arbitrary $m \geq t$, making $R((s_0), (s_1), \ldots, (s_m)) \rightarrow s$.

The advantage of secret sharing is that secrets are not really shared by every part, but they are used to compute in order to get result which could be shared together. Secret sharing is a computation in multiparty. Taking addition for example, if the sum of $x + y + z = c$ should be obtained, there requires three data suppliers and four computation nodes, which is illustrated in Fig. 8.22.

Each data of supplier should slice some shares according to the number of computation party. Then, these shares should be allocated to every computation node which should compute sum of every receiving share and get the middle result. All secrets of every part are garbled together. Finally, the result is the sum of every middle result. In this situation, each could only get the share which sent to it and not get others so that the secret is shared in certain aspect but shared entirely. Secure threshold is

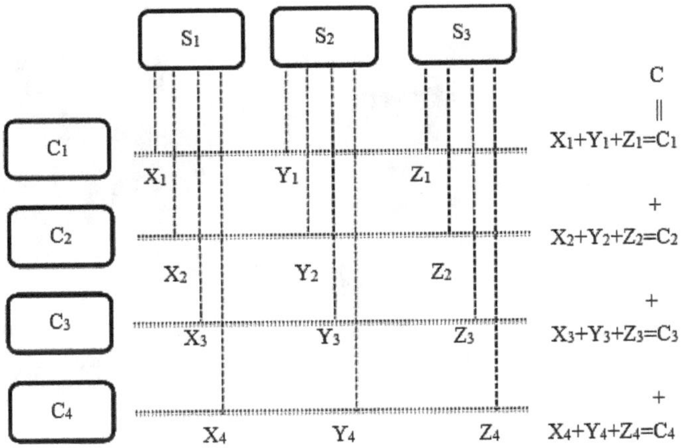

Figure 8.22 The demonstration of Secret Sharing.

important factor for secret sharing, i.e., $n - 1$, where n is the number of parts. So, secret sharing is secure only when $n > 2$, which is namely multiparty.

(4) **Neural network training:** It was reported that a novel three-party secure computation protocols for various NN building blocks, such as matrix multiplication, convolutions, rectified linear units, Maxpool, normalization, and so on for better computation avoiding conflicts with data privacy. Moreover, a secure training solution which should solve the problem that multiple contributors such that plaintext data is kept hidden from training entities in N server model, was provided. The details are a set of M data owners who wish to execute training over their joint data using N servers; theses M parties send "secret shares" of their input data to the N servers, and the servers collectively run an interactive protocol to train a neural network over the joint data to produce a trained model that could be used for inference. No individual party or server learns any information about any other party's training data in this protocol. This was called N server model. $N = 3$ and M is arbitrary are mostly discussed in this chapter.

No single party could learn any information about the data in this protocol. With the communicating through the elimination of expensive garbled circuits and oblivious transfer protocols, the state-of-the art of secure computation for neural networks was advanced in the following three ways:

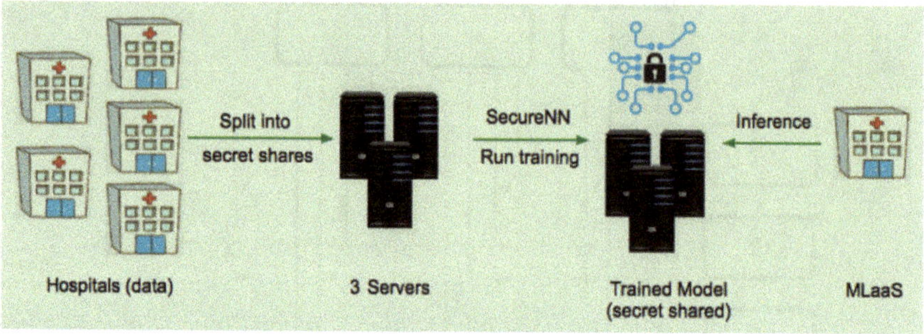

Figure 8.23 Horizontal architecture of trained model.

- ***Scalability***: Convolutional neural networks that have an accuracy of >99% on the MNIST dataset was firstly trained by this protocol.
- ***Performance***: For secure inference (see Section 5.8.5 and 7.6.2, ML as an inference service) or secure training, this protocol is faster than other protocols.
- ***Security***: Full security (privacy and correctness) against one semi-honest corruption and the notion of privacy against malicious corruption were provided by this protocol.

For better understanding, a system illustrated in Fig. 8.23 is set up in which the patient's sensitive input and predicted output are only revealed to the patient and remains hidden from everyone else. This protocol provided an interesting solution for solving a series of questions, such as how to defeat malicious adversaries model, how to increase the efficiency of two-parity computation, and so on.

8.7.3 *Edge security model*

The right of privacy is an important civil right that people enjoy to personal information and decide private affairs. It includes the right to keep personal information confidential, the right to keep personal life undisturbed, and so on. In real life, people have different privacy states at different occasions. For example, in a private home, only you or your family know what you are doing; in public places (such as shops, restaurants, and amusement parks), others can see what you are doing but they do not know who you are (anonymity). Your boss may be very concerned about where you are on business occasions, and your family may just think about whether you are at home or not.

Once personal information is leaked, it is an afterthought to maintain the original privacy state, so for any IoT application scenario, we should try to prevent the leakage of any personal information. Some promising personalized services mostly require customers to provide some personal information. However, once the merchants have mastered the customer information, they may carry out compulsory sales promotion, which will affect the customers' life choices. Therefore, in securing the IoT grid, we try to explore the strategy of distributed security in edge security grids.

8.7.3.1 *Security grid elements and trust management*

As discussed in Section 6.2, IoT grid, the three elements of PIoT in an IoT grid are things, relationship set, and service. These can be reflected in the security grid center as security manager. Grid intelligent gateway/edge device as HW of grid center is the core of edge security grid and plays the role of security manager (SM, including the above AM and Trust Manager (TM)). It owns all the resources in the grid and its allocation, and can be used as the agent to deal with the trust relationship between grids, as follows:

- Objects in a secure grid: Grid members.
- Relationships in security grid: Grid members and their relationships with secure services (a kind of PIoT service).
- Services in security grid: Security services, etc.

The responsibilities of grid edge center (e.g., intelligent gateway device) include but are not limited to grid member management, relationship management, and trust management. The trust management includes

- Internal security management: Manage privacy and resources, and
- External security management: Responsible for external or upward data protection (e.g., edge to cloud) and security authentication. It would be furthered as trust interaction policy resources in an IoT security grid refer to the grid internal resources, such as computing, storage, interconnection (communication protocols), and other resources.

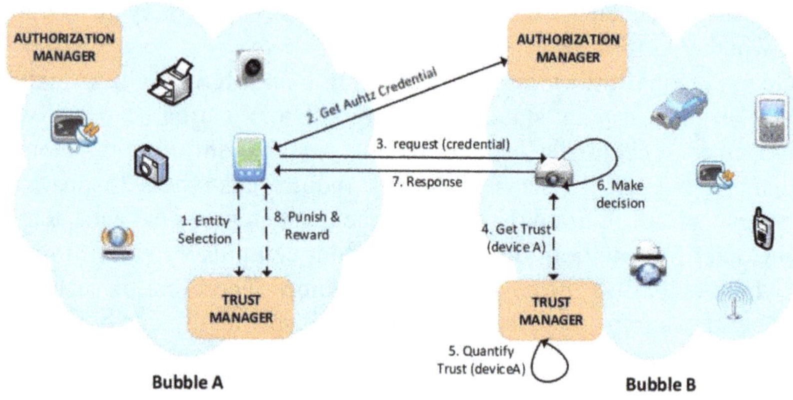

Figure 8.24 Trust exchange of two edge IoT grid, or edge-cloud.

"Things" in the grid: Device members in the grid (like a family), as shown in Fig. 8.24.

(1) **Trust management in secure grids**: In the security environment, all behaviors involved in "things, relationships, and services" should meet the security requirements of trust management. Trust management issues include but are not limited to, such as "who can share my information", "who can I allow to see my privacy", "who can guarantee the safe sharing when exchanging secrets", and so on. It includes the following aspects:

(a) ***Trust framework***: This is the component responsible for defining the trust mechanism of "things, relationship, and service", in which all security related activities are recorded and updated. When the large-scale applications and services of the IoT grid (through integration or joint, expansion) will cross the security domain, or the ownership of its resources belongs to different entities, a trust framework that can form a consensus is needed. Make the IoT grid users believe: the security of information and services is credible, which can be built up by data protection, access control, and other security technology.

(b) ***Trust interaction***: Under the constraint of trust framework, the trust of IoT grid can be established, transferred (partial transfer), inherited (partial inheritance), and the state can be changed to semi-trust or no trust. In the discussion of privacy protection services, the IoT grid (see Fig. 8.24) can be used as the trusted bubble boundary, i.e., the most basic function group but scalable edge units in the trust interaction IoT secure grid model or trust management model.

In the scenario analysis of trust interaction, an example of trust establishment between grids is used to illustrate the trust interaction model of access control system. As shown in Fig. 8.24, the Bubble A and Bubble B are used to implement the secure and reliable interaction in a trust model, which can be deployed in different types of grid bubble entities (such as edge sites/MEC, families, offices, or communities) by forming the trust contact among different intelligent objects.

According to Fig. 8.24, each grid bubble is a set of smart objects, within an IoT edge grid. Security manager of each is divided into an AM and a TM, and the smart object authorization credentials is generated by the AM. TM is responsible for evaluating the credibility of the entities involved, such as smart phone, printer, camera, and sensor, and each of them can be used as a PIoT services provider or client (services such as temperature and location) through IoT protocols (such as COAP).

AM as a function of edge grid center, is responsible for generating and sending authorization tokens (credentials) for smart objects. In addition, it is composed of two sub parts: policy decision point (PDP) and token management (generate authorization credentials according to the decision).[6]

TM is also a function of edge grid center, in the trust model; on the one hand, it allows the requester (the smart phone in the figure) know the most reliable service provider (PIoT provider) in a set of devices that can provide the same service. On the other hand, the service provider (the projector in the figure) uses it to obtain the trust value level, which is used together with the authorization credentials previously obtained by the AM to make access control decisions.

As shown in Fig. 8.24, the process of trust-based access control is summarized as follows.

First of all, the device accesses its TM and finds the most trusted service provider in the neighboring bubble B. This requires computing the trust value level of available provider in grid bubble B. Then, in step 2, the device obtains the authorization credentials to access the device in grid bubble B. In step 3, the requester sends the request according to the obtained authorization credentials; In steps 4 and 5, the trusted devices in grid bubble A are evaluated and the trusted level is quantified. The trusted

[6] In the process, PIP and PEP will be exposed from a service platform on the edge.

level is calculated in real time based on previous evidence. Then, in step 6, the device in grid bubble B accepts the service request or not according to the PDP of bubble B. In step 7, the interaction takes place and the evidence of reliability is formed, and the quantitative value of mutual trust (representing the trust level) is updated in real time for the next instance of trust interaction between grids.

(2) **The third partner in case of cloud security**: The interaction of trust sometimes needs a trusted third party, as shown in Fig. 8.25. In the application of grid collaboration, the three-part grid (father node) needs to obtain the trust of its children node (both of the bubble grids) by a security demonstration of a trust chain, such as PKI/PKC infrastructure, mentioned above, blockchain, and other cloud security mechanics which can be extended to cover an extended IoT security domain (such as the right part of Fig. 8.25, a star topology of trusted cloud).

The security domain has its own autonomous trust management. Trans-security domains trustworthiness requires third-party organizations as auditors to ensure neutrality and "credibility".

(3) **Cloud security infrastructure technology**: For the consumers of cloud infrastructure (the right part of Fig. 8.25), if the cloud supplier can also be held responsible for its security, it will at least increasing the confidence of the consumers in cloud infrastructure.

Structural integrity and secure cloud as a trusted infrastructure need certification. For example, an agreement or SLAs for the integrity proof

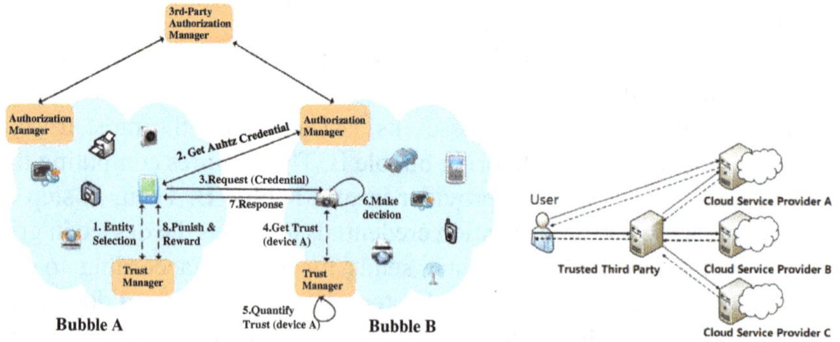

Figure 8.25 Tree and star topologies when considering third trust link for secure exchange.

of component structure (the claimed credibility or trusted value of cloud/edge-cloud infrastructure) and the actual security guarantee of cloud topology (the integrity of connected components). This is the task of structural integrity and virtual infrastructure certification (which needs to be formed under the framework of public recognition). Specifically, it includes trusted infrastructure certification and cloud topology security authentication. Cloud topology security authentication refers to the proof that it can provide certain security (e.g., network isolation).

Recently, the concept of graph signatures is expected to solve these problems. Graph signatures allow a trusted third party to act as an auditor to verify the zero-knowledge properties of graphs, such as the connection or isolation properties of topological graphs.

Graph signature can be used to convince a user that he is already in a multi-tenant cloud environment with certain security of infrastructure, although the (confidential) drawings of the virtualization infrastructure are not disclosed to him. In short, the cloud needs to prove that the customer's infrastructure is isolated from other users who rent the cloud, without disclosing the details of other users' infrastructure. An infrastructure that allows authentication can make the cloud infrastructure meet a certain level of security performance.

In summary, we need a strong trust management modular security mechanism. Devices and service should not only imitate human's handling of trust but also consider how devices can protect users' privacy. What's more, according to the "physical security" of devices themselves in Maslow's security analysis model (mentioned above), devices should not be damaged and can work normally while avoiding its malicious use (e.g., denial of sleep in power attack).

(4) **PIoT service design example in an access control model:** The access control based on policy management of "the security toolkit (Seckit)" access control model is taken as an example to illustrate the "privacy by design", which can be directly used for privacy access control of edge security grid. Here is only a brief introduction of its ideas. Access control itself is an exploration direction of IoT security policy, such as hierarchical access control (e.g., ABAC) and private key protection scheme of hierarchical nodes.

Under the policy management framework (ICORE project) of SecKit, as shown in Fig. 8.26, Seckit model design is divided into an entity grid

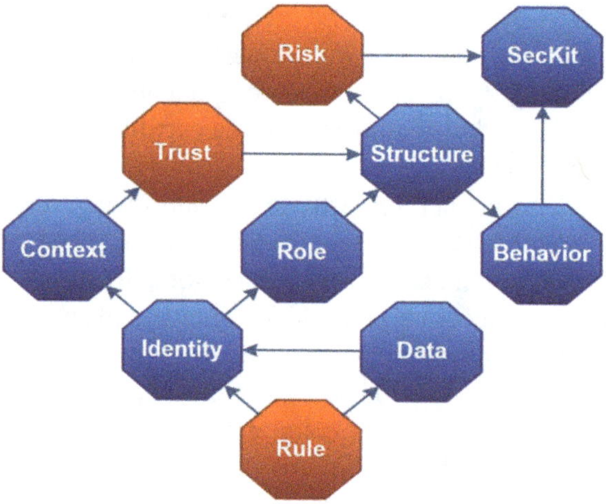

Figure 8.26 SecKit meta model for building a trusted chain.

element and a set of security related PIoT service to meet the requirements of secure sharing data and the access control of a given system:

- **Entity grid**: The communication mechanism between entities and entities that allow them to exchange information.
  (a) ***Risk (assessment) service***: Detailed information of each entity, including action, interaction, causality, and information attributes, which can be valued by PDP in AM of a grid center.
  (b) ***Trusk***: Specify with data protection, identity, context, role of trust, risk, and security rules. Aiming at the structure vector for risk assessment of PDP and behavior analysis. Figure 8.26 illustrates the SecKit MetaModel and its dependencies.
  (c) ***Rule*:** An HMI setting, from ML, or human preference. The specification of policy rules referencing identities is done using an abstract identity design model that can be mapped to the specific technical choice. The evaluation of the policies by the PDP is done using events signaled by the policy enforcement point (PEP) deployed as service provider for request/response to PDP in the same AM.
- **PDP service:** PDP-based trust service depends on the context (trust exchange bubble or cloud of figure), which can be limited in a time period, e.g., the context meta model specifies the background

information and context type. Background information is a simple type of information of an entity, which obtains the type of background situation that starts and ends at a specific time in a specific period of time. For example, "body temperature" is a type of background situation, while "fever" is a time when the target patient has a temperature higher than 37°C. The entity is associated with the role (e.g., patient) used in the context type.

PDP monitors and registers events when the context starts and ends. These events contain references to entities participating in the context and can be used to support the specification of policy rules. Policy rules can include authorization access at the beginning of a situation, data protection obligations after the beginning and at the end. For example, when an emergency starts, it can allow access to patient data and fulfill data protection obligations; when the emergency is over, all data is deleted. A security policy should include that the access data is allowed at the beginning of the situation and the data is deleted at the end of the situation. When considering the security policy being from a human as an administrator, another PDP relative policies-specifying service is PAP (policy administration point), as the service of TM.

8.7.3.2 *Trust management and rule on the edge*

The security and access control use case in Fig. 8.27 is the secure edge use case based on the Swarm platform, which includes both the use of appropriate algorithms and protocols to protect exchanged messages and a flexible access control mechanism to govern which interactions are allowed.

The Swarm approach to access control uses attribute-based access control (ABAC), a flexible and comprehensive system in which subject requests to perform operations on objects are "granted or denied based on assigned attributes of the subject, assigned attributes of the object, environment conditions, and a set of policies specified in terms of those attributes and conditions".

The security rule/policy model in Fig. 8.27 is composed of two parts: the AM working in authorization phase and the TM working in policy management phase. The model supports: rule template policy's standardized formulation, execution, rule configuration, and instantiation template. These policy templates are designed to imitate the trust behavior and trust architecture between people and groups and take into account the

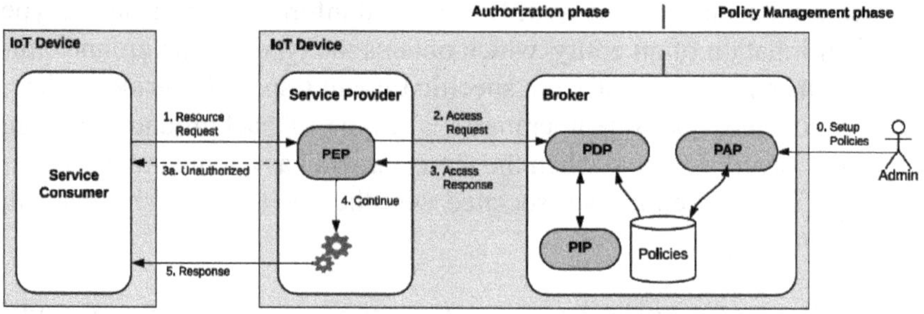

Figure 8.27 Security and access control architecture on the Swarm using ABAC policies. PIoT service designed on a secure edge platform of the Swarm using ABAC policies.

non-functional requirements of security and privacy, such as data protection, integrity, authorization, and non-repudiation.

Four main types of security PIoT service are defined in the edge grid: PDP, PEP, PIP, and PAP, and their interworking is described as follows:

The PDP is for the valuation of the policies using events signaled by the policy enforcement point (PEP) as mentioned above. The PDP evaluates policies managed through the PAP, while the policy information point (PIP) accounts for gathering context and other attributes, and the PEP intercepts requests and verifies their permission with the PDP.

The security policy of PAP must consider the devices used to collect data in a secure manner. According to the security policy, the device has an appropriate mechanism for triggering and sending data. This includes three steps: first, the device has been mapped to a specific data collection strategy. Second, the policy should determine the encryption/security level of the data to determine the appropriate transmission mechanism, while considering the energy efficiency requirements of the device (such as adaptive encryption scheme). Third is the setting preference of security events (e.g., sensitivity and encryption level).

For example, in the traffic monitoring scenario, car users can send information to the application. In this scenario, only the traffic flow of each district (or block area) should be known. The user's in-vehicle communication module (e.g., T-box or OBU) has the ability to send all kinds of traffic-related data, i.e., the accurate position, speed, movement direction per second (to/from an edge map server or RSUs). If the application wants to estimate the traffic flow, it should consider the user's relevant strategies, i.e., the average speed of each time period and its block can be sent, so as to avoid the leakage of the user's precise location at a certain time (privacy by design view). In fact, the intermediate node (edge gateway device or server) should also consider these policies and only send the aggregated or average processed data to the application server, so as to protect the user's location privacy. When other applications do need to know the exact location of users (according to their access control policies), they will be able to send the exact location. For example, if a person's car is stolen, he can track his car.

Therefore, it is very important to implement the security policy to ensure the security and privacy protection of the whole system. The system should be able to identify the integrity of the security policy sent to the device so that unauthorized applications cannot access privacy-sensitive data.

When considering the above edge security policy templates designed to imitate the trust behavior from human groups and further improve the trust establishment between two IoT sectors (or domain), a policy-sharing mechanism must be developed. In a previous work, shown in Fig. 8.28, a trust interaction service is designed to exchange the security policy templates at the PAP level for two IoT domains bridging (for details, see the reference of the figure. For the secure edge and trust collaboration, a policy distribution algorithm was implemented, which allowed devices to gather policies from surrounding devices (e.g., ML algorithms), and the policy would be edited by a human user (e.g., the negotiation between PAPs in each IoT grid/domain) and then pushed the policies to the appropriate devices again.

The SecKit as a model-based security toolkit is an EU-funded project of Internet Connected Objects for Reconfigurable Ecosystem (iCore).

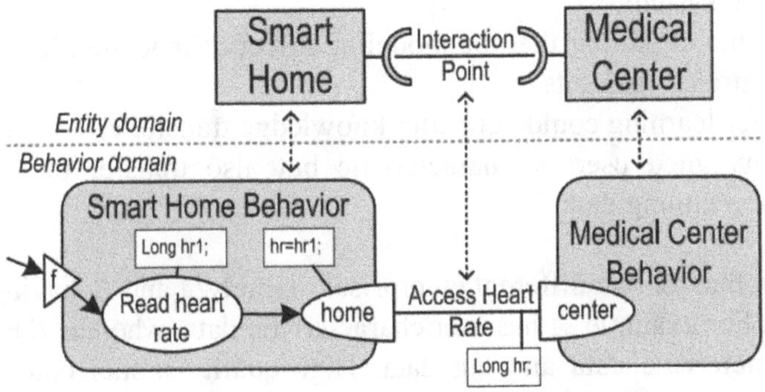

Figure 8.28 Entity and behavior between IoT domains for trust policies interaction.

The followed section will focus on the federated learning model, which is used in secure cloud computing when the user side is on sites and its data process or model training is in the cloud or on the edge.

8.7.4 *The rule training by federated learning model*

With the development of big data, data privacy and security also are on the development trend around the world. A series of accidents of leaked data bring big challenges in the future. It is a development trend that managing privacy and security of user data strictly is issued in General Data Protection Regulation (GDPR, (https://gdpr-info.eu/)). However, there is a common phenomenon that the collecting data party is not the using data party in research and industry field. For instance, data were collected by A and transferred to B for cleaning, then modeled by C and sold to D. So, a puzzle emerges: how to make sure data privacy and security to validate forever when data were used by different parties?

There is an important thesis that a machine learning framework was designed by which intelligent system could use every data efficiently and accurately satisfying data privacy, security, and regulation. Perhaps, federated learning is a nice solution.

The characteristics of federated learning are as follows:

- All data are stored at a local storage so that data privacy would not be leaked.
- Virtual mutual model and mutual beneficial system are constructed with joint data of every party.
- Identity and status of every party are the same under the federated learning system.
- It is same or similar that the modeling effect of federated learning and concentrated data sets.
- Transfer learning could get better knowledge transfer effect not only in the unaligned user or characteristic but also transfer of encrypted function among data.

Hypothesize two different enterprises, namely *A* and *B*, having different data. For example, *A* has user characteristic data, whereas *B* has product characteristic data and tag data. High-quality model could not be constructed because of incomplete or insufficient data in each party, i.e.,

A lacks product characteristic data and tag data and *B* lacks user characteristic data. However, federated learning could construct a virtual mutual model by encrypted parameter transfer method by which all the data is also stored in local storage.

8.7.4.1 *The definition of federated learning*

When the machine learning model could be trained by D_i $i = 1,\ldots, N$ which possessed by E_i, $i = 1,\ldots, N$, model *M_SUM* would be trained by combination data sets $D = \{D_i, i = 1,\ldots, N\}$ in traditional way, which is influenced by data privacy and security easily. However, model *M_FED* could be trained by other data without D_i which is possessed by E_i in federated learning method. The difference of model effect *V_SUM* of *M_SUM* and *V_FED* of *M_FED* is quite small. This could be described that given an arbitrary value δ, then $|V\_FED - V\_SUM| < \delta$.

8.7.4.2 *The classes of federated learning*

The classification of federated learning could be classified with data distributed characteristics. Every data set D_i could be represented by a matrix. Every row represents a user, and every column represents a kind of user characteristic. Perhaps, some data sets include tag data which is the necessary data to model user's behavior. User characteristic were flagged as *X*, tag characteristic was flagged as *Y*. User characteristic *X* and tag characteristic *Y* make up the complete training data (X,Y) mutually. Data distribution form is probable as follows in the instance of two possessed data users through federated learning scheme:

(a) The overlap of user characteristic (X_1,Y_2) of two data sets is more, but the overlap of user (U_1,U_2) is smaller.
(b) The overlap of user (U_1,U_2) is more, but the overlap of user characteristic (X_1,Y_2) is smaller.
(c) The overlap of user (U_1,U_2) and user characteristic (X_1,Y_2) are both small.

The classification of federated learning could be concluded as horizontal federated learning (HFL), vertical federated learning (VFL), and federated transfer learning (FTL), according to the above different distributed forms of user and user characteristic.

(1) **HFL**: With the situation of more overlap of user characteristic and smaller overlap of user of two data sets, data sets should be sliced along with horizontal direction or user dimension, the overlap data of user characteristics but not the user could be trained for parameters of model with federated learning. This is HFL. An example will be employed for explaining the principle of HFL. There are two banks in different regions. For the customers of the two banks coming from each region, the overlap of customers is small, but the business is very similar. So, the records of customer are similar, and HFL should be employed for modeling. Figure 8.29 is the illustration of HFL, where X_A are the data of bank A, X_B are the data of bank B, Y_B are the tag data, and HFL are the overlap business data of the two banks.

(2) **VFL**: With the situation on more overlaps of user but smaller overlap of user characteristic, data sets should be sliced along the vertical direction or characteristic dimension, the overlap data of same user but not same characteristic should be trained for parameters of model with federated learning. This is VFL. For instance, consider two different entities: one is a bank and another is an electronic business at the same region. The overlap of customer is more for the customer coming from the same region. The payment records and credit evaluation are always the special characteristic of bank behavior, but the browsing and purchasing records were stored by the electronic business. So, the overlap of customer characteristic is small. All these different encrypted characteristics were clustered in order to train the necessary parameters of model by VFL. Figure 8.30 shows **VFL**.

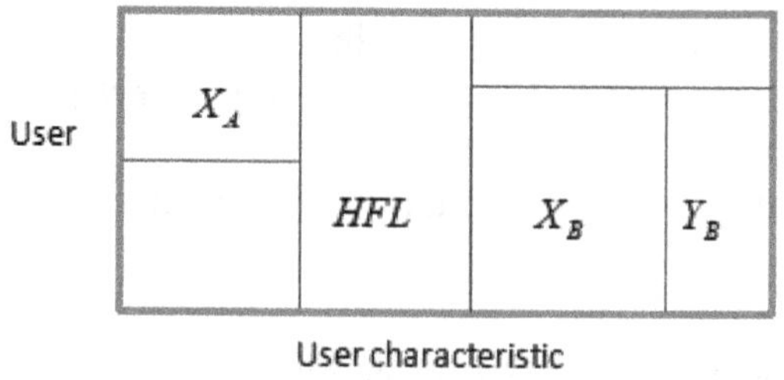

Figure 8.29 Horizontal federated learning (HFL).

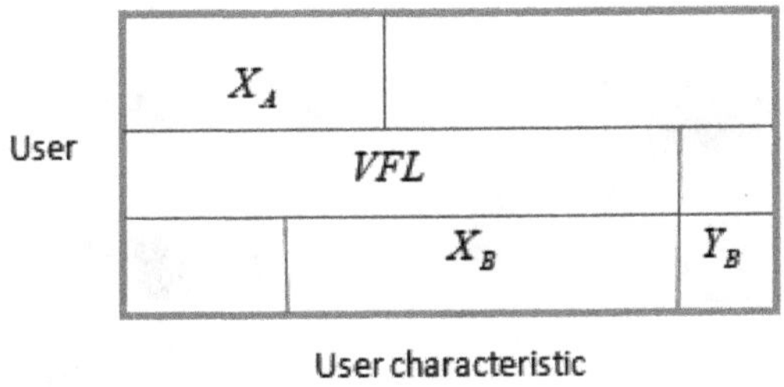

Figure 8.30 Vertical federated learning (VFL).

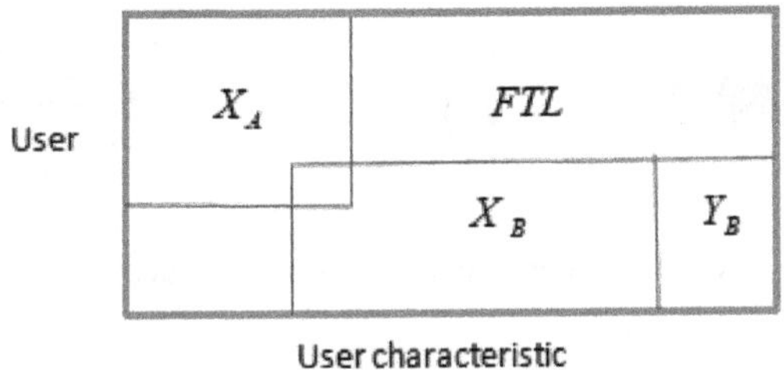

Figure 8.31 Federated transfer learning (FTL).

(3) **FTL:** The data sets should not be sliced under the situation of data sets of user and user characteristic are smaller. The transfer learning should be employed for solving the insufficiency data or tags by FTL. For instance, consider a Chinese bank located in China and an American electronic business located in America; the overlap of customers of these two entities may be smaller and the data characteristic also may be small for the different type of these two entities, Thus, the FTL should be employed for training the valid parameter of model. Figure 8.31 shows FTL.

8.7.4.3 *The system architecture of federated learning*

There are two data-possessed users on the system architecture of federated learning, which is illustrated in Fig. 8.32. It could extend to many data-possessed users. It is assumed that a combination machine learning model would be trained by enterprise A and B mutually. The relative data are possessed by them, and B also has the tag data. However, the data could not be swapped by A and B for the data privacy and security. But the necessary model could be constructed by federated learning. The system architecture of federated learning contains two parts as shown on Fig. 8.32.

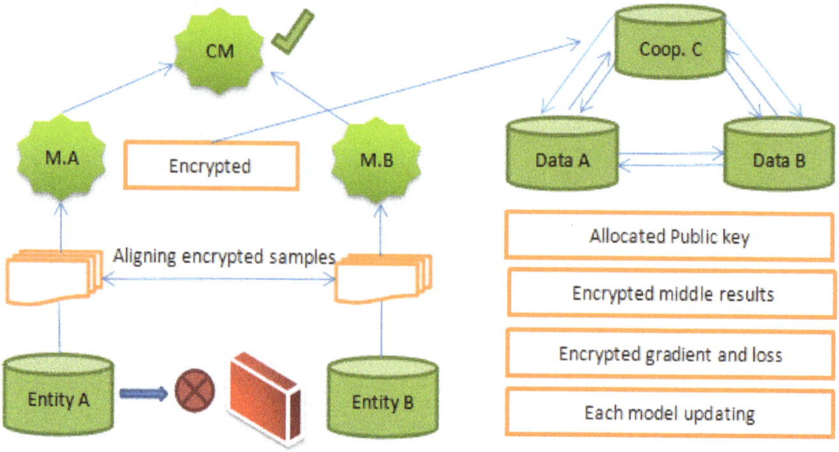

Figure 8.32 System architecture of federated learning.

The training steps of federated learning are as follows:

(1) **Aligning the encrypted samples**: If the overlap of two entities are not always same, the aligning encrypted samples technology is employed for confirming the mutual users on the premise that all data of A and B are not disclosed and the non-overlapping users are not revealed, so that the model combining these user characteristic could be made.

(2) **Encrypted model training**: The machine learning model could be trained by these data after mutual users were confirmed. The third cooperator C should be employed at training process in order to protect the data privacy and security. The training steps would be divided into the following four steps with the instance of linear regression:

(a) Public key should be allocated for A and B by cooperator C in order to encrypt the data by swapping during training process.
(b) The middle result which would be employed for computing gradient should be swapped as a form of encryption.
(c) The encrypted gradient of A and B should be calculated by each other. The loss of gradient should be calculated by B according to its tag data meantime. All results should be clustered to C. The total gradient would be calculated and cracked by C.

(d) The cracked gradient would be transmitted to A and B by C; the relative model parameters should be updated by A and B.

All of the above steps should not be iterated until loss function is converged. The data of A and B all stored at local storage, and the data privacy and security could be protected completely at the all-training process. So, the combination machine learning model of A and B could be trained with the help of federated learning.

(3) **Effect incentive**: It is important that every entity wishes to participate in federated mutual model in federated learning method. The model effect would be revealed during exercise after model was constructed and should be recorded at forever data record mechanism, such as blockchain. The more the data supplied, the better the model effect. It means that the contributions for its own and for others. The effect of this model for others would be contributed to every entity and encourages more and more entities participating in federated learning model.

Acknowledgment

For this chapter, the author would like to thank Dr. Hai-tao LIU for his assistance. He received the B.S. degree in Information and Computation Science from Shandong University, China, in 2005 and Ph.D. degree in Pattern Recognition and Intelligence System from University of Science and Technology of China in 2010. He has two titles of Senior Engineer and Senior Economist of China. He was as a visiting scholar at University of North Carolina in Charlotte in 2017. He was the deputy president of state owner corporation, deputy president of financial holdings corporation, and executive director of Hong Kong corporation. He has published 14 papers in journals and international conferences.

Appendix

An instance of Elgamal encryption scheme to explain multiplying homomorphism (see Fig. 8.19) is shown as the following steps.

When the form of cyphertext is,

$$CK = (C_1, C_2) = (g^r, h^r \cdot m) \tag{8.1}$$

where r is a random number, g is an infinitesimal generator, h is a public key, and m is a constant.

$$CK_1 = (g^{r1}, h^{r1} \cdot m_1), CK_2 = (g^{r2}, h^{r2} \cdot m_2), \tag{8.2}$$

where CK_1 and CK_2 are two cyphertexts; the first part of CK_1 is multiplied by the first part of CK_2, and the second part of CK_1 is multiplied by the second part of CK_2. Then, the results are

$$CK = (g^{r_1} \cdot g^{r_2}, h^{r_1} \cdot m_1 \cdot h^{r_2} \cdot m_2) = (g^{r_1+r_2}, h^{r_1+r_2} \cdot m_1 \cdot m_2). \tag{8.3}$$

It means that the cyphertext of CK_1 multiplied by CK_2 equals the encrypted result of m_1 multiplied by m_2. So, Elgamal has the characteristic of multiplying homomorphism.

Chapter 9

Conclusions and Expectations

An overview of the next generation Internet of Things (IoT), Internet of Everything (IoE) is provided in this book, in the scope of research, innovation, development priorities, to enabling technologies in a global context. It is intended as a standalone series covering the activities of the IoT over the past few years, including technological innovation, practical application, and security.

Innovation is made from social and technical perspectives which, to some extent, lay the foundation for the interactive play among scientists, engineers, and artists and new knowledge and technologies are introduced, in accordance with actual social and market demands. In other words, this book aims to benefit IoT researchers and practitioners by merging scientific and artistic research & development (R&D) practices into production of new philosophical knowledge and technologies as well as making R&D practitioners aware that the above combined knowledge may produce new methodologies as well as an upcoming market of IoT, based on new business models, products, and services.

The chapters built on the developments and innovative ideas as proposed by IoT sense, RFID/WSN, 5G, and the ubiquitous connections, data analysis and ML models, edge/cloud computing, and the new models such as tactile IoT (TIoT), industrial IoT (Industrial 4.0), sat. IoT (or satellite-IoT), and digital twins (DTs). A generic presentation of concept, characteristics, and history is given in Chapters 1 to 3. Based on the layered architecture of IoT itself, the pervasive perception technologies, ubiquitous communication technologies, platforms, and diversity applications are introduced one by one from Chapters 4 to 7.

New concepts, ideas, and the future IoT trends mentioned in this book provides great facilities for researchers, developers, integrators, and other stakeholders, with engineering, technology, practice, framework from comprehensive and developmental perspectives, and also helps develop the open data, open platforms, and IoT marketplaces into a larger deployment ecosystem. All chapters have covered the framework of the diverse IoT solutions as the generic architecture (ITU or reference architectural four layers in Chapter 3), the edge/cloud oriented architecture, the Industrial 4.0 architecture (RAMI4.0), M2M architecture (ETSI M2M, LwM2M, and so on), and architectures of the TIoT, sat. IoT, DT, and IoT security (in Section 7.2).

In Chapter 5, technologies of communication and network layer, the topics cover the capillary LAN/PAN, the end-to-end M2M, proprietary/cellular LPWAs, 5G IoT, sat. IoT, and TIoT. The latter three show potentials from the views of 3GPP/ITU, and the application angles as AR/VR, V2X/autonomous driving, massive MTC (mMTC), and IIoT/TSNs (time-sensitive communications).

Chapters 6 and 7 expand the application of consumer, business, industrial, and tactile IoT requirements in view of platforms and applications, which further develop hyper automated IoT concepts for human–machine solutions to expand augmented creativity at the shared (or in a given specific IoT sector/domain) platforms, the smart service (e.g., ML as-a-service), and the collaborative (collective) applications, either vertically or horizontally. The smart service, smart IoT solutions, and technological details covered in the two chapters can create new value for a giant number of devices and data at our hands, for analysis, demonstration, and understanding (either for us at knowledge or wisdom level, or for AI/ML methods in the closed loop of control, prediction, and collaboration).

In Chapter 8, topics cover the evolution of architectures and technologies in the security and privacy of IoT. In short, this book focuses on bringing all IoT related technologies into one source, so that students, researchers, and practitioners can refer to this book in order to easily understand IoT methodology and deployment in their respective practices. In recent IoT practical applications, more attention should be paid to the topics referred in Fig. 9.1.

Together with the above enlightenments, the adoption of application practices, such as research methodologies and deployment in different projects, are critical to promote the generation of scientific, reproducible knowledge (including imagination and expansion of re-constructive and

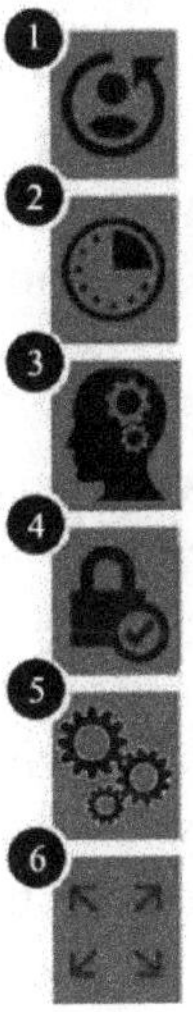

Organizational, cultural, and environmental change influences may be often underestimated. People have to face all kinds of restrictions that change their mentality and behaviors especially in post-pandemic era. It is a good adapting manner to integrate the transformational ICTs well into IoT sections merged into our lives.

IoT projects usually take longer than expected, and the more the consideration about IoT security, the more the details are involved.

The unique combination of software, hardware, and ICTs is as important as the necessary skills required for IoT deployment and developers.

Security is usually an afterthought. If we can eliminate the concerns of users in advance by giving priority to security, it will help promote the IoT products to markets earlier.

Interconnection is a complex problem. Fortunately, many groups, organizations, and industrial institutions have been formulating corresponding standards and the legitimate devices and connections are to be used.

Considering thousands of device connections, especially in IIoT scenarios, scalability poses new challenges to data/service models, middleware/platform design, and dedicated deployment.

Figure 9.1 Some enlightenments in the IoT projects.

the design for re-use and composable components, e.g., the PIoT/IoT grid) allowing a holistic approach, not only the introducing the future science, but also future technology, especially the intersection of the IoT engineering and information & communication technologies (ICTs).

Additionally, the book also nurtures social, technological, and humanistic innovations through its mediation between the digital ICTs and traditional cultural enlightenment and considers the present-day benefits and the sustainable development in a long run. By promoting the intersection of scientific and technological practices, the book opens a window to new methodologies and processes of generating new knowledge, to extensive research and development communities, and to achieve their relevant research goals: let them be open-minded to novelty, explorative mechanisms, creativity, and imagination, concentrated on concrete research outputs; meanwhile, the product design/deployment of close-to-market prototyping (see Sections 3.4, 6.2, and 6.6) can come true.

Secure and safe approaches are fundamental in making technological innovation in a profound and continuous way. As shown in Fig. 9.1, technical considerations for IoT security can fill in the gap between what is feasible from a pure technological point of view and what people can afford and enjoy in their daily lives for a better, trust-worthy life. At the same time, more humanistic viewpoints are discussed along with the progress of IoT and further introduction, especially in the relevant IoT security sections of Chapter 8. These provide tools and motivate us to climb the wisdom pyramid (see Chapter 2), and the Maslow's pyramid for both ourselves and intelligent things (see Chapter 8), with no worry about security at all.

To integrate the technological and humanistic views, the author has immersed himself with much reading including psychology lectures, e.g., *Harvard Open Class*, *Yale Open Class* (even including courses on "death", some of which can be easily obtained on the Internet, such as MOOC, Bilibili.com), and the series of *David's Brain Science*, trying to grasp the concept of "IoT security" as a whole while separately ignoring certain portions, such as certain key words of security, privacy, encryption, network/cyber security, etc., but trying not to focus merely on the sole interest of human beings, while "taking the sit" subject to the opposition of "things" for granted. In addition, Chapter 8 employs security analysis and security-by-design principles to discuss the security of IoT ecosystem and to implement cyber-security solutions from different levels. This chapter takes the readers on a journey beginning with understanding the security issues in IoT-enabled technologies to how it can be applied in various situations. It explains how to cope with the security challenges and address a secure infrastructure for IoT devices and solutions. The chapter helps readers gain an overall understanding of security architecture through IoT and offers state-of-the-art IoT countermeasures.

Nowadays, to improve a fully secured economy with all stakeholders and new markets online as well as all connecting and automated business processes, one can talk about a "post-pandemic economy" pushed and pulled by the innovation of the IoE era, where products and services can be fully and flexibly tailored to individual needs. For example, when writing the last part, in June 2021, the netizens around Adelaide central market, Australia, begin to buy fresh vegetables online (@https://shop.adelaidecentralmarket.com.au) in a no-personal-contact environment.

Likewise, the security of IoT is not only a technical issue but also a complementary humanistic issue including cognition, trust, and social responsibility. The above security-associated chapter is only an attempt to explore the so-called "Grand IoT security" (partly inspired by a lecture on clinical psychology about the dual process theory at Stanford University), and Chapter 8 starts with the humanistic analysis of IoT security, then after hierarchical discussion at a technical level, it attempts to unify humanistic analysis and technical application in the IoT security framework model.

However, under the construction of "Grand IoT security", people will accept and embrace the IoT in an appreciative way. People are sure that the IoT will not keep them vulnerable, nor their privacy be disclosed or misused, nor negatively affect their lives. In short, technical solutions just solve problems in a technical way. Design of beneficial and harmless security architecture for IoT, while ensuring a certain level of security in deployment, implementation and application, perhaps can only be achieved under the dual security protection of technology and humanity.

Finally, in the new IoE era, the actual relationship between ICT and IoT allows for an unprecedented integration in the context of technological research and practical application. The transformational innovation in the integration of things, IoT, and ICTs is bringing forth new business outcomes, enhancing the efficiency of workers with automation process, creating new digital products based on information-fueled insights and actions, or scaling the business by activating an ecosystem to enhance the individual capabilities through a unified solution. What we all look forward to are the following:

Toward the blossom of IoT ecosystem, through our long-term, unswerving efforts, the highly secure, long lasting, and comprehensive values will be created in the concurrent world of things around us, an appropriate security and safety framework established, the evolution strategy of IoT be optimized and a promising future with sufficient protection and growth potential will show up for given technology, morality, and law conditions.

Bibliography

3GPP TS 23.501. System architecture for the 5G system; Stage 2(R16). Available at https://www.3gpp.org/DynaReport/23501.htm.

3GPP. 3GPP TS 36. 305-2017, Evolved universal terrestrial radio access network (E-UTRAN); stage 2 functional specification of user equipment (UE) positioning in E-UTRAN V14. 1. 0. Dubrovnik: 3GPP Press, p. 78, 2017.

3GPP. NR and overall description. 3rd Generation Partnership Project (3GPP), TS 23.501, September 2020, v16.0. Available at http://www.3gpp.org/ftp/Specs/archive/.

3GPP. Study on using satellite access in 5G; Stage 1; Technical Report 38.822 v16.0.0, 2019. Available at https://portal.3gpp.org/desktopmodules/Specifications/SpecificationDetails.aspx?specificationId=3372.

3GPP. TR 22.822 — Study on Using Satellite Access in 5G. Sophia-Antipolis, France: 3GPP, 2018.

3GPP. TR 36.888, Study on Provision of Low-Cost Machine-Type Communications (MTC) User Equipments (UEs) Based on LTE V1200. 3GPP Press, 2013, p. 17.

3GPPP. Solutions for NR to support non-Terrestrial Networks *(NTN)*. Technical Report 38.821 v0.7.0, 2019. Available at https://portal.3gpp.org/. desktopmodules/Specifications/SpecificationDetails.aspx?specificationId=3525.

5G Americas White Paper. Cellular V2X Communications Towards 5G. March 2018.

5G Americas. *V2X Cellular Solutions*. October 2016.

5G Americas. LTE progress leading to the 5G massive Internet of Things, 2017, December 6, 2017. Available at http://www.5gamericas.org/files/8415/1250/0673/LTE_Progress_Leading_to_the_5G_Massive_Internet_of_Things_Final_12.5.pdf.

5G Network Architecture a High-Level Perspective. White Paper, HUAWEI Technologies Co. Ltd., 2016. Available at https://www-file.huawei.com/-/media/CORPORATE/PDF/mbb/5gnetworkarchitecturewhitepaperen.pdf?la=en&source=corp_comm.

5G Americas White Paper. The 5G-Evolution-3GPP Releases 16–17, 2020. Available at https://www.5gamericas.org/wp-content/uploads/2020/01/5G-Evolution-3GPP-R16-R17-FINAL.pdf.

A. Alarifi, A. Al-Salman, M. Alsaleh, A. Alnafessah, S. Al-Hadhrami, M. A. Al-Ammar, and H. S. Al-Khalifa. Ultra wideband indoor positioning technologies: Analysis and recent advances. *Sensors* 16: 707, 2016.

A. Azzara, S. Bocchino, P. Pagano, G. Pellerano, and M. Petracca. Middleware solutions in WSN: The IoT oriented approach in the ICSI project. In *Proceedings of the 21st International Conference Software Telecommunications and Computer Networks*. pp. 1–6, 2013.

A. Botta, W. de Donato, V. Persico, and A. Pescapé. Integration of cloud computing and Internet of Things: A survey. *Future Generation Computer Systems* 56: 684–700, March 2016.

A. C. Yao. Protocols for secure computation. In *Proceedings of the 23rd IEEE Symposium on Foundation of Computer Science*, Los Alamitos, CA, USA, IEEE Computer Society Press, pp. 160–164, 1982.

A. Fragkiadakis, E. Tragos, and A. Traganitis. Lightweight and secure encryption using channel measurements. In *2014 4th International Conference on Wireless Communications, Vehicular Technology, Information Theory and Aerospace & Electronic Systems (VITAE)*, IEEE, 2014.

A. Ghosh, A. Maeder, M. Baker and D. Chandramouli. 5G Evolution: A view on 5G cellular technology beyond 3GPP Release 15. *IEEE Access* 7: 127639–127651, 2019, doi: 10.1109/ACCESS.2019.2939938.

A. Gluhak, O. Vermesan, R. Bahr, F. Clari, T. Macchia, M. T. Delgado, A. Hoeer, F. Boesenberg, M. Senigalliesi, and V. Barchetti. Report on IoT platform activities, 2016. Available at http://www.internet-of-things-research.eu/pdf/D03_01_WP03_H2020_UNIFY-IoT_Final.pdf.

A. Grizhnevich. IoT architecture: Building blocks and how they work. April 1, 2018. Available at https://www.scnsoft.com/blog/iot-architecture-in-a-nutshell-and-how-it-works.

A. Hamam, A. El Saddik, and J. Alja'am. A quality of experience model for haptic virtual environments. *ACM Transactions on Multimedia Computing, Communications, and Applications* 10(3): 28, 2014.

A. Herutomo, M. Abdurohman, N. A. Suwastika, S. Prabowo, and C. W. Wijiutomo. Forest fire detection system reliability test using wireless sensor network and OpenMTC communication platform. In *2015 3rd International Conference on, Information and Communication Technology (ICoICT)*, pp. 87–91, May 27–29, 2015.

A. Hussien, N. Hamza, and H. A. Hefny. Attacks on anonymization-based privacy-preserving: A survey for data mining and data publishing. *Journal of Information Security* 4(2): 101–112, 2013.

A. Ikezoe, H. Nakamoto, and M. Nagase. Development of RTmiddleware for image recognition module. In *Proceedings of SICA-ICASE International Joint Conference 2006*, 2006.

A. Jerichow *et al.* 3GPP non-public network security. *Journal of ICT Standardization* January 2020. https://doi.org/10.13052/jicts2245-800X.815.

A. K. Jain, P. Flynn, and A. A. Ross. *Handbook of Biometrics*. Springer Science & Business Media, 2008.

A. Karaagac, P. Suanet *et al.* Light-weight integration and interoperation of localization systems in IoT. *Sensor*. MDPI.

A. L. Murphy, G. P. Picco, and G. Roman. LIME: A middleware for physical and logical mobility. In *Proceedings of the 21st International Conference on Distributed Computer Systems*. pp. 524–533, 2001.

A. P. Haripriya and K. Kulothungan. Secure-MQTT: An efficient fuzzy logic-based approach to detect DoS attack in MQTT protocol for Internet of Things. *EURASIP Journal on Wireless Communications and Networking* 2019(1): 1–15, 2019.

A. Loutfi, S. Coradeschi, G. Kumar Manib, P. Shankarb, and J. B. Balaguru Rayappanb. Electronic noses for food quality: A review. *Journal of Food Engineering* 144: 103–111, 2015.

A. Reyna, C. Martín, J. Chen, E. Soler, and M. Díaz. On blockchain and its integration with IoT. Challenges and opportunities. *Future Generation Computer Systems* 88: 173–190, 2018.

A. W. Al-Dabbagh, Y. Li, and T. Chen. An intrusion detection system for cyber-attacks in wireless networked control systems. *IEEE Transactions on Circuits and Systems II. Express Briefs* 65(8): 1049–1053, 2018.

A. W. Colombo, S. Karnouskos, O. Kaynak, Y. Shi, and S. Yin. Industrial cyber physical systems: A backbone of the fourth industrial revolution. *IEEE Industrial Electronics Magazine* 11(1): 6–16, 2017. https://doi. org/10.1109/mie.2017.2648857.

A. W. Colombo, T. Bangemann, S. Karnouskos, J. Delsing, P. Stluka, R. Harrison, F. Jammes, and J. Lastra (Eds.). *Industrial Cloud-based Cyber-Physical Systems: The IMC-AESOP Approach*. Springer, 2014.

A. Weitzendfeld, S. Gutierrez-Nolasco *et al.* MIRO: An embedded distributed architecture for biologically inspired mobile robots. In *11th IEEE International Conference on Advanced Robotics (ICAR'03)*, 2003.

Accenture 2016 Consumer Survey. Available at https://www.accenture.com/us-en/insight-ignite-growth-consumer-technology.

Adaptive attack means that an attacker tries to pass the security authentication of the system by collecting a large number of normal authentication session information (or even acting as a legitimate RFID reader or tag) in order to intrude into the system.

Amazon. Amazon planning 3,236-satellite constellation for Internet connectivity. 2019. Available at https://www.space.com/amazon-plans- 3236-satellite-constellation-for-internet.html. (Accessed July 29, 2019).

Analysys Mason. M2M and Internet of Things (IOT) opportunities for telecoms operators 2017, p. 6. Available at https://www.analysysmason.com/globalassets/x_migrated-media/media/analysys_mason_iot_operator_opportunities_vol3_jun20177.pdf.

Art. 6 GDPR — Lawfulness of processing | General Data Protection Regulation (GDPR) (gdpr-info.eu). Available at https://gdpr-info.eu/art-6-gdpr/.

Augmentation systems, such as Wide Area Augmentation System (WAAS) in the US, European Geo Navigation Overlapping System (EGNOS) in Europe, and Multi-Function Satellite Augmentation System (MSAS) in Japan.

B. Dieber *et al.* Ella: Middleware for multi-camera surveillance in heterogeneous visual sensor networks. *Conference Paper*, October 2013. https://doi.org/10.1109/ICDSC.2013.6778223.

B. Evans, N. Wang, Y. Rahulan *et al.* An integrated satellite–terrestrial 5G network and its use to demonstrate 5G use cases. *International Journal of Satellite Communication Network* 1–22, 2021. https://doi.org/10.1002/sat.1393.

B. Han, V. Gopalakrishnan, L. Ji, and S. Lee. Network function virtualization: Challenges and opportunities for innovations. *IEEE Communications Magazine* 53(2): 90–97, February 2015.

B. Nunes, M. Mendonca, X. -N. Nguyen, K. Obraczka, and T. Turletti. A survey of software-defined networking: Past, present, and future of programmable networks. *IEEE Communications and Surveys Tutorials* 16(3): 1617–1634, 2014.

B. Schilit, N. Adams, and R. Want. Context-aware computing applications. In *Proceedings of IEEE Workshop on Mobile Computing Systems and Applications, 1994*, Santa Cruz, CA, pp. 85–90, 1994. Foundations of Location Based Services. Available at https://www.research-gate.net/publication/230777155_Foundations_of_Location_Based_Services. (Accessed June 16, 2020).

B. Varga, J. Farkas *et al.* Integration of 5G and TSN. January 2020. Available at https://www.itu.int/en/ITU-T/Workshops-and-Seminars/202001/Documents/3_JanosFarkas_BalazsVargas.pdf.

Big Data triggers personal privacy related location. How to solve the security problem. January 27, 2016. Available at http://www.boiots.com/news/show-14665.html.

Blog ID: Wo13142yanyouxin. AdaBoost algorithm in face detection. CSDN blog. 2017. Available at https://blog.csdn.net/wo13142yanyouxin/article/details/76572119.

BodyCloud: A Cloud-assisted Software Platform for Pervasive and Continuous Monitoring of Assisted Livings using Wearable and Mobile Devices. Available at http://bodycloud.dimes.unical.it.

C. Bock, M. Marquardt, A. Martens, O. Simanski, and O. Hagendorf. Smart sensors and actors with BACnetTM and Mbed OS on Cortex-M micro-controllers. In *2019 IEEE 5th World Forum on Internet of Things (WF-IoT)*, Limerick, Ireland, pp. 937–942, 2019. https://doi.org/10.1109/WF-IoT.2019.8767341.

C. Curino, M. Giani, M. Giorgetta, A. Giusti, A. L. Murphy, and G. P. Picco. Mobile data collection in sensor networks: The TinyLime middleware. *Pervasive and Mobile Computing* 1(4–5): 446–469.

C. Fernndez-Llatas, A. Martinez-Romero, A. M. Bianchi, J. Henriques, P. Carvalho, and V. Traver. Challenges in personalized systems for Personal HealthCare. In *IEEE-EMBS International Conference on Biomedical and Health Informatics* (*BHI*), IEEE, pp. 356–359, 2016.

C. Gang and L. Huiqi. An analysis of the age of the Internet of things from the perspective of the relationship between man and nature. *Guide to Economic Research* (10): 189–190, 2012. Available at http://www.docin.com/p-456656473.html.

C. Gentry. Fully homomorphic encryption using ideal lattices. STOC 2009. Also, see A fully homomorphic encryption scheme, PhD thesis, Stanford University, 2009.

C. Gutierrez. Boeing improves operations with blockchain and the Internet of Things, 2017. Available at https://www.altoros.com/blog/boeing improves-operations-with-blockchain-and-the-internet-of-things/.

C. Lu, X. Rui *et al.* Feedback control real-time scheduling in ORB middleware. In *Proceedings of the 9th IEEE Real-Time and Embedded*

C. Magerkurth, A. S. Segura, N. Vicari, M. Boussard, and S. Meyer. IoT-A deliverable D6.3 — Final requirements list, Internet of Things Architecture IoT-A. EC Research Project. Available at http://www.meet-iot.eu/deliverables-IOTA/D6_3.pdf, 2013.

C. Ruixin, Z. Chuanyun, and H. Jingwu. RFID Cryptographic protocol based on mutual Hash authentication. *Microcomputer Information* 26(11): 149–151, 2010.

C. Steinbach, N. Ge, S. Wang, S. Member, I. Selinis, J. Cahill, M. Kavanagh, K. Liolis, C. Politis, J. Nunes, B. Evans *et al.* QoE-assured live streaming via satellite backhaul in 5G networks. *IEEE Transactions on Broadcast* 1–11, 2019.

C. Valasek. IOActive Technical White Paper. Remote exploitation of an unaltered passenger vehicle. 2015. Available at https://ioactive.com/pdfs/ IOActive_ Remote_Car_Hacking.pdf.

C. Y. Chow, M. F. Mokbel, and T. He. Tinycasper: A privacy-preserving aggregate location monitoring system in wireless sensor networks. In *SIGMOD*

'08 Proceedings of the 2008 ACM SIGMOD International Conference on Management of Data, Vancouver, BC, Canada; New York, USA: ACM, pp. 1307–1310, 2008.

C.-L. Fok, G. C. Roman, and C. Lu. Agilla: A mobile agent middleware for self-adaptive wireless sensor networks. *ACM Transactions on Autonomous & Adaptive Systems* 4(3): 1–26, 2009.

Cellular Internet of Things: From Massive Deployments to Critical 5G Applications. 2nd edn. Academic Press, 2020.

Cisco. White Paper. Time-sensitive networking: A technical introduction. Available at https://www.cisco.com/c/dam/en/us/solutions/collateral/industry-solutions/white-paper-c11-738950.pdf.

Cloud IoT Edge. Available at https://cloud.google.com/iot-edge/.

Credentials Community Group (W3C). A primer for decentralized identifiers. Draft Community Group Report 29 December 2020. Available at https://w3c-ccg.github.io/did-primer/.

D. Biswas *et al.* CorNET: Deep learning framework for PPG-based heart rate estimation and biometric identification in ambulant environment. *IEEE Transactions on Biomedical Circuits & Systems*, 2019.

D. Evans. The Internet of Things: How the next evolution of the Internet is changing everything. Cisco White Paper. April 11, 2011. Available at https://www.cisco.com/c/dam/en_us/about/ac79/docs/innov/IoT_IBSG_0411FINAL.pdf.

D. Freeman. Market trends: The five phases that smart lighting providers must address to be successful in the Internet of Things. Gartner, June 2, 2015. Available at https://www.gartner.com/en/documents/3067420.

D. Gelernter. Generative communication in Linda. *TOPLAS* 7(1): 80–112, 1985.

D. Henrici and P. M. Müller. Hash-based enhancement of location privacy for radio-frequency identification devices using varying identitiers. In *Proceedings of the IEEE International Conference on Pervasive Computing and Communications*, pp. 149–153, 2004.

D. I. Portillo, B. G. Cameron, and E. F. Crawley. A technical comparison of three low earth orbit satellite constellation systems to provide global broad- band. *Acta Astronautica* 159: 123–135, 2019.

D. Molnar, A. Soppera, and D. Wagner. A scalable, delegatable pseudonym protocol enabling ownership transfer of RFID tags. In *Proceedings of the Workshop on Selected Areas in Cryptography (SAC 2005)*, Vol. 3897 of LNCS, Springer, 2006.

D. Ramel. Microsoft makes run at 5G, edge computing with Azure edge zones. April 02, 2020. Available at https://rcpmag.com/articles/2020/04/02/microsoft-makes-run-at-5g-edge.aspx.

D. Yacchirema, R. Gonzalez-Usach, M. Esteve, and C. Palau. IoT interoperability applied to the domain of port and logistics. In *Transport Research Arena Conference 2018*, April 2018.

D6.3 Virtual Factory Experimentation Report. Available at https://cordis.europa.eu/docs/projects/cnect/4/604674/080/deliverables/001-D63FITMANVirtual-FactoryExperimentationReportv10.pdf.

Deloitte. Secure IoT by design Cybersecurity capabilities to look for when choosing an IoT platform. 2018. Available at https://www2.deloitte.com/content/dam/Deloitte/us/Documents/us-IoT-platform-security.pdf and https://www2.deloitte.com/us/en/pages/operations/articles/iot-platform-security.html.

Deloitte. Technology Trends 2019. Available at https://www2.deloitte.com/cn/en/pages/technology/articles/tech-trends-2019.html.

desktopmodules/Specifications/SpecificationDetails.aspx?specificationId=3525.

Discussing the construction of Internet of Things security mechanism from a biological perspective. Available at http://www.cnii.com.cn/thingsnet/2014-12/08/content_1492401.htm.

E. Candes and M. Wakin. An introduction to compressive sampling. *IEEE Signal Processing Magazine* 25(2): 21–30, 2008.

E. Cau, M. Corici, P. Bellavista, L. Foschini, G. Carella, A. Edmonds, and T. M. Bohnert. Efficient exploitation of mobile edge computing for virtualized 5G in EPC architectures. In *Proceedings of the 4th IEEE International Conference on Mobile Cloud Computing, Services, and Engineering*, Mobile Cloud, Oxford, UK, 29 March–1 April 2016, pp. 100–109.

E. Fourgeau, E. Gomez, H. Adli *et al*. System engineering workbench for multi — Views systems methodology with 3D-EXPERIENCE platform. The aircraft radar use case. In *Complex Systems Design & Management Asia*. Berlin, Germany: Springer International Publishing, 2016.

E. Kaljic *et al.* A survey on data plane flexibility and programmability in software-defined networking. *IEEE Access* 7: 47804–47840, 2019.

E. Steinbach *et al.* Haptic codecs for the tactile Internet. In *Proceedings of the IEEE*, pp. 1–24, 2018.

Enhancements and Performance Improvements, IEEE Standard 802.1Qcc-2018, October 2018.

Ericsson Mobility Report, June 2020, Available at https://www.ericsson.com/49da93/assets/local/mobility-report/documents/2020/june2020-ericsson-mobility-report.pdf.

E-Spion is presented by Dr. Elisa Bertino and her working group@ A. Mudgerikar, P. Sharma, and E. Bertino. E-Spion: A system-level intrusion detection system for IoT devices. In *Asia CCS*, pp. 493–500, 2019.

ETSI ISG Multi-access Edge Computing. Available at https://portal.etsi.org/MEC.

ETSI Technical Specification 102 690 Machine to Machine communications (M2M) Functional Architecture. V2.1.1. Available at http://www.etsi.org/deliver/etsi_ts/102600_102699/102690/02.01.01_60/ts_102690v020101p. pdf.

ETSI. "IPv6-based Tactile Internet", International Telecommunication Union (ITU), Group Specification GR IP6 0014, 2017.

ETSI. Network Functions Virtualization (NFV); architectural framework, 2013.

ETSI. TR 103 611 — Satellite Earth Stations and Systems (SES); Seamless Integration of Satellite and/or HAPS (High Altitude Platform Station) Systems into 5G System and Related Architecture Options, ETSI, Sophia Antipolis, France, 2019.

European Commission. An EU strategy on cooperative, connected and automated mobility. November 2016.

European Commission. Available at http://ec.europa.eu/economyfinance/articles/structuralreforms/2012-05-15ageingreporten.html.

F. Aiello, G. Fortino, and A. Guerrieri. Using mobile agents as enabling technology for wireless sensor networks. In *Proceedings of the SENSORCOMM*, August 2008.

F. Behmann and K. Wu. *Collaborative Internet of Things (C-IoT) for Future Smart Connected Life and Business*. John Wiley & Sons Ltd., 2015.

F. Bonomi, R. Milito, J. Zhu, and S. Addepalli. Fog computing and its role in the Internet of Things. In *Proceedings of the 1st Edition MCC Workshop Mobile Cloud Computing*. Helsinki, Finland, 2012, pp. 13–16.

F. Carrez, M. Bauer, M. Boussard, N. Bui, C. Jardak, J. D. Loof *et al*. SENSEI deliverable D1.5 — Final architectural reference model for the IoT v3.0, Internet of Things Architecture IoT-A. EC research project, 2013. Available at http://www.meet-iot.eu/deliverables-IOTA/D1_5.pdf.

F. James, S. Karnouskos, B. Bony, P. Nappey, A. W. Colombo, J. Delsing *et al.* Promising technologies for SOA-based industrial automation systems. In *Industrial Cloud-based Cyber-Physical Systems: The IMC- AESOP Approach*. Springer, 2014, pp. 89–109.

F. Tao, Y. Zuo, L. Xu *et al*. Internet of Things and BOM based life cycle assessment of energy-saving and emission-reduction of products. *IEEE Transactions on Industrial Informatics* 10(2): 1252–1261, 2014.

F. Völk, R. T. Schwarz, M. Lorenz, A. Knopp, and M. Landmann. Concept and evaluation of mobile cell connectivity over a satellite backhaul for future 5G networks. In *Proceedings of the IEEE Global Conference on Signal and Information Processing (GlobalSIP)*, Anaheim, CA, USA, November 26–29, 2018, pp. 1025–1029.

F. Völk. Satellite integration into 5G: Accent on first over-the-air tests of an edge node concept with Integrated satellite backhaul. *Future Internet* 11(9), 2019. DOI:10.3390/fi11090193.

F.-Y. Wang, J. Jason Zhang, X. Zheng, X. Wang, Y. Yuan, X. Dai, J. Zhang, and L. Yang. Where does AlphaGo go: From Church-Turing Thesis to AlphaGo Thesis and beyond. *IEEE/CAA Journal of Automatica Sinica* 3(2): 113–120, 2016.

Fraunhofer-FOKUS. Open5GCore, 2019. Available at http://www.open5gcore.org. (Accessed February 20, 2019).

From "Changes of Zhou" or "Zhou Yi".

FTC report on Internet of Things urges companies to adopt best practices to address consumer privacy and security risks. Federal Trade Commission, January 27, 2015. Accessed October 23, 2016.

G. Asharov and Y. Lindell. A full proof of the BGW protocol for perfectly secure multiparty computation. *Journal of Cryptology* 30: 1–94, 2015.

G. Baldini. Improving Internet of Things device certification with policy based management. Report of DG.JRC.E3. Available at https://iotweek.blob.core.windows.net/slides2017/GIoTS/GIoTS%20Paper%20Session-%20IoT%20Security%20and%20Privacy/G.%20Baldini%20Improving%20 Internet%20of%20Things%20Device%20Certification.pdf.

G. F. Anastasi, E. Bini, A. Romano, and G. Lipari. A service-oriented architecture for QoS configuration and management of wireless sensor networks. In *Proceedings of the IEEE Conference on Emerging Technologies and Factory Automation (ETFA)*. pp. 1–8, 2010.

G. Fedrecheski *et al.* Attribute-based access control for the swarm with distributed policy management. *IEEE Transactions on Consumer Electronics* 65(1): 90–98, 2019.

G. Fortino, C. Savaglio, C. E. Palau *et al.* Towards multi-layer interoperability of heterogeneous IoT platforms: The INTER-IoT approach. In *Integration, Interconnection, and Interoperability of IoT Systems*, 2018.

G. H. Merabet, M. Essaaidi, H. Talei, M. R. Abid, N. Khalil, M. Madkour, and D. Benhaddou. Applications of multi-agent systems in smart grids: A survey. In *Proceedings of the IEEE 2014 International Conference on Multimedia Computing and Systems (ICMCS)*, Marrakech, Morocco, April 14–16, 2014, pp. 1088–1094.

G. Kambourakis *et al.* A state-of-the-art review on the security of mainstream IoT wireless PAN protocol stacks. *Symmetry* 12(4): 579, 2020.

G. P. Fettweis, W. Lehner, and W. Nagel. Pathways to servers of the future: Highly Adaptive Energy Efficient Computing (HAEC). In *Proceedings of DATE-Conference*, pp. 1161–1166, 2013.

G. Sziebig, A. Gaudia, P. Korondi, N. Ando, and B. Solvang. Robotvision for RT-Middleware framework. In *2007 IEEE Instrumentation & Measurement Technology Conference IMTC 2007*, Warsaw, Poland, May 2007, pp. 1–6. (Accessed November 1, 2020).

G. Tsudik. YA-TRAP: Yet another trivial RFID authentication protocol. In *Proceedings of the IEEE International Conference on Pervasive Computing and Communications (PerCom 2006)*, IEEE Press.

G. V. Lioudakis, E. A. Koutsoloukas, N. Dellas *et al.* A proxy for privacy: The discreet box. In *Proceedings of the IEEE Eurocon2007*, Warsaw, Poland, 2007, IEEE, pp. 966–973, 2007.

G. Villarrubia, J. Bajo, J. F. De Paz, and J. M. Corchado. Monitoring and detection platform to prevent anomalous situations in home care. *Sensors* 14(6): 9900–9921, 2014. https://doi.org/10.3390/s140609900.

Google AR technology see "Google ARCore", which is available at https://developers.google.com/ar/. And Apple AR technology see "Apple ARKit", which is available at https://developer.apple.com/arkit/.

GSMA. Understanding the Internet of Things (IoT). July 2014. Available at https://www.gsma.com/iot/wp-content/uploads/2014/08/cl_iot_wp_07_14.pdf.

H. Chourabi, T. Nam, S. Walker, J. R. Gil-Garcia, S. Mellouli, K. Nahon, T. A. Pardo, and H. J. Scholl. Understanding smart cities: An integrative framework. In *Proceedings of the 2012 45th Hawaii International Conference on System Sciences*, IEEE, New York, pp. 2289–2297, 2012.

H. Haas. LiFi is a paradigm-shifting 5G technology. *Reviews in Physics* 3: 26–31, 2018.

H. Karimi and S. Jadid. Optimal energy management for multi-microgrid considering demand response programs: A stochastic multi-objective framework. *Energy* 195: 116992, 2020.

H. Ning *et al.* Physical unclonable function: Architectures, applications and challenges for dependable security. *IET Circuits Devices and Systems*, 2020.

H. Ning, F. Farha, A. Ullah, and L. Mao. Physical unclonable function: Architectures, applications and challenges for dependable security. *IET Circuits Devices and Systems* 14: 407–424, 2020. https://doi.org/10.1049/iet-cds.2019.0175.

H. Song *et al.* Analysis of AI development and the relationship of AI to IoT security. *DEStech Transactions on Computer Science and Engineering AITA*, 2017.

H. Song, S. Yanqiang *et al.* An improved location algorithm based on TDOA for wireless sensor networks[C]. In *2016 International Conference on Control and Automation (ICCA2016)*, January 15.

H. Song. *IoE: Core Technology and Security of IoT.* Tsinghua Press, another book of the author, pp. 214–215, 2019.

H. Song. *The Technology and Military Application of Internet of Things*. National Defense Industry Press, pp. P45–P60, 2013.

H. Urlings. Satellite IoT: A game changer for the industry? 2019. Available at http://satellitemarkets.com/satellite-iot-game-changer-industry.

HAEC. SFB 912: Highly adaptive energy-efficient computing. 2015. Available at http://tu-dresden.de/sfb912.

I. Corredor, J. F. Martinez, M. S. Familiar *et al.* Knowledge-aware and service-oriented middleware for deploying pervasive services. *Journal of Network & Computer Applications* 35(2): 562–576, 2012.

I. Corredor, J. F. Martnez, M. S. Familiar, and L. López. Knowledgeware and service-oriented middleware for deploying pervasive services. *Journal of Network and Computer Applications* 35: 562–576, 2012.

I. Marques, J. Ronan, and N. Rosa. A register-based virtual machine for wireless sensor networks. In *Proceedings of Sensors*. pp. 1423–1426, 2009.

I. Sittón-Candanedo, R. S. Alonso, J. M. Corchado, S. Rodríguez-González, and R. Casado-Vara. A review of edge computing reference architectures and a new global edge proposal. *Future Generation Computer Systems* 99: 278–294, 2019.

I. Sittón-Candanedo, R. S. Alonso, Ó. García, L. Muñoz, and S. Rodríguez-González. Edge computing, IoT and social computing in smart energy scenarios. *Sensors* 19(15): 3353, 2019. https://doi.org/10.3390/s19153353.

IBM and Samsung bet on Bitcoin Tech to save the Internet of Things. Available at https://securityledger.com/2015/01/ibm-and-samsung-bet-on-bitcoin-to-save-iot/.

ID TechEx. Comparison of Low Power Wide Area Networks (LPWAN) for IoT 2018–2019, Available at https://www.idtechex.com/research/articles/comparison-of-low-power-wide-area-networks-lpwan-for-iot-2018-2019-00014777.asp.

IEEE 1918.1. Available at http://grouper.ieee.org/groups/1918/1/.

IEEE P1901. Draft standard for broadband over power line networks: Medium access control and physical layer specifications. Available at http://grouper.ieee.org/groups/1901/index.html.

IEEE Standard for Local and Metropolitan Area Networks — Bridges and Bridged Networks — Amendment 31: Stream Reservation Protocol (SRP)

IEEE Std 2030.7. *IEEE Standard for the Specification of Microgrid Controllers*. Piscataway, NJ, USA: IEEE Standards Association, 2018.

IEEE Standard for Wireless Medium Access Control (MAC) and Physical Layer (PHY) Specifications for Peer Aware Communications.

IEEE Std 802.15.8-2017, 2017. 3GPP, "NR and NG-RAN overall description", 3rd Generation Partnership Project (3GPP), TS 38.300. December 2017, v2.0. Available at http://www.3gpp.org/ftp/Specs/archive/38series/38.300/.

IEEE. Tactile Internet emerging technologies subcommittee. Available at http://ti.committees.comsoc.org/.

Industrial Internet Consortium. The industrial Internet Consortium and OpenFog Consortium join forces. September 13, 2019. Available at http://www.iiconsorium.org/press-romm/12-18-18.html.

Industrial Internet of Things. Available at https://en.wikipedia.org/wiki/Industrial_Internet of Things.

INTER-IoT Ontology. Available at http://docs.inter-iot.eu/ontology.

International Journal of Wavelets, Multiresolution and Information Processing 19: 2050064:1–2050064:30, 2021.

International Telecommunication Union Telecom. Overview of the Internet of Things, ITU-T recommendation Y. 2060. Available at https://www.itu.int/rec/T-REC-Y.2060-201206-I, 2012.

Internet of Things: A vision for the future. Available at https://otalliance.org/IoT.

Introducing Fujisawa SST — A town sustainably evolving through living ideas, Panasonic. Available at http://panasonic.net/es/fujisawasst/.

IoT-A. Initial Architectural Reference Model for IoT. D1.2, June 2011.

IPSO Alliance. Internet Protocol for Smart Objects (IPSO). Available at https://www.ipso-alliance.org.

ITU Report. The Internet of Things, 2015. https://www.itu.int/osg/spu/publications/internetofthings/InternetofThings_summary.pdf.

J. Delsing. *IoT Automation: Arrowhead Framework*. CRC Press, 2017.

J. Farkas, B. Varga, G. Miklós, and J. Sachs. 5G-TSN integration meets networking requirements for industrial automation. *Ericsson Technology Review* 7, 2019.

J. Follett. *Designing for Emerging Technologies*. O'Reilly Media, 2014.

J. Fu, Y. Liu, H. Chao, B. K. Bhargava, and Z. Zhang. Secure data storage and searching for industrial IoT by integrating fog computing and cloud computing. *IEEE Transactions on Industrial Informatics* 14(10): 4519–4528, October 2018. https://doi.org/10.1109/TII.2018.2793350.

J. Höller, V. Tsiatsis, and C. Mulligan. Toward a machine intelligence layer for diverse industrial IoT use cases. *IEEE Intelligent Systems* 32(4): 64–71, 2017.

J. Ilmarinen. Promoting active ageing in the workplace. *European Agency for Safety and Health at Work (OSHA),* 2012.

J. J. Kang, T. H. Luan, and H. Larkin. Enhancement of sensor data transmission by inference and efficient data processing. In *International Conference on Applications and Techniques in Information Security*, Springer. Singapore, 2016.

J. Jimenez, K. Koster, and H. Tschofenig. *IPSO Smart Objects*. San Diego, CA, USA: IPSO Alliance, 2016.

J. Kim and S. Sukkarieh. Real-time implementation of airborne inertial-SLAM. *Robotics and Autonomous Systems* 55(1): 62–71, January 2007.

J. Kohnstamm and D. Madhub. Mauritius declaration on the Internet of Things. In *36th International Conference of Data Protection and Privacy Commissioners*, 2014.

J. Ma. Research on hierarchical access control mechanism of the IoT perception environment. Doctoral Dissertation of XiDian University, 2014.

J. Morrish, M. Hatton, and M. Arnott. Global IoT forecast insight report 2020. Transforma Insights, 2020. Available at https://transformainsights.com/research/reports/global-iot-forecast-insight-report-2020.

J. Popper, C. Harms, and M. Ruskowski. Enabling reliable visual quality control in smart factories through TSN. *Procedia CIRP* 88: 549–553, 2020.

J. Rong, C. Lai, J. Luo *et al.* EAP-based group authentication and key agreement protocol for machine-type communications. *International Journal of Distributed Sensor Networks* 2013(6), November 5, 2013.

J. Strömbergson. Some notes on the lightweight Block Cipher PRINCE. Available at https://www.assured.se/2020/04/24/some-notes-on-the-lightweight-block-cipher-prince/.

J. Virtanen, J. Virkki *et al.* Inkjet-printed UHF RFID tags on renewable materials. *Advances in Internet of Things* 2: 79–85, 2012. http://dx.doi.org/10.4236/ait.2012.24010.

J. Wang and P. Zhang. Research of industrial robot open service middle-ware based on SOA. *Journal of Shanghai Jiao Tong University* 50(S1): 23–26, 2016.

J. Wolfert, C. G. Sørensen, and D. Goense. A future Internet collaboration platform for safe and healthy food from farm to fork. In *Global Conference (SRII), 2014 Annual SRII*, IEEE, San Jose, CA, USA, pp. 266–273, 2014.

June 2004. Available at http://www.cl.cam.ac.uk/techreports/UCAMCL-TR-590.pdf.

K. Aberer, M. Hauswirth, and A. Salehi. A middleware for fast and flexible sensor network deployment. In *Proceedings of the 32nd International Conference on Very Large Data Bases*, p. 1199, 2006.

K. Briodagh. STMicroelectronics and Valencell reveal biometric IoT sensor platform. Iotevolutionworld. 2016. Available at http://www. iotevolutionworld.com/m2m/articles/428233-stmicroelectronics-valencell-reveal-biometric-iot-sensor-platform.htm and http://www.iotevolutionworld.com/m2m/articles/428233-stmicroelectronics-valencell-reveal-biometric-iot-sensor-platform.htm.

K. Chiew, Y. Li, T. Li, and R. H. Deng. On false authentications for C1G2 passive RFID tags. In *Radio Frequency Identification System Security*, pp. 50–65.

K. D. Vavelidis, C. P. Kapnistis, and I. F. Vassiliou. Method and system for RF front-end calibration scheme using fractional-N frequency synthesized signals and RSSI. 2010.

K. Ding *et al.* Defining a digital twin-based cyber-physical production system for autonomous manufacturing in smart shop floors. *International Journal of Production Research* 1–23, 2019.

K. E. Skouby I. Williams, and A. Gyamfi. *Handbook on ICT in Developing Countries: Next Generation ICT Technologies. River Publishers Series in Communications*. Denmark: Aalborg University, May 2019.

K. Goerlich. IoT 2.0: Rewiring To Create Live, Digital Businesses. LinkedIn 2016. Available at http://www.linkedin.com/pulse/iot-20-rewiring-create-live-digital-businesses-kai-goerlich.

K. Henricksen and R. Robinson. A survey of middleware for sensor networks: State-of-the-art and future directions. In *Proceedings of the Middleware Sensor Networks*. pp. 60–65, 2006.

K. Katsuragawa, J. Wang, Z. Shan *et al.* Tip-Tap: Battery-free discrete 2D fingertip input. In *UIST'19 Proceedings of the 32nd Annual ACM Symposium on User Interface Software and Technology*, pp. 1045–1057.

K. Liolis, A. Geurtz, R. Sperber, D. Schulz, S. Watts, G. Poziopoulou, B. Evans, N. Wang, O. Vidal, B. Tiomela *et al.* Use cases and scenarios of 5G integrated satellite-terrestrial networks for enhanced mobile broadband: The SaT5G approach. *International Journal of Satellite Communications and Networking* 91–112, 2018.

K. N. Lianos, J. L. Schönberger, M. Pollefeys, and T. Sattler. VSO: Visual semantic odometry. In *Lecture* Notes *in Computer Science (Including Subseries Lecture* Notes *in Artificial Intelligence and Lecture* Notes *in Bioinformatics)*, 11208 LNCS, pp. 246–263, 2018. https://doi.org/10.1007/978-3-030-01225-015.

L. Atzori, A. Iera, and G. Morabito. The Internet of Things: A survey.*Computer Networks* 54(15): 2787–2805, 2010.

L. Cheng. Research on authentication technology and key management in Internet of things. Doctoral dissertation, Central South University, 2013.

L. Gao, B. Chen, and L. Yu. Fusion-based FDI attack detection in cyberphysical systems. IEEE Transactions on *Circuits and Systems II: Express Briefs* (99): 1–1, 2019.

L. Jorge *et al.* A proof-of-concept for semantically interoperable federation of IoT experimentation facilities. *Sensors* 16(7): 1006, 2016.

L. Juhani, I. Antti, V. Paul *et al.* A survey on M2M service Networks. *Computers* 3(4): 130–173, 2014.

L. Mottola, A. L. Murphy, and G. P. Picco. Pervasive games in a moteenabled virtual world using tuple space middleware. In *Proceedings of the 5th ACM SIGCOMM*. p. 29, 2006.

L. Tightiz, H. Yang, and M. J. Piran. A survey on enhanced smart micro-grid management system with modern wireless technology contribution. *Energies* 13(9): 2258, 2020. https://doi.org/10.3390/en13092258.

L. Ying, X. Yong, Z. Yanping, and K. Yan. The design and implement of Hilbert location k-Anonymity algorithm based on Spatial Quadtree. *Journal of Wuhan University (Natural Science)* 64(3), 2018.

L. Z. Li, P. L. Zhou, P. Cheng, Z. G. Shi. Architecture, challenges and applications of edge computing. *Big Data Research* 5(2): 3–16, 2019.

L. Zhai and Q. Hu. The research of double-biometric identification technology based on finger geometry & palm print. *Communications in Information Science and Management Engineering* 3(2): 100–105, February 2013.

L. Zhu. Internet of Things, quietly into your life. *Science and Technology Daily*, May 13, 2016. Available at: http://www.cac.gov.cn/2016-05/13/c_1118858885.htm.

M. A. Razzaque, M. Milojevic-Jevric, A. Palade *et al.* Middleware for Internet of Things: A survey. *IEEE Internet of Things Journal* 3(1): 70–95, 2017.

M. Abdurohman *et al.* M2M middleware based on OpenMTC platform for enabling smart cities solution. ICST Institute for Computer Sciences, Social Informatics and Telecommunications Engineering 2016. A. Leon-Garcia *et al.* (eds.), *Smart City 2015*, LNICST, Vol. 166, pp. 239–249, 2016. https://doi.org/10.1007/978-3-319-33681-7_20.

M. Abdurohman, A. Herutomo, V. Suryani, A. Elmangoush, and T. Magedanz. Mobile tracking system using OpenMTC platform based on event driven method. In *2013 IEEE. 38th Conference on Local Computer Networks Workshops (LCN Workshops)*, pp. 856–860, October 21–24, 2013.

M. Abdurohman, A. Sasongko, and A. Herutomo. *M2M Middleware Based on OpenMTC Platform for Enabling Smart Cities Solution*. Springer International Publishing, 2016.

M. Aly, F. Khomh, Y. Guéhéneuc, H. Washizaki, and S. Yacout. Is fragmentation a threat to the success of the Internet of things? *IEEE Internet of Things Journal* 6(1): 472–487, February 2019. https://doi.org/10.1109/JIOT.2018.2863180.

M. Corici, I. Gheorghe-Pop, E. Cau, K. Liolis, C. Politis, A. Geurtz, F. Burkhardt, S. Covaci, J. Koernicke, F. Völk *et al.* SATis5 solution: A comprehensive practical validation of the satellite use cases in 5G. In *Proceedings of the 24th Ka and Broadband Communications Conference*, Niagara Falls, ON, Canada, October 15–18, 2018.

M. Corici, K. Liolis *et al.* Satellite is 5G: SATis5 Whitepaper, November 2020.

M. Eisenhauer *et al. The Next Generation Internet of Things — Hyperconnectivity and Embedded Intelligence at the Edge*. River Publishers, 2018.

M. Fowler. Microservices: A definition of this new architectural term. 2014. Available at https://martinfowler.com/articles/microservices.html.

M. Frey *et al.* Security for the industrial IoT: The case for information-centric networking. In *2019 IEEE 5th World Forum on Internet of Things (WF-IoT), Limerick,* Ireland. pp. 424–429, 2019. https://doi.org/10.1109/WF-IoT.2019.8767183.

M. Ganzha, M. Paprzycki, W. Pawłowski, P. Szmeja, and K. Wasielewska. Alignment-based semantic translation of geospatial data. In *Advances in Computing, Communication and Automation (ICACCA)*. September 2017.

M. Grieves. *Virtually Perfect: Driving Innovative and Lean Products through Product Lifecycle Management*. 2011.

M. Gunasekaran. Adaptive neural network with hybrid optimization oriented localization in wireless sensor network: A multi-objective model.

M. Gupta, J. Gao, C. C. Aggarwal, and J. Han. Outlier detection for temporal data: A survey. *IEEE Transactions on Knowledge and Data Engineering* 26(9): 2250–2267, September 2014, https://doi.org/10.1109/TKDE.2013.184.

M. Kranz, R. B. Rusu, A. Maldonado, M. Beetz, and A. Schmidt. A player/stage system for context-aware intelligent environments. In *Proceedings of the System Support for Ubiquitous Computing Workshop (UbiSys 2006), at the 8th Annual Conference on Ubiquitous Computing (Ubicomp 2006)*, Orange County, CA, September 2006.

M. Langheinrich. Privacy by design — Principles of privacy-aware ubiquitous systems. Version: 2001. In *Ubicomp 2001: Ubiquitous Computing Bd. 2201*, G. D. Abowd, B. Brumitt, and S. Shafer (eds.), Berlin, Heidelberg: Springer, pp. 273–291, 2001. http://dx.doi.org/10.1007/3-540-45427-6-23.

M. Li. Framework analysis of open source vector similarity search engine-Milvus.

M. Mamei and F. Zambonelli. *Field-Based Coordination for Pervasive Multiagent Systems*. Berlin, Germany: Springer-Verlag, 2005.

M. Marchese, A. Moheddine, and F. Patrone. IoT and UAV integration in 5G hybrid terrestrial-satellite networks. *Sensors* 19(17): 3704, 2019.

M. Mizukawa, H. Matsuka, T. Koyama, T. Inukai, A. Noda, H. Tezuka, Y. Noguchi, and N. Otera. ORiN: Open robot interface for the network — The standard and unified network interface for industrial robot applications. In *Proceedings of the 41st SICE Annual Conference (SICE 2002)*, Tokyo, Japan, Vol. 2, pp. 925–928.

M. Nadeski. Bringing machine learning to embedded systems. Available at https://www.ti.com/lit/wp/sway020a/sway020a.pdf.

M. Roberts. Serverless architectures. 2016. Available at https://martin-fowler.com/articles/serverless.html.

M. Romanato, D. Drozdov, S. Patil, J. Delsing, and V. Vyatkin. Arrowhead Datamanager integration with Eclipse 4DIAC environment. In *2020 25th IEEE International Conference on Emerging Technologies and Factory Automation (ETFA)*. Vienna, Austria, 2020, pp. 1377–1380. https://doi.org/10.1109/ETFA46521.2020.9212004.

M. Satyanarayanan, P. Bahl, R. Caceres, and N. Davies. The case for VM-based cloudlets in mobile computing. *IEEE Pervasive Computing* 8(4): 14–23, October/December 2009.

M. Scott and R. Whitney. The industrial Internet of Things, 2014. Available at http://www.mcrockcapital.com/uploads/1/0/9/6/10961847/mcrock_industrial_ internet_of_things_report_2014.pdf.

M. Sharif, J. Skowronek, and G. Lueckemeyer. HPC (High Performance Computing) diagnostics list of use-cases for standardization. BMW. COaaS: Continuous integration and delivery framework for HPC. In *Conference: BDIOT 2020*, Singapore, 2020.

M. Simsek, A. Aijaz, M. Dohler, J. Sachs, and G. Fettweis. 5G-enabled tactile Internet. *IEEE Journal on Selected Areas in Communications* February 2016. https://doi.org/10.1109/JSAC.2016.2525398.

M. Simsek, A. Aijaz, M. Dohler, J. Sachs, and G. Fettweis. 5G-enabled tactile Internet. *IEEE Journal on Selected Areas in Communications* 34(3): 460–473, March 2016. https://doi.org/10.1109/JSAC.2016.2525398.

M. Singh, M. A. Rajan, V. L. Shivraj, and P. Balamuralidhar. Secure MQTT for Internet of Things (IoT). In *2015 Fifth International Conference on Communication Systems and Network Technologies*, pp. 746–751, 2015. https://doi.org/10.1109/CSNT.2015.16.

M. Strese, R. Hassen, A. Noll, and E. Steinbach. A tactile computer mouse for the display of surface material properties. *IEEE Transactions on Haptics* 12(1): 18–33, January–March 2019. https://doi.org/10.1109/TOH.2018.2864751. Epub August 10, 2018.

M. Su, B. Zhou, A. Fu *et al.* PRTA: A proxy re-encryption based trusted authorization scheme for nodes on cloud IoT. *Information Sciences*, January 28, 2019. https://doi.org/10.1016/j.ins.2019.01.051.

M. Vinyals, J. A. Rodriguez-Aguilar, and J. Cerquides. A survey on sensor networks from a multi-agent perspective. *The Computer Journal* 54(3): 455–470, March 2011. https://doi.org/10.1093/comjnl/bxq018.

M. W. M. G. Dissanayake, P. Newman, S. Clark, H. F. Durrant-Whyte, and M. Csorba. A solution to the Simultaneous Localization and Map Building (SLAM) problem. *IEEE Transactions on Robotics and Automation* 17(3): 229–241, June 2001.

MEC in 5G networks. ETSI White Paper. Available at https://www.etsi.org/images/files/ETSIWhitePapers/etsi_wp28_mec_in_5G_FINAL.pdf.

Moor Insights and Strategy. Behaviorally segmenting the Internet of Things (IoT), 2013. Available at http://www.moorinsightsstrategy.com/wp-content/uploads/2013/10/Behaviorally-Segmenting-the-IoT-by-Moor-Insights-Strategy.pdf.

N. Bennani, C. Ghedira-Guegan, M. A. Musicante, and G. Vargas-Solar. SLA-Guided Data Integration on Cloud Environments. CLOUD, June 2014, Alaska, United States, pp. 934–935. https://doi.org/10.1109/CLOUD.2014.130. hal-01006238.

N. Gruschka, D. Gessner, A. Serbanati, A. S. Segura, A. Olivereau, Y. B. Saied *et al.* SENSEI deliverable D4.2 — Concepts and solutions for privacy and security in the resolution infrastructure, Internet of Things.

N. M. Kou, C. Peng *et al.* Idle time optimization for target assignment and path finding in sortation centers. In *Proceedings of the AAAI Conference on Artificial Intelligence* 34(6): 9925–9932, 2020. https://doi.org/10.1609/aaai.v34i06.6547.

N. Sakr, N. Georganas, J. Zhao, and X. Shen. Motion and force prediction in haptic media. In *Proceedings of the IEEE International Conference on Multimedia and Expo*. pp. 2242–2245, July 2007.

Next_Generation_Internet_of_CRACKed_Distributed_Intelligence_at_the_Edge_IERC_2018_Cluster_eBook_978-87-7022-007-1_P_Web.pdf.

Ó. García, R. S. Alonso, J. Prieto, and J. M. Corchado. Energy efficiency in public buildings through context-aware social computing. *Sensors* 17(4): 826, 2017. https://doi.org/10.3390/s17040826.

O. Gunther. Security challenges of the EPCglobal network Beam in Fabian. *Communications of the ACM* 7(52): 121–125, 2009.

O. Savry and F. Vacherand. Security and privacy protection of contactless devices. In *The Internet of Things: 20th Tyrrhenian Workshop on Digital Communications*, New York: Springer New York, pp. 409–418, 2010.

O. Vermesan and J. Bacquet. *Next Generation Internet of Things Distributed Intelligence at the Edge and Human Machine-to-Machine Cooperation.* River Press, 2018. pp. 38, 87, 148.

O. Vermesan and P. Friess. *Building the Hyperconnected Society IoT Research and Innovation Value Chains, Ecosystems and Markets*. River Publishers, p. 159, 2019.

O. Vermesan and P. Friess. *Building the Hyperconnected Society IoT Research and Innovation Value Chains, Ecosystems and Market.* River Publishers, Vol. 43, pp. 80, 192–195, 203, 2015.

O. Vermesan and P. Friess. Digitising the industry Internet of things connecting the physical, digital and virtual worlds. In *River Publishers Series in Communications*. Vol. 49, pp. 22, 89–92, 162, 206, 2016.

O. Vermesan and P. Friess. *IoT Digital Value Chain Connecting Research, Innovation and Deployment. River Publishers Series in Communications*. Vol. 49, pp. 206–207, 2016.

O. Vermesan *et al.* Internet of energy — Connecting energy anywhere any- time. In *Advanced Microsystems for Automotive Applications 2011: Smart Systems for Electric, Safe and Networked Mobility*, Springer, Berlin, 2011.

O. Vermesan *et al. Internet of Things — The Call of the Edge — Everything Intelligent Everywhere.* DK: River Publishers, October 2020.

OASIS Devices Profile for Web Services (DPWS). Available at http://docs.oasis-open.org/ws-dd/ns/dpws/2009/01.

OMA Lightweight M2M. Available at https://www.omaspecworks.org.

OPC UA for Field Level Communication — A Theory of Operation. (v1.2020). Available at https://opcfoundation.org/wp-content/uploads/2020/11/OPCF-FLC-Technical-Paper-C2C.pdf.

OPC-UA Security Model for Administrators. (v.1.2014) Available at https://opcfoundation.org/wp-content/uploads/2014/05/OPC-UA_Security_Model_for_ Administrators_V1.00.pdf.

OPC-UA. Available at https://opcfoundation.org/about/opc-technologies/opc-ua/.

Open Mobile Alliance (OMA). Lightweight machine to machine technical specification V1.0.2. 2018. Available at http://www.openmobilealliance.org/release/LightweightM2M/V1_0_2-20180209-A/OMA-TS-LightweightM2MV1_0_2-20180209-A.pdf.

OTA Research September 8, 2016. https://otalliance.org/IoTvulnerabilities.

P. A. L. Besari, M. Abdurohman, and A. Rakhmatsyah. Application of M2M to detect the air pollution. In *2015 3rd International Conference on Information and Communication Technology (ICoICT)*, pp. 87–91, 27–29, 2015.

P. A. Levis. Application specific virtual machines: Operating system sup- port for user-level sensor net programming. Ph.D. dissertation, Berkeley, CA, USA, 2005.

P. Adolphs, H. Bedenbender, D. Dirzus, M. Ehlich, U. Epple, M. Hankel *et al.* Reference architecture model industrie 4.0 (RAMI4.0). Tech. Rep., 2015. Available at https://goo.gl/3DcvkQ.

P. Andreou, D. Zeinalipour-Yiazti, P. Chrysanthis, and G. Samaras. Towards a network-aware middleware for wireless sensor networks. In *Proceedings of the International Workshop on Data Management for Sensor Networks (DMSN)*, 2011.

P. C. Calcina-Ccori *et al.* Enabling semantic discovery in the Swarm. *IEEE Transactions on Consumer Electronics* 65(1): 57–63, 2018.

P. Costa *et al.* The runes middleware for networked embedded systems and its application in a disaster management scenario. In *Proceedings of the 5th Annual IEEE International Conference on Pervasive Computing and Communications* (PerCom'07). pp. 69–78, 2007.

P. Kang, C. Borcea, G. Xu *et al.* Smart messages: A distributed computing platform for networks of embedded systems. Special issues on mobile and pervasive computing. *The Computer Journal* 2004.

P. M. Papadopoulos, V. Reppa, M. M. Polycarpou, and C. G. Panayiotou. Scalable distributed sensor fault diagnosis for smart buildings. *IEEE/CAA Journal of Automatica Sinica* 7(3): 638–655, May 2020.

P. Mogensen, A. Ghosh, A. Maeder, M. Uusitalo, and S. Redana. 5G evo- lution: A view on cellular technology beyond 5G. Presented at the 6G Conf., Levi, Finland, March 2019. Available at http://www.6gsummit.com/speakers/preben-mogensen/. (Accessed September 2019).

P. N. Karamolegkos *et al.* User-profile based communities assessment using clustering methods. In *Proceedings of 18th International Symposium on Personal, Indoor and Mobile Radio Communications*, PIMRC IEEE, 2007.

P. R. Pietzuch. Hermes: A scalable event-based middleware. University of Cambridge, Computer Laboratory, Technical Report. UCAM-CL-TR-590,

P. Zhi-juan. Hierarchical analysis of Internet of Things security. *Computer Knowledge and Technology* 12(16): 71–72, June 2016.

P. Zhisong and S. Bing. Research and simulation of intelligent robot visual in obstacle recognition method. *Computer Simulation* 33(1), 2016.

Path. Hawking (Hawking): The earth has only 1000 years left. Fast Technology. 2016. Available at http://news.mydrivers.com/1/507/507985. htm (Hawking delivered a speech on the universe and the future of humanity at the Oxford Union on November 14, 2016).

Pew Research Center. Americans' attitudes about privacy, security and surveillance, 2015. Available at http://www.pewinternet.org/2015/05/20/americans-attitudes-about-privacy-security-and-surveillance/.

Polaris RTLS. Available at http://www.nebusens.com/en/products/polaris.

Proceedings Volumes 42(4): 2131–2136, 2009. https://doi.org/10.3182/20090603-3-ru-2001.0551.

Q. F. Yan, H. Y. Hu, T. P. Hang *et al.* Path tracking of INS AGV corrected by double magnetic nails based on fuzzy controller. In *2019 IEEE 3rd Advanced Information Management, Communicates, Electronic and Automation Control Conference (IMCEC)*, IEEE, 2019.

Q. Hong. Research on RFID Security Protocol and Implementation of General Test Platform. University of Electronic Science and Technology of China, June 2015.

Q. Lou, W.-J. Lu *et al. Falcon: Fast Spectral Inference on Encrypted Data*. NIPS 2020.

Q. Tong, P. Li, and S. Shen. VINS-Mono: A robust and versatile monocular visual-inertial state estimator. *IEEE Transactions on Robotics* (99): 1–17, 2017.

Q. Wang, X. Xiong, W. Tian *et al.* Low-cost RFID: Security problems and solutions. In *Proceedings of the 2011 International Conference on Management and Service Science.* IEEE, Piscataway, pp. 1–4, 2011.

Qualcomm. Accelerating C-V2X Commercialization, September 2017.

R. Balani, C.-C. Han, R. K. Rengaswamy, I. Tsigkogiannis, and M. Srivastava. Multi-level software reconfiguration for sensor networks. In *Proceedings of the 6th ACM IEEE International Conference on Embedded Software*. pp. 112–121, 2006.

R. Dreves, F. Hällmayer, L. Haunert, B. Sechser, and A. Rieß. A method to realize traceability in development processes. *Journal of Software Evolution and Process* 28: 1011–1019, 2016. https://doi.org/10.1002/smr.1828.

R. Gravina, C. Ma, P. Pace, G. Aloi, W. Russo, W. Li, and G. Fortino. Cloudbased Activity-as-a-Service cyber physical framework for human activity monitoring in mobility. *Future Generation Computer Systems*, 2016.

R. Mick and C. Polsonetti. Collaborative automation: The platform for operational excellence. Arc Advisory Group. ARC White Paper-2003.

R. Neisse, G. Steri, I. N. Fovino *et al.* SecKit: A model-based security toolkit for the Internet of Things. *Computers & Security*, 2015.

R. Neisse, I. Nai Fovino, G. Baldini *et al.* A model-based security toolkit for the Internet of things. In *International Conference on Availability, Reliability and Security (ARES)*, University of Fribourg, Switzerland, 2014.

R. Pinto, G. Gonçalves, E. Tovar, and J. Delsing. Attack detection in cyber-physical production systems using the deterministic dendritic cell algorithm. In *2020 25th IEEE International Conference on Emerging Technologies and Factory Automation (ETFA)*, Vienna, Austria. pp. 1552–1559, 2020. https://doi.org/10.1109/ETFA46521.2020.9212021.

R. Rivest, L. Adleman, and M. L. Dertouzos. On data banks and privacy homomorphisms. *Foundations of Secure Computation*, 1978.

R. Roman, J. Zhou, and J. Lopez. On the features and challenges of security and privacy in distributed Internet of Things. *Computer Networks* 57(10): 2266–2279. Towards a Science of Cyber Security Security and Identity Architecture for the Future Internet, 2013.

Reference Architecture Foundation for Service-Oriented Architecture Version 1.0. 04 December 2012. OASIS Committee Specification 01.

Revised WID: Integrated Access and Backhaul for NR, document RP-190712, 3GPP, Shenzhen, China, March 2019.

RFID Security issues-Generation2 Security. Available at: http://www.thingmagic.com/index.php/rfid-security-issues.

S. Boschert and R. Rosen. Digital twin-the simulation aspect. In *Mechatronic Futures*. Berlin, Germany: Springer Verlag, 2016.

S. H. Nethravathi. Implementation of AUTOSAR ASW and I/O abstraction layer. In *2015 International Conference on Innovations in Information, Embedded and Communication Systems (ICIIECS)*. Coimbatore, pp. 1–5, 2015, https://doi.org/10.1109/ICIIECS.2015.7193003.

S. Howell, Y. Rezgui, J. L. Hippolyte, B. Jayan, and H. Li. Towards the next generation of smart grids: Semantic and holonic multi-agent management of distributed energy resources. *Elsevier Renewable and Sustainable Energy Reviews* 77: 193–214, 2017.

S. K. Lo *et al.* Analysis of blockchain solutions for IoT: A systematic literature review. *IEEE Access* 99: 1–1, 2019.

S. K. Sharma, I. Woungang *et al.* Toward tactile Internet in beyond 5G era: Recent advances, current issues, and future directions. *IEEE Access* 8: 56948–56991, 2020. https://doi.org/10.1109/ACCESS.2020.2980369.

S. Karnouskos, A. W. Colombo, T. Bangemann, K. Manninen, R. Camp, M. Tilly, P. Stluka, F. Jammes, J. Delsing, and J. Eliasson. A SOA-based architecture for empowering future collaborative cloud-based industrial automation. In *38th Annual Conference of the IEEE Industrial Electronics Society (IECON 2012)*. Montréal, Canada, 2012.

S. Karnouskos, D. Guinard, D. Savio, P. Spiess, O. Baecker, V. Trifa *et al.* Towards the real-time enterprise: Service based integration of heterogeneous SOA-ready industrial devices with enterprise applications. *IFAC*

S. Karnouskos, D. Savio, P. Spiess, D. Guinard, V. Trifa, and O. Baecker. Real world service interaction with enterprise systems in dynamic manufacturing environments. In *Artificial Intelligence Techniques for Networked Manufacturing Enterprises Management*, L. Benyoucef and B. Grabot (Eds.), Springer, 2010.

S. Lin, H. F. Cheng, W. Li, Z. Huang, P. Hui, and C. Peylo. Ubii: Physical world interaction through augmented reality. *IEEE Transactions on Mobile Computing* 16: 872–885.

S. Lucero (IHS Whitepaper). IoT platforms: Enabling the Internet of Things, 2016. Available at http://cdn.ihs.com/www/pdf/enabling-IOT.pdf.

S. Mijovic, E. Shehu, and C. Buratti. Comparing application layer protocols for the internet of things via experimentation. In *2016 IEEE 2nd International Forum on Research and Technologies for Society and Industry Leveraging a Better Tomorrow (RTSI)*, 978-1-5090-1131- 5/16/$31.00.

S. Nangare. What's next: 5G network slicing with ETSI OSM 5 and OpenStack. May 24, 2019. Available at https://superuser.openstack.org/articles/5g-network-slicing-etsi-osm-5-and-openstack/.

S. Newman. *Building Microservices: Designing Fine-Grained Systems*. Press of O'Reilly Media, 2014.

S. Sukhmani *et al.* Edge caching and computing in 5G for mobile AR/VR and tactile Internet. *IEEE MultiMedia* 26(1): 21–30, 2019.

S. Wagh, D. Gupta, and N. Chandran. SecureNN: 3-Party secure computa- tion for neural network training. In *Proceedings on Privacy Enhancing Technologies*, pp. 1–24, 2018.

SATis5. Demonstrator for Satellite-Terrestrial Integration in the 5G Context, 2018. Available at https://satis5.eurescom.eu/.

SCHADE H J. CEN — ETSI Progress Report. Available at https://www.etsi.org/images/files/technologies/Final_Joint_Mandate_M453_Report_2013-07-15.pdf.

See Connected Factory Global. Manufacturing Control System Cybersecurity: Risk Assessment & Mitigation Strategies. 2016. Available at http://www.connectedfactoryglobal.com/resources/cybersecurity-report/.

See ENISA. Baseline security recommendations for IoT. 2017. Available at https://www.enisa.europa.eu/publications/baseline-security-recommendations-for-iot/at_download/fullReport.

Sensors 18: 2142, 2018. https://doi.org/10.3390/s18072142.

SES. SES ASTRA 2F Satellite, 2019. Available at https://www.ses.com/our-coverage/satellites/344.

Sevone. How will the Internet of Things disrupt your performance monitoring strategy? White Paper. 2015. Available at https://www.sevone.com/

whitepaper/how-will-internetthings-disrupt-your-performance-monitoring-strategy 2015.

Sino-German White Paper on Functional Safety for Industrie 4.0 and Intelligent Manufacturing. 2020.

SpaceX. SpaceX's Starlink Constellation Construction Begins. 2200 Satellites Will go up Over the Next five years, 2019. Available at https://www.universetoday.com/141980/spacexs-starlink-constellation-construction-begins-2200-satellites-will-go-up-over-the-next-5-years/. (Accessed July 29, 2019).

Specification Group Services and System Aspects; Release 14 Description; Summary of Rel-14 Work Items Release 14 (2018-03).

State of the IoT 2018: Number of IoT devices now at 7B — Market accelerating, IoT analytics, Available at https://iot-analytics.com/state-ofthe-iot-update-q1-q2-2018-number-of-iot-devices-now-7b/.

STMicroelectronics. Neural Networks on STM32. Available at https://www.st.com/content/st_com/en/about/innovation---technology/artificial-intelligence.html.

Study on Architecture Aspects for Using Satellite Access in 5G, document SP-181253, 3GPP, Reno, NV, USA, May 2019.

Study on Enablers for Network Automation for 5G — Phase 2, document SP-190557, 3GPP, Sapporo, Japan, June 2019.

Study on Enhanced Support of Industrial IoT, document S2-1908585, 3GPP, Sapporo, Japan, June 2019.

Study on Enhanced Support of Non-Public Networks, document SP-190453, 3GPP, May 2019.

Study on Enhancement of Support for 5G LAN-Type Service, document SP-190454, Reno, NV, USA, May 2019.

Study on Enhancement of Support for Edge Computing in 5GC, document SP-190185, 3GPP, Reno, NV, USA, May 2019.

Study on Enhancement to the 5GC Location Services-Phase 2, document SP-190452, 3GPP, Reno, NV, USA, May 2019.

Study on Solutions Evaluation for NR to Support Non Terrestrial Network, document RP-181370, 3GPP, La Jolla, CA, USA, June 2018.

Study on Supporting Unmanned Aerial Systems Connectivity, Identification, and Tracking, document SP-181114, 3GPP, Reno, NV, USA, May 2019.

Sun Java System RFID Software 3.0 Administration Guide. Available at https://docs.oracle.com/cd/E19486-01/819-4685/819-4685.pdf.

Symantec Internet Security Threat Report. Available at https://www.symantec.com/content/dam/symantec/docs/reports/istr-21-2016-en.pdf.

System Architecture for the 5G System, document TS 23.501 V16.1.0, 3GPP, June 2019.

T. Carmenate, M. M. Rahman, D. Leante *et al.* Modeling and analyzing occupant behaviors in building energy analysis using an information space approach.

In *IEEE International Conference on Automation Science and Engineering*. IEEE, 2015.

T. de Cola and I. Bisio. QoS optimization of eMBB services in converged 5G-satellite networks. *IEEE Transactions on Vehicular Technology* 69(10): 12098–12110, October 2020. https://doi.org/10.1109/TVT.2020.3011963.

T. E. Elgamal. A public key cryptosystem and a signature scheme based on discrete logarithms. *IEEE Transactions on Information Theory* 31: 469–472, 1985.

T. Groß. Certification and efficient proofs of committed topology graphs. In *CCSW*, ACM, 2014.

T. Groß. Signatures and efficient proofs on committed graphs and NP-statements. In *Financial Cryptography and Data Security*, LNCS, Springer, 2015.

T. Liu and M. Martonosi. Impala: A middleware system for managing autonomic, parallel sensor systems. In *Proceedings of the 9th ACM SIGPLAN Symposium on Principles and Practice of Parallel Programming (PPoPP '03)*, ACM, pp. 107–118, 2003.

T. Ryberg. BERG INSIGHT, NB-IoT networks are here, now it's time to make business. Available at https://www.iot-now.com/2018/07/04/85156-nb-iot-networks-now-time-make-business/.

T. Suganuma, T. Oide *et al.* Multiagent-based flexible edge computing architecture for IoT. *IEEE Network*, January/February 2018.

T. Yamashita *et al.* Emma middleware: An application-level multicast infrastructure for multi-party video communication. In *Proceedings of the 15th International Conference Parallel and Distributed Computing and Systems. (PDCS '03)*. pp. 416–421, 2003.

Technology and Applications Symposium, 2003. https://doi.org/10.1109/RTTAS.2003.1203035.

Test Considerations for 5G New Radio, White Paper, Keysight Technologies, April 2018. Available at http://literature.cdn.keysight.com/litweb/pdf/5992-2921EN.pdf.

The IETF DetNet Working Group is standardizing Deterministic Networking, and the DetNet Architecture (draft) can be available at https://datatracker.ietf.org/doc/html/draft-ietf-detnet-architecture.

The Tactile Internet. ITU-T technology watch report. 2014. Available at https://www.itu.int/dms_pub/itu-t/oth/23/01/T23010000230001PDFE.pdf.

TinyOS Available at http://www.tinyos.net/. Other examples as Contiki (http://www.contiki-os.org/); Brillo (https://developers.google.com/brillo/); RIOT (http://www.riot-os.org/); Embedded Linux (http://elinux.org) and OpenWSN (http://openwsn.atlassian.net).

Toward a Tactile Internet Reference Architecture: Vision and Progress of the IEEE P1918.1 Standard.

U. Raza, P. Kulkarni, and M. Sooriyabandara. Low power wide area networks: An overview. *IEEE Communications Surveys and Tutorials* 19: 855–873, 2017.

V. C. Hu *et al.* Guide to attribute-based access control (ABAC) definition and considerations (draft). NIST Special Publication 800.162, 2013.

V. Ovidiu and F. Peter. *Internet of Things: Converging Technologies for Smart Environments and Integrated Ecosystems*. 2013.

V. Tsiatsis, S. Karnouskos *et al. Internet of Things Technologies and Applications for a New Age of Intelligence.* 2nd edn. Academic Press, 2018.

Vodafone White Paper. IoT Barometer 2016. Available at https://www.vodafone.com/business/news-and-insights/white-paper/the-iot-barometer-2016.

W. Chuan-Kun. An overview on the security techniques and challenges of the Internet of Things. *Journal of Cryptologic Research* 2(1): P40–P53, 2015.

W. D. Eggers and J. Skowron. Forces of change: Smart cities, Deloitte Insights, March 22, 2018.

W. Jun, H. Guixian, Y. Yong, and Z. Yibin. Application research progress of electronic nose and electronic tongue in food monitoring. *Transactions of the Chinese Society of Agricultural Engineering* 3, 2004.

W. Mahnke, S. H. Leitner, and M. Damm. *OPC Unified Architecture*. Heidelberg: Springer, 2009.

W. Shi, J. Cao, Q. Zhang, Y. Li, and L. Xu. Edge computing: Vision and challenges. *IEEE Internet of Things Journal* 3(5): 637–646, 2016. https://doi.org/10.1109/JIOT.2016.2579198.

W. Xue-Tao. Research of secure JTAG technique in cryptographic SoC. Master Degree Dissertation Submitted to PLA Information Engineering University for the Degree of Master, April 2015.

Websphere mq. Available at http://www-03.ibm.com/software/products/en/websphere-mq.

White Paper by Government of the HKSAR. RFID SECURITY. February 2008. Available at https://www.tceic.com/l2hhg369g45177232l60g294.html.

Wi-Sun Fan Overview. Available at https://tools.ietf.org/id/draft-heilelp-wan-wisun-overview-00.html.

X. Jin, W. M. Haddad, and T. Yucelen. An adaptive control architecture for mitigating sensor and actuator attacks in cyber-physical systems. *IEEE Transactions on Automatic Control* 62: 6058–6064, November 2017.

X. Lin and J. G. Andrews. An Overview on 3GPP Device to Device Proximity Services.

X. Liu, J. Yin, and S. Zhang 等. Range-based localization for sparse 3D sensor networks. *Internet of Things Journal IEEE* 6(1): 753–764, 2019.

X. Liu. Let the imagination fly (2nd) — 'Popular Science' launches 2014 invention of the year. *Science and Technology Daily*, May 13, 2014.

Y. C. Hu, M. Patel, D. Sabella *et al.* Mobile edge computing-A key technol- ogy towards 5G. *ETSI White Paper* 11(11): 1–16, 2015.

Y. Chunqing. Internet of Things security needs scalable solutions. *Fintech Times*, April 2016. Available at http://www.cnki.com.cn/Article/CJFDTotal-HNRD201604040.htm.

Y. LeCun, Y. Bengio, and G. Hinton. Deep learning. *Nature* 521: 436–444, May 28, 2015.

Y. Liu *et al.* Blockchain-based identity management systems: A review. *Journal of Network and Computer Applications* 166: 102731, 2020.

Y. Xinchun and X. Yebin. Universal radio frequency identification security authentication protocol classification model. *Journal of Computer Applications* 35(S2): 57–61, 2015.

Y. Xinchun and X. Yebin. Universal radio frequency identification security authentication protocol. *Journal of Computer Applications* 35(S2): 57–61, 2015.

Z. Qu, G. Zhang, H. Cao, and J. Xie. LEO satellite constellation for Internet of Things. *IEEE Access* 5: 18391–18401, 2017.

Z. Zou, K. J. Li, R. Li *et al.* Smart home system based on IPV6 and ZIGBEE technology. *Procedia Engineering* 15: 1529–1533, 2011.

Website References

http://baike.baidu.com/link?url=3dr_NgS9NxLdFX-8aY_k0U6d2nsnPa1d9ZW9yJlf9qOIMqxqVwQKEt0sONIbVwDYWgold3oQtHuoaR57I8i80ea58tjrzZZpw5AZk2WdOGyiSs3Kmk03HFEFciUl9ToDdbtUFT3usqVf0mCjg5FZsq.

http://baike.baidu.com/link?url=MCksb3LGcuTZdJxOljJFz9ummvtvDPbryFiAZ-AkyidOV0hSphffD3ba-FbG92XYu7KTsG8qvbBOVH83Dc0An_.

https://en.wikipedia.org/.

http://en.wikipedia.org/wiki/Virtual_power_plant.

http://freshmeat.net/projects/rfdump/?branch_id=61265&release_id=264928.

http://ietf.org/topics/iot/.

http://industry.beidou.gov.cn/WebUI/News?NewsId=702&NewsTypeId=4.

http://member.onem2m.org/Application/documentapp/downloadLatestRevision/?docId=10507.

http://microinteractions.com/what-is-a-microinteraction/.

http://paper.cnii.com.cn/rmydb/html/2016-10/26/nw.D110000rmydb_20161026_3-05.htm?div=-1. (EU will formulate new Internet of things security regulations, Source: China Information Industry Network-People's Post and Telecommunications, October 26, 2016).

http://scholar.lib.vt.edu/theses/available/etd-04042008-152245/unrestricted/raymond_dissertation.pdf.

http://science.china.com.cn/2020-11/26/content_41373016.htm.

http://v.youku.com/v_show/id_XMTQ3NDg2NzAwMA==.html?firsttime=0.

http://www.3gpp.org/release-13.

http://www.autosec.org/pubs/cars-usenixsec2011.pdf.www.3gpp.org/DynaReport/33501.htm.

http://www.biometric-solutions.com/face-recognition.html.

http://www.biometric-solutions.com/iris-recognition.html.

http://www.chinanews.com/gj/2012/05-16/3893684.shtml.

http://www.eurosmart.com/Update/07-10/Eurosmart_White_paper_on_RFID_Oct07.pdf.

http://www.gartner.com/newsroom/id/3165317.

http://www.nytimes.com/2006/10/23/business/23card.html?pagewanted=1&_r=1.

http://www.open5gcore.org.

http://www.open-mtc.org.

http://www.orbweb.com.

http://www.qdaily.com/articles/43586.html.

http://www.qidic.com/51765.html.

http://www.qnx.com/developers/docs/660/index.jsp?topic=%2Fcom.qnx.doc.neutrino.sys_arch%2Ftopic%2Ffsys_ETFS.html.

http://www.rfidvirus.org/.

http://www.senseg.fi/.

http://www.sickinsight-online.de/diagnosedaten-frei-haus/.

http://www.ti.com/ww/en/wireless_connectivity/sensortag.

http://www.weightless.org/.

http://www.wyzxwk.com/e/DoPrint/index.php?classid=22&id=102383.

https://aijourn.com/what-is-machine-vision-everything-you-need-to-know/.

https://azure.microsoft.com/en-us/overview/what-is-middleware/.

https://blogs.intel.com/iot/tag/intelligent-systems/.

https://datatracker.ietf.org/doc/draft-ietf-ace-oauth-authz/.

https://docs.microsoft.com/en-us/azure/rtos/netx-duo/netx-duo-lwm2m/chapter3.

https://docs.microsoft.com/en-us/previous-versions/aa480021(v=msdn.10)?redirectedfrom=MSDN#principles-and-definitions.

https://docs.oracle.com/cd/B28359_01/appdev.111/b28424/adfns_idcode.htm#BCGBAHIJ.

https://docs.oracle.com/cd/E19486-01/819-4685/sw-overview.html.

https://en.t-h.de/portfolio/sap-mii.html.

https://en.wikipedia.org/wiki/Dual_process_theory_(moral_psychology).

https://en.wikipedia.org/wiki/Electronic_Product_Code.

https://en.wikipedia.org/wiki/Lie_to_Me.

https://en.wikipedia.org/wiki/Zero-knowledge_proof.

https://enterpriseiotinsights.com/20191016/channels/fundamentals/what-is-mmtc-in-5g-nr-and-how-does-it-impact-nb-iot-and-lte-m.

https://epic.org/privacy/.

https://etech.iec.ch/issue/2020-04/iec-62443-standards-a-cornerstone-of-industrial-cyber-security.

https://github.com/alexe100/OpenMTC.

https://haltian.com/resource/nb1-vs-nb2-complete-comparison-table-and-overview/.

https://iot-analytics.com/product/digital-twin-insights-report-2020/.

https://labs.integrity.pt/articles/from-0-day-to-exploit-buffer-overflow-in-belkin-n750-cve-2014-1635/.

https://martinfowler.com/articles/microservices.html.

https://mashable.com/category/andreessen-horowitz/.

https://mobilab.cse.wustl.edu/projects/agilla/.

https://mp.weixin.qq.com/s/0484MsLOFf_yiaL2JxRQMQ.

https://opcconnect.opcfoundation.org/2020/06/exploring-opc-ua-security-concepts/.

https://opcfoundation.org/.

https://opcfoundation.org/news/opc-foundation-news/update-iec-62541-opc-ua-published/.

https://opcfoundation.org/wp-content/uploads/2017/11/OPC-UA-Security-Advise-EN.pdf.

https://rcpmag.com/articles/2020/04/02/microsoft-makes-run-at-5g-edge.aspx.

https://reference.opcfoundation.org/v104/Safety/docs/#8.

https://smart.columbus.gov/.

https://software.org/press-release/connecting-to-new-opportunities-through-connected-devices/.

https://standards.ieee.org/standard/802_11ah-2016.html.

https://techcrunch.com/2017/08/03/edge-computing-could-push-the-cloud-to-the-fringe/.

https://techxplore.com/news/2020-05-scalable-method-hvac-sensor-faults.html.

https://thecustomizewindows.com/2017/05/function-service-faas/.

https://ww2.frost.com/frost-perspectives/new-opportunities-and-vehicle-architectures-how-upcoming-cybersecurity-regulations-will-transform-the-connected-car-ecosystem/.

https://www.163.com/dy/article/FUP9IB5B0511DV4H.html.

https://www.actility.com/what-is-lorawan/.

https://www.businesswire.com/news/home/20120716006158/en/BI2-Technologies%E2%80%99-MORIS%E2%84%A2-Multi-modal-Biometric- Mobile-ID.

https://www.cnblogs.com/ibrahim/p/microsoft-azure-iot.html.

https://www.darpa.mil/program/active-authentication.
https://www.en-standard.eu/iec-tr-63069-2019-industrial-process-measurement-control-and-automation-framework-for-functional-safety-and- security/.
https://www.fokus.fraunhofer.de/en/edge_computing_forum_2019.
https://www.ge.com/digital/blog/what-edge-computing#to-section-index=section-3.
https://www.gs1.org/standards/epc-rfid. More details can be found at "http://www.epcglobalinc.org/".
https://www.gs1.org/standards/id-keys.
https://www.ibm.com/topics/what-is-a-digital-twin.
https://www.investopedia.com/terms/i/internet-energy-ioe.asp.
https://www.kongsberg.com/maritime/products/vessel-reference-systems/position-systems/non-differential-position-sensors.
https://www.marketsandmarkets.com/PressReleases/digital-twin.asp.
https://www.metaswitch.com/knowledge-center/reference/what-is-session-initiation-protocol-sip.
https://www.nist.gov/programs-projects/digital-thread-smart-manufacturing.
https://www.nist.gov/publications/nist-definition-cloud-computing.
https://www.nobelprize.org/prizes/medicine/1981/hubel/facts/.
https://www.omg.org.
https://www.onem2m.org/getting-started/onem2m-overview.
https://www.plattform-i40.de/PI40/Redaktion/EN/Downloads/Publikation/industrie-4-0-sino-german-white-paper-on-functional-safety-for-industry-4-0-and-intelligent-manufacturing.pdf? blob=publicationFile&v=2.
https://www.plattform-i40.de/PI40/Redaktion/EN/Downloads/Publikation/hm-2018-manufacturing.html.
https://www.researchgate.net/publication/228844364_Methods_and_soft-ware_architecture_for_managing_a_system_for_verifying_the_authenticity_of_branded_products/figures.
https://www.sick.com/cn/zh/networking-and-digitization-in-production/w/industry40-connectivity/.
https://www.storaenso.com/en/products/intelligent-packaging/eco-rfid-tag-technology.
https://www.tceic.com/l2hhg369g45177232l60g294.html.
https://www.tcs.com/blogs/the-role-of-augmented-reality-and-iot-in-the-connected-digital-enterprise.
https://www2.deloitte.com/content/dam/insights/us/articles/4748_Smart-buildings/DI_Smart-buildings.pdf.
https://xmpp.org.
https://xueqiu.com/6659575183/134686815.
Packet cleaning, in another word.
www.gdpr-info.eu/.

https://www.ericsson.com/en/reports-and-papers/ericsson-technologyreview/articles/5g-tsn-integration-for-industrial-automation.
https://www.etsi.org/deliver/etsi_ts/129500_129599/129520/15.00.00_60/ts_129520v150000p.pdf.

Index